3. The Doctrine of Implied Prohibition in Practice....................2–10

4. Statutory Interpretation...2–14

5. Conditional Agreements
   (a) Compliance with Legal Requirements 2–19
   (b) Contractual Allocation of Responsibility 2–23

3. UNLAWFUL PERFORMANCE

1. Scope of the Chapter 3–01

2. Executory Contracts and Ignorance of the Law
   (a) Illegality Irrelevant 3–02
   (b) Illegality Confused With Other Concepts
       (i) *Waugh v Morris* Lost Sight of................................3–04
       (ii) *Mistake* 3–05
       (iii) *Failure of Consideration*.................................3–07
       (iv) *Restitution to the Rescue?* 3–11

3. Position of the Party Responsible for Unlawful
   Performance...3–12

4. Position of the "Innocent" Party 3–19

4. KNOWLEDGE AND PARTICIPATION

1. Introduction 4–01

2. Extent of Claimant's Involvement
   (a) Mere Awareness...4–04
   (b) Participation 4–07
       (i) *Profiting from the Illegality* 4–08
       (ii) *Providing Assistance* 4–09
   (c) Contractual Obligation Not Required.........................4–12
   (d) Involvement in a Related Transaction
       (i) *Participation Still Relevant*..............................4–14
       (ii) *Claimant's Motive* 4–16
       (iii) *Insurance*..4–19

3. Where the Illegal Scheme is Especially Grave 4–22

4. Performance Unlawful from the Outset
   (a) Rights of the "Innocent" Party 4–27
   (b) "Excusable Ignorance" 4–30
   (c) "Promises" and "Warranties" 4–33

5. INDEMNITY AND FORFEITURE

1. Introduction 5–01

2. Recovery of Criminal Penalties and Costs......................5–02

3. RECOVERY OF DAMAGES
    (a) Policy Issues 5–10
    (b) Intentional Wrongdoing 5–14
    (c) Exemplary Damages...5–19

4. SUICIDE AND LIFE INSURANCE
    (a) Enforceability by the Deceased's Estate 5–23
    (b) Assignment of Life Policies 5–26

5. SUCCESSION AND FORFEITURE
    (a) At Common Law 5–30
    (b) By Statute...5–35

6. "NO BENEFIT FROM A CRIME" 5–40

PART 2
Public Policy

6. POLICY AND MORALITY

1. INTRODUCTION 6–01

2. PUBLIC POLICY IN THE COURTS
    (a) Nature of Public Policy 6–03
    (b) Factors to be Taken into Account...................................6–11

3. MARRIAGE AND SEXUAL MORALITY
    (a) Marriage...6–15
    (b) Sexual Relationships Outside Marriage 6–21

4. PUBLIC POLICY IN PRACTICE 6–27

7. FRAUD AND CORRUPTION

1. INTRODUCTION 7–01

2. FRAUDULENT CONTRACTS 7–03

3. DEFRAUDING THE REVENUE
    (a) General Applicability...7–09
    (b) Deceptive Documentation..7–10
    (c) Evading Income Tax 7–12
    (d) Degrees of Blameworthiness 7–19

4. CORRUPT BARGAINS 7–24

5. CONFIDENTIALITY AGREEMENTS
    (a) Payment for Silence...7–28
    (b) Libellous Communications..7–29
    (c) Concealment of Criminality 7–32

(d) Disclosure and the Public Interest...7–35

8. COMPROMISING THE LEGAL PROCESS

1. CATEGORIES OF CASES...8–01

2. CONTRACTS TO STIFLE PROSECUTIONS
    (a) Introduction..8–04
    (b) Offences of Differing Gravity 8–05
    (c) Concealing an Arrestable Offence...8–10
    (d) Existing Liabilities..8–12
    (e) Illegality and Duress...8–17

9. MAINTENANCE AND CHAMPERTY

1. INTRODUCTION 9–01

2. LAWFUL MAINTENANCE 9–06

3. CHAMPERTY 9–11

4. ASSIGNMENT...9–15

5. THE LEGAL PROFESSION 9–21

6. THE EFFECTS OF MAINTENANCE AND CHAMPERTY 9–26

7. IMPLICATIONS FOR PUBLIC POLICY GENERALLY 9–28

10. PEACE AND WAR

1. INTRODUCTION 10–01

2. INTERNATIONAL COMITY
    (a) Contracts Governed by English Law 10–02
    (b) Contracts Governed by Foreign Law 10–09

3. TRADING WITH THE ENEMY
    (a) The Principles 10–14
    (b) Questions of General Relevance to Illegality
        (i)   *Policy and Flexibility*...10–21
        (ii) *Conceptual Issues*..10–25

PART 3
Restraint of Trade

11. NATURE OF THE DOCTRINE

1. INTRODUCTION...11–01

2. CONCEPTS AND CATEGORIES...11–04

3. SANCTIONS AND BENEFITS 11–08

4. CONTINUING RELATIONSHIPS 11–13

5. LEGISLATIVE PROMOTION OF COMPETITION
    (a) Nature of the Statutory Provisions 11–19
    (b) Prohibited Agreements..11–22
    (c) Abuse of Dominant Position 11–26

12. FRONTIERS OF PROTECTION

1. CONFIDENTIALITY AND SECRECY
    (a) Scope of Protection..12–01
    (b) Trade Secrets..12–03
    (c) Confidential Information 12–06
    (d) Relationship to Breach of Confidence 12–08

2. "PUBLIC INTEREST"
    (a) The Issues 12–10
    (b) Relationship to the Interests of the Parties...............................12–11
    (c) Circumstances in which Public Interest will
         Invalidate..12–13
    (d) Criteria for Assessment..12–15

3. VENDOR AND PURCHASER 12–17

4. EXCLUSIVE SUPPLY CONTRACTS...12–24

13. CONSTRUCTION AND SCOPE OF COVENANTS

1. INTERPRETATION: LITERAL OR CONTEXTUAL? 13–01

2. AREA COVENANTS..13–09

3. DURATION 13–16

4. MODIFICATION BY STATUTE IN OTHER JURISDICTIONS
    (a) New Zealand..13–21
    (b) New South Wales..13–22

14. CUSTOMERS, RIVALS AND THE PROFESSIONS

1. INTRODUCTION 14–01

2. SOLICITATION OF CUSTOMERS...14–02

3. RIVAL EMPLOYERS
    (a) Covenants Against Joining Other Organisations.....................14–08
    (b) "Poaching" by Former Employee..14–13

4. MEDICAL PRACTITIONERS 14–15

5. SOLICITORS...14–18

15. OPPRESSION, REPUDIATION AND INTERIM INJUNCTIONS

   1. INTRODUCTION 15–01

   2. OPPRESSION 15–02

   3. REPUDIATION 15–07

   4. INTERIM INJUNCTIONS 15–15

PART 4
Relief from the Consequences

16. THE ENFORCEABILITY OF PROPRIETARY INTERESTS

   1. PASSING OF PROPERTY 16–01

   2. THE "NO-RELIANCE" DOCTRINE AND ITS DEMISE
      (a) At Common Law 16–04
      (b) In Equity 16–07
          (i) Resulting Trusts 16–08
          (ii) Presumption of Advancement 16–10
          (iii) Windfalls 16–12
          (iv) Presumption of Advancement Rebutted ..16–14

   3. CONCLUSIONS 16–17

17. ILLEGALITY AND RESTITUTION

   1. INTRODUCTION 17–01

   2. WHERE RESTITUTIONARY RELIEF WAS FORMERLY
      DENIED 17–04

   3. MISTAKE, FAILURE OF CONSIDERATION AND OPPRESSION 17–06
      (a) Mistake 17–07
      (b) Failure of Consideration 17–09
      (c) Oppression 17–11

   4. RESTITUTION AND ENFORCEMENT 17–14

   5. FRAUD AND NEGLIGENCE 17–19

18. UNDOING THE TRANSACTION

   1. THE LOCUS POENITENTIAE DOCTRINE 18–01

   2. PROTECTION OF THE CLAIMANT 18–04

19. THE DOCTRINE OF SEVERANCE

1. INTRODUCTION 19–01

2. WORDING OF THE PROVISION 19–04

3. SCOPE OF THE CONSIDERATION....................................19–10

4. CHARACTER OF THE CONTRACT 19–13

5. POLICY FACTORS 19–16
   (a) Restraint of Trade 19–17
   (b) "Tainted" Contracts..19–22

6. CONCLUSION...19–26

PART 5
Reform

20. THE NEW ZEALAND ILLEGAL CONTRACTS ACT 1970

1. INTRODUCTION 20–01

2. PROVISIONS OF THE ACT
   (a) Definition and Scope 20–02
   (b) Nullification and Validation................................20–04
   (c) Property Rights 20–06
   (d) Discretion 20–08

3. THE OPERATION OF THE ACT 20–09
   (a) Adjusting Rights 20–10
   (b) Potential Conflict with Legitimate Policies 20–13

21. REFORM PROPOSALS IN COMMONWEALTH JURISDICTIONS

1. INTRODUCTION 21–01

2. BRITISH COLUMBIA 21–02

3. ONTARIO 21–08

4. SOUTH AUSTRALIA 21–11

5. SINGAPORE 21–14

6. PROPOSALS OF THE LAW COMMISSION IN ENGLAND
   (a) Background...21–15
   (b) 2010 Recommendations.......................................21–17

7. REFORM BY THE JUDICIARY
   (a) Canada..21–23

(b) Australia 21–26

8. CURRENT STATE OF ENGLISH LAW 21–28

PART 6
Cases and Comments

22. HYPOTHETICAL SITUATIONS INVOLVING ILLEGALITY

1. ILLEGALITY IN PERFORMANCE 22–02

2. STATUTORY ILLEGALITY 22–04

3. DEFRAUDING THE REVENUE 22–06

4. BREACH OF LICENSING REQUIREMENTS 22–08

5. EFFECT OF KNOWLEDGE OF OTHER PARTY'S ILLEGALITY 22–10

6. DEFRAUDING INSURERS 22–12

7. TAX EVASION IN EMPLOYMENT 22–14

8. TRANSFERRING PROPERTY TO DECEIVE CREDITORS 22–16

9. RESTRAINTS UPON FORMER EMPLOYEES...22–18

10. COVENANTS BETWEEN VENDOR AND PURCHASER 22–20

                                                                      PAGE
Index 343

TABLE OF CASES

21st Century Logistic Solutions Ltd (In Liquidation) v Madysen Ltd [2004] EWHC 231
   (QB); [2004] 2 Lloyd's Rep. 92; [2004] S.T.C. 1535; [2004] B.T.C. 5720; [2004] B.V.C.
   779; [2004] S.T.I. 497; (2004) 101(12) L.S.G. 35 7–11
A Schroeder Music Publishing Co Ltd v Macaulay (formerly Instone); sub nom. Macaulay
   (formerly Instone) v A Schroeder Music Publishing Co Ltd [1974] 1 W.L.R. 1308;
   [1974] 3 All E.R. 616; (1974) 118 S.J. 734 HL 11–04, 15–02, 15–03,
                                       15–04, 15–05, 15–06
A Smith & Son (Bognor Regis) v Walker [1952] 2 Q.B. 319; [1952] 1 All E.R. 1008; [1952]
   1 T.L.R. 1089; (1952) 96 S.J. 260 CA 2–25
A v Hoyden (1984) 156 C.L.R. 532 .... 7–32, 8–11
Abraham v Thompson [1997] 4 All E.R. 362; [1997] C.L.C. 1370; (1997) 94(37) L.S.G. 41;
   (1997) 141 S.J.L.B. 217 CA (Civ Div) 9–26
Adamson v Jarvis 130 E.R. 693; (1827) 4 Bing. 66 CCP 5–12
Ailion v Spiekermann [1976] Ch. 158; [1976] 2 W.L.R. 556; [1976] 1 All E.R. 497; (1976)
   31 P. & C.R. 369; (1975) 238 E.G. 48; (1975) 120 S.J. 9 Ch D 2–12
AL Barnes Ltd v Time Talk (UK) Ltd [2003] EWCA Civ 402; [2003] B.L.R. 331; (2003)
   147 S.J.L.B. 385 7–07
Al-Kishtaini v Shanshal; sub nom. Shanshal v Al-Kishtaini [2001] EWCA Civ 264; [2001] 2
   All E.R. (Comm) 601; [2001] Lloyd's Rep. Bank. 174; (2001) 98(17) L.S.G.
   38 1–04
Alabaster v Harness [1895] 1 Q.B. 339 CA 9–09
Alec Lobb Garages Ltd v Total Oil Great Britain Ltd [1985] 1 W.L.R. 173; [1985] 1 All
   E.R. 303; [1985] 1 E.G.L.R. 33; (1985) 273 E.G. 659; (1985) 82 L.S.G. 45; (1985) 129
   S.J. 83 CA (Civ Div) 12–27, 12–28, 15–06,
                                         19–10, 19–11, 19–14
Alexander v Rayson [1936] 1 K.B. 169; 114 A.L.R. 357 CA 7–10, 7–11, 7–23,
                                         10–10, 16–04, 18–02
Allan (Merchandising) v Cloke [1963] 2 Q.B. 340; [1963] 2 W.L.R. 899; [1963] 2 All E.R.
   258; 61 L.G.R. 304; (1963) 107 S.J. 213 CA 3–05, 3–06, 4–07,
                                         4–34, 4–35
Allan Janes LLP v Johal [2006] EWHC 286 (Ch); [2006] I.C.R. 742; [2006] I.R.L.R. 599;
   (2006) 156 N.L.J. 373 .... 14–19, 14–22
Allen v Hounga; Hounga v Allen [2014] UKSC 47; [2014] 1 W.L.R. 2889; [2014] 4 All
   E.R. 595; [2014] I.C.R. 847; [2014] I.R.L.R. 811; [2014] H.R.L.R. 23; 39 B.H.R.C. 412;
   [2014] Eq. L.R. 559 .... I–01, 1–08, 7–16,
                                         21–18
Allen v Rescous (1676) 2 Lev. 174 1–01
Alliance Paper Group Plc v Prestwich (No.1) [1996] I.R.L.R. 25 Ch D 12–19, 14–14
Allied Dunbar (Frank Weisinger) Ltd v Frank Weisinger [1988] I.R.L.R. 60 ...... 11–12, 12–19
Amar Singh v Kulubya [1964] A.C. 142; [1963] 3 W.L.R. 513; [1963] 3 All E.R. 499;
   (1963) 107 S.J. 616 PC (EA) 18–04
American Cyanamid Co v Ethicon Ltd (No.1) [1975] A.C. 396; [1975] 2 W.L.R. 316; [1975]
   1 All E.R. 504; [1975] F.S.R. 101; [1975] R.P.C. 513; (1975) 119 S.J. 136
   HL 15–15, 15–16, 15–18
Amicable Society v Boland (1830) 4 Bligh. (N.S.) 194 5–24
Amoco Australian Pty Ltd v Rocca Bros Motor Engineering Co Pty Ltd; sub nom. Amoco
   Australia Pty v Rocco Bros Motor Engineering Co Pty [1975] A.C. 561; [1975] 2 W.L.R.
   779; [1975] 1 All E.R. 968; (1975) 119 S.J. 301 PC (Aus) 12–26, 19–13, 19–14
Anderson Ltd v Daniel [1924] 1 K.B. 138 CA 1–16, 2–05, 22–05
Andrews v Parker [1973] Qd.R. 93 6–22
Anglo Petroleum Ltd v TFB (Mortgages) Ltd; TFB (Mortgages) Ltd v Sutton; TFB
   (Mortgages) Ltd v Anglo Petroleum Ltd [2007] EWCA Civ 456; [2007] B.C.C. 407;
   [2008] 1 B.C.L.C. 185 .... 3–03, 4–07
Annandale Engineering v Samson [1994] I.R.L.R. 59 EAT 7–22
Annesley v Earl of Anglesea (1743) 17 State Trials 1139 7–38

Antoni v Antoni [2007] UKPC 10; [2007] W.T.L.R. 1335 PC (Bah) 16–10
Arab Bank Ltd v Barclays Bank (Dominion, Colonial and Overseas) [1954] A.C. 495;
    [1954] 2 W.L.R. 1022; [1954] 2 All E.R. 226; (1954) 98 S.J. 350 HL 10–14, 10–26
Aratra Potato Co Ltd v Taylor Joynson Garrett [1995] 4 All E.R. 695; (1995) 145 N.L.J.
    1402 QBD 9–22, 9–27, 17–09
Archbolds (Freightage) Ltd v S Spanglett Ltd [1961] 1 Q.B. 374; [1961] 2 W.L.R. 170;
    [1961] 1 All E.R. 417; (1961) 105 S.J. 149 CA 1–11, 2–10, 2–12,
                                                    2–26, 3–18, 3–19, 4–31, 4–32, 22–09,
                                                    22–11
Argos, Cargo ex (No.2) (1872-75) L.R. 4 A. & E. 13 Ct of Admiralty 3–03
Arkin v Borchard Lines Ltd (Costs Order) [2005] EWCA Civ 655; [2005] 1 W.L.R. 3055;
    [2005] 3 All E.R. 613; [2005] 2 Lloyd's Rep. 187; [2005] C.P. Rep. 39; [2005] 4 Costs
    L.R. 643; (2005) 155 N.L.J. 902 9–26
Armhouse Lee Ltd v Chappell, Times, 7 August 1996; Independent, 26 July 1996 CA (Civ
    Div) 6–24, 6–25, 6–30
Arnold v Britton [2015] UKSC 36; [2015] A.C. 1619; [2015] 2 W.L.R. 1593; [2016] 1 All
    E.R. 1; [2015] H.L.R. 31; [2015] 2 P. & C.R. 14; [2015] L. & T.R. 25; [2015] C.I.L.L.
    3689 13–01
Ashcourt Rowan Financial Planning Ltd v Hall [2013] EWHC 1185 (QB); [2013] I.R.L.R.
    637 . . . . 11–17, 14–12, 15–17
Ashmore Benson Pease & Co Ltd v AV Dawson Ltd [1973] 1 W.L.R. 828; [1973] 2 All E.R.
    856; [1973] 2 Lloyd's Rep. 21; [1973] R.T.R. 473; (1973) 117 S.J. 203 CA (Civ
    Div) 2–10, 3–19, 3–21,
                                                    4–07, 4–08, 7–17, 22–11
Askey v Golden Wine Co Ltd [1948] 2 All E.R. 35; 64 T.L.R. 379; (1948) 92 S.J. 411
    KBD 5–07
Atkinson v Denby (1862) 7 H. & N. 934 . . . . 8–20, 17–11
Attorney General of Australia v Adelaide Steamship [1913] A.C. 781 PC
    (Aus) 12–11, 12–16
Attorney General of New Brunswick v St John [1948] 3 D.L.R. 693 Sup Ct
    (NB) 2–22
Attorney General v Observer Ltd; Attorney General v Times Newspapers Ltd (No.2);
    Attorney General v Guardian Newspapers Ltd (No.2) [1990] 1 A.C. 109; [1988] 3
    W.L.R. 776; [1988] 3 All E.R. 545; [1989] 2 F.S.R. 181; (1988) 85(42) L.S.G. 45;
    (1988) 138 N.L.J. Rep. 296; (1988) 132 S.J. 1496 HL 7–35, 7–38
Attwood v Lamont [1920] 3 K.B. 571 CA 19–04, 19–05, 19–07,
                                                    19–13, 19–18, 19–19, 19–20, 19–21
Australian Broadcasting Corporation v Redmore Proprietary (1988-89) 166 C.L.R.
    454 2–04
Australian Competition and Consumer Commission v Baxter Healthcare (2007) 232 C.L.R.
    1 2–16
Awwad v Geraghty & Co; sub nom. Geraghty & Co v Awwad [2001] Q.B. 570; [2000] 3
    W.L.R. 1041; [2000] 1 All E.R. 608; [2000] 1 Costs L.R. 105; [1999] N.P.C. 148 CA
    (Civ Div) 9–23, 9–29, 17–16
Ayerst v Jenkins (1873) L.R. 16 Eq. 275 Lord Chancellor 16–01
B and B Viennese Fashions v Losane [1952] 1 All E.R. 909; [1952] 1 T.L.R. 750
    CA 1–16, 2–05, 22–05
Baker v Jones [1954] 1 W.L.R. 1005; [1954] 2 All E.R. 553; (1954) 98 S.J. 473
    QBD 9–09
Baker v Lintott (1981) 141 D.L.R. (3d) 571 CA (Alberta) 12–16
Bakewell Management Ltd v Brandwood; sub nom. Brandwood v Bakewell Management
    Ltd [2004] UKHL 14; [2004] 2 A.C. 519; [2004] 2 W.L.R. 955; [2004] 2 All E.R. 305;
    [2004] R.T.R. 26; [2005] 1 P. & C.R. 1; [2004] 2 E.G.L.R. 15; [2004] 20 E.G. 168;
    [2004] 15 E.G. 104 (C.S.); (2004) 101(18) L.S.G. 34; (2004) 154 N.L.J. 553; (2004) 148
    S.J.L.B. 418; [2004] N.P.C. 53; [2004] 2 P. & C.R. DG6 5–40
Balston Ltd v Headline Filters Ltd (No.1) [1987] F.S.R. 330 Ch D 12–04, 12–08, 12–09
Barclays Bank Plc v O'Brien [1994] 1 A.C. 180; [1993] 3 W.L.R. 786; [1993] 4 All E.R.
    417; [1994] 1 F.L.R. 1; [1994] 1 F.C.R. 357; (1994) 26 H.L.R. 75; (1994) 13 Tr. L.R.
    165; [1994] C.C.L.R. 94; [1994] Fam. Law 78; [1993] E.G. 169 (C.S.); (1993) 143
    N.L.J. 1511; (1993) 137 S.J.L.B. 240; [1993] N.P.C. 135 HL 6–22
Bardsell v Kerr [1979] 2 N.Z.L.R 731 20–15

Barker v Westmorland CC, 56 L.G.R. 267 DC 10–02
Barrett Builders v Miller (1990) 76 Ad.2 455 2–05
Batra v Ebrahim [1982] 2 Lloyd's Rep. 11 (Note) CA (Civ Div) 2–26
Beckett Investment Management Group v Glyn Hall [2007] EWCA Civ 613 . 13–04, 13–20, 19–04
Bedford Insurance Co Ltd v Instituto de Resseguros do Brasil [1985] Q.B. 966; [1984] 3
    W.L.R. 726; [1984] 3 All E.R. 766; [1984] 1 Lloyd's Rep. 210; [1985] Fin. L.R. 49;
    (1985) 82 L.S.G. 37; (1984) 134 N.L.J. 34; (1984) 128 S.J. 701 QBD
    (Comm) 1–13, 1–15, 2–16,
                                                                                        21–29
Beer v Townsgate (1997) 152 D.L.R. (4th) 671 2–09
Begbie v Phosphate Sewage Co Ltd (1875-76) L.R. 1 Q.B.D. 679 CA 17–10
Bell v Lever Brothers Ltd; sub nom. Lever Bros Ltd v Bell [1932] A.C. 161
    HL 3–06
Belvoir Finance Co Ltd v Harold G Cole & Co Ltd [1969] 1 W.L.R. 1877; [1969] 2 All E.R.
    904 QBD 16–03
Belvoir Finance Co Ltd v Stapleton [1971] 1 Q.B. 210; [1970] 3 W.L.R. 530; [1970] 3 All
    E.R. 664; (1970) 114 S.J. 719 CA (Civ Div) 16–03
Ben Hashem v Al Shayif [2008] EWHC 2380 (Fam); [2008] Fam. Law 1179 6–17
Benedetti v Sawiris; sub nom. Sawiris v Benedetti [2013] UKSC 50; [2014] A.C. 938;
    [2013] 3 W.L.R. 351; [2013] 4 All E.R. 253; [2013] 2 All E.R. (Comm) 801; 149 Con.
    L.R. 1 17–14
Bennett v Bennett [1952] 1 K.B. 249; [1952] 1 All E.R. 413; [1952] 1 T.L.R. 400
    CA 8–02, 19–10, 19–14,
                                                                                        19–16, 19–23
Beresford v Royal Insurance Co Ltd [1938] A.C. 586 HL 4–23, 5–23, 5–24,
                                                                                        5–25, 5–26
Berg v Sadler and Moore [1937] 2 K.B. 158 CA 17–10
Berrett v Smith [1965] N.Z.L.R. 460 . . . . 20–05, 22–05
Best v Glenville [1960] 1 W.L.R. 1198; [1960] 3 All E.R. 478; 58 L.G.R. 333; (1961) 12 P.
    & C.R. 48; (1960) 104 S.J. 934 CA 2–22
Betts v Gibbins (1834) 2 Ad. & El. 57 5–12
Bevan Ashford v Geoff Yeandle (Contractors) Ltd (In Liquidation) [1999] Ch. 239; [1998] 3
    W.L.R. 172; [1998] 3 All E.R. 238; 59 Con. L.R. 1; [1998] 2 Costs L.R. 15; (1998)
    95(16) L.S.G. 27; (1998) 148 N.L.J. 587; (1998) 142 S.J.L.B. 151; [1998] N.P.C. 69 Ch
    D 9–22, 9–29
Bevan v Bevan (No.1) [1955] 2 Q.B. 227; [1955] 2 W.L.R. 948; [1955] 2 All E.R. 206;
    (1955) 99 S.J. 306 QBD 10–17, 10–27
Bevin v Smith [1994] 3 N.Z.L.R. 648 . . . . 20–12, 20–14
Biggs v Hoddinott; Hoddinott v Biggs [1898] 2 Ch. 307 CA 12–29
Biggs v Lawrence (1789) 3 Term.R. 454 4–10
Bigos v Bousted [1951] 1 All E.R. 92 KBD 18–02, 22–17
Bilbie v Lumley (1802) 2 East. 469 17–08
Bilta (UK) Ltd (In Liquidation) v Nazir; sub nom. Jetivia SA v Bilta (UK) Ltd (In
    Liquidation) [2015] UKSC 23; [2016] A.C. 1; [2015] 2 W.L.R. 1168; [2015] 2 All E.R.
    1083; [2015] 2 All E.R. (Comm) 281; [2015] 2 Lloyd's Rep. 61; [2015] B.C.C. 343;
    [2015] 1 B.C.L.C. 443; [2015] B.V.C. 20 . . . . I–01, 1–08, 5–08,
                                                                                        5–40, 21–18
Binder v Alachouzos [1972] 2 Q.B. 151; [1972] 2 W.L.R. 947; [1972] 2 All E.R. 189;
    [1972] 1 Lloyd's Rep. 524; (1972) 116 S.J. 139 CA (Civ Div) 8–03
Birkett v Acorn Business Machines Ltd [1999] 2 All E.R. (Comm) 429; (1999) 96(31)
    L.S.G. 35 CA (Civ Div) 7–08, 22–13
Birmingham City Council v Forde; sub nom. sub nom. Forde v Birmingham City Council
    [2009] EWHC 12 (QB); [2009] 1 W.L.R. 2732; [2010] 1 All E.R. 802; [2009] 2 Costs
    L.R. 206; [2009] N.P.C. 7 17–16
Bishop v Kitchin (1868) 38 L.J.Q.B. 20 11–10
Blackburn Bobbin Co Ltd v TW Allen & Sons Ltd [1918] 2 K.B. 467; 3 A.L.R. 11
    CA 19–11
Blackburn v YV Properties Ltd [1980] V.R. 290 16–07
Bloxsome v Williams 107 E.R. 720; (1824) 3 B. & C. 232 KB 2–16, 2–17
Boissevain v Weil [1950] A.C. 327; [1950] 1 All E.R. 728; 66 T.L.R. (Pt. 1) 771; (1950) 94
    S.J. 319 HL 1–16, 17–16

Bonnard v Dott [1906] 1 Ch. 740 CA 18–07
Bostel Bros v Hurlock [1949] 1 K.B. 74; [1948] 2 All E.R. 312; 64 T.L.R. 495; [1948]
    L.J.R. 1846; (1948) 92 S.J. 361 CA 1–16, 2–25
Bouchard Servais v Princes Hall Restaurant (1904) 20 T.L.R. 574 11–15
Bourne v Colodense [1985] I.C.R. 291; [1985] I.R.L.R. 339; (1985) 82 L.S.G. 923; (1985)
    129 S.J. 153 CA (Civ Div) 9–19
Boussmaker, Ex p. (1806) 13 Ves. 71 10–25
Bowmakers Ltd v Barnet Instruments Ltd [1945] K.B. 65 CA 3–06, 16–03, 16–04,
                                        16–05, 16–06, 16–07, 16–08, 16–09,
                                                      16–10, 16–17
Bowman v Secular Society Ltd; sub nom. Secular Society Ltd v Bowman; Bowman, Re
    [1917] A.C. 406 HL 6–33
Bowry v Bennett (1808) 1 Camp. 348 6–23
Bradlaugh v Newdegate (1882-83) L.R. 11 Q.B.D. 1 QBD 9–06
Bradstreets British Ltd v Mitchell; Bradstreets British Ltd v Carapanayoti & Co Ltd [1933]
    Ch. 190 Ch D 7–30
Braganza v BP Shipping Ltd; British Unity, The [2015] UKSC 17; [2015] 1 W.L.R. 1661;
    [2015] 4 All E.R. 639; [2015] 2 Lloyd's Rep. 240; [2015] I.C.R. 449; [2015] I.R.L.R.
    487; [2015] Pens. L.R. 431 5–25
Braham v Walker [1960-61] 104 C.L.R. 366 2–20
Brake Bros Ltd v Ungless [2004] EWHC 2799 (QB) 12–01, 13–20
Brand Studio Ltd v St John Knits Inc; sub nom. Brand Studio Ltd v St Johns Knits Inc
    [2015] EWHC 3143 (QB); [2016] 1 All E.R. (Comm) 1163; [2015] Bus. L.R. 1421;
    [2016] 1 Lloyd's Rep. 179; [2016] E.C.C. 1 19–14
Bridge v Deacons [1984] A.C. 705; [1984] 2 W.L.R. 837; [1984] 2 All E.R. 19; (1984) 81
    L.S.G. 1291; (1984) 134 N.L.J. 723; (1984) 128 S.J. 263 PC (HK) 12–12, 12–16, 13–16,
                                        13–19, 14–14, 14–18, 14–19, 14–22
Briggs v Oates [1991] 1 All E.R. 407; [1990] I.C.R. 473; [1990] I.R.L.R. 472; (1990) 140
    N.L.J. 208 Ch D 11–12, 15–09
British Cash & Parcel Conveyors Ltd v Lamson Store Service Co Ltd [1908] 1 K.B. 1006
    CA 9–07, 9–08
British Homophone v Kunz and Crystalline Gramaphone Record Manufacturing Co (1935)
    152 L.T. 589 1–01
British Motor Trade Association v Gilbert [1951] 2 All E.R. 641; [1951] 2 T.L.R. 514;
    [1951] W.N. 454; (1951) 95 S.J. 595 Ch D 12–16
British Reinforced Concrete Engineering Co Ltd v Scheliff [1921] 2 Ch. 563 Ch
    D 12–21, 19–09, 19–13,
                                                      22–21
Broadlands Rentals Ltd v R.D. Bull Ltd [1976] 2 N.Z.L.R. 595 20–12
Brodie, Re; sub nom. Brodie v Brodie [1917] P. 271 PDAD 6–18
Brooks v Burns Philp Trustee Co (1969) 121 C.L.R. 432 19–01
Brown Jenkinson & Co Ltd v Percy Dalton (London) Ltd [1957] 2 Q.B. 621; [1957] 3
    W.L.R. 403; [1957] 2 All E.R. 844; [1957] 2 Lloyd's Rep. 1; (1957) 101 S.J. 610
    CA 5–11, 5–12
Brown v Brown [1980] 1 N.Z.L.R. 484 . . . . 11–12, 13–21
Brown v Duncan 109 E.R. 385; (1829) 10 B. & C. 93 KB 2–08
Browning v Floyd [1946] K.B. 597; [1946] 2 All E.R. 367; 62 T.L.R. 405; (1946) 110 J.P.
    308; [1947] L.J.R. 245; 175 L.T. 135; (1946) 90 S.J. 332 KBD 3–10
Browning v Morris 98 E.R. 1364; (1778) 2 Cowp. 790 KB 18–04
Brownton Ltd v Edward Moore Inbucom Ltd [1985] 3 All E.R. 499; (1985) 82 L.S.G. 1165
    CA (Civ Div) 9–16, 9–19
Brumau v Laliberte (1901) 19 S.C. 425 (Quebec) 4–21, 6–24
Buckle & Son Pty v McAllister (1986) 4 N.S.W.L.R. 426 13–22
Buckley v Tutty (1971) 125 C.L.R. 353 11–23
Bull v Pitney Bowes Ltd [1967] 1 W.L.R. 273; [1966] 3 All E.R. 384; 1 K.I.R. 342; (1967)
    111 S.J. 32 QBD 11–09, 19–11
Burrows v Rhodes; sub nom. Burroughs v Rhodes [1899] 1 Q.B. 816 QBD 5–07, 5–10, 7–30
Business Seating (Renovations) v Broad [1989] I.C.R. 713 . . . . 14–07, 19–18
C Battison & Sons v Mauti (1986) 34 D.L.R. (4th) 700 (Ontario) 2–05
Callaghan v O'Sullivan [1925] V.L.R. 664 8–21

Camdex International Ltd v Bank of Zambia (No.1) [1998] Q.B. 22; [1996] 3 W.L.R. 759;
    [1996] 3 All E.R. 431; [1996] C.L.C. 1477 CA (Civ Div) 9–16, 9–17, 9–19,
                                                                                9–20
Canadian American Financial Corp v King (1989) 60 D.L.R. (4th) 293 CA (British
    Columbia) 19–13
Candler v Candler (1821) Jac. 225 14–22
Cannan v Bryce (1819) 3 B. & Ald. 179 4–17
Cantol v Brodi Chemicals (1969) 94 D.L.R. (3d) 265 .11–12
Carewatch Care Services Ltd v Focus Caring Services Ltd [2014] EWHC 2313
    (Ch) 12–19
Caribonum Co Ltd v Le Couch (1913) 109 T.L.R. 385 .12–03
Carnduff v Rock [2001] EWCA Civ 680; [2001] 1 W.L.R. 1786; [2001] Po. L.R. 142;
    (2001) 98(25) L.S.G. 47; (2001) 145 S.J.L.B. 141 7–33
Carney v Herbert [1985] A.C. 301; [1984] 3 W.L.R. 1303; [1985] 1 All E.R. 438; (1984) 81
    L.S.G. 3500 PC (Aus) 19–01, 19–24
Caterpillar Logistics Services (UK) Ltd v Huesca de Crean [2012] EWCA Civ 156; [2012] 3
    All E.R. 129; [2012] C.P. Rep. 22; [2012] I.C.R. 981; [2012] F.S.R. 33 12–09
Catley v Herbert [1988] 1 N.Z.L.R 606 20–14
Cavalier Insurance Co Ltd, Re [1989] 2 Lloyd's Rep. 430 Ch D 2–03
Cavendish Square Holdings BV v Makdessi [2012] EWHC 3582 (Comm); [2013] 1 All E.R.
    (Comm) 787 12–19
Cayne v Global Natural Resources Plc [1984] 1 All E.R. 225 CA (Civ Div) 15–17
CEF Holdings Ltd c City Electrical Factors Ltd [2012] EWHC 1525 . . . . .14–14, 15–17
Cevern v Ferbish 666 A.2d 17 (1995) 2–09
Chafer v Lilley [1947] L.J.R. 231; 176 L.T. 22 11–18
Chandris v Argo Insurance Co Ltd [1963] 2 Lloyd's Rep. 65; (1963) 107 S.J. 575 QBD
    (Comm) 2–13
Chapman v Michaelson [1909] 1 Ch. 238 CA 18–07
Charlton v Fisher; sub nom. Churchill Insurance v Charlton [2001] EWCA Civ 112; [2002]
    Q.B. 578; [2001] 3 W.L.R. 1435; [2001] 1 All E.R. (Comm) 769; [2001] R.T.R. 33;
    [2001] Lloyd's Rep. I.R. 387; [2001] P.I.Q.R. P23; (2001) 98(10) L.S.G.
    45 . . . . .5–14, 5–16, 5–17,
                                                                                5–18, 5–21, 5–22
Chartbrook Ltd v Persimmon Homes Ltd [2009] UKHL 38; [2009] 1 A.C. 1101; [2009] 3
    W.L.R. 267; [2009] 4 All E.R. 677; [2010] 1 All E.R. (Comm) 365; [2009] Bus. L.R.
    1200; [2009] B.L.R. 551; 125 Con. L.R. 1; [2010] 1 P. & C.R. 9; [2009] 3 E.G.L.R. 119;
    [2009] C.I.L.L. 2729; [2009] 27 E.G. 91 (C.S.); (2009) 153(26) S.J.L.B. 27; [2009]
    N.P.C. 87; [2009] N.P.C. 86 13–01
Chemidus Wavin Ltd v Societe pour la Transformation et l'Exploitation des Resines
    Industrielles SA [1978] 3 C.M.L.R. 514; [1977] F.S.R. 181 CA (Civ Div) 19–03
Chester City Council v Arriva Plc [2007] EWHC 1373 (Ch); [2007] U.K.C.L.R. 1582;
    (2007) 151 S.J.L.B. 855 11–26
Chettiar (ARPL Palaniappa) v Chettiar (PLAR Arunasalam); sub nom. Chettiar v Chettiar
    [1962] A.C. 294; [1962] 2 W.L.R. 548; [1962] 1 All E.R. 494; (1962) 106 S.J. 110 PC
    (FMS) 16–10, 22–17
Chrispen v Topham (1986) 28 D.L.R. (4th) 754 (Saskatchewan) 6–22
Clapham Steamship Co Ltd v Naamlooze Vennootschap Handels-En Transport-Maatschappij
    Vulcaan of Rotterdam [1917] 2 K.B. 639 KBD 10–29
Clark v Electronic Applications (Commercial) [1963] R.P.C. 234 13–04
Clark v Hagar (1894) 22 S.C.R. 510 . . . . .4–07, 6–24
Clarke v Newland [1991] 1 All E.R. 397 CA (Civ Div) 13–01, 13–05, 14–16,
                                                                                14–17
Cleaver v Mutual Reserve Fund Life Association [1892] 1 Q.B. 147 CA 5–30
Clelland v Clelland [1944] 4 D.L.R. 703 (Can) 4–28
Cleveland Petroleum Co Ltd v Dartstone Ltd (No.1) [1969] 1 W.L.R. 116; [1969] 1 All E.R.
    201; (1969) 20 P. & C.R. 235; (1968) 112 S.J. 962 CA (Civ Div) 12–25, 12–26
Clifford Davis Management Ltd v WEA Records Ltd [1975] 1 W.L.R. 61; [1975] 1 All E.R.
    237; (1974) 118 S.J. 775 CA (Civ Div) 15–04
Clubb v Hutson (1865) 18 C.B.N.S. 414 . . . . .8–04, 8–14
Clugas v Penaluna (1791) 4 Term.R. 466 4–10

Clunis v Camden and Islington HA [1998] Q.B. 978; [1998] 2 W.L.R. 902; [1998] 3 All
E.R. 180; (1997-98) 1 C.C.L. Rep. 215; (1998) 40 B.M.L.R. 181; [1998] P.N.L.R. 262;
(1998) 95(2) L.S.G. 23; (1998) 142 S.J.L.B. 38 CA (Civ Div) 5–02, 5–40
Cohen v J Lester Ltd [1939] 1 K.B. 504 KBD 18–07
Cointat v Myham & Son [1913] 2 K.B. 220 KBD .5–04, 5–05, 5–06,
5–08
Colburn v Patmore 149 E.R. 999; (1834) 1 Cr. M. & R. 73; (1834) Tyr. 677 Ex
Ct 5–06
Cole v Booker (1913) T.L.R. 295 9–11
Coleman v Myers [1977] 2 N.Z.L.R 225 20–14
Colen v Cebrian (UK) Ltd [2003] EWCA Civ 1676; [2004] I.C.R. 568; [2004] I.R.L.R. 210;
(2004) 101(2) L.S.G. 27) 3–13, 7–16, 7–17
Collier v Collier [2002] EWCA Civ 1095; [2002] B.P.I.R. 1057; [2003] W.T.L.R. 617;
(2003-04) 6 I.T.E.L.R. 270; [2003] 1 P. & C.R. DG3 . . . . .1–07, 16–10, 16–14,
18–02
Collins v Blantern (1767) 2 Wils. 341 8–06
Commercial Plastics Ltd v Vincent [1965] 1 Q.B. 623; [1964] 3 W.L.R. 820; [1964] 3 All
E.R. 546; (1964) 108 S.J. 599 CA 12–03, 13–01, 13–08,
14–09, 14–12
Compania Colombiana de Seguros v Pacific Steam Navigation Co (The Colombiana);
Empressa de Telefona de Bogota v Pacific Steam Navigation Co (The Colombiana)
[1965] 1 Q.B. 101; [1964] 2 W.L.R. 484; [1964] 1 All E.R. 216; [1963] 2 Lloyd's Rep.
479; (1964) 108 S.J. 75 QBD (Comm) 9–16
Condliffe v Hislop [1996] 1 W.L.R. 753; [1996] 1 All E.R. 431; [1996] E.M.L.R. 25 CA
(Civ Div) 9–10
Connor Bros v Connors [1940] 4 All E.R. 179 .11–05, 11–12, 11–16,
12–19, 13–17, 22–21
Consolidated Exploration and Finance Co v Musgrave [1900] 1 Ch. 37 Ch D 8–02
Continental Bank Leasing Corp v Canada (1998) 163 D.L.R. (4th) 385 2–05
Cook v Black (1842) 1 Hare 390 5–28
Cooke v Head (No.1) [1972] 1 W.L.R. 518; [1972] 2 All E.R. 38; (1972) 116 S.J. 298 CA
(Civ Div) 6–22
Cooke v Routledge [1998] N.I. 174 CA (NI) 5–13
Coplan v Coplan (19585) 14 D.L.R. (2d) 426 (Can.) 16–07
Coppage v Safety Net Security Ltd. See Safetynet Security Ltd v Coppage
Coral Leisure Group v Barnett [1981] I.C.R. 503; [1981] I.R.L.R. 204; (1981) 125 S.J. 374
EAT 3–13, 22–03
Corby v Morrison (t/a the Card Shop) [1980] I.C.R. 564; [1980] I.R.L.R. 218
EAT 7–13, 7–14
Corr v IBC Vehicles Ltd [2008] UKHL 13; [2008] 1 A.C. 884; [2008] 2 W.L.R. 499; [2008]
2 All E.R. 943; [2008] I.C.R. 372; [2008] P.I.Q.R. P11; (2008) 105(10) L.S.G. 28;
(2008) 152(9) S.J.L.B. 30 5–26
Costello v Chief Constable of Derbyshire [2001] EWCA Civ 381; [2001] 1 W.L.R. 1437;
[2001] 3 All E.R. 150; [2001] 2 Lloyd's Rep. 216; [2001] Po. L.R. 83 . . . . .16–01, 16–06
Cotronic (UK) Ltd v Dezonie (t/a Wendaland Builders Ltd) [1991] B.C.C. 200; [1991]
B.C.L.C. 721 CA (Civ Div) 2–05
Coulson v News Group Newspapers Ltd [2012] EWCA Civ 1547; [2013] 1 Costs L.O. 117;
[2013] I.R.L.R. 116 5–09
County Hotel & Wine Co Ltd v London & North Western Railway Co [1921] 1 A.C. 85
HL 9–16
Cowan v Milbourn (1866-67) L.R. 2 Ex. 230 Ex Ct 4–26, 22–11
Crage v Fry (1903) J.P. 240 . . . . .5–05, 5–06
Credit Suisse Asset Management Ltd v Armstrong [1996] I.C.R. 882; [1996] I.R.L.R. 450;
(1996) 93(23) L.S.G. 35; (1996) 140 S.J.L.B. 141 CA (Civ Div) 11–17, 13–20
Credit Suisse v Allerdale BC [1997] Q.B. 306; [1996] 3 W.L.R. 894; [1996] 4 All E.R. 129;
[1996] 2 Lloyd's Rep. 241; [1996] 5 Bank. L.R. 249; (1997) 161 J.P. Rep. 88 CA (Civ
Div) 19–13
Crehan v Inntrepreneur Pub Co (CPC); sub nom. Inntrepreneur Pub Co (CPC) v Crehan
[2006] UKHL 38; [2007] 1 A.C. 333; [2006] 3 W.L.R. 148; [2006] 4 All E.R. 465;
[2006] U.K.C.L.R. 1232; [2007] E.C.C. 2; [2006] Eu. L.R. 1189; [2006] I.C.R. 1344;
[2006] 30 E.G. 103 (C.S.); (2006) 150 S.J.L.B. 983; [2006] N.P.C. 85 11–25

Crisp v Churchill Unreported 6–24
Croesus Financial Services Ltd v Bradshaw [2013] EWHC 3685 (QB) 13–20
Cunard v Hyde (No.1) (1858) El. & B1 . . . . 3–16, 4–20
Cunard v Hyde (No.2) (1859) 2 El. & B.1 . . . . 3–16, 4–20, 22–03
Cunigunda, In the Estate of; sub nom. Crippen, In the Estate of [1911] P. 108
    PDAD 5–30, 5–40
Curragh Investment v Cook; sub nom. Curragh Investments, Ltd v Cook [1974] 1 W.L.R.
    1559; [1974] 3 All E.R. 658; (1974) 28 P. & C.R. 401; (1974) 118 S.J. 737 Ch
    D 2–01
Cuthbertson v Lowes (1870) 8 M. 1073 CSIH (1st Div) 17–02
Cutler v Wandsworth Stadium Ltd [1949] A.C. 398; [1949] 1 All E.R. 544; 65 T.L.R. 170;
    [1949] L.J.R. 824; (1949) 93 S.J. 163 HL 18–08
D Bates & Co v Dale [1937] 3 All. E.R. 650 12–20
D v M [1996] I.R.L.R. 192 QBD 15–09, 15–10
D&C Builders Ltd v Rees [1966] 2 Q.B. 617; [1966] 2 W.L.R. 288; [1965] 3 All E.R. 837;
    (1965) 109 S.J. 971 CA 11–11
Daimler Co Ltd v Continental Tyre & Rubber Co (Great Britain) Ltd; Continental Tyre &
    Rubber Co (Great Britain) Ltd v Thomas Tilling Ltd; sub nom. Continental Tyre &
    Rubber Co (Great Britain) Ltd v Daimler Co Ltd [1916] 2 A.C. 307 HL 10–18
Dairy Crest v Pigott [1989] I.C.R. 92 CA (Civ Div) 15–16
Dalton v Latham; sub nom. Murphy (Deceased), Re [2003] EWHC 796 (Ch); [2003]
    M.H.L.R. 271; [2003] W.T.L.R. 687; (2003) 147 S.J.L.B. 537; [2003] N.P.C.
    54 5–38
Dann v Curzon (1910) 104 L.T. 66 8–01
Dart Holdings Pty Ltd v Total Concept Group Pty Ltd [2012] QSC 158 (Aus) 2–25
David Securities Pty v Commonwealth Bank of Australia 175 C.L.R. 353 HC
    (Aus) 17–08
Davidson v Pillay [1979] I.R.L.R. 275 EAT 7–16
Davies v Davies (1887) L.R. 36 Ch. D. 359 CA 19–15
Davies v London and Provincial Marine Insurance Co (1878) L.R. 8 Ch. D. 469; (1878) 26
    W.R. 794 Ch D 17–13
Davitt v Titcumb [1990] Ch. 110; [1990] 2 W.L.R. 168; [1989] 3 All E.R. 417 Ch
    D 5–29
Dawnay Day & Co Ltd v de Braconier d'Alphen [1998] I.C.R. 1068; [1997] I.R.L.R. 442;
    (1997) 94(26) L.S.G. 30; (1997) 141 S.J.L.B. 129 CA (Civ Div) 12–12, 12–19, 13–20,
                                                                                                    14–14
Dawson v Great Northern & City Railway Co [1905] 1 K.B. 260 CA 9–16
Daymond v Enterprise South Devon, 2007 7–19
Deacons v Bridge. See Bridge v Deacons
Defries v Milne [1913] 1 Ch. 98 CA 9–15, 9–16
Dennis & Co v Munn [1949] 2 K.B. 327; [1949] 1 All E.R. 616; 65 T.L.R. 251; [1949]
    L.J.R. 857; (1949) 93 S.J. 181 CA 1–16, 2–04, 2–23,
                                                                                                    2–25, 22–11
Dentmaster (UK) Ltd v Kent [1997] I.R.L.R. 636 CA (Civ Div) 13–20, 14–07
Deutsche Morgan Grenfell Group Plc v Inland Revenue Commissioners; sub nom. Inland
    Revenue Commissioners v Deutsche Morgan Grenfell Group Plc; Deutsche Morgan
    Grenfell Group Plc v Revenue and Customs Commissioners [2006] UKHL 49; [2007] 1
    A.C. 558; [2006] 3 W.L.R. 781; [2007] 1 All E.R. 449; [2007] S.T.C. 1; [2007] 1
    C.M.L.R. 14; [2007] Eu. L.R. 226; 78 T.C. 120; [2006] B.T.C. 781; 9 I.T.L. Rep. 201;
    [2006] S.T.I. 2386; (2006) 103(43) L.S.G. 29; (2006) 150 S.J.L.B. 1430 17–08
Dickson v Jones [1939] 3 All E.R. 182 . . . . 13–10, 13–14, 14–19
Dimond v Lovell [2002] 1 A.C. 384; [2000] 2 W.L.R. 1121; [2000] 2 All E.R. 897; [2000]
    R.T.R. 243; [2000] C.C.L.R. 57; 2000 Rep. L.R. 62; (2000) 97(22) L.S.G. 47; (2000)
    150 N.L.J. 740 HL 9–12
Dimskal Shipping Co SA v International Transport Workers Federation (The Evia Luck)
    (No.2) [1992] 2 A.C. 152; [1991] 3 W.L.R. 875; [1991] 4 All E.R. 871; [1992] 1 Lloyd's
    Rep. 115; [1992] I.C.R. 37; [1992] I.R.L.R. 78 HL 10–12
Dodge v Eisenman 68 B.C.L.R. 327 CA (BC) 2–21
Dorma UK Ltd v Bateman [2015] EWHC 4142 (QB); [2016] I.R.L.R. 616 14–14
Dott v Brickwell (1906) 23 T.L.R. 61 . . . . 17–19, 17–20

Dowling & Rutter v Abacus Frozen Foods Ltd (No.2) 2002 S.L.T. 491; 2001 G.W.D.
1-19 . . . . 3–18, 17–02
Drage v Ibberson (1798) 2 Esp. 643 8–06
Dranez Anstalt v Hayek [2002] EWCA Civ 1729; [2003] 1 B.C.L.C. 278; [2003] F.S.R. 32;
(2002) 146 S.J.L.B. 273 . . . . 12–12, 12–23
Dreadon v Fletcher Development Co Ltd [1974] 2 N.Z.L.R. 11 20–13
Dromorne Linen Co v Ward [1963] N.Z.L.R. 614 20–05
Duarte v Black & Decker Corp [2007] EWHC 2720 (QB); [2008] 1 All E.R. (Comm)
401 . . . . 13–20, 14–12
Dubowski & Sons v Goldstein [1896] 1 Q.B. 478 CA 14–03
Dunbar v Plant [1998] Ch. 412; [1997] 3 W.L.R. 1261; [1997] 4 All E.R. 289; [1998] 1
F.L.R. 157; [1997] 3 F.C.R. 669; [1998] Fam. Law 139; (1997) 94(36) L.S.G. 44; (1997)
141 S.J.L.B. 191 CA (Civ Div) 5–34, 5–37
Duncan v McDonald [1997] 3 N.Z.L.R. 669 20–11
DWS (Deceased), Re; EHS (Deceased), Re; TWGS (A Child) v JMG; sub nom. S
(Deceased), Re; S (A Child) v G [2001] Ch. 568; [2000] 3 W.L.R. 1910; [2001] 1 All
E.R. 97; [2001] 1 F.C.R. 339; [2001] W.T.L.R. 445; (2000) 97(46) L.S.G. 39; (2000) 150
N.L.J. 1788 CA (Civ Div) 5–30
East England Schools CIC (t/a 4MySchools) v Palmer [2013] EWHC 4138 (QB); [2014]
I.R.L.R. 191 19–03
Eastham v Newcastle United Football Club [1964] Ch. 413; [1963] 3 W.L.R. 574; [1963] 3
All E.R. 139; (1963) 107 S.J. 574 Ch D 11–23
Edler v Auerbach [1950] 1 K.B. 359; [1949] 2 All E.R. 692; 65 T.L.R. 645; (1949-51) 1 P.
& C.R. 10; (1949) 93 S.J. 727 KBD 2–21
Edwards v O'Connor [1989] 3 N.Z.L.R 448 20–14
Egerton v Brownlow 10 E.R. 359; (1853) 4 H.L. Cas. 1 QB 6–11, 6–12, 6–13,
8–01
Eisen v M'Cabe (1920) 57 Sc.L.R. 126 2–24
Elias v Walsam Investments (1964) 45 D.L.R. (2d) 561 2–22
Elsevier Ltd v Munro [2014] EWHC 2648 (QB); [2014] I.R.L.R. 766 . . . . 11–15, 14–09
Elsey v J.G. Collins Insurance Agencies (1978) 83 D.L.R. (3d) 1 12–19
Empire Meat Co v Patrick [1939 2 All E.R. 85 13–13
Enfield Technical Services Ltd v Payne; Grace v BF Components Ltd [2008] EWCA Civ
393; [2008] I.C.R. 1423; [2008] I.R.L.R. 500 7–18
English Hop Growers v Dering; sub nom. English Hop Growers Ltd v Dering [1928] 2 K.B.
174 CA 11–08, 12–16
Equuscorp Pty Ltd v Haxton [2012] HCA 7 17–17
Ernest's Char Pit v Demendeiros (1970) 15 D.L.R. (3d) 663 (Ontario) 13–15
Ertel Bieber & Co v Rio Tinto Co Ltd; Dynamit AG (Vormals Alfred Nobel Co) v Rio Tinto
Co Ltd; Vereingte Koenigs v Rio Tinto Co Ltd [1918] A.C. 260 HL 10–29
Esposito v Bowden (1857) 7 El. & Bl. 763 10–16
Esso Petroleum Co Ltd v Harper's Garage (Stourport) Ltd [1968] A.C. 269; [1967] 2 W.L.R.
871; [1967] 1 All E.R. 699; (1967) 111 S.J. 174 HL 11–01, 11–04, 11–05,
11–06, 11–13, 11–16, 11–17, 11–25,
12–11, 12–12, 12–13, 12–24, 12–25,
12–26, 12–27, 12–28, 12–30, 15–02,
15–03
Estate of Arnandh v Barnet Primary Health Care Trust [2004] EWCA Civ 5 2–17
Euro-Diam Ltd v Bathurst [1990] 1 Q.B. 1; [1988] 2 W.L.R. 517; [1988] 2 All E.R. 23;
[1988] 1 Lloyd's Rep. 228; [1988] F.T.L.R. 242; [1988] Fin. L.R. 27; (1988) 85(9)
L.S.G. 45; (1988) 132 S.J. 372 CA (Civ Div) 2–26, 4–12, 4–15,
4–19, 4–20, 10–04, 21–30
Euro-National Corporation v NZI Bank Ltd [1992] 2 N.Z.L.R 739 20–14
Evans v Credit Services [1975] 2 N.Z.L.R. 560 20–12
Everet v Williams (1893) 9 L.Q.R. 106 . . . . 1–01, 17–04
Excalibur Ventures LLC v Texas Keystone Inc; Texas Keystone Inc v Psari Holdings Ltd;
sub nom. Psari Holdings Ltd v Association of Litigation Funders of England and Wales
[2016] EWCA Civ 1144; [2016] 6 Costs L.O. 999; [2017] C.I.L.L. 3919 9–26
Explora Group Plc v Hesco Bastion Ltd; Explora Group Ltd v Trading Force Ltd [2005]
EWCA Civ 646; (2005) 149 S.J.L.B. 924 15–11
Express Dairy Co v Jackson (1929) 99 L.J.K.B. 181 14–03

Faccenda Chicken Ltd v Fowler; Fowler v Faccenda Chicken Ltd [1987] Ch. 117; [1986] 3
    W.L.R. 288; [1986] 1 All E.R. 617; [1986] I.C.R. 297; [1986] I.R.L.R. 69; [1986] F.S.R.
    291; (1986) 83 L.S.G. 288; (1986) 136 N.L.J. 71; (1986) 130 S.J. 573 CA (Civ
    Div) 12–04, 12–08, 12–09
Factortame Ltd v Secretary of State for the Environment, Transport and the Regions (Costs)
    (No.2); sub nom.: R. (on the application of Factortame Ltd) v Secretary of State for
    Transport, Local Government and the Regions (Costs: Champertous Agreement) [2002]
    EWCA Civ 932; [2003] Q.B. 381; [2002] 3 W.L.R. 1104; [2002] 4 All E.R. 97; [2003]
    B.L.R. 1; [2002] 3 Costs L.R. 467; (2002) 99(35) L.S.G. 34; (2002) 152 N.L.J. 1313;
    (2002) 146 S.J.L.B. 178 . . . . .9–13, 9–24, 9–25,
                                                                                                                       9–29
Fallowes v Taylor (1798) 7 T.R. 475 8–06
Farmers Mart Ltd v Milne [1915] A.C. 106; 1914 S.C. (H.L.) 84; 1914 2 S.L.T. 153
    HL 7–05
Farrow v Edgar (1993) 114 A.L.R. 1 18–07
Fender v St John Mildmay; sub nom. Fender v Mildmay [1938] A.C. 1 HL 6–10, 6–11, 6–14,
                                                                                                                  6–15
Fentem (Deceased), Re; sub nom. Cockerton v Fentem [1950] 2 All E.R. 1073; [1950] W.N.
    543; (1950) 94 S.J. 779 Ch D 6–18
Fenton v Scotty's Car Sales [1968] N.Z.L.R. 929 . . . . .20–05, 22–05
Feret v Hill, 139 E.R. 400; (1854) 15 C.B. 207 Comm Pl 16–01, 16–04
Fibrosa Spolka Akcyjna v Fairbairn Lawson Combe Barbour Ltd; sub nom. Fibrosa Societe
    Anonyme v Fairbairn Lawson Combe Barbour Ltd [1943] A.C. 32; [1942] 2 All E.R.
    122; (1942) 73 Ll. L. Rep. 45; 144 A.L.R. 1298 HL 17–09
Field v Leeds City Council [1999] C.P.L.R. 833; [2001] C.P.L.R. 129; (2000) 32 H.L.R.
    618; [2000] 1 E.G.L.R. 54; [2000] 17 E.G. 165 CA (Civ Div) 9–25
Fielding & Platt Ltd v Selim Najjar [1969] 1 W.L.R. 357; [1969] 2 All E.R. 150; (1969) 113
    S.J. 160 CA (Civ Div) 4–12, 19–25
Fisher & Co v Apollinaris Co (1874-75) L.R. 10 Ch. App. 297 CA in
    Chancery 8–07, 8–08
Fisher v Bridges 118 E.R. 1283; (1854) 3 El. & Bl. 642 QB 4–14, 4–15
Fitch v Dewes; sub nom. Dewes v Fitch [1921] 2 A.C. 158 HL 13–14, 14–18, 14–19,
                                                                                                                 14–22
Fitzgerald v F.J. Leonardt (1997) 189 C.L.R. 215 . . . . .1–05, 1–10, 2–26,
                                                                                                                3–16, 21–27
Fitzroy v Cave [1905] 2 K.B. 364 CA 9–16
Flower v Sadler (1882-83) L.R. 10 Q.B.D. 572 CA 8–13
Force India Formula One Team Ltd v 1 Malaysia Racing Team Sdn Bhd; sub nom. Force
    India Formula One Team Ltd v Aerolab SRL (an Italian company) [2013] EWCA Civ
    780; [2013] R.P.C. 36 12–09
Foster v Driscoll; Lindsay v Attfield; Lindsay v Driscoll [1929] 1 K.B. 470
    CA 4–09, 10–05, 10–06,
                                                                                                                10–13
France v Might [1987] 2 N.Z.L.R. 38 20–12
Francotyp-Postalia Ltd v Whitehead [2011] EWHC 367 (Ch) 19–04, 19–13
Fried Krupp Aktiengesellashaft v Orconera Iron Ore Co [1918] 88 L.J. Ch.
    304 10–29
FSS Travel & Leisure Systems Ltd v Johnson [1998] I.R.L.R. 382; [1999] I.T.C.L.R. 218;
    [1999] F.S.R. 505 CA (Civ Div) 12–04, 22–19
Fuji Finance Inc v Aetna Life Insurance Co Ltd [1997] Ch. 173; [1996] 3 W.L.R. 871;
    [1996] 4 All E.R. 608; [1996] L.R.L.R. 365; [1997] C.L.C. 141 CA (Civ
    Div) 2–14, 21–29
Galsworthy v Strutt (1848) 1 Exch. 659 11–08
Gardner v Moore [1984] A.C. 548; [1984] 2 W.L.R. 714; [1984] 1 All E.R. 1100; [1984] 2
    Lloyd's Rep. 135; [1984] R.T.R. 209; (1984) 81 L.S.G. 1444; (1984) 128 S.J. 282
    HL 5–15, 5–21
Gartside v Outram (1856) 26 L.J. Ch. 113 Ch D 7–36, 7–38
Gas and Light Coke Co v Turner (1839) 5 Bing. N.C. 666 . . . . .4–14, 16–04

Geismar v Sun Alliance and London Insurance Ltd [1978] Q.B. 383; [1978] 2 W.L.R. 38;
    [1977] 3 All E.R. 570; [1977] 2 Lloyd's Rep. 62; [1977] Crim. L.R. 475; (1977) 121 S.J.
    201 QBD 3–16, 4–20, 4–21,
                                                                                                      10–04
General Billposting Co Ltd v Atkinson [1909] A.C. 118 HL 15–07, 15–08, 15–09,
                                                                                    15–10, 15–11, 15–12, 15–14
Generics (UK) Ltd v Yeda Research and Development Co Ltd [2012] EWCA Civ 726;
    [2013] Bus. L.R. 777; [2012] C.P. Rep. 39; [2013] F.S.R. 13 12–08
George v Greater Adelaide Land Development Co (1929) 43 C.L.R. 91 . . . . . . .2–19, 2–20, 2–21,
                                                                                                      2–24
Geraghty v Minter 142 C.L.R. 177 13–19
Geys v Societe Generale; sub nom. Societe Generale (London Branch) v Geys [2012] UKSC
    63; [2013] 1 A.C. 523; [2013] 2 W.L.R. 50; [2013] 1 All E.R. 1061; [2013] I.C.R. 117;
    [2013] I.R.L.R. 122. 15–07
Giles v Thompson; Devlin v Baslington; Sanders v Templar [1994] 1 A.C. 142; [1993] 2
    W.L.R. 908; [1993] 3 All E.R. 321; [1993] R.T.R. 289; (1993) 143 N.L.J. 884; (1993)
    137 S.J.L.B. 151 HL 9–02, 9–03, 9–04,
                                                                                    9–12, 9–13, 9–26, 9–28, 9–31
Giles, Re; sub nom. Giles v Giles [1972] Ch. 544; [1971] 3 W.L.R. 640; [1971] 3 All E.R.
    1141; (1971) 115 S.J. 428 Ch D 5–31
Gilford Motor Co Ltd v Horne [1933] Ch. 935 CA. 13–17, 13–18, 14–04,
                                                                                    14–05, 22–21
Gillespie Management Corp v Terrace Properties (1989) 62 D.L.R. (4th) 221 CA (British
    Columbia). 10–02
Gillingham BC v Medway (Chatham Docks) Co Ltd [1993] Q.B. 343; [1992] 3 W.L.R. 449;
    [1992] 3 All E.R. 923; [1993] Env. L.R. 98; 91 L.G.R. 160; (1992) 63 P. & C.R. 205;
    [1992] 1 P.L.R. 113; [1992] J.P.L. 458; [1991] E.G. 101 (C.S.); [1991] N.P.C. 97
    QBD 11–19
Gledhow Autoparts v Delaney [1965] 1 W.L.R. 1366; [1965] 3 All E.R. 288; (1965) 109 S.J.
    571 CA 11–12, 13–08, 13–10,
                                                                                                      14–07
Glegg v Bromley [1912] 3 K.B. 474 CA 9–15, 9–16
Globex Foreign Exchange Corp v Kelcher (2011) 337 DLR (4th) 202, 2011 ABCA
    240 15–12
Gnych v Polish Club Ltd [2015] HCA 23 2–05
Golden Eye (International) Ltd v Telefonica UK Ltd [2012] EWHC 723 (Ch); [2013]
    E.M.L.R. 1; [2012] R.P.C. 28 9–13
Goldsoll v Goldman [1915] 1 Ch. 292 CA 19–06, 19–07, 19–18,
                                                                                    19–20, 22–21
Goodinson v Goodinson [1954] 2 Q.B. 118; [1954] 2 W.L.R. 1121; [1954] 2 All E.R. 255;
    (1954) 98 S.J. 369 CA 8–02, 19–10, 19–16,
                                                                                                      19–23
Gordon v Commissioner of Police of the Metropolis [1910] 2 K.B. 1080 CA 7–11, 16–01
Gray v Barr [1971] 2 Q.B. 554; [1971] 2 W.L.R. 1334; [1971] 2 All E.R. 949; [1971] 2
    Lloyd's Rep. 1; (1971) 115 S.J. 364 CA (Civ Div) 5–16, 5–17, 5–18,
                                                                                    5–21, 5–22, 5–24, 5–31, 22–03
Gray v Southouse [1949] 2 All E.R. 1019 KBD 18–05
Gray v Thames Trains Ltd [2009] UKHL 33; [2009] 1 A.C. 1339; [2009] 3 W.L.R. 167;
    [2009] 4 All E.R. 81; [2009] P.I.Q.R. P22; [2009] LS Law Medical 409; (2009) 108
    B.M.L.R. 205; [2009] M.H.L.R. 73; [2009] Po. L.R. 229; (2009) 159 N.L.J. 925; (2009)
    153(24) S.J.L.B. 33 . . . . .5–02, 5–10, 5–40
Great Peace Shipping Ltd v Tsavliris Salvage (International) Ltd [2002] EWCA Civ 1407;
    [2003] Q.B. 679; [2002] 3 W.L.R. 1617; [2002] 4 All E.R. 689; [2002] 2 All E.R.
    (Comm) 999; [2002] 2 Lloyd's Rep. 653; [2003] 2 C.L.C. 16; (2002) 99(43) L.S.G. 34;
    (2002) 152 N.L.J. 1616; [2002] N.P.C. 127 3–06
Green v Portsmouth Stadium [1953] 2 Q.B. 190; [1953] 2 W.L.R. 1206; [1953] 2 All E.R.
    102; (1953) 97 S.J. 386 CA 18–08
Green v Stanton (1969) 6 D.L.E. (3d) 680 . . . . .12–16, 14–17
Greer v Sketchley Ltd [1979] I.R.L.R. 445; [1979] F.S.R. 197 CA (Civ Div) . 12–01, 12–06, 13–05,
                                                                                                      13–07

Griffin v UHY Hacker Young & Partners (A Firm) [2010] EWHC 146 (Ch); [2010] P.N.L.R.
20 5–09
Group Josi Re Co SA v Walbrook Insurance Co Ltd; sub nom. Group Josi Re (formerly
Group Josi Reassurance SA) v Walbrook Insurance Co Ltd; Deutsche Ruckversicherung
AG v Walbrook Insurance Co Ltd [1996] 1 W.L.R. 1152; [1996] 1 All E.R. 791; [1996]
1 Lloyd's Rep. 345; [1995] C.L.C. 1532; [1996] 5 Re. L.R. 91 CA (Civ
Div) 2–14
Grovewood Holdings Plc v James Capel & Co Ltd [1995] Ch. 80; [1995] 2 W.L.R. 70;
[1994] 4 All E.R. 417; [1995] B.C.C. 760; [1994] 2 B.C.L.C. 782; [1994] E.G. 136
(C.S.); (1994) 144 N.L.J. 1405 Ch D 9–26
Gurwicz Ex p. Trustee, Re [1919] 1 K.B. 675 KBD 8–01
GW Plowman & Son Ltd v Ash; sub nom. Plowman (GW) & Son v Ash [1964] 1 W.L.R.
568; [1964] 2 All E.R. 10; (1964) 108 S.J. 216 CA 13–02, 13–20, 14–05,
14–06, 14–07
H (Deceased), Re [1990] 1 F.L.R. 441; [1990] Fam. Law 175 . . . . 5–31, 5–34, 5–36
H & R Block v Sanott [1976] 1 N.Z.L.R. 213 . . . . 11–08, 13–21
Hall v Woolston Hall Leisure Ltd [2001] 1 W.L.R. 225; [2000] 4 All E.R. 787; [2001] I.C.R.
99; [2000] I.R.L.R. 578; (2000) 97(24) L.S.G. 39; (2000) 150 N.L.J. 833 CA (Civ
Div) 7–16, 22–15
Hall's Estate, Re [1914] P.1 CA 5–30
Halsey v Lowenfeld [1916] 2 K.B. 707 CA 10–19
Hamilton v Al-Fayed (Costs); sub nom. Hamilton v Fayed (Costs); Al-Fayed v Hamilton
(Costs) [2002] EWCA Civ 665; [2003] Q.B. 1175; [2003] 2 W.L.R. 128; [2002] 3 All
E.R. 641; [2002] C.P. Rep. 48; [2002] 3 Costs L.R. 389; [2002] E.M.L.R. 42; (2002)
99(25) L.S.G. 34; (2002) 146 S.J.L.B. 143 9–25
Hanover Insurance Brokers Ltd v Schapiro [1994] I.R.L.R. 82 CA (Civ Div) . 13–06, 14–03, 14–13,
14–14
Harding v Coburn [1976] 2 N.Z.L.R. 577 . . . . 20–13, 20–14
Hardy v Motor Insurers Bureau [1964] 2 Q.B. 745; [1964] 3 W.L.R. 433; [1964] 2 All E.R.
742; [1964] 1 Lloyd's Rep. 397; (1964) 108 S.J. 422 CA 5–14, 5–15, 5–16,
5–21
Harse v Pearl Life Assurance Co [1904] 1 K.B. 558 CA 17–08
Haseldine v Hosken [1933] 1 K.B. 822; (1933) 45 Ll. L. Rep. 59 CA 5–18
Haugesund Kommune v Depfa ACS Bank [2010] EWCA Civ 579; [2012] Q.B. 549; [2012]
2 W.L.R. 199; [2011] 1 All E.R. 190; [2011] 1 All E.R. (Comm) 985; [2012] Bus. L.R.
1; [2010] 1 C.L.C. 770 . . . . 17–08, 17–09
Haynes v Doman [1899] 2 Ch. 13 CA 13–04, 13–20
Haywood v Whitaker (1887) 3 T.L.R. 537 8–19
Hazell v Hammersmith and Fulham LBC [1992] 2 A.C. 1; [1991] 2 W.L.R. 372; [1991] 1
All E.R. 545; 89 L.G.R. 271; (1991) 3 Admin. L.R. 549; [1991] R.V.R. 28; (1991) 155
J.P.N. 527; (1991) 155 L.G. Rev. 527; (1991) 88(8) L.S.G. 36; (1991) 141 N.L.J. 127
HL 17–01
Heglibiston Establishments v Heyman (1978) 36 P. & C.R. 351; (1977) 246 E.G. 567;
(1977) 121 S.J. 851 CA (Civ Div) 6–22
Hensman v Traill (1980) 124 S.J. 776 14–17
Hentig v Staniforth (1816) 5 M. & S. 122 17–07
Herbert Morris Ltd v Saxelby [1916] 1 A.C. 688 HL 11–01, 11–02, 11–05,
12–01, 12–02, 12–11
Herman v Jeuchner (1884-85) L.R. 15 Q.B.D. 561 CA 8–01
Hermann v Charlesworth [1905] 2 K.B. 123 CA 6–19, 6–20
Hewcastle Catering v Ahmed and Elkamah [1992] I.C.R. 626; [1991] I.R.L.R. 473 CA (Civ
Div) 7–15, 7–16, 22–15
Hewison v Meridian Shipping Services Pte Ltd; sub nom. Hewison v Meridian Shipping Pte
[2002] EWCA Civ 1821; [2003] I.C.R. 766; [2003] P.I.Q.R. P17; (2003) 147 S.J.L.B.
24 5–40
HF Clarke v Thermidaire Corp (1974) 5 D.L.R. (3d) 385 SC (Can) 11–08
Hickman v Turner and Waverley Ltd [2012] NZSC 72; [2013] 1 NLZR 741 20–05
Hill v Archbold [1968] 1 Q.B. 686; [1967] 3 W.L.R. 1218; [1967] 3 All E.R. 110; 3 K.I.R.
40; (1967) 111 S.J. 543 CA (Civ Div) 9–09
Hill v Missouri Pacific Railway Co (1933) 8 F.Supp (W.D.La) 18–06

Hinton & Higgs (UK) Ltd v Murphy 1988 S.C. 353; 1989 S.L.T. 450; 1989 S.C.L.R. 42
    OH 19–15
Hitchcock v Coker (1836) 6 Ad. & El. 438 11–11
Hodgson v Temple (1813) 5 Taunt. 181 . . . . 4–09, 4–10
Holdcraft v Market Garden Produce [2000] Q.C.A. 396 7–11
Holland v Hall (1817) 1 B. & Ald. 53 2–21
Hollis & Co v Stocks [2000] U.K.C.L.R. 658; [2000] I.R.L.R. 712 CA (Civ
    Div) 14–19
Holman v Johnson 98 E.R. 1120; (1775) 1 Cowp. 341 KB 4–10, 10–04
Home Counties Dairies v Skilton [1970] 1 W.L.R. 526; [1970] 1 All E.R. 1227; 8 K.I.R.
    691; (1970) 114 S.J. 107 CA (Civ Div) 13–02, 13–07, 14–05
Hoop, The (1799) 1 Ch.Rob. 196 . . . . 10–16, 10–21
Horwood v Millar's Timber & Trading Co Ltd [1917] 1 K.B. 305 CA 15–05
Hounga v Allen. See Allen v Hounga
Hoverd Industries Ltd v Supercool Refrigeration Ltd [1994] 3 N.Z.L.R 300 20–14
Howard v Odhams Press Ltd [1938] 1 K.B. 1 CA 7–32, 7–33, 8–21
Howard v Shirlstar Container Transport [1990] 1 W.L.R. 1292; [1990] 3 All E.R. 366 CA
    (Civ Div) 1–02, 1–05, 21–30
Howick Building Co Ltd v Howick Parklands Ltd [1993] 1 N.Z.L.R. 759 20–13
Hubbard v Vosper [1972] 2 Q.B. 84; [1972] 2 W.L.R. 389; [1972] 1 All E.R. 1023; (1972)
    116 S.J. 95 CA (Civ Div) 7–36
Hugh Stephenson & Sons Ltd v Carton Nagen Industrie AG; sub nom. Hugh Stevenson &
    Sons Ltd v Cartonnagen-Industrie AG [1918] A.C. 239 HL 10–20
Hughes v Asset Managers Plc [1995] 3 All E.R. 669; [1994] C.L.C. 556 CA (Civ
    Div) 2–15, 21–29
Hughes v Kingston upon Hull City Council [1999] Q.B. 1193; [1999] 2 W.L.R. 1229;
    [1999] 2 All E.R. 49; [1999] Env. L.R. 579; (1999) 31 H.L.R. 779; (1998) 95(44) L.S.G.
    36; (1999) 143 S.J.L.B. 54 DC 9–23, 9–29
Hughes v Liverpool Victoria Legal Friendly Society [1916] 2 K.B. 482 CA 17–19
Hurrell v Townend [1976] 2 N.Z.L.R. 577 20–14
Husak v Imperial Life Assurance Co of Canada (1970) 9 D.L.R. 602 5–24
Hyland v JH Barker (North West) [1985] I.C.R. 861; [1985] I.R.L.R. 403; (1985) 82 L.S.G.
    2740 EAT 7–13
Hyman v Hyman; Hughes v Hughes [1929] A.C. 601 HL 8–02, 19–10
IBM United Kingdom Holdings Ltd v Dalgleish [2015] EWHC 389 (Ch); [2015] Pens. L.R.
    99 19–12
ICT Pty v Sea Containers (1995) N.S.W.L.R. 640 13–22
IMG Pension Plan, Re; sub nom. HR Trustees Ltd v German International Management
    Group (UK) Ltd v German [2009] EWHC 2785 (Ch); [2010] Pens. L.R.
    237 8–03
Ingham v ABC Contract Services Ltd Unreported CA (Civ Div) 14–14
Initial Services v Putterill [1968] 1 Q.B. 396; [1967] 3 W.L.R. 1032; [1967] 3 All E.R. 145;
    2 K.I.R. 863; (1967) 111 S.J. 541 CA (Civ Div) 7–37
Investors Compensation Scheme Ltd v West Bromwich Building Society (No.1); Investors
    Compensation Scheme Ltd v Hopkin & Sons; Alford v West Bromwich Building
    Society; Armitage v West Bromwich Building Society [1998] 1 W.L.R. 896; [1998] 1 All
    E.R. 98; [1998] 1 B.C.L.C. 531; [1997] C.L.C. 1243; [1997] P.N.L.R. 541; (1997) 147
    N.L.J. 989 HL 13–01
Israel Discount Bank of New York v Hadjipateras [1984] 1 W.L.R. 137; [1983] 3 All E.R.
    129; [1983] 2 Lloyd's Rep. 490; (1984) 81 L.S.G. 37; (1983) 127 S.J. 822 CA (Civ
    Div) 10–12
J v ST (formerly J) (Transsexual: Ancillary Relief); sub nom. ST v J (Transsexual: Void
    Marriage) [1998] Fam. 103; [1997] 3 W.L.R. 1287; [1998] 1 All E.R. 431; [1997] 1
    F.L.R. 402; [1997] 1 F.C.R. 349; [1997] Fam. Law 239 CA (Civ Div) 5–41, 6–10, 6–17
JA Mont (UK) Ltd v Mills [1993] I.R.L.R. 172; [1993] F.S.R. 577 CA (Civ
    Div) 12–04, 13–06
Jackson Stansfield & Sons v Butterworth [1948] 2 All E.R. 558; 64 T.L.R. 481; (1948) 112
    J.P. 377; 46 L.G.R. 410; [1948] W.N. 315; (1948) 92 S.J. 469 CA 1–16
Jajbhay v Cassim [1939] A.D. 537 . . . . 16–17, 17–02, 17–16
James v British General Insurance Co Ltd [1927] 2 K.B. 311; (1927) 27 Ll. L. Rep. 328
    KBD 5–10, 5–13

Jamieson v Watt's Trustee, 1950 S.C. 265; 1950 S.L.T. 232 2–25
Janson v Driefontein Consolidated Mines Ltd; West Rand Central Gold Mines Co Ltd v De
    Rougemont; sub nom. Driefontein Consolidated Gold Mines Ltd v Janson [1902] A.C.
    484 HL. 6–05, 6–06, 6–10,
                                                                                              10–21
Jebara v Ottoman Bank; sub nom. Jebara v Imperial Ottoman Bank; Ottoman Bank v Jebara;
    Jebara v Imperial Ottoman Bank; Jebara v Imperial Ottoman Bank [1928] A.C. 269;
    (1928) 31 Ll. L. Rep. 37 HL 10–27
Jenkins Deed of Partnership, Re; sub nom. Jenkins v Reid [1948] 1 All E.R. 471; [1948]
    W.N. 98; (1948) 92 S.J. 142 Ch D 13–19, 14–15, 14–17
JM Finn & Co Ltd v Holliday [2013] EWHC 3450 (QB); [2014] I.R.L.R. 102 11–17
John Michael Design Plc v Cooke [1987] 2 All E.R. 332; [1987] I.C.R. 445; [1987] F.S.R.
    402; (1987) 84 L.S.G. 1492; (1987) 131 S.J. 595 CA (Civ Div). 14–05, 15–16, 15–19
Johnson v Hudson (1809) 11 East 180 2–08
Johnson v Musselman (1917) 37 D.L.R. 162 (Can). 8–16
Johnson v Ogilby (1734) 3 P. Wins. 277 8–06
Jones (John Keith) v Roberts (John Ronald) [1995] 2 F.L.R. 422; [1995] Fam. Law 673 Ch
    D 5–31, 5–34, 22–03
Jones v Kernott; sub nom. Kernott v Jones [2011] UKSC 53; [2012] 1 A.C. 776; [2011] 3
    W.L.R. 1121; [2012] 1 All E.R. 1265; [2012] 1 F.L.R. 45; [2011] 3 F.C.R. 495; [2011]
    B.P.I.R. 1653; [2012] H.L.R. 14; [2012] W.T.L.R. 125; 14 I.T.E.L.R. 491; [2011] Fam.
    Law 1338; [2011] 46 E.G. 104 (C.S.); (2011) 155(43) S.J.L.B. 35; [2011] N.P.C. 116;
    [2012] 1 P. & C.R. DG9 16–08
Jones v Merionethshire Permanent Benefit Building Society [1892] 1 Ch. 173
    CA 8–04, 8–15, 8–16,
                                                                                          8–19, 17–11
Joseph Evans & Co v Heathcote [1918] 1 K.B. 418 CA 11–10
Joseph v Spiller; sub nom. Spiller v Joseph [2010] UKSC 53; [2011] 1 A.C. 852; [2010] 3
    W.L.R. 1791; [2011] 1 All E.R. 947; [2011] I.C.R. 1; [2011] E.M.L.R. 11; (2010)
    107(48) L.S.G. 13; (2010) 160 N.L.J. 171 2–05
K (Deceased), Re [1986] Ch. 180; [1985] 3 W.L.R. 234; [1985] 2 All E.R. 833; [1986] Fam.
    Law 19; (1985) 82 L.S.G. 2242; (1985) 135 N.L.J. 655; (1985) 129 S.J. 364 CA (Civ
    Div) 5–36
KA & C Smith Pty v Ward (1998) 45 N.S.W.L.R. 702 . . . . .13–22, 13–23
Kasumu v Baba-Egbe [1956] A.C. 539; [1956] 3 W.L.R. 575; [1956] 3 All E.R. 266; (1956)
    100 S.J. 600 PC (West Africa) 18–07
Kaufman v Gerson [1904] 1 K.B. 591 CA 8–19, 10–11, 10–12
Kearley v Thomson (1890) L.R. 24 Q.B.D. 742 CA 18–02
Kearney v Whitehaven Colliery Co [1893] 1 Q.B. 700 CA 19–10
Keir v Leeman (1846) 9 L.J. Q.B. 371 . . . . .8–06, 8–07
Kemp v Glasgow Corp [1920] A.C. 836; 1920 S.C. (H.L.) 73; 1920 2 S.L.T. 6
    HL 7–26
Kerchiss v Colora Printing Inks [1960] R.P.C. 235 . . . . .11–18, 12–03
Kerr v Morris [1987] Ch. 90; [1986] 3 W.L.R. 662; [1986] 3 All E.R. 217; (1986) 83 L.S.G.
    2570; (1986) 130 S.J. 665 CA (Civ Div) 14–17
Kerridge v Simmonds (1906) 4 C.L.R. 253 . . . . .7–32, 7–34, 8–08,
                                                                                          8–09
Kiddus v Chief Constable of Leicestershire Constabulary [2001] 3 All E.R.
    193 5–19
Kingshott v Brunskill [1953] O.W.N. 133 . . . . .21–09, 21–10
Kiriri Cotton Co Ltd v Dewani; sub nom. Kiriri Cotton Ct v Dewani [1960] A.C. 192;
    [1960] 2 W.L.R. 127; [1960] 1 All E.R. 177; (1960) 104 S.J. 49 PC (EA) 18–05
Kleinwort Benson Ltd v Lincoln City Council; Kleinwort Benson Ltd v Birmingham City
    Council; Kleinwort Benson Ltd v Southwark LBC; Kleinwort Benson Ltd v Kensington
    and Chelsea RLBC [1999] 2 A.C. 349; [1998] 3 W.L.R. 1095; [1998] 4 All E.R. 513;
    [1998] Lloyd's Rep. Bank. 387; [1999] C.L.C. 332; (1999) 1 L.G.L.R. 148; (1999) 11
    Admin. L.R. 130; [1998] R.V.R. 315; (1998) 148 N.L.J. 1674; (1998) 142 S.J.L.B. 279;
    [1998] N.P.C. 145 HL 3–06, 3–10, 4–32,
                                                                                          17–01, 17–08, 18–08

Kores Manufacturing Co Ltd v Kolok Manufacturing Co Ltd [1959] Ch. 108; [1958] 2
    W.L.R. 858; [1958] 2 All E.R. 65; [1958] R.P.C. 200; (1958) 102 S.J. 362
    CA 11–23, 14–13
Kremen v Agrest [2013] EWCA Civ 41; [2013] 2 F.L.R. 187; [2013] 2 F.C.R. 181; [2013]
    B.P.I.R. 497; [2013] Fam. Law 669 6–18
Kuenigl v Donnersmarck [1955] 1 Q.B. 515; [1955] 2 W.L.R. 82; [1955] 1 All E.R. 46;
    (1955) 99 S.J. 60 QBD 10–18
Lamb v Cotogno (1987) 164 C.L.R. 1 . . . . 5–20, 5–21, 5–22
Lancashire CC v Municipal Mutual Insurance Ltd [1997] Q.B. 897; [1996] 3 W.L.R. 493;
    [1996] 3 All E.R. 545; [1996] C.L.C. 1459; (1996) 160 L.G. Rev. 612; (1996) 93(21)
    L.S.G. 27; (1996) 140 S.J.L.B. 108 CA (Civ Div) 5–19
Land v Land (Deceased); sub nom. Land, In the Estate of [2006] EWHC 2069 (Ch); [2007]
    1 W.L.R. 1009; [2007] 1 All E.R. 324; [2006] W.T.L.R. 1447 . . . . 5–32, 5–35, 5–39
Landall v Bogaers [1980] W.A.R. 33 2–20
Langton v Hughes 105 E.R. 222; (1813) 1 M. & S. 593 KB 4–09
Lansing Linde Ltd v Kerr [1991] 1 W.L.R. 251; [1991] 1 All E.R. 418; [1991] I.C.R. 428;
    [1991] I.R.L.R. 80; (1990) 140 N.L.J. 1458 CA (Civ Div) 12–06, 15–17, 15–18
Launchbury v Morgans; sub nom. Morgans v Launchbury [1973] A.C. 127; [1972] 2 W.L.R.
    1217; [1972] 2 All E.R. 606; [1972] 1 Lloyd's Rep. 483; [1972] R.T.R. 406; (1972) 116
    S.J. 396 HL 6–04
Laurent v Sale & Co [1963] 1 W.L.R. 829; [1963] 2 All E.R. 63; [1963] 1 Lloyd's Rep. 157;
    (1963) 107 S.J. 665 QBD 9–15, 9–17, 9–27
Lavelle v Lavelle [2004] EWCA Civ 223; [2004] 2 F.C.R. 418 16–10
Lawrence David Ltd v Ashton [1991] 1 All E.R. 385; [1989] I.C.R. 123; [1989] I.R.L.R. 22;
    [1989] 1 F.S.R. 87; (1988) 85(42) L.S.G. 48 CA (Civ Div) 11–12, 15–14, 15–16,
                                                                                  15–18
Lediaev v Vallen; sub nom. Ladyaev v Vallen [2009] EWCA Civ 156; (2009) 106(11) L.S.G.
    20 1–09
Leith v Gould [1986] 1 N.Z.L.R 760 20–14
Lemenda Trading Co Ltd v African Middle East Petroleum Co Ltd [1988] Q.B. 448; [1988]
    2 W.L.R. 735; [1988] 1 All E.R. 513; [1988] 1 Lloyd's Rep. 361; [1988] 1 F.T.L.R. 123;
    (1988) 132 S.J. 538 QBD (Comm) 10–07, 10–09
Les Laboratoires Servier v Apotex Inc [2012] EWCA Civ 593; [2013] Bus. L.R. 80; [2013]
    R.P.C. 21 3–16
Les Laboratoires Servier v Apotex Inc [2014] UKSC 55; [2015] A.C. 430; [2014] 3 W.L.R.
    1257; [2015] 1 All E.R. 671; [2014] Bus. L.R. 1217; [2015] R.P.C. 10 . . . . . I–01, 1–04, 1–08,
                                                                                  21–18
Lion Laboratories Ltd v Evans [1985] Q.B. 526; [1984] 3 W.L.R. 539; [1984] 2 All E.R.
    417; (1984) 81 L.S.G. 1233; (1984) 81 L.S.G. 2000; (1984) 128 S.J. 533 CA (Civ
    Div) 7–35, 7–36
Lipkin Gorman v Karpnale Ltd [1991] 2 A.C. 548; [1991] 3 W.L.R. 10; [1992] 4 All E.R.
    512; (1991) 88(26) L.S.G. 31; (1991) 141 N.L.J. 815; (1991) 135 S.J.L.B. 36
    HL 17–01, 17–09
Lister v Romford Ice and Cold Storage Co Ltd; sub nom. Romford Ice & Cold Storage Co v
    Lister [1957] A.C. 555; [1957] 2 W.L.R. 158; [1957] 1 All E.R. 125; [1956] 2 Lloyd's
    Rep. 505; (1957) 121 J.P. 98; (1957) 101 S.J. 106 HL 5–12
Littlewoods Organisation Ltd v Harris [1977] 1 W.L.R. 1472; [1978] 1 All E.R. 1026;
    (1977) 121 S.J. 727 CA (Civ Div) 12–07, 12–08, 13–04,
                                                                   13–06, 13–23, 14–08, 14–09, 14–12,
                                                                                  22–21
Liverpool Roman Catholic Archdiocesan Trustees Inc v Goldberg (No.3); sub nom.
    Liverpool Roman Catholic Archdiocesan Trust v Goldberg (No.3); Liverpool Roman
    Catholic Archdiocese Trustees Inc v Goldberg (No.3) [2001] 1 W.L.R. 2337; [2001] 4
    All E.R. 950; [2001] B.L.R. 479; [2002] T.C.L.R. 4; (2001) 98(32) L.S.G. 37; (2001)
    151 N.L.J. 1093 Ch D 9–25
Living Design (Home Improvements) Ltd v Davidson 1994 S.L.T. 753; [1994] I.R.L.R. 67
    OH 15–09
Lloyd v Johnson (1798) 1 Bos. & P. 340 6–24
Lloyds Bank Ltd v Bundy [1975] Q.B. 326; [1974] 3 W.L.R. 501; [1974] 3 All E.R. 757;
    [1974] 2 Lloyd's Rep. 366; (1974) 118 S.J. 714 CA (Civ Div) 15–06

Lock International Plc v Beswick [1989] 1 W.L.R. 1268; [1989] 3 All E.R. 373; [1989]
　I.R.L.R. 481; (1989) 86(39) L.S.G. 36; (1989) 139 N.L.J. 644; (1989) S.J. 1297 Ch
　D 12–03
Lodge v National Union Investment Co Ltd [1907] 1 Ch. 300 Ch D 18–07
Lound v Grimwade (1888) L.R. 39 Ch. D. 605 Ch D 8–15, 8–21, 19–10
Love's Realty and Financial Services Ltd v Coronet Trust (1989) 57 D.L.R. (4th)
　606 21–25
Lower Hutt City Council v Martin [1987] 1 N.Z.L.R 321 20–14
Lowson v Coombes [1999] Ch. 373; [1999] 2 W.L.R. 720; [1999] 1 F.L.R. 799; [1999] 2
　F.C.R. 731; [1999] Fam. Law 91; (1999) 96(1) L.S.G. 23; (1999) 77 P. & C.R. D25 CA
　(Civ Div) 16–08, 16–11
Lu v Lim (1993) 30 N.S.W.L.R. 332 14–20
Lumley v Wagner 42 E.R. 687; (1852) 1 De G.M. & G. 604 QB 11–15
Lyne-Pirkis v Jones [1969] 1 W.L.R. 1293; [1969] 3 All E.R. 738; (1969) 113 S.J. 568 CA
　(Civ Div) 13–01, 14–15, 14–16,
　14–17, 14–20
M&S Drapers (A Firm) v Reynolds [1957] 1 W.L.R. 9; [1956] 3 All E.R. 814; (1957) 101
　S.J. 44 CA 13–16, 13–18, 13–20,
　14–03
MacDonald v Myerson [2001] EWCA Civ 66; [2001] 6 E.G. 162 (C.S.); (2001) 98(6)
　L.S.G. 47; [2001] N.P.C. 20 16–01
MacDonald v Prudential Assurance Co (1971) 24 D.L.R. (3d) 185 (Can) 5–15
MacLeod v MacLeod [2008] UKPC 64 PC (IoM) 6–18
Madson Estate v Saylor 2007 SCC 18; [2007] W.T.L.R. 1579; (2006-07) 9 I.T.E.L.R. 903
　Sup Ct (Can) 16–10
Maggbury Pty v Hafele Australia Pty (2001) 210 C.L.R. 181 11–13
Mahmoud and Ispahani, Re; sub nom. Mahmoud v Ispahani; Arbitration between Mahmoud
　and Ispahani, Re [1921] 2 K.B. 716; (1921) 6 Ll. L. Rep. 344 CA 1–13, 1–15, 1–16,
　2–02, 2–04, 2–11, 2–12, 2–17, 3–15,
　4–30, 22–11
Mahonia Ltd v JP Morgan Chase Bank (No.1) [2003] EWHC 1927 (Comm); [2003] 2
　Lloyd's Rep. 911 . . . . 10–02, 19–23
Makdessi v Cavendish Square Holdings BV; ParkingEye Ltd v Beavis; sub nom. Cavendish
　Square Holding BV v Makdessi; El Makdessi v Cavendish Square Holdings BV [2015]
　UKSC 67; [2016] A.C. 1172; [2015] 3 W.L.R. 1373; [2016] 2 All E.R. 519; [2016] 2 All
　E.R. (Comm) 1; [2016] 1 Lloyd's Rep. 55; [2015] 2 C.L.C. 686; [2016] B.L.R. 1; 162
　Con. L.R. 1; [2016] R.T.R. 8; [2016] C.I.L.L. 3769 11–08
Mall Finance & Investment Co Ltd v Slater [1976] 2 N.Z.L.R 685 20–15
Mallalieu v Hodgson (1851) 16 Q.B. 689 7–04
Man; Duchess of Sutherland, Re (1915) 31 T.L.R. 3954 CA 10–17
Mansell v Robinson [2007] EWHC 101 QBD 9–13, 19–10
Mapleback Ex p. Caldecott, Re (1876-77) L.R. 4 Ch. D. 150 CA 8–21, 17–13
Marchon Products v Thornes (1954) 71 R.P.C. 445 11–18
Marles v Philip Trant & Sons Ltd (No.2) [1954] 1 Q.B. 29; [1953] 2 W.L.R. 564; [1953] 1
　All E.R. 651; (1953) 97 S.J. 189 CA 2–06, 2–12, 4–23
Marley Tile Co v Johnson [1982] I.R.L.R. 75 CA (Civ Div) 14–07
Marshall v NM Financial Management Ltd; sub nom. NM Financial Management Ltd v
　Marshall [1997] 1 W.L.R. 1527; [1997] I.C.R. 1065; [1997] I.R.L.R. 449 CA (Civ
　Div) 11–09, 11–10, 19–03,
　19–11, 19–12
Martell v Consett Iron Co Ltd [1955] Ch. 363; [1955] 2 W.L.R. 463; [1955] 1 All E.R. 481;
　(1955) 99 S.J. 148; (1955) 99 S.J. 211 CA 9–08, 9–26, 9–28
Martoo v MacDonald (1947) Q.S.R. 263 FC (Queensland) 2–10
Marvin v Marvin (1976) 557 P.2d 106 6–22
Maschinenfabrik Seydelman K-G v Presswood Bros (1964) 47 D.L.R. (2d) 214 HC
　(Ont) 2–22
Mason v Clarke [1955] A.C. 778; [1955] 2 W.L.R. 853; [1955] 1 All E.R. 914; (1955) 99
　S.J. 274 HL 4–05, 4–06, 4–12
Mason v Provident Clothing & Supply Co Ltd. See Provident Clothing & Supply Co Ltd v
　Mason
Master Education Services Pty Ltd v Ketchell [2008] HCA 38 2–06

Maxwell v Gibsons Drugs (1979) 103 D.L.R. (3d) 433 (British Columbia) 15–14
May v Lane (1894) 64 L.J. Q.B. 236 9–15
Mayor of Norwich v Norfolk Railway (1855) 4 El.B. & El. 397 2–21
McClatchie v Haslam (1891) 65 L.T. 691 8–19
McEllistrim v Ballymacelligott Cooperative Agricultural & Dairy Society Ltd [1919] A.C.
  548 HL (UK-Irl) 12–12
McFarlane v Daniell (1938) 38 S.R. (N.S.W.) 337 19–22
McFarlane v Kent [1965] 1 W.L.R. 1019; [1965] 2 All E.R. 376; (1965) 109 S.J. 497 Ch
  D 14–17
Meah v McCreamer (No.1) [1985] 1 All E.R. 367; (1985) 135 N.L.J. 80 QBD 5–02
Meah v McCreamer (No.2) [1986] 1 All E.R. 943; (1986) 136 N.L.J. 235
  QBD 5–02, 5–16
Melliss v Shirley Local Board of Health; sub nom. Melliss v Shirley and Freemantle Local
  Board of Health (1885-86) L.R. 16 Q.B.D. 446 CA 1–13, 1–16
Merryweather v Nixan 101 E.R. 1337; (1799) 8 Term Rep. 186 KB 5–12
Miah v Islam [2010] EWHC 1569 (Ch) 7–11
Michael Richards Properties Ltd v Corp of Wardens of St Saviour's Parish (Southwark)
  [1975] 3 All E.R. 416 Ch D 2–22
Miller v Karlinski (1946) 62 T.L.R. 85 CA 7–12, 7–17, 19–25,
                                                                                                              22–07, 22–15
Mills v Dunham [1891] 1 Ch. 576 CA 13–04
Millward v Littlewood 155 E.R. 339; (1850) 5 Ex. 775 Ex Ct 6–16
Milner v Staffordshire Congregational Union Inc [1956] Ch. 275; [1956] 2 W.L.R. 556;
  [1956] 1 All E.R. 494; (1956) 100 S.J. 170 Ch D 2–19
Mineral Water Bottle Exchange and Trade Protection Society v Booth (1887) L.R. 36 Ch. D.
  465 CA 12–13
Missouri Steamship Co, Re (1889) L.R. 42 Ch. D. 321 CA 10–09
Mitchel v Reynolds (1711) 1 P. Wins. 181 11–01
Mitsubishi Corp v Alafouzos [1988] 1 Lloyd's Rep. 191; [1988] 1 F.T.L.R. 47 QBD
  (Comm) 10–10
Mobil Oil Australia Pty v Trendlen Pty [2006] H.C.A. 42 9–04
Moenich v Fenestre (1892) 67 L.T. 602 13–04
Mohamed v Alaga & Co; sub nom. Mohammed v Alaga & Co [2000] 1 W.L.R. 1815;
  [1999] 3 All E.R. 699; [2000] C.P. Rep. 87; [1999] 2 Costs L.R. 169 CA (Civ
  Div) 2–14, 17–15, 17–17,
                                                            17–18, 17–21, 18–06, 21–16, 22–07
Montefiore v Menday Motor Components Co Ltd [1918] 2 K.B. 241 KBD 7–25, 7–26, 10–08
Moore v Wolsey (1854) 4 El. & Bl. 243 . . . . 5–28, 5–29
Morris v Colman (1812) 18 Ves. 437 11–15
Mortgage Express v McDonnell; sub nom. Mortgage Express v Robson [2001] EWCA Civ
  887; [2001] 2 All E.R. (Comm) 886; [2002] 1 F.C.R. 162; (2001) 82 P. & C.R.
  DG21 16–01
Morton v Riley (1843) 11 M. & W. 492 17–11
Morton v Supreme Council of Royal League (1903) 100 Mo. App. 76 5–24
Mouflet v Cole (1872-73) L.R. 8 Ex. 32 Ex Chamber 13–15
Mountain Village Developments v Engineered Homes (1985) 64 B.C.L.R.
  195 2–22
MSC Mediterranean Shipping Co SA v Cottonex Anstalt [2016] EWCA Civ 789; [2016] 2
  Lloyd's Rep. 494 15–07
MSL Group Holdings Ltd v Clearwell International Ltd; sub nom. Clearwell International
  Ltd v MSL Group Holdings Ltd [2012] EWHC 3707 (QB); [2013] 3 E.G. 87
  (C.S.) 13–04
Mulcaire v News Group Newspapers Ltd [2011] EWHC 3469 (Ch); [2012] Ch. 435; [2012]
  2 W.L.R. 831; (2012) 109(3) L.S.G. 14 5–09
Multiservice Bookbinding Ltd v Marden [1979] Ch. 84; [1978] 2 W.L.R. 535; [1978] 2 All
  E.R. 489; (1978) 35 P. & C.R. 201; (1978) 122 S.J. 210 Ch D 6–04
Murray Vernon Holdings Ltd v Hassall [2010] EWHC 7 (Ch) 18–04
Mutual Finance Ltd v John Wetton & Sons Ltd [1937] 2 K.B. 389 KBD 8–17, 17–11
Nakata v Dominion Fire Insurance Co (1915) W.W.R. 1084 SC (Canada) 4–21
Napier v National Business Agency Ltd [1951] 2 All E.R. 264; 44 R. & I.T. 413; (1951) 30
  A.T.C. 180; [1951] W.N. 392; (1951) 95 S.J. 528 CA 7–12, 7–13, 7–17

Nash v Stevenson Transport Ltd [1936] 2 K.B. 128 CA 3–09
National Surety Co v Larsen [1929] 4 D.L.R. 918 10–11
Nayyar v Denton Wilde Sapte [2009] EWHC 3218 (QB); [2010] Lloyd's Rep. P.N. 139;
    [2010] P.N.L.R. 15 7–24
Neal v Avers (1940) 63 C.L.R. 524 17–20
Nelson v Nelson (1995) 184 C.L.R. 538 . . . . 16–12, 16–13, 16–14,
                                                                     21–26, 21–27, 21–17
Nelson v Nelson 185 C.L.R. 538 22–17
Neville v Dominion of Canada News Co Ltd [1915] 3 K.B. 556 CA 7–28, 7–29, 12–14
Neville v London Express Newspaper Ltd; sub nom. Neville v London Express Newspapers
    Ltd [1919] A.C. 368 HL 9–01, 9–26, 9–28
New Zealand Shipping Co Ltd v AM Satterthwaite & Co Ltd (The Eurymedon); sub nom.:
    AM Satterthwaite & Co Ltd v New Zealand Shipping Co Ltd [1975] A.C. 154; [1974] 2
    W.L.R. 865; [1974] 1 All E.R. 1015; [1974] 1 Lloyd's Rep. 534; (1974) 118 S.J. 387 PC
    (NZ) 11–11
Newcombe v Yewen and Croydon RDC (1913) T.L.R. 299 5–12
Newell v Royal Bank of Canada (1997) 147 D.L.R. (4th) 268 8–16
Newland v Simons & Willer (Hairdressers) [1981] I.C.R. 521; [1981] I.R.L.R. 359
    EAT 7–14
Niemann v Smedley [1973] V.R. 769 19–25
Nizamuddowlah v Bengal Cabaret (1977) 399 N.Y.S. 2d 854 18–06
Noble & Wolfe, Re (1951) 1 D.L.R. 321 6–30
Nora Beloff v Pressdram Ltd [1973] 1 All E.R. 241; [1973] F.S.R. 33; [1973] R.P.C. 765 Ch
    D 7–36
Norbrook Laboratories (GB) Ltd v Adair [2008] EWHC 978 (QB) 13–20, 14–07, 14–12
Nordenfelt v Maxim Nordenfelt Guns & Ammunition Co Ltd; sub nom. Maxim Nordenfelt
    Guns & Ammunition Co v Nordenfelt [1894] A.C. 535 HL 6–09, 6–10, 11–01,
                                                   11–05, 12–10, 12–18, 12–19, 13–17,
                                                                             22–21
Norglen Ltd (In Liquidation) v Reeds Rains Prudential Ltd; Mayhew-Lewis v Westminster
    Scaffolding Group Plc; Levy v ABN AMRO Bank NV; Circuit Systems Ltd (In
    Liquidation) v Zuken-Redac (UK) Ltd [1999] 2 A.C. 1; [1997] 3 W.L.R. 1177; [1998] 1
    All E.R. 218; [1998] B.C.C. 44; [1998] 1 B.C.L.C. 176; 87 B.L.R. 1; (1997) 94(48)
    L.S.G. 29; (1997) 147 N.L.J. 1773; (1998) 142 S.J.L.B. 26; (1998) 75 P. & C.R. D21
    HL 9–26
Norman v Cole 170 E.R. 606; (1800) 3 Esp. 253 Assizes 7–25, 10–08
North v Marra Developments (1981) 148 C.L.R. 42 7–06
Northwestern Mutual Life Assurance Co v Johnson (1920) 254 U.S. 96 5–23
NWL Ltd v Woods (The Nawala) (No.2); NWL Ltd v Nelson and Laughton [1979] 1 W.L.R.
    1294; [1979] 3 All E.R. 614; [1980] 1 Lloyd's Rep. 1; [1979] I.C.R. 867; [1979]
    I.R.L.R. 478; (1979) 123 S.J. 751 HL 15–16
O'Hearn v Yorkshire Insurance Co (1921) 67 D.L.R. 735 (Can) 5–13
OAMPS Insurance Brokers Ltd v Hanna 2010] NSWSCA 267 13–22
Oasis Merchandising Services Ltd (In Liquidation), Re; sub nom. Ward v Aitken [1998] Ch.
    170; [1997] 2 W.L.R. 764; [1996] 1 All E.R. 1009; [1997] B.C.C. 282; [1997] 1
    B.C.L.C. 689; (1996) 146 N.L.J. 1513 CA (Civ Div) 9–02, 9–26
Office Angels v Rainer-Thomas [1991] I.R.L.R. 214 CA (Civ Div) 13–05, 13–09, 13–09,
                                                                         14–07
Office Overload Ltd v Gunn [1977] F.S.R. 39; (1976) 120 S.J. 147 CA (Civ
    Div) 15–15
OMM v RIA Financial Services. See One Money Mail Ltd v RIA Financial Services
One Money Mail Ltd v RIA Financial Services [2015] EWCA Civ 1084 . . . . 12–30, 13–14, 13–20
Oom v Bruce (1810) 12 East. 225 17–07
Oppenheimer v Cattermole (Inspector of Taxes); sub nom. Nothman v Cooper [1976] A.C.
    249; [1975] 2 W.L.R. 347; [1975] 1 All E.R. 538; [1975] S.T.C. 91; 50 T.C. 159; [1975]
    T.R. 13; (1975) 119 S.J. 169 HL 10–03, 10–04
Orakpo v Manson Investments Ltd [1978] A.C. 95; [1977] 3 W.L.R. 229; (1978) 35 P. &
    C.R. 1; (1977) 121 S.J. 632 HL 18–07
Oram v Hun [1914] 1 Ch. 98 CA 9–09
Orton v Melman [1981] 1 N.S.W.L.R. 583 13–23

Osborne v Amalgamated Society of Railway Servants (No.1); sub nom. Amalgamated
    Society of Railway Servants v Osborne (No.1) [1910] A.C. 87 HL 7–26
Osman v Moss (J Ralph) [1970] 1 Lloyd's Rep. 313 CA (Civ Div) 5–03, 5–05, 5–07,
                                                    5–08
Oswald Hickson Collier & Co v Carter-Ruck [1984] A.C. 720; [1984] 2 W.L.R. 847; [1984]
    2 All E.R. 15; (1983) 133 N.L.J. 233; (1982) 126 S.J. 120 CA (Civ Div) 14–22
Ouston v Zurowski [1985] 5 W.W.R. 169 CA (BC) 18–02
P Samuel & Co Ltd v Dumas; sub nom. P Samuel & Co Ltd v Motor Union Insurance Co
    Ltd [1924] A.C. 431; (1924) 18 Ll. L. Rep. 211 HL 5–15
Papera Traders Co Ltd v Hyundai Merchant Marine Co Ltd (The Eurasian Dream) (No.2)
    [2002] EWHC 2130 (Comm); [2002] 2 All E.R. (Comm) 1083; [2002] 2 Lloyd's Rep.
    692 9–13
Parker v Rock Finance Corporation Ltd [1981] 1 N.Z.L.R. 488 20–13
Parkin v Dick (1809) 11 East 502 4–20
ParkingEye Ltd v Somerfield Stores Ltd [2012] EWCA Civ 1338; [2013] Q.B. 840; [2013]
    2 W.L.R. 939; [2012] 2 Lloyd's Rep. 679 3–17
Parkinson v College of Ambulance Ltd [1925] 2 K.B. 1 KBD 7–27, 10–08
Partabmull Rameshar v KC Sethia (1944) Ltd; sub nom. KC Sethia (1944) Ltd v Partabmull
    Rameshwar [1951] 2 All E.R. 352 (Note); [1951] 2 Lloyd's Rep. 89; [1951] W.N. 389;
    (1951) 95 S.J. 528 HL 2–24
Passmore v Morland Plc [1999] 3 All E.R. 1005; [1999] 1 C.M.L.R. 1129; [1999] E.C.C.
    367; [1999] Eu. L.R. 501; [1999] I.C.R. 913; [1999] 1 E.G.L.R. 51; [1999] 15 E.G. 128;
    [1999] E.G. 14 (C.S.); [1999] N.P.C. 14 CA (Civ Div) 11–25
Patel v Mirza [2016] UKSC 42; [2016] 3 W.L.R. 399; [2016] 2 Lloyd's Rep. 300; [2016]
    Lloyd's Rep. F.C. 435 . . . . .I–01, I–02, I–03,
                              I–04, I–07, I–08, 1–05, 1–06, 1–07,
                              1–08, 2–06, 2–13, 2–06, 2–13, 3–03,
                              3–11, 3–17, 4–03, 4–07, 5–15, 6–02,
                              6–07, 7–19, 7–20, 7–23, 7–27, 7–28,
                              8–21, 9–27, 10–26, 16–01, 16–04,
                              16–06, 16–11, 16–14, 16–15, 16–16,
                              16–17, 17–03, 17–05, 17–06, 17–09,
                              17–10, 17–14, 17–18, 17–20, 18–01,
                              18–02, 18–03, 18–04, 18–06, 21–01,
                              21–18, 21–23, 21–31, 22–03, 22–07,
                              22–13, 22–17
PatSystems Holdings Ltd v Neilly; sub nom. Pat Systems v Neilly [2012] EWHC 2609
    (QB); [2012] I.R.L.R. 979 13–08
Pavey & Matthews Pty v Paul (1987) 162 C.L.R. 221 17–17
PCO Services v Rumleski [1963] 38 D.L.R. (2d) 390 11–12
Pearce v Brooks (1865-66) L.R. 1 Ex. 213 Ex Ct 4–08, 4–09, 4–23,
                                      6–04, 6–23, 6–24
Pecore v Pecore 2007 SCC 17; [2007] W.T.L.R. 1591; (2006-07) 9 I.T.E.L.R. 873 Sup Ct
    (Can) 16–10, 22–17
Pellecat v Angel (1835) 2 Cr.M. & R. 311 4–09
People v United National Life Insurance Co (1967) 427 P.2d 199 2–12
Pepper (Inspector of Taxes) v Hart [1993] A.C. 593; [1992] 3 W.L.R. 1032; [1993] 1 All
    E.R. 42; [1992] S.T.C. 898; [1993] I.C.R. 291; [1993] I.R.L.R. 33; [1993] R.V.R. 127;
    (1993) 143 N.L.J. 17; [1992] N.P.C. 154 HL 2–14
Personnel Hygiene Services Ltd v Rentokil Initial UK Ltd (t/a Initial Medical Services)
    [2014] EWCA Civ 29 12–09
Peter Cassidy Seed Co v Osuustukkukauppa IL [1957] 1 W.L.R. 273; [1957] 1 All E.R. 484;
    [1957] 1 Lloyd's Rep. 25; (1957) 101 S.J. 149 QBD (Comm) 2–24
Peters (WA) v Petersville (2001) 205 C.L.R. 126 11–13
Peters v Collinge [1993] 2 N.Z.L.R 554 20–15
Petrofina (Great Britain) Ltd v Martin [1966] Ch. 146; [1966] 2 W.L.R. 318; [1966] 1 All
    E.R. 126; (1965) 109 S.J. 1009 CA 11–07, 12–28
Peyton v Mindham [1972] 1 W.L.R. 8; [1971] 3 All E.R. 1215; (1971) 115 S.J. 912 Ch
    D 14–15

Pharmaceutical Society of Great Britain v Dickson; sub nom. Dickson v Pharmaceutical
    Society of Great Britain [1970] A.C. 403; [1968] 3 W.L.R. 286; [1968] 2 All E.R. 686;
    (1968) 112 S.J. 601 HL 11–05
Phillips v Foster [1991] 3 N.Z.L.R 263 20–15
Phoenix General Insurance Co of Greece SA v Halvanon Insurance Co Ltd; sub nom.:
    Phoenix General Insurance Co of Greece SA v Administratia Asigurarilor de Stat [1988]
    Q.B. 216; [1987] 2 W.L.R. 512; [1987] 2 All E.R. 152; [1986] 2 Lloyd's Rep. 552;
    [1987] Fin. L.R. 48; (1987) 84 L.S.G. 1055; (1987) 131 S.J. 257 CA (Civ
    Div) 1–15, 2–03, 2–05,
                                       2–07, 2–11, 2–12, 2–14, 2–17, 21–29
Photo Production Ltd v Securicor Transport Ltd [1980] A.C. 827; [1980] 2 W.L.R. 283;
    [1980] 1 All E.R. 556; [1980] 1 Lloyd's Rep. 545; (1980) 124 S.J. 147
    HL 15–11
Picton Jones v Arcadia Developments [1989] 03 E.G. 85 DC 9–14
Pigney v Pointer's Transport Services Ltd [1957] 1 W.L.R. 1121; [1957] 2 All E.R. 807;
    (1957) 101 S.J. 851 Assizes (Norwich) 5–25
Plating Co v Farquharson (1881) L.R. 17 Ch. D. 49 CA 9–06
Polymasc Pharmaceutical Plc v Charles [1999] F.S.R. 711 Ch D (Patents Ct) 15–15
Polymer Developments Group v Tilialo [2002] 3 N.Z.L.R 8–07, 20–15
Porter v Freudenberg; Kreglinger v S Samuel & Rosenfeld; sub nom. Merten's Patents, Re
    [1915] 1 K.B. 857 CA 10–17, 10–19
Potomac Leasing Co v Vitality Centers 718 S.W. 2d 928 (1986) 4–25
PR Consultants Scotland Ltd v Mann 1997 S.L.T. 437; [1996] I.R.L.R. 188
    OH 15–09
Praxis Capital Ltd v Burgess [2015] EWHC 2631 (Ch) 15–11
Printers & Finishers Ltd v Holloway (No.2) [1965] 1 W.L.R. 1; [1964] 3 All E.R. 731;
    [1965] R.P.C. 239; (1965) 109 S.J. 47 Ch D 12–03, 12–08
Printing and Numerical Registering Co v Sampson (1874-75) L.R. 19 Eq. 462 Ct of
    Chancery 6–29
Proactive Sports Management Ltd v Rooney [2011] EWCA Civ 1444; [2012] 2 All E.R.
    (Comm) 815; [2012] I.R.L.R. 241; [2012] F.S.R. 16 . . . . 11–16, 15–04, 15–06,
                                                17–14
Proops v Chaplin (1920) 37 T.L.R. 112 5–05
Prophet Plc v Huggett [2014] EWCA Civ 1013; [2014] I.R.L.R. 797 13–06
Provident Clothing & Supply Co Ltd v Mason; sub nom. Mason v Provident Clothing &
    Supply Co Ltd [1913] A.C. 724 HL 13–01, 13–10, 13–11,
                                      19–07, 19–17, 19–18, 19–20
Provident Financial Group and Whitegates Estate Agency v Hayward [1989] 3 All E.R. 298;
    [1989] I.C.R. 160; [1989] I.R.L.R. 84 CA (Civ Div) 11–17
Prudential Assurance Co v Rodrigues [1982] 2 N.Z.L.R. 54 11–07
Prudential Assurance Co's Trust Deed, Re; sub nom. Horne v Prudential Assurance Co Ltd
    [1934] Ch. 338 Ch D 11–10, 19–11
PSG Franchising Ltd v Lydia Darby Ltd [2012] EWHC 3707 (QB); [2013] 3 E.G. 87
    (C.S.) 13–04
Putsman v Taylor [1927] 1 K.B. 741 CA 13–14, 14–12, 19–04,
                                                19–07, 19–20
Pye Ltd v BG Transport Service Ltd [1966] 2 Lloyd's Rep. 300; 116 N.L.J. 1713
    QBD 4–12, 4–19
QBE Management Services (UK) Ltd v Dymoke [2012] EWHC 80 (QB); [2012] I.R.L.R.
    458; (2012) 162 N.L.J. 180 14–14
Quadramain Pty v Sevastopol Investments (1975-6) 133 C.L.R. 390 12–24
Queensland Cooperative Milling Association v Pamag Property 133 C.L.R. 260 HC
    (Aus) 12–29
Quinlan v University of British Columbia [2009] BCCA 248 2–22
R. v Chief National Insurance Commissioner Ex p. Connor [1981] Q.B. 758; [1981] 2
    W.L.R. 412; [1981] 1 All E.R. 769; [1980] Crim. L.R. 579; (1980) 124 S.J. 478
    QBD 5–40
R. v Porter [1910] 1 K.B. 369 CCA 8–01
R. v Reeves, *Times*; 17 January 2006 (Maidstone Crown Court) 1–01

R. v Registrar General Ex p. Smith [1991] 2 Q.B. 393; [1991] 2 W.L.R. 782; [1991] 2 All
  E.R. 88; [1991] 1 F.L.R. 255; [1991] F.C.R. 403; [1991] C.O.D. 232; (1991) 88(2)
  L.S.G. 32; (1991) 135 S.J. 52 CA (Civ Div) 5–41
R. v Secretary of State for the Home Department Ex p. Puttick [1981] Q.B. 767; [1981] 2
  W.L.R. 440; [1981] 1 All E.R. 776; (1981) 125 S.J. 201 QBD 5–41
R. v Simmonds (Bernard Harry); R. v Barrington-Coupe (William Holford); R. v Cohen
  (Henry); R. v Hamden Co (Sales) Ltd; R. v Hamden Co (Electronics) Ltd; R. v Orwell
  (Terence William) [1969] 1 Q.B. 685; [1967] 3 W.L.R. 367; [1967] 2 All E.R. 399;
  (1967) 51 Cr. App. R. 316; (1967) 131 J.P. 341; (1967) 111 S.J. 274 CA (Crim
  Div) 1–18
R. (on the application of Best) v Chief Land Registrar; sub nom. Best v Chief Land
  Registrar [2015] EWCA Civ 17; [2016] Q.B. 23; [2015] 3 W.L.R. 1505; [2015] 4 All
  E.R. 495; [2015] C.P. Rep. 18; [2015] H.L.R. 17; [2015] 2 P. & C.R. 1 .... 5–40, 21–18
R Leslie Ltd v Reliable Advertising & Addressing Agency Ltd [1915] 1 K.B. 652
  KBD 5–06, 5–07, 5–08,
                                                                                    5–09
Radmacher v Granatino; sub nom. G v R (Pre-Nuptial Contract) [2010] UKSC 42; [2011] 1
  A.C. 534; [2010] 3 W.L.R. 1367; [2011] 1 All E.R. 373; [2010] 2 F.L.R. 1900; [2010] 3
  F.C.R. 583; [2010] Fam. Law 1263; (2010) 107(42) L.S.G. 18; (2010) 160 N.L.J. 1491;
  (2010) 154(40) S.J.L.B. 37 6–18
Rainy Sky SA v Kookmin Bank; sub nom. Kookmin Bank v Rainy Sky SA [2011] UKSC
  50; [2011] 1 W.L.R. 2900; [2012] 1 All E.R. 1137; [2012] 1 All E.R. (Comm) 1; [2012]
  Bus. L.R. 313; [2012] 1 Lloyd's Rep. 34; [2011] 2 C.L.C. 923; [2012] B.L.R. 132; 138
  Con. L.R. 1; [2011] C.I.L.L. 3105 13–01
Ralli Bros v Compania Naviera Sota y Aznar; sub nom. Compania Naviera Sota Y Aznar v
  Ralli Bros [1920] 2 K.B. 287; (1920) 2 Ll. L. Rep. 550 CA 2–23, 10–02, 10–13
Rampal v Rampal (Ancillary Relief); sub nom. Rampal v Rampal (No.2) [2001] EWCA Civ
  989; [2002] Fam. 85; [2001] 3 W.L.R. 795; [2001] 2 F.L.R. 1179; [2001] 2 F.C.R. 552;
  [2001] Fam. Law 731; (2001) 98(29) L.S.G. 37; (2001) 151 N.L.J. 1006; (2001) 145
  S.J.L.B. 165 6–17
Ramsey v Hartley [1977] 1 W.L.R. 686; [1977] 2 All E.R. 673; (1977) 121 S.J. 319 CA (Civ
  Div) 9–26
Re Still v Minister of National Revenue (1997) 154 D.L.R. (4th) 229 21–24
Rees v Gateley Wareing (A Firm) [2014] EWCA Civ 1351; [2015] 1 W.L.R. 2179; [2015] 3
  All E.R. 403; [2015] 2 All E.R. (Comm) 117; [2014] 6 Costs L.O. 953 9–24
Regazzoni v KC Sethia (1944) Ltd; sub nom. Regazzoni v Sethia (KC) (1944) [1958] A.C.
  301; [1957] 3 W.L.R. 752; [1957] 3 All E.R. 286; [1957] 2 Lloyd's Rep. 289; (1957)
  101 S.J. 848 HL.. 10–02, 10–03, 10–04,
                                                                          10–06, 10–13
Reynolds v Kinsey 1959 (4) S.A. 60 .... 3–07, 3–09
Rich (TP) Investments v Calderon [1964] N.S.W.R. 709 2–21
Richardson v Mellish (1824) 2 Bing. 229 6–03
Ritter v Mutual Life Assurance Co (1897) 169 U.S. 139 5–24
Robinson v Continental Insurance Co of Mannheim [1915] 1 K.B. 155 10–19
Robson v Premier Oil & Pipe Line Co Ltd [1915] 2 Ch. 124 CA 10–18
Rock Refrigeration Ltd v Jones [1997] 1 All E.R. 1; [1997] I.C.R. 938; [1996] I.R.L.R. 675;
  (1996) 93(41) L.S.G. 29; (1996) 140 S.J.L.B. 226 CA (Civ Div) 15–08, 15–09, 15–10,
                                                                          15–12, 15–13
Rodriguez v Speyer Bros [1919] A.C. 59 HL 6–02, 6–06, 6–10,
                                                                          10–22, 10–24, 10–27
Romero Insurance Brokers Ltd v Templeton [2013] EWHC 1198 (QB) 13–20
Ronbar Enterprises Ltd v Green [1954] 1 W.L.R. 815; [1954] 2 All E.R. 266; (1954) 98 S.J.
  369 CA 12–17, 12–22, 19–07,
                                                                          19–20, 22–21
Rourke v Mealy (1879) 41 L.T. 168 (Ir.Ex.Div) 8–20
Rousillon v Rousillon (1880) L.R. 14 Ch. D. 351 Ch D 10–11
Routh v Jones [1947] 1 All E.R. 758; [1947] W.N. 205; (1947) 91 S.J. 354
  CA 13–01, 14–15, 14–16
Royal Bank of Canada v Grobman (1977) 83 D.L.R. (3d) 415 21–24

Royal Boskalis Westminster NV v Mountain [1999] Q.B. 674; [1998] 2 W.L.R. 538; [1997]
    2 All E.R. 929; [1997] L.R.L.R. 523; [1997] C.L.C. 816 CA (Civ Div) . . 10–06, 10–12, 10–13,
    19–23
Royse (Deceased), Re; sub nom. Royse v Royse [1985] Ch. 22; [1984] 3 W.L.R. 784;
    [1984] 3 All E.R. 339; [1985] Fam. Law 156; (1984) 81 L.S.G. 2543 CA (Civ
    Div) 5–31, 5–39
RTA (Business Consultants) Ltd v Bracewell [2015] EWHC 630 (QB); [2015] Bus. L.R.
    800; [2015] Lloyd's Rep. F.C. 357; [2015] C.T.L.C. 221 . . . . 1–16, 2–05
Ruttle Plant Hire Ltd v Secretary of State for Environment Food and Rural Affairs [2008]
    EWHC 238 (TCC); [2008] B.P.I.R. 1395 9–26
Sadler v Imperial Life Assurance Co of Canada Ltd [1988] I.R.L.R. 388 QBD 11–09, 11–10,
    19–03
Safetynet Security Ltd v Coppage; sub nom. Coppage v Safety Net Security Ltd [2013]
    EWCA Civ 1176; [2013] I.R.L.R. 970 . . . . 14–05, 14–07
Safeway Stores Ltd v Twigger [2010] EWCA Civ 1472; [2011] 2 All E.R. 841; [2011] Bus.
    L.R. 1629; [2011] 1 Lloyd's Rep. 462; [2011] 1 C.L.C. 80; [2011] U.K.C.L.R.
    339 5–08
Salvesen v Simons [1994] I.C.R. 409; [1994] I.R.L.R. 52 EAT 7–13, 7–19, 22–15
Saunders v Edwards [1987] 1 W.L.R. 1116; [1987] 2 All E.R. 651; [2008] B.T.C. 7119;
    (1987) 137 N.L.J. 389; (1987) 131 S.J. 1039 CA (Civ Div) 21–30, 22–07
Saunders v Edwards [2008] EWCA Civ 393 . . . . 7–19, 7–21, 7–22,
    7–23
Saunders v Seyd and Kelly's Credit Index (1896) 75 L.T. 193 7–31
Savage v Chief Constable of Hampshire; sub nom. Savage v Hoddinot [1997] 1 W.L.R.
    1061; [1997] 2 All E.R. 631 CA (Civ Div) 7–33
Savill Bros v Langman (1898) 79 L.T. 44 9–14
SBJ Stephenson Ltd v Mandy [2000] I.R.L.R. 233; [2000] F.S.R. 286 QBD . . 11–17, 11–18, 12–07,
    14–14, 15–14
SCF Finance Co Ltd v Masri (No.2) [1987] Q.B. 1002; [1987] 2 W.L.R. 58; [1987] 1 All
    E.R. 175; [1986] 2 Lloyd's Rep. 366; [1986] Fin. L.R. 309; (1987) 84 L.S.G. 492;
    (1987) 131 S.J. 74 CA (Civ Div) 2–04
Schaffenius v Goldberg [1916] 1 K.B. 284 CA 10–17
Schering Ltd v Stockholms Enskilda Bank Aktiebolag [1946] A.C. 219 HL 10–25, 10–26
Schostall v Johnson (1919) 36 T.L.R. 75 10–17
Scorer v Seymour Jones [1966] 1 W.L.R. 1419; [1966] 3 All E.R. 347; 1 K.I.R. 303; (1966)
    110 S.J. 526 CA 12–16, 13–14, 13–20,
    19–08, 19–19
Scott v Avery 10 E.R. 1121; (1856) 5 H.L. Cas. 811 HL 8–02
Scott v Brown Doering McNab & Co; Slaughter & May v Brown Doering McNab & Co
    [1892] 2 Q.B. 724 CA 7–06
Scully UK Ltd v Lee [1998] I.R.L.R. 259 CA (Civ Div) 13–01, 13–06, 14–11
Seear v Cohen (1882) 45 L.T. (N.S.) 589 8–20
Sempra Metals Ltd (formerly Metallgesellschaft Ltd) v Inland Revenue Commissioners
    [2007] UKHL 34; [2008] 1 A.C. 561; [2007] 3 W.L.R. 354; [2008] Bus. L.R. 49; [2007]
    4 All E.R. 657; [2007] S.T.C. 1559; [2008] Eu. L.R. 1; [2007] B.T.C. 509; [2007] S.T.I.
    1865; (2007) 104(31) L.S.G. 25; (2007) 157 N.L.J. 1082; (2007) 151 S.J.L.B.
    985 17–09
Sewell v Royal Exchange Assurance Co (1813) 4 Taunt. 856 2–21
SG&R Valuation Service Co LLC v Boudrais [2008] EWHC 1340 (QB); [2008] I.R.L.R.
    770 11–17
Shackell v Rosier (1836) 2 Bins. N.C. 634 5–11
Shaw v DPP; sub nom. R. v Shaw (Frederick Charles) [1962] A.C. 220; [1961] 2 W.L.R.
    897; [1961] 2 All E.R. 446; (1961) 45 Cr. App. R. 113; (1961) 125 J.P. 437; (1961) 105
    S.J. 421 HL 6–04
Shaw v Groom [1970] 2 Q.B. 504; [1970] 2 W.L.R. 299; [1970] 1 All E.R. 702; (1970) 21
    P. & C.R. 137; (1969) 114 S.J. 14 CA (Civ Div) 1–17, 2–05, 2–06,
    2–17, 22–05
Shaw v Shaw [1954] 2 Q.B. 429; [1954] 3 W.L.R. 265; [1954] 2 All E.R. 638; (1954) 98
    S.J. 509 CA 2–12, 4–28, 4–28,
    6–16

Shelley v Paddock [1980] Q.B. 348; [1980] 2 W.L.R. 647; [1980] 1 All E.R. 1009; (1979)
 123 S.J. 706 CA (Civ Div) 17–19, 17–20, 22–07
Sheridan v Dickson [1970] 1 W.L.R. 1328; [1970] 3 All E.R. 1049; (1970) 114 S.J. 474 CA
 (Civ Div) 2–26, 3–15
Short v Bullion-Beck and Champion Mining Co (1899) 20 Utah 20 . . . . .2–18, 18–06
Sibthorpe v Southwark LBC; Morris v Southwark LBC [2011] EWCA Civ 25; [2011] 1
 W.L.R. 2111; [2011] 2 All E.R. 240; [2011] C.P. Rep. 21; [2011] 3 Costs L.R. 427;
 [2011] H.L.R. 19; (2011) 108(6) L.S.G. 18; (2011) 161 N.L.J. 173; [2011] N.P.C.
 11 . . . . .9–11, 9–24, 9–29
Sidmay v Whettam Investments (1967) 61 D.L.R. (2d) 358 .18–07
Simpson v Norfolk and Norwich University Hospital NHS Trust [2011] EWCA Civ 1149;
 [2012] Q.B. 640; [2012] 2 W.L.R. 873; [2012] 1 All E.R. 1423; [2012] 1 Costs L.O. 9;
 [2012] P.I.Q.R. P2; (2012) 124 B.M.L.R. 1; (2011) 108(41) L.S.G. 24; (2011) 161 N.L.J.
 1451 9–16
Sinclair v Brougham; sub nom. Birkbeck Permanent Benefit Building Society, Re [1914]
 A.C. 398; [1914-15] All E.R. Rep. 622 HL 17–02
Singh v Ali [1960] A.C. 167; [1960] 2 W.L.R. 180; [1960] 1 All E.R. 269; (1960) 104 S.J.
 84 PC (FMS) 16–01, 16–02
Skelton v Baxter [1916] 1 K.B. 321 CA 9–26
Smith v Cuff (1817) 6 M. & S. 160 . . . . .8–20, 17–11, 17–12
Smith v Mawhood 153 E.R. 552; (1845) 14 M. & W. 452 Ex Ct 2–07, 2–08
Snell v Unity Finance Co Ltd [1964] 2 Q.B. 203; [1963] 3 W.L.R. 559; [1963] 3 All E.R.
 50; (1963) 107 S.J. 533 CA 1–16
Soleimany v Soleimany [1999] Q.B. 785; [1998] 3 W.L.R. 811; [1999] 3 All E.R. 847;
 [1998] C.L.C. 779 CA (Civ Div) 10–04
Solle v Butcher [1950] 1 K.B. 671; [1949] 2 All E.R. 1107; 66 T.L.R. (Pt. 1) 448
 CA 3–06
Soteriou v Ultrachem Ltd [2004] EWCA Civ 1520 . . . . .I–04
South Australia Cold Stores v Electricity Trust of South Australia (1965) 115 C.L.R.
 247 18–08
South Western Mineral Water Co Ltd v Ashmore [1967] 1 W.L.R. 1110; [1967] 2 All E.R.
 953; (1967) 111 S.J. 453 Ch D 19–24
Sovfracht (V/O) v Van Udens Scheepvaart en Agentuur Maatschappij (NV Gebr); sub nom.
 NV Gerb Van Udens Scheepvaart en Agentuur Maatschappij v V/O Sovfracht [1943]
 A.C. 203; (1942) 74 Ll. L. Rep. 59; 1943 A.M.C. 445 HL 10–18, 10–24
Spector v Ageda [1973] Ch. 30; [1971] 3 W.L.R. 498; [1971] 3 All E.R. 417; (1971) 22 P. &
 C.R. 1002; (1971) 115 S.J. 426 Ch D 4–18
Spence v Mercantile Bank of India (1921) 37 T.L.R. 745 CA 11–09
Spiers v Hunt [1908] 1 K.B. 720 KBD 6–15
Spink (Bournemouth) Ltd v Spink [1936] Ch. 544 Ch D 11–12, 12–19, 13–17
SST Consulting Services Pty Ltd v Rieson (2006) 225 C.L.R. 516 2–04
St Helens Smelting Co v Tipping 11 E.R. 1483; (1865) 11 H.L. Cas. 642 HL 11–19
St John Shipping Corp v Joseph Rank Ltd [1957] 1 Q.B. 267; [1956] 3 W.L.R. 870; [1956]
 3 All E.R. 683; [1956] 2 Lloyd's Rep. 413; (1956) 100 S.J. 841 QBD 1–03, 1–05, 1–10,
 1–11, 1–14, 2–05, 3–13, 3–14, 3–16,
 3–17, 5–41, 20–14, 22–03, 22–09
Stack v Dowden; sub nom. Dowden v Stack [2007] UKHL 17; [2007] 2 A.C. 432; [2007] 2
 W.L.R. 831; [2007] 2 All E.R. 929; [2007] 1 F.L.R. 1858; [2007] 2 F.C.R. 280; [2007]
 B.P.I.R. 913; [2008] 2 P. & C.R. 4; [2007] W.T.L.R. 1053; (2006-07) 9 I.T.E.L.R. 815;
 [2007] Fam. Law 593; [2007] 18 E.G. 153 (C.S.); (2007) 157 N.L.J. 634; (2007) 151
 S.J.L.B. 575; [2007] N.P.C. 47; [2007] 2 P. & C.R. DG11 .16–08
Stein v Blake (No.1) [1996] A.C. 243; [1995] 2 W.L.R. 710; [1995] 2 All E.R. 961; [1995]
 B.C.C. 543; [1995] 2 B.C.L.C. 94; (1995) 145 N.L.J. 760 HL 9–26
Stenhouse Australia v Phillips [1974] A.C. 391; [1974] 2 W.L.R. 134; [1974] 1 All E.R. 117;
 [1974] 1 Lloyd's Rep. 1; (1973) 117 S.J. 875 PC (Aus) 11–07, 14–07
Stephens v Avery [1988] Ch. 449; [1988] 2 W.L.R. 1280; [1988] 2 All E.R. 477; [1988]
 F.S.R. 510; (1988) 85(25) L.S.G. 45; (1988) 138 N.L.J. Rep. 69; (1988) 132 S.J. 822 Ch
 D 6–26
Stephens v Gulf Oil Canada Ltd (1975) 65 D.L.R. (3d) 193 .12–15
Stevens v Allied Freightways [1968] N.Z.L.R. 1195 . . . . .12–19, 13–16, 14–04

Stevenson Jordan & Harrison v McDonnell & Evans [1952] 1 T.L.R. 101; (1952) 69 R.P.C.
   10 CA 12–04
Stewart v Oriental Fire & Marine Insurance Co Ltd [1985] Q.B. 988; [1984] 3 W.L.R. 741;
   [1984] 3 All E.R. 777; [1984] 2 Lloyd's Rep. 109; (1984) 1 B.C.C. 99127; [1984]
   E.C.C. 564; [1985] Fin. L.R. 64; (1984) 81 L.S.G. 1915; (1984) 134 N.L.J. 584; (1984)
   128 S.J. 645 QBD (Comm) 2–07, 21–29
Stocznia Gdanska SA v Latvian Shipping Co (Abuse of Process) [1999] 3 All E.R. 822;
   [1999] C.L.C. 1451 QBD (Comm) 9–26
Stone & Rolls Ltd (In Liquidation) v Moore Stephens (A Firm); sub nom. Moore Stephens
   (A Firm) v Stone & Rolls Ltd (In Liquidation) [2009] UKHL 39; [2009] 1 A.C. 1391;
   [2009] 3 W.L.R. 455; [2009] 4 All E.R. 431; [2010] 1 All E.R. (Comm) 125; [2009]
   Bus. L.R. 1356; [2009] 2 Lloyd's Rep. 537; [2009] 2 B.C.L.C. 563; [2009] 2 C.L.C.
   121; [2009] Lloyd's Rep. F.C. 557; [2009] B.P.I.R. 1191; [2009] P.N.L.R. 36; (2009) 159
   N.L.J. 1218; (2009) 153(31) S.J.L.B. 28 5–40
Streatham Cinema Ltd v John McLauchlan Ltd [1933] 2 K.B. 331 KBD 3–06
Strongman (1945) v Sincock [1955] 2 Q.B. 525; [1955] 3 W.L.R. 360; [1955] 3 All E.R. 90;
   (1955) 99 S.J. 540 CA 2–23, 2–25
Sunrise Brokers LLP v Rodgers; sub nom. Sunrise Brokers LLP v Rogers [2014] EWCA
   Civ 1373; [2015] I.C.R. 272; [2015] I.R.L.R. 57 11–15
SW Strange v Mann [1965] 1 W.L.R. 629; [1965] 1 All E.R. 1069; (1965) 109 S.J. 352 Ch
   D 13–10, 13–12, 14–17,
                                                                                        15–14
Swain v Law Society [1983] 1 A.C. 598; [1982] 3 W.L.R. 261; [1982] 2 All E.R. 827;
   (1982) 79 L.S.G. 887; (1982) 126 S.J. 464 HL 9–23, 17–15
Sykes (Basil Landon) v DPP; sub nom. R. v Sykes (Basil Landon) [1962] A.C. 528; [1961]
   3 W.L.R. 371; [1961] 3 All E.R. 33; (1961) 45 Cr. App. R. 230; (1961) 125 J.P. 523;
   (1961) 105 S.J. 566 HL 8–10
Systems Reliability Holdings v Smith [1990] I.R.L.R. 377 Ch D 12–09, 12–19, 12–20
T Lucas & Co Ltd v Mitchell [1974] Ch. 129; [1972] 3 W.L.R. 934; [1972] 3 All E.R. 689;
   (1972) 116 S.J. 711 CA (Civ Div) 19–05, 19–09, 19–19,
                                                                                        19–20, 19–21
Tank Lining Corp v Dunlop Industrial (1982) 140 D.L.R. (3d) 659 12–12
Tanner v Tanner (No.1) [1975] 1 W.L.R. 1346; [1975] 3 All E.R. 776; (1975) 5 Fam. Law
   193; (1975) 119 S.J. 391 CA (Civ Div) 6–22
Taylor v Bhail [1996] C.L.C. 377; 50 Con. L.R. 70 CA (Civ Div) 1–01, 7–07, 7–08,
                                                                                        22–13
Taylor v Bowers (1875-76) L.R. 1 Q.B.D. 291 CA 22–13, 22–17
Taylor v Chester (1868-69) L.R. 4 Q.B. 309 QB 16–06
Taylor v McQuilkin (1968) 2 D.L.R. (3d) 463 11–09
Tekron Resources Ltd v Guinea Investment Co Ltd [2003] EWHC 2577; [2004] 2 Lloyd's
   Rep. 26 7–27
Texaco v Mulberry Filling Station [1972] 1 W.L.R. 814; [1972] 1 All E.R. 513; (1971) 116
   S.J. 119 Ch D 12–15
TFS Derivatives Ltd v Morgan [2004] EWHC 3181 (QB); [2005] I.R.L.R.
   246 ....13–20, 19–03
Thackwell v Barclays Bank Plc [1986] 1 All E.R. 676 QBD 21–30
Thai Trading Co v Taylor [1998] Q.B. 781; [1998] 2 W.L.R. 893; [1998] 3 All E.R. 65;
   [1998] 1 Costs L.R. 122; [1998] 2 F.L.R. 430; [1998] 3 F.C.R. 606; [1998] P.N.L.R. 698;
   [1998] Fam. Law 586; (1998) 95(15) L.S.G. 30; (1998) 142 S.J.L.B. 125 CA (Civ
   Div) 9–11, 9–22, 9–23,
                                                                                        9–24, 9–29
Thomas Bates & Son's Application, Re 176 E.G. 163; [1960] J.P.L. 650 Lands
   Tr 13–14
Thomas Brown & Sons v Fazal Deen 108 C.L.R. 391 ....16–04, 19–24
Thomas v Farr Plc [2007] EWCA Civ 118; [2007] I.C.R. 932; [2007] I.R.L.R. 419; (2007)
   151 S.J.L.B. 296 13–20
Thomson v Thomson, 1981 S.C. 344; 1982 S.L.T. 521 CSIH (Div 1) 6–18
Ting Siew May v Boon Lay Choo [2014] SGCA 28 ....1–11, 7–10
Tingley v Muller; sub nom. Tingley v Mš ller [1917] 2 Ch. 144 CA 10–25
Tinline v White Cross Insurance Association Ltd [1921] 3 K.B. 327 KBD 5–10, 5–13, 5–14

Tinsley v Milligan [1994] 1 A.C. 340; [1993] 3 W.L.R. 126; [1993] 3 All E.R. 65; [1993] 2
    F.L.R. 963; (1994) 68 P. & C.R. 412; [1993] E.G. 118 (C.S.); [1993] N.P.C. 97
    HL 1–07, 1–08, 4–25,
                                                    7–11, 7–16, 7–20, 7–21, 7–22, 16–06,
                                                    16–08, 16–10, 16–11, 16–12, 16–13,
                                                    16–14, 16–15, 16–16, 16–17, 18–02,
                                                    18–03, 19–25, 21–22, 21–28, 21–30,
                                                    21–31, 22–07, 22–17
Tomlinson v Dick Evans U Drive Ltd [1978] I.C.R. 639; [1978] I.R.L.R. 77
    EAT 7–13, 22–15
Torrez, Re (1987) 827 F.2d 1299 16–14
Tracy v Talmage, 14 N.Y. 162; 67 Am. Dec. 132 (1856) 4–23, 4–24, 4–25
Trego v Hunt [1896] A.C. 7 HL 12–18
Trendtex Trading Corp v Credit Suisse [1982] A.C. 679; [1981] 3 W.L.R. 766; [1981] 3 All
    E.R. 520; [1981] Com. L.R. 262; (1981) 125 S.J. 761 HL 9–01, 9–15, 9–16,
                                                    9–17, 9–19, 9–21
Trepca Mines Ltd (No.2), Re; sub nom. Radomir Nicola Pachitch (Pasic)'s Application, Re
    [1963] Ch. 199; [1962] 3 W.L.R. 955; [1962] 3 All E.R. 351; (1962) 106 S.J. 649
    CA 9–05
Tribe v Tribe [1996] Ch. 107; [1995] 3 W.L.R. 913; [1995] 4 All E.R. 236; [1995] C.L.C.
    1474; [1995] 2 F.L.R. 966; [1996] 1 F.C.R. 338; (1996) 71 P. & C.R. 503; [1996] Fam.
    Law 29; (1995) 92(28) L.S.G. 30; (1995) 145 N.L.J. 1445; (1995) 139 S.J.L.B. 203;
    [1995] N.P.C. 151; (1995) 70 P. & C.R. D38 CA (Civ Div) 16–12, 16–13, 16–14,
                                                    16–15, 18–02
Triplex Safety Glass Ltd v Scorah [1938] Ch. 211; [1937] 4 All E.R. 693; (1938) 55 R.P.C.
    21 Ch D 12–04
Troja v Troja [1994] 33 N.S.W.L.R. 269 . . . . 5–33, 5–34
TSC Europe (UK) Ltd v Massey [1999] I.R.L.R. 22 Ch D 11–18, 14–14
Tucker v Gillis (1988) 53 D.L.R. (4th) 688 CA (New Brunswick) 16–11
Turner v Commonwealth & British Minerals Ltd [2000] I.R.L.R. 114 CA (Civ
    Div) 11–11, 13–04
United States v Farrar (1930) 2 U.S. 624 2–11
Upfill v Wright [1911] 1 K.B. 506 KBD 6–21, 6–22, 6–23
V v V (Ancillary Relief: Pre-Nuptial Agreement); sub nom. V v V (Prenuptial Agreement)
    [2011] EWHC 3230 (Fam); [2012] 1 F.L.R. 1315; [2012] 2 F.C.R. 98; [2012] Fam. Law
    274; (2012) 109(4) L.S.G. 17 6–18
Vancouver Malt & Sake Brewing Co Ltd v Vancouver Breweries Ltd [1934] A.C. 181 PC
    (Can) 11–03, 11–04, 11–06,
                                                    11–10, 12–16
Vandervell Products v McLeod [1957] R.P.C. 185 CA 14–10, 14–12
Vellino v Chief Constable of Greater Manchester [2001] EWCA Civ 1249; [2002] 1 W.L.R.
    218; [2002] 3 All E.R. 78; [2002] P.I.Q.R. P10; [2001] Po. L.R. 295; (2001) 151 N.L.J.
    1441 5–40
Vervaeke v Smith [1983] 1 A.C. 145; [1982] 2 W.L.R. 855; [1982] 2 All E.R. 144; (1982)
    126 S.J. 293 HL 6–18, 10–09
Vestergaard Frandsen S/A (now called MVF3 APS) v Bestnet Europe Ltd [2013] UKSC 31;
    [2013] 1 W.L.R. 1556; [2013] 4 All E.R. 781; [2013] I.C.R. 981; [2013] I.R.L.R. 654;
    [2013] E.M.L.R. 24; (2013) 157(21) S.J.L.B. 31 12–05
Victorian Daylesford Syndicate Ltd v Dott [1905] 2 Ch. 624 Ch D 2–07, 18–07
Vinall v Howard [1954] 1 Q.B. 375; [1954] 2 W.L.R. 314; [1954] 1 All E.R. 458; (1954) 98
    S.J. 143 CA 1–16
Vita Food Products Inc v Unus Shipping Co Ltd (In Liquidation) [1939] A.C. 277; (1939)
    63 Ll. L. Rep. 21 PC (Can) 1–14
W Dennis & Sons Ltd v Tunnard Bros and Moore (1911) 56 S.J. 162 15–14
Wallace v Hardacre (1807) 1 Camp. 45 8–13
Wallis v Day (1837) 2 M. & W. 273 11–10
Walton (Grain and Shipping) Ltd v British Italian Trading Co Ltd [1959] 1 Lloyd's Rep. 223
    QBD (Comm) 2–23, 2–24, 10–02
Ward v Lloyd (1843) 6 Man. & G. 785 8–13
Warm Zones v Thurley [2014] EWHC 988 (QB); [2014] I.R.L.R. 791 15–15
Warner Bros Pictures Inc v Nelson [1937] 1 K.B. 209 KBD 11–15, 11–16

Warren v Mendy [1989] 1 W.L.R. 853; [1989] 3 All E.R. 103; [1989] I.C.R. 525; [1989]
 I.R.L.R. 210; (1989) 133 S.J. 1261 CA (Civ Div) 11–15
Wasel Bros v Laskin [1934] 2 D.L.R. 798 . . . . .2–10, 3–18, 22–09
Watson v Prager [1991] 1 W.L.R. 726; [1991] 3 All E.R. 487; [1991] I.C.R. 603; [1993]
 E.M.L.R. 275 Ch D 11–16
Waugh v Morris (1872-73) L.R. 8 Q.B. 202 QBD 3–03, 3–04, 3–05
Waymell v Read (1794) 5 Term.R. 599 4–10
WC Leng & Co Ltd v Andrews [1909] 1 Ch. 763 CA 13–16
Webb v Chief Constable of Merseyside; Chief Constable of Merseyside v Porter; sub nom.:
 Porter v Chief Constable of Merseyside [2000] Q.B. 427; [2000] 2 W.L.R. 546; [2000] 1
 All E.R. 209; (1999) 96(47) L.S.G. 33; (2000) 144 S.J.L.B. 9 CA (Civ
 Div). 16–01, 16–06
Weld-Blundell v Stephens [1920] A.C. 956 HL 7–29, 7–31
Welwyn Hatfield Council v Secretary of State for Communities and Local Government; sub
 nom. R. (on the application of Welwyn Hatfield BC) v Secretary of State for
 Communities and Local Government; Secretary of State for Communities and Local
 Government v Welwyn Hatfield BC [2011] UKSC 15; [2011] 2 A.C. 304; [2011] 2
 W.L.R. 905; [2011] 4 All E.R. 851; [2011] P.T.S.R. 825; [2011] B.L.G.R. 459; [2011] 2
 P. & C.R. 10; [2011] 2 E.G.L.R. 151; [2011] J.P.L. 1183; [2011] 15 E.G. 93 (C.S.);
 (2011) 108(16) L.S.G. 16; (2011) 161 N.L.J. 550; (2011) 155(14) S.J.L.B. 30; [2011]
 N.P.C. 40 5–40
Westdeutsche Landesbank Girozentrale v Islington LBC; Kleinwort Benson Ltd v Sandwell
 BC; sub nom. Islington LBC v Westdeutsche Landesbank Girozentrale [1996] A.C. 669;
 [1996] 2 W.L.R. 802; [1996] 2 All E.R. 961; [1996] 5 Bank. L.R. 341; [1996] C.L.C.
 990; 95 L.G.R. 1; (1996) 160 J.P. Rep. 1130; (1996) 146 N.L.J. 877; (1996) 140 S.J.L.B.
 136 HL. 17–01, 17–02, 17–09
Westlaw Services Ltd v Boddy [2010] EWCA Civ 929; [2010] 6 Costs L.R. 934; [2011]
 P.N.L.R. 4; (2010) 160 N.L.J. 1153; (2010) 154(31) S.J.L.B. 30 2–14
Wetherell v Jones; sub nom. Wetherall v Jones 110 E.R. 82; (1832) 3 B. & Ad. 221
 KB 3–13, 22–03
WH Smith v Clinton (1908) 25 T.L.R. 34 5–11
Wheeler v Quality Deep Ltd (t/a Thai Royale Restaurant); sub nom. Wheeler v Qualitydeep
 Ltd (t/a Thai Royale Restaurant) [2004] EWCA Civ 1085; [2005] I.C.R. 265; (2004)
 101(35) L.S.G. 33 . . . . .7–17, 22–15
Whiston v Whiston [1995] Fam. 198; [1995] 3 W.L.R. 405; [1998] 1 All E.R. 423; [1995] 2
 F.L.R. 268; [1995] 2 F.C.R. 496; [1995] Fam. Law 549 CA (Civ Div) 5–41, 6–17
White (Marion) v Francis [1972] 1 W.L.R. 1423; [1972] 3 All E.R. 857; (1972) 116 S.J. 822
 CA (Civ Div) 13–03, 13–07, 13–14
White v British Empire Mutual Life Assurance Co (1868-69) L.R. 7 Eq. 394 Ct of
 Chancery 5–28
Whitehill v Bradford [1952] Ch. 236; [1952] 1 All E.R. 115; [1952] 1 T.L.R. 66; (1952) 96
 S.J. 42 CA 13–16, 13–19, 14–16,
                                                                                          14–17
Whitmore v Farley (1880) 43 L.T. (N.S.) 192 8–14
Whitmore v King (1918) 87 L.J. Ch. 647 CA 13–01
Whittaker v Howe (1841) 3 Beav. 383 . . . . .14–21, 14–22
Wiggins v Lavy (1928) xliv T.L.R. 721 9–01
Wild v Harris 137 E.R. 395; (1849) 7 C.B. 999 QB 6–16
Wild v Simpson [1919] 2 K.B. 544 CA 9–26
William E Thomson Associates v Carpenter (1989) 61 D.L.R. (2nd) 1 21–25
William Hill Organisation Ltd v Tucker [1999] I.C.R. 291; [1998] I.R.L.R. 313; (1998)
 95(20) L.S.G. 33; (1998) 142 S.J.L.B. 140 CA (Civ Div) 11–17
Williams v Bayley (1866) L.R. 1 H.L. 200 HL 8–18, 17–11
Williams v Gibbons [1994] 1 N.Z.L.R 273 20–14
Willis v Baldwin (1780) 2 Doug. 450 7–03
Willow Oak Developments Ltd (t/a Windsor Recruitment) v Silverwood [2006] EWCA Civ
 660; [2006] I.C.R. 1552; [2006] I.R.L.R. 607; (2006) 103(23) L.S.G. 29 13–05
Wilson v Carnley [1908] 1 K.B. 729 CA 6–15, 6–16

Wilson v First County Trust Ltd (No.2); sub nom. Wilson v Secretary of State for Trade and
   Industry [2003] UKHL 40; [2004] 1 A.C. 816; [2003] 3 W.L.R. 568; [2003] 4 All E.R.
   97; [2003] 2 All E.R. (Comm) 491; [2003] H.R.L.R. 33; [2003] U.K.H.R.R. 1085;
   (2003) 100(35) L.S.G. 39; (2003) 147 S.J.L.B. 872 . . . . I-03, I-04
Wilson v Rankin (1865-66) L.R. 1 Q.B. 162 Ex Chamber 3-16
Windhill Local Board of Health v Vint (1890) L.R. 45 Ch. D. 351 CA 8-06, 8-08
Woolwich Equitable Building Society v Inland Revenue Commissioners [1993] A.C.
   709 18-08
Wright v Gasweld Pty (1991) 22 N.S.W.L.R. 317 13-22
Wrn Ltd v Ayris [2008] EWHC 1080 (QB); (2008) 152(23) S.J.L.B. 29 14-07
Wyatt v Kreglinger [1933] 1 K.B. 793 CA 11-09, 11-10, 19-11
Wylie v Lawrence Wright Music Co (1932) T.L.R. 295 . . . . 2-18, 18-06
Yango Pastoral Co Pty v First Chicago Australia 139 C.L.R. 41 . . . . 2-05, 2-06, 2-07,
                                                                                                                      22-09
Yin (Chai Sau) v Sam (Liew Kwee) [1962] A.C. 304; [1962] 2 W.L.R. 765; (1962) 106 S.J.
   217 PC (FMS) 2-02, 2-11, 2-17
Young v Timmins (1831) Cr. & J. 331 11-16
Z v Z (Financial Remedy: Marriage Contract) [2011] EWHC 2878 (Fam); [2012] 1 F.L.R.
   1100; [2012] Fam. Law 136 6-18
Zimmermann v Letkeman (1977) 79 D.L.R. (3d) 508 . . . . 7-10, 18-02
Zinc Corp Ltd v Hirsch [1916] 1 K.B. 541 CA 10-29

TABLE OF STATUTES

1677 Sunday Observance Act (c.7)
    s.1 2–16
1845 Gaming Act (8 109) 1–15
1853 Customs Consolidation Act
    (c.107) 3–16
1873 Supreme Court of Judicature Act
    (c.66) 9–15
    s.1 9–15
1875 Sale of Food and Drugs Act (c.63)
    s.28 5–05
1892 Gaming Act (c.9) 1–15
1906 Fertiliser and Feeding Stuffs
    Act 2–05
    Marine Insurance Act
    (c.41) 2–26
1914 Trading with the Enemy
    Act 10–14
1920 Seeds Act (c.54) 2–06
1925 Law of Property Act (c.20)
    s.136 9–15
    Honours (Prevention of Abuses) Act
    (c.72) 7–27
1930 Road Traffic Act (c.43) 5–13
1932 Merchant Shipping (Safety and Load
    Line Conventions) Act
    (c.9) 3–14
1933 Road and Rail Traffic Act
    (c.53) 3–09
1934 Betting and Lotteries Act
    (c.58) 18–08
1939 Trading with the Enemy Act
    (c.89) 10–14, 10–27
1947 Exchange Control Act
    (c.14) 17–19, 18–02
    Town and Country Planning Act
    (c.51) 11–19
1952 Defamation Act (c.66)
    s.11 . . . . 5–11, 7–31
1956 Restrictive Trade Practices Act
    (c.68) 7–37, 11–20
1958 Prevention of Fraud (Investments) Act
    (c.45) 2–15
1960 Betting and Gaming Act . . . 3–05, 4–34
1961 Suicide Act (c.60) 5–24
    s.1 5–23
1965 Monopolies and Mergers Act
    (c.50) 11–20
1967 Misrepresentation Act (c.7)
    s.2(1) 17–21
    Merchant Shipping (Load Lines) Act
    (c.27) 3–14
    Criminal Law Act (c.58) . . . 8–11, 9–01
    s.1(2) 8–05, 8–10
    s.4(1A) 8–10
    s.5(1) 7–33, 8–10, 8–11

    s.13 9–01
    s.14(1) 8–11
    (2) 8–11, 9–01, 9–02
1968 Trade Descriptions Act (c.29)
    s.35 2–05
    Theft Act (c.60) 4–24, 7–32
1970 Law Reform (Miscellaneous Provisions)
    Act (c.33) 4–29
    s.1 4–29
    s.6 4–29
1972 European Communities Act
    (c.68) 11–20
1973 Matrimonial Causes Act
    (c.18) 8–02
    s.25 6–18
    s.37 16–08
    Employment Agencies Act
    (c.35) 2–05
1974 Consumer Credit Act (c.39)
    s.127(3) I–03
    Solicitors Act (c.47) 1–09
    Insurance Companies Act
    (c.49) 1–15, 2–03, 2–07,
                        2–12
    Rehabilitation of Offenders Act
    (c.53) 7–33
1975 Inheritance (Provision for Family and
    Dependants) Act (c.63) 5–39
    s.1(1A) 4–29
1977 Criminal Law Act (c.45)
    s.1 1–18
1979 Banking Act (c.37)
    s.1(8) 2–05
1982 Forfeiture Act (c.34) . . 5–33, 5–35, 5–39
    s.2(1) 5–35
    (2) 5–35
    (3) 5–34, 5–35
    s.3(1) 5–39
    s.5 5–35
1984 Road Traffic Regulation Act (c.27)
    s.81(1) 1–13
    Food Act (c.30) 2–12
1986 Insolvency Act (c.45)
    s.216 5–09
    Financial Services Act (c.60)
    s.132 . . . . 2–03, 2–14, 21–29
    (6) 1–15
1988 Criminal Justice Act (c.33)
    s.141(1) 1–13
    Road Traffic Act (c.52) 5–13, 5–14
    s.17(2) 1–13
1990 Town and Country Planning Act
    (c.8) 11–19

1990   Contracts (Applicable Law) Act
         (c.36) 10–01
         s.2(2) 10–13
       Courts and Legal Services Act (c.41)
         s.58 . . . . 9–04, 9–21, 9–24
           (1) 9–24
           (3) 9–24
         s.58AA 9–21
1993   Criminal Justice Act (c.36)
         s.52 17–03
1995   Merchant Shipping Act (c.21)
         s.98 3–15
1996   Employment Rights Act (c.18)
         s.43B 7–38
       Arbitration Act (c.23) 8–02
       Defamation Act (c.31)
         s.2 7–31
         s.5(1) 7–34
         s.11 7–32
1998   European Communities (Amendment)
         Act (c.21) 11–20
       Public Interest Disclosure Act
         (c.23) 7–35, 7–38
         s.1 7–38
       Competition Act (c.41) . . 11–20, 11–21,
                                        11–25,
                                        12–16
         s.2 11–22
           (1) 5–08, 11–22
           (2) 11–22
           (4) 11–22
           (8) 11–22
         ss.3—16 11–22
         s.18(1) 11–26
           (4) 11–26
         s.36 . . . . 11–22, 11–24
         s.39 11–24
         s.50(1) 11–25
         s.60(1) 11–21
           (2) 11–21

       Human Rights Act (c.42) . . . I–03, I–04,
                                            6–31
1999   Access to Justice Act (c.22)
         s.27 . . . . 9–04, 9–21, 9–24
2000   Financial Services and Markets Act (c.8)
         s.26(1) 1–13
         s.28 . . . . 2–03, 2–14
           (3) 21–29
           (4) 21–29
           (5) 21–29
           (6) 21–29
2002   Proceeds of Crime Act 2002
         (c.29) 5–40
       Enterprise Act (c.40) 11–20
2005   Constitutional Reform Act
         (c.4) 6–32
2009   Coroners and Justice Act (c.25)
         s.154 9–21
2010   Equality Act (c.15)
         s.199 22–17
           (1) 16–16
           (2) 16–16
       Bribery Act (c.23) 7–24
         s.1 7–24
2011   Estates of Deceased Persons (Forfeiture
         Rule and Law of Succession) Act
         (c.7) 5–30
2012   Legal Aid, Sentencing and Punishment
         of Offenders Act (c.7)
         s.45 9–21
2013   Enterprise and Regulatory Reform Act
         (c.24) 11–20
         s.17 7–38
2014   Transparency of Lobbying, Non-party
         Campaigning and Trade Union
         Administration Act
         (c.4) 7–26

TABLE OF STATUTORY INSTRUMENTS

1987 Consumer Protection (Cancellation of
     Contracts Concluded away from
     Business Premises) Regulations (SI
     1987/2117)
     reg.4(1) 1–13

TABLE OF EUROPEAN CASES

Delimitis v Henninger Brau AG (C-234/89) [1991] E.C.R. I-935; [1992] 5 C.M.L.R.
210 11–25
Suiker Unie v Commission of the European Communities (40/73) [1975] E.C.R.
1663 11–23
Volk v Etablissements J Vervaecke SPRL (5/69) [1969] E.C.R. 295; [1969] C.M.L.R.
273 11–24

TABLE OF COURT OF HUMAN RIGHTS CASES

Osman v United Kingdom (23452/94) [1999] 1 F.L.R. 193; (2000) 29 E.H.R.R. 245; 5
    B.H.R.C. 293; (1999) 1 L.G.L.R. 431; (1999) 11 Admin. L.R. 200; [2000] Inquest L.R.
    101; [1999] Crim. L.R. 82; [1998] H.R.C.D. 966; [1999] Fam. Law 86; (1999) 163
    J.P.N. 297 . . . . I–03
Z v United Kingdom (29392/95) [2001] 2 F.L.R. 612; [2001] 2 F.C.R. 246; (2002) 34
    E.H.R.R. 3; 10 B.H.R.C. 384; (2001) 3 L.G.L.R. 51; (2001) 4 C.C.L. Rep. 310; [2001]
    Fam. Law 583 . . . . I–03

TABLE OF TREATIES AND CONVENTIONS

1950   European Convention for the Protection of Human Rights and Fundamental Freedoms I–03
      Art.6(1) I–03, I–04
      Protocol 1 art.1 . . . . I–04
1957   Treaty establishing the European Community (renumbered by the Treaty of Amsterdam)
      Art.1 11–22
      Art.39 (ex Art.48) 11–23
1980   Convention on the Law applicable to Contractual Obligations 1980 (Rome Convention) 10–01
      Art.7(1) 10–13
      (2) 10–09

      Art.16 10–09
1997   Treaty of Amsterdam 11–20, 11–23
2008   Treaty on the Functioning of the European Union
      art.101 (ex art.81 TEC) 11–20, 11–22, 11–23, 11–24, 11–25
      (3) 11–25
      art.102 (ex art 82 TEC) . 11–20, 11–26

GENERAL INTRODUCTION

1.   NATURE AND SCOPE OF ILLEGALITY

Complexity.   The aim of this book is to set out the law relating to illegality and   **I–01**
public policy, in the context of contract, as fully and clearly as the authorities
allow. Illegality forms an exceptional body of doctrine within the law of contract,
since it is not concerned primarily with the interests and expectations of the
parties. It is focused instead upon possible undesirable consequences which their
agreement may have for society at large, and it has long been seen as a difficult
branch of the law. The underlying conflict between public and private interest is
not readily conducive to the formulation of clear rules and principles, especially
given the range and complexity of the differing types of situation in which such
conflict can arise. As a result, judgments in illegality cases have often been
expressed in the familiar language of the general law of contract combined,
somewhat uneasily, with well-worn phrases and maxims which are intended to
highlight the public policy dimension. Unfortunately, the underlying issues do not
readily lend themselves to conventional contractual analysis, with its inevitable
preoccupation with the parties' dealings with each other as distinct from wider
considerations. And the maxims deployed, such as "no person may benefit from
his own wrong", or "no cause of action may be founded on an illegal act", are
inherently vague and even question-begging. The overall effect was therefore apt
to be one of confusion rather than illumination. Fortunately the process of
exposition has been rendered more straightforward than formerly as result of the
radical and far-reaching 2016 decision of the Supreme Court in *Patel v Mirza*.[1] In
this case a nine-member Court substituted, by a majority, a more transparent
approach to situations involving illegality than had been adopted hitherto. The
new approach calls for overt consideration of a number of factors, including the
underlying policies of the rules giving rise to the illegality in the particular case.
Patel v Mirza was itself the final case in an extraordinary sequence of Supreme
Court decisions in which that court addressed illegality issues on no fewer than
four separate occasions within two years[2], and reflected profound differences of
judicial approach in the process.

---

[1] [2016] UKSC 42.
[2] See *Hounga v Allen* [2014] UKSC 47; [2014] 1 W.L.R. 2889; *Les Laboratoires Servier v Apotex*
[2014] UKSC 55; [2014] 3 W.L.R. 1257; *Bilta (UK) Ltd (in liquidation) v Nazir* [2015] UKSC 23;
Patel v Mirza [2016] UKSC 42. The cases concerned illegality respectively in discrimination law
(*Hounga*), patent law (*Les Laboratoires Servier*), company law (*Bilta (UK) Ltd*), and contract (*Patel v
Mirza*).

I–02   **Blunt instrument.**   When the law of contract is used as a vehicle for the pursuit of broad objectives determined by the interests of the public, as distinct from those of the parties, it is inevitably a somewhat blunt instrument. If the outcome is the denial of enforceability, there is the obvious danger that one party may suffer a loss far greater than any penalty which a criminal court might have imposed, even assuming that what occurred would have come within the purview of the criminal law. At the same time, the other party will gain a corresponding windfall even though he may have been at least equally responsible for the illegality. In some cases it is possible to mitigate such adverse consequences by combining unenforceability with, for one of the parties, a degree of restitutionary relief. Such relief will now, in fact, be more readily available after *Patel v Mirza* in which the actual decision of the Court, upon which it was unanimous, was to grant such relief in the case before it. The even more radical solution contemplated occasionally, of abandoning illegality *as a part of the law of contract altogether*: enforcing all agreements and leaving it to the criminal law to impose such sanctions on the parties as it considers appropriate, is clearly both impractical and intuitively unacceptable. No court is going to allow a contract killer to soften the blow of life imprisonment by suing for his fee. Important issues can therefore arise, particularly where the conduct of the parties did not directly involve criminal activity, both as to the scope of the illegality doctrine and its capacity for change. How far the law of contract does, or should, continue to concern itself with questions of sexual morality, for example, has been a matter of some interest in recent times.

I–03   **Human Rights Act.**   The need for the development of clarity and coherence, within the law relating to illegality and public policy, has been made greater by the implementation of the Human Rights Act 1998. The Act does not apply directly to litigation between individuals, as distinct from cases brought by individuals against public authorities. Nevertheless, even the common law now has to be applied and developed in a manner consistent with the European Convention on Human Rights. Accordingly, the UK would be in breach if the reasoning underlying rejection of a private law claim could be shown to have been inconsistent with the Convention. Article 6(1) of the Convention guarantees a "right to a fair trial" in "the determination of . . . civil rights and obligations". The jurisprudence surrounding the Convention, developed by the European Court of Human Rights, has involved concepts such as proportionality, and the need to avoid arbitrariness. These developments raise the possibility that the illegality doctrine, with its apparent lack of predictability and tendency to produce harsh results in some cases, could be questioned for its consistency with art.6(1). In Strasbourg the European Court itself has already considered cases which raised policy issues not wholly dissimilar from those sometimes raised by illegality. These include the operation of common law immunities, enjoyed in certain circumstances by the police and local authorities, from liability in tort for negligence. The results of these cases have not been wholly unambiguous.[3] But it seems to be clear that concepts which could be perceived as denying, for a priori

---

[3] Compare *Osman v United Kingdom* (1999) 29 E.H.R.R. 245 with the later case of *Z v United Kingdom* [2001] 2 F.L.R. 603.

reasons, the right of a party to have his or her case considered "on the merits", may be vulnerable to challenge under art.6(1). Nevertheless, attempts to mount Human Rights Act challenges in the English courts to decisions based on common law illegality, or analogous statutory provisions, have so far ultimately proved unsuccessful. Although the Court of Appeal once held, in *Wilson v First County Trust*,[4] that a provision in consumer protection legislation was incompatible with the rights guaranteed by art.6(1), their decision was reversed by the House of Lords.[5] The provision operated automatically to prohibit a creditor from recovering the sum loaned, in the event of certain requirements as to documentation being not complied with,[6] but Lord Nicholls observed in the House of Lords that that was insufficient to "bring Article 6(1) into play". It did not "bar access to court to decide whether the case [was] caught by the restriction".[7] Their Lordships emphasised that art.6(1) was confined to procedural, as distinct from substantive, law and that since the statutory provision was concerned with the latter it did not contravene the Article. Nevertheless, as their Lordships also acknowledged,[8] the distinction between procedural and substantive provisions is not always straightforward, or easy to draw. It therefore remains a possibility that some aspect of common law illegality, or analogous statute law, might eventually be held to contravene art.6(1). This possibility is, however, somewhat reduced by *Patel v Mirza*, the reasoning in which both clarifies the law on illegality and emphasises that it is predominantly a matter of substantive, rather than procedural, law.

Protection of property. In addition to art.6(1), another aspect of the Human Rights convention which may be relevant in illegality cases is art.1 of the First Protocol. This deals with the "Protection of Property", and provides that no one "shall be deprived of his possessions except in the public interest and subject to the conditions provided for by law". Alongside the consideration of art.6(1), art.1 of the First Protocol was also considered in *Wilson v First County Trust*. Nevertheless, the House of Lords, reversing the Court of Appeal on this point as well as on the art.6(1) point, held that the challenged consumer protection provision did not contravene this Article either. The vulnerability of debtors, and the consequent need to regulate moneylending transactions, meant that the legislature was justified in imposing drastic controls on creditors and preventing them from recovering the money loaned if they failed to comply with the statutory restrictions.[9] In another case the compatibility of the common law illegality rules was considered by the Court of Appeal, and survived the challenge. In *Al-Kishtaini v Shanshal*[10] the issue concerned the recovery of money which had been transferred in breach of exchange controls imposed as a

I–04

---

[4] See *Wilson v First County Trust* [2001] 3 All E.R. 229 at 244, per Sir Andrew Morrit VC delivering the judgment of the court.
[5] See *Wilson v First County Trust* [2003] UKHL 40; [2003] 4 All E.R. 97.
[6] See the Consumer Credit Act 1974 s.127(3).
[7] See [2003] UKHL 40 at [36].
[8] [2003] UKHL 40 especially per Lord Scott, at [165].
[9] See [2003] UKHL 40 at [74]–[75] (Lord Nicholls); [138] (Lord Hobhouse) and [169] (Lord Scott).
[10] [2001] EWCA Civ 264. See also *Soteriou v Ultrachem* [2004] EWHC 983 (affmd [2004] EWCA Civ 1520).

result of United Nations sanctions then in force against Iraq. Although the controls themselves were statutory, the Court accepted that the irrecoverability of the money was a consequence of the common law. But the Court held that the common law rules fell within the "public interest" exception to art.1 and that there had therefore been no contravention of the Article.[11] The decision was, however, based on the high public policy background to the controls,[12] and the possibility that common law aspects of illegality might fall foul of art.1 in other circumstances can never be wholly discounted. Nevertheless, the actual decisions in illegality cases usually possess a degree of rationality even if in the past this has not always been apparent from the reasoning advanced to support them. And the relative merits of the parties are seldom in practice wholly ignored, even if they necessarily play a subordinate role. As a result of the Human Rights Act, the latent rationality of the illegality doctrine needs to be made more evident, and the greatest possible precision in the formulation of doctrine is desirable. The approach facilitated by *Patel v Mirza* should contribute to this process.

I–05   **"Illegal contracts".** In order to avoid the appearance, or actuality, of arbitrariness and disproportionality, it is particularly important to avoid falling into the trap of denominating every agreement, which is affected in some way by illegality, as an "illegal contract": enforceable by neither party to it regardless of any differences in their relative degrees of involvement. Since the notion of reciprocity is central to the English law of contract, it is apt to appear curious to accord different rights to the parties on some basis other than discrepancies in their dealings with each other. In the special context of illegality, however, careful analysis of the relevant public interest, and how it can most appropriately be protected, may well lead to the conclusion that it is legitimate to afford a degree of relief to one party, and deny it to the other, even though this would not be justified if their behaviour towards each other was considered in isolation. The gravity of what each of the parties achieved, or attempted to achieve, is also an important factor.

2. STRUCTURE OF THE BOOK

I–06   **Criminal law and civil law.** The book is divided into six parts. Among the issues dealt with in the opening chapters of the first Part is the distinction between "statutory illegality" and illegality derived purely from the common law. Other chapters highlight the need to distinguish between an agreement itself, and the circumstances which surround it, when ascribing responsibility to the parties for their respective degrees of involvement in any illegality. The final chapter in this Part considers a cluster of issues arising out of the relationship between the criminal law and the civil law. These include the recovery by claimants in actions for breach of contract of fines and damages previously awarded against them in other proceedings; the effect of suicide upon life insurance policies; and the forfeiture rule in the law of succession. The second Part is devoted to the nature and scope of the doctrine of "Public Policy" itself. One chapter deals with the

[11] See [2001] EWCA Civ 264 at [50]–[62] per Mummery LJ and at [90]–[99] per Rix LJ.
[12] See [2001] EWCA Civ 264 at [58]–[59] per Mummery LJ and at [97] per Rix LJ.

important topic of contracts affected by fraud or corruption, including the evasion of tax. Other chapters address issues relating to the integrity of the legal process, including the doctrines of maintenance and champerty, and the stifling of prosecutions. The application of public policy to cases with an international dimension is also considered.

Restraint of trade; and the consequences of illegality.   The third Part of the   I–07
book examines the doctrine of restraint of trade. This doctrine is of obvious practical importance as well as theoretical interest. It is significant not least for the way in which the courts interfere openly with the enforceability of contracts, without any of the deference normally shown towards the terms of concluded agreements. The various aspects of the doctrine are explored, including the nature of the distinction between public and private interest; how covenants entered into by employees are treated differently from those involving some element of protection of goodwill; and the contrasting approaches sometimes adopted towards the actual *construction* of covenants. The doctrine of severance often plays an important role in restraint of trade cases. But it is also applicable in many other types of situation, and the chapter devoted to it is included in the fourth Part of the work, which is concerned generally with relief against the consequences of illegality. Another chapter in this Part deals with the passing of property under contracts unenforceable for illegality, and the difficulties which have arisen with respect to the transfer of limited interests. Restitutionary relief can mitigate the harshness often associated with a finding of illegality, and secure more proportionate and policy-oriented outcomes. Two chapters deal with this increasingly important branch of the law; highlighting the recent substantial broadening in the availability of such relief in illegality cases brought about by *Patel v Mirza*.

Reform.   The fifth Part explores possible reforms of the law relating to   I–08
illegality and public policy. One chapter is devoted to New Zealand, the only Commonwealth jurisdiction which has so far actually legislated across the whole field. The last chapter of the book examines the issues raised by reports of official bodies in several jurisdictions, including the UK, which have addressed the many concerns associated with the way in which the illegality doctrine has operated in practice; especially its perceived uncertainty and rigidity. One possible approach to reform which has found considerable, but not universal, support is that of conferring a statutory discretion on the court, enabling it to balance conflicting interests in a variety of different situations. The radical transformation in favour of flexibility and transparency brought about in the UK by *Patel v Mirza* in fact represents the response of the common law itself to the pressure for reform.

Examples.   The final part of the book, Part 6, provides a number of   I–09
hypothetical examples of illegality situations, together with commentary on possible approaches to their resolution which might commend themselves to the court.

[5]

PART 1

CONTRAVENING THE LAW

CHAPTER 1

CRIME, TORT AND STATUTORY ILLEGALITY

1. INTRODUCTION

Fundamental questions. If parties agree, with full knowledge both of the surrounding factual circumstances and the relevant law, to do something which constitutes a serious criminal offence, there can be no doubt that the courts will deny their agreement the status of an enforceable contract.[1] It is also clear that, at least in some circumstances, agreements to commit a tort upon a third party will similarly be denied enforceability.[2] In a broad sense, any refusal to enforce a contract for reasons not related primarily to the merits of the parties to it may be said to be a decision derived from "public policy". Nevertheless, situations in which that decision is based upon criminal or tortious behaviour by the parties may legitimately be regarded as conceptually distinct from those involving issues such as "morality", or restraint of trade, in which the law of contract has developed "policies" of its own which may result in enforceability being denied. Both types of situation can, of course, give rise to similar questions: in particular, how far differing degrees of "guilt" or "innocence" by the parties may justify their being treated differently. These questions are dealt with in subsequent chapters. Nevertheless, there are two fundamental issues which relate specifically to contracts involving criminal or tortious behaviour, and it is with these that this first chapter is mainly concerned. First, what constitutes a serious crime or tort for the purposes of enforceability? Or to put it more generally, are there any circumstances in which deliberate criminal or tortious behaviour or intention in relation to a contract may leave the rights of the party or parties involved unaffected and intact? Secondly, what precisely is to be understood by expressions such as "statutory illegality", or "implied statutory prohibition"; and how far do such notions relate to contracts involving contravention of the criminal law in general? In so far as statutory prohibition can properly be regarded as a discrete area, what does it comprise?

1-01

---

[1] See, e.g. *Taylor v Bhail* [1996] C.L.C. 377 (fraud on a third party); *Everet v Williams* (1725) highway robbery: (see (1893) 9 L.Q.R. 106 and 197, confirming that the case, long thought to have been fictional, actually occurred); *Allen v Rescous* (1676) 2 Lev. 174 (assault). cf. the criminal case of *R. v Reeves* (2006) *The Times*, January 17 (Maidstone Crown Court) in which someone who wished to end her own life paid substantial sums to the defendant in return for an (unfulfilled) promise to kill her: for discussion, see Michael L. Nash in (2006) 156 N.L.J. 280.
[2] Thus it has been argued that an agreement which constitutes the tort of inducing breach of contract, by virtue of its known inconsistency with an earlier agreement, will normally be unenforceable for illegality: see H. Lauterpacht, "Contracts to Break a Contract" (1936) 52 L.Q.R. 494. See also, per du Parcq J in *British Homophone v Kunz and Crystalline Gramophone Record Manufacturing Co* (1935) 152 L.T. 589 at 592.

2. SERIOUSNESS

(a) Deliberate Acts

1–02   **Successful claim.** In *Howard v Shirlstar Container Transport Ltd*[3] the claimant, a qualified pilot, agreed to try and retrieve for the defendants an aircraft which belonged to them, but which was being detained in Nigeria in breach of the provisions of the contract under which it had been let out on hire. In the course of the operation, which was successful, the claimant committed a statutory offence against Nigerian law by taking off from Lagos without obtaining permission from air traffic control. This was because the enterprise, which involved the claimant placing himself in considerable personal danger, was contrary to the wishes of the Nigerian military authorities, who even sent up a fighter in apparent pursuit. Despite the successful recovery of their aircraft the defendants sought to avoid paying the claimant's fee by relying upon illegality. They contended that his breach of the air traffic control regulations meant that his claim was unenforceable. The Court of Appeal rejected this argument and found for the claimant. Staughton LJ said that "the plaintiff's claim should not fail, because the conscience of the court is not affronted". He continued[4]:

> "For the avoidance of doubt, I would add that I would have reached the same conclusion if a similar offence or offences had been committed in England under English law in similar circumstances. It would have been for the criminal courts to consider what penalties should be imposed, and I say nothing as to whether they should have been substantial or lenient. But, if the offences had been committed to escape danger to life, I would not have held that Captain Howard was disqualified from claiming his fee in a civil action here."[5]

1–03   **Overloading.** In the earlier case of *St John Shipping Corporation v Joseph Rank*[6] a cargo-ship was overloaded while crossing the Atlantic, and the load-line was submerged. This was a criminal offence for which the Captain was convicted and fined. Although the cargo had been delivered safely the cargo-owners, possibly anxious that this might not have been the outcome on a future occasion, sought to teach the ship-owners a lesson by refusing to pay for the cost of carriage. They argued that the carriers' unlawful performance of the contract meant that they were barred by public policy from enforcing the contract to recover payment. Devlin J rejected this argument and held that the ship-owners could sue despite the offence which had been committed, and despite the fact that, in the words of Devlin J himself, it was "not at all improbable" that the overloading had been "deliberate".

1–04   **Conscious intention.** Thus, even if a contract was entered into with the conscious intention, by one or both parties, of committing a criminal offence or a

---

[3] [1990] 1 W.L.R. 1292; [1990] 3 All E.R. 366.
[4] [1990] 1 W.L.R. 1292 at 1301; [1990] 3 All E.R. 366 at 374.
[5] cf. Treitel, *The Law of Contract*, edited by Peel, 14th edn, 2015, para.11-113, emphasising that the aircraft had been empty and had flown over the sea: "A different view might have been taken if an aircraft with passengers on board had (in breach of air traffic regulations) been flown low over a densely populated area."
[6] [1957] 1 K.B. 267.

tort, it appears that there can be exceptional situations in which the contract could be enforced even by the party primarily responsible for the illegality. As far as tort is concerned, Sir Percy Winfield was of the opinion that an agreement to enter the land of a third party in order to test the legality of a claimed right of way could constitute an enforceable contract even if it ultimately transpired that a trespass had been committed.[7] As far as criminal behaviour is concerned, the *Second American Restatement of Contracts* makes the following suggestion[8]:

"A and B make an agreement for the sale of goods for $10,000, in which A promises to deliver the goods in his own truck at a designated time and place. A municipal parking ordinance makes unloading of a truck at that time and place an offense punishable by a fine of up to $50. A delivers the goods to B as provided. Because the public policy manifested by the ordinance is not sufficiently substantial to outweigh the interest in the enforcement of B's promise, enforcement of his promise is not precluded on grounds of public policy."

(b)   The approach after Patel v Mirza

Proportionality.   It seems not unlikely that the English courts in *St John Shipping Corporation v Joseph Rank* and *Howard v Shirlstar Container Transport Ltd* were adopting a not dissimilar approach, albeit in rather different circumstances, to that contemplated by the *Restatement*. In effect, enforceability was permitted because refusal would have imposed a penalty upon the party responsible which was perceived as disproportionate to the offence which he had committed. Thus, in the *St John Shipping* case Devlin J said[9]:

1–05

"It is a misfortune for the defendants that the legal weapon which they are yielding is so much more potent than it need be to achieve their purpose. Believing, rightly or wrongly, that the plaintiffs have deliberately committed a serious infraction of the Act and one which has placed their property in jeopardy, the defendants wish to do no more than to take the profit out of the plaintiffs' dealing. But the principle which they invoke for this purpose cares not at all for the element of deliberation or for the gravity of the infraction, and does not adjust the penalty to the profits unjustifiably earned. The defendants cannot succeed unless they claim the right to retain the whole freight and to keep it whether the offence was *accidental or deliberate, serious or trivial*. The application of this principle to a case such as this is bound to lead to startling results."[10]

Patel v Mirza.[11]   In this case a majority of the Supreme Court for the first time expressly recognised that proportionality is one of the factors to be taken into account in determining whether or not a claim should fail on grounds of illegality and, moreover, that the purpose of the rule giving rise to the illegality should also be considered. Although it is unlikely that many of the actual decisions in

1–06

---

[7] See *Winfield on Tort* (6th edn, 1954), p.31 (cited in Furmston, "The Analysis of Illegal Contracts" (1966) 16 U.T.L.J. 267 at p.263). cf *Les Laboratoires Servier v Apotex* [2014] UKSC 55; [2014] 3 W.L.R. 1257 (infringement of a foreign patent right not sufficiently serious to give rise to a defence of illegality).
[8] At para.178.
[9] [1957] 1 K.B. 267 at 280–281 (italics supplied).
[10] See also *Fitzgerald v F. J. Leonardt* (1997) 189 C.L.R. 215, especially at 249, per Kirby J: "It would be absurd if a trivial breach of a statutory provision constituting illegality, connected in some way with a contract or contracting parties, could be held to justify the total withdrawal of the facilities of the courts."
[11] [2016] UKSC 42.

previous cases involving illegality would be decided differently as a result of it, the reasoning of the majority in this case represents a radical change in approach from that generally adopted earlier. Flexibility and transparency are the hallmarks of this approach, and all previous judgments must now be read in the light of it. The case itself concerned a claim for unjust enrichment, which the defendant sought to resist on the ground that both parties had been involved in a plan to profit by inside information, and hence unlawfully, from movements in share prices. The Supreme Court held unanimously that the defence of illegality would fail and that the claim would therefore succeed. The effect of the decision on illegality as a defence to unjust enrichment is dealt with in subsequent chapters. Although the three members of the Court who were effectively in the minority[12] confined their reasoning largely to unjust enrichment, the six who were in the majority[13] ranged much more widely to address the defence of illegality in broad terms. Lord Toulson, who delivered the leading majority judgment, said[14]:

> "The essential rationale of the illegality doctrine is that it would be contrary to the public interest to enforce a claim if to do so would be harmful to the integrity of the legal system…In assessing whether the public interest would be harmed in that way, it is necessary a) to consider the underlying purpose of the prohibition which has been transgressed and whether that purpose will be enhanced by denial of the claim, b) to consider any other relevant public policy on which the denial of the claim may have an impact and c) to consider whether denial of the claim would be a proportionate response to the illegality, bearing in mind that punishment is a matter for the criminal courts. Within that framework, various factors may be relevant, but it would be a mistake to suggest that the court is free to decide a case in an undisciplined way. The public interest is best served by a principled and transparent assessment of the considerations identified…"

As far as the "various factors" of possible relevance are concerned, Lord Toulson said that he "would not attempt to lay down a prescriptive or definitive list because of the infinite possible variety of cases". Nevertheless, he did say that[15]:

> "Potentially relevant factors include the seriousness of the conduct, its centrality to the contract, whether it was intentional and whether there was marked disparity in the parties' respective culpability."

1–07 **Overruling of *Tinsley v Milligan*.** Both the majority and the minority in *Patel v Mirza* were unanimous not only as to the actual result in the case but also in concluding that the reasoning in the much-criticised case of the House of Lords, more than 20 years earlier, in *Tinsley v Milligan*[16] should "no longer be followed".[17] In that case the House, by a bare majority,[18] rejected a defence of illegality which had been advanced in an attempt to resist enforcement of a resulting trust in circumstances in which the parties had been involved in criminal

---

[12] Lord Mance, Lord Clarke and Lord Sumption.
[13] Lord Toulson, Lady Hale, Lord Kerr, Lord Wilson, and Lord Hodge. Lord Neuberger also agreed ultimately with the majority despite admitting that he had had reservations.
[14] See [2016] UKSC 42 at [120].
[15] See [2016] UKSC 42 at [107].
[16] [1994] 1 A C 340.
[17] See [2016] UKSC 42 at [110] (Lord Toulson).
[18] Lord Browne-Wilkinson, Lord Jauncey and Lord Lowry, Lord Goff and Lord Keith dissenting.

deception as to the ownership of a house in order to obtain welfare benefits. Criticism of the case had focused not so much on the actual result as to the highly formalistic way in which it had been reached.[19] It was held that the claimant avoided the effect of the illegality defence because she did not need to "rely" on the deception in order to enforce the trust. Unfortunately this approach rendered the outcome in similar cases essentially arbitrary: if the purchasers of the house had been married, the presumption of advancement could have led to the case being decided the other way, for reasons wholly unrelated to the underlying issue of illegality.[20] Although the minority in *Patel v Mirza* considered that the "problem about the reliance test [was] not so much the test itself as the way in which it was applied in *Tinsley v Milligan*",[21] the majority rejected the "test" itself.

Dispute resolved. The effect of the decision of the Supreme Court in *Patel v Mirza* was to resolve a long-standing judicial dispute as to the appropriate approach which should be adopted by the court to cases involving illegality. On the one hand there were those who favoured a "strictly rule-based approach", and those who favoured "a more flexible approach by which the court would look at the policies underlying the doctrine.[22] This difference came to a head in the remarkable quartet of Supreme Court cases culminating in *Patel v Mirza* itself[23]; but it actually stretches back at least to the decision in *Tinsley v Milligan* and, from a broader common law perspective, to 1970 and beyond: the year in which this branch of the law was reformed in New Zealand by the conferring on the judiciary of a statutory discretion.[24] It also included several Law Commission consultation papers and reports culminating in *The Illegality Defence*, 2010.[25] This Report in fact recommended that the courts should, as a matter of common law, adopt a flexible approach broadly similar to that which eventually succeeded in *Patel v Mirza*. Although the three minority judgments in that case argued in favour of "rules", and contended that the flexible approach favoured by the majority would lead uncertainty and lack of predictability,[26] it is submitted that the majority view is much the more persuasive.[27] As Lord Toulson put it at the conclusion of the passage quoted above[28]:

1–08

> "The public interest is best served by a principled and transparent assessment of the considerations identified, *rather than by the application of a formal approach capable of producing results which may appear arbitrary, unjust or disproportionate.*"

---

[19] See Ch.16, below.

[20] cf. *Collier v Collier* [2002] EWCA Civ 1095.

[21] See [2016] UKSC 42 at [236] per Lord Sumption.

[22] See [2016] UKSC 42 at [81] per Lord Toulson.

[23] See *Hounga v Allen* [2014] UKSC 47; [2014] 1 W.L.R. 2889; *Les Laboratoires Servier v Apotex* [2014] UKSC 55; [2014] 3 W.L.R. 1257; *Bilta (UK) Ltd (in liquidation) v Nazir* [2015] UKSC 23; *Patel v Mirza* [2016] UKSC 42.

[24] See the New Zealand Illegal Contracts Act 1970 (discussed in Chapter 20 below).

[25] See Law Com No. 320. See also Ch.21 below.

[26] See eg per Lord Sumption in [2016] UKSC 42 at [261]-[265].

[27] "A rule-based approach to the question of the effect of illegality on the availability of a remedy has failed to deliver on what some have claimed to be its principal virtues *viz* ease of application and predictability of outcome": per Lord Kerr in [2016] UKSC 42 at [134].

[28] See [2016] UKSC 42 at [108 (italics supplied).

In any event, however, the matter has now fortunately been put beyond doubt by the judgments of six members of a nine-member Supreme Court, and the lower courts have been left in no doubt as to the appropriate approach to adopt in future cases.

1–09   **Facts uncertain?**   The court will sometimes invoke factual uncertainty as a reason for rejecting a defence of illegality. Thus in *Lediaev v Vallen*[29] the Court of Appeal held that in order to determine whether a contract was rendered unenforceable by virtue of contravention of the Solicitors Act 1974, which made it a criminal offence for unqualified persons to carry out certain legal processes for reward, it would be necessary to investigate not only the precise scope of the duties to be undertaken by the unqualified person but also the state of knowledge of the respective parties to the contract, including whether the lack of legal qualifications was known to the other party for whom the services were provided. Since those facts had not been investigated at trial the Court of Appeal held that the contract for reward would be enforced, since it was not considered to be illegal "on its face" (which would have obliged the court to refuse enforcement of its own motion) and it was too late on appeal for the facts to be investigated.[30]

3.   THE NATURE OF STATUTORY ILLEGALITY

(a)   Separate from "Common Law" Illegality

1–10   **A necessary distinction.**   It is important to distinguish situations in which the general principles of public policy, relating to transactions which involve criminal or tortious activity, apply from those in which a contract is affected by "statutory illegality".[31] It is the former which have just been considered, and we now turn to the latter. Unfortunately, however, drawing the distinction is often far from straightforward. This is because many situations in the former category, as cases such as *St John Shipping Corporation v Joseph Rank* illustrate, concern the commission of statutory criminal offences and, as a result, the distinction between that category and "statutory illegality" in the narrow sense is not as clearly developed in the authorities as would be desirable. Thus, in some situations in which contracts have been held to be unenforceable on grounds of illegality, on account of the perceived relevance of a statutory provision to the circumstances of the case, confusion has arisen from a failure to draw the distinction between "statutory" and "common law" illegality.

1–11   **Confusion of categories.**   It is important to appreciate that a claim which failed might still have done so on account of "common law" illegality, notwithstanding that a legislative provision provided the background to the failure.[32] The significance of this is that in such a case the court will have had an unconstrained

---

[29] [2009] EWCA Civ 156.
[30] See ibid. per Aikens LJ at [55]–[61].
[31] See *Fitzgerald v F. J. Leonardt* (1997) 189 C.L.R. 215 at 245 and 247, per Kirby J.
[32] See *Ting Siew May v Boon Lay Choo* [2014] SGCA 28 at [38] et seq., per Andrew Phang Boon Leong JA (referring to the 3rd edition of the present work).

choice, save only for the operation of the normal rules of precedent, in deciding whether or not to invalidate the claim. In cases of "statutory illegality", on the other hand, the court is in theory constrained, by the priority accorded to statute by constitutional theory, to reach only one possible conclusion. Even in cases of this type, however, there will often be a need for a precise analysis both of the statutory provision itself, and of its relationship to the contractual situation, before a conclusion is reached which can appropriately be regarded as inescapable. Nevertheless, since the court's freedom of manoeuvre is inevitably greater in the common law category it is unfortunate that the two categories should be confused by the not uncommon approach which is prepared to ascribe a finding of illegality in any statutory context to the statute itself.[33]

The issues.   Exposition and analysis of this branch of the law therefore requires examination of the approaches which the courts have so far adopted, explicitly or otherwise, in expressing the relationships perceived to exist between statutory provisions and contractual claims. What is the difference, for example, between so-called "express prohibition of contracts" and "implied prohibition"? How does the latter concept relate generally to situations in which the activities of the contracting parties risk contravention of the criminal law, including non-statutory crimes such as murder? Finally, what machinery provides the best framework for dealing with illegality problems in this area? These are some of the issues to be addressed.

1–12

Three types of statutory provision.   Although the notion of "express statutory prohibition" sounds self-evident it has actually turned out to be rather ambiguous. It is necessary to distinguish broadly between three types of statutory provision. First, a criminal statute may prohibit certain activities and render them punishable. Those activities, which constitute the great majority of crimes, may not necessarily have any obvious relationship with contracts; that is it may be perfectly possible and usual for them to be engaged in without entering into any kind of contract.[34] Secondly, a statute may refer to contracts or to commercial activity in defining the conduct to be penalised; but fail to state whether contravention of the statute is to have any effect upon the enforceability of the contracts in question, or whether the criminal penalties stipulated should be the only sanctions to be imposed.[35] Thirdly, a statute may provide that contracts to which it refers should, as such, actually be "void" or unenforceable.[36] The better

1–13

---

[33] cf. *St John Shipping Corporation v Joseph Rank* [1957] 1 Q.B. 267. See also *Archbold's Freightage v S. Spanglett & Co* [1961] 1 Q.B. 374.
[34] See, e.g. Road Traffic Regulation Act 1984 s.81(1): "It shall not be lawful for a person to drive a motor vehicle on a restricted road at a speed exceeding 30 miles an hour".
[35] See, e.g. Road Traffic Act 1988 s.17(2): "If a person sells or offers for sale [a motor-cycle crash helmet not of an approved type] he is guilty of an offence"; see also the Criminal Justice Act 1988 s.141(1): "Any person who ... sells or hires or offers for sale or hire [an offensive weapon] shall be guilty of an offence."
[36] See, e.g. Financial Services and Markets Act 2000 s.26(1): certain contracts made by unauthorised persons to be "unenforceable against the other party"; Consumer Protection (Cancellation of Contracts Concluded away from Business Premises) Regs 1987, (SI 1987/2117), reg.4(1) (since repealed): "No contract to which these Regulations apply shall be enforceable against the consumer unless…".

view is that *only* provisions of this last type are properly to be regarded as instances of "express prohibition". Nevertheless, judges sometimes refer to contractual claims falling properly within the second category as having been "expressly prohibited"'; presumably on the ground that the statute refers expressly to contracts, even though it makes no express provision for consequences within the *law* of contract.[37] This usage is confusing and should be avoided.[38]

1–14   **Result not always to be ascribed to statute.**   Even more undesirable is the usage which would treat cases in which contravention of a provision in the first category just happens to have involved a contractual situation as instances of "implied prohibition". Devlin J once said, for example, that "you can hardly make sense of a statute which forbids an act and yet permits to be made a contract to do it; that is a clear implication".[39] Taken literally, this would seem to treat any situation in which the enforceability of a contract is in doubt, because it involved contravention of the statutory criminal law, as a case of "statutory" illegality. This would be so even if the case involved, say, criminal damage or contravention of parking or speeding restrictions. Whether or not contracts which involve contravention of such provisions are denied enforceability, it does not follow that the result should always be ascribed to the statute which created the criminal liability. This is not a merely semantic issue. Whatever the true scope of "statutory" illegality, it will inevitably be perceived as according the courts less flexibility in its application than is available to them when fashioning and applying doctrines developed by the common law itself. And the infinite variety of differing factual situations which may arise in illegality cases makes a degree of flexibility in their resolution highly desirable.[40]

(b) Contractual Context

1–15   **Necessary contemplation by the statute.**   If the narrow definition of express statutory prohibition or invalidity suggested above is accepted, the small number of cases within that category will seldom give rise to debate about the nature of the issues involved; even though complex questions of construction may still arise in particular contexts.[41] The main problem for present purposes is to determine the existence and scope of an *implied* statutory prohibition. Notwithstanding confusion in the reasoning in some cases, a close reading of the

---

[37] See, e.g. *Re Mahmoud and Ispahani* [1921] 2 K.B. 716 at 731, per Atkin LJ; *Bedford Insurance v Resseguros do Brasil* [1985] Q.B. 966 at 984; [1984] 3 All E.R. 766 at 774, per Parker J See also *Melliss v Shirley Local Board* (1885) 16 Q.B.D. 446 at 453, per Cotton L.J.; and at 454, per Bowen LJ.

[38] The better view is that such cases involve the doctrine of *implied* prohibition: see below, Ch.2.

[39] See *St John Shipping Corporation v Joseph Rank* [1957] 1 Q.B. 267 at 288.

[40] cf. *Vita Food Products v United Shipping Co* [1939] A.C. 277, per Lord Wright at 293: "Nor must it be forgotten that the rule by which contracts not expressly forbidden by statute or declared to be void are in proper cases nullified for disobedience to a statute is a rule of public policy only, and public policy understood in a wider sense may at times be better served by refusing to nullify a bargain save on serious and sufficient grounds".

[41] cf. the Gaming Acts 1845 and 1892.

authorities supports the view that a contractual claim can only properly be said to have been impliedly prohibited by statute when the legislation which imposes criminal penalties upon activities necessarily contemplates those activities being done in a contractual context, i.e. the second of the three categories outlined above. Thus in *Bedford Insurance Co v Instituto de Resseguros do Brasil*[42] the claimant insurers sought to enforce marine reinsurance contracts which they had entered into with the defendants. Unfortunately, however, the claimant did not possess authorisation from the Department of Trade to carry on marine insurance business. In consequence, in writing the business which they had sought to reinsure they had committed an offence under legislation then in force[43] which made it an offence, punishable by fine and imprisonment, for persons lacking the relevant authorisation "to carry on ... insurance business". Parker J held that the claimants were precluded by illegality from enforcing the reinsurance.[44] Similarly in the well-known case of *Re Mahmoud and Ispahani*[45] a vendor was unable to sue on a contract of sale with an unlicensed purchaser on account of the Seeds, Oils and Fats Order 1919 which provided that:

"a person shall not ... *buy or sell or otherwise deal in*, any of the articles specified in the schedule hereto ... except under and in accordance with the terms of a licence." (Italics supplied).

Where activities are usually non-contractual.   It is submitted that there is a   1–16
significant difference between statutory provisions which penalise "sales" or "business",[46] and provisions which merely prohibit acts which can be done, and indeed usually are done, without involving *contractual* activity at all. It is, for example, unlikely to be profitable to consider whether the terms of a statute laying down speed limits "impliedly prohibit" the enforcement of claims arising out of contracts, the performance of which necessarily involve the breaking of the limit. Depending upon the court's perception of the gravity of the case,[47] and the extent of the individual involvement of each of the parties,[48] such contracts may or may not be unenforceable for illegality. But to describe them as having been

---

[42] [1985] Q.B. 966.
[43] Insurance Companies Act 1974.
[44] The actual decision was promptly reversed by subsequent legislation (the Financial Services Act 1986 s.132(6) provided that contravention of the relevant provisions "shall not affect the validity of any re-insurance contract ..."). cf. *Phoenix Insurance v Helvanon Insurance* [1988] Q.B. 216, discussed in Ch.2, below.
[45] [1921] 2 K.B. 716.
[46] See, e.g. *Mellis v Shirley Local Board* (1885) 16 Q.B.D. 446: "any bargain or contract"; *Re Mahmoud and Ispahani* [1921] 2 K.B. 716: "buy or sell": *Anderson v Daniel* [1924] 1 K.B. 138: "Every person who sells"; *B. & B. Viennese Fashions v Losanne* [1952] 1 All E.R. 909: "contract of sale"; *Vinall v Howard* [1953] 1 W.L.R. 987 (revsd. on other grounds [1954] 1 Q.B. 375): "to sell". Similar language is to be found in licensing regulations which have rendered building contracts unenforceable for illegality in the event of non-compliance: see, e.g. *Jackson Stansfield & Sons v Butterworth* [1948] 2 All E.R. 558; *J. Dennis and Co v Munn* [1949] 2 K.B. 327; *Bostel Bros v Hurlock* [1949] 1 K.B. 74. See also *Snell v Unity Finance* [1964] 2 Q.B. 203 (violation of hire-purchase credit restrictions); *Boissevain v Weil* [1950] A.C. 327 (exchange controls); *RTA Business Consultants v Bracewell* [2015] EWHC 630 (unlicensed estate agent) See generally Buckley, "Implied Statutory Prohibition of Contracts" (1975) 38 M.L.R. 535.
[47] See para.1–05, above.
[48] See Chs 3 and 4, below.

"impliedly prohibited" by a statute which is wholly silent as to contractual situations is an exceptionally artificial, and unnecessary, use of the concept of legislative intention.

(c) Statutory Duties in Tort and Crime

1–17   **Breach of statutory duty.**   One possible reason for the confused approach which would so broaden the scope of implied prohibition as to seek a legislative intention with respect to contracts in statutes which make no mention of them, is a comparison sometimes made between this area of the law of contract and the doctrine of the law of tort that breach of statutory duty may in certain circumstances give rise to a civil action.[49] In the latter context, however, the statute cannot contemplate a civil law tort since *ex hypothesi* there was no tort in existence prior to the passing of the statute.[50] The issue is different in the contractual sphere where some statutes do contemplate commercial activity as the basis for the imposition of criminal liability. The comparison is therefore misleading.

1–18   **Conspiracy.**   Another possible source of confusion is the fact that contracts for the deliberate commission of crimes will normally be illegal as amounting to criminal conspiracies. In view of this it is pertinent to emphasise that conspiracy originated as a common law crime.[51] No one ever felt it necessary to resort to a fiction which would have regarded the criminality of a conspiracy to commit any given statutory crime as being derived from the statute which made the actual commission of that crime punishable. On the contrary, the juristic basis of the crime of conspiracy was the same whether the conspirators planned to commit a statutory offence, a common law offence or even an act which, if done by an individual, would not be an offence at all. It was the common law.[52]

(d) Conclusion

1–19   **Limited scope of implied prohibition.**   The doctrine of implied statutory prohibition should therefore be *confined* to situations in which the language of a statute which imposes penalties necessarily envisages the activities which it penalises being carried out against a contractual background, but does not stipulate what the consequences of its infringement should be for the enforceability of the contracts in question. If such a stipulation *is* included, the situation may be one of express prohibition. All other situations involving

---

[49] See, e.g. per Sachs LJ in *Shaw v Groom* [1970] 2 Q.B. 504 at 523 ("a parallel problem").
[50] See, generally, Stanton. *Breach of Statutory Duty in Tort* (Sweet & Maxwell, London, 1986); Stanton and others, *Statutory Torts* (Sweet & Maxwell, London, 2003), Ch.2; Buckley, "Liability in Tort for Breach of Statutory Duty" (1984) 100 L.Q.R. 204.
[51] See Ormerod and Laird eds, *Smith and Hogan's Criminal Law* 14th edn, (Oxford University Press, 2015), Ch.13, para.13.3 (p.484 et seq.). For the history of the doctrine see Holdsworth, *History of English Law* (Vol. 8). pp.378–384.
[52] See *R. v Simmonds* [1969] 1 Q.B. 685. The crime of conspiracy is now on a largely statutory footing: see the Criminal Law Act 1977 s.1. But this does not affect the analogy in the text.

illegality in the law of contract are governed by the common law's own perception of the requirements of public policy in the particular circumstances. The ways in which the important doctrine of implied statutory prohibition operates in practice will be examined in the next chapter.

CHAPTER 2

IMPLIED PROHIBITION OF CONTRACTS

1. NATURE OF THE DOCTRINE

Contractual context.   In *Curragh Investments v Cook*[1] Megarry J observed,   **2–01**
obiter, "that where a contract is made in contravention of some statutory
provision then, in addition to any criminal sanctions, the courts may in some
cases find that the contract itself is stricken with illegality". He continued[2]:

> "If the statute prohibits the making of contracts of the type in question, or provides that one of
> the parties must satisfy certain requirements (e.g. by obtaining a licence or registering some
> particulars) before making any contract of the type in question, then the statutory prohibition
> or requirement may well be sufficiently linked to the contract for questions to arise of the
> illegality of any contract made in breach of the statutory requirement."

Merits often irrelevant.   In resolving the question of illegality in cases falling   **2–02**
within the scope of this doctrine, the prevailing judicial tendency is to adopt a
rather formal approach in deference to the statutory origin of the prohibition. It is
often assumed that broad consideration of policy issues, or of the relative merits
of the parties, would be inappropriate in such circumstances. An illustration is
provided by the decision of the Privy Council in *Yin v Sam*.[3] A Malayan statute[4]
provided that:

> "no person shall purchase . . . rubber . . . unless he shall have been duly licensed in that behalf
> under this enactment."

   Criminal penalties were imposed for breach of this provision. The defendant
purchaser, who did not possess a licence, was able successfully to rely on his own
illegality in order to defeat a claim for the price of rubber delivered to him. The
Privy Council followed the familiar decision of the Court of Appeal in *Re
Mahmoud* and *Ispahani*[5] in which a similar result had been reached.

Both parties affected.   The same approach was adopted by the Court of Appeal   **2–03**
in the more recent case of *Phoenix General Insurance Co of Greece v Helvanon*

---

[1] [1974] 1 W.L.R. 1559; [1974] 3 All E.R. 658.
[2] [1974] 1 W.L.R. 1559 at 1563; [1974] 3 All E.R. 658 at 661.
[3] [1962] A.C. 294.
[4] The Rubber Supervision Enactment 1937.
[5] [1921] 2 K.B. 716. See Ch.1, above. See also Glanville Williams, "The Legal Effects of Illegal
Contracts" (1942) 8 C.L.J. 51.

Insurance,[6] in which *Re Mahmoud and Ispahani* was again cited. The defendants in the *Phoenix* case were reinsurers who claimed that the plaintiffs, in entering into the primary insurance contracts, had done so in contravention of a statute[7] then in force which imposed penalties upon the "effecting and carrying out" of such contracts without authorisation. The Court of Appeal held that the true effect of complex transitional provisions was that the plaintiffs had in fact been authorised anyway. The illegality point therefore did not arise, but it was discussed extensively by Kerr LJ who delivered the only judgment. He indicated that had the transitional provisions not applied the primary insurance contracts would have been unenforceable, not only by the plaintiffs themselves but also by the other parties. It would have followed from this that the reinsurance contracts would themselves have been unenforceable.[8] The conclusion that claims under the original insurance contracts would not have been enforceable by the innocent parties to them is harsh, and Kerr LJ reached it with reluctance.[9]

2–04   **Rationale.**   At least in some cases, the doctrine of implied statutory prohibition will therefore result in a forfeiture of contractual rights which will be strict in the sense that ignorance of the prohibition, or of the facts bringing the particular contractual situation within it, will not provide an escape.[10] In such cases, statutory interference with freedom of contract is assumed by the courts to reflect a legislative decision to regulate, in the broader public interest, some aspect of trade at the expense of justice as between the parties to the agreement. If the intervention could be circumvented by pleas of ignorance or inadvertence such schemes of regulation might be significantly less effective. Moreover the stigma associated with a criminal conviction is absent from a finding that a contractual claim is unenforceable for illegality, so the need for the protection afforded a defendant by the doctrine of mens rea may be regarded as unnecessary. On the other hand, contractual forfeiture may often result in the imposition of a financial penalty upon the party affected more severe than any fine that a criminal court might have imposed. It is therefore important that, in every case in which the presence of an implied prohibition is contended for, the court should analyse the particular statute with precision in order to prevent unnecessary harshness or avoidable injustice.[11] The cases reveal several approaches which have been adopted towards the construction of statutes in this area, usually in order to limit the scope of the prohibition.[12]

---

[6] [1988] Q.B. 216. See Malcolm Clarke, "Illegal Insurance" [1987] 1 L.M.C.L.Q. 201, for a penetrating analysis of the issues involved in the case.
[7] Insurance Companies Act 1974.
[8] See also *Re Cavalier Insurance* [1989] 2 Lloyd's Rep. 430.
[9] [1988] Q.B. 216 at 276; [1987] 2 All E.R. 152 at 178c: "If this conclusion is correct . . . it is of course a most unfortunate state of affairs . . ." The decision, which is discussed further below, was reversed by the Financial Services Act 1986 s.132. See now the Financial Services and Markets Act 2000 s.28.
[10] See, especially, per Atkin LJ in *Re Muhmoud and Ispahani* [1921] 2 K.B. 716 at 731–732; see also *J. Dennis & Co v Munn* [1949] 2 K.B. 327.
[11] If no criminal penalty is imposed by the Act, the court might construe even a provision clearly designed to regulate contractual activity as merely directory, and hence as not giving rise to invalidity:

2. TECHNIQUES OF CONSTRUCTION

Small fines. In some cases the courts have felt able to conclude that the imposition of criminal sanctions was all that was intended, so that the agreement remained fully enforceable.[13] A distinction is sometimes drawn between statutes which provide for fixed penalties, such as a limited fine, and those which provide for an unlimited fine or imprisonment: prohibition of the contract being more readily made out in the latter[14] than the former.[15] Thus if the statute imposes only a small fixed fine for breach of its provisions, the court *may* be willing to allow the party responsible for the infringement to enforce the contract even against a party belonging to the class of persons for whose benefit the statute would appear to have been enacted. The outcome in these cases is, however, often difficult to predict.[16] In *Shaw v Groom*[17] a landlord who attempted to sue for rent was met with a defence of illegality based on the fact that she had failed to supply a rent book, which complied with statutory regulations intended to protect tenants by requiring the inclusion of information in the book about the rights of tenants against their landlords. But the maximum fine for a first offence was only £50. The Court of Appeal stressed that the value of any contractual forfeiture could have been far in excess of that figure, and permitted the landlord to enforce the contract notwithstanding the contravention. In other cases, however, contravention of criminal provisions imposing small penalties *has* been held to deprive a party of his contractual rights.[18] Thus the conclusion reached in *Shaw v Groom* involved the Court of Appeal in distinguishing narrowly the well-known decision of the same court,[19] nearly half a century earlier, in *Anderson v Daniel*.[20] In that case a vendor of fertiliser who failed to give the purchaser an invoice containing certain particulars relating to its composition, as required by the Fertiliser and Feeding Stuffs Act 1906, was unable to sue for the price.[21] The approach adopted

2–05

---

see, e.g. the decision of the High Court of Australia in *Australian Broadcasting Corporation v Redmore Proprietary* (1988–89) 166 C.L.R. 454, but cf. the dissenting judgment of Brennan and Dawson JJ, at 460 et seq.

[12] Of course the Act may itself provide that contracts penalised are not to be invalid: see, e.g. the Banking Act 1979 s.1(8) applied in *SCF v Masri (No.2)* [1987] Q.B. 1002. See also the Trade Descriptions Act 1968 s.35. Cf. *SST Consulting Services Pty Ltd v Rieson* (2006) 225 CLR 516 on the Trade Practices Act 1974 s.4L (Aus).

[13] For an example see the majority decision of the Canadian Supreme Court in *Continental Bank Leasing Corp v Canada* (1998) 163 D.L.R. (4th) 385.

[14] See e.g. per Hobhouse J at first instance in *Phoenix Insurance v Helvanon Insurance* [1988] Q.B. 216 at 235; [1986] 1 All E.R. 908 at 920.

[15] See e.g. *St John Shipping Corporation v Joseph Rank* [1957] 1 Q.B. 267; *Yango Pastoral Co Pty v First Chicago Australia* (1978) 139 C.L.R. 410; *Gnych v Polish Club Ltd* [2015] HCA 23.

[16] See e.g. *C. Battison & Sons v Mauti* (1986) 34 D.L.R. (4th) 700 (Ontario): breach of a by-law requiring a building renovator to provide a customer with a detailed written contract did not prevent the renovator from recovering payment. But cf. *Barrett Builders v Miller* (1990) 76 A.2d 455 in which the Supreme Court of Connecticut decided the other way (by a four-three majority) a case which involved parallel legislation, and similar facts, to those in the *Battison* case.

[17] [1970] 2 Q.B. 504. See also *Cotronic (UK) Ltd v Dezonie* [1991] B.C.L.C. 721, CA.

[18] See e.g. *RTA Business Consultants v Bracewell* [2015] EWHC 630 (unlicensed estate agent).

[19] Composed of Bankes, Atkin and Scrutton LJJ.

[20] [1924] 1 K.B. 138. See also *B. and B. Viennese Fashions v Losane* [1952] 1 All E.R. 909, CA.

[21] See, especially, per Scrutton LJ in [1924] 1 K.B. 138 at 147: "When the policy of the Act in question is to protect the general public or a class of persons by requiring that a contract shall be

in this case is, on the whole, less likely to commend itself to a modern court than that adopted in *Shaw v Groom*.[22] Nevertheless, the notional dependence of each case upon its own particular statute inevitably gives the court a degree of covert discretion to take into account the relative merits of the parties. Wherever possible, however, it is preferable for such factors to be considered openly on the basis of "common law" illegality rather than hidden behind a rather artificial exercise in statutory interpretation.

2–06   **Importance of common law illegality.**   In *Shaw v Groom* Sachs LJ emphasised[23] that there was "not the slightest suggestion" that the landlord's breach had been "knowingly or wilfully committed".[24] It would seem to follow that, if the breach in *Shaw's* case had been deliberate, the result in the case would have been different. This would presumably have been on the basis that, at common law, rather than by virtue of any prohibition in the statute itself, public policy required the imposition of an additional deterrent upon such a landlord. A combination of high potential profits, and fines that might have become absurdly low, might provide a positive incentive to law-breaking. It may well therefore be appropriate for the law of contract to discourage the anti-social conduct at which the statute is directed, without necessarily ascribing that result to the statute itself. This was emphasised by the High Court of Australia in *Yango Pastoral Co Pty Ltd v First Chicago Australia Ltd*,[25] in which a statute[26] provided that "a body corporate shall not carry on any banking business in Australia unless the body corporate is in possession of an authority . . . to carry on banking business". A penalty of AUS $10,000 was imposed "for each day while the contravention continues". The High Court of Australia held that there was no implied prohibition of contracts, and that even an unauthorised banker could recover under a mortgage and guarantee. Mason J said[27]:

> ". . . in the present case Parliament has provided a penalty which is a measure of the deterrent which it intends to operate in respect of non-compliance with section 8. In this case it is not for the court to hold that further consequences should flow, consequences which in financial terms could well far exceed the prescribed penalty . . . In saying this I am mindful that there could be a case where the facts disclose that the plaintiff stands to gain by enforcement of rights gained

---

accompanied by certain formalities or conditions, and a penalty is imposed on the person omitting those formalities or conditions, the contract and its performance without those formalities or conditions is illegal, and cannot be sued upon by the person liable to the penalties."

[22] See, e.g. *Craig Joseph v Jason Spiller and 1311 Events Ltd* [2009] EWCA 1075 (breach by an employment agency of a documentation requirement specified by regulations made under the Employment Agencies Act 1973 did not render a contract with the Agency unenforceable). See also the decision of the High Court of Australia in *Master Education Services Pty Ltd v Ketchell* [2008] HCA 38.

[23] [1971] 2 Q.B. at 519.

[24] See also *Marles v Trant (Philip) & Sons* [1954] 1 Q.B. 29 in which a vendor of seeds, who had been held liable to a purchaser for breach of warranty, was able to recover an indemnity from his own original supplier despite the fact that when reselling the seeds the vendor had contravened the Seeds Act 1920 by omitting to deliver prescribed particulars (and could not himself have enforced the contract of sale with the purchaser). Denning LJ observed that the omission had been "an act of inadvertence . . . not a deliberate breach of the law".

[25] (1978) 139 C.L.R. 410.

[26] Commonwealth Banking Act 1959 s.8. (Aus.).

[27] (1978) 139 C.L.R. 410 at 429.

through an illegal activity far more than the prescribed penalty . . . On this basis the common law principle of ex turpi causa can be given an operation consistent with, though subordinate to, the statutory intention, denying relief in those cases where a plaintiff may otherwise evade the real consequences of a breach of a statutory prohibition."

It is also important to remember that, since the far-reaching change in approach to the doctrine of common law illegality brought about by the decision of the Supreme Court in *Patel v Mirza*, in favour of transparency and flexibility, the actual intentions of the parties, and the seriousness of what occurred, are among the factors expressly to be taken into account as well as the underlying purpose of the statute in question.[28]

Whether each individual contract is penalised.   Importance is sometimes   2–07
attached to whether the criminal statute merely penalises generally the carrying on of a certain type of commercial activity, or whether it appears to impose penalties in relation to each individual *contract*. If the former is the case, this has sometimes been treated as an indication that no implied prohibition of enforceability was intended at all. This was the main ground of decision in *Yango Pastoral Co Pty Ltd v First Chicago Australia Ltd*[29] itself. Gibbs ACJ said that "the language of section 8 indicates that it is directed, not at the making or performance of particular *contracts*, but at the carrying on of any banking business".[30] Similarly in *Stewart v Oriental Fire & Marine Insurance Co*,[31] which involved a statutory provision similar in some respects to that in the *Yango* case, Leggatt J said that "the fact that insurance business was carried on in contravention of the Act of 1974 is not on its face directed either at the contracts themselves or performance of them". In the old case of *Smith v Mawhood*[32] a statute imposed penalties on dealers in tobacco in certain circumstances. In holding that a dealer liable to the penalties could nevertheless enforce contracts for the sale of tobacco Alderson B observed that "there is no addition to his criminality if he makes fifty contracts for the sale of tobacco". In *Victorian Daylesford Syndicate v Dott*[33] the distinction was applied in a case in which it pointed to the opposite conclusion. Buckley J observed:

"Not a bad test [i.e. for implied prohibition] to apply is to see whether the penalty in the Act is imposed once for all, or whether it is a recurrent penalty imposed as often as the act is done. If it be the latter, then the act is a prohibited one. Now here the penalty is imposed every time the act is done."

Although this "test" has its merits, it can never be more than a loose guideline and needs to be used with caution. There could well be situations in which the legislature contemplated contracts, and intended them to be unenforceable, while at the same time desiring, for reasons of policy peculiar to the criminal law, not to impose a separate punishment for each individual agreement entered into.

---

[28] See *Patel v Mirza* [2016] UKSC 42 at [107] per Lord Toulson.
[29] (1978) 139 C.L.R. 410.
[30] See (1978) 139 C.L.R. 410 at 415 (italics supplied).
[31] [1985] Q.B. 988 (overruled in *Phoenix Insurance v Helvanon Insurance* [1988] Q.B. 216).
[32] (1845) 14 M. & W. 452.
[33] [1905] 2 Ch. 624.

2–08   **Protecting the public or the revenue.**   A distinction was sometimes drawn in the older cases between statutes passed for the protection of the revenue and statutes passed for the protection of the public,[34] with the former not giving rise to prohibition of contracts. A crude distinction of this kind is not, as such, tenable nowadays. The notion that penalties imposed by *criminal* statutes could be intended *merely* to boost the public purse is clearly insupportable. The distinction between a fine and a tax on conduct is fundamental; there being a legislative intention to discourage conduct "punished" but not, or not necessarily, to discourage conduct "taxed".[35] Nevertheless it may still be legitimate for the court to infer, from the social purpose of a given statute, that Parliament did not intend that that purpose should always be pursued to the extent of invalidating contracts; irrespective of any disproportionality between the severity of the forfeiture and the importance of the statutory purpose. The point is particularly likely to arise in relation to licensing provisions.

2–09   **Health and safety.**   The commentary to para.181 of the American Law Institute's Second *Restatement of Contracts*[36] suggests that the court will attach greater significance "to a measure intended to protect the public health or safety than one intended to have only an economic effect". The *Restatement* goes on to contrast a statute "enacted to prevent the public from being victimised by incompetent plumbers and to protect the public health", with one requiring milk dealers to be licensed "for the purpose of economic regulation of the milk industry". It is suggested that, whereas an unlicensed plumber may be prevented from suing for his fees, an unlicensed milk dealer may be able to sue for the price of milk delivered. At first blush a distinction between health and safety on the one hand, and economic management on the other, seems to be more sophisticated than a distinction between "revenue" statutes and others. It is less clear, however, that it represents a significant advance analytically. Moreover, if it were to be treated as a firm distinction, it certainly does not represent English law: in which a great many of the cases on implied prohibition, possibly the majority, have concerned what may very loosely be termed the "economic" sphere. Furthermore, many statutes combine both safety and organisational issues in such a way as to make it difficult to separate them.[37] Nevertheless, in a context in which the

---

[34] See, e.g. *Smith v Mawhood* (1845) 14 M. & W. 452; *Brown v Duncan* (1829) 10 B. & C. 93; *Johnson v Hudson* (1809) 11 East 180. See also *Cheshire, Fifoot and Furmston on Contract*, 16th edn, edited by Furmston, (Butterworths, 2012), pp.451–452

[35] See Hart, *Concept of Law* (1961), p.39. The occasional imposition of taxation with an incidental broader social purpose, such as discouragement of tobacco consumption or promotion of the use of lead-free petrol, does not detract from this.

[36] The Paragraph itself reads as follows: "If a party is prohibited from doing an act because of his failure to comply with a licensing, registration or similar requirement, a promise in consideration of his doing that act or of his promise to do it is unenforceable on grounds of public policy if (a) the requirement has a regulatory purpose, and (b) the interest in the enforcement of the promise is clearly outweighed by the public policy behind the requirement."

[37] e.g. the fully-qualified plumber who inadvertently fails to renew his licence on the annual expiry date: see illustration 4 to para.181 of the *Restatement*. See also the decision of the District of Columbia Court of Appeals in *Cevern v Ferbish* 666 A.2d 17 (1995), in which the *Restatement* was cited and the Court was divided. The majority refused to allow a home improvement contractor who was fully qualified, but only obtained a licence shortly after the work had begun, to sue on the ground that "anything but an unyielding rule would put temptation in the way of unqualified" contractors.

absence of any clear indication in the statute inevitably makes the process of construction somewhat speculative, a broad distinction between health and safety on the one hand, and financial or managerial concerns on the other, has an undeniable appeal. The factor would seem to be one which it may occasionally be appropriate to weigh in the balance; especially since even if the provision falls into the latter category, *deliberate* contravention can still lead to contractual forfeiture by virtue of the doctrine of "common law" illegality.[38]

3.   THE DOCTRINE OF IMPLIED PROHIBITION IN PRACTICE

Type of contract.   In determining whether a statute has given rise to an implied   **2–10**
prohibition, it will sometimes be necessary to distinguish between different types of contract. The provision may not have been directed at the kind of agreement in question. One area in which this can be important is that relating to the licensing of motor-vehicles. The precise impact of licensing provisions on a contract may depend upon the nature of the agreement in question. Thus there is a basic distinction in the law of transport between a contract for the carriage of goods in a vehicle, and a contract for the hire of a vehicle.[39] This may be crucial in determining the legality of an agreement in which a vehicle alleged to have been improperly licensed was involved.[40] A carrier who performs a contract of *carriage* in an unlicensed vehicle may be unable, in any event, to enforce the contract to recover his charges.[41] But the owner of the goods will normally be able to sue if the goods are lost[42]; unless he actively encouraged the unlawful performance, in which case the principles of "common law" illegality will be fatal to his claim.[43] If the contract was one for the hire of a vehicle, on the other hand, it may be that the absence of the appropriate licence will have a wider impact: both parties being under an implied statutory obligation to ensure that the relevant provisions are complied with, regardless of the precise instance of criminal liability.[44]

The dissentient emphasised that the claimant "had done all that was necessary to qualify for the requisite licence, except pay the licensing fee", and castigated the majority for "precisely the sort of rigidity that gives government regulation a bad name", cf. *Beer v Townsgate* (1997) 152 D.L.R. (4th) 671 (Ontario Court of Appeal) at 676–679 (". . . contracts should not be rendered unenforceable merely because of technical deficiencies".)

[38] See para.2–06, above.

[39] See Professor Kahn-Freund in (1961) J.B.L. 299 at 301 (Note on *Archbolds (Freightage) v S. Spanglett*).

[40] See, e.g. *Martoo v MacDonald* (1947) Q.S.R. 263 (Full Court of Queensland). Noted in (1948) 22 Aust. LJ 233.

[41] See *Wasel Bros v Laskin* [1934] 2 D.L.R. 798 (reported more fully in [1934] 2 W.W.R. 577: Saskatchewan Court of Appeal). See also, per Devlin LJ in *Archbolds (Freightage) v S. Spanglett* [1961] 1 Q.B. 374 at 388.

[42] See *Archbolds (Freightage) v S. Spanglett* [1961] 1 Q.B. 374. For further discussion of this case see Ch.3.

[43] See *Ashmore, Benson, Pease & Co v A. v Dawson* [1973] 1 W.L.R. 828. See also Ch.3, below.

[44] See below, para.2–17.

2–11   **Position of "innocent" parties.**   In *Re Mahmoud and Ispahani*,[45] *Yin v Sam*,[46] *Phoenix Insurance v Helvanon Insurance*,[47] and many other cases, the claims held to be unenforceable for illegality were brought not by the party subject to the criminal penalty, but by the *other* party. In *Re Mahmoud and Ispahani* and *Yin v Sam* licences were necessary to trade in the relevant commodities. In each case the buyer falsely asserted that he possessed one and succeeded in relying on his own illegality to defeat a claim brought by the "innocent" vendor. In the *Phoenix* case the authorisation procedure only applied to insurers, but it was held, obiter, that absence of authorisation would defeat claims by innocent insureds. The harshness of these decisions renders this area the most difficult aspect of the law relating to implied prohibition. The "licence" cases can be supported on the basis that the statutory scheme imposed a duty upon both parties to verify the status of each other by actual inspection of the licences.[48] The dicta in the *Phoenix* case present greater difficulties.

2–12   **Literal interpretation: "carrying out".**   In *Phoenix Insurance v Helvanon Insurance*[49] Kerr LJ conceded that "the statutory prohibitions [were] to protect the insured" and even that "good public policy and common sense required[d] that contracts of insurance, even if made by unauthorised insurers, should not be invalidated". Nevertheless, he "reluctantly" saw "no convincing escape" from the "unfortunate"' conclusion that "contracts of insurance [were] prohibited by the 1974 Act in the sense that they [were] illegal and void, and therefore unenforceable" even by the innocent parties.[50] He emphasised that the statutory wording was not confined to "effecting contracts of insurance" but also referred specifically to the "carrying out" of such contracts. He expressed himself as follows:

> "Since the statute prohibits the insurer from carrying out the contract (of which the most obvious example is paying claims), how can the insured require the insurer to do an act which is expressly forbidden by statute? And how can a court enforce a contract against an unauthorised insurer when Parliament has expressly prohibited him from carrying it out? In that situation there is simply no room for considerations of public policy."

---

[45] [1921] 2 K.B. 716, see fn.10, above.
[46] [1962] A.C. 294.
[47] [1988] Q.B. 216, see fn.14, above.
[48] The imposition of penalties on one party only does not, of course, necessarily imply that the illegality was intended for the *benefit* or protection of the other party. One possible reason might be to facilitate detection by removing a disincentive to testify from one of the parties: see *US v Farrar* (1930) 2 U.S. 624 at 634.
[49] [1988] Q.B. 216, see para.2–03, above.
[50] A more satisfactory approach has been adopted in cases involving the same type of situation by the courts in the majority of states in the US. See, e.g. the Supreme Court of California in *People v United National Life Insurance Co* (1967) 427 P.2d 199 at 214: "The insurance industry is regulated primarily for the benefit of those who make use of the services the industry offers. Penalties are imposed on those members of the industry who violate the regulatory scheme . . . but the Insurance Code places no penalties, or even duties, on insured persons . . . We reject imposition of the minority rule that would allow an insurer . . . to avoid obligations to the detriment of innocent members of the protected class". (Quoted in Fraser P. Davidson, "Unauthorised Insurers and Prohibited Contracts" (1986) Juridical Review 38 at 44.)

This reasoning seems to involve reading too much into the words "carrying out". It also seems to be at variance with several earlier cases which indicate that, at least in the case of executed contracts, the courts are sometimes prepared to award damages in favour of innocent parties in circumstances in which entry into the contract by the defendant, or his chosen manner of performance, involved the commission of a criminal offence.[51] Indeed Kerr LJ conceded that this would be permitted where food unfit for human consumption had been sold contrary to the Food Act 1984.

Secondary obligation. It is apparent that the distinction between executory and executed contracts is more significant in illegality than it is elsewhere, and that the courts will occasionally find it easier to provide a remedy in the latter situation than in the former.[52] But to treat insurance cases as executory for this purpose, on the ground that the insurer has yet to "carry out" his obligations by satisfying the claim, seems difficult to support when the facts giving rise to the claim have already occurred. There is much to be said for the view of Hobhouse J, at first instance in the *Phoenix* case, who held that although the statute precluded the insurers from enforcing the original contracts, and hence also the reinsurance contracts, it would not have precluded the other parties to the original contracts, the insureds, from enforcing them.[53] He too had been faced with the argument based on "carrying . . . out", but had rejected it. He pointed out that "an action by an assured under a policy is an action for unliquidated damages"[54] and observed that "what the plaintiff is enforcing is not the primary obligation of performance, but the secondary obligation to pay damages in the absence of performance".[55] The better view is that the phrase "carrying out" was intended merely to add emphasis to the statutory prohibition imposed upon the "guilty" insurers themselves, rather than drastically to extend the consequences of that prohibition to their innocent victims.

2–13

---

[51] See *Archbold's Freightage v S. Spanglett* [1961] 1 Q.B. 374; *Shaw v Shaw* [1954] 2 Q.B. 429; *Marles v Trant (Philip) & Sons* [1954] 1 Q.B. 29. cf. *Ailion v Spieckerman* [1976] Ch. 158. See also *Re Mahmoud and Ispahani* [1921] 2 K.B. 716 at 731, per Atkin LJ. See further para.2–16, below.

[52] Sometimes the distinction will favour *executory* contracts, e.g. resiling from the unlawful purpose was formerly only possible before the contract had been performed (see now *Patel v Mirza* [2016] UKSC 42 and Ch.18, below). But where performance has taken place the court may be less embarrassed, than it would be if the contract were still executory, by the suggestion that a readiness to award damages to an innocent party might encourage the performance of unlawful acts.

[53] Unless they had been aware of the illegality, in which case they might have been precluded from suing by the principles of common law illegality, and might also theoretically have incurred criminal liability for aiding and abetting.

[54] *Chandris v Argo Insurance* (1963) Lloyd's Rep. 65.

[55] [1988] Q.B. 216 at 233.

4.   STATUTORY INTERPRETATION

2–14   **Legislative purpose.**   The actual decision of the Court of Appeal in the *Phoenix Insurance v Helvanon Insurance* case was promptly reversed by legislation.[56] But this reversal does not affect the authority of the case as an example of the rigid approach often adopted towards situations involving statutory illegality. A similar approach was also adopted by the Court of Appeal in the later case of *Fuji Finance Inc v Aetna Life Insurance Co Ltd*.[57] The Court considered, obiter, whether an insurance company could rely upon its own breach of statutory provisions to avoid liability. Although the Court of Appeal was divided on the point, it appeared united in approaching the issue on the basis of literal interpretation of the statutory wording rather than upon "public policy".[58] It is certainly appropriate for such cases to be treated as giving rise to questions of implied prohibition, rather than "common law" illegality. Nevertheless, it is submitted that an approach which accords greater weight to the *purposes* of the statute would be more appropriate. Nor, given that the statutes concerned are silent as to the effect of their provisions upon the contracts to which they refer, would such an approach seem to violate established canons of construction: that silence creates an ambiguity which requires a wider frame of reference for its resolution.[59]

2–15   **Flexible approach.**   A more flexible approach to statutory interpretation in this context was demonstrated by the Court of Appeal in *Hughes v Asset Managers Plc*.[60] An investor sought unsuccessfully to recover losses he had incurred on the stock market, on the ground that his agreement with the company which had managed the investments for him had been void because their representative had not held the requisite licence under the Prevention of Fraud (Investments) Act 1958. Saville LJ said[61] that on its true construction the statute did not render the agreement void but, significantly, he added that even "if there were other indications that Parliament intended to strike down deals made by unlicensed representatives. I would not myself regard this point as conclusive, since to do so would be to prefer the form to the substance". He concluded that there was nothing "to indicate any good reason or public need for such a result". Similarly, Hirst LJ observed that, to have allowed the claim to succeed, "would be inimical to public policy, which is the ultimate test to be applied".[62]

---

[56] See the Financial Services Act 1986 s.132. For the effect of this provision see *Deutsche Ruckversicherung v Walbrook Insurance* [1996] 1 W.L.R. 1152. See now the Financial Services and Markets Act 2000 s.28, and Ch.21, below.

[57] [1997] Ch. 173 reversing [1995] Ch. 122.

[58] See [1997] Ch. 173 at 192, per Morritt LJ. For another example of the adoption of the literal interpretation approach, so as to render the innocence of the claimant irrelevant, see the decision of Lightman J at first instance in *Mohamed v Alaga & Co* [1998] 2 All E.R. 720 (reversed in part, [2000] 1 W.L.R. 1815. CA); see also *Westlaw Services v Boddy* [2010] EWCA Civ 929.

[59] cf. *Pepper v Hart* [1993] A.C. 593.

[60] [1995] 3 All E.R. 669.

[61] [1995] 3 All E.R. 669 at 673–674.

[62] [1995] 3 All E.R. 669 at 675.

Successful claim by innocent party. Interpretation of statutes in this area should also focus wherever possible upon contractual *rights*, rather than conceptually upon prohibited *contracts*.[63] In illegality, despite the pervasive influence of reciprocity elsewhere in contract, it will often be legitimate to permit enforceability by one party alone, even though such a course would be inappropriate if the relative merits of the parties were considered in isolation. In the old case of *Bloxsome v Williams*[64] the purchaser of a horse which had turned out to be defective claimed damages from the vendor. The latter relied on his own illegality, alleging that the contract had been made on a Sunday and citing s.1 of the Sunday Observance Act 1677, which prohibited persons from pursuing their "ordinary callings" upon the "Lord's Day". The situation would appear to qualify as one of implied statutory prohibition since pursuit of ordinary callings would frequently involve trading activity and hence, as in the case itself, the making of contracts. Although it is unlikely that the vendor could have enforced the agreement, Bayley J allowed the innocent purchaser to sue: he had not known that the defendant's "ordinary calling" was horse-trading and hence was ignorant of the facts giving rise to the prohibition. It is submitted that this decision was correct.[65]

2–16

A possible presumption. As has already been demonstrated, it is always possible that a particular statutory formulation, unlike that in *Bloxsome v Williams*, might strike at *both* parties to a contract even while imposing criminal penalties upon only one.[66] But the courts should not be as zealous as the Court of Appeal was in *Phoenix Insurance v Helvanon Insurance* to identify such broad prohibitions unless that conclusion is inescapable. It is suggested that an underlying principle can be derived from the majority of the cases as follows: there is a rebuttable presumption that a criminal statute which defines the offence it creates in terms of contractual activity (a) impliedly prohibits enforceability of contracts by the party subject to the penalty but (b) leaves unaffected the rights of the other party.[67] As *Shaw v Groom* and *Yin v Sam* illustrate, both limbs of this presumption are rebuttable: the party penalised was able to sue in the former, while in the latter even the party not penalised was unable to do so.

2–17

---

[63] "There is nothing unusual about a circumstance in which making or giving effect to a contract involves an offence by one party but not by the other. The consequences of such illegality for the rights of the respective parties will not necessarily be the same": per the majority of the High Court of Australia in *Australian Competition and Consumer Commission v Baxter Healthcare* (2007) 232 C.L.R. 1 at [44].

[64] (1824) 3 B. & C. 232.

[65] In *Bedford Insurance Co v Resseguros do Brasil* [1985] Q.B. 966 at 985; [1984] 3 All E.R. 766 at 774, Parker J suggested that *Bloxsome v Williams* was wrongly decided: sed quaere.

[66] See above, "Position of innocent parties", and cases there cited, especially *Re Mahmoud and Ispahani* [1921] 2 K.B. 716.

[67] In *Anandh v Barnet Primary Health Care Trust* [2004] EWCA Civ 5, the Court of Appeal held that while the carrying out of eye-tests by unlicensed persons was statutorily prohibited, this did not render the formation of contracts for eye-tests by such persons unlawful: "If the making of contracts for eye tests to be provided by an unqualified person is also impliedly prohibited, neither a paying customer nor the public purse could recover the cost . . . This result would be to the detriment of innocent parties" (per Arden LJ, at [36]).

2–18　**Protection of one of the parties.**[68]　One variable of particular importance, which may affect the application of the general presumption suggested above, is whether the statutory provision was intended to *protect* one of the parties against the other and, if so, whether the contract had been performed. If, for example, the agreement was still executory the court may be reluctant to award damages for non-performance even in favour of a party the statute was intended to protect. To hold otherwise would be tantamount to holding that the statutory protection could be waived,[69] and could also encourage the "guilty" party to perform. But if performance has already occurred, it may well be appropriate to allow the other party to enforce the contract.[70] The presumption in favour of the party not penalised will then apply unrebutted. Otherwise employers of underage workers, for example, might be positively encouraged to continue their activities knowing that they could never be compelled to pay remuneration.[71] The result may be the same even if, exceptionally, the employee is penalised as well as the employer. The following illustration is provided by the Second American *Restatement of Contracts* as follows[72]:

> "A employs B to work in his factory and promises to pay him double for the overtime if B works ten hours a day instead of the usual eight. A state statute, designed to protect the health of workers in such factories, provides a maximum period of employment of eight hours a day and makes violation a crime for both employer and employee. B works ten hours a day but A refuses to pay him extra for the overtime. A court may decide that the statute was enacted to protect a class of persons to which B belongs against a class to which A belongs and that therefore enforcement of A's promise is not precluded on grounds of public policy."

5.　CONDITIONAL AGREEMENTS

(a)　Compliance with Legal Requirements

2–19　**Wording of the statute.**　In certain circumstances parties may reach prior agreement in situations in which the obtaining of licences, or compliance with other statutory requirements which depend upon factors not in the hands of the parties themselves, is necessary for legal performance. Provided that agreement is reached on the assumption that the licences or the like are to be obtained prior to performance, the contract will not normally be considered to be unenforceable for illegality. There is no objection in principle to conditional contracts of this kind, or to agreements in which one party undertakes to ensure that all legal requirements affecting performance are complied with. The wording of the particular statute might, however, provide otherwise. In *George v Greater*

---

[68] See also Ch.18, below, on protection as a basis for restitution.

[69] cf. *Wylie v Lawrence Wright Music Co* (1932) T.L.R. 295 (shop assistant who agrees to forego holidays, resulting in his exceeding the maximum number of hours permitted by statute, cannot recover damages in lieu of the holidays).

[70] e.g. where food unfit for human consumption has been sold and caused poisoning.

[71] cf. *Short v Bullion-Beck and Champion Mining Co* (1899) 20 Utah 20; 57 Pac.720, discussed by Gellhorn in "Contracts and Public Policy" (1935) 35 Col. L.R. 679. Restitutionary relief may not always provide an adequate substitute for enforceability in such cases: see generally, Ch.18 below.

[72] At para.179.

Adelaide Land Development Co,[73] the parties reached an agreement for the sale of certain land in circumstances governed by the South Australia Town Planning and Development Act 1920. The contract contemplated expressly that the requirements of the Act would be fulfilled and they were, in fact, subsequently complied with. Nevertheless the High Court of Australia held that compliance after the formation of the contract was not good enough, and that the contract was unenforceable for illegality. Starke J said[74]:

> "Selling, in the case of land, includes the making of agreements for its conveyance in consideration of a price in money: and this is so whether the agreement be absolute or conditional, for a conditional agreement for the sale of land is none the less a sale of land, and therefore a selling of it."

Flawed approach. The highly conceptual approach adopted in this case would appear to be flawed. In the absence of much more specific statutory wording to the contrary than was present in this case, there is no good reason for holding that agreements which contemplate subsequent compliance with legal requirements should be treated as being unenforceable for illegality providing that those requirements are in fact satisfied prior to performance. It is significant that the tendency in subsequent Australian cases, when considering *George v Greater Adelaide Land Development Co*, has been to distinguish the case narrowly and "confine it to its particular legislation".[75]

2–20

Where compliance not expressly provided for. A further question which can arise concerns the status of executory contracts which, unlike that in *George v Greater Adelaide Land Development Co*, do not expressly provide that the statutory requirements are to be complied with before performance, but are simply silent on the matter. Should the law presume in favour of legality, so that conditional agreements will be effective in the absence of proof of a positive intention not to comply with the relevant provisions; or will the contracts be unenforceable in any event if they do not expressly provide that the statutory requirements are to be fulfilled?[76] The former is the more desirable view.[77] The older English authorities on the point are, however, conflicting. In *Sewell v Royal Exchange Assurance Co*[78] a question arose as to the legality of a voyage under charterparty whereby certain cargo was to be landed in England of a kind which required a statutory licence before it could be landed from the type of ship in question. Mansfield CJ found in favour of the charterparty, and said[79] that it was sufficient if the licence was obtained "just before the act of importation". But in

2–21

---

[73] (1929) 43 C.L.R. 91. cf. *Milner v Staffordshire Congregational Union* [1956] Ch. 275.
[74] See (1929) 43 C.L.R. 91 at 104.
[75] See, per Wallace J in *Landall v Bogaers* [1980] W.A.R. 33 referring to the judgment of Dixon CJ in the High Court of Australia in *Braham v Walker* [1960–61] 104 C.L.R. 366.
[76] On the special situation where the parties only enter into the contract through ignorance of the existence of a legal provision which actually undermines their purpose in so doing see Ch.3, below.
[77] See, e.g. *Dodge v Eisenman* (1985) 22 D.L.R. (4th) 711 (British Columbia Court of Appeal), per Macfarlane JA at 720–721: "The acquisition of a licence was a routine and trivial matter . . . Each of the parties must be taken to have contemplated that this routine requirement would be fulfilled as and when it was necessary".
[78] (1813) 4 Taunt. 856.
[79] (1813) 4 Taunt. 856 at 865.

Holland v Hall,[80] decided shortly afterwards, and in which *Sewell's* case was cited, a different result was reached. Abbott J said[81]:

> "If there be, on the face of the agreement, an illegal intention, is it too much to say, that the burden lies on the party who uses expressions prima facie importing an illegal purpose, to shew that the intention was legal?"[82]

2–22 **Canadian decisions.** Two Canadian cases show that uncertainty as to what presumption should operate in cases of this type can still occur. In *Elias v Walsam Investments*[83] Ferguson J, in a decision which was later upheld by the Ontario Court of Appeal, held that the contract before him was unenforceable for illegality and said[84]:

> "It was argued in the present case that the parties intended to comply with the statute, but no such provision appears in the agreement. Whatever their intentions were with respect to the company which they proposed to incorporate to take a transfer or conveyance of the land no intention to comply with the Act before transfer to that company is to be found anywhere in the agreement, and evidence tending to add to or vary the terms of the agreement was inadmissible."

In *Maschinenfabrik Seydelmann K-G v Presswood Bros*,[85] however, the Ontario Court of Appeal reversed the decision of a judge at first instance who had pronounced in favour of illegality stressing that he had been unable to find any indication from the documents in the transaction that the agreement was conditional upon compliance with the relevant statutory requirements. Shroeder JA, delivering the judgment of the Appeal Court, said that the trial judge had "failed to take into account the well-settled presumption of law in favour of the legality of a contract; that if a contract can be reasonably susceptible of two meanings . . . one legal and the other not, that interpretation is to be put upon it which will support it and give it operation".[86] It is to be hoped that this approach will be adopted in any future English cases. In *Mountain Village Developments v Engineered Homes*,[87] however, the British Columbia Court of Appeal chose, by a majority, to distinguish the *Maschinenfabrik* case and to hold a contract unenforceable for illegality in not dissimilar circumstances. Significantly the decision provoked a strongly worded dissenting judgment in which it was said

---

[80] (1817) 1 B. & Ald. 53. cf. *Mayor of Norwich v Norfolk Railway* (1855) 4 El. Bl. & El. 397.

[81] (1817) 1 B. & Ald. at 56. It is possible that the court was doubtful about the intention of the parties and suspected that they intended to go ahead regardless of whether the requisite statutory consent was obtained or not. cf. *Edler v Auerbach* [1950] 1 K.B. 359; *Rich (T. P.) Investments v Calderon* [1964] N.S.W.R. 709.

[82] cf. Pollock, *Principles of Contract* Winfield ed. (Stevens, 13th edn, 1950), p.263: "Whenever it is desired to contract for the doing of something which is not certainly lawful at the time, or the lawfulness of which depends on some event not within the control of the parties, the terms of the contract should make it clear that the thing is not to be done unless it becomes or is ascertained to be lawful".

[83] (1964) 45 D.L.R. (2d) 561 affirmed [1965] 2 O.R. 672.

[84] See (1964) 45 D.L.R. (2d) 561 at 568.

[85] (1966) 53 D.L.R. (2d) 224, reversing (1965) 47 D.L.R. (2d) 216.

[86] See also *Att-Gen for New Brunswick v St John* [1948] 3 D.L.R. 693 (Can), cf. *Best v Glenville* [1960] 1 W.L.R. 1198; *Michael Richards Properties v St Saviours Parish* [1975] 3 All E.R. 416.

[87] (1985) 64 B.C.L.R. 195.

that "literal effect should not be given to the words of a statute if the result would be absurd or unreasonable".[88] Moreover, the *Maschinenfabrik* case has been cited with approval in subsequent Canadian judgments in support of the presumption of legality favoured in it.[89]

(b)   Contractual Allocation of Responsibility

Before performance.   In some cases the parties may choose to allocate by their agreement the duty of fulfilling any necessary statutory conditions. The enforceability of such an undertaking, however, may depend crucially upon whether or not the contract remained executory. If performance took place without the conditions being fulfilled, so that the mischief at which the statute was aimed must be taken to have occurred, the outcome will depend upon whether the Act, on its true construction, imposed a duty with respect to licensing on both parties or upon only one. Even if only one party was statutorily required to possess a licence, the other one may have been under an obligation to ensure, prior to performance, that this requirement had been complied with.[90] If no licence was obtained, so that legal performance of the contract was impossible, both parties will be excused performance.[91] But the party who agreed to be responsible for obtaining a licence may be liable for his failure to do so. In *Walton (Grain) Ltd v British Italian Trading Co*,[92] Diplock J said:

> "Prima facie there is, in my view, an implied condition in a contract that at the time of performance it shall be legal for the promisor to do the act which he has contracted to do . . . There may, of course, be cases . . . where, upon the true construction of the contract, the promisor warrants that the doing of the act he has contracted to do will be legal . . .; but the true nature of such a warranty is that it is a collateral warranty, that is to say. an undertaking collateral to the main contract, and if the act which he has contracted to do is illegal and, therefore, impossible of performance, his failure to perform the main contract is not a breach of the main contract, but a breach of the collateral undertaking that performance of the main contract shall not become illegal."

Depending upon the nature of the undertaking the party giving it will be liable in any event,[93] or only in the event of his having failed to use due diligence.[94]

2–23

---

[88]   (1985) 64 B.C.L.R. 195 at 213, per Esson JA.
[89]   For a recent example see the decision of the British Columbia Court of Appeal itself in *Quinlan v University of British Columbia* [2009] BCCA 248 at [23].
[90]   Post-war control, by licensing, of building operations led to a number of cases on this point. See, e.g. *J. Dennis & Co v Munn* [1949] 2 K.B. 327 at 331–332, per Denning LJ: "Builders who undertake work nowadays do so at their risk, unless there is a licence to cover it . . . It is, therefore, incumbent on them, before they undertake any work, to see that there is a licence covering their undertaking . . . They must not simply take the owner's word that there is a licence. They should ask to see it. If they do not do so, and it turns out that he has no licence at all, they have acted illegally and can recover nothing". But cf. *Strongman (1945) Ltd v Sincock* [1955] 2 Q.B. 525, discussed below.
[91]   See *Ralli Bros v Campania Naviera Sota Y Aznar* [1927] 2 K.B. 287.
[92]   [1959] 1 Lloyd's Rep. 223 at 236.
[93]   See, e.g. *Peter Cassidy Seed Co v Osuustukkukauppa LL* [1957] 1 W.L.R. 273 (Devlin J); see also *Portabmbull Rameshwar v K. C. Sethia (1944) Ltd* [1951] 2 Lloyd's Rep. 89, HL.
[94]   See *Walton (Grain) Ltd v British Italian Trading Co* [1959] 1 Lloyd's Rep. 223.

2–24   **Contingency of refusal.**   In cases of failure to use due diligence, it may be unclear whether a licence would in practice have been granted even if the appropriate steps to secure one had actually been taken. This possibility was considered at first instance in the Scottish case of *Eisen v M'Cabe*.[95] The parties to a contract for the sale of timber stipulated that their agreement was subject to a condition that the buyers should obtain a permit from the Timber Controller, pursuant to a statutory order which provided that timber should be sold only to holders of such permits. In an action for breach of contract it was alleged that the buyers had refused to give the Controller certain information required by him and as a result had failed to obtain a permit. The claim ultimately failed, in the Court of Session and the House of Lords, on the ground, similar to that in *George v Greater Adelaide Land Development Co*, that the statutory wording prohibited even a conditional contract which anticipated that an application to the Timber Controller would be made. The Lord Ordinary, however, had been prepared to treat a conditional contract as outside the prohibition, and to award damages subject to "an allowance . . . in respect of the contingency that the permit might have been refused".[96]

2–25   **"Warranties of legality".**   The proposition that parties may be permitted to reach agreement before the fulfilment of statutory conditions, and even determine where the burden of satisfying those conditions should fall, must be distinguished from the proposition that the *legal consequences* of performance going ahead, in the event of the conditions remaining unsatisfied, can also be allocated. The principles relating to illegality in contract exist to protect the public interest, they are therefore beyond the reach of the parties and cannot be amended by agreement. Nevertheless, in *Strongman (1945) Ltd v Sincock*[97] the Court of Appeal allowed a party to a contract, which had been performed unlawfully without compliance with relevant statutory conditions, to recover damages for breach of a collateral warranty that the conditions had been satisfied. The claimants were builders who had undertaken certain work on the defendant's premises. Under regulations then in force[98] a licence was required to cover the work but was never obtained, and when it had been completed the defendant sought to avoid payment. Similar pleas of illegality had been successful in several earlier cases of the same type.[99] In the present case, however, the defendant, who was an architect, had admitted in evidence that it was the "universal practice" in the trade, if an architect was involved, "for the architect and not the builder to get the licence". The Court of Appeal held that the building contract itself had been illegal, but that "there was a warranty, or (putting it more accurately) a promise by the architect that he would get supplementary licences, or that if he failed to

---

[95] (1920) 57 Sc.L.R. 126; reversed (1920) 57 Sc.L.R. 534.
[96] See (1920) 57 Sc.L.R. 126 at 129.
[97] [1955] 2 Q.B. 525.
[98] See the Defence (General) Regulations 1939, reg.56A.
[99] See, e.g. *J. Dennis and Co v Munn* [1949] 2 K.B. 327: *Bostel Bros v Hurlock* [1949] 1 K.B. 74; *A. Smith and Son v Walker* [1952] 2 Q.B. 319; *Jamieson v Watt's Trustee* [1950] SC 265 (Scotland) See also the much more recent decision of the Queensland Supreme Court in *Dart Holdings Pty Ltd v Total Concept Group Pty Ltd* [2012] QSC 158 (Aus).

get them he would stop the work".[100] The claimant was allowed to recover, as damages for breach of that warranty, exactly the sums due to him under the building contract which was unenforceable for illegality. The decision has inevitably proved controversial,[101] and would have been easier to understand if the contract had been left unperformed; damages being sought merely for failure to procure the licences which would have facilitated lawful performance.[102] Once the contract was no longer executory the enforceability of the warranty is not easy to reconcile with the finding of illegality.[103]

Misleading terminology. The very terminology of "warranty", with its connotation of the free allocation of risk, is a potential source of confusion in illegality cases.[104] Although it is unobjectionable if the constraints imposed on the parties by the law are borne in mind, it needs to be used with caution. The notion is particularly misleading if invoked to justify *rejection* of a defence of illegality which was misconceived in any event. The reasoning of Devlin LJ in *Archbold's (Freightage) v S. Spanglett*,[105] in which an unlicensed earner attempted unsuccessfully to rely on his own illegality in order to defeat a claim by the goods owner for losing his property in transit, provides an unfortunate example of this process. He said[106]:

> "I think there is much to be said for the argument that in a case of this sort there is, unless the circumstances exclude it, an implied warranty that the van is properly licensed for the service for which it is required."

This dictum was not necessary for the decision in *Archbold's* case, since the statutory duty with respect to licensing was imposed not on the claimant but only on the defendant. The former was therefore able to sue even though "performance" had taken place, and a contravention of the statute had

2–26

---

[100] [1955] 2 Q.B. 525 at 534, per Denning LJ. But cf. *J. Dennis & Co v Munn* [1949] 2 K.B. 327 at 331–332, also, per Denning LJ (quoted above, fn.87).

[101] See Treitel, in *Essays in Memory of Sir Rupert Cross* (Tapper ed., Butterworths, 1981), pp.98–99.

[102] cf. the American Law Institute's Second *Restatement of Contracts*, Para.180, Illustration 4: "A and B make an agreement under which A, a builder, promises to build a house for B for $100,000. The plan and specifications involve violations of local planning ordinances of which B neither knows nor has reason to know. *On discovering the violations, B promptly refuses to allow A to proceed with the work*. Enforcement of A's promise to build the house is not precluded on grounds of public policy and B has a claim against A for damages" (italics supplied).

[103] cf. *Batra v Ephraim* [1982] 2 Lloyd's Rep 11 (Note), per Bridge LJ at 14: "The other way the argument was put was to suggest that the plaintiff should now be able to reconstitute the action and obtain damages for a breach of warranty . . . To do that would enable the plaintiff by a roundabout route to do precisely what the law forbids, namely, to enforce a contract which the law says is unenforceable".

[104] The concept has actually been incorporated into one branch of the law by statute: see the Marine Insurance Act 1906 s.4l. But see also criticism in *Chalmers on the Marine Insurance Act* (10th edn, E.R. Hardy Ivamy ed., Butterworths, 1993), p.64, fn.1: "'Warranty' is not an apt term in this context, inasmuch as a warranty can be waived, but illegality cannot", cf. *Euro-Diam v Bathurst* [1990] 1 Q.B. 1 at 40–41; [1988] 2 All E.R. 23 at 33, per Kerr LJ.

[105] [1961] 1 Q.B. 374. For further discussion of this case see Ch.7, below.

[106] See [1961] 1 Q.B. at 392.

occurred.[107] If, however, a statutory duty had been imposed on the plaintiff, or if he had been aware of the illegality and participated in it,[108] no attempt in the contract to allocate the risk of illegality to the defendant would have been effective to enable the plaintiff to sue.[109]

---

[107] See also the recent decision of the High Court of Australia in *Fitzgerald v F.J. Leonardt* (1997) 189 C.L.R. 215.
[108] See Chs 3 and 4, below.
[109] cf. *Sheridan v Dickson* [1970] 1 W.L.R. 1328.

CHAPTER 3

UNLAWFUL PERFORMANCE

1.   SCOPE OF THE CHAPTER

Where primary object lawful.   This chapter is concerned with the
enforceability, or otherwise, of contracts in situations in which the primary
objective of the contract is lawful, but one or both of the parties intends to
commit, or does commit, an unlawful act in the course of performance.

3–01

2.   EXECUTORY CONTRACTS AND IGNORANCE OF THE LAW

(a)   Illegality Irrelevant

Abandonment of original intention.   In some cases one or both of the parties
may intend that an otherwise lawful contract should be performed in a manner
which would in fact involve contravention of the law. If this intention was formed
through ignorance of the surrounding circumstances, and was abandoned
immediately the true position was ascertained so that the agreement was
performed lawfully, illegality as such should not, in principle, be relevant to the
resolution of any dispute which might subsequently occur between the parties.

3–02

Waugh v Morris.   In the important nineteenth century case of *Waugh v Morris*[1]
the Court of Queen's Bench held that this is indeed the position. Moreover, they
did so in a situation in which the parties' initial ignorance had related not merely
to factual circumstances but to the law itself. A charterparty provided that the ship
under charter should carry a cargo of hay from France to London, where it was to
be unloaded. Unknown to the parties, however, the unloading of French hay in
the UK was illegal; having been recently prohibited by an Order in Council made
under legislation to prevent the spread of contagious diseases among animals.
Fortunately, the intention to unload the hay in London was not spelt out in the
charterparty, which merely provided that the cargo should be taken from the ship
"alongside". When the existence of the Order in Council was discovered the
original intention was abandoned; the hay was taken from the ship into another
vessel and exported. Although no violation of the Order in Council ever took
place, relations between the parties became sour, and the claimant shipowners
brought an action for demurrage. The defendants contended that the claim should
fail, on the ground that the original intention to unload the hay in London had

3–03

---

[1] (1873) L.R. 8 Q.B. 202.

rendered the entire charterparty unenforceable for illegality. Blackburn J conceded "that a contract, lawful in itself, is illegal if it be entered into with the object that the law should be violated",[2] but emphasised that the law had never actually been violated in the case and that the intention to perform in a manner in fact unlawful had been abandoned immediately the Order in Council had been discovered. He continued[3]:

> "In order to avoid a contract which can be legally performed, on the ground that there was an intention to perform it in an illegal manner, it is necessary to show that there was the wicked intention to break the law; and if this is so, the knowledge of what the law is becomes of great importance."[4]

In the result, the defence of illegality was rejected. The reasoning, and the decision, in this case are surely unimpeachable.

(b) Illegality Confused With Other Concepts

(i) Waugh v Morris Lost Sight of

3–04 **Failure to explore other avenues of escape.** Of course, disputes may still arise between the parties, as in *Waugh v Morris* itself, in principle unrelated to illegality; and it is important that the appropriate conceptual basis for the resolution of such disputes should be correctly identified. Unfortunately, however, this has not always been done in subsequent cases. As a result, illegality has occasionally been successfully relied on in order to escape from obligations from which more legitimate avenues of escape may or may not have existed. Failure to explore those avenues, and to deploy "illegality" instead, has sometimes resulted in the important principle embodied in *Waugh v Morris* being lost sight of. The confusion usually arises because it is the abandonment of the intended method of performance which has rendered the contract less attractive or profitable to the party who wishes to escape from it: so that illegality is perceived to be relevant when in truth it is not.

(ii) Mistake

3–05 ***Allan (Merchandising) v Cloke.*** It is interesting to contrast *Waugh v Morris* with the much more recent decision of the Court of Appeal in *Allan (Merchandising) v Cloke*.[5] A roulette wheel was let on hire for playing at a

---

[2] (1873) L.R. 8 Q.B. 202 at 207.

[3] (1873) L.R. 8 Q.B. 202 at 208. This passage was quoted with approval by Toulson LJ in *Anglo-Petroleum v TFB (Mortgages)* [2007] EWCA Civ 456 who said (at [63]): "130 years later, this statement of the law has added importance because of the explosion in the number of statutory regulations of one kind or another under English and European law". See also the same judge (as a Justice of the Supreme Court) in *Patel v Mirza* [2016] UKSC 42 at [70]-[71].

[4] See also *Cargo Ex Argos* (1873) L.R. 5 P.C. 134 in which a similar decision was reached; and in which Sir Montague E. Smith said (at 163): "It is admitted that both parties, when they made the contract, were ignorant of the prohibition against landing petroleum, and therefore no question of intentional infraction of the law of France arises".

[5] [1963] 2 Q.B. 340.

country club a particular form of roulette which in fact, but unknown to the parties, violated the provisions of the Betting and Gaming Act 1960. Although the wheel could have been used for playing ordinary, perfectly lawful, forms of roulette the hirers did not wish to use it in that way. Accordingly, as soon as they discovered that the original intention happened to be illegal, they returned the wheel to the owners. As in *Waugh v Morris* the law was therefore never actually contravened. The owners refused, however, to accept the termination of the contract and sued for rent. Despite the possibility that the wheel could have been used perfectly lawfully the action, unlike that in *Waugh v Morris*, failed. The hirers managed successfully to defeat the claim by relying on illegality. Lord Denning MR, in a passage which is in sharp contrast to that of Blackburn J quoted above, expressed himself as follows[6]:

"I desire to say that where two people together have the common design to use a subject-matter for an unlawful purpose, so that each participates in the unlawful purpose, then that contract is illegal in its formation: and it is no answer for them to say that they did not know the law on the matter."

Incorrect proposition. It is submitted that this proposition is incorrect, and that the principle stated by Blackburn J is to be preferred. A different approach to the problem in *Allan (Merchandising) v Cloke* might have been to consider whether the contract was void for mistake on the ground that its subject-matter was fundamentally different from that which the parties had assumed.[7] Given the demise of relief in equity for mistakes insufficiently fundamental to render contracts void at common law,[8] the chances of an avenue of escape emerging via the doctrine of "mistake" would probably not be very high if a similar case were to occur today.[9] But, irrespective of the likely outcome via that approach, the crucial point is that the case should be perceived as having raised an issue on the law which applies when a state of affairs exists which is different from that which was in contemplation when the contract was made.[10] To invoke "illegality" in such circumstances, with its focus upon the public interest rather than that of the parties, could potentially have quite inappropriate consequences. Difficulties might arise in a similar case, for example, in relation to recovery by the owner of goods transferred under the contract of hire.[11]

3–06

(iii) Failure of Consideration

Reynolds v Kinsey. The proposition that it is important carefully to distinguish illegality from mistake, and other branches of the law of contract governing the relationship of the parties with each other, was made expressly in a dissenting

3–07

[6] [1963] 2 Q.B. 340 at 348.
[7] See *Bell v Lever Bros* [1932] A.C. 161.
[8] See *Great Peace Shipping v Tsavaliris Salvage* [2002] EWCA Civ 1407; [2002] 4 All E.R. 689 disapproving *Solle v Butcher* [1950] 1 K.B. 671.
[9] The mistake had been one of law but, for what it is worth, this would no longer present a difficulty even if it might have done at the time when the case was actually decided: see now *Kleinwort Benson Ltd v Lincoln City Council* [1999] 2 A.C. 349; [1998] 4 All E.R. 513, HL.
[10] cf. *Streatham Cinema v John MacLauchlan* [1933] 2 K.B. 331.
[11] cf. *Bowmakers v Barnet Instruments* [1945] K.B. 65, and see generally, Ch.16, below.

judgment in a case in the then Federal Supreme Court of Rhodesia and Nyasaland. In *Reynolds v Kinsey*[12] the claimant agreed to sell a mining business to the defendant. Both parties entered into the transaction on the assumption that it would be possible for the defendant to house the African labour force on the site of the business. Subsequent events were indeed to prove that this was the only way in which to render the business economically viable. Unfortunately, although neither party was aware of it at the time of making the contract, to house African employees in the manner contemplated was illegal as constituting an offence under the Southern Rhodesia Land Apportionment Act of 1941. When the defendant began to comply with the law he found that the Africans left his employment, and he resisted a claim by the claimant for an outstanding portion of the purchase-price by relying on illegality.

3–08   **Other remedies.**   By a majority the Court held that the defence, based on the ground that both parties had contemplated that the business was to be operated in a manner which turned out to be unlawful, would succeed; the parties' ignorance of the law being considered irrelevant. Tredgold CJ, expressing the majority view, observed that it "would obviously be unjust to enforce the contract" when "the establishment of the illegality might completely frustrate the contract from the point of view of the other party, who might well have been equally ignorant of the law".[13] The fallacy in this reasoning was sharply expressed by the dissentient, Clayden FJ, who said[14]:

> "... it is, I think necessary not to confuse failure of consideration with illegality of consideration. If the failure of the substantial consideration for the contract, the right to house employees on the claims, was such as to make performance of the contract impracticable, the [defendant] might have other remedies to rid himself of his obligations."

3–09   *Nash v Stevenson Transport.*   Traces of the confusion in the reasoning of the majority in *Reynolds v Kinsey* can also be detected in an earlier decision of the English Court of Appeal. In *Nash v Stevenson Transport*[15] the claimant was entitled by statute to take out licences in respect of goods vehicles. Since he did not wish to use the licences himself he attempted to profit from his statutory right by contracting to allow the defendant company to use his name, for the purpose of operating goods vehicles under the licences. The agreement was made in the honest belief that this arrangement would be effective, in law, to enable the defendant company to enjoy the benefit of the licences. But the defendants refused to pay the sums due from them under the agreement, and the Court of Appeal held that they were entitled to do so. On the construction of the Road and Rail Traffic Act 1933, which conferred the right to the licences on the claimant, the Court held that the licences granted were personal to the licensee and that the claimant could not transfer the benefit of them by allowing the defendants to use his name.

---

[12] 1959 (4) S.A. 50; (1959) 2 R. & N. 289.
[13] 1959 (4) S.A. 50 at 50–51; (1959) 2 R. & N. 289 at 295.
[14] 1959 (4) S.A. 50 at 63; (1959) 2 R. & N. 289 at 313.
[15] [1936] 2 K.B. 128.

Incorrect analysis. The actual result is clearly correct, since if the defendants   **3–10**
had operated vehicles in reliance on the licences they would have incurred
criminal liability for putting unlicensed vehicles on the road.[16] If the claimant had
been allowed to recover from the defendants he would therefore have got his
money for nothing. Nevertheless, the basis of the decision was not that the
defendants succeeded on the ground of total failure of consideration, but that the
contract was one which could not be legally performed. But this does not seem to
have been a correct analysis. The defendants would only have committed an
offence if they had put the vehicles on the road, and the agreement did not impose
an obligation on them to use the vehicles in this or in any other way. The contract
was simply one which, for reasons of law, lacked content. In the event of the
contract having been fully executed, an attempt to recover back any money
transferred in return for the "licences" might have faced difficulties if the
transaction was treated as "illegal". But it is not obvious that such difficulties
should face someone who, in good faith, had simply made a payment under a
mistake of law.[17]

(iv)   Restitution to the Rescue?

Relief despite misclassification.   In practice the possible adverse conse-   **3–11**
quences of wrongly classifying situations, such as those in the cases just
discussed, may be unlikely to occur. The expanding law of restitution might still
enable relief to be granted, despite the inappropriate premise that the transactions
in question had been unlawful. This should not, however, be taken for granted.
The perceived presence of "illegality" can still be a complicating factor in
restitution cases,[18] as well as in those in which actual enforcement of the contract
is sought.

3.   POSITION OF THE PARTY RESPONSIBLE FOR UNLAWFUL
PERFORMANCE

Relative positions of the parties.   What if a contract capable of lawful   **3–12**
performance is, unlike the agreements considered above, actually performed
unlawfully? It will often be important in such cases to differentiate carefully
between the relative positions of the parties, and to avoid the conceptual approach
reflected in the notion of the "illegal contract"; supposedly enforceable by neither
party regardless of the circumstances. Failure to do this is apt to lead to curious
propositions; ranging from the suggested forfeiture of contractual rights by
wholly innocent parties, to the full validation of claims by parties implicated in
deliberate law-breaking.

Can performance ever preclude recovery?   The view is expressed occasion-   **3–13**
ally that the manner in which a contract is performed can have no effect upon its

---

[16] cf. *Browning v Floyd* [1946] K.B. 597.
[17] cf. *Kleinwort Benson Ltd v Lincoln City Council* [1999] 2 A.C. 349; [1998] 4 All E.R. 513, HL.
[18] But see now *Patel v Mirza* [2016] UKSC 42 which has greatly expanded the scope of recovery for
unjust enrichment in cases involving illegality. See, generally, Chs 17 and 18 below.

inherent validity, which must be determined, once and for all, at the time of its formation. In *Coral Leisure Group v Burnett*[19] Browne-Wilkinson J, delivering the judgment of the Employment Appeal Tribunal, said[20]:

> "The fact that a party has in the course of performing a contract committed an unlawful or immoral act will not by itself prevent him from further enforcing that contract unless the contract was entered into with the purpose of doing that unlawful or immoral act or the contract itself (as opposed to the mode of his performance) is prohibited by law."

The authorities cited in support of this statement included *Wetherell v Jones*,[21] in which Lord Tenterden CJ expressed himself in very similar terms[22]; and *St John Shipping Corporation v Joseph Rank*,[23] in which Devlin J in turn referred to what Lord Tenterden had said as "a clear and decisive statement of the law".[24] Nevertheless, the proposition cannot be right.[25] If a shipowner, realising that he would incur penalties for late delivery because a yachting regatta was blocking his vessel's entry to port, ordered the ship to plough through the regatta drowning many of the participants, it is difficult to believe that he would be permitted to enforce the contract. Rigid application of the conventional distinction between an agreement itself on the one hand, and its performance on the other, could soon lead to absurdity in the context of illegality. The statement of Browne-Wilkinson J can conveniently be contrasted with the more cautious formulation of Waller LJ in *Colen v Cebrian (UK) Ltd*[26]:

> "If at the date of the contract the contract was perfectly lawful and it was intended to perform it lawfully, the effect of some act of illegal performance is not automatically to render the contract unenforceable. If the contract is ultimately performed illegally and the party seeking to enforce takes part in the illegality, that *may* render the contract unenforceable at his instigation. But not every act of illegality in performance . . . will have that effect."

3–14   **The *St John Shipping* case.**   In *St John Shipping Corporation v Joseph Rank*[27] the holders of bills of lading, representing part of a cargo carried by sea from the US to England, attempted to avoid paying a proportion of the freight demanded of them by pointing out that, during her crossing of the Atlantic, the ship in question had been submerged up to eleven inches over the load line. This overloading involved the commission of an offence under the Merchant Shipping

---

[19] (1981) I.C.R. 503.

[20] (1981) I.C.R. 503 at 509.

[21] (1832) 3 B. & Ad. 221.

[22] ". . . where the consideration and the matter to be performed are both legal, we are not aware that a plaintiff has ever been precluded from recovering by an infringement of the law, not contemplated by the contract, in the performance of something to be done on his part." (1832) 3 B. & Ad. 221 at 226.

[23] [1957] 1 Q.B. 267. This case is discussed further below.

[24] [1957] 1 Q.B. 267 at 286.

[25] The actual decision in the *Bennett* case, that an employee who spent part of his time procuring prostitutes for his employer's customers did not forfeit his right to protection against unfair dismissal, can perhaps be supported on the ground that the conduct was not actually illegal and that, in the circumstances, contemporary public policy did not consider it sufficiently serious to warrant depriving the employee of his rights. But what if the employee's zeal had extended to hiring assassins to eliminate his employer's business rivals?

[26] See [2003] EWCA Civ 1676; [2004] I.C.R. 568 at [23] (the italics are in the original).

[27] [1957] 1 Q.B. 267.

(Safety and Load Line Convention) Act 1932[28] for which the master of the ship was fined. This case really raised two separate questions. First, whether the shipowners were impliedly prohibited by the 1932 Act itself from enforcing the contract; and secondly, if they were not, whether they were nevertheless precluded by the common law from enforcing it by virtue of having committed an illegal act in the course of performance. The judge, Devlin J, answered the first question correctly in the negative. The statute did not refer to contractual situations, and it would have been artificial to have inferred from it that the legislature had had such situations in contemplation when the Act was passed. Unfortunately Devlin J failed to identify the second question as a separate issue. Indeed he assumed that a contract could only become unenforceable by virtue of the commission of a statutory offence committed in the course of its performance if the particular statute impliedly so provided.[29] Since the state of the parties' minds is normally irrelevant in statutory illegality,[30] it seemed to follow that this factor was of no relevance in the *St John Shipping* case itself. Devlin J then pointed to the absurd consequences of holding that any infringement of a statute, however inadvertent, committed in the course of performing a contract, rendered it unenforceable by the party responsible.[31] He concluded that the unlawful overloading in the course of performance did not render the contract statutorily prohibited, and the shipowners were able to recover. This reasoning is, with respect, unconvincing.

Sacrifice of safety for profit?   If it had been proved that the ship-owners had taken a deliberate decision to subordinate safety to profit, it is at least arguable that they should have forfeited their contractual rights. The cargo-owners would have received a windfall, but the result would have been salutary in a case in which the deterrent value of the criminal law had been seriously eroded by the effect of inflation upon the level of fines which could be imposed.[32]   **3–15**

Relevance of state of mind.   It is therefore important that the common law aspects of illegality in performance are not overlooked. Without them the courts will be unable to deal adequately with situations in which the illegality has no statutory foundation at all. If murder were committed in the course of performing a contract,[33] it is difficult to believe that this would be ignored by a court which   **3–16**

---

[28] See now the Merchant Shipping (Load Lines) Act 1967.

[29] ". . . whether it is the terms of the contract or the performance of it that is called in question, the test is just the same: is the contract, as made or as performed, a contract that is prohibited by the statute?" [1957] 1 Q.B. 267 at 284.

[30] ". . . the court will not enforce a contract which is expressly or impliedly prohibited by statute. If the contract is of this class it does not matter what the intent of the parties is: if the statute prohibits the contract, it is unenforceable whether the parties meant to break the law or not" [1957] 1 Q.B. 267 at 283. See also *Re Mahmoud and Ispahani* [1921] 2 K.B. 716; *Sheridan v Dickson* [1970] 1 W.L.R. 1328. For discussion see generally Ch.2, above.

[31] See [1957] 1 Q.B. 267 at 281.

[32] See [1957] 1 Q.B. 267 at 279. The maximum penalties for overloading have been increased since the case was decided: see now the Merchant Shipping Act 1995 s.98 (£50,000 line and two years' imprisonment).

[33] i.e. as distinct from an agreement actually to commit murder, which is obviously unenforceable: see Ch.1, above.

found itself trying an action for breach of contract brought by the murderer, even though murder is a common law crime and there is therefore no statutory wording from which an intention to strike at contracts could be construed.[34] In so far as questions of unlawful performance can be approached from a common law standpoint, even when the offences concerned *are* statutory in origin, absurd results can be avoided because it is possible for all the surrounding circumstances to be taken into account. Unlike the position in statutory illegality properly so called, a technical infringement caused inadvertently will not result in contractual forfeiture.[35] On the other hand, a serious offence deliberately committed might well do so. In *Cunard v Hyde (No.2)*[36] underwriters succeeded in avoiding liability on a policy covering cargo and freight which had been carried on the deck of the ship contrary to the Customs Consolidation Act 1853. This legislation, which was intended to protect life and property at sea,[37] made it a criminal offence for a ship wholly or partly laden with timber to leave any British port in North America or the Honduras during the winter months, unless the whole of the cargo was carried below deck. The case was expressly decided on the basis that the illegality had not been merely a unilateral act on the part of the master of the ship but, on the contrary, "that the insured knew of the master's act, in the sense of consenting to it and wanting it to be done".[38]

3–17   **Formidable task.**   Although the decision concerned insurance, it would seem to follow from it that the contract for the carriage of the cargo, which the policy was intended to cover, would also have been unenforceable for illegality. This case appears to have been overlooked when *St John Shipping Corporation v Joseph Rank* was decided. Those who seek to profit from deliberate contravention of provisions governing safety or similar matters should, it is submitted, be liable to forfeiture of their contractual rights. The number of cases involving such forfeiture is never likely to be large. The formidable task of proving the necessary

---

[34] Invocation of the vague maxim that "no person may benefit from a crime" is not a viable alternative approach to the problem of unlawful performance of contracts. The maxim proves too much since not every offence committed in the course of performance will deprive the party responsible of his rights under the agreement, cf. *St John Shipping Corporation v Joseph Rank* (1957) 1 Q.B. 267 at 293. See further, Ch.5, below.

[35] See *Fitzgerald v F. J. Leonardt* (1997) 189 C.L.R. 215 at 249, per Kirby J: "It would be . . . absurd if the courts closed their doors to a party seeking to enforce its contractual rights without having regard to the degree of that party's transgression, the deliberateness or otherwise of its breach of the law and its state of mind generally relevant to the illegality". See also per Etherton LJ in *Les Laboratoires Servier v Apotex* [2012] EWCA Civ 593 at [74]: ". . . the illegality defence does not or may not arise where the unlawful act is merely trivial or where the illegality is the result of an inadvertent breach of some law or regulation."

[36] (1859) 2 El. & Bl. 1.

[37] See, per Lord Campbell CJ in *Cunard v Hyde (No.1)* (1858) El. & Bl. 1 at 676.

[38] The insurer's plea was originally held defective precisely because it did not allege knowledge and involvement in the illegality on the part of the insured: see *Cunard v Hyde (No.1)* (1858) El. & Bl. 670 from which the quotation in the text is in fact taken (per Coleridge J at 677). cf. *Wilson v Rankin* (1865) L.R. 1 Q.B. 162. See also, per Talbot J in *Geismar v Sun Alliance* [1978] Q.B. 383 at 395, distinguishing situations involving "a deliberate breach of the law" from those involving unintentional illegality or innocence.

degree of knowledge and deliberation should deter the majority of parties from seeking to escape from their contractual obligations by relying upon the other party's unlawful performance.[39]

Parkingeye Ltd v Somerfield Stores Ltd. The reluctance of the courts to decline enforcement of a contract even by the party responsible for illegal performance is illustrated by the recent case of *Parkingeye Ltd v Somerfield Stores Ltd.*[40] The defendants entered into a contract with the claimants, Parkingeye, whereby the latter operated a parking scheme at the defendants' stores. The defendants repudiated the contract several months early. The scheme involved charging motorists who parked for longer than a stipulated period, with the claimants benefiting from the resultant income. The claimants planned to send various inaccurate letters of a threatening nature to motorists who had overstayed, the wording of which sought to deceive the recipients as to the legal proceedings which could be taken against them, and which allegedly involved the claimants in various breaches of the criminal law, as well as commission of the tort of deceit. Although the trial judge held that no criminal offences had ultimately been committed, the defendants argued that the claimant's plans constituted an intention to perform the contract unlawfully, which rendered it unenforceable. The defendants' contention failed and Parkingeye were awarded damages for breach of contract. Sir Robin Jacob said that to have allowed the defence to succeed "would be unduly sanctimonious" and would have produced a "disproportionate result".[41] Toulson LJ said that "the illegality was incidental to part of the performance of the contract but far from central to it".[42] This reasoning clearly leaves open the possibility that in other circumstances, especially where the illegality *was* central to the contract, and especially if matters such as health and safety were involved, the courts *will* refuse enforceability on the ground of deliberate unlawful performance.[43]

3–18

4. POSITION OF THE "INNOCENT" PARTY

***Archbold's* case.** If a contract capable at the outset of legal performance was nevertheless performed by one of the parties to it in an unlawful manner, this should not affect the rights of the other party unless he was in some way

3–19

---

[39] In *St John Shipping Corporation v Joseph Rank* itself no attempt was made to establish that the overloading had been deliberate, but Devlin J appears to have believed that it might well have been: see [1957] 1 Q.B. 267 at 280 ("not at all improbable").

[40] [2012] EWCA Civ 1338.

[41] See ibid at [38].

[42] See [2012] EWCA Civ at [75], and the same judge (as a Justice of the Supreme Court) in *Patel v Mirza* [2016] UKSC 42 at [67]-[69] See also *Dowling & Rutter v Abacus Frozen Foods Ltd* [2002] SLT 491 at [19] per Lord Johnston: ". . . just because illegality enters into a contract, that does not necessarily make it unenforceable . . . there has to be some scope for considerations of inadvertence, irrelevance, immateriality, innocence and so on . . .".

[43] "*ParkingEye* is a good example of a case where denial of claim would have been disproportionate. The claimant did not set out to break the law. *If it had realised that the letters which it was proposing to send were legally objectionable, the text would have been changed*": per Lord Toulson in *Patel v Mirza* [2016] UKSC 42 at [108] (italics supplied).

implicated in the illegality. In *Archbold's (Freightage) v S. Spanglett*[44] the defendants had undertaken to carry the claimants' cargo of whisky from Leeds to London when it was stolen en route. To an action for breach of contract the defendants argued that since the contract had been performed by them in an unlicensed vehicle even the innocent claimants were precluded from suing on it. The trial judge and the Court of Appeal held that the contract itself did not implicitly identify a particular van for use in its performance and that the agreement was therefore not one which, contrary to the submission of the defendants, was incapable from the outset of legal performance. This was sufficient, once a separate point concerning statutory illegality had been disposed of,[45] to conclude the case in favour of the claimants. The Court differentiated specifically between the positions of the parties, by emphasising that the carrier could not have sued for payment if the whisky had not been lost.[46] But to have rejected the claimants' claim would perversely have provided an incentive to illegality: carriers would only have had to risk the fines payable for not licensing their vehicles in order to earn immunity from liability to their customers for breach of contract.

3–20 **Shared guilt.** *Archbold's (Freightage) v S. Spanglett* should be contrasted with a later decision of the Court of Appeal, decided in a somewhat similar fact situation, but in which the carriers succeeded in relying on a defence of illegality to a claim by a customer whose property they had damaged in transit. The decision was nevertheless appropriate because the claimants' involvement in the manner of performance precluded them from arguing that it had been a matter for the defendants alone. In *Ashmore, Benson, Pease & Co v A. v Dawson*[47] the claimants had manufactured a large piece of engineering equipment called a "tube bank", which weighed 25 tons, and they entered into a contract with the defendant carriers in which the latter undertook to transport it to the port of Hull for shipment. Unfortunately, the vehicle used by the defendants to perform the contract had a maximum laden weight of 30 tons. As the unladen weight of the vehicle itself was 10 tons the total weight exceeded the prescribed maximum by five tons, and this involved the commission of an offence under the Motor Vehicles (Construction and Use) Regulations then in force. It so happened that the claimants' transport manager, a Mr Bulmer, had been present when the defendants loaded the "tube bank" on to their vehicle. Although he was familiar with the regulations governing the carriage of heavy loads, and realised that the only vehicle suitable for carrying the "tube bank" was a specially constructed "low loader", Mr Bulmer raised no objection to the way in which the defendants were performing the contract. Subsequently, while en route for Hull, the defendants' vehicle toppled over and the "tube bank" was damaged.

---

[44] [1961] 1 Q.B. 374. See also Ch.4, below.

[45] See [1961] 1 Q.B. 374 at 384–387 (Pearce LJ), and at 389–390 (Devlin LJ).

[46] "[the defendants] cannot themselves enforce the contract because they intended to perform it unlawfully with a van they knew was not properly licensed for the purpose": [1961] 1 Q.B. 374 at 388, per Devlin J. For a Canadian case in which a claim for payment brought by an unlicensed carrier failed for illegality see *Wasel Bros v Laskin* [1934] 2 D.L.R. 798. (The case is more fully reported in [1934] 2 W.W.R. 577.)

[47] [1973] 1 W.L.R. 828.

Claim rejected. The Court of Appeal, reversing the trial judge, rejected the   **3–21**
claimants' claim for negligence and breach of contract. The Court held that the
claimants, through Mr Bulmer, had been implicated in the unlawful performance
of the contract by the defendants and that their claim therefore failed. Lord
Denning MR stated that the cost of carrying the "tube bank" on a "low loader"
would have been £30 greater than the actual price agreed with the defendants;
and Phillimore LJ indicated strongly that, in his view, Mr Bulmer had been trying
to save money on transportation and had given the task to the defendants for that
reason. He concluded that the evidence was "consistent and consistent only with
this contract having been deliberately given to Dawsons in the knowledge that it
involved a breach of these regulations and in order to economise on the job".[48]

Extent of involvement. *Ashmore, Benson, Pease & Co v A. v Dawson* was   **3–22**
therefore a clear case of involvement by the otherwise "innocent" party in the
unlawful performance of a contract which, at the outset, had been "legal".
Difficult questions may nevertheless arise in other cases concerning the nature
and extent of such involvement. These are addressed in the next chapter.

---

[48] [1973] 1 W.L.R. 828 at 834.

CHAPTER 4

KNOWLEDGE AND PARTICIPATION

1. INTRODUCTION

Two categories.   In many cases the illegal scheme will have been designed and   **4–01**
perpetrated by one of the parties to the contract, primarily for his benefit. This
chapter is concerned with the extent to which the enforceability of the contract by
the *other* party to it can become jeopardised in such situations. Two types of case
are involved. First, those in which the illegality takes the form of an ulterior
motive to use the agreement to facilitate some unlawful purpose. Occasionally
this will relate to the actual carrying out of the agreement itself, but more often it
will not have any necessary connection with the actual performance of the
contract. The second type of case is that in which performance was itself
unlawful from the outset, but only as a result of surrounding circumstances of
which one party was aware but the other was not.

Source of the illegality.   Both categories concern cases which fall outside the   **4–02**
scope of the doctrine of implied statutory prohibition, otherwise they would be
governed by the principles considered in Ch.2. Nevertheless, in most of them, but
not in all, the source of the illegality will be the criminal law, or the law of tort. In
situations involving contracts contrary to the common law's own conception of
public policy in the broad sense, such as those involving restraint of trade or
interference with the administration of justice, the issue usually surrounds the
legitimacy of the agreement itself rather than any question of differentiation
between the parties.

Effect of *Patel v Mirza*.   Most of the cases considered in this Chapter were   **4–03**
decided before the ground-breaking decision of the Supreme Court in *Patel v
Mirza*.[1] It is not unlikely that at least some of the situations discussed would now
be analysed using the more flexible and policy-oriented approach which now
governs the law in this area, with its emphasis upon proportionality and
transparency. This contrasts with the rather more rigid approach which often
assumed that the contracts themselves were "illegal", and then proceeded to
consider the relationship of the respective parties to that illegality by using such
concepts as "participation". No doubt in many cases where the unenforceability
of the contract by at least one of the parties to it is likely to be beyond question
this approach will still be adopted. Moreover it is too early to predict precisely
how far-reaching the consequences of *Patel v Mirza* will turn out to be in

---

[1] [2016] UKSC 42.

practice. Nevertheless the possibility of adopting a more broadly-based analysis of the situation from the outset is one which all those dealing with cases allegedly involving "illegality" should now bear in mind.

2.   EXTENT OF CLAIMANT'S INVOLVEMENT

(a)   Mere Awareness

4–04   **Claimant's knowledge.**   One party to it may set out deliberately to use a contract, including its documentation, the fact of its existence, or anything else to which it relates, as a means of promoting some illegal scheme of his own. It is clear that such a party will normally lose the right to enforce the agreement. What is much less clear, however, is how far the *other* party has to be implicated in the unlawful purpose for his right to enforcement to be forfeited as well. If that party is unaware of the illegality, had no reason to become aware of it, and remains unaware of it throughout, there can be no doubt that his rights will be unaffected. In other situations, however, the position is more complex. It is likely to vary in relation not only to the precise extent of the claimant's involvement, but also the gravity of the defendant's unlawful scheme itself. One extreme view is that the crucial test is merely that of awareness: did the claimant know of the scheme? If so, he will fail regardless of that scheme's nature or seriousness. Support for this view can be found in the authorities,[2] and it would have the virtue of simplicity. Nevertheless, the difficulties to which such a blanket approach can give rise is well-illustrated by an important case in which it was sought to be applied.

4–05   *Mason v Clarke.*   In *Mason v Clarke*[3] a receipt in acknowledgment of a payment given for the purchase of certain shooting rights was invoiced "for bailiffs' wages on Hogthorpe estate". When a dispute arose between the parties, it was argued that being given this receipt fixed the otherwise innocent party, to whom it was given, with knowledge of a scheme on the part of the other party to defraud the Inland Revenue. The House of Lords, reversing the Court of Appeal which had upheld the defence of illegality raised,[4] held that on the facts the mere giving of the receipt in the form stated was insufficient evidence on which to hold that even the party giving it had any intention of defrauding the revenue. But even if this had not been the case, the House indicated that merely receiving the receipt thus invoiced would not have been sufficient to taint the otherwise innocent party with such knowledge of the fraudulent scheme as would debar him from recovering.[5] The consideration of the evidence in *Mason*'s case was thus based on the assumption that mere knowledge of the illegal purpose, without more, was sufficient to defeat an action on the contract brought by an otherwise innocent party.[6]

---

[2] See also Enonchong, *Illegal Transactions* (LLP Ltd, 1998), Ch.15, esp. pp.290–291.
[3] [1955] A.C. 778.
[4] See [1954] 1 Q.B. 460.
[5] [1955] A.C. 778 per Viscount Simonds at 793; per Lord Reid at 804–5 and per Lord Keith at 806.
[6] [1955] A.C. 778 e.g. per Lord Reid at 800.

Unworkable rule.   The significance of the decision, however, is that it shows **4–06** the lengths to which the court will go, when acting on that assumption, to deny the existence of "knowledge".[7] A strained interpretation is put on the evidence in order to conceal departure from an unworkable rule of law. It would have been unjust if the claimant in *Mason v Clarke* had been defeated merely as a result of his acceptance of the falsely invoiced receipt and yet, on the facts, there is much to be said in favour of the view accepted by the Court of Appeal that the receipt could hardly have been invoiced in the way that it was except to further some unlawful purpose; and that any person accepting the receipt must therefore be taken to have notice of that purpose.[8] The Court of Appeal's decision highlights the unsatisfactory nature of a rule which would debar an otherwise innocent party from suing on a contract, on account of mere notice of an intention on the part of the other party to engage in conduct similar to that alleged in *Mason v Clarke* itself: defrauding the revenue.

(b)   Participation

Knowledge insufficient.   An alternative approach to that based on awareness **4–07** would require something more than mere knowledge before the "innocent" party was disqualified, at least if the illegal scheme fell short of very serious criminal activity. This approach can also be found in the cases. In *Ashmore, Benson, Pease & Co v A. V. Dawson*, the facts of which were given in the previous chapter, it was emphasised that the claimants were obliged to forfeit their rights not because their representative, Mr Bulmer, had known of what was happening, that alone would have been insufficient, but because he had actively involved himself in it.[9] "[K]nowledge by itself", observed Scarman LJ in his judgment, "is not, I think, enough. There must be knowledge plus participation". In the earlier case of *Allan (Merchandising) v Cloke*,[10] Lord Denning MR was even more explicit. "With an unlawful purpose", he said, "active participation debars, but knowledge by itself does not".[11] Participation takes many forms.[12] It is the kind of notion which is easier to recognise than to define.[13] Indeed it will usually be a question of fact.[14]

---

[7] In *Mason*'s case the House of Lords took the view that the invoicing of the receipt was merely equivocal and did not necessarily entail the consequence that it was to be used unlawfully; *sed quaere*.

[8] The possibility of deciding the case on the short ground that the transaction was already completed by the time that the receipt was handed over, making it too late for the claimant to attempt to unscramble it, was not considered. Perhaps the relevant events were regarded as contemporaneous and inseparable, ruling out that analysis.

[9] [1973] 1 W.L.R. 828 at 836.

[10] [1963] 2 Q.B. 340 at 348.

[11] See also the decision of the Supreme Court of Canada in *Clark v Hugar* (1894) 22 S.C.R. 510. especially, per Gwynne J at 540: "Knowledge in the mind of the transferor that the transferee intended to apply the property when transferred to him to an illegal purpose will not avoid a contract . . . unless . . . a just inference can be drawn from the facts in evidence that the property was so transferred *with the intent and for the purpose*, operating in the mind of the transferor, that the property when transferred should be applied by the transferee to the illegal purpose" (italics supplied).

[12] See R. A. Buckley, "Participation and Performance in Illegal Contracts" (1974) 25 N.I.L.Q. 421.

[13] cf. per Lord Mance in *Patel v Mirza* [2016] UKSC 42 at [208] (criticising the reasoning of the majority in the same case): "...the question what constitutes knowing participation sufficient to render

Nevertheless, it is possible to identify at the outset at least two distinct situations which both qualify for membership of the general category which the notion represents.

(i) Profiting from the Illegality

4–08   **Claimant saves money.** The first type of case in which participation may be said to be present is that of seeking to profit from the illegality.[15] The typical situation, involving actual unlawful performance, is where the claimant saves money by entrusting a job to a cut-price operator well aware that he is unlicensed, or that he will "cut corners" and perhaps breach safety regulations. The reasoning in *Ashmore, Benson, Pease & Co v A. V. Dawson*[16] makes it very clear that that was such a case.[17]

(ii) Providing Assistance

4–09   **"Sharer in the illegal transaction".** Another instance of participation is the doing of some act by the claimant, not necessarily required by the contract, which assists the defendant's unlawful scheme. The search for illustrations of this principle is made easier by the fact that the distinction between knowledge and participation is not a new one. Before it fell into disuse,[18] with knowledge alone being the favoured test, it was drawn in a number of cases decided at the end of the eighteenth century and the beginning of the nineteenth. In *Hodgson v Temple*[19] it was applied in favour of a vendor who was able to sue for the price of spirits despite knowing that the purchaser, who was licensed to sell spirits by retail, intended to use the spirits in a distillery owned by him. His ownership contravened a statute[20] which forbade licensed retailers from being interested in the trade or business of distilling. Mansfield CJ said:

> "This would be carrying the law much further than it has ever yet been carried. The merely selling goods, knowing that the buyer will make an illegal use of them, is not sufficient to deprive the vendor of his just right of payment, but to effect that, it is necessary that the vendor should be a sharer in the illegal transaction."[21]

---

a contract unenforceable is a discrete problem, which is unlikely to be resolved any more simply under the 'range of factors' approach now advocated".

[14] See e.g. *Anglo-Petroleum v TFB (Mortgages)* [2007] EWCA Civ 456 in which the authorities, including *Allan (Merchandising) v Cloke*, are discussed. But in which *Allan*'s case was distinguished and it was held that there was no participation on the facts.

[15] There are dicta in the cases to the effect that seeking payment from the proceeds is not a necessary condition of illegality in this context (see, e.g. *Pearce v Brooks* (1866) L.R. 1 Exch 213, per Pollock CB and Bramwell B, at 218 and 221 respectively) but this only serves to highlight that it is a sufficient condition.

[16] [1973] 1 W.L.R. 828.

[17] See Ch.3, above.

[18] Partly as a result of dicta in *Pearce v Brooks* (1866) L.R. 1 Exch 213.

[19] (1813) 5 Taunt. 181.

[20] 26 Geo, c.73, s.54.

[21] The decision of the Court of Common Pleas in *Hodgson's* case is in conflict with another case decided the same year. In *Langton v Hughes* (1813) 1 M. & S. 593, the Court of King's Bench held, on indistinguishable facts, that mere knowledge of the other party's intended illegality was sufficient

Actually facilitating the unlawful purpose.   It is instructive to compare   4–10
Hodgson v Temple with the earlier case of *Waymell v Read*.[22] In this case the
claimant attempted to sue for the price of a quantity of lace which had been sold
and delivered to the defendants in France, but subsequently smuggled by them
into England. It appeared from the evidence, however, that the claimant had
packed the lace in a special manner in order to facilitate the smuggling, and this
was held to be fatal to his claim.[23] His counsel relied on *Holman v Johnson*[24] in
which, like *Hodgson v Temple*, the distinction between knowledge and
participation had been applied in favour of a vendor who had been aware of the
illegal purpose, but had not himself assisted in it. This argument was however, of
no avail. Buller J said:

> "In *Holman v Johnson*, the seller did not assist the buyer in the smuggling; he merely sold the
> goods in the common and ordinary course of trade. But this case does not rest merely on the
> circumstance of the plaintiff's knowledge of the use intended to be made of the goods; for he
> actually assisted the defendants in the act of smuggling, by packing the goods up in a manner
> most convenient for that purpose."

Restatement.   The approach adopted in these old cases is reflected in the   4–11
American Law Institute's Second *Restatement of Contracts*. The commentary to
para.182 states that, providing "the improper use does not involve grave social
harm, the promisee is not barred from recovery unless he not only knew of the
use but acted for the purpose of furthering it". The following example is given:

> "A sells and delivers to B a quantity of plants. The sale of such plants is legal, but B plans to
> transport them to a country where quarantine regulations forbid their importation. A not only
> knows this, but so packs and marks them as to conceal their character in order to aid B's plan.
> B's promise to pay the price is unenforceable on grounds of public policy."[25]

(c)   Contractual Obligation Not Required

Fielding and Platt v Najjar.   If the claimant is contractually obliged to assist in   4–12
the defendant's illegal purpose, the agreement will have been incapable from the
outset of wholly lawful performance. Such contracts are governed by separate
principles from those applicable where one party only is seeking independently to
pursue some improper objective. But even in the absence of such an obligation, a
"participating" party may still be so involved that his rights ought to be forfeit. It
is important not to narrow the concept of participation to such an extent that
claimants who were fully implicated in the unlawful scheme manage to escape

---

to deprive the "innocent" party of his rights. But the approach adopted in *Hodgson's* case was also
applied in *Pellecat v Angel* (1835) 2 Cr. M. & R. 311, and approved by the Court of Appeal in *Foster
v Driscoll* [1929] 1 K.B. 470. See Glanville Williams, *Criminal Law: the General Part* (2nd edn,
Stevens, 1961), p.373.
[22] (1794) 5 Term. R. 599.
[23] See also *Biggs v Lawrence* (1789) 3 Term. R. 454: *Clugas v Penaluna* (1791) 4 Term. R. 466.
[24] (1775) 1 Cowp. 341. A case remembered less for its facts than for a well known dictum by Lord
Mansfield: "No Court will lend its aid to a man who founds his cause of action upon an immoral or an
illegal act".
[25] See also *Williston on Contracts* (Lawyers Co-operative Pub. Co, 4th edn, 1998), ss.19.14–19.15
and cases there cited.

the consequences of their actions, and thereby retain their rights of enforceability to the full. In order to avoid this danger, it is necessary to ensure that the notion of what constitutes a contractual "term" is not analysed incorrectly. In *Fielding and Platt v Najjar*[26] an action on a contract was met with a defence of illegality based on the claim that the claimants, an English company, had been implicated in a scheme devised by the defendants, a Lebanese company, to deceive the Lebanese import authorities. The scheme was allegedly based on the giving of a false invoice for the goods sold.[27] The Court of Appeal held that the defence had not been made out and that the claimant should succeed. Both Lord Denning MR and Widgery L appropriately applied the test of participation rather than that of mere knowledge,[28] and the actual decision was no doubt correct. At one point in his judgment, however, Lord Denning MR said the following:

> "In order for this to be any kind of defence, [the defendant] must show first of all that the contract contained a term that the English company were to give a false invoice: so that it could not lawfully be performed. For if it could be lawfully performed (by giving a correct invoice) the English company can certainly sue upon it."

4–13   **Participation not to be confused with "term".**   This dictum is misleading. By confusing the presence of participation with that of a contractual term it potentially narrows the former in an unprincipled way. A contractual term is pre-eminently concerned to regulate the rights and duties of the parties towards each other. In the context of illegality, however, it may often be appropriate that a participant in an unlawful scheme should be deprived of his contractual rights on grounds of public policy despite the fact that his readiness to "participate" in the scheme, for example by packing some object to which the agreement related in a special way, could not be said to satisfy the criteria normally required for an enforceable contractual promise. An actual obligation to break the law is not a necessary condition of a party's forfeiting his contractual rights on the ground of illegality.

(d)   Involvement in a Related Transaction

(i)   Participation Still Relevant

4–14   *Fisher v Bridges.*   The question may arise whether an agreement which is ostensibly separate from an illegal transaction, but which may involve at least one of the parties to it, is so closely related to that transaction that the parties to the other agreement have themselves become implicated in the original illegality. If so, their rights under the separate agreement may also become unenforceable. In *Fisher v Bridges*[29] the claimant sold land to the defendant who proposed to re-sell

---

[26] [1969] 1 W.L.R. 357.

[27] cf. *Mason v Clarke* [1954] 1 Q.B. 460, [1955] A.C. 778, discussed above. See also *Euro-Diam v Bathurst* [1990] 1 Q.B. 1; [1988] 2 All E.R. 23 and *Pye v BG Transport Service* [1966] 2 Lloyd's Rep. 300, discussed in para.4.19, below.

[28] [1969] 1 W.L.R. 357 at 362 and 363.

[29] (1854) 3 El. & B1. 642, reversing the decision of the Court of Queen's Bench reported in 2 El. & B1. 118.

it by lottery. Sales of land by lottery were, however, forbidden by statute. After the conveyance had taken place, the defendant executed a covenant in favour of the claimant as security for payment, at the previously agreed price. When the claimant sued on the covenant, however, he was met with a successful defence of illegality. Although consideration is not required to support a covenant, it will nevertheless be unenforceable if clearly given in order to secure payment of the consideration for a separate illegal transaction.[30] Jervis CJ said[31]:

> "It is clear that the covenant was given for the payment of the purchase money. It springs from, and is a creature of, the illegal agreement; and, as the law would not enforce the original illegal contract, so neither will it allow the parties to enforce a security for the purchase money, which by the original bargain was tainted with illegality."

"Tainting".   It has become conventional, as a result of this passage, to use the language of "tainting" when considering the effect of the illegality of one transaction upon another.[32] That expression is not, however, entirely appropriate since it is apt to convey an impression of some kind of automatic mechanism, or organic process, which operates independently of the knowledge and intentions of the parties themselves.[33] It is submitted that the issue should really be analysed in terms of the notion of "participation". The distinction between participation and knowledge was, in fact, referred to expressly early in the judgment of Jervis CJ in *Fisher v Bridges* itself. The claimant had argued that the defendant's plea "did not sufficiently affect the plaintiff with a participation" in the defendant's unlawful scheme because it alleged "that the plaintiff merely knew of the intent". The Court rejected this submission, however, on the ground that the overall wording of the plea sufficiently averred that "the sale was to the intent and for the purpose of the future lottery".[34] It would seem to be clear from the facts of *Fisher v Bridges* that the claimant sought at least to provide assistance for the defendant's illegal scheme, if not to profit from it. It was this deliberate participation in the scheme that defeated his claim, rather than any purely technical doctrine about relationships between separate transactions.

4–15

---

[30] The Court distinguished the familiar principle that a deed given in respect of past consideration (e.g. in favour of a former mistress) is enforceable since past consideration is no consideration: see (1854) 3 El. & Bl. 642 at 650–651, per Jervis CJ.

[31] See (1854) 3 El. & Bl. 642 at 649. See also *Gas and Light Coke Co v Turner* (1839) 5 Bing. N.C. 666 at 675, per Tindal CJ.

[32] See, e.g. *Chitty on Contracts*, 32nd edn, (London: Sweet & Maxwell, 2015), para.16–182; *Halsbury's Laws of England*, 5th edn, (London: Butterworths, 2012), Vol.22, para.460. The terminology is also used in the context of severance, in which it is perhaps more appropriate: Ch.19, below.

[33] cf. per Staughton J at first instance in *Euro-Diam v Bathurst* [1990] 1 Q.B. 1 at 15; [1987] 2 All E.R. 113 at 120: "'Tainted' in its literal sense means contaminated with something poisonous, or with incipient putrefaction. As a metaphor in the context of a contract and illegality I think it means that, while the contract is not itself illegal, it has a connexion with some other illegal transaction which renders it obnoxious".

[34] See (1854) 3 El. & Bl. 642 at 647–648.

(ii)   Claimant's Motive

4–16   **Residual category.**   Seeking to profit from the illegality, and providing assistance in the furtherance of it, are not the only situations which can render a party guilty of "participation". Particularly where related transactions are concerned, a broader, residual, category can be identified. This concerns the *motive* of the claimant in entering into the transaction. There can be other motives for entering into a contract apart from the desire for profit, or other immediate benefit. The claimant may, for example, be anxious to enable the other party to confer a benefit upon some third person, whom the claimant wishes to assist.

4–17   **Repayment of loans.**   The notion that motive may be relevant is particularly helpful in cases involving the loan of money, which is subsequently used by the borrower to further an unlawful purpose. These cases give rise to special difficulties. The lender may have had no particular source in mind for the repayment of his loan, so it cannot be said that he sought to share in the proceeds of the illegality, nor will the ideas of physical assistance demonstrated in the smuggling cases normally be applicable. In *Cannan v Bryce*[35] the motive of the lender was used to resolve this dilemma. Money which had been lent to enable the borrower to make good losses incurred on illegal stock-jobbing transactions was held to be irrecoverable. It was clear that the transaction had been entered into to enable the borrower to make good the stock-jobbing debt, and that it would not have been entered into otherwise. Abbott CJ, delivering the judgment of the Court, said:

> "As the statute in question has absolutely prohibited the payment of money for compounding differences, it is impossible to say that the making of such payment is not an unlawful act; and if it be unlawful in one man to pay, how can it be lawful for another to furnish him with the means of payment? It will be recollected that I am speaking of a case wherein the means were furnished with a full knowledge of the object to which they were to be applied, *and for the express purpose of accomplishing that object.*"[36]

4–18   ***Spector v Ageda.***   A somewhat similiar, but much more recent, example is provided by the decision of Megarry J in *Spector v Ageda*.[37] A creditor was unable to sue on a loan when she made it to enable the borrower to repay an earlier loan to the creditor's own sister. The creditor knew, but the borrower did not, that the earlier loan was unenforceable for illegality; and it seems to have been clear that the creditor's motive was to circumvent the illegality which barred her sister from enforcing the earlier loan.

(iii)   Insurance

4–19   ***Euro-Diam v Bathurst.***   The question can arise whether a contract of insurance is affected by the illegality of an earlier transaction, to which it may be perceived

---

[35] (1819) 3 B. & Ald. 179.
[36] Italics supplied.
[37] [1973] Ch. 30; [1971] 3 All E.R. 417.

to be related. In *Euro-Diam v Bathurst*[38] the claimants, an English company, sent diamonds to Germany on a sale or return basis. At the request of the importers, the claimants sent an invoice which stated a lower value for the diamonds than the correct one; the importers' intention being to deceive the German customs authorities. When the diamonds were stolen, while still the property of the claimants, the latter sought to recover the full value of the diamonds from the defendant underwriter who had insured them. The defendant contended the misstatement in the invoice meant that the claim was "tainted", and that the claimants should therefore recover nothing. The defence failed, and the claimants recovered in full. The Court of Appeal emphasised that the misleading invoice had been issued solely for the benefit of the importers; any benefit accruing to the claimants, attributable to preserving the importers' goodwill, was intangible and "virtually negligible".[39] The Court approved the decision in the earlier case of *Pye v BG Transport Service*[40] in which carriers, who had lost the claimants' goods while in transit, sought unsuccessfully to rely on a false invoice, given by the claimants to their purchasers in Persia, in very similar circumstances to those in the *Euro-Diam* case itself.

Deliberate defiance. On the other hand, in *Geismar v Sun Insurance*[41] a **4–20** claimant who had smuggled goods into England in order to avoid paying customs duties, thereby rendering the goods liable to possible confiscation, was unable to recover their value from his insurers when they were stolen.[42] This decision was in the forefront of the arguments for the defendant underwriter in *Euro-Diam v Bathurst*. But the Court of Appeal in the latter case had no difficulty both in agreeing with the earlier decision and in distinguishing it.[43] The claimant in *Geismar* had deliberately acted in defiance of the law solely for his own benefit.[44]

Limits to the Geismar principle. The *Geismar* principle must, however, have **4–21** limits. The smuggled goods were at the heart of the contract in that case. Merely because an unlawful activity has been deliberately carried on, it does not follow that an insurance policy which could be said to facilitate that activity will necessarily be unenforceable for illegality. Although there are Commonwealth cases in which fire insurance policies effected on premises used for prostitution have been held to be unenforceable,[45] those decisions would appear to be questionable.[46] The appropriate question to ask may be whether taking out

[38] [1990] 1 Q.B. 1; [1988] 2 All E.R. 23. See Y. L. Tan, "Stolen Diamonds and Ex Turpi Causa" (1988) 104 L.Q.R. 523.
[39] See [1990] 1 Q.B. 1 at 38; [1988] 2 All E.R. 23 at 31, per Kerr LJ.
[40] [1966] 2 Lloyd's Rep. 300.
[41] [1978] Q.B. 83.
[42] See also *Parkin v Dick* (1809) 11 East. 502.
[43] [1990] 1 Q.B. 1 at 39–40; [1988] 2 All E.R. 23 at 32, per Kerr LJ.
[44] See also *Cunard v Hyde* (No.2) (1859) 2 El. & Bl. 1. cf. *Cunard v Hyde* (No. 1) (1858) El. & Bl. 670. Both these cases are discussed in Ch.3.
[45] See *Nakata v The Dominion Fire Insurance Co* (1915) 9 W.W.R. 1084 (Supreme Court of Canada); *Brumau v Laliberte* (1901) 19 S.C. 425 (Quebec).
[46] cf. per Duff J, dissenting in *Nakata* (fn.45 above) "One would not think of describing a policy of insurance upon his office furniture taken out by a promoter whose chief business was to effect

insurance would have been a routine and common practice irrespective of the nature of the activity. If so, the policy should in most cases be unobjectionable.

3. Where the Illegal Scheme is Especially Grave

4–22   **Degrees of turpitude.** The insistence that mere "knowledge" is insufficient, in the absence of participation, to warrant forfeiture of an "innocent" party's claim, is only tenable if the other party's illegal scheme is not of such gravity that anyone becoming aware of it should immediately refuse to proceed with the transaction. It is always regrettable to deprive an otherwise "innocent" party of his contractual rights, when the primary responsibility for wrongdoing rests with the other. But it will sometimes be inevitable. The owner of a garden centre who sells weed killer on credit, knowing that the purchaser intends using it to commit murder by poisoning, cannot expect to be able to sue for payment. On the other hand, if a customer buys a hose from the garden centre, and happens to mention while doing so that he proposes to use it to water his garden in contravention of drought restrictions then in force, it is at least questionable whether the owner of the centre should be obliged to refuse to proceed with the sale; at risk of being prevented from suing for the price if the purchaser refuses to pay for the hose. Such a result might itself be considered an affront to ordinary commercial morality. In exceptional cases, it will therefore be impossible to achieve acceptable results in this unusual area of the law without adopting a flexible approach to the seriousness of the particular situation.

4–23   **"No moral justification".** The point was made with exceptional clarity by an American judge, Comstock J, in the nineteenth century case of *Tracy v Talmage*.[47] The vendor of certain shares knew that the purchaser, a bank, planned to resell them speculatively in a manner which happened to be contrary to applicable banking legislation. An attempt by the receiver of the bank to resist payment for the shares, on the ground of illegality, failed. But the Court distinguished expressly cases "of poison, or of a deadly weapon purchased for the purpose of murder". In such situations no one knowing what was intended could "remain neutral without being in a just sense a criminal himself". It followed that where the other party intended "to violate the fundamental laws of society, a positive duty of intervention may arise to prevent the perpetration of crime". Finally Comstock J said[48]:

> ". . . if the question should ever be thoroughly examined, it will, I think be found to have been far too broadly asserted in respect to illegal contracts, that the law does not distinguish between acts criminal in their essential nature, and those which are wrong, only because they are prohibited. This distinction cannot be made where the contract itself is prohibited, and the question is directly upon its validity. The inquiry, then, depends not so much upon the ethics as the logic of the law, which cannot both affirm and prohibit the same contract. But in respect to many incidental questions, the moral feeling and common sense of every man does discriminate, and so I apprehend does the law."

---

mergers obnoxious against the provisions of the Criminal Code as an agreement to indemnify against loss incurred in the course of his illegal business; and yet the parallel if not exact is approximate".

[47] 14 N.Y. 162; 67 Am. Dec. 132 (1856).

[48] See 14 N.Y. 162 at 215.

In a similar vein, Lord Wright once said[49] of the Latin maxim ex turpi causa non oritur actio that "in these days there are many statutory offences which are the subject of the criminal law, and in that sense are crimes, but which would, it seems afford no moral justification for a Court to apply the maxim".[50]

"Mala in se" and "mala prohibita". The proposition that the court should   **4–24**
consider whether or not there would be a "moral justification" for denial of a remedy on grounds of illegality, should not be confused with the ancient distinction, derived from Roman Law and supported by Blackstone, between *mala prohibita* and *mala in se*.[51] Nor should the language of Comstock J in *Tracy v Talmage* be read in precisely that light. As Leon E. Trakman wrote[52]:

> "The Roman law classification which distinguished between . . . illegality and immorality, would undoubtedly force the conventional judge to rigid, even arbitrary decisions on issues of morality. Nevertheless, it is firmly contended that there is still scope in all legal systems for due consideration of degrees of illegality. Indeed, if a judicial system purports to grant relief to any illegal arrangements, the character of the illicit act is of fundamental importance."

The gravity of the situation in any given case will depend upon the particular circumstances, rather than upon some abstract issue of moral classification. Some cases of *mala prohibita*, for example, would properly be regarded as necessitating the severest censure: trading with the enemy being an obvious example.[53] As Trakman concluded[54]:

> ". . . it is imperative that courts do not adopt unbending classifications and rules in relation to the degrees of morality, public policy and illegality. To do so would only lead to inequitable and imperceptive results. Each decision must be carefully evolved from its particular factual framework. In this way, having been reasoned on an informed basis, judicial decisions which involve notions of public policy and morality will acquire a greater sense of credibility."

Intuitive decision.   When it comes to distinguishing between the gravity of   **4–25**
different crimes, for the purpose of disqualifying those merely with knowledge from enforcing their contracts, the court will therefore have of necessity to approach the question on a broad basis.[55] Whatever the position in other situations involving illegality,[56] in this context an appeal to the "public conscience" is, in effect, inescapable to avoid absurdity. Any fears that this will

---

[49] *Beresford v Royal Insurance Co* [1937] 2 K.B. 197 at 220.
[50] Cited with approval by Denning LJ in *Marles v Philip Trant* [1954] 1 Q.B. 29 at 37, and also by Lord Devlin in *The Enforcement of Morals* (Oxford University Press, 1965). In *Pearce v Brooks* (1866) L.R. 1 Exch. 213, Pollock CB denied that "any distinction [could] be made between an illegal and an immoral purpose", but only in order to deny that any point could be taken *in favour* of enforceability in that case on the ground that prostitution was not contrary to positive law.
[51] cf. Bentham in *Comment on the Commentaries*: "That acute distinction between *mala in se* and *mala prohibita*, which being so shrewd and sounding so petty, and being in Latin, has no sort of an occasion to have any meaning to it; accordingly it has none" (quoted by Trakman, see fn.52 below).
[52] "The Effect of Illegality in the Law of Contract: Suggestions for Reform" (1977) 55 Canadian Bar Review 625 at p.638.
[53] See Trakman, cited at fn.52 above, at p.638.
[54] See Trakman, cited at fn.52 above, at pp.638–639.
[55] cf. the concept of "dishonesty" in the Theft Act 1968. Ormerod and Laird eds, *Smith and Hogan's Criminal Law*, 14th edn, (Oxford University Press, 2015), Ch.19, para.19.4 (p.939 et seq.).
[56] cf. *Tinsley v Milligan* [1994] 1 A.C. 340.

cause significant uncertainty are almost certainly exaggerated. In practice intuition is likely to produce a high degree of consensus in the small number of cases in which the issue arises.[57] No great difficulty appears to have been experienced in those American jurisdictions in which the approach adopted in *Tracy v Talmage* has been applied.[58] Thus s.182 of the American Law Institute's Second *Restatement of Contracts* draws a distinction between situations involving "grave social harm" and others. The following illustration is given:

> "A sells and delivers to B a shotgun on credit, but B plans to use the gun in hunting without a license required by law and A knows this. Enforcement of B's promise to pay the price is not precluded on grounds of public policy. If B planned to use the gun to commit a robbery and A knew this, B's promise to pay the price would be unenforceable on those grounds."

The *Restatement* was cited, and the distinction drawn in it applied, in the 1986 case of *Potomac Leasing Co v Vitality Centers*.[59] A finance company leased an automated telephone system knowing that the lessee intended using it to make random calls for advertising purposes, a practice which happened to be contrary to an Arkansas statute. Despite the fact that the equipment was capable of being put to a legal use, the lessee was successful in the lower court in relying on its own illegality to resist an action on the contract by the finance company. But that decision was reversed on appeal by the Supreme Court of Arkansas. Holt CJ said that, except in cases involving "the commission of a serious crime or an act of great moral turpitude . . . the seller's knowledge does not prevent his enforcement of the bargain, if he in no way participates in the purpose and does not act in furtherance of it aside from making the sale".

4–26   **Where information is acquired later.**   What if the "innocent" party only learns of the other party's gravely illegal scheme after the formation of the contract has been completed, but *before* performance has taken place? In principle, he should be both entitled and obliged to refuse to carry out any act ascribed to him by the agreement. He should be immune from any attempt by the other party to enforce the contract; and if he continues with performance after acquisition of the relevant knowledge, he should forfeit any right to contractual remuneration which might already have accrued. The nineteenth century case of *Cowan v Milbourn*[60] suggests that this is indeed the law; even though the context, blasphemy, would no longer be regarded as involving illegality of the utmost gravity. The defendant contracted to let rooms to the claimant who intended to use them for the purpose of delivering blasphemous lectures. At the time of the making of the contract the defendant had been unaware of the claimant's intention, but he discovered it subsequently, and on so doing refused to carry out the contract. It was held that he was able to so without becoming liable for breach. Kelly CB observed that "the defendant was not only entitled, but was

---

[57] See Enonchong, *Illegal Transactions* (LLP Ltd, 1998), Ch.17.
[58] See *Williston on Contracts* 4th edn (Lawyers Co-operative Pub. Co, 1998) s.19.13. See also *Corbin on Contracts* (West Publishing Co, 1963), s.1519: "Just how serious the crime or immorality must be in order that the seller's mere knowledge will prevent his enforcement of the bargain is a matter of degree, such as to make it undesirable to attempt to draw an exact line".
[59] 718 S.W.2d 928 (1986).
[60] (1867) L.R. 2 Exch. 230.

called upon and bound by the law to refuse his sanction to the use of the rooms".[61] It is implicit in this statement that if, on subsequently acquiring his knowledge of the hirer's purpose, the defendant had allowed the hirer to use the rooms then he would have been unable to sue on the contract if the latter had refused to pay.

4. PERFORMANCE UNLAWFUL FROM THE OUTSET

(a) Rights of the "Innocent" Party

Entire contract not necessarily unenforceable. If an agreement simply happens to be incapable of legal performance owing to a peculiar factual situation of which only one party is actually aware, and of which the other party could not reasonably be expected to be aware, the rights of the innocent party should be unaffected by illegality. And this will be so whether or not the agreement is still executory. The only rights liable to forfeiture should be those of the party who knew the facts. In this context, illegality strikes primarily at contracting parties, and their rights, not usually at contracts as such.

4–27

Shaw v Shaw. The situation which arose in the case of *Shaw v Shaw*[62] is instructive. A married man represented himself to be a widower and went through a form of marriage with the claimant. The two parties lived together for 15 years, and the claimant assumed throughout that the ceremony of marriage had been valid. She only discovered the truth when her "husband" died intestate, and she sought to recover damages from his estate for breach of an implied warranty that he had been in a position to marry her; the object being to recover compensation for her inability to prove in the intestacy. The action succeeded. The Court of Appeal held, first, that the alleged warranty existed[63] and, secondly, that since the claimant was unaware of the first marriage her claim was not excluded on grounds of public policy. Of course, if the claimant had actually known the true facts no warranty to the effect that they were otherwise could have prevented her claim from failing. Her claim would also have failed if the law imposed a duty upon potential spouses to make inquiries as to their prospective partners' existing marital status. But the law does not do so. A bigamous marriage is invalid as a marriage,[64] but no offence is committed by the innocent party if he or she is unaware of his or her partner's existing status.

4–28

Abolition of actions for breach of promise. The significance of the decision in *Shaw*'s case, in relation to the rights of innocent parties where contracts are incapable of legal performance, obviously goes beyond the particular situation

4–29

---

[61] See (1867) L.R. 2 Exch. 230 at 234.

[62] [1954] 2 Q.B. 429.

[63] "Every man who proposes marriage to a woman impliedly warrants that he is in a position to marry her, and that he is not himself a married man": per Denning LJ in [1954] 2 Q.B. 429 at 440.

[64] cf. *Clelland v Clelland* [1944] 4 D.L.R. 703 (Can) (presumption of advancement inapplicable where a man transfers property to a woman when the parties are in fact unmarried, even though both mistakenly believed themselves to be married).

which occurred in the case itself. Since the abolition of actions for breach of promise of marriage, by s.1 of the Law Reform (Miscellaneous Provisions) Act 1970, it is unclear whether a contractual claim could still be mounted on similar facts. On one view, the implied warranty that the other party was free to marry would remain as a basis for liability, notwithstanding the abolition of the primary obligation.[65] But this view has not gone unchallenged.[66] The 1970 Act itself did, however, provide for a more limited, and less valuable, remedy by enabling the survivor of the "marriage" to be treated as a "dependent" of the deceased, for the purposes of seeking the exercise of the court's statutory discretion to make provision out of an estate.[67]

(b) "Excusable Ignorance"

4–30 **Limited scope of statutory illegality.** If an express or implied statutory duty is imposed on a party, and is not complied with, ignorance of the law, or even of the facts, giving rise to the existence of the duty will normally afford no excuse.[68] It is therefore important to bear in mind the limited scope of statutory illegality. A contract incapable from the outset of legal performance is not necessarily prohibited by the statute which makes performance unlawful, even though enforceability by the party responsible for the contravention may be disallowed.

4–31 **No compulsion to unsatisfactory conclusion.** In *Archbold's (Freightage) v S. Spanglett*[69] a carrier, who had lost the goods being carried, sought to defend an action for breach by arguing that his own failure to possess an appropriate vehicle licence rendered the contract of carriage incapable of legal performance, and also prohibited by statute. The Court of Appeal found for the claimant. The contract itself was not prohibited by statute; nor was it incapable of legal performance, because no particular vehicle had been identified in the contract as the one to be used. The significance of the case for present purposes, however, is that the Court felt that even if the contract had been incapable of legal performance from the outset, because a particular vehicle *had* been identified, the outcome in favour of the "innocent" party should still have been the same. Pearce LJ said[70]:

> "The case has been argued with skill and care on both sides, and yet no case has been cited to us establishing the proposition that where a contract is on the face of it legal and is not forbidden by statute, but must in fact produce illegality by reason of a circumstance known to one party only, it should be held illegal so as to debar the innocent party from relief. In the absence of such a case I do not feel compelled to so unsatisfactory a conclusion, which would injure the innocent, benefit the guilty, and put a premium on deceit. Such a conclusion (in cases like this where a contract is not forbidden by statute) can only derive from public policy

---

[65] See J. M. Thomson "The End of Actions for Breach of Promise?" (1971) 87 L.Q.R. 158.

[66] See L.C.B. Gower in (1971) 87 L.Q.R. 314.

[67] See the Law Reform (Miscellaneous Provisions) Act 1970 s.6. (See now the Inheritance (Provision for Family and Dependants) Act 1975 s.1 (1A)).

[68] See cases discussed in Chs 1 and 2, above, especially *Re Mahmoud and Ispahani* [1921] 2 K.B. 716.

[69] [1961] 1 Q.B. 374. See also Ch.3, above, where the case is discussed on the basis of illegality merely in performance.

[70] [1961] 1 Q.B. 374 at 387.

... No question of moral turpitude arises here. The alleged illegality is, so far as the plaintiffs were concerned, the permitting of their goods to be carried by the wrong carrier, namely, a carrier who, unknown to them, was not allowed by his licence to carry that particular class of goods. The plaintiffs were never in delicto since they did not know the vital fact that would make performance of the contract illegal."[71]

Fact and law. In *Archbold*'s case the claimant's ignorance was not as to the law but only the facts: non-possession of a licence by the defendant carrier. The Second American *Restatement of Contracts*, however, contains the attractive suggestion that the relevant principle should extend also to questions of law.[72] Paragraph 180 is as follows:

> "**Effect of Excusable Ignorance**
> If a promisee is excusably ignorant of facts or of legislation of a minor character, of which the promisor is not excusably ignorant and in the absence of which the promise would be enforceable, the promisee has a claim for damages for its breach but cannot recover damages for anything that he has done after he learns of the facts or legislation."

4–32

(c) "Promises" and "Warranties"

Need for careful categorisation. The "innocent" party to a contract incapable of legal performance from the outset may therefore be able to sue for damages.[73] Nevertheless, a party to such a contract is still potentially in a less advantageous position than that of the "innocent" party to a contract which is capable of legal performance, but which the defendant intends to perform unlawfully or to use in the furtherance of some ulterior illegal purpose. This is because, as explained above, mere knowledge of the illegality is not enough to disqualify in the latter case. Providing that the defendant's purpose is not especially grave, the claimant must be a "participant" before forfeiting his rights. If a contract is incapable of legal performance, however, mere knowledge that that is the case should and does render the contract unenforceable, even by the party not obliged to carry out the unlawful performance. Knowingly to enter into a contract which cannot be legally performed is an affront to the law which cannot be overlooked. If the claimant is in fact aware of what the defendant proposes to do, it may therefore be crucial to determine whether the case falls into the category of contracts incapable from the outset of legal performance, or merely into that of a defendant choosing to promote an unlawful scheme by means of the contract or its performance. The need to distinguish between the two categories may require, in borderline cases, careful analysis of different types of contractual "term".

4–33

---

[71] See also Professor Otto Kahn-Freund, who wrote in a note on *Archbold*'s case: "This makes good sense. If a person charters a vehicle, he ought to inquire into the licensing position, but if he merely contracts for the carriage of goods, he should not be concerned with this matter. Otherwise businessmen would bear a burden of inquiry which would be quite intolerable" (1961) J. B. L. 299 at 302.

[72] cf. *Kleinwort Benson v Lincoln City Council* [1999] 2 A.C. 349; [1998] 4 All E.R. 513, HL (recovery back of money paid under a mistake of law).

[73] But not for specific performance.

4–34   **Not all terms relate to "performance".**   It will be recalled that in *Allan (Merchandising) v Cloke*,[74] which was criticised earlier,[75] a contract for the hire of a roulette wheel was held to be unenforceable for illegality because of a shared intention that it should be used in a particular manner, which happened to contravene the Betting and Gaming Act 1960. The Court of Appeal appears to have treated the agreement as incapable of legal performance from the outset, even though no obligation to use the roulette wheel in any particular way was actually imposed upon the hirers by the contract. Davies LJ said[76]:

> "The county court judge has made an express finding that the contract here could not be performed without breaking the law and that the intention of the parties when they made the contract was to do the very thing which the county court judge has held, and which this court is of opinion, is prohibited by law."

This statement is misleading because it fails to draw a significant but neglected distinction between two different types of contractual "term": that between those which govern the *performance* of the contract, and those which relate merely to a state of fact unrelated to actual performance. This distinction can be seen in a contract for the sale of goods. The vendor might undertake to deliver the goods to the purchaser and such delivery would, in an important sense, constitute "performance" of the agreement. In addition, however, the vendor will normally have undertaken that the goods delivered are of merchantable quality, but this undertaking is quite separate from the physical act of delivery. This distinction was expressed with great clarity in *Salmond and Williams on Contracts*,[77] where the authors contrasted "promises" with "warranties"[78]:

> "Contractual undertakings . . . are . . . of two kinds . . . promises and warranties. A promise is a term whereby a party to the contract undertakes to do a certain act. A warranty is a term whereby he undertakes that a certain fact exists, or that a certain event has occurred or will occur. A promise is a contractual undertaking as to the future acts of him who makes it; a warranty is a contractual undertaking as to any other fact or event whatever."

4–35   **Distinction important in illegality cases.**   In some cases it will be difficult to distinguish between terms which govern performance of the agreement and those which relate merely to a state of fact unrelated to performance. Moreover, in the majority of cases the distinction will be immaterial since the court will only be concerned to determine whether or not the contract has been broken and, if so, what the legal consequences of the breach should be. For this purpose it will rarely matter whether the particular term broken did, or did not, govern "performance" in the present sense. In the context of illegality, however, the distinction can be of great importance because of the special position of agreements which are incapable of lawful performance. In *Allan (Merchandising) v Cloke*, for example, the mere fact that the claimant company had undertaken

---

[74] [1993] 2 Q.B. 340.
[75] See Ch.3, above.
[76] [1963] 2 Q.B. 340 at 351.
[77] 2nd edn (Sweet & Maxwell, 1945), at p.44.
[78] The expression "warranty" is, of course, not used here in the more familiar sense in which it is contrasted with a "condition", nor in the sense in which it is used in the law of insurance.

expressly to provide a roulette wheel for the purpose of playing a forbidden type of game was not sufficient to render the agreement incapable of legal performance. It would only have been thus incapable if the defendants had been obliged to use the equipment for that game *specifically*, or if transactions involving roulette wheels as such had been prohibited by law.

CHAPTER 5

INDEMNITY AND FORFEITURE

1. INTRODUCTION

Range of issues.   This chapter is concerned, first, with situations in which a   **5–01**
claimant seeks to avoid the financial consequences of legal liability, criminal or
civil, by enforcing an indemnity against a third party. Insofar as they may "soften
the blow" suffered by the claimant as a result of his own unlawful activities, and
compromise the deterrent or denunciatory effect of the law, the enforceability of
such indemnities has long been seen to raise an illegality issue. The chapter also
deals with the effect upon the enforceability of life insurance policies of the
insured's committing suicide, and with the effect of homicide in the law of
succession. These two areas raise policy issues not dissimilar from those faced by
the law relating to the enforceability of indemnities, and therefore also warrant
consideration. This is notwithstanding the fact that cases involving succession do
not concern illegality in *contract* as such.

2. RECOVERY OF CRIMINAL PENALTIES AND COSTS

Absence of fault.   In principle it would seem curious if the full impact of   **5–02**
sanctions imposed by a criminal court could be avoided by means of a civil action
brought by the person convicted. Nevertheless, there is a very small number of
exceptional cases in which convicted claimants have succeeded in "softening the
blow", by suing third parties said to have been really to blame for what had
occurred. In one case a brain-damaged claimant was awarded damages in tort for
negligence to compensate him for the fact that he had been sentenced to a long
term of imprisonment.[1] But this decision, which appears to be unique,[2] was
subsequently effectively overruled by the House of Lords in a case involving
similar facts.[3] Nevertheless, other cases, which have not been overruled, have
involved the recovery, in actions for breach of contract, of fines imposed for
relatively minor offences. While such decisions still appear anomalous, they no
doubt reflect the intense pragmatism of the common law in its desire to avoid
injustice.

---

[1] See *Meah v McCreamer* [1985] 1 All E.R. 367.
[2] cf. *Meah v McCreamer* (No.2) [1986] 1 All E.R. 493.
[3] See *Gray v Thames Trains* [2009] UKHL 33, [2009] 4 All ER 81. See also *Clunis v Camden and Islington Health Authority* [1998] Q.B. 978; [1998] 3 All E.R. 180.

5–03   **Driving while uninsured.**   The cases include one relatively recent decision of the Court of Appeal. In *Osman v J. Ralph Moss*[4] the defendant was an insurance broker who had insured the claimant with a cut-price motor insurance company, which had subsequently failed. As a result of his ignorance of the company's failure the claimant was convicted by magistrates for driving while uninsured, and fined £25 plus costs. In an action against the broker in contract and tort the County Court found that he had been at fault in placing the insurance with a company which he ought to have known was unsafe, and that he had also been culpable in failing to advise the claimant sufficiently of the company's collapse. In consequence he was ordered to pay the value of the fines and costs to the claimant. This decision was upheld by a unanimous Court of Appeal. The Court held that recovery of a fine in a civil action is only prohibited when the person convicted has been at fault, and does not apply to cases of "absolute" liability "unless it is shown that there was on the part of the person fined a degree of mens rea or of culpable negligence in the matter which resulted in the fine".[5] Phillimore LJ said[6]:

> "This man incurred ... liability through no fault, no negligence or dishonesty on his part. He incurred it because he was grossly misled by the insurance brokers whose duty it was to advise him. It would, as I think, be quite wrong in such circumstances if he was not able to recover the amount of this fine as a just debt."

5–04   **Bad meat.**   In the earlier case of *Cointat v Myham*[7] the defendants sold the claimant butcher a tuberculous pig to sell in his shop. The claimant was not aware of the state of the meat, which was in due course seized by an inspector and ordered to be destroyed. The claimant was convicted and fined £20, plus costs, for having bad meat on his premises. Lord Coleridge J gave judgment for the claimant in an action for breach of warranty. He awarded damages in respect of the fine and costs, as well as for loss of trade. His Lordship emphasised that the crime was one of strict liability, observing that although "no doubt in one sense the plaintiff was in default in rendering himself liable to the law, yet absence of knowledge, absence of negligence, is no defence to the charge, and his conviction does not imply that he was negligent".[8]

5–05   **Size of the fine.**   In both *Osman v J. Ralph Moss*[9] and *Cointat v Myham*[10] importance was attached to the fact that the respective fines were not perceived to have been "heavy": the implication being that, if they had been, this might have provided some indication of the claimant's culpability and resulted in the dismissal of his claim. In another case involving food unfit for consumption, the

---

[4] [1970] 1 Lloyd's Rep. 313.
[5] See, per Sachs LJ in [1970] 1 Lloyd's Rep. 313 at 316.
[6] See [1970] 1 Lloyd's Rep. 313 at 320.
[7] [1913] 2 K.B. 220.
[8] See [1913] 2 K.B. 220 at 222. The decision of Lord Coleridge J was subsequently reversed by the Court of Appeal (see (1914) 84 L.J.K.B. 2253). But the illegality point was not mentioned, the case being sent back for a new trial on the general issue of warranty (no subsequent proceedings were reported).
[9] [1970] 1 Lloyd's Rep. 313 at 318 per Edmund Davies LJ.
[10] See [1913] 2 K.B. 220 at 222.

size of the fine was the basis of the decision. In *Crage v Fry*[11] the defendants sold the claimant a quantity of tinned mackerel which turned out to be "not fit for the ordinary purposes of food", and was seized by the authorities. The claimant was convicted, and fined £20 plus costs. He sought to recover the fine and costs from the defendants in an action for breach of warranty.[12] On the claim for the fine Kennedy J gave judgment for the defendant, but only because "it was a heavy fine, and it might [have been] that the magistrate was led to impose it because he thought that the plaintiff had not been as diligent, or as careful, as he ought to have been in periodically examining his stock".[13] The claimant was, however, allowed to recover the prosecution costs which he had been ordered to pay, and his own defence costs.[14]

Recovery refused.   The much more orthodox view that criminal penalties **5–06** cannot be recovered over in a civil action is reflected in two cases,[15] decided later than *Crage v Fry* and *Cointat v Myham*. In *R. Leslie v Reliable Advertising and Addressing Agency*[16] the defendants agreed to address advertising circulars for the claimants, who were money-lenders. They agreed to "take every precaution" to ensure that no minor was circularised, because inviting a minor to borrow money was a criminal offence in the absence of reasonable grounds for believing that the minor was of full age. Unfortunately the precautions proved insufficient and, having been convicted and fined, the claimants sought to recover the fine and costs from the defendants. The claim failed. Rowlatt J made clear his belief that the action was "misconceived on the broad ground that a person convicted of a criminal offence could never have the assistance of a civil court to ease himself of the punishment by the recovery over" of any fine or costs. Moreover, there should not be any difference, in his Lordship's view, "between cases where the legislature had made an act or default punishable as a crime without the existence of a guilty mind and any other class of offence". In deference to *Cointat v Myham*, however, Rowlatt J decided the case on the narrow ground that the conviction of the claimants had not been based on strict liability, but on their failure to prove that they had had reasonable grounds for believing the minor in question to be of full age: "They knew what ground they had—namely their contract with the defendants—and it was insufficient".

[11] (1903) J.P. 240.
[12] cf. the curious (repealed) Food and Drugs Act 1875 s.28 which provided expressly that fines and costs imposed under the act on "innocent" defendants could be recovered by them from the persons ultimately responsible. This provision was not relevant in *Cointat v Myham* and *Crage v Fry*, but it may have influenced the climate in which those two cases were decided.
[13] It is interesting to note that the fine was the same size as the one regarded as not heavy in *Cointat v Myham* a decade later (£20).
[14] See also *Proops v Chaplin* (1920) 37 T.L.R. 112 in which the costs of defending a prosecution were held to be recoverable in a civil action. In that case, however, the defence had succeeded and the claimant had been acquitted.
[15] See also the nineteenth century case of *Colburn v Patmore* (1834) 1 Cr. M. & R. 73, especially per Lord Lyndhurst CB at 83.
[16] [1915] 1 K.B. 652.

5–07   ***Askey v Golden Wine Co.***   The same result was reached in *Askey v Golden Wine Co*[17] a decision of Denning J. In this case the claimant, who had been convicted of selling cocktails unfit for human consumption, sought unsuccessfully to recover the value of his fine, costs, and other damages, from his suppliers. Although Denning J pointed out that the claimant had been grossly negligent, he preferred to decide the case on broader grounds[18]:

> "It is, I think, a principle of our law that the punishment inflicted by a criminal court is personal to the offender, and that the civil courts will not entertain an action by the offender to recover an indemnity against the consequences of that punishment. In every criminal court the punishment is fixed having regard to the personal responsibility of the offender in respect of the offence, to the necessity for deterring him, and, in cases such as the present, to make him and others more careful in their dealings, to make him choose with more discrimination his suppliers or his servants, and to make him more exact and scrupulous in the supervision of the matters for which he is responsible. All these objects would be nullified if the offender could recover the amount of the fine and costs from another by process of the civil courts."

Despite the persuasiveness of this reasoning, the Court of Appeal in *Osman v J. Ralph Moss*[19] distinguished *Askey's* case on the ground that the claimant in that case had been at fault. Edmund Davies LJ also indicated,[20] in *Osman's* case, that he considered *Cointat v Myham* to be "preferable" to *R. Leslie v Reliable Advertising and Addressing Agency*.

5–08   ***Safeway Stores v Twigger.***   In the recent case of *Safeway Stores v Twigger*[21] the claimant company sought to recover a penalty which it had been ordered to pay by the Office of Fair Trading for illegal sharing of pricing information with competitors, contrary to s.2(1) of the Competition Act 1998. The defendants were former employees of the company itself, who had actually been responsible for the illegal activity. The case proceeded on the basis that the penalty was equivalent to a fine imposed by a criminal court, and the Court of Appeal emphasised that the company was, as such, itself liable for the penalty: it was not a case of its being held liable vicariously for the employees who had instigated the illegality. In judgments which referred, inter alia, to *R. Leslie v Reliable Advertising and Addressing Agency, Askey v Golden Wine Co* and *Osman v J. Ralph Moss*, the Court of Appeal held unanimously that the claimant company would fail. The Competition Act predicated liability on the illegal activity having been "committed intentionally or negligently", and the Court held that this was sufficient to preclude recovery.[22] It was therefore unnecessary to express a concluded view on the strict liability cases and the Court declined to do so. But Pill LJ did acknowledge that "other situations may be more complex", and observed that it "is not easy to provide a single, simple rule which applies to the wide range of situations in which civil claims may follow a conviction or

---

[17] [1948] 2 All E.R. 35.
[18] [1948] 2 All E.R. 35 at 38.
[19] [1970] 1 Lloyd's Rep. 313, see para.5–03, above.
[20] [1970] 1 Lloyd's Rep. 313 at 318.
[21] [2010] EWCA Civ 1472.
[22] In *Bilta (UK) Ltd (in liquidation) v Nazir* the Supreme Court briefly considered the reasoning in *Safeway Stores v Twigger* but declined to express a concluded view as to the correctness of the decision, see [2015] UKSC 23 at [31] and [156]-[162].

quasi-conviction".[23] The position would therefore appear to be that, unless and until *Osman v J. Ralph Moss* is overruled, claimants convicted on the basis of strict liability in circumstances in which they were not in any way at fault, may very occasionally succeed in recovering fines and costs in a civil action.[24]

Contractual indemnities against costs in criminal cases. If the claimant is not seeking to recover costs imposed by a criminal court, but to enforce an express indemnity against the costs incurred by himself during criminal proceedings, it appears that there is no objection to enforcing such an indemnity even if serious criminal charges are involved. In *Coulson v News Group Newspapers*[25] the claimant had been editor of one of the defendant's newspapers. On the cessation of his employment the defendants expressly agreed to pay any reasonable "legal and accounting costs" incurred by the claimant as a result of his having to "defend or appear in" any legal proceedings arising out of his former post. When the claimant was subsequently arrested and charged with the offence of conspiracy to intercept communications the defendants declined to pay the claimant's defence costs. They argued that criminal offences involving personal misconduct were outside the scope of the indemnity and that, even if they were not, indemnities against such costs would be unenforceable for illegality. Counsel for the defendants relied, inter alia, on *R. Leslie v Reliable Advertising and Addressing Agency*. The Court of Appeal rejected the defendant's contentions and held, in broad terms, that the indemnity extended to the proceedings in question and that the claimant was entitled to enforce it. McCombe LJ said[26]:

5–09

> "The cases to which we were referred related to attempts by wrongdoers to recover under an indemnity fines and costs imposed for breach of the law. They did not relate to indemnities for the costs of defending oneself. There is nothing contrary to public policy in one person providing funds to another for that other to defend himself against a criminal charge: the Criminal Defence Service does it all the time. I can see no objection to private persons agreeing to do so for consideration.[27]"

---

[23] See ibid. at [51]–[52].

[24] See also *Burrows v Rhodes* [1899] 1 Q.B. 817, in which the claimant was awarded damages for injuries suffered during a military expedition despite the fact that in joining it he had committed a criminal offence. The defendants had fraudulently misrepresented to him that the expedition was legal, and had the support of the Crown. Although the claimant was never in fact convicted, and claimed only for personal injuries and related losses, the case was treated "as if the plaintiff had been convicted and was claiming an indemnity for the penal consequences of a criminal offence": at 834, per Kennedy J cf. *Griffin v UHY Hacker Young & Partners* [2010] EWHC 146 (claim for damages flowing, inter alia, from conviction for an offence under s.216 of the Insolvency Act 1986 allowed to go to trial to determine the extent of the claimant's moral culpability).

[25] [2012] EWCA Civ 1547.

[26] See ibid. at [61].

[27] See also *Mulcaire v News Group Newspapers* [2011] EWHC 3469 at [43]–[45] per Morritt C.

3. RECOVERY OF DAMAGES

(a) Policy Issues

5–10 **Social interests.** The reasoning which normally prevents criminal penalties from being recovered over clearly does not apply in the same way to the recovery, from the persons ultimately responsible, of damages awarded against the claimants in civil actions. In this area, unlike that of the criminal law, there is a substantial element of loss distribution and the punitive aspect is much less pronounced.[28] When claimants have sought to enforce contracts of indemnity, or of liability insurance, the law has therefore been able to examine less rigidly the social interests and policies for and against enforceability.[29] Even if the claimant had incurred, or could have incurred, criminal liability as a result of the activity in question this will not, in itself, preclude him from recovering over any civil damages awarded against him[30]; although any criminal penalties will remain irrecoverable unless the case falls into the exceptional category discussed above.

5–11 **Discouraging misrepresentation.** On the other hand, claimants shown to have knowingly taken a risk of liability, while engaging with the defendant in deliberate activities, may be unable to enforce an indemnity agreed with the latter.[31] In *Brown Jenkinson & Co v Percy Dalton (London) Ltd*[32] the defendants wished to ship a quantity of orange juice to Hamburg. The shipowners informed the defendants that it would be necessary to issue a claused bill of lading because the barrels which contained the orange juice were old, frail and leaking. But the defendants requested that a clean bill of lading should be given and, at the shipowners' request, undertook to indemnify them against any losses which they might incur as a result of the issue of a clean bill. Accordingly, bills of lading were signed stating that the barrels were "shipped in good order and condition". The shipowners incurred, as a result, liability to the receivers of the orange juice in Hamburg, and sought to enforce the indemnity. Their claim failed. The Court of Appeal held, by a majority,[33] that since the consideration for the giving of the indemnity was the making by the shipowners of a representation known to them to be fraudulent, they could not recover. Morris LJ said[34]:

---

[28] cf. per Lord Hoffman in *Gray v Thames Trains* [2009] UKHL 33, [2009] 4 All ER 81 at [29] et seq., distinguishing between "narrower" and "wider" forms of the public policy rule against a claimant benefiting from his own wrong.

[29] See McNeely, "Illegality as a Factor in Liability Insurance" (1941) 41 Col. L.R. 26.

[30] See *Tinline v White Cross Insurance Association* [1921] 3 K.B. 327 and *James v British General Insurance Co* [1927] 2 K.B. 311 (motor manslaughter), discussed in para.5–13, below, cf. *Burrows v Rhodes* [1899] 1 Q.B. 817.

[31] This gave rise to particular difficulty in relation to the enforceability of libel indemnities in publishing contracts, and resulted in statutory intervention: see the Defamation Act 1952 s.11: "An agreement for indemnifying any person against civil liability for libel in respect of the publication of any matter shall not be unlawful unless at the lime of the publication that person knows that the matter is defamatory, and does not reasonably believe that there is a good defence to any action brought upon it." cf. *Shackell v Rosier* (1836) 2 Bins. N.C. 634: *W. H. Smith v Clinton* (1908) 25 T.L.R. 34.

[32] [1957] 2 Q.B. 621, CA.

[33] Morris and Pearce LJ, Lord Evershed MR dissenting.

[34] [1957] 2 Q.B. 621 at 635.

"Can A, who does what B asks him to do, enforce against B a promise made in the following terms: 'If you will at my request make a statement which you know to be false and which you know will be relied on by others and which may cause them loss, then if they hold you liable, I will indemnify you'? In my judgment the assistance of the courts should not be given to enforce such a promise."

Pearce LJ drew attention to the practical disadvantages which would accrue if the practice the parties had adopted became widespread.[35]

Claimant's awareness. The Court in the *Percy Dalton* case did emphasise, however, that the claim did not fail because the giving of a clean bill of lading was misleading in itself, but only because the claimants were aware of the actual condition of the barrels. The distinction between the situation in cases such as that, and cases in which the real responsibility lay with the defendant even if the essentially innocent claimant had been the one actually held liable,[36] was established in early cases on contribution at common law between tortfeasors; in which indemnities accepted bona fide were enforced. Thus in 1827, *Adamson v Jarvis*[37] established that an auctioneer who sells goods under order of the defendant, when he has no reason to doubt the latter's title, can claim an indemnity if he has to pay damages to the true owner.[38] Best CJ observed that a decision to the opposite effect "would create great alarm".[39]

5–12

Protecting third parties. A powerful factor favouring the enforceability of contracts of indemnity or insurance is that refusal of such recovery could prejudice the original victim, whose claim might go uncompensated if the person held liable to him would otherwise have insufficient funds to satisfy the judgment. In the sphere of motor insurance this was recognised by the courts even before the legislature intervened and provided for a compulsory third party insurance scheme.[40] In *Tinline v White Cross Insurance Association*,[41] Bailhache J[42] held that a person who had been convicted of manslaughter after a serious accident, in which by driving at excessive speed he had injured two people and killed a third, could enforce a liability insurance policy so as to obtain an

5–13

---

[35] "Trust is the foundation of trade; and bills of lading are important documents. If purchasers and banks fell that they could no longer trust bills of lading, the disadvantage to the commercial community would far outweigh any conveniences provided by the giving of clean bills of lading against indemnities" [1957] 2 Q.B. 621 at 639.

[36] See, e.g. *Newcombe v Yewen and Croydon RDC* (1913) T.L.R. 299; *Lister v Romford Ice and Cold Storage Co* [1957] A.C. 535.

[37] (1827) 4 Bing. 66.

[38] See also *Betts v Gibbins* (1834) 2 Ad. & El. 57. Cf. *Merryweather v Nixan* (1799) 8 Term Rep.186.

[39] (1827) 4 Bing. 66 at 72.

[40] See, especially, per Roche J in *James v British General Insurance Co* (1927) 137 L.T. 156 at 158 noting that it had been "advocated, that persons should be obliged to insure against these risks on the ground that with the spread of motoring the risks to other persons are so great, and the risk or chance of injury from any impecunious person is so great, that it really is unfair that people should be driving when they are not covered against third-party risks" (passage omitted from the report in [1927] 2 K.B. 311). Such insurance became compulsory shortly thereafter with the passing of the Road Traffic Act 1930, see now the Road Traffic Act 1988.

[41] [1921] 3 K.B. 327.

[42] "[A] judge of great experience in matters of insurance", per Roche J in *James v British General Insurance Co* [1927] 2 K.B. 311 at 321.

indemnity in respect of damages claims made against him by the victims of the accident. The same result was reached in *James v British General Insurance Co*[43] in which the claimant, who sought an indemnity under his insurance policy, had been convicted of manslaughter following an accident caused by his driving while intoxicated. Roche J rejected an argument to the effect that *Tinline*'s case was distinguishable on the ground that "the drunkenness involved a degree of deliberation or intention which was not present"[44] in the earlier decision.[45]

(b)   Intentional Wrongdoing

5–14   **Motor vehicle cases.**   In *Tinline v White Cross Insurance*, Bailhache J emphasised that the claimant could not have enforced the insurance policy if he had committed murder by intentionally driving at his victims. Although his Lordship ascribed that result to the wording of the insurance policy itself,[46] illegality would apparently preclude recovery in such circumstances in any event. In *Hardy v Motor Insurers' Bureau*[47] a driver who was uninsured drove his van in such a way as deliberately to injure the claimant, and was later convicted of maliciously inflicting grievous bodily harm on him. The claimant obtained a judgment against the driver for his injuries which was, however, unsatisfied. He therefore proceeded against the Motor Insurers' Bureau pursuant to their well-known agreement with the Minister of Transport.[48] The Bureau argued, however, that it was not liable; contending that the direct right of action against insurers conferred upon motor accident victims by the Road Traffic Act would not, on the facts of the case, have been available even if the driver had been insured. They argued that compulsory third party cover applied only to negligence, and did not extend to intentional infliction of injury. The Court of Appeal[49] agreed that the fact that the injuries had been inflicted intentionally would have prevented the driver himself from recovering an indemnity from his insurers if he had been insured.[50] This was, in the words of Lord Denning MR,[51] "for the good and sufficient reason that no person can claim reparation or indemnity for the consequences of a criminal offence where his own wicked and deliberate intent is an essential ingredient in it".

5–15   **Bureau liable.**   The Court of Appeal went on, however, to hold the Bureau liable on the ground that the enforceability by third parties of their statutory right

---

[43] [1927] 2 K.B. 311.

[44] [1927] 2 K.B. 311 at 323, per Roche J cf. *O'Hearn v Yorkshire Insurance Co* (1921) 67 D.L.R. 735 (Can).

[45] See also *Cooke v Routledge* [1998] N.I. 174, CA in which a motorist who crashed his car, while driving when in excess of double the prescribed alcohol limit, was permitted to enforce his comprehensive motor insurance policy for his own benefit in order to replace the vehicle.

[46] "Manslaughter is the result of an accident and murder is not, and it is against accident and accident only that this policy insures" [1921] 3 K.B. 327 at 332.

[47] [1964] 2 Q.B. 745.

[48] The text of the then current version of the agreement is set out in full in the report: see [1964] 2 K.B. 745 at 771–775.

[49] Lord Denning MR, Pearson and Diplock LTJ.

[50] See also *Charlton v Fisher and another* [2001] EWCA Civ 112, [2002] QB 578.

[51] [1964] 2 Q.B. 745 at 760.

of action was independent of any such defence of illegality which the insurer might enjoy against the policy-holder himself. Moreover, the "risk" of their causing intentional injury was one against which motorists were compulsorily required to insure—thus precluding reliance on the principle of insurance law that the insurer is not liable where the policy-holder has intentionally caused the act insured against.[52] The result was therefore that he was able to obtain compensation,[53] but only by virtue of the special legislative provisions relating to motor-vehicles and the existence of the Motor Insurers' Bureau. In the subsequent case of *Gardner v Moore*[54] which was decided on effectively identical facts, the House of Lords was invited to overrule *Hardy v Motor Insurers' Bureau*, but chose instead expressly to affirm its correctness.[55]

Acts of violence. In the absence of special legislative provisions such as those which applied in *Hardy's* case, the court's refusal to allow persons guilty of deliberate criminality to enforce indemnities will leave their victims dependent for compensation upon the depth of the defendant's own pocket. It is at least questionable whether this is a satisfactory position. In *Gray v Barr*[56] a husband, who was the holder of a "hearth and home" insurance policy, set out to frighten a man who was having an affair with his wife. He did so by threatening him with a shotgun. Unfortunately, a struggle broke out between the two men and the gun went off, killing the wife's lover. The insured was held liable to pay damages to the widow of the deceased under the Fatal Accidents Acts, and sought to obtain an indemnity by enforcing his policy. The Court of Appeal held that his claim would fail. He had been acquitted of manslaughter at his criminal trial; but Lord Denning MR described that as a "merciful verdict" and indicated that his actions would nevertheless be regarded, for the purposes of his claim for an indemnity, as having been "wilful and culpable". It followed that his claim was barred by public policy, irrespective of any other defence enjoyed by the insurance company based on the wording of the agreement itself.[57] "Crimes of violence", observed Salmon LJ,[58] "are amongst the worst curses of this age"; and "public policy undoubtedly requires that no one who threatens unlawful violence with a

5–16

---

[52] See *MacGillivray on Insurance Law*, 13th edn, (Sweet & Maxwell, 2015), Ch.14, para.14.030. cf. Lord Sumner in *P Samuel & Co v Dumas* [1924] A.C. 431 at 474 (suggesting that "the lawyer's ethical objection to allowing a man to profit by his own wrong" might itself be the historical basis of what is now treated as an implied term in contracts of insurance).

[53] See also the similar case of *MacDonald v Prudential Assurance Co* (1971) 24 D.L.R. (3d) 185 (Can), in which the same result was reached.

[54] [1984] 1 All E.R. 1100. Lord Hailsham of St Marylebone LC delivered the only substantive speech, with which the other members of the House agreed.

[55] See also *Patel v Mirza* [2016] UKSC 42 at [102] per Lord Toulson.

[56] [1971] 2 Q.B. 554, CA affirming [1970] 2 Q.B. 626 (Geoffrey Lane J). For comment on the upheld decision at first instance see Fleming (1971) 34 M.L.R. 176. and Jolowicz (1970) 28 C.L.T. 194.

[57] i.e. that the fatality had not been an "accident" within the terms of the policy. Lord Denning MR and Phillimore LJ expressed the view that this defence would have availed the insurers even if illegality had not. cf. *Charlton v Fisher and another* [2001] EWCA Civ 112, [2002] QB 578, in which there were conflicting dicta in the Court of Appeal on the question whether the deliberate ramming of one motor vehicle, by the driver of another, would constitute an "accident": Kennedy and Laws LJJ considered that it would, Rix LJ that it would not. On accident policies see generally, *MacGillivray on Insurance Law*, 13th edn, (Sweet & Maxwell 2015), Ch.27.

[58] [1971] 2 Q.B. 554 at 581.

loaded gun should be allowed to enforce a claim for indemnity against any liability he may incur as a result of having so acted".[59]

5–17   Danger of leaving victims uncompensated.   There is no indication in the report of *Gray v Barr* whether the insured was able personally to satisfy the judgment against him. It must be doubtful whether the risk that judgments will go unsatisfied in such cases, leaving victims uncompensated, is justified by any benefit to the public generally of declining to enforce indemnities. It is fanciful to suppose that those not otherwise deterred from criminal activity will be inhibited by fear that their liability insurance policies may be unenforceable.[60] Nevertheless, in the more recent case of *Charlton v Fisher and another*,[61] the Court of Appeal again held that an indemnity would be unenforceable, because the insured had acted intentionally, notwithstanding that the insured's victim would almost certainly remain uncompensated as a result. The decision is all the more striking since it was a motor-vehicle case. The claimant had been injured when the car in which she was a passenger had been deliberately rammed by a car driven by the defendant, the insured. Because the incident happened in a hotel car-park, and not on a public road, the claimant was unable to benefit from the statutory provisions in the Road Traffic Acts giving third party victims direct recourse against the defendant's insurers. The Court of Appeal held unanimously that the insured was prevented by public policy from enforcing his insurance policy; and that it followed that there was no basis upon which the claimant could obtain compensation indirectly from the insurance company.

5–18   Professional indemnity.   The principle of public policy underlying *Gray v Barr* and *Charlton v Fisher and another* is not confined to intentional physical acts. In *Haseldine v Hosken*[62] a solicitor committed champerty, at a time when such activity was still criminal and tortious. As a result damages were awarded against him, and he sought to enforce his professional indemnity policy to obtain reimbursement. His attempt failed. The Court of Appeal[63] held that he had not been negligent in the course of his professional duty, but had instead entered into a personal speculation. Accordingly, his activities had probably been outside the scope of the policy in any event but, if even that were not the case, the Court indicated that the claim for indemnity was unenforceable for illegality.

---

[59] See also *Meah v McCreamer* (No.2) [1986] 1 All E.R. 943 in which *Gray v Barr* was applied. A rapist was held unable to recover from the defendant, whose negligence had turned the claimant into a rapist by inflicting brain injuries upon him, damages which he had been ordered to pay to his rape victims.

[60] See Dr Malcolm Clarke, "Illegal Insurance" (1987) Lloyd's M.C.L.Q. 201 at 209: "One may wonder whether a husband, inflamed by jealousy, is likely to be deterred from attacking his wife's lover by thoughts of insurance? Has there been any significant drop in the number of spouses shot since 1971?".

[61] [2001] EWCA Civ 112 [2002] QB 578.

[62] [1933] 1 K.B. 822.

[63] Scrutton, Greer and Slesser LJJ.

(c) Exemplary Damages

Where the liability is vicarious.   In *Lancashire CC v Municipal Mutual*   **5–19**
Insurance[64] the claimant authority sought to enforce a liability insurance policy
so as to obtain an indemnity in respect of exemplary damages. The Authority,[65]
and its Chief Constable, had become vicariously liable for such damages as a
result of assaults by police officers, and also as a result of child abuse in homes
run by the Authority. The defendant insurers argued that, irrespective of the
wording of the contract itself, an indemnity against exemplary damages was
unenforceable as a matter of public policy since it would negate the punitive and
deterrent reasoning which underlies such damages. The Court of Appeal found in
favour of the Authority. Simon Brown LJ said[66]:

> "In my judgment there is nothing either in the authorities or in logic to justify extending this
> principle of public policy so as to deny insurance cover to those whose sole liability is one
> which arises vicariously, whether as employers or, as here, under an equivalent statutory
> provision."

Possibility of recovery by claimants directly liable.   Although the basis of the   **5–20**
Court's decision in the *Lancashire CC* case was therefore that those who find
themselves vicariously liable may enforce indemnities against exemplary
damages,[67] its reasoning did not wholly exclude the possibility of claimants who
had been held directly liable also recovering.[68] Simon Brown LJ noted that the
Court had been told that "newspapers ... regularly insure against exemplary
damages for defamation".[69] He also considered that increased premiums, and the
difficulty of obtaining cover in the future, meant that "even though the
defendant's liability be insurable, an exemplary damages award is still likely to
have punitive effect".[70]

Compulsory insurance.   Of course if the situation is such that, as in *Gray v*   **5–21**
Barr and *Charlton v Fisher and another*, a claimant is precluded by his conduct
from enforcing an indemnity against an award of merely compensatory damages,
it follows a fortiori that an indemnity against exemplary damages will similarly
be unenforceable. It is noteworthy, however, that just as compulsory insurance
schemes may enable a policy-holder's victims to recover damages even where the

---

[64] [1997] Q.B. 897, CA.
[65] cf. *Kiddus v Chief Constable of Leicestershire Constabulary* [2001] 3 All E.R. 193 in which the
House of Lords left open the question whether vicarious liability should not, as a matter of principle,
extend to exemplary damages.
[66] [1997] Q.B. 897, at 908.
[67] [1997] Q.B. 897, at 911 per Staughton LJ.
[68] The American cases, which had been cited to the Court of Appeal, apparently reveal three different
approaches. Simon Brown LJ said: "Some states prohibit recovery of exemplary damages in all cases
which involve intentionally inflicted wrong; other states have no such rule in any case; others yet have
a rule prohibiting recovery where the insured is personally liable, but not where he is only vicariously
so" ([1997] Q.B. 897 at 908). See also the judgment of the High Court of Australia in *Lamb v Cotogno*
(1987) 164 C.L.R. 1 at 10, and references there given.
[69] [1997] Q.B. 897 at 908.
[70] [1997] Q.B. 897 at 909.

policy could not have been enforced by the holder himself,[71] such schemes may also be effective to enable the victims to recover exemplary damages, in those jurisdictions in which such awards are regularly made. In the Australian case of *Lamb v Cotogno*[72] exemplary damages had been awarded against a motorist following an incident in which his driving had inflicted serious injuries upon someone outside his car, following an argument between the two of them. The validity of the award was challenged on the ground that it was inappropriate where the damages would effectively be borne by the compulsory insurance scheme. This challenge was, however, rejected by the High Court of Australia in the following terms[73]:

"So far as the object of deterrence is concerned, not only does it extend beyond the defendant himself to other like-minded persons, but it also extends generally to conduct of the same reprehensible kind. Whilst an award of exemplary damages against a compulsorily insured motorist may have a limited deterrent effect upon him or upon other motorists also compulsorily insured, the deterrent effect is undiminished for those minded to engage in conduct of a similar nature which does not involve the use of a motor vehicle. Moreover, whilst the smart or sting will obviously not be the same if the defendant does not have to pay an award of exemplary damages, it does serve to mark the court's condemnation of the defendant's behaviour and its effect is not entirely to be discounted by the existence of compulsory insurance."

5–22   **Interests of the victims.**   The limited availability of exemplary damages means that the precise situation in *Lamb v Cotogno* would be unlikely to occur in England. Nevertheless, it is striking that both the Court of Appeal in the *Lancashire CC* case, and the High Court in *Lamb v Cotogno*, regarded the interests of the victims in exemplary damages cases as relevant and important. Thus, in the latter, the High Court observed that, "it is an aspect of exemplary damages that they serve to assuage any urge for revenge felt by victims and to discourage any temptation to engage in self-help".[74] And in the former Simon Brown LJ expressed himself as follows in the Court of Appeal:[75]

"Whilst it is true that to allow a defendant liable for exemplary damages to be held harmless against them by insurance must undoubtedly reduce the deterrent and punitive effect of the order upon him, it will greatly improve the plaintiff's prospects of recovering the sum awarded. It is, of course, this consideration—the interests of those harmed by the torfeasor—which has prompted the law in certain circumstances to require compulsory insurance."

It is ironic that the courts are prepared to treat the interests of the victim as significant in exemplary damages cases, when those interests were apparently disregarded in *Gray v Barr* and *Charlton v Fisher and another* in relation to compensatory awards. It is to be hoped that this contrast will not be overlooked if an opportunity to consider the correctness of those two cases ever presents itself.

---

[71] i.e. as in *Hardy v Motor Insurer's Bureau* [1964] 2 Q.B. 745 and *Gardner v Moore* [1984] A.C. 548.
[72] (1987) 164 C.L.R. 1.
[73] (1987) 164 C.L.R. 1 at 10.
[74] (1987) 164 C.L.R. 1 at 9.
[75] [1997] Q.B. 897 at 909.

4. SUICIDE AND LIFE INSURANCE

(a) Enforceability by the Deceased's Estate

Beresford's case. In *Beresford v Royal Insurance Co*[76] the holder of a life   **5–23**
insurance policy, who had got badly into debt, shot himself with the intention of
making the policy moneys available for his creditors. The policy provided by
necessary implication that the insurance company would be liable upon it even in
the event of suicide, provided that this took place more than twelve months after
the policy had commenced. At the time of his death the deceased's policy had
been running for nine years, so no objection to its enforceability could be based
on the terms of the agreement itself. The insurers nevertheless sought to deny
liability to the representatives of the deceased by relying on illegality. It had been
found as a fact that the deceased had been of sound mind, and suicide by such a
person was in those days a criminal offence.[77] In a robust judgment at first
instance Swift J held that the company was liable, but his decision was reversed
by the Court of Appeal, which was upheld by the House of Lords. The Court of
Appeal, in a judgment delivered by Lord Wright MR, did not attempt any
systematic analysis of precisely how enforceability ran counter to the public
interest; nor did the two speeches delivered in the House of Lords, by Lords
Atkin and Macmillan, seek to do so. The deceased's estate could be in no better
position than the deceased himself, and the claim was therefore considered to be
defeated by what Lord Atkin described as "the absolute rule . . . that the Courts
will not recognize a benefit accruing to a victim from his crime".[78]

Suicide no longer a crime. This reasoning is no longer applicable, since   **5–24**
suicide ceased to be a crime with the passing of the Suicide Act 1961, and it is
unclear whether or not *Beresford's* case might still be decided the same way
today; but on other grounds.[79] Since insurance companies are obviously free to
make suicide an excepted risk if they so choose,[80] the only possible rational
justification for the preservation of the rule in *Beresford's* case, as an independent

---

[76] [1938] A.C. 586.
[77] See now the Suicide Act 1961 s.1.
[78] [1938] A.C. 586 at 599. cf. *Northwestern Mutual Life Assurance Co v Johnson* (1920) 254 U.S. 96,
in which the US Supreme Court held that it would enforce life policies in circumstances similar to
those in *Beresford's* case, unless it appeared that a different view was taken by the law of the State in
which the contract was made. This liberal ruling departed from an earlier ruling in which the Supreme
Court itself had favoured the opposite view: see *Ritter v Mutual Life Assurance Co* (1897) 169 U.S.
139. See generally, on the American cases down to 1935: Goodhart, "Suicide and Life Insurance"
(1936) 52 L.Q.R. 575.
[79] cf. *Gray v Burr* [1971] 2 Q.B. 554 at 582, per Salmon LJ: "Public policy is not static. Even if the
crime of suicide had not been abolished by statute, it may be that today *Beresford's* case would have
been differently decided".
[80] There have been conflicting decisions in the US and Canada on whether or not policies in which
there is no mention of suicide should be presumed to have made it impliedly an excepted risk. The
majority of the cases favour such an implication: see, e.g. *Husak v Imperial Life Assurance Co of
Canada* (1970) 9 D.L.R. 602 (noted by Furmston in [1969] A.S.C.L. 754). But cf. the Missouri case of
Morton v Supreme Council of Royal League (1903) 100 Mo. App. 76: ". . . self-destruction always
indicates, if not insanity, at least an irresponsible state of mind, and may be considered part of the risk
assumed, if not specifically excluded" (cited by Goodhart in (1936) 52 L.Q.R. 575 at 583).

doctrine of public policy, would appear to be that it might discourage self-slaughter.[81] It is of course clear that, in *Beresford v Royal Insurance Co* itself, the deceased was motivated to take his own life in the hope that his estate would benefit from the policy moneys. Nevertheless, the House of Lords appears to have been content to regard these circumstances as quite exceptional. Lord Atkin and Lord Macmillan both admitted that they saw no real tendency to encourage suicide in the policy before them, and both insisted that they did not base the decision on this ground.[82]

5–25   **A possible distinction.**   The better view is therefore clearly that, at least in the overwhelming majority of cases, suicide by persons of sound mind will no longer render insurance policies taken out by the deceased on his life unenforceable, unless the policy itself so provides. The only conceivable exception might be cases in which it could be proved that the deceased had committed suicide in order to secure the proceeds of the policy for his estate.[83] If such an exception were established, and well-publicised, it would overcome any remaining objection to enforceability based upon the danger of encouraging self-slaughter. It would, of course, also mean that the actual decision in *Beresford v Royal Insurance Co* would still be correct. But the drawing of such a distinction between deceased policy-holders, according to their motives for suicide, has apparently been discounted through fear of uncertainty.[84] At least in principle, however, such a distinction would appear to have something to commend it; and a heavy burden of proof on the insurance company, equivalent to that for proving fraud, could ensure that significant uncertainty was avoided.[85] Moreover, if the deceased was insane his "motive" would become irrelevant: there never appears to have been any public policy objection to recovery by the estates of persons who had committed suicide while insane.[86]

---

[81] cf. *Amicable Society v Boland* (1830) 4 Bligh. (N.S.) 194, in which a policy taken out by someone who later suffered judicial execution was held to be void, against assignees of the deceased, on the ground (per Lord Lyndhurst at 211) that enforceability would "take away one of those restraints operating on the minds of men against the commission of crimes", sed quaere. For criticism of the decision see Devlin, *The Enforcement of Morals* (Oxford University Press, 1959), pp.53–54.

[82] "The instinct of self-preservation may be said to provide a stronger motive against suicide than the desire to benefit relatives or creditors can be said to provide a motive to commit suicide": [1938] A.C. 586 at 604, per Lord Macmillan; see also, per Lord Atkin at 601.

[83] See (1935) 49 Harv. L.R. 304 at 309.

[84] See Goodhart, "Suicide and Life Insurance" (1936) 52 L.Q.R. 575 at 585.

[85] cf. *Braganza v BP Shipping and another* [2015] UKSC 17, [2015] All ER (D) 185 (Mar).

[86] cf. *Pigney v Pointer's Transport Services* [1957] 1 W.L.R. 1121 in which, at a time when suicide was still a crime, a widow was able to recover damages under the Fatal Accidents Acts when her husband committed suicide as a result of depression caused by an accident for which the defendants were responsible. The same result was reached by the House of Lords (without the complication of suicide being a crime) in the recent case of *Corr v IBC Vehicles* [2008] UKHL 13; [2008] 2 All E.R. 943.

(b) Assignment of Life Policies

Security. An important question arising out of the possible invalidity of life   **5–26**
insurance policies, in the event of suicide, concerns the common practice of using
such policies as a form of security in loan transactions. Since an assignee cannot
normally be in a better position than his assignor, does it follow that a creditor
who lent money on the strength of a life policy would lose his security in the
event of the debtor's suicide? In so far as it can be argued that the decision in
Beresford v Royal Insurance Co might still be good law, even though suicide is
no longer a crime, the issue remains a live one. At first instance in *Beresford*'s
case,[87] Swift J emphasised that "the negotiable value of an assurance policy is
obviously much less if it relieves the assurors from liability in case of suicide",
and observed that it was presumably in order to meet this objection that the
wording of the policy in the case before him had not made suicide an excepted
risk.[88] In the House of Lords, Lord Atkin and Lord Macmillan both noted the
commercial importance of protecting the assignability of life policies.[89] Although
Lord Macmillan reserved his opinion on the point, Lord Atkin felt able to state
positively that the decision of the House would not affect assignees. He expressed
himself as follows:

> "I consider myself free to say that I cannot see that there is any objection to an assignee for
> value before the suicide enforcing a policy which contains an express promise to pay upon a
> sane suicide, at any rate so far as the payment is to extend to the actual interest of the
> assignee."

Surrender value. Since life policies are normally only acceptable to creditors   **5–27**
as security for loans up to the level of their surrender value, it clearly makes good
sense that the law should be in accordance with Lord Atkin's dictum.[90]
Assignment should provide no incentive to suicide because the policy-holder can
clear the debt simply by surrendering the policy.[91] There is therefore no
convincing reason for holding that assignees for value of life policies should be
under a disability, even if it is accepted that the personal representatives of a
deceased who committed suicide should be.

Moore v Wolsey. Lord Atkin's dictum is supported by the nineteenth century   **5–28**
case of *Moore v Wolsey*.[92] The policy in that case provided that it should be

---

[87] See (1936) 52 T.L.R. 650 at 654.
[88] See also, [1938] A.C. 586 at 604, per Lord Macmillan: "It is of the first importance . . . that policies
of life assurance, which are among the most useful instruments of credit, should not be subject to
contingent invalidity, and the present form of clause was no doubt adopted by the respondents . . .
solely with a view to rendering their policies attractive by reason of their stipulated incontestability".
[89] [1938] A.C. 586 at 599–600, per Lord Atkin and at 604, per Lord Macmillan.
[90] The statement was apparently made to reassure building societies, and other creditors, who had
been alarmed that the decision of the Court of Appeal may have rendered their security of uncertain
value.
[91] It is noteworthy that some policies actually provide that in the event of suicide the surrender value
of the policy, as distinct from the full sum provided for by the contract, shall be paid to the estate of
the deceased: see Colinvaux and Merkin's *Insurance Contract Law*, vol.2 para.B-0690.
[92] (1854) 4 El. & Bl. 243. cf. *Cook v Black* (1842) 1 Hare. 390; *White v British Empire and Mutual
Life Assurance Co* (1868) L.R. 7 Eq. 394.

"void" in the event of suicide, as far as the personal representatives of the deceased were concerned, but that it would "remain in force . . . to the extent of any bona fide interest which may have been acquired by any other person under an actual assignment by deed for a valuable consideration". The policy-holder having taken his own life, the defendant insurance company sought to have their own provision in favour of assignees declared illegal as offering an inducement to commit suicide. But the Court of Queen's Bench rejected their argument. Lord Campbell CJ said[93]:

> "When we are called upon to nullify a contract on the ground of public policy, we must take care that we do not lay down a rule which may interfere with the innocent and useful transactions of mankind. That the condition under discussion may promote evil by leading to suicide is a very remote and improbable contingency; and it may frequently be very beneficial by rendering a life policy a safe security in the hands of an assignee."

5–29   **Debtor not prejudiced.**   Even in the absence of a specific provision such as that in *Moore v Wolsey*, it would still seem possible to distinguish the position of assignees, in the event of the insured's suicide, from that of personal representatives. Since the "defence" enjoyed against the latter is based purely upon public policy, the debtor cannot legitimately claim to be prejudiced by his inability to invoke it against the assignee.[94] As elsewhere in illegality, the ordinary principles of the law of contract, in this instance those relating to assignment, do not operate as they would in cases where adjudication is based solely on the merits of the parties.

5.   SUCCESSION AND FORFEITURE

(a)   At Common Law

5–30   **The forfeiture rule.**[95]   In *Cleaver v Mutual Reserve Fund Life Association*[96] Lord Esher MR said[97]:

> "That the person who commits murder, or any person claiming under him or her, should be allowed to benefit by his or her criminal act, would no doubt be contrary to public policy."

In that case a widow convicted of the murder of her husband was precluded from recovering the proceeds of an insurance policy taken out for her benefit by the deceased, and the sums due became part of his estate instead. Similarly, in the well-known case of *Re Crippen (dec'd)*,[98] the estate of a notorious executed murderer was unable to benefit from his late wife's intestacy, she having been his victim. In the latter case Sir Samuel Evans P. put the underlying principle on the very broad basis of the supposed doctrine "that no person can obtain, or enforce,

---

[93] See (1854) 4 El. & Bl. 243 at 255.
[94] cf. *Davitt v Titcumb* [1990] Ch.110.
[95] See Enonchong, *Illegal Transactions* (LLP Ltd, 1998), Pt Two.
[96] [1892] 1 Q.B. 147, CA.
[97] [1892] 1 Q.B. 147 at 152.
[98] [1911] P. 108.

any rights resulting to him from his own crime".[99] Such a formulation clearly implied that the forfeiture rule was not confined to murder; and in *Re Hall's Estate*[100] the Court of Appeal confirmed that it could also apply to cases of manslaughter.[101]

Manslaughter by diminished responsibility. In view of the widely differing types of situation in which manslaughter can occur, indiscriminate application of the rule began to seem intuitively unattractive; and in *Gray v Barr*[102] Salmon LJ implied, obiter, that there could be circumstances in which someone who had committed manslaughter might inherit under the will or on the intestacy of the person he had killed.[103] Nevertheless, attempts to persuade the court to explore the extent of blameworthiness in each case were largely unsuccessful. In *Re Giles (dec'd)*[104] Pennycuick VC asserted that "the deserving of punishment and moral culpability" were "not necessary ingredients of the type of crime to which this rule applies, that is, culpable homicide, murder or manslaughter".[105] In that case a widow detained under the Mental Health Act, after pleading guilty to the murder of her husband by reason of diminished responsibility, was unable to benefit from his will. The decision was referred to with approval by the Court of Appeal in *Re Royse (dec'd)*,[106] which was decided on very similar facts and in which the same result was reached. On the other hand, in *Re H (dec'd)*[107] Peter Gibson J refused to follow *Re Giles* and held "that it would not be just to apply the forfeiture rule in every case of proof of manslaughter".[108] In *Re H* a devoted husband killed his wife while suffering from hallucinations caused by a drug which he had been prescribed for depression, and pleaded guilty to manslaughter on the ground of diminished responsibility. Peter Gibson J said that the test for application of the forfeiture rule was the commission of "deliberate, intentional and unlawful violence or threats of violence",[109] and concluded that it therefore did not apply to the case before him. But *Re H* itself was not followed, and the forfeiture rule

5–31

---

[99] [1911] P. 108 at 112. See also, per Fry LJ in *Cleaver v Mutual Reserve Fund Life Association* [1892] 2 Q.B. 147 at 156.

[100] [1914] P. 1, CA.

[101] The effect of the rule was formerly to prevent not only the killer, but also his descendants (such as his children) from taking under the deceased's will or intestacy: (see *Re DWS (dec'd)* [2001] Ch. 568, CA). But following recommendations made by the Law Commission in 2005 (see The Forfeiture Rule and the Law of Succession, Law Com. 295) the law was changed by the Estates of Deceased Persons (Forfeiture Rule and Law of Succession) Act 2011, which deems the killer to have died immediately *before* his victim (thereby limiting the effect of the disqualification to the killer himself).

[102] [1971] 2 Q.B. 544.

[103] See [1971] 2 Q.B. 544 at 552. See also T. G. Youdan. "Acquisition of Property by Killing" (1973) 89 L.Q.R. 235, especially at p.240: "The principle suggested is that the killer should only be deprived when he does or causes a dangerous act *intending* harm to the person whose death occasions his acquisition, and that person dies as a result of that act" (italics supplied).

[104] [1972] Ch. 544.

[105] See [1972] Ch. 544 at 552. It has long been accepted that persons found not guilty of murder on account of insanity are not subject to the forfeiture rule.

[106] [1985] Ch. 22; [1984] 3 All E.R. 339.

[107] [1990] 1 F.L.R. 441.

[108] [1990] 1 F.L.R. 441 at 446.

[109] [1990] 1 F.L.R. 441 at 447.

was applied, in a very similar manslaughter case in which a paranoid schizophrenic, suffering from delusions, killed his parents.[110]

5–32   **Manslaughter by gross negligence.**   The rule has even been applied to a case of manslaughter by gross negligence, in which no act of violence had been involved. In *Re Land (dec'd)*[111] a son who failed appropriately to care for his sick mother, resulting in her death, was held to be disqualified by the rule from taking under her will.[112]

5–33   **Need for flexibility.**   A conflict of approaches, not dissimilar from that reflected in the English cases, can also be seen in the majority decision of the New South Wales Court of Appeal in *Troja v Troja*.[113] The wife of the testator had been convicted of manslaughter on the basis of diminished responsibility, after shooting her husband following what she claimed had been a period of prolonged harassment. The deceased had bequeathed all his property to his wife but the majority, Mahoney and Meagher JJA, held that this would be forfeit on the ground that "where a person who would otherwise obtain a benefit by the death of another, has brought about that other's death by violent means, he shall not be entitled to take that benefit".[114] Kirby P dissented. He asserted that the moral culpability of the wife, against the background of her diminished responsibility, was not such that the public would be "outraged" if she were to benefit from the husband's estate; especially as she had contributed over many years to its accumulation. He also claimed that the court, in its equitable jurisdiction, could fashion a constructive trust to enable the wife to take some, but not all, of the estate.[115]

5–34   **Legislative intervention.**   The majority in *Troja v Troja* rejected the suggestion of Kirby P, however, on the ground that it would require legislative intervention. Legislation to mitigate the harshness of the forfeiture rule was, in fact, enacted in England in 1982; and although cases on the scope of the common law principle can still arise,[116] the statutory provisions should now apply in the majority of

---

[110] See *Jones (John Keith) v Roberts (John Ronald)* [1995] 2 F.L.R. 422.

[111] [2006] EWHC 2069 (Ch.); [2007] 1 All E.R. 324.

[112] Relief from the full consequences of the forfeiture was, however, granted on other grounds: see below para.5–39.

[113] [1994] 33 N.S.W.L.R. 269.

[114] See ibid, at 299, per Meagher JA.

[115] On the potential usefulness of the constructive trust in forfeiture cases generally, as a means of determining the incidence of the property, see T. G. Youdan (writing before the 1982 Act) in "Acquisition of Property by Killing" (1973) 89 L.Q.R. 235 at 256, et seq.: "As the English courts have worked out no suitable justification for depriving the wrongdoer of property acquired as the result of the killing so no rational theory has been devised for working out who becomes entitled to the property. However, if it is accepted that it is the constructive trust which is used to prevent the unjust enrichment of the wrongdoer the confusion is reduced and the person who is entitled to the property—the beneficiary of the constructive trust—is the person who, in the eyes of equity, has the best right to it".

[116] See, e.g. *Re H (dec'd)* [1990] 1 F.L.R. 441 and *Jones (John Keith) v Roberts (John Ronald)* [1995] 2 F.L.R. 422; the Act was not mentioned in the latter case (possibly because the strict time-limit provided for its application under s.2(3) had been exceeded). In *Dunbar v Plant* [1998] Ch.412 at 436;

cases. The common law nevertheless remains relevant in such cases, since it provides the necessary precondition for the operation of the statutory machinery.

(b)   By Statute

Forfeiture Act 1982.   The Forfeiture Act 1982 provides that "where a court determines that the forfeiture rule has precluded a person . . . who has unlawfully killed another from acquiring any interest in property", the court can make an order "modifying the effect of that rule".[117] There is a strict time-limit for the application of the Act where the person concerned has actually been convicted of unlawful killing: proceedings have to be brought not later than three months after the conviction.[118] Crucially, s.2(2) provides as follows:

> "The court shall not make an order under this section modifying the effect of the forfeiture rule in any case unless it is satisfied that, having regard to the conduct of the offender and of the deceased and to such other circumstances as appear to the court to be material, the justice of the case requires the effect of the rule to be so modified in that case."

The Act also makes clear that convictions for murder are outside its scope,[119] so that the common law rule will continue to apply with full vigour in such cases.

The Act applied.   The first application to come before the court under the Act was apparently *Re K (dec'd).*[120] A loyal wife, who had been subjected to a long period of domestic violence, tried to protect herself from another anticipated assault by picking up her husband's own shotgun to frighten him off. Unfortunately the gun went off accidentally, killing the husband, and a manslaughter conviction resulted. Vinelott J held that the forfeiture rule applied, but emphasised that the Act then required the court to form a view "of the degree of moral culpability attending the killing". He concluded[121] "that in the very unusual circumstances of [the] case it would be unjust that the widow should be deprived of any of the benefits which the deceased chose to confer on her by his will or which accrued to her by survivorship". The Court of Appeal, in the same case, upheld Vinelott J and commended his judgment. Ackner LJ noted[122] that the judge had borne in mind that the widow had given up "a worthwhile and satisfying career" in order to marry her husband, "that her conduct towards him to the very end of his life was not open to criticism, and to the fact that there was no other person for whom he was under any moral duty to provide". Similarly, in *Re H (dec'd),*[123] Peter Gibson J indicated that, had he held that the forfeiture rule

5–35

5–36

[1997] 4 All E.R. 289 at 310, Phillips LJ said that the "pressure for judicial intervention" to modify the common law rule "was removed by the Forfeiture Act", sed quaere.

[117] Forfeiture Act 1982 s.2(1).

[118] Forfeiture Act 1982 s.2(3). See e.g. *Re Land (dec'd)* [2006] EWHC 2069 (Ch.); [2007] 1 All E.R. 324: no relief under the Act as the application was four days out of time (but relief granted on other grounds, see below para.5–39).

[119] Forfeiture Act 1982 s.5.

[120] [1985] Ch. 85; affirmed [1986] Ch. 180.

[121] See [1985] Ch. 85 at 102.

[122] [1986] Ch. 180 at 193.

[123] [1991] 1 F.L.R. 441 at 447–448. The facts of the case are given in para.5–31, above.

applied, he would have exercised the discretion under the Act to accord full relief from the rule to the widower. His reasons included the fact that the killing had been brought about by circumstances beyond the widower's control, the happiness of the marriage, the wishes of the deceased, and the fact that there were "no other moral claims on the assets in question".

5–37 **Suicide pact.** In *Dunbar v Plant*[124] the Court of Appeal had to consider the application of the Act in particularly tragic circumstances. A devoted young couple, in their early twenties, made a suicide pact. Although the survivor was never prosecuted, the court held that she had committed the offence of aiding and abetting suicide and that the forfeiture rule applied. At first instance the judge had exercised his discretion under the Act to grant only partial relief against the rule, thereby enabling some of the assets to be recovered by the parents of the deceased, who opposed the application for relief. The Court of Appeal was unanimous in holding that the judge had adopted the wrong approach in seeking, as he had put it, to do "justice between the parties". The Court of Appeal was therefore free to exercise the discretion itself, but was divided as to the result. Mummery LJ would have upheld the judge's actual decision, but the majority awarded the survivor total relief against the rule so that she received all the assets. Phillips LJ, with whom Hirst LJ agreed, noted that the assets, which included the proceeds of an insurance policy and an interest in a house, "were in no way derived" from the parents of the deceased. The main emphasis of Phillips LJ, however, was on the circumstances of the death, and the fact that the survivor had not been prosecuted. He observed that "where two people are driven to attempt, together, to take their lives and one survives, the survivor will normally attract sympathy rather than prosecution". He concluded[125] that "where the public interest requires no penal sanction ... strong grounds are likely to exist for relieving the person who has committed the offence from all effect of the forfeiture rule".

5–38 **Relief denied.** In *Dalton v Latham*[126] an application for relief under the Act was unsuccessful. The claimant had been convicted of manslaughter on the ground of diminished responsibility, and sentenced to six years imprisonment. He had strangled his elderly homosexual partner while under the influence of drink, and while suffering from a depressive illness. The deceased had left most of his property by will to the claimant. Following a thorough examination of "all the relevant factors", including the abusive behaviour of the claimant towards the deceased in his lifetime, Patten J held that the "justice of the case" did not require any modification of the effect of the forfeiture rule.[127] The claimant was therefore disqualified from taking under the will.

---

[124] [1998] Ch. 412; [1997] 4 All E.R. 289.
[125] [1998] Ch. 412 at 437; [1997] 4 All E.R. 289 at 312.
[126] [2003] EWHC 796 (Ch).
[127] [2003] EWHC 796 at [45].

Inheritance (Provision for Family and Dependants Act) 1975. In *Re Land*   **5–39**
(dec'd)[128] the claimant's mother had left all her property to him in her will. He
was convicted of her manslaughter in circumstances which rendered the
forfeiture rule applicable, but his application for modification of the rule under
the 1982 Act was out of time. Nevertheless the High Court[129] held that substantial
provision could be made for the claimant out of the deceased's estate under the
Inheritance (Provision for Family and Dependants) Act 1975. Section 3(1) of the
Forfeiture Act itself provides that the forfeiture rule shall not prevent an order
being made in favour of a claimant under the 1975 Act,[130] but that Act is
primarily directed towards situations in which deceased persons have failed to
provide adequately for their families in their wills. The Court held, however, that
the 1982 provision enables applicants to be granted relief under the 1975 Act
notwithstanding that adequate provision *had* been made for them in the will of
the deceased, and that only the forfeiture rule prevented them from taking under
it.[131] In so holding the Court declined to follow earlier dicta in the Court of
Appeal which had apparently favoured a narrow construction of s.3(1), confining
the applicability of the 1975 Act in forfeiture cases to situations in which neither
the will nor the intestacy rules sought to confer any benefit upon the claimant.[132]

6. "NO BENEFIT FROM A CRIME"

An unhelpful maxim in contract cases. The maxim that "no person may   **5–40**
benefit from his or her crime" is commonly invoked in judgments on the
forfeiture rule.[133] Nevertheless, as the cases which have sought to modify the
common law rule illustrate, the aphorism is inherently question-begging and
misleadingly wide. Lord Lane CJ drew attention to the inadequacy of a
mechanistic approach in *R v Chief National Insurance Commissioner Ex p.
Connor*,[134] when he said that "in each case it is not the label which the law
applies to the crime which has been committed but the nature of the crime itself
which in the end will dictate whether public policy demands the court to drive the
applicant from the seat of justice".[135] But provided this injunction is borne in
mind, the maxim does have some utility in the context of the forfeiture rule itself,
and in some other non-contractual contexts[136] such as actions in tort,[137] planning

---

[128] [2006] EWHC 2069 (Ch.); [2007] 1 All E.R. 324.
[129] Judge Alastair Norris QC sitting as a judge of the High Court.
[130] "The forfeiture rule shall not be taken to preclude any person from making an application under
[the 1975 Act] or the making of any order on the application".
[131] See [2006] EWHC 2069 (Ch.) at [18]–[23].
[132] See *Re Royse (dec'd)* [1984] 3 All E.R. 339 at [344d-e], per Slade LJ, see also per Ackner LJ at
[343b].
[133] See especially *Re Crippen (dec'd)* [1911] P. 108.
[134] [1981] 1 Q.B. 758 at 765.
[135] See also *Bakewell Management Ltd v Brandwood* [2004] UKHL 14; [2004] 2 A.C. 519 (criminal
conduct capable of giving rise to prescriptive rights in exceptional cases). Cf *R (on the application of
Best) v Chief Land Registrar* [2015] EWCA Civ 17,
[136] There is elaborate statutory machinery for depriving "persons who benefit from criminal conduct"
of their assets: see the Proceeds of Crime Act 2002 (preamble).
[137] In two cases, both decided in 2009, the House of Lords subjected the application of the maxim in
tort to extensive analysis: see *Gray v Thames Trains* [2009] UKHL 33, [2009] 4 All ER 81 and *Moore*

law[138], or claims for the conferment of statutory benefits.[139] This is because, in those contexts, there is less danger of the maxim generating confusion by overlapping with other principles. This is not the case, however, in the context of illegality in *contract* itself; where denial of enforceability depends upon the elaborate rules and concepts examined elsewhere in this book.

5–41   **Redundant notion.**   The supposed "no benefit" principle is a fifth wheel on the coach in contract cases, and is calculated to muddy the waters. This effect is seen particularly vividly in the well-known decision of Devlin J in *St John Shipping Corporation v Joseph Rank*,[140] which concerned the relatively straight forward situation of an overloaded ship. Devlin J approached the case from three separate angles.[141] First, he considered what he described as the "general proposition that a person who performs a legal contract in an illegal manner cannot sue upon it". Secondly, he turned to the submission "that a plaintiff cannot recover money if in order to establish his claim to it, he has to disclose that he committed an illegal act"; and, finally, he came to "the principle that a person cannot enforce rights which result to him from his own crime".[142] The consequence of approaching the case through what might almost be described as a thicket of catch-phrases, was that the central issues, which should have been addressed, were rendered obscure. These were whether the overloading had been deliberate and whether, even if it had not, the doctrine of implied statutory prohibition might operate to preclude enforceability. These questions, and the decision of Devlin J in favour of enforceability, have been examined in earlier chapters.[143] But the case demonstrates how maxims such as the supposed "no benefit" principle can impede analysis.

5–42   **Counter-productive precision.**   The manner in which Devlin J dealt with the argument based on the maxim is particularly instructive. He decided the point in favour of recovery on the ground "that in this type of case no claim or part of a claim for freight can be clearly identified as being the excess illegally earned".[144] This reasoning does, with respect, come perilously close to sophistry.[145] Many

---

Stephens v Stone Rolls [2009] UKHL 39, [2009] 4 All ER 451. cf. *Bilta (UK) Ltd (in liquidation) v Nazir* [2015] UKSC 23; [2015] 2 All ER 1083, In *Gray's* case , Lord Hoffman said that the maxim "expresses not so much a principle as a policy" ([2009]) UKHL 33 at [30]. See also *Vellino v Chief Constable of Greater Manchester* [2002] 3 All E.R. 78, C.A. especially per Sir Murray Stuart-Smith at 62 et seq.; *Hewison v Meridian Shipping Services* [2002] EWCA Civ 1821; [2003] I.C.R. 766, *Clunis v Camden and Islington Health Authority* [1998] Q.B. 978; [1998] 3 All E.R. 180.
[138] See *Welwyn Hatfield BC v Secretary of State for Communities and Local Government* [2011] UKSC 15.
[139] See *R. v Home Secretary Ex p. Puttick* [1981] 1 Q.B. 767 (British citizenship); *R. v Registrar-General Ex p. Smith* [1991] 2 Q.B. 393 (Adoption Act application for identity of natural mother). See also *Whiston v Winston* [1995] 2 F.L.R. 268 (ancillary relief in matrimonial cases), cf. *J v S-T* [1997] 1 F.L.R. 402.
[140] [1957] 1 Q.B. 267.
[141] [1957] 1 Q.B. 267 at 282.
[142] [1957] 1 Q.B. 267 at 283.
[143] See Chs 1–3, above.
[144] See [1957] 1 Q.B. 267 at 293.
[145] For criticism, see Grunfeld (1957) 20 M.L.R. 172 at p.177; Bateson (1957) J.B.L. 79 at pp.81–82; and Furmston (1965) University of Toronto LJ 267 at p.273.

contracts which should, on the basis of illegality, rightly be denied enforceability, would slip through the net if the objectionable component had to be identified with such microscopic precision. In truth, a bizarre answer was being given to an irrelevant question.

PART 2

PUBLIC POLICY

CHAPTER 6

POLICY AND MORALITY

1.   INTRODUCTION

Fundamental questions.   The doctrine whereby the court may refuse to   **6–01**
enforce a contract solely on the ground of "public policy" raises a number of
interwoven issues.[1] The most fundamental concerns the legitimacy, from a
separation of powers standpoint, of essentially legislative activity on the part of
the judges. Furthermore, once a particular aspect of public policy has assumed a
settled form, does it have to be applied with the rigidity customarily associated
with rules of law? If not, do different branches of the doctrine enjoy a greater, or
lesser, degree of flexibility in this respect than others? A related issue concerns
the ease, or otherwise, with which particular aspects of public policy can be
changed by the courts to reflect changing social conditions or attitudes. Can "new
heads" of public policy be created? If so, is it appropriate for the court to
stigmatise contracts not only on the basis of proven harm, but also on that of a
mere "tendency" to facilitate undesirable social consequences? These issues will
be examined in this chapter, along with the approach of the courts to moral
questions surrounding sexual matters and the institution of marriage. Such
questions are particularly sensitive with respect to the role of the judiciary in
society, and it is therefore appropriate that they should feature prominently in any
general discussion of the functioning of the doctrine of public policy.

Change and transparency.   This Chapter is clearly concerned with contracts   **6–02**
which the common law declines to enforce in order to promote "policies" which
are of its own making. Accordingly, the question which now arises in other
contexts, following the decision of the Supreme Court in *Patel v Mirza*,[2] of
whether denial of enforceability would "enhance"[3] the underlying policy of a
specific rule of the (usually) criminal law will seldom arise directly.[4]
Nevertheless, the emphasis in *Patel*'s case upon transparency and flexibility
could influence indirectly the way in which the courts approach the common
law's own policies. They may be readier to ask not merely whether deciding a
case in a particular way would help to promote a given policy, but also whether
that policy is one which should be pursued at all. A degree of scepticism is
therefore appropriate when evaluating the older decisions in which contracts have

---

[1] For a wide-ranging discussion of the nature of the judicial function in relation to policy questions
see John Bell, *Policy Arguments in Judicial Decisions* (Oxford University Press, 1983).
[2] 2016] UKSC 42.
[3] See ibid at [120] per Lord Toulson,
[4] But see *Rodriguez v Speyer Bros* [1919] A.C. 59 discussed in para.6–06 below.

been held to be "contrary to public policy". Nevertheless, as has been indicated in the previous paragraph, the question how far it is permissible for the courts to change the common law in this special area was debated well before the recent developments elsewhere in illegality, so that issue is by no means a new one.

2.   PUBLIC POLICY IN THE COURTS

(a)   Nature of Public Policy

6–03   **Courts and the legislature.**   A classic statement of the need for judicial caution in the public policy area is to be found in the early nineteenth century case of *Richardson v Mellish*.[5] An unsuccessful attempt was made to persuade the court that an agreement whereby the claimant had been promised command of a ship, if certain eventualities should occur, was contrary to public policy. Various grounds were suggested, including corruption and an analogy with the statutorily prohibited sale of certain "offices" of profit. All failed. The court found nothing "corrupt, illegal, or impolitic" in the agreement. It was in this case that Burrough J famously protested "against arguing too strongly upon public policy; it is a very unruly horse, and when once you get astride it you never know where it will carry you".[6] But a more reasoned explanation for judicial reticence is to be found in the judgment of Best CJ. He said[7]:

> "I am not much disposed to yield to arguments of public policy: I think the courts . . . have gone much further than they were warranted in going in questions of policy; and they are always in danger of so doing, because courts of law look only at the particular case, and have not the means of bringing before them all those considerations which ought to enter into the judgment of those who decide on questions of policy. I therefore say, it is not a doubtful matter of policy that will decide this, or that will prevent the party from recovering: if once you bring it to that, the plaintiff is entitled to recover; and let that doubtful question of policy be settled by that high tribunal, namely, the legislature, which has the means of bringing before it all the considerations that bear on the question, and can settle it on its true and broad principles."

6–04   **Ambiguity of "public policy".**   There is a decidedly modern ring to this insistence upon the importance of respecting the differing functions and capacities of the legislature on the one hand, and the courts on the other.[8] It also serves, incidentally, to highlight part of the ambiguity inherent in the notion of "public policy" itself. Developments which might have a widespread, and possibly controversial, impact on commercial or social life generally should certainly be left to the legislature, especially if much information needs to be

---

[5] (1824) 2 Bing. 229.

[6] (1824) 2 Bing. 229 at 252.

[7] (1824) 2 Bing. 229 at 242–243.

[8] See also, per Browne-Wilkinson J in *Multiservice Bookbinding v Marden* [1979] Ch. 84 at 104: "It would, in my judgment, be wrong for the courts to declare that a particular class of transaction is against the public interest even though there is a body of better-informed opinion that takes the view that no harm is caused. It is for Parliament, with all its facilities for weighing the complex issues involved, to make a policy decision of this kind". In this case the Court rejected a submission that an index-linked repayment obligation in a mortgage should be held contrary to public policy in the belief that such obligations might help to cause inflation.

obtained and analysed before that impact can be predicted.[9] On the other hand, however, not all considerations of "public policy" as applied in the courts fall into this category. Some are questions of moral intuition which are unlikely to yield to analysis, except of the never-ending philosophical variety. The common law has, for example, always refused to allow prostitutes to sue for services rendered[10]; although the legislature has never made prostitution as such into a criminal offence. There is nothing incongruous or inappropriate in this dichotomy. The fundamental libertarian and practical objections to the criminalisation of consensual sexual activity do not apply to the mere denial of contractual enforceability. Many would find it just as repugnant for the civil courts to legitimise the commercialisation of such activity, as they would find it offensive for the criminal courts to stigmatise and punish it.

Flexible or rigid?   The lack of any clearly defined doctrinal basis for declining to enforce contracts on public policy grounds can give rise to difficult questions, when application of an established principle of public policy would produce a result at variance with the underlying rationale of that principle. In *Janson v Driefontein Mines*[11] the government of the South African Republic, known as the Transvaal, seized a quantity of gold belonging to one of its subjects. The seizure took place very shortly before the outbreak of hostilities between the Republic and the UK, which came to be known as the Boer War, and was clearly intended to help the Republic to finance the war. The gold had been insured in the UK, and the question arose whether the underwriters were liable for the loss. They would clearly *not* have been liable if the seizure had taken place after war had actually been declared, since enforcement of the policy in those circumstances would have become illegal under familiar principles of public policy relating to trading with the enemy.[12] Should enforcement be permitted at any time up to the actual outbreak of hostilities, even though it would render just as much assistance to the eventual "enemy" as would enforcement afterwards? Vaughan Williams LJ, in the Court of Appeal, believed that the claim against the British underwriters should fail: "if it is made out", he said,[13] "that it would be injurious generally to the State to allow such a contract by a British subject to be valid, the principle must be applied, although there may be no previous instance of its application to this particular case". Vaughan Williams LJ was, however, a lone voice. A unanimous House of Lords, along with the majority in the Court of Appeal, held that the formal declaration of war was decisive in drawing a clear line between contracts made before it which were valid, and those made after it which were not.[14] Lord Lindley said that "public policy is a very unstable and dangerous foundation on which to build until made safe by decision".[15]

6–05

---

[9] cf. *Morgans v Launchbury* [1973] A.C. 127.
[10] cf. *Pearce v Brooks* (1866) L.R. 1 Exch. 213. See also *Shaw v D.P.P.* [1962] A.C. 220.
[11] [1902] A.C. 484.
[12] See Ch.10, below.
[13] See [1901] 2 K.B. 419 at 432.
[14] "It is war, and war alone, that makes trading illegal": per Lord Halsbury LC in [1902] A.C. 484 at 494.
[15] [1902] A.C. 484 at 507. See also, per Lord Davey at 500: "Public policy appears to me to be always unsafe and treacherous ground of legal decision".

6–06 **Where rigidity would result in unenforceability.** What if, conversely to the situation in *Janson v Driefontein Mines*, insistence upon the letter, rather than the spirit, of the relevant principle of public policy would result in a contract being held to be unenforceable rather than the reverse? In a sense this is a truer test of whether public policy, once established, yields firm rules which leave no room for judicial subjectivity; since a positive answer will result in claims actually failing rather than, as in *Janson*'s case, normal enforcement taking place by default. The question arose in another case concerning the public policy against trading with the enemy, but this time it found the House of Lords sharply divided. In *Rodriguez v Speyer Bros*[16] a claim by a partnership to recover a debt during the First World War was met with the essentially technical defence that the action was not competently constituted, since one of the six partners happened to be an enemy alien. Enforcement would not have directly benefited the enemy, but its denial would have caused loss to the British claimant. Lord Atkinson and Lord Sumner would nevertheless have refused the claim, on the ground that the incapacity of an enemy alien was an inescapable barrier. The former considered that it would be "wholly illegitimate for any judicial tribunal which may disapprove of the principles of public policy so embodied in the rigid rule to disregard that rule in any particular case and base its decision on other principles of public policy of which it more approves". For a court to act in that way would, in his view, "usurp the prerogative and powers of the legislature".[17]

6–07 **Three classes.** Lord Atkinson and Lord Sumner were, however, dissenting. Lord Haldane, who was one of those in the majority, divided public policy cases into three classes.[18] First, those in which "the law, although originally based on public policy, has become so crystallised that only a statute can alter it": he gave the rule against perpetuities as an example. Secondly, those "in which the principle of public policy has never crystallised into a definitive or exhaustive set of propositions", such as the common law relating to wagers. Thirdly, cases "in which public policy has partially precipitated itself into recognised rules which belong to law properly so called, but where these rules have remained subject to the moulding influence of the real reasons of public policy from which they proceeded". Trading with the enemy fell into the third category, enabling the "balance of public convenience" to be invoked, and the claim to be enforced, notwithstanding the technical objection.[19]

6–08 **Where existing doctrine has been relied on.** It is submitted that Lord Haldane's approach is to be preferred to that of the minority, and that his analysis is instructive. Leaving aside his second category, into which few situations nowadays are likely to fall, the critical distinction is between those areas of existing public policy which can only be altered by statute, and those which can still be "moulded" by the court. The application of the distinction probably

---

[16] [1919] A.C. 59.
[17] [1919] A.C. 59 at 90.
[18] [1919] A.C. 59 at 81.
[19] The refusal of the majority to allow rigidity to prevail over the underlying purpose of the rule against trading with the enemy could be said to anticipate the flexibility now introduced into illegality in general by the decision of the Supreme Court in *Patel v Mirza* [2016] UKSC 42.

depends primarily upon the extent to which the particular doctrine in question has been relied upon in transactions over the years, especially transactions of an on-going nature. In the nature of things such reliance is likely to be in marginal cases, and to be in respect of what is *not* regarded as contrary to public policy rather than what is so regarded. Parties rarely make contracts with the intention that they should fail, but sometimes find it necessary to stay only just within the limits of what the law will allow.

Reliance and restraint of trade. One of the few areas of public policy which 6–09 might be thought to fall into this "reliance" category is that of restraint of trade. In practice, however, the freedom of manoeuvre enjoyed by the courts, in construing the actual wording of the covenant in any given case, means that the assumption that there is a high degree of reliance on supposedly clear rules in this context is perhaps rather misleading.[20] Moreover, in the leading case of *Nordenfelt v Maxim Nordenfelt Guns and Ammunition Co*,[21] Lord Watson expounded eloquently upon the power of the court to develop the law in this area as follows[22]:

> "A series of decisions based upon grounds of public policy, however eminent the judges by whom they were delivered, cannot possess the same binding authority as decisions which deal with and formulate principles which are purely legal. The course of policy pursued by any country, in relation to and for promoting the interest of its commerce, must, as time advances, and as its commerce thrives, undergo change and development from various causes which are altogether independent of the action of its courts. In England at least it is beyond the jurisdiction of her tribunals to mould and stereotype national policy. Their function when a case like the present is brought before them is, in my opinion, not necessarily to accept what was held to have been the rule of policy a hundred or a hundred and fifty years ago, but to ascertain with as near an approach to accuracy as circumstances permit, what is the rule of policy for the then present time. When that rule has been ascertained, it becomes their duty to refuse to give effect to a private contract which violates the rule, and would, if judicially enforced, prove injurious to the community."

Fluidity or novelty? In his dissenting speech in *Rodriguez v Speyer Bros*[23] 6–10 Lord Atkinson argued vehemently, and at length, that the *Nordenfelt* case was not, as he put it, an example of "the adoption and application of new principles". On the contrary, it was "a conspicuous example of the adherence to and application of the principles established by old authorities to the new and peculiar facts of the particular case". There was "not a syllable in any of the judgments delivered to suggest that their Lordships were applying any new rule or principle of public policy to these new facts". Lord Atkinson's argument was based on the use of the fluid concept of "reasonableness" in both the *Nordenfelt* formulation, and in the older authorities. In a different context, but in a similiar vein, Lord Halsbury LC denied, in *Janson v Driesfontein Mines*,[24] "that any court can invent a new head of public policy".[25]

---

[20] See Ch.13, below.
[21] [1894] A.C. 535.
[22] [1894] A.C. 535 at 553–554.
[23] [1919] A.C. 59 at 107.
[24] [1902] A.C. 484 at 491.
[25] cf. *J. v S-T* [1997] 1 F.L.R. 402 at 441, per Ward LJ: ". . . we must reflect, not form, public policy". See also *Fender v Mildmay* [1937] 3 All E.R. 402 at 425–426, per Lord Wright: "What is, I think, now

(b) Factors to be Taken into Account

6–11 **Question of degree.** In a sense, of course, the debate whether a particular case developed new principles, or merely applied old ones in a new context, is always a sterile one; it is apt to depend upon differing perceptions of matters which are, in themselves, usually questions of degree. A more helpful approach is to try and identify some of the factors which a court should, or should not, take into account when assessing the merits, or otherwise, of an argument based upon public policy. The fullest attempts at such an exercise are to be found in two decisions of the House of Lords nearly a century apart: *Egerton v Earl Brownlow*[26] and *Fender v St John Mildmay*.[27] Both were concerned, in different contexts, with the question whether a stipulation could be contrary to public policy; not because its performance would in itself have adverse consequences, but merely because it might "tend" to encourage or promote such consequences as an indirect result.

6–12 **Dangerous "tendencies"?** *Egerton v Earl Brownlow* was not, strictly speaking, a contract case. Nevertheless, the general judicial discussion of the principles of public policy to which it gave rise is equally relevant to such cases. By his will the Earl of Bridgewater devised his estates to his heir, but did so subject to the condition that the estates would only devolve in turn to the heirs of the recipient if the latter, before his own death, succeeded in obtaining from the Crown the title of *Duke* of Bridgewater. The question arose whether this condition was valid, or whether it was void as contrary to public policy. All the common law judges were consulted by the House of Lords, before the House gave its decision, and a majority of them advised in favour of the condition's validity. But the House rejected that view and held that the condition was contrary to public policy. A variety of reasons were given, but most were based on the fear that the condition would tend to encourage undesirable behaviour. It was suggested that the recipient, being already a member of the peerage, might be tempted to discharge his legislative and other duties in that role in such a manner as to avoid jeopardising his chances of preferment; thus compromising his independence. It was also thought that the condition could embarrass the Crown itself, when the latter became aware that the refusal of a title could have such dire consequences for the aspirant.

6–13 **Decision unfavourably received.** The central ground of decision, however, was that in order to gain his dukedom, the recipient would be tempted to bribe, or otherwise corrupt, those public servants who advised the Crown on the grant of honours. Lord Brougham said[28]:

> "The tendency is alone to be considered; and unless the possibility is so remote as to justify us in affirming that there is no tendency at all . . . gifts, bequests, conditions, contracts, are illegal from their tendency to promote unlawful acts, without regard to the amount of the

---

clear is that public policy is not a branch of the law to be extended . . . I find it difficult to conceive that, in these days, any new head of public policy could be discovered".

[26] (1853) 4 H.L. Cas. 1.
[27] [1938] A.C. 1.
[28] (1853) 4 H.L. Cas. 1 at 174.

inducements held out or interest created, the position of the parties, or any other circumstances which go to affect the probability of the unlawful act being done."

The reasoning and decision in *Egerton's* case have not, on the whole, been favourably received by subsequent generations of judges. The opinion of Park B, one of the judges consulted, whose view was rejected by the House of Lords, has more often been quoted with approval in later cases. His Lordship castigated an earlier decision as "ridiculous" for the far-fetched basis upon which it detected the possibility of harm arising out of one particular contract, and continued[29]:

"in short, there are few contracts in which a suspicious mind might not find a tendency to produce evil; and to hold all such contracts to be void would, indeed, be an intolerable mischief."

Fender v Mildmay. The question of mere undesirable "tendencies", as a basis for illegality on the ground of public policy, was again explored by the House of Lords in *Fender v Mildmay*.[30] The defendant, who was in the process of getting divorced, proposed marriage to the claimant before the pronunciation of the degree absolute, but after the grant of the decree nisi. The defendant in fact went on to marry someone else, and was sued by the claimant for breach of promise; such actions having yet to be abolished. This time the House of Lords itself was sharply divided. By a bare majority it held that the promise was not invalidated by public policy, and that the defendant was therefore liable. The latter had argued that enforceability would discourage reconciliation, and also promote "immorality", by encouraging parties to commit what would, prior to the actual dissolution of the claimant's marriage, be adultery. These arguments were forcefully rejected by the majority.[31] Lord Atkin said[32]:

6–14

"... assuming, as we must, that the harmful tendency of a contract must be examined, what is meant by tendency? It can only mean, I venture to think, that, taking that class of contract as a whole, the contracting parties will generally, in a majority of cases, at any rate in a considerable number of cases, be exposed to real temptation, by reason of the promises to do something harmful, i.e. contrary to public policy, and that it is likely that they will yield to it. All kinds of contracts provide motives for improper actions, e.g. benefits deferred until the death of a third party, and contracts of insurance. To avoid a contract, it is not enough that it affords a motive to do wrong: it must be shown that such a contract generally affords a motive, and that it is likely to be effective."[33]

The dissentients, Lord Russell and Lord Roche, placed emphasis not so much on the "tendency" aspect of the case as on a priori considerations relating to the status of marriage. The approach which the public policy doctrine has adopted

[29] (1853) 4 H.L. Cas. 1 at 128.
[30] [1938] A.C. 1.
[31] See, especially, per Lord Atkin reacting as follows "with some indignation" to the adultery argument: "No doubt a promise to marry is one of the weapons of the seducer, but no one has yet sought to invalidate on this ground a promise to marry made by unmarried persons, and I am quite unable to see why any different view should be taken of promises to marry which differ only in respect of the short period, six months or less, which must elapse between promise and performance" [1938] A.C. 1 at 17–18.
[32] [1938] A.C. 1 at 13.
[33] See also [1938] A.C. 1 at 25, per Lord Thankerton: "Public policy is not concerned with tendencies that may exist in a very limited number of cases".

towards marriage, and more generally to sexual matters, is of special interest in view both of the importance of the issues and of the changing attitudes of society towards them.

3. MARRIAGE AND SEXUAL MORALITY

(a) Marriage

6–15   **Anticipating death of spouse.**   In his speech in *Fender v Mildmay*[34] Lord Russell of Killowen said that "it is in the interest of the State that, if possible, the marriage tie should remain stable and be maintained". He deplored the extent to which the institution of marriage had "long been on a slippery slope", and was "steadily assuming the characteristics of a contract for a tenancy at will". He placed great emphasis, as did Lord Roche, upon the 1908 decision of the Court of Appeal in *Wilson v Carnley*.[35] Since both Lord Russell and Lord Roche were dissenting, however, what is more significant is that the majority also accepted that that earlier decision was correct, albeit distinguishable. *Wilson's* case also concerned an action for breach of promise and, along with *Fender v Mildmay*, the actual decision is no longer of practical importance since the abolition of actions for breach of promise. In so far, however, as the law continues to refuse totally to assimilate the obligations of unmarried cohabitees with those of married persons, *Wilson v Carnley* remains relevant as an indication of the general approach of the common law to the status of marriage, an approach which cannot be said to be wholly obsolete even though a century has passed since the case was decided. In 1894 the defendant promised to marry the claimant, both parties being aware that the former was already married. It appears that the defendant's existing wife was unwell, and was expected not to survive. When her death eventually occurred, which was not until 1906, the defendant refused to marry the claimant, who sued him for breach of promise. The Court of Appeal was emphatic in holding that contract was, in the words of Vaughan Williams LJ,[36] "void *ab initio*" as being "against public morality", and could "never be enforced". Kennedy LJ said[37]:

> "I should have thought that discussion was needless to show that such a promise is against public policy as tending to immorality, and that nothing but mischief could follow from upholding such an unhallowed bargain, which would always be a temptation to bring about the dissolution of the marriage tie which hindered the defendant from carrying out his promise."

6–16   **Ignorance of existing marriage.**   The claimant in *Wilson v Carnley* relied upon two earlier cases in support of her claim,[38] but in both of them the claimant had been unaware that the defendant was already married, and the Court of Appeal distinguished them on this ground without indicating clearly whether or not it agreed with them. That issue did, however, arise in the much more recent

---

[34] [1938] A.C. 1 at 33.
[35] [1908] 1 K.B. 729. See also *Spiers v Hunt* [1908] 1 K.B. 720.
[36] [1908] 1 K.B. 729 at 734.
[37] [1908] 1 K.B. 729 at 742 (wording as quoted from 98 L.T. 265 at 268).
[38] See *Wild v Harris* (1849) 7 C.B. 999; *Millward v Littlewood* (1850), 5 Exch. 775.

case of *Shaw v Shaw*.[39] In that case the deceased, having left his wife, had falsely represented to the claimant that he was a widower. He went through a ceremony of marriage with her, and lived with her as her husband. The claimant did not discover the truth until her "husband" died intestate 14 years later. The claimant then brought an action for breach of promise to recover from the estate a similar sum to that to which she would have been entitled if she had, in fact, been the widow of the deceased. Pilcher J, at first instance, held that the claim was contrary to public policy, but the Court of Appeal unanimously reversed his decision.[40] It was, however, an essential condition of the claimant's recovery that she was at all times wholly unaware of the true position; otherwise her claim would have been barred by the rule in *Wilson v Carnley*.

Bigamy and ancillary relief.   As recently as 1996, a judgment delivered in the Court of Appeal included the following[41]:

6–17

> ". . . it seems to me that the status of married persons, the sanctity of the marriage union, and the institution of marriage itself are all objects of public policy requiring our protection."

In *Whiston v Whiston*,[42] decided in 1995, a bigamist was held by the Court of Appeal, reversing the court below, to be disqualified from obtaining ancillary relief on the nullification of her bigamous marriage. Ward LJ said[43] that to grant such relief would give "scant effect to the seriousness of bigamy", a crime which "undermines our fundamental notions of monogamous marriage". It is significant, however, that in *Rampal v Rampal (No.2)*,[44] decided in 2001, the Court of Appeal held that there is no absolute rule that a bigamist can never claim ancillary relief; and allowed such a claim to proceed. Thorpe LJ said[45] that "the rule in *Whiston v Whiston* . . . does not preclude this court from having regard to the nature of the crime and all the surrounding circumstances".[46]

Wills and contracts.   It is a long established principle that the court will not enforce any condition in a will which would operate as a restraint upon the devisee's freedom to marry.[47] The importance which the common law attached to the traditional concept of marriage was also highlighted by the fact that agreements between husband and wife for future separation, including agreements entered into before marriage that the parties would live separate and apart from the outset,[48] were contrary to public policy and void. Indeed, "pre-nuptial contracts", whereby parties about to marry agree how their assets should be

6–18

---

[39] [1954] 2 Q.B. 429.
[40] See Ch.4, above, for further discussion of this case, and of the likely impact upon it of the statutory abolition in 1970 of actions for breach of promise.
[41] See *J. v S-T* [1997] 1 F.L.R. 402 at 438, per Ward LJ.
[42] [1995] 2 F.L.R. 268.
[43] [1995] 2 F.L.R. 268 at 274.
[44] [2001] 2 F.L.R. 1179.
[45] [2001] 2 F.L.R. 1179 at 1188.
[46] See also *Faiza Ben Hashem v Abdulhadi Ali Shayif* [2008] EWHC 2380 (Fam) per Mumby J at 303–322.
[47] cf. *Re Fentem* [1950] 2 All E.R. 1073.
[48] See *Brodie v Brodie* [1917] P. 271. See also *Vervaeke v Smith* [1983] A.C. 145.

divided in the event of divorce, are still not automatically enforceable in England.[49] Their position was reviewed by the Judicial Committee of the Privy Council in 2008 in *MacLeod v MacLeod*,[50] in which the Board concluded that it was not open to it "to reverse the long-standing rule that ante-nuptial agreements are contrary to public policy and thus not valid or binding in the contractual sense".[51] The Board considered that any change "was more appropriate for legislative than judicial development".[52] Nevertheless, two years later such agreements were subjected to extensive consideration by the Supreme Court in *Radmacher v Granantino*,[53] and a significantly different approach was adopted. By a majority of eight to one[54] the Court introduced, in effect, a rebuttable presumption to the effect that they would be binding unless the court, in its overall jurisdiction relating to the distribution of assets on divorce,[55] considered them to be unfair.[56] In the case itself the pre-nuptial agreement which the parties had entered into was held to bind the parties.[57] Furthermore, separation agreements entered into between persons *already married*, are valid. Prior to the decision of the Privy Council in *MacLeod v MacLeod* they were in general only considered to be valid if they were to take effect immediately. In *MacLeod*'s case, however, it was held that such agreements should be valid even if entered into while the parties were still living together with no immediate intention to separate.[58]

6–19   **Marriage brocage.**   Contracts whereby one party agrees to bring about a marriage between the other party to the contract, and another person, have long been held to be void.[59] "[A]t the root of the question of the illegality of a marriage brocage contract", said Collins M.R. in *Hermann v Charlesworth*,[60] "is the introduction of the consideration of a money payment into that which should be free from any such taint". In *Hermann*'s case the defendant, who was the proprietor of a newspaper called "The Matrimonial Post and Fashionable Marriage Advertiser", agreed to introduce the claimant to several potential partners in return for an advance payment, and a larger sum in the event of marriage actually taking place. It did not do so, and the claimant sued to recover

---

[49] For the very different position in Scotland, where the prima facie validity of pre-nuptial contracts has long been accepted, see Kate Molan and Sarah Caroline Boyle, "North and South, Marital agreements: who's got it right?" *2012 New Law Journal* 1304 (October 19) and cases there cited, especially *Thomson v Thomson* 1982 SLT 521.

[50] [2008] UKPC 64.

[51] [2008] UKPC 64 at 31 per Baroness Hale, delivering the judgment of the Board.

[52] [2008] UKPC 64 at 35. In 2011 the Law Commission published a Consultation Paper (No.198) on *Marital Property Agreements* and a Supplementary Consultation Paper in 2012. In 2014 the Commission issued its final report: *Matrimonial Property: Needs and Agreements*.

[53] [2010] UKSC 42.

[54] Lady Hale dissented.

[55] See the Matrimonial Causes Act 1973 s.25.

[56] See [2010] UKSC 42 per Lord Phillips P at [75].

[57] See also *Z v Z (Financial Remedy: Marriage Contract)* [2011] EWHC 2878; *V v V (Prenuptial Agreement)* [2011] EWHC 3230. Cf. *Kremen v Agrest* [2012] EWHC 45.

[58] See [2008] UKPC 64 at 36–40.

[59] See, generally, the valuable comparative and historical study by Raphael Powell, "Marriage Brocage Agreements" [1953] C.L.P. 254.

[60] See [1905] 2 K.B. 123 at 130.

the advance payment on the ground that the agreement had been illegal as constituting a marriage brocage contract, and that as the less guilty party she was entitled to relief.[61] The defendant contended that only contracts to bring about a marriage with a specific third party were objectionable but the Court of Appeal, reversing the Divisional Court, rejected this argument and held that the claimant's claim would succeed. "[N]o such distinction exists", said Mathew LJ.[62] "between a contract for reward to introduce a number of persons with a view to procuring a marriage with one or other of them and the case of a contract the object of which is to procure the marriage with a particular person".

Is *Hermann v Charlesworth* still good law?   There is now a substantial and profitable industry devoted to the finding of spouses, or other life-partners, for those who take advantage of its services. In view of the decision in *Hermann v Charlesworth*, it must be at least questionable whether the agencies operating in this field could successfully resist claims for the return of fees received by them. The position does not, however, appear to have been tested in the century since *Hermann's* case was decided. It is therefore possible that the court could distinguish that case by confining it to introductions with a view to *marriage* as such, as distinct from life-long friendship. Alternatively, and perhaps preferably, it might be held that *Hermann v Charlesworth* does not reflect contemporary public policy.[63]   **6–20**

(b)   Sexual Relationships Outside Marriage[64]

Upfill v Wright.   The importance which the common law traditionally attached to the institution of marriage was long accompanied by a somewhat sceptical attitude towards sexual partnerships between persons who were not married to each other. In practice, however, issues involving such partnerships usually only come before the courts as a result of disputes about such matters as the ownership of property. In the 1911 case of *Upfill v Wright*[65] the claimant landlord let a flat to the defendant knowing that she was the mistress of a certain man, and that the rent was probably being paid indirectly by him. In an action for arrears of rent the defendant contended that the flat had been let to her for an "immoral purpose", and that the claim should therefore fail. The Divisional Court, reversing the county court judge, held that this defence would succeed. The Court rejected the claimant's argument that "prostitution is one thing, and living as one man's mistress is quite a different thing". Bucknill LJ responded that they "may differ in degree, but they both stand upon the same plane".[66]   **6–21**

Cohabitation no longer contrary to public policy.   In theory it might have been possible to contend that the decision in *Upfill v Wright* prevented landlords   **6–22**

---

[61] See Ch.18, below.
[62] See [1905] 2 K.B. 123 at 135.
[63] cf. Powell, [1953] C.L.P. 254 at p.273.
[64] See John Dwyer, "Immoral Contracts" (1977) 93 L.Q.R. 386.
[65] [1911] 1 K.B. 506.
[66] [1911] 1 K.B. 506.

from suing for rent in any case involving a letting to an unmarried couple, in which only one of them provided the income out of which the rent was paid. It has long been clear, however, that such an argument would be wholly untenable.[67] The massive increase in cohabitation in recent decades has meant that the courts routinely deal with disputes involving cohabiting couples, without any suggestion of there being any legally relevant impropriety in the background.[68] It can therefore be taken that such cohabitation is no longer regarded as being "contrary to public policy".[69] In the 1977 case of *Heglibiston Establishments v Heyman*[70] a landlord sought to argue that a statutory tenancy should be forfeit on the ground, inter alia, of immoral user in that the tenant permitted his son and girlfriend to occupy one of the bedrooms as man and wife. In rejecting the landlord's application for possession, the Court of Appeal referred to his argument on this point as having "lacked substance or merit". Moreover, *Upfill's* case itself was not a straightforward one of long-term cohabitation, but involved instead occasional visits to a mistress in return for money to pay the rent; it could therefore be distinguished from the cohabitation cases in any event. Nowadays, however, it seems very unlikely that, even on facts similiar to those assumed in *Upfill v Wright*, the court would hold that "immorality" had any relevance to enforceability of the tenancy agreement.[71]

6–23 **Prostitution.** As it happens the defendant in *Upfill v Wright* had in fact been a prostitute, but since she was unable to establish that the landlord had been aware of this, the case proceeded on the narrower ground indicated above. It is evident that, had she been able to establish such knowledge on the part of the landlord, it would have been even clearer, on the authorities as they then stood, that his claim for arrears of rent would fail. In the very well-known case of *Pearce v Brooks*[72] a coach-builder was unable to enforce what appears, in effect, to have been a contract for the hire-purchase of an ornamental carriage when, to his knowledge, the other party to the contract was a prostitute who intended to use the carriage as part of her display to attract men. The Court of Exchequer Chamber expressly

---

[67] Lord Devlin, writing in 1976, said: "Ideas about sexual behaviour have recently changed with abnormal rapidity and the common law is quite out of touch . . . Some people . . . regard living out of wedlock as socially undesirable. But it is unreasonable now to treat every such association with abhorrence of the ex turpi causa type and for the law to insist that all unmarried couples should either be ejected or live rent-free". See "Judges and Lawmakers" (1976) 39 M.L.R. 1 at p.12. See also *Chrispen v Topham* (1986) 28 D.L.R. (4th) 754 (Saskatchewan).

[68] See, e.g. *Tanner v Tanner* [1975] 1 W.L.R. 1346; [1975] 3 All E.R. 776, CA. See also *Cooke v Head* [1972] 1 W.L.R. 389 (resulting trust).

[69] cf. per Lord Browne-Wilkinson in *Barclays Bank Plc v O'Brien* [1994] 1 A.C. 180 at 198; [1993] 4 All E.R. 417 at 431: "Now that unmarried cohabitation, whether heterosexual or homosexual, is widespread in our society, the law should recognise this". In the US an important decision which marked recognition of the property rights of unmarried cohabitees was that of the California Supreme Court in *Marvin v Marvin* (1976) 557 P.2d 106. See "Property Rights upon Termination of Unmarried Cohabitation" (1976–7) 90 Harv. L.R. 1708.

[70] (1978) 36 P. & C.R. 351, CA.

[71] cf. the robust judgment of Stable J in the Australian case of *Andrews v Parker* [1973] Qd.R. 93 at 104 (quoted in John Dwyer, "Immoral Contracts" (1977) 93 L.Q.R. 386 at 395): ". . . the social judgments of today upon matters of 'immorality' are as different from those of last century as is the bikini from a bustle".

[72] (1866) L.R. 1 Exch. 213.

rejected a suggestion, based on Lord Ellenborough's decision in *Bowry v Bennett*,[73] that it was necessary to prove that the claimant actually sought payment out of the proceeds of the defendant's activities, and not merely that he had knowledge of her purposes.

Narrow compass.   Even today, the law would almost certainly refuse to   6–24
enforce a contract between a prostitute and one of her clients, in the highly unlikely event of the former launching legal proceedings to secure payment for her services.[74] It must be very doubtful, however, whether other contracts related to her activities would nowadays be regarded as "contrary to public policy".[75] To hold that they were unenforceable for illegality could in theory give rise to questions of considerable difficulty. How far would the principle go?[76] In *Pearce v Brooks* itself Bramwell B observed in argument[77] that:

> ". . . in some sense everything which [is] supplied to a prostitute is supplied to enable her to carry on her trade, as, for instance, shoes sold to a street walker."

Similarly, Eyre CJ is said to have pointed out that "both an infant and a prostitute must have a lodging".[78] The nature of a prostitute's trade is such that many of the contracts into which she might enter, particularly those relating to the necessities of life, could be said to be of benefit to her in her line of business.[79] The better view is therefore that, on grounds of pragmatism as well as principle, the category of contracts considered contrary to public policy on grounds of "immorality" should be kept within a narrow compass: with *Pearce v Brooks* being regarded as a doubtful authority.

Sexual services falling short of prostitution.   The Court of Appeal recently   6–25
had occasion to consider the application of the doctrine of public policy to contracts allegedly involving sexual immorality, in the 1996 case of *Armhouse Lee v Chappell*.[80] The defendants provided over the telephone pre-recorded sex messages and also opportunities for live conversation of a sexual nature. In a defence described by the court as "hypocrisy writ large", the defendants sought to avoid liability to the publishers of the magazines which had advertised their telephone services, for the cost of the advertisements. They contended, as Simon Brown LJ put it, "that their promotional material [was] so immoral . . . that they ought not to have to pay for it". It is notable that the Court accepted as its starting

---

[73] (1808) 1 Camp. 348.
[74] See, per Simon Brown LJ in *Armhouse Lee v Chappell, The Times*, 7 August 1996, discussed in para.6–25, below.
[75] For a recent attempt to regulate prostitution in New Zealand see the Prostitution Reform Act 2003 (NZ), especially s.7: "No contract for the provision of or arranging the provision of commercial sexual services is illegal or void on public policy or other similar grounds".
[76] See M. P. Furmston, "The Analysis of Illegal Contracts" (1965) 16 Toronto L.J. 267 at pp.307–308.
[77] See (1866) L.R. 1 Exch. 213 at 214.
[78] *Crisp v Churchill* (unreported but cited in *Lloyd v Johnson* (1798) 1 Bos. & P. 340). See also *Clark v Hagar* (1894) 22 S.C.R. 510 at 541, per Gwynne J (Supreme Court of Canada).
[79] In *Bruneau v Laliberte* (1901) 19 Que. S.C. 425, the Superior Court of Quebec held that a contract of insurance on the furniture in a brothel was unenforceable, *sed quaere*.
[80] *The Times*, 7 August 1996. The quotations which follow are from the LEXIS (Smith Bernal) transcript.

point that "on any view of the law, public policy still precludes the enforcement of contracts for the promotion of an undoubtedly immoral purpose such as prostitution". The defendants' contention was nevertheless rejected, and their liability to pay for their own advertisements was confirmed. The Court rejected a submission that the telephone services themselves constituted "prostitution", on the ground that so to hold would unduly widen the definition of that activity. Of greater significance, however, was the rejection of a more wider and more general submission to the effect that the Court should refuse "to lend itself to the enforcement of any contract involving the supply of services of a sexual nature for reward". The submission was rejected for two reasons. First, there was the need to distinguish the advertisements from the telephone services themselves. The contract between the telephone subscriber and the defendants might well have been unenforceable; preventing the former from complaining, for example, that the content had been disappointingly benign rather than pornographic. But it did not follow that the contracts with the publishers were similarly afflicted. Simon Brown LJ expressed himself as follows:

"Is it to be said that the models should not be paid? Or the rent? What was supplied by the Respondents here were not sexual services but rather advertising services: the sexual services were at one remove."

6–26 **Consensus approach.** It was the second reason for rejecting the submission, however, which went to the heart of the approach of the contemporary judiciary to moral questions. It was far from clear that public opinion as a whole regarded telephone sex lines as immoral, and in those circumstances it was not appropriate for the court to step in and condemn them. Simon Brown LJ said that "any relevant public policy must be found in the uncertain climate of sexual morality prevailing today", and continued:

"Distasteful though these advertisements and the services they invite may be, in my judgment they come nowhere near the point where the court should feel morally obliged to abjure its usual jurisdiction over contractual disputes. I simply cannot accept that these services (even assuming they were to be supplied in the full measure promised) cause incontestable public harm. Nor do I feel confident that my own subjective reactions to various types of sexual conduct necessarily represent a clear public consensus as to today's properly tolerable bounds of behaviour".

It is therefore clear that the judges usually seek to operate on a "consensus" basis when deciding public policy cases,[81] at least in the area of sexual morality.[82] The implications of this approach will be returned to in the context of more general consideration of the nature of public policy, and of the judicial role in its exercise.

---

[81] See John Bell, *Policy Arguments in Judicial Decisions* (Oxford University Press, 1983), Ch.1, pp.10–14, and Ch.7, passim.
[82] See also *Stephens v Avery* [1988] Ch.449 at 454, per Sir Nicolas Browne-Wilkinson VC: "If it is right that there is now no generally-accepted code of sexual morality applying to this case, it would be quite wrong in my judgment for any judge to apply his own personal moral views, however strongly held, in deciding the legal rights of the parties. The court's function is to apply the law, not personal prejudice. Only in a case where there is still a generally accepted moral code can the court refuse to enforce rights in such a way as to offend that generally accepted code".

4.   PUBLIC POLICY IN PRACTICE

Judicial reticence.   Although the fiction that judges do not exercise discretion   **6–27**
when deciding novel points of law has long since been discredited, the explicit
recognition of "public policy" as a distinct concept in relation to unlawful
transactions still renders this corner of the law a somewhat unusual one.
Elsewhere, the use of the term "policy" is usually accompanied by a degree of
judicial reticence, and a reluctance to acknowledge that its influence is anything
other than marginal.[83] Even in the present sphere, where the notion is openly
accepted, its deployment is usually negative in effect, and invariably cautious.
The sterile controversy over whether "new heads" of public policy can be created
is symptomatic of an aversion to treating the category as an opportunity for
constructive and imaginative approaches to novel situations, or to situations in
which social changes have rendered existing legal doctrines anachronistic.

Uncharted territory.   While the judicial unease in dealing with "public policy"   **6–28**
no doubt does partly reflect concerns about the separation of powers, it is
probable that this is accompanied by a more general intellectual discomfort at
being obliged to explore uncharted territory. In his important study of the topic
half a century ago, Professor Lord Lloyd drew attention to the significance in this
area of the methodological differences between the common law and continental
systems, and the implications for the former of its "haphazard" approach.[84] To
achieve a degree of coherence the concept of "public policy" would seem to need
a general philosophical framework within which to operate; and the overt
adoption of such a framework would be difficult to reconcile with the deeply
pragmatic nature of the common law.[85]

Possible influences.   In the absence of a framework to guide the formulation of   **6–29**
principle, there is a danger that "public policy" decisions may be unduly
idiosyncratic, or excessively influenced by vocal pressure groups anxious to
protect their own particular interests.[86] There is also the danger of obsolete
theories surviving beyond their sell-by date. In so far as the judicial approach to
"public policy" favours the enforceability of contracts, rather than their
nullification, it is usually on the ground that there is a strong public interest in
keeping people to their agreements. This is considered to outweigh any other
concerns to which a particular contract might give rise, in respect of its fairness
or social consequences.[87] Lloyd posed the question whether traditional judicial

---

[83] See, e.g. the law of negligence.
[84] See Dennis Lloyd, *Public Policy* (1953), p.149.
[85] See, generally, Winfield, "Public Policy in the English Common Law" (1928) 42 Harv. L.R. 76,
especially at 99: ". . . public policy is emphatically no ideal standard to which law ought to conform
. . . when the founders of our common law spoke of 'reason', 'the law of reason', 'the law of nature',
they doubtless had a vision of some abstraction and wished to make the law harmonize with that. *That
vision has long passed from public policy as we now understand the phrase*" (italics supplied).
[86] See C. R. Symmons, "The Function and Effect of Public Policy in Contemporary Common Law"
(1977) 51 Aust. L.J. 185 at 190–191.
[87] The classic statement is that of Sir George Jessel MR in *Priming and Numerical Registering Co v
Sampson*, (1875) L.R. 19 Eq. 462 at 465: "It must not be forgotten that you are not to extend
arbitrarily those rules which say that a given contract is void as being against public policy, because if

adherence to laissez faire economics was merely a reflection of the dominant economic theory during the formative years of the common law's development, or whether it reflected a stronger adherence resulting from the fact that the social origins of the judges lay largely in the entrepreneurial class.[88]

6–30   **Caution or conservatism?**   It is clear from cases such as *Armstrong Lee v Chappell*[89] that the judges will invoke the notion of consensus, or its absence, to justify presuming in favour of the status quo when they wish to avoid declaring a contract to be void on grounds of public policy.[90] On the whole this caution would seem to be desirable, as it was in *Armstrong Lee v Chappell* itself. Nevertheless, ambiguities in the very notion of consensus create the danger that, in less straightforward cases, the courts may simply, under the guise of preserving the status quo, inadvertently reinforce possibly widespread, but crude and dangerous, prejudices such as racism.[91] Moreover, even if it is assumed, for the purposes of argument, that judicial caution is to be applauded when it results in challenges to the validity of contracts on the ground of public policy being rejected, it does not follow that it is equally attractive when the question is not whether invalidity should be extended, but whether it should be removed. In such cases there is an obvious danger that the decision-making can become loaded in favour not of a contemporary "consensus", but of one which commended itself to an earlier generation. In truth, the notion of "consensus", although valuable as a loose presumption, raises as many questions as it answers when it is invoked to rationalise the working of the public policy doctrine. There is no escaping the fact that no mechanical artifice can wholly abrogate the degree of discretion which the judges inevitably enjoy in these cases.

6–31   **Confidence in the judiciary.**   The dilemma with which the concept of "public policy" presents the courts in this area is a challenge to judicial statesmanship, the resolution of which is apt to reflect the distinctive culture and preoccupations of each new generation. The pressures on the contemporary judiciary are particularly acute. On the one hand, expectations generated by such legislation as the Human Rights Act, and by looser European techniques of statutory drafting, call for the courts to adopt a higher profile than formerly on sensitive issues. On the other hand, a public better informed than ever before, allied with a not overly sympathetic media, is apt to scrutinise closely the ways in which the judges

---

there is one thing which more than another public policy requires it is that men of full age and competent understanding shall have the utmost liberty of contracting, and that their contracts when entered into freely and voluntarily shall be held sacred and shall be enforced by Courts of Justice. Therefore, you have this paramount public policy to consider-that you are not lightly to interfere with this freedom of contract".

[88] See Dennis Lloyd, *Public Policy* (Athlone Press, 1953), p.142.
[89] *The Times*, 7 August 1996, discussed above.
[90] cf. Lord Devlin, "Judges and Lawmakers" (1976) 39 M.L.R. 1 at p.1: ". . . law is the gatekeeper of the status quo . . . New policies must gather strength before they can force an entry".
[91] cf. *Re Noble & Wolfe* (1949) 4 D.L.R. 375 (reversed on other grounds in (1951) 1 D.L.R. 321), in which the Ontario courts refused to declare a covenant prohibiting the sale of a property to members of certain races invalid as contrary to public policy. See Dennis Lloyd, *Public Policy* (1953), pp.58 et seq. See also J. F. Garner, "Racial Restrictive Covenants in England and the United States" (1972) 35 M.L.R. 478.

exercise their power. Any perceived narrowness in the background of the judges themselves, which may be thought to have influenced the development of their views on social questions, is likely to come in for particular criticism.

Sensitivity of the appointment system.   The concept of "public policy", and   **6–32**
the opportunities which it provides for the law to keep abreast of changing times, nevertheless remains valuable and worth preserving. Nor is the absence of an over-arching philosophical framework necessarily to be deplored. The overt exercise of a soundly-based judicial intuition is still capable of commanding public confidence and respect. An alternative approach, based upon an extended empirical investigation by the court of the implications of possible develop- ments,[92] would be inconsistent with the nature of the judicial process in England; and would itself raise critical issues of legitimacy. But in order for their conclusions to be perceived as having been "soundly-based", those empowered to make intuitive decisions must be drawn from as wide a cross-section of society as possible.[93] "The value of the doctrine", as Winfield put it over 80 years ago, "depends on the men [*sic*] who administer it".[94] One important factor in the development and acceptance of a healthy "public policy" is therefore public confidence in the institutional arrangements for the appointment of judges. Since the passing of the Constitutional Reform Act 2005 responsibility for judicial appointments has been transferred from the former Lord Chancellor's Depart- ment to an independent Judicial Appointments Commission which, other things being equal, is seeking to achieve greater diversity in the judiciary.

Need for variability.   Sir Percy Winfield once said[95]:   **6–33**

> "Public policy is necessarily variable. It may be variable not only from one century to another, not only from one generation to another, but even in the same generation ... This variability of public policy is a stone in the edifice of the doctrine, and not a missile to be flung at it. Public policy would be almost useless without it."

There is clearly a danger, however, that the operation of the doctrine of precedent within the common law system may lead to "public policy" becoming ossified. On the whole the courts have been alive to this danger, and have recognised that judgments on public policy questions do not have the same precedential force as decisions on points of law".[96] A degree of danger nevertheless remains that undue deference to "authority" will allow rigidity to creep in. Even the treatment of public policy issues as questions of "fact" will not guarantee flexibility.[97] The notorious difficulty of drawing a clear distinction

---

[92] cf. the "Brandeis brief" of US law.
[93] But cf. Lord Devlin, "Judges and Lawmakers" (1976) 39 M.L.R. 1 at p.8: "Let the practice of the law be opened up by all means and let the judiciary be composed of the best that the practice of the law can produce. You will find, I am sure, that judges will still be of the same type whether they come from major or minor public schools, grammar schools or comprehensives, and whether they like to spend their leisure in a library or in a club".
[94] See Winfield, "Public Policy in the English Common Law" (1928) 42 Harv. L.R. 76 at p.100.
[95] See Winfield, "Public Policy in the English Common Law" (1928) 42 Harv. L.R. 76 at pp.93–95.
[96] See, e.g. *Bowman v Secular Society* [1917] A.C. 406.
[97] See Dennis Lloyd, *Public Policy* (1953), p.117.

between fact and law only too easily leads to decisions on the former being treated as the latter. Statutory intervention would therefore be desirable in order to put the matter as far beyond doubt as is practically possible. In accordance with this view, the Law Commission in 1999 recommended provisionally as follows[98]:

> ". . . a legislative provision should make it clear that the courts are to judge whether a contract is contrary to public policy in the light of policy matters of the present day and that contracts which were previously considered to be contrary to public policy may no longer be so and *vice versa*."

In its more recent Consultation Paper on illegality, however, the Law Commission retreated from the view that such a general legislative provision would be appropriate, concluding that "the courts remain the best arbiters of which transactions, while not involving unlawful conduct, should be regarded as contrary to public policy, with Parliament intervening only in particular areas as and when appropriate".[99]

6–34   **Lessons from maintenance and champerty.**   The state of the law relating to maintenance and champerty is particularly instructive in relation to the capacity of public policy to change as circumstances change, as well its tendency to crystallise on occasion into undesirable rigidity. Recent cases in that area have also highlighted the differing possible approaches which are available towards the relationship between statutory and judge-made law in the public policy field. These matters are dealt with below, at the conclusion of the chapter on maintenance and champerty itself.[100]

---

[98] See Law Commission Consultation Paper No.154, *Illegal Transactions: The Effect of Illegality on Contracts and Trusts* (1999), p.98 (para.7–16).
[99] See Law Commission Consultation Paper No.189, *The Illegality Defence, A Consultative Report* (2009), p.3 (para.1–11). The point is not mentioned in the Commission's final report *The Illegality Defence* (2010), Law Com No.320, but it is clear that the views in the 2009 paper remain those of the Commission.
[100] See Ch.9.

CHAPTER 7

FRAUD AND CORRUPTION

1.   INTRODUCTION

Purpose of the agreement.   One or both of the parties to a contract may intend   **7–01**
to use the agreement to defraud another person or institution. This intention may
exist at the time when the agreement is formed, or only be developed
subsequently; the whole purpose of the agreement may itself have been
fraudulent, or the contract may simply have provided a convenient opportunity to
secure an illicit collateral advantage subordinate to its main purpose. The latter
category typically includes situations in which information is concealed, or
documentation manipulated, in order to avoid the payment of tax lawfully due as
a result of an otherwise legitimate contract. Similar to contracts entered into with
the intention of committing fraud are those entered into with a purpose which is
inherently corrupt. These include attempts to secure, usually in return for the
payment of money, advantages or benefits ostensibly dependent upon objective
criteria free from financial inducement. Yet another related category of cases is
that in which the enforceability of confidentiality agreements may be considered
to be contrary to the public interest.

Illegality based on public policy.   In many of the cases examined in this   **7–02**
chapter, the conduct of the parties will probably have involved them in the
commission of criminal offences. In practice, however, prosecutions are rare, and
the courts do not regard their possible criminality as the reason for depriving the
parties of their contractual rights. The position is therefore rather different from
cases in which the infringement, often of regulatory or other "technical"
provisions, is the sole justification for the suggestion that enforcement should be
denied. On the contrary, in this area the language and concepts of "public policy"
typically provide the basis upon which the courts approach the issues.

2.   FRAUDULENT CONTRACTS

"Fraud upon the public".   There are, not surprisingly, few reported instances   **7–03**
of one member of a fraudulent conspiracy actually launching proceedings against
his co-conspirator, in the event of the latter failing to keep his part of the bargain.
One such is the old case of *Willis v Baldwin*.[1] The claimant was a supplier of
provisions to four army regiments, and this entitled him to obtain free oats and

---

[1] (1780) 2 Doug. 450.

hay from a depot controlled by the defendant who, in turn, was entitled to charge the Government for them. The defendant and claimant struck a bargain whereby the latter would not take his full quota of rations, but receive a payment from the former in their place. The defendant could then sell the oats elsewhere, while still claiming the full cost from the Government. The defendant failed, however, to make the requisite payments to the claimant, and the latter sued him. An ingenious argument by his counsel to the effect that the claimant might simply have spent the money he received from the defendant in obtaining supplies from elsewhere, and so still keep the regiments fully provisioned, understandably did not meet with a favourable response. Lord Mansfield castigated the case as "a foul agreement between the parties" and "a clear fraud upon the public".[2]

7–04   **Fraudulent preferences.**   A more familiar type of fraudulent transaction to appear in the law reports is that in which an insolvent debtor transfers, or promises to transfer, assets to one of his creditors with the intention, to the knowledge of both parties, of defeating the legitimate claims of the remaining creditors. Fraudulent preferences were outlawed by the common law before they became the subject of statutory control. As Erle J put it in *Mallalieu v Hodgson*,[3] a case in which a composition agreement had been reached between the debtor and his creditors, "where any creditor, in fraud of the agreement to accept the composition, stipulates for a preference to himself, his stipulation is altogether void: not only can he take no advantage from it, but he is also to lose the benefit of the composition". The actual decision in *Mallalieu v Hodgson* illustrates that fraudsters who are, in the same overall transaction, themselves the victims of fraud, will attract little sympathy from the court. A creditor sought to avoid the composition agreement, and recover the full amount owed to him, on the ground that it had been falsely represented to him that no preferences had been accorded to other creditors. His claim failed, notwithstanding the fraudulent misrepresentation, because he had, in fact, secretly negotiated a preference for himself, and had merely sought an assurance that no-else had done so as well!

7–05   ***Farmers' Mart v Milne.***   In the twentieth century case of *Farmers' Mart v Milne*[4] the House of Lords was faced with a rather more sophisticated illegal scheme arising out of insolvency. A firm of land agents agreed with one of their employees that he could accept appointment as a trustee in bankruptcy providing he pooled his fees with the firm in such a way that, in cases in which the firm itself happened to be one of the creditors, its share of the proceeds of the payout exceeded that enjoyed by the other creditors. Lord Atkinson had "not the slightest hesitation in holding that such an agreement [was] a fraud upon the bankruptcy laws, the great object of which . . . is not merely to secure that the assets of a bankrupt shall be distributed amongst his creditors, but that they shall also be distributed equally".[5]

---

[2] (1780) 2 Doug. 450 at 451.
[3] (1851) 16 Q.B. 689 at 711–712.
[4] [1915] A.C. 106.
[5] [1915] A.C. 106 at 115.

Ulterior motive. It has been held that the parties to an otherwise legitimate contract may forfeit any rights under it if they entered into the agreement in the hope that its existence would create a misleading impression in the minds of third parties. In *Scott v Brown, Doering, McNab & Co*[6] a contract for the purchase of shares in a company was held to come into this category on the ground that it had been entered into in order to create the impression that shares in the company were at a premium, when they were not.[7] Although their intention had been to attract investors by giving a false impression to the public, the actual agreement for the purchase of the shares had been genuine and the price had been paid. Nevertheless, the Court of Appeal described the agreement as "a deceitful and fraudulent means whereby to cheat and defraud those who might buy shares in the company".[8] Although it has been suggested that the consequences of this decision could be far-reaching, since any large-scale investor must be aware that his transactions might have a disproportionate effect on the market,[9] in practice it does not appear to have caused uncertainty and its correctness has never been questioned. There was clear evidence of a conspiracy "to make a market",[10] which distinguished the case from orthodox transactions.

7–06

Insurance fraud. In the more recent case of *Taylor v Bhail*[11] the Court of Appeal took the opportunity to make it clear that those who engage in a widespread form of fraud will find that their contracts will be unenforceable for illegality. As a result of storm damage, against which he was insured, the defendant wished to have building work carried out to the value of approximately £12,000. He approached the claimant builder, pointed out that an insurance company was to pay, and said: "You put an extra £1,000 on the price for me and I'll make sure you get the job". It was therefore clear that, in return for being awarded the contract, the claimant was required to assist the defendant in defrauding the latter's insurance company out of £1,000. The claimant duly obliged and the work went ahead. When a dispute subsequently arose between the parties, the builder sued to enforce the contract, but the defendant contended that it was unenforceable for illegality. The Court of Appeal, reversing the county court judge, found for the defendant and dismissed the action. The claimant's argument that the contract to defraud the insurers was separate from the building contract, leaving the latter enforceable, was rejected. Noting that the builder had been a "willing participant" in the intended fraud, Millett LJ said that it was "time that a clear message was sent to the commercial community", and continued:

7–07

> "Let it be clearly understood if a builder or a garage or other supplier agrees to provide a false estimate for work in order to enable its customer to obtain payment from his insurers to which he is not entitled, then it will be unable to recover payment from its customer and the customer will be unable to claim on his insurers even if he has paid for the work."[12]

---

[6] [1892] 2 Q.B. 724.
[7] See also *North v Marra Developments* (1981) 148 C.L.R. 42.
[8] [1892] 2 Q.B. 724 at 734, per A. L. Smith LJ.
[9] See Furmston, "Analysis of Illegal Contracts" (1965) 16 Toronto L.J. 267 at pp.284–285.
[10] [1892] 2 Q.B. 724 at 726.
[11] (1995) 50 Con. L.R. 70.
[12] *Taylor v Bhail* was distinguished by the Court of Appeal in *A L Barnes Ltd v Time Talk (UK) Ltd* [2003] EWCA Civ 402, in which the defendants unsuccessfully sought to resist payment for services

7–08   **Deceiving finance company.**   Another relatively recent case in which the deliberate deception of a third party resulted in a claim failing for illegality, is the decision of the Court of Appeal in *Birkett v Acorn Business Machines*.[13] In this case it was unclear whether the third party had actually suffered any loss as a result, but that was irrelevant. The claimant wished to hire a photocopier machine with the assistance of a finance company, which would purchase the machine and hire it out to the claimant. In order to satisfy limitations imposed by the finance company as to the type of equipment which it would acquire, the defendants and claimant together deliberately misrepresented that the machine in question had a fax facility, and was not an ordinary photocopier. As in *Taylor v Bhail* this misrepresentation was instigated by the defendants, who were office equipment suppliers, for their own benefit, and then advanced by them as a defence to an otherwise legitimate claim against them. Sedley LJ accordingly observed that this was "one of those cases where . . . law and justice part company", but felt obliged to conclude that, as the contract between the claimant and the defendant "was founded upon an intended fraud on a third party", it was unenforceable.

3.   DEFRAUDING THE REVENUE

(a)   General Applicability

7–09   In a considerable number of reported cases, attempting to defraud the tax authorities has been put forward as a basis upon which to hold that a contract was unenforceable for illegality. It is convenient to consider these cases together, even though the issues to which they give rise will rarely be exclusive to revenue frauds and will also be applicable, at least in theory, to other types of situation in which illegality is involved.

(b)   Deceptive Documentation

7–10   *Alexander v Rayson.*   In the well-known case of *Alexander v Rayson*[14] a landlord who attempted to sue for rent was met with a defence of illegality based on the fact that he had executed two separate documents in connection with the letting, and had done so with the intention of showing only one of them to the local rating authorities. This was done in order to mislead the authorities as to the level of rent being received, so that they would assess the rateable value of the

---

rendered on the ground that one of the claimants' directors had been aware of a dishonest arrangement whereby the defendants' own agent had obtained payment twice over for work done in relation to the contract between the claimants and the defendants. But in the absence of evidence that the claimants themselves had sought actively to bribe the defendant's agent, the Court held that the claim for services rendered was unaffected by the dishonest arrangement: see per Longmore LJ at paras 8–15.

[13] [1999] 2 All E.R. Comm. 429.
[14] [1936] 1 K.B. 169, du Parcq J and CA.

premises at a lower figure than was appropriate.[15] The Court of Appeal, reversing du Parcq J, held that the defence of illegality would succeed.[16]

Tenuous connection? The decision in this case has prompted speculation as to how far the principle in it extends.[17] There was nothing improper in the letting itself, nor was the actual information contained in the documents inaccurate. Du Parcq J, at first instance, had compared the situation with the hypothetical case of a party to a valid contract who subsequently alters the contractual documentation by forgery to promote some illicit scheme quite unconnected with the original agreement itself. Du Parcq J considered that the forgery would not affect the forger's rights under the original contract.[18] Significantly, the Court of Appeal agreed with that conclusion, and only differed from du Parcq J as to whether the facts of the actual case before them were comparable. When use is made of an already existing contract to promote an illegal scheme, there must clearly come a point at which the connection between the scheme and the contract becomes too tenuous for the enforceability of the agreement to be adversely affected.[19] Thus in *21st Century Logistic Solutions v Madysen*[20] Field J distinguished *Alexander's* case and held that the fact that a supplier of goods intended to defraud the Revenue of VAT did not prevent the supplier from recovering the price of the goods, which had been delivered to the defendants. Although the existence of the contract of sale had provided the opportunity for the claimant to act upon his intention to defraud the Revenue, that intention was too remote from the contract to render it unenforceable for illegality.[21] The decision of the Court of Appeal in *Alexander v Rayson* itself would, however, seem to be correct because the intention to deceive the rating authorities was present in the claimant's mind at the time when the contract of letting was formed, and the documentation was drawn up at the outset in such a way as to facilitate that deception.[22] It would be going too far to insist that the requirements of contemporaneity and overt action should be necessary conditions for a finding of illegality in similar circumstances. Nevertheless, where they are absent, the court should proceed with considerable caution before making such a finding. The principles relating to illegality must

7–11

---

[15] cf. *Ting Siew May v Boon Lay Choo* [2014] SGCA 28 in which the Singapore Court of Appeal held that backdating an option to purchase land to evade subsequently enacted restrictions on the availability of credit rendered the option unenforceable for illegality.
[16] See also *Zimmermann v Letkeman* (1977) 79 D.L.R. (3d) 508, in which the principle in *Alexander v Rayson* was applied by the Supreme Court of Canada.
[17] See Furmston, "Analysis of Illegal Contracts" (1965) 16 Toronto L.J. 267 at 287: "near to the limit of the law".
[18] [1936] 1 K.B. 169 at 171.
[19] See *Williston on Contracts* (4th ed., 1998), para.19.11: "merely collaterally connected". See also, per Lloyd LJ in *Tinsley v Milligan* [1992] 2 All E.R. 391 at 415, CA: ". . . general depravity has never been a bar".
[20] [2004] EWHC 231 (QB); [2004] 2 Lloyd's Rep 92. See also *Miah v Islam* [2010] EWC 1569.
[21] It should be noted that the claimant company was in liquidation and the consequence of rejecting the defence of illegality was that the Revenue was able to recover the VAT, which it would have lost if recovery of the price of the goods supplied had been barred by illegality.
[22] See also the Australian case of *Holdcraft v Market Garden Produce* [2000] QCA 396 in which a sale of shares was disguised as an employment contract to secure tax advantages, and the Queensland Court of Appeal held the sale to be unenforceable for illegality.

not be allowed to degenerate into unprincipled stigmatisation of contracting parties so that they become, in effect, "outlaws".[23]

(c) Evading Income Tax

7–12   **Fictitious expenses.**   In two cases decided in the middle of the twentieth century the Court of Appeal emphasised that those who contrived improperly to avoid the payment of income tax would receive little sympathy from the court. In *Miller v Karlinski*[24] the claimant and his employer agreed that part of what was, in fact, the former's remuneration would be falsely described as "expenses", in order to avoid payment of tax on the part thus identified. An action by the claimant to recover arrears of salary was dismissed. "It is too plain for argument", said du Parcq LJ, "that this agreement to charge tax to expenses is against public policy".[25] In the very similar case of *Napier v National Business Agency*,[26] decided a few years later, and in which the same result was reached, the Court of Appeal made clear that there was no question of severing the "expenses" part of such agreements so as to leave the remainder enforceable. Denning LJ said[27]:

> "The insertion of a fictitious figure for expenses in order to defraud the revenue is illegal. It vitiates the whole remuneration and disentitles the servant from recovering any part of it. He cannot recover either the part described as expenses or even the part described as salary."

7–13   **Unfair dismissal.**   In a series of cases decided by the Employment Appeal Tribunal, that tribunal chose to apply the *Miller* and *Napier* decisions to situations involving the statutory right to compensation for unfair dismissal or redundancy. The necessity for a claimant to be a party to a contract of employment was held to render those decisions directly applicable, notwithstanding the statutory basis of the claim itself. The English authorities were very fully reviewed by Lord Coulsfield, delivering the judgment of the tribunal in the Scottish case of *Salvesen v Simons*.[28] In that case an employee who asked for part of his salary to be paid as a consultancy fee outside the PAYE scheme, even though his salaried employment was a full-time one which rendered the arrangement illegitimate, was denied compensation for constructive dismissal. Similarly, employees who knew that their full income was not being disclosed to the Inland Revenue by their employers because, for example, it was paid out of petty cash,[29] or was notionally in the form of an unclaimable lodging allowance,[30] found their claims for statutory compensation dismissed.

---

[23] cf. *Gordon v Metropolitan Police Chief Commissioner* [1910] 2 K.B. 1080, CA (police not allowed to seize and retain claimant's property merely on the ground that it represented the proceeds of illegal street betting).

[24] (1946) 62 T.L.R. 85.

[25] (1946) 62 T.L.R. 85 at 86.

[26] [1951] 2 All E.R. 264.

[27] At 266.

[28] [1994] I.C.R. 409.

[29] See *Tomlinson v Dick Evans "U" Drive* [1978] I.C.R. 639. See also *Corby v Morrison (t/a the Card Shop)* [1980] I.C.R. 564.

[30] See *Hyland v J.H. Barker (North West)* [1985] I.C.R. 861.

Harsh decisions. The Employment Appeal Tribunal often chose to apply the general rule of unenforceability to unfair dismissal cases in a particularly harsh manner. It appeared to take little account of the relative positions of employer and employee, and to adopt an unrealistic approach in expecting the latter effectively to resist arrangements which were usually instigated by the former. Mere knowledge of those arrangements was apparently enough to disqualify the employee.[31] In one case Bristow J, delivering the judgment of the Tribunal, expressly stated that the rule would be applied with full rigour even in "cases in which a junior employee goes along with an employer's tax fraud knowing it to be dishonest, in circumstances where more blame attaches to the employer than to him".[32]

7–14

More enlightened approach. Although none of the relevant decisions of the Employment Appeal Tribunal have been overruled, so that employees would still be unwise to be confident of leniency, two relatively recent decisions at Court of Appeal level suggest fortunately that a more enlightened approach might sometimes be adopted. In *Hewcastle Catering v Ahmed and Elkamah*[33] the dismissed employees were waiters who passively, and without benefit to themselves, assisted in a value added tax fraud perpetrated by their employers. The waiters simply carried out instructions to give different types of bill to customers depending upon whether or not they indicated that they wished to pay in cash. The dismissal of the waiters followed criminal proceedings in which they had given evidence against their employers, and which had resulted in the latter being sentenced to imprisonment. The Court of Appeal upheld the award of damages for unfair dismissal. Beldam LJ emphasised that "the obligation to make returns for value added tax and to ensure that proper records are kept is that of the employer",[34] and pointed out that dismissal of the claims could discourage employees from assisting the authorities in similiar cases in the future.[35]

7–15

Participation. The *Hewcastle* case was referred to in the decision of the Court of Appeal in *Hall v Woolston Hall Leisure Ltd*,[36] which was handed down in May 2000. The employers in this case responded to a claim for dismissal, arising out of sex discrimination, by pointing out that the applicant had been aware that the payslips she was given showed a lower net figure than the amount which she actually received; from which she should have inferred that the full amount of tax due was not being paid. The Court of Appeal nevertheless found in the applicant's favour, reversing the decision to the contrary of the Employment Appeal Tribunal. The main ground of the Court of Appeal's decision was that sex

7–16

---

[31] cf. *Newland v Simons and Willer (Hairdressers)* [1981] I.C.R. 521.
[32] See *Tomlinson v Dick Evans "U" Drive* [1978] I.C.R. 639 at 642.
[33] [1992] I.C.R. 626.
[34] [1992] I.C.R. 626.
[35] Beldam LJ also invoked the "public conscience" test later rejected by the House of Lords in *Tinsley v Mittigan* [1994] 1 A.C. 340, but this does not invalidate the overall approach of Beldam LJ: see *Hall v Wooolston Hall Leisure* [2001] 1 W.L.R. 225 at 249; [2000] 4 All E.R. 787, at 809–810, per Mance LJ.
[36] [2001] 1 W.L.R. 225; [2000] 4 All E.R. 787. See also *Colen v Cebrian (UK) Ltd* [2003] EWCA Civ 1676; [2004] I.C.R. 568.

discrimination claims are not based upon the contract of employment in the same immediate sense as claims for unfair dismissal arising out of the employment protection legislation. Irregularities in the tax situation which might lead to the dismissal of claims in that context would therefore not necessarily do so in the context of sex discrimination, in which the claims were perceived to be more analogous to actions in tort than in contract.[37] It is significant, however, that the Court of Appeal indicated that, contrary to the views of both the industrial tribunal and the Employment Appeal Tribunal, even an ordinary unfair dismissal claim would not necessarily have failed on the facts of the case. The applicant had actually queried the payslips, but the employers had replied that that was "the way they did business".[38] In those circumstances the Court of Appeal adopted an approach more familiar in illegality cases not involving revenue frauds, and emphasised that the contract of employment had not been illegal from the outset but had merely been *performed* unlawfully.[39] Peter Gibson LJ said[40]:

> "In cases where the contract of employment is neither entered into for an illegal purpose nor prohibited by statute, the illegal performance of the contract will not render the contract unenforceable unless in addition to knowledge of the *facts* which make the performance illegal, the employee actively *participates* in the illegal performance. It is a question of fact in each case whether there has been a sufficient degree of participation by the employee."

7–17   **Need to avoid rigidity and literalism.** Mance LJ associated himself expressly with this analysis,[41] emphasising that "both knowledge and participation on her part in the illegal method of performance" had to be shown before the employers' failure to make the appropriate deductions "could disable the appellant from enforcing her contract of employment".[42] Although Peter Gibson LJ said of the judge in the Employment Appeal Tribunal that "his view of the unfair dismissal cases [was] an over-simplified one",[43] in reality the Court of Appeal was substituting a more satisfactory approach for the harsh one which appeared to have become established by earlier decisions of the Employment Appeal Tribunal. In revenue cases the fundamental importance of the distinction between participation and mere knowledge,[44] where the other party to the contract had simply performed improperly an agreement which had been lawful at the outset, appears to have been lost sight of. There is no doubt that the leading cases of

---

[37] See also the important decision of the Supreme Court in *Hounga v Allen* [2014] UKSC 47; [2014] 1 W.L.R. 2889 in which the Court held that a claimant who had entered the country illegally was not thereby barred by illegality from obtaining compensation from her former employer under the "statutory tort" of (racial) discrimination.

[38] See [2001] 1 W.L.R. 225 at 229; [2000] 4 All E.R. 787, at 791.

[39] cf. *Davidson v Pillay* [1979] I.R.L.R. 275.

[40] See [2001] 1 W.L.R. 225, at 236; [2000] 4 All E.R. 787, at 797 (italics supplied).

[41] See [2001] 1 W.L.R. 225, at 248; [2000] 4 All E.R. 787, at 809. See also *Ashmore, Benson, Pease & Co v A. V. Dawson* [1973] 1 W.L.R. 828 (cited by Mance LJ).

[42] See also *Wheeler v Quality Deep Ltd* [2004] EWCA Civ 1085; [2005] I.C.R. 265 in which *Hall's* case was followed and a claim for unfair dismissal succeeded, but Hooper LJ cautioned as follows at 71: "This is a very unusual case concerning as it does a foreign national working in this country in her own language with limited knowledge of the English language and of the tax and national insurance provisions of this country. Had she not had that limited knowledge, she may well not have succeeded."

[43] See [2001] 1 W.L.R. 225, at 236; [2000] 4 All E.R. 787, at 797.

[44] See Ch.4, above.

Miller v Karlinski and *Napier v National Business Agency* were decided correctly. The employees in those cases appear to have been fully implicated in the fraudulent schemes from the beginning. But some of the unfair dismissal cases appear to have applied those decisions with a degree of rigidity and literalism not warranted by the decisions themselves, once their facts are taken fully into account.[45]

Erroneous categorisation of contract.   One recent decision in which   **7–18**
excessive rigidity was fortunately avoided was that of the Court of Appeal in
Enfield Technical Services v Payne.[46] In this case the Court of Appeal held that
merely because employer and "employee" categorise their relationship *in good
faith* as one of employer and independent contractor, resulting in PAYE tax not
being deducted at source by the employer, that will not prevent the employee
from subsequently taking advantage of the unfair dismissal legislation if the
categorisation turns out to have been incorrect: so that the claimant had not
actually been self-employed but had been an employee instead. Since there can,
in borderline cases, be an unavoidable degree of uncertainty in classifying a
contract as one of employment or self-employment, the Court held that illegality
would only become relevant if one or both of the parties had sought deliberately
to *mislead* the Revenue. In the *Enfield* case the Court decided two appeals in
favour of employees, allowing them to sue for unfair dismissal despite the fact
that their contracts had been perceived, albeit mistakenly, by both them and their
employers as having given them self-employed status. Pill LJ said[47]:

> "A contract of employment may, as the cases show, be unlawfully performed if there are misrepresentations, express or implied, as to the facts. An obvious example occurs when what is in fact taxable salary is claimed to be non-taxable expenses. That is, however, distinguishable from an error of categorisation (as in the present cases) unaccompanied by such false representations, even if the employee had claimed the advantages of self-employment before the dispute arose. ... This is not a case of ignorance of the law providing a defence. A genuine claim to self-employment, unaccompanied by false representations as to the work being done or the basis on which payment is being made, does not necessarily amount to unlawful performance of a contract of employment."

The claimants in the *Enfield* cases had sought to comply with their tax obligations during their perceived period of self-employed status. The Court of Appeal emphasised that had there been any attempt at improper exploitation of that status the decisions would have been different.[48] On this basis the Court distinguished earlier cases in which such exploitation appears to have been likely, even though the wide reasoning adopted in those cases could be interpreted as rendering it unnecessary.[49]

---

[45] For a review by the Court of Appeal of the applicable principles in the context of unfair dismissal see *Colen v Cebrian (UK) Ltd* [2003] EWCA Civ 1676; [2004] I.C.R. 568, in which an allegation of tax evasion failed on the facts.

[46] [2008] EWCA Civ 393.

[47] [2008] EWCA Civ 393 at paras 28–29.

[48] See [2008] EWCA Civ 393 at paras 24–25 per Pill LJ, and per Lloyd LJ in paras 37 and 41.

[49] See especially *Daymond v Enterprise South Devon* [2007] UKEAT 005 07 0606. See also *Salvesen v Simons* [1994] I.C.R. 409.

(d) Degrees of Blameworthiness

7–19   **"Relative moral culpability".**   Even if a claimant was fully implicated in a fraudulent scheme, or was even its instigator, it does not follow that a defence of illegality will always succeed regardless of the circumstances. In *Saunders v Edwards*[50] the claimant, who agreed to purchase a flat for £45,000, asked that the price should be recorded as £40,000, with the extra £5,000 being attributed to certain chattels included in the sale. Both parties were aware that the chattels were not worth anything approaching that sum; the claimant's aim being fraudulently to reduce the extent of his liability to stamp duty on the transaction. It so happened, however, that the defendant vendor had himself been guilty of fraudulent misrepresentation with respect to the transaction, and the flat was worth considerably less than it would have been had his representations been true. The claimant brought an action against him in tort for deceit, which the defendant sought to resist by pointing to the unlawful scheme relating to stamp duty. The Court of Appeal held that the claimant would succeed, notwithstanding his own deliberate illegality. Although Kerr LJ emphasised that the claimant's claim was based in tort rather than contract, he also insisted that "the conduct and relative moral culpability of the parties"[51] was relevant in public policy cases generally; a proposition with which Nicholls and Bingham LJJ agreed. The correctness of this approach has now been confirmed by the far-reaching decision of the Supreme Court in *Patel v Mirza*,[52] in which *Saunders v Edwards* was referred to with approval.[53]

7–20   **Proportionality.**   It will be recalled that in the well-known case of *Tinsley v Milligan* the parties had combined to conceal the true ownership of a property jointly owned by them, in order to perpetrate a deliberate fraud on the Department of Social Security, with respect to the provision of housing benefit. Although the scheme had been fully carried out the courts, up to and including the House of Lords, declined to hold that the fraud disqualified the parties from invoking the ordinary law governing property jointly purchased, once a dispute had arisen between them. An attempt by one of them to retain all the proceeds of the sale of the property for herself, on the ground that public policy precluded intervention to enforce the distribution which would otherwise have been insisted upon, was therefore unsuccessful. Although the much-criticised *reasoning* in *Tinsley v Milligan* has now been overruled by the Supreme Court in *Patel v Mirza* it is significant that the actual *decision* was *not* criticised and appears, on the contrary, to have been accepted undoubtedly as correct. It is submitted that the underlying basis of the intuition, which led six out of the nine judges who heard *Tinsley v Milligan* to decide it in the way in which they did, is best encapsulated in the judgment of Nicholls LJ in the Court of Appeal. He said[54]:

---

[50] [1987] 1 W.L.R. 1116; [1987] 2 All E.R. 651, CA.
[51] [1987] 1 W.L.R. 1116 at 1127; [1987] 2 All E.R. 651 at 660.
[52] [2016] UKSC 42.
[53] See [2016] UKSC 42 at [106] (Lord Toulson), 156 (Lord Neuberger), and 228 (Lord Sumption).
[54] [1992] Ch.310, at 326; [1992] 2 All E.R. 391, at 403 (italics supplied).

"Both parties are liable for whatever criminal penalties may flow from their fraudulent conduct. But in this case the civil court ought not, by refusing relief to one party, whether plaintiff or defendant, to impose on that party a one-sided and *disproportionate* confiscatory sanction."

The importance of proportionality as a relevant factor in illegality cases has now been emphatically affirmed by the majority of the Supreme Court in *Patel v Mirza*.

Subordinate purpose. Defrauding the revenue can never be condoned.   **7–21**
Nevertheless, the arguments for confining sanctions to the criminal law, or to analogous means of redress open to the revenue or other State authority itself, will often be somewhat stronger in this area than in many other situations involving illegality. This is because the fraudulent scheme will usually have been a very subordinate part of the overall contractual purpose. The primary purpose of the agreements in both *Saunders v Edwards* and *Tinsley v Milligan* was the pre-eminently legitimate one of securing living accommodation for owner-occupation. Accordingly, the sum representing the tax evaded, or benefit gained, will normally be a great deal smaller than the value of the contract itself. It is in those circumstances that to deprive one party of the value of the contract, which in *Tinsley*'s case would probably have been the entire capital of the person concerned, is apt to seem grossly disproportionate and hence unjust: especially when the amount forfeited is simply handed as a gratuitous windfall to the other, usually equally guilty, party.

Facts and circumstances. The sentiment seen in the *Saunders* and *Tinsley*   **7–22**
decisions is probably also reflected in the decision of the Employment Appeal Tribunal in the Scottish case of *Annandale Engineering v Samson*.[55] The defendant, who trained greyhounds, made intermittent payments to his employees out of sums given to the defendant himself by owners of greyhounds which had been successful in races. No tax was paid on these sums, and the defendant sought to rely on this fact to defend a claim for unfair dismissal brought by one of his former kennel hands. Although the payments were admittedly taxable, being analogous to tips earned by waiters in the catering trade, the Tribunal upheld a decision in favour of the applicant rejecting the defence of illegality. Lord Coulsfield, delivering the judgment of the Appeal Tribunal, concluded that "the mere making of an occasional payment without deduction of tax" did not automatically render the contract of employment unenforceable. It was necessary in each case to take into account "the particular facts and circumstances, including the amount and frequency of the payments and the reasons for which they are made".[56]

Flexibility. Notwithstanding the clarity, and salutary effect, of *Alexander v*   **7–23**
Rayson and similiar cases, it seems impossible to deny, especially after the decision of the Supreme Court in *Patel v Mirza*, that the courts retain a degree of

---

[55] [1994] I.R.L.R. 59.
[56] [1994] I.R.L.R. 59 at 60.

flexibility to disapply the general doctrine of unenforceability if the circumstances so warrant. That doctrine itself therefore seems to be more in the nature of a rebuttable presumption than an inflexible rule. There is much to be said for the way in which Bingham LJ expressed the general judicial approach in *Saunders v Edwards*, when he said[57]:

> "Where issues of illegality are raised, the courts have (as it seems to me) to steer a middle course between two unacceptable positions. On the one hand it is unacceptable that any court of law should aid or lend its authority to a party seeking to pursue or enforce an object or agreement which the law prohibits. On the other hand, it is unacceptable that the courts should, on the first indication of unlawfulness affecting any aspect of a transaction, draw up its skirts and refuse all assistance to the plaintiff, no matter how serious his loss or how disproportionate his loss to the unlawfulness of his conduct."

This passage by Bingham LJ was quoted with approval by both the majority and minority in *Patel v Mirza*.[58]

4. CORRUPT BARGAINS

7-24 **Bribery.** The making of a payment, or the intention to make a payment, in order improperly to secure preference over rivals in a competitive situation ostensibly based purely on the merits of the various bids, will result in any related contract being unenforceable at the instance of the person responsible. In *Nayyar v Sapte*,[59] decided in 2009, the claimant travel agents paid nearly £4,000 on the understanding that it would secure a lucrative concession from an airline. When the concession failed to materialise an attempt to recover the money, which had been described as a "deposit", was unsuccessful. Hamblen J said he considered that "proof of a payment which is intended to be a civil law bribe is sufficient to engage the ex turpi causa principle".[60] His Lordship added that, in the circumstances, it was unnecessary to determine whether any criminal offence had actually been committed.[61] Legislation now exists which expressly creates "offences of bribing another person".[62] Contravention of the provisions of the Bribery Act 2010 can clearly be expected to result in forfeiture of contractual rights, as well as criminal penalties of up to 10 years imprisonment.

7-25 **Procuring influence.** It has been held that an agreement to pay someone, in order to influence the outcome of a supposedly objective decision-making process, can be an unenforceable contract. In the old case of *Norman v Cole*[63] an attempt to obtain payment for trying to secure clemency for someone under sentence of death was dismissed. Lord Eldon said:

---

[57] [1987] 1 W.L.R. 1116, at 1134; [1987] 2 All E.R. 651, at 665–666.
[58] See [2016] UKSC 42 at [106] per Lord Toulson and [228] per Lord Sumption. See also per Lord Neuberger at [150].
[59] [2009] EWHC 3218.
[60] See ibid. at [118].
[61] See [2009] EWHC 3218 at [119].
[62] See the Bribery Act 2010 s1.
[63] (1800) 3 Esp. 253.

"I am of opinion that this action is not maintainable; where a person interposes his interest and good offices to procure a pardon it ought to be done gratuitously, and not for money. The doing of an act of that description should proceed from pure motives, not from pecuniary ones."

This decision was cited with approval in the early twentieth century case of *Montefiore v Menday Motor Components Co.*[64] The claimant claimed to have the ear of persons responsible for the allocation of Government finance to develop the aircraft industry, which was then in its infancy. He agreed to use his connections to try and obtain Government finance for the defendant company, which wished to develop a business of making aircraft components. In return he was promised a 10 per cent commission on the amount received. The company did, in fact, receive an allocation of capital from the Government, although it was unclear whether or not this was as a result of the claimant's efforts. The claimant sued for the commission which he had been promised, but Shearman J held that the claim would fail regardless of whether or not the allocation was as a result of the claimant's intervention. His Lordship said[65] that it was "contrary to public policy that a person should be hired for money or valuable consideration when he has access to persons of influence to use his position and interest to procure a benefit from the government". Such a contract was "illegal and void", since "it would tend to corrupt the public service".

Implications and regulation. The implications of the *Montefiore* decision **7–26** have not been explored in depth in subsequent cases.[66] The relative dearth of authority is perhaps surprising in view of the substantial industry built up in recent times by "lobbyists", and others, who promote for reward the interests of their clients in the parliamentary sphere and elsewhere. In June 2013 the Government announced that it intended to introduce a statutory register of lobbyists. The following year the Transparency of Lobbying, Non-party Campaigning and Trade Union Administration Act 2014 was passed which introduced such a register, and in 2015 the Office of the Registrar of Consultant Lobbyists was set up to administer it. There has also been much public concern over the extent to which Members of Parliament may have exposed themselves to influence by receiving payment for acting as parliamentary "advisors", or "consultants", to particular interest groups. This resulted in the setting up of the Register of Members' Interests, and more specific concerns led to the setting up of such bodies as the Committee on Standards in Public Life. The activities of Members of Parliament are not affected in any way by the 2014 Act, but if the position were ever to be fully tested, it may be that agreements whereby Members of Parliament obtain payment from particular organisations will turn out not to be enforceable contracts.[67]

---

[64] [1918] 2 K.B. 241.
[65] [1918] 2 K.B. 241, at 244–246.
[66] cf. *Kemp v Glasgow Corporation* [1920] A.C. 836.
[67] It has long been clear that a Member of Parliament cannot validly undertake, for reward, to vote in a particular way: see, per Fletcher Moulton LJ in *Osborne v Amalgamated Society of Railway Servants* [1909] 1 Ch.163 at 186, CA.

7–27   **Recovery of payments.**   Although contracts which are contrary to public policy as corrupt bargains will obviously never be enforced in the sense of an award of damages for breach, or order for specific performance, it does not follow that payments made in pursuit of the improper objective will be irrecoverable. On the contrary, the Supreme Court in *Patel v Mirza*[68] has unanimously held that such recovery will now normally be permissible as a matter of course. This far-reaching change in the law, which is dealt with below,[69] is based on the idea that such recovery should assist in discouraging, as distinct from furthering, the unlawful purpose. In so holding the Supreme Court overruled the well-known decision of Lush J in *Parkinson v College of Ambulance*.[70] In that case the claimant was persuaded to make a substantial donation to a charity by the fraudulent representation of one of its employees, that the charity could, and would, ensure that he immediately received a knighthood. When the honour was not forthcoming, and the fraud had become apparent, the claimant sued for the return of his "donation". His claim was dismissed by Lush J who had no doubt that the contract was against public policy and therefore illegal at common law.[71] "No Court", he said, "could try such an action ... with any propriety or decency".[72] It is now clear, however, that Lush J was wrong to allow his distaste at the nature of the contract to lead him to decline to draw any distinction between enforceability and restitution.[73]

5.   CONFIDENTIALITY AGREEMENTS

(a)   Payment for Silence

7–28   **Abstaining from comment.**   In *Neville v Canada News Co*[74] the defendants, who owned a newspaper, owed money to the claimant, who was a prominent and controversial business man involved in selling land in Canada. The parties agreed that the newspaper would abstain from commenting in its pages on the defendants' companies, in return for the claimant foregoing part of the debt. Although the newspaper was not a specialist financial journal, it included a column headed "Gold and Glitter" in which it purported fearlessly to give honest advice about investing in Canadian land. The claimant alleged that the defendants had published material which contravened the agreement, and sued for the balance of the debt. Atkin J, and the Court of Appeal, dismissed his claim. The owners of the newspaper had, in the words of Warrington LJ,[75] "accepted a bribe" which could inhibit them in discharging their self-espoused duty to their readers,

---

[68] [2016] UKSC 42.
[69] See Chs 17 and 18.
[70] [1925] 2 K.B. 1.
[71] Criminal liability was subsequently attached to such agreements by statute: see the Honours (Prevention of Abuses) Act 1925.
[72] [1925] 2 K.B. 1 at 13.
[73] See *Patel v Mirza* [2016] UKSC 42 at [95]-[96] (Lord Toulson), [150] (Lord Neuberger), and [245] (Lord Sumption).
[74] [1915] 3 K.B. 556. See also Ch.12, below.
[75] [1915] 3 K.B. 556 at 568.

even if the claimant's activities had been fraudulent. Pickford LJ[76] quoted with approval the words of Atkin J, who had said:

> "To my mind, for a newspaper to stipulate for a consideration that it will refrain from exercising its right of commenting upon fraudulent schemes when it is the ordinary business of the [newspaper] . . . to comment upon fraudulent schemes is in itself a stipulation which is quite contrary to public policy, and it cannot be enforced in a court of law."

(b)   Libellous Communications

Weld-Blundell v Stephens.   While the decision in *Neville v Canada News Co* is unquestionably correct, the precise extent of the principle which precludes the enforceability of contracts to remain silent about matters of legitimate interest and concern to third parties is not altogether clear. In *Weld-Blundell v Stephens*[77] the claimant employed the defendant chartered accountant to investigate the financial affairs of a company in which he was interested. The claimant gave a letter of instructions to the defendant which, owing to carelessness, was left at the company's office where it was found by the manager. The letter referred in defamatory terms to two officers of the company, and its contents were communicated by the manager to the persons mentioned in it. As a result the claimant found himself sued for libel; he relied on qualified privilege, but was found to have been malicious and was ordered to pay substantial damages. He sought to recover these damages from the defendant, contending that the latter had broken an implied term of the contract by negligently causing the contents of the confidential letter to be disclosed.

7–29

Nominal damages?   The Court of Appeal,[78] reversing Darling J,[79] held unanimously that the defendant had indeed been under a contractual duty to keep the letter secret, and emphasised that the implied term to this effect was not contrary to public policy.[80] By a majority, however, the Court confined the claimant to nominal damages for breach of the contract, on the ground that to compensate him for the libel damages which he had been compelled to pay would be "in the nature of an indemnity against the consequences of his own wilful and deliberate wrongdoing".[81] Scrutton LJ dissented with characteristic vigour, arguing that denial of substantial damages contradicted the finding in the claimant's favour on liability.[82] Nevertheless the House of Lords agreed that the claimant, having been a victim of "his own wrongful act in indulging in malicious libel",[83] should be confined to nominal damages.[84] It is noteworthy, however, that

7–30

---

[76] [1915] 3 K.B. 556 at 567.

[77] [1920] A.C. 956.

[78] [1919] 1 K.B. 520.

[79] [1918] 2 K.B. 742.

[80] [1919] 1 K.B. 520, at 527–529 (Bankes LJ); at 533–535 (Warrington LJ): and at 547–548 (Scrutton LJ).

[81] [1919] 1 K.B. 520, at 531. See also Warrington LJ at 536 referring to the dictum of Kennedy J in *Burrows v Rhodes* [1899] 1 Q.B. 816, at 833.

[82] [1919] 1 K.B. 520, at 549.

[83] [1920] A.C. 956 at 998, per Lord Wrenbury.

[84] See also *Bradstreets British v Mitchell* [1933] Ch.190.

two members of the House dissented and, since one member of the majority decided the case on a different ground,[85] this meant that there was, in effect, an even split on the present point. Viscount Finlay, in his dissenting speech, said[86]:

> "It is no part of the policy of the law that immunity should be extended to breaches of trust committed by an agent in revealing information which has been given to him in confidence as to facts on which possible claims for damages might be preferred against his principal."

7–31   **Malice.**   There is much to be said for Viscount Finlay's view. It cannot be the law that claimants will never be able to recover, as damages for breach of confidence, sums representing civil liabilities which they have themselves been compelled to discharge in favour of third parties as a result of that breach. In so far as dicta in the majority speeches suggest that such sums will always be irrecoverable on a priori grounds, they are too wide.[87] There is no absolute objection to a claimant seeking to recover, in an action for breach of contract, damages already awarded against him. Indemnities against civil liability, including tortious liability, are routinely enforced. Claims on liability insurance policies are an obvious example. On the other hand, however, contractual attempts to conceal serious wrongdoing must be contrary to public policy and unenforceable. If the result in *Weld-Blundell v Stephens* can be supported at all, it is probably on the basis that the claimant had been found to have been malicious. There seems to be no reason why a claimant who has been compelled to pay compensation for libel, in circumstances in which he was largely free from blame,[88] should not be able, in an appropriate case, to recover those damages in an action for breach of confidence.[89] Contracts of indemnity in respect of libel are enforceable by statute, unless the claimant knew that the matter was libellous and did not believe that a good defence existed.[90]

(c)   Concealment of Criminality

7–32   *Howard v Odham's Press.*   If a defendant agrees to treat as confidential information to the effect that the claimant had engaged in criminal behaviour, it must be doubtful whether the latter can recover, unless the circumstances are exceptional, substantial damages from the defendant if the agreement is broken and disclosure takes place.[91] In one case, *Howard v Odham's Press*,[92] the Court of

---

[85] Lord Sumner considered that the particular sequence of events broke the chain of causation between the defendant's negligent breach of confidence and the claimant's loss: see [1920] A.C. 956, at 979, et seq.

[86] [1920] A.C. 956, at 968. See also, per Lord Parmoor, at 994–995.

[87] See e.g. [1920] A.C. 956 per Lord Wrenbury at 997: "Weld-Blundell . . . suffered no damage at all. He had to pay money, but a defendant is in no sense damaged by being compelled by legal process to satisfy his legal obligation".

[88] e.g. in circumstances involving an accepted offer to make amends under Defamation Act 1996 s.2.

[89] In *Saunders v Seyd and Kelly's Credit Index* (1896) 75 L.T. 193, a Court of Appeal consisting of Lindley, Lopes and Rigby LJJ appeared, obiter, to contemplate that a contract not to disclose a libellous communication might be binding in some circumstances.

[90] See the Defamation Act 1952 s.11.

[91] cf. *A. v Hoyden* (1984) 156 C.L.R. 532. But see also *Kerridge v Simmonds* (1906) 4 C.L.R. 253, discussed in Ch. 8, below (compromising of prosecutions for very minor offences).

Appeal did contemplate a possible situation in which such a claim might succeed. The observations were, however, obiter and are open to question. In the case itself the defendants agreed not to disclose that the claimant had confessed to fraud. The consideration for this agreement was not the payment of money but the giving of information by the claimant, which it was hoped would enable the defendants to prevent the commission of further frauds against them.[93] Subsequently, however, relations between the parties went sour, partly because the defendants believed that the claimant had not been as co-operative as he had promised to be in helping to clear up the frauds. As a result the defendants took the view that they were no longer bound by the obligation of secrecy, and disclosed the claimant's confession to third parties. The claimant's employment prospects suffered as a result, and he sued for breach of contract to recover this financial loss.

Narrow ground. The Court of Appeal held that the claim would fail, but did so on very narrow grounds. The agreement was held to be unenforceable for illegality only on the ground that it required the defendants to keep silent about frauds already committed, and possibly to be committed in the future, against *third parties*. The implication was that had the defendants merely agreed in return for information to stay silent about past or future frauds against *themselves*, the contract would have been enforceable. Indeed Greene LJ said[94]: 7–33

> "It may well be permissible for a person against whom frauds have been and are intended to be committed to give a promise of secrecy in order to obtain information relating to them which will enable him, by taking steps himself, to prevent the commission of future frauds."

This dictum is difficult to follow. It is probable that bargains similiar in principle to that in *Howard v Odham's Press* are frequently made by the police in order to procure informers, and to extract confessions to other offences. It seems to be clear, however, that these agreements do not have any binding force.[95] Why should they become enforceable contracts simply because they are made with prospective victims?[96] On the other hand, if the alleged criminal behaviour had been relatively minor, had occurred long ago and had not resulted in conviction,

---

[92] [1938] 1 K.B. 1. There is a useful note on the decision at first instance, which was, however, reversed by the Court of Appeal in (1936–7) 50 Harv. L.R. 693.

[93] The frauds took the form of obtaining prizes in a crossword competition by removing the correct solution from entries submitted by bona fide competitors. Although apparently only misdemeanours at common law, such frauds would now seem to involve the commission of an offence contrary to the Theft Act 1968.

[94] [1938] 1 K.B. 1 at 42.

[95] Such agreements should not be confused with agreements by the police to pay informers for information received, unrelated to criminal activities by the informers themselves. It appears that such claims might succeed in clear cases. See, e.g. per Laws LJ in *Carnduff v Rock* [2001] EWCA Civ. 680 ("I do not say there can never be a claim in contract by an informer against a police force to recover agreed remuneration for the delivery of information"). Although the Court of Appeal (by a majority) struck out the particular claim in *Carnduff's* case, in an earlier case the Court allowed a claim by an informer to proceed: see *Savage v Chief Constable of Hampshire* [1997] 1 W.L.R. 1061.

[96] Quaere whether the agreement in *Howard's* case would now, in any event, be unenforceable pursuant to the Criminal Law Act 1967 s.5(1) (concealing "a relevant offence" for "consideration"—a term which is not limited to the taking of money and could therefore extend to receiving information). On s.5(1) see, generally, Ch.8, below.

the possibility of an enforceable claim for breach of a contract of confidentiality should not be ruled out. The issue could arise in a situation in which a claimant lost his job as a result of some youthful indiscretion being revealed. Since actual convictions are in the public domain, however, it is difficult to see how a claim for damages could ever be based on disclosure of such a conviction, unless the conviction was a "spent" one for the purposes of the Rehabilitation of Offenders Act 1974. Indeed the provisions of that Act might provide a useful analogy if a case *should* ever arise in which an unconvicted claimant seeks substantial damages for disclosure of his activities in breach of confidence.

7–34   **Stifling prosecutions.**   If there is any question of a contract being entered into to conceal information in order to prevent a prosecution from taking place, the enforceability of the agreement presents special difficulties which are dealt with in another chapter.[97]

(d)   Disclosure and the Public Interest

7–35   **Where activity was neither criminal nor tortious.**   The broad question of the extent to which public interest may be relied upon as a defence to the disclosure of information belongs to the law relating to breach of confidence, and is beyond the scope of this book.[98] Nevertheless, it is now clear that public policy may in some cases bar a claim based on breach of confidence even if the revealed activity was not criminal, or even tortious. In *Att. Gen. v Guardian Newspapers (No.2)*,[99] which arose out of the publication in the 1980s of a book called *Spycatcher*, Lord Goff of Chieveley referred with approval to a passage from the judgment of Griffiths LJ in the Court of Appeal in the earlier case of *Lion Laboratories v Evans*.[100] His Lordship had said that he was "quite satisfied that the defence of public interest is now well-established in actions for breach of confidence" and continued:

> "I can see no sensible reason why this defence should be limited to cases in which there has been wrongdoing on the part of the plaintiffs. I believe that the so-called iniquity rule evolved because in most cases where the facts justified a publication in breach of confidence the plaintiff had behaved so disgracefully or criminally that it was judged in the public interest that his behaviour should be exposed. No doubt it is in such circumstances that the defence will usually arise, but it is not difficult to think of instances where, although there has been no wrongdoing on the part of the plaintiff, it may be vital in the public interest to publish a part of his confidential information."

7–36   **"Disclosure of iniquity".**   The *Lion Laboratories* case concerned an unsuccessful attempt to prevent employees of a company, which manufactured breath-testing machines used by the police, from disclosing serious reservations within the company as to the accuracy and reliability of the machines. The public

---

[97] See Ch.8, below.
[98] See Gurry, *Breach of Confidence* 2nd edn, Aplin, Bentley, Johnson and Malynicz (eds), (Oxford University Press, 2012) Ch.15; Cripps, *The Legal Implications of Disclosure in the Public Interest* 2nd edn, (Sweet & Maxwell, 1994), Ch.2. Cf. Public Interest Disclosure Act 1998.
[99] See [1990] 1 A.C. 109, at 282; [1988] 3 All E.R. 545, at 659.
[100] [1985] Q.B. 526, at 550; [1984] 2 All E.R. 417, at 432–433.

interest in disclosure has also been applied to "medical quackeries of a sort which may be dangerous if practised behind closed doors".[101] The reference of Griffiths LJ, quoted above from *Lion Laboratories v Evans*, to the "so-called iniquity rule" is derived from the old case of *Gartside v Outram*,[102] which was one of the originating authorities in this area. The claimants sought an injunction to restrain a former employee from disclosing their business methods to third parties. The defendant argued that those methods were fraudulent, and that he was therefore entitled to disclose them. His case was that the claimants, while acting as brokers for the sale of wool, were in the habit of misrepresenting to their clients the prices at which the wool had been sold, and themselves pocketing the difference between the real and fictitious prices. The defendant filed interrogatories in support of his plea, but the defendants declined to answer them on the ground that the defence itself was misconceived. Wood VC overruled the claimants' objections and asserted the legitimacy of the defence in strong terms. "The true doctrine", he said, "is that there is no confidence as to the disclosure of iniquity".

Initial Services v Putterill. This "vivid" statement was quoted with approval by Lord Denning MR in the important modern case of *Initial Services v Putterill*.[103] An attempt was made in this case to restrain an employee of a laundry business from disclosing that his employers had participated in secret agreements with other firms to keep up prices, contrary to the Restrictive Trade Practices Act 1956. Such agreements were unenforceable unless they were registered with the Registrar of Restrictive Trading Agreements, and made subject to the jurisdiction of the Restrictive Practices Court. The employee's defence was that disclosure of the agreements was in the public interest, and that he was therefore entitled to disclose them despite the contractual relationship with his employers. The Court of Appeal rejected the claimants' attempt to have the defence struck out. Lord Denning MR rejected a suggestion that the defence "was limited to the proposed or contemplated commission of a crime or a civil wrong" and continued[104]:

7–37

> "I should have thought that that was too limited. The exception should extend to crimes, frauds and misdeeds, both those actually committed as well as those in contemplation, provided always—and this is essential—that the disclosure is justified in the public interest ... The disclosure must, I should think, be to one who has a proper interest to receive the information ... There may be cases where the misdeed is of such a character that the public interest may demand, or at least excuse, publication on a broader field, even to the press."

The Public Interest Disclosure Act 1998. The cases already discussed should be read in the light of the provisions of the Public Interest Disclosure Act 1998. These provisions are limited to protecting employees, who reasonably believe that it is in the public interest to disclose matters relating to their employment,

7–38

---

[101] See *Hubbard v Vosper* [1972] 2 Q.B. 84, at 96; [1972] 1 All E.R. 1023, at 1029, CA. See also *Beloff v Pressdram Ltd* [1973] 1 All E.R. 241, at 260, per Ungoed-Thomas J: "matters ... destructive of the country or its people, including matters medically dangerous to the public; and doubtless other misdeeds of similiar gravity".

[102] (1856) 26 LJ Ch. 113.

[103] [1968] 1 Q.B. 396.

[104] [1968] 1 Q.B. 396, at 405–406; [1967] 2 All E.R. 145 at 148.

from victimisation by their employers in the event of such disclosure. The matters listed are therefore not directly relevant to attempts to use the law to restrain disclosure on grounds of confidentiality, nevertheless they provide some indication of the kinds of situation in which the court is unlikely to be prepared to enforce secrecy. The list is as follows[105]:

(a)   that a criminal offence has been committed, is being committed or is likely to be committed,

(b)   that a person has failed, is failing or is likely to fail to comply with any legal obligation to which he is subject,

(c)   that a miscarriage of justice has occurred, is occurring or is likely to occur,

(d)   that the health or safety of any individual has been, is being or is likely to be endangered,

(e)   that the environment has been, is being or is likely to be damaged...

In matters not included in this list striking the appropriate balance between the protection of confidentiality on the one hand, and preventing the concealment of matters which should be revealed on the other,[106] will not be straightforward in borderline cases. The overall impression left by the authorities, however, is that a claim based upon confidentiality is unlikely to meet with a particularly sympathetic response if the claimant's activities can be said to have been characterised by a significant degree of impropriety, or otherwise to be a matter of legitimate public concern.[107]

---

[105] See s.1 of the Public Interest Disclosure Act 1998 (and s.17 of the Enterprise and Regulatory Reform Act 2013) inserting s.43B into the Employment Rights Act 1996.

[106] See *Att.-Gen. v Guardian Newspapers (No.2)* [1990] 1 A.C. 109, at 282; [1988] 3 All E.R. 545, at 659 per Lord Goff of Chieveley.

[107] cf. dictum, per counsel, arguendo, in *Annesley v Earl of Anglesea* (1743) 17 State Trials 1139 at 1229, cited with approval in *Gartside v Outram* and *Initial Services v Putterill*: "... no private obligations can dispense with that universal one which lies on every member of the society to discover every design which may be formed, contrary to the laws of the society, to destroy the public welfare".

CHAPTER 8

COMPROMISING THE LEGAL PROCESS

1. CATEGORIES OF CASES

Wide scope.   A vital area of public policy is that which denies enforceability to   **8–01**
contracts likely to undermine the integrity of the legal process.[1] It is impossible to
subject the agreements which are invalid on this ground to any water-tight
classification, since the courts retain their inherent jurisdiction to strike down
novel forms of objectionable contract whenever they appear.[2] The existing cases
do, however, fall into a number of broadly defined categories which raise specific
issues. The focus of the present chapter is largely upon issues arising out of
agreements to stifle prosecutions, while a following chapter deals at length with
the law relating to maintenance and champerty.[3] Another category of cases
concerns the enforceability of agreements which might weaken the force of the
bail system in criminal proceedings. It is now clear, from well-established
authorities of long-standing, that such practices are contrary to public policy.[4] In
Herman v Jeuchner[5] a defendant in a criminal case, who transferred funds to
someone on a temporary basis so that the recipient could become his surety, was
unsuccessful when he sought to get the money back afterwards.[6] Moreover, the
principle is not confined to funds provided by the defendant himself, but also
extends to agreements by third parties to indemnify the surety.[7]

Ousting the jurisdiction.   The right of access to the courts has always been   **8–02**
jealously guarded by the common law, and the general principle remains that
contracts which seek to oust the jurisdiction of the courts are invalid.[8] Ever since
the famous decision of the House of Lords in *Scott v Avery*[9] however, it has been
possible for parties to bind themselves to submit their disputes to arbitration, at
least in the first instance. Precisely how far arbitration procedures can be made
exclusive of judicial intervention is now the subject of detailed statutory

---

[1] cf. per Lord Lyndhurst in *Egerton v Earl Brownlow* (1853) 4 H.L. Cas. 1 at 163: "Any contract or
engagement having a tendency, however slight, to affect the administration of justice, is illegal and
void".
[2] See, e.g. *Dann v Curzon* (1910) 104 L.T. 66 (institution of bogus proceedings as a publicity stunt).
[3] See Ch.9, below.
[4] cf. *R v Porter* [1910] 1 K.B. 369 (agreement between accused and his surety to indemnify the latter
is a criminal conspiracy).
[5] (1885) 15 Q.B.D. 561.
[6] See also *Re Gurwicz* [1919] 1 K.B. 675.
[7] See *Consolidated Exploration and Finance Co v Musgrave* [1900] 1 Ch. 37.
[8] See *Scott v Avery* (1855) 5 H.L. Cas. 811.
[9] (1855) 5 H.L. Cas. 811.

provisions,[10] and is beyond the scope of this book. The law governing access to the courts in matrimonial disputes also produced a number of important twentieth century appellate decisions on attempts at ouster of the jurisdiction.[11] This area too, however, is now governed largely by its own detailed statute[12] and case-law, exposition of which properly belongs to works on Family Law rather than Illegality.

8–03 **Out of court settlements.** An issue somewhat analogous to that of ouster of the jurisdiction is raised by the situation in which a case involving a defence of illegality is settled out of court. Can the defendant seek subsequently to deny the validity of the compromise, and revive the defence, on the ground that illegality is beyond the reach of the parties and therefore cannot be made the subject of a binding compromise? The point was considered in *Binder v Alachouzos*,[13] in which such an attempt to evade a settlement, and reopen the question of illegality, received short shrift from the Court of Appeal. The original claim had been one for the recovery of a debt, which the defendant had alleged was unenforceable under the Moneylenders Acts. The claimant, however, denied that he was a moneylender, and it was this factual dispute which was settled at the door of the court. A new agreement was drawn up as a result, the effect of which was largely to give the defendant more time to pay. When the claimant sought to enforce the new agreement, the defendant again sought to argue that the claimant was a moneylender and that the settlement was unenforceable. The Court of Appeal refused to entertain the argument, and upheld a summary judgment in the claimant's favour. "In such a case", said Roskill LJ,[14] "it seems to me clear that the court should encourage and when appropriate enforce any bona fide compromise arrived at". *Binder's* case should not, however, be interpreted too widely. The Court of Appeal emphasised that the dispute had merely been one of fact rather than law, and that both parties had had the benefit of advice from competent lawyers. The factual basis for the defendant's contention also appears to have been relatively weak.[15] But in any event, it would not be right to allow the public interest, as reflected in the principles of illegality, to be circumvented merely by an agreement between the parties.[16] If there is any serious likelihood of that interest being adversely affected, it would be the duty of the court, notwithstanding the undoubted strength of the policy of encouraging settlements, to allow the issue to be reopened.[17]

---

[10] See the Arbitration Act 1996.

[11] See, e.g. *Hyman v Hyman* [1929] A.C. 601; *Bennett v Bennett* [1952] 1 K.B. 249; *Goodinson v Goodinson* [1954] 2 Q.B. 118.

[12] See especially, the Matrimonial Causes Act 1973.

[13] [1972] 2 Q.B. 151.

[14] [1972] 2 Q.B. 151 at 160.

[15] [1972] 2 Q.B. 151 at 158–159, per Phillimore LJ.

[16] See *IMG Pension Plan Trustees v German* [2009] EWHC 2785 per Arnold J. at [230].

[17] cf. per Lord Denning M.R. at 158: "It cannot be reopened *unless there is evidence that the lender has taken undue advantage of the situation of the borrower*. In this case no undue advantage was taken" (italics supplied).

2. CONTRACTS TO STIFLE PROSECUTIONS

(a) Introduction

Difficult questions.   The issues which have produced one of the most   **8–04**
substantial bodies of case-law relating to the administration of justice, are those
arising out of contractual attempts to prevent criminal prosecutions from taking
place. In *Clubb v Hutson*,[18] Erle CJ observed that: "It is to the interest of the
public that the suppression of a prosecution should not be made the matter of a
private bargain". Thus, in *Jones v Merionethshire Permanent Benefit Building
Society*,[19] the secretary of the claimant society embezzled moneys paid to him on
its behalf; and a contract whereby his relatives promised to repay the money, in
return for an agreement not to prosecute, was held to be unenforceable for
illegality. The principle exemplified by this decision has generated a number of
difficult questions. These include the extent to which the existence and nature of
pre-existing liabilities, involving one or both of the parties, may affect the legality
of the agreement. This question is itself closely connected with that concerning
the precise relationship between the concepts of illegality and duress. Before
examining these issues, however, important questions arising out of legislative
reforms of the criminal law in the 1960s, which still await authoritative
resolution, will be addressed first. These questions will be considered against the
background of the pre-existing law, without which the likely consequences of the
reforms for the law of contract cannot be understood or assessed.

(b) Offences of Differing Gravity

Felonies and misdemeanours.   The Criminal Law Act 1967 s.1(2) provides as   **8–05**
follows:

> ". . . on all matters on which a distinction has previously been made between felony and
> misdemeanour . . . the law and practice in relation to all offences recognizable under the law of
> England and Wales . . . shall be the law and practice applicable at the commencement of this
> Act in relation to misdemeanour."

At common law it was a settled rule that all agreements to compromise
prosecutions for felony were unenforceable for illegality. The position as
regarded misdemeanours, however, was rather less certain. It was sometimes held
that a prosecution for a misdemeanour which was merely of a "private", as
distinct from a "public" nature could be validly compromised. If the distinction
deployed in these old cases is still valid, it will be evident that s.1(2) renders it
potentially relevant to the validity of any contract to compromise a criminal
prosecution.

---

[18] (1865) 18 C.B.N.S. 414 at 417.
[19] [1892] 1 Ch.173.

8–06   **"Public" and "private" offences.**   In *Johnson v Ogilby*[20] and *Drage v Ibberson*,[21] it was held that prosecutions for common law frauds had been validly compromised, although in the former it is clear that Lord Chancellor Talbot had doubts about his own decision.[22] Moreover, these two eighteenth century decisions were criticised in the better known nineteenth century case of *Keir v Leeman*.[23] Several individuals were alleged to have committed the misdemeanours of riot and assault, while impeding an attempt to levy execution of a judgment debt on the goods of one of them. The defendant third parties promised to pay the balance outstanding on the debt, in consideration of the claimant's agreeing not to prosecute for these offences. The Court of Exchequer Chamber refused, however, to enforce this agreement. Tindal CJ, delivering the judgment of that court, said that had it not been for the authorities to the contrary, he would have had no doubt that "any compromise of a misdemeanour, or indeed of any public offence, [could] be otherwise than illegal".[24] There is inevitably a sense in which the use of the word "public" in this passage begs the question at issue. Moreover, the observation, which was clearly obiter, has to be read in the light of the basis upon which the case was actually decided. This was clearly expressed by Lord Denman CJ in the Court of Queen's Bench. His Lordship said that "the result of the cases makes it clear that some indictments for misdemeanour may be compromised, and equally so that some cannot". He then continued[25]:

> "In the present instance the offence is not confined to personal injury, but is accompanied with riot and obstruction of a public officer in the execution of his duty. These are matters of public concern, and therefore not legally the subject of a compromise."[26]

Similarly, in *Windhill Local Board of Health v Vint*,[27] a compromise of a prosecution for public nuisance arising out of an obstruction of a public road was held to be illegal.[28] Cotton LJ observed that the prosecution involved "a matter which concerned the public" and that the obstruction had been "an interference with the public highway in a very serious manner".[29]

---

[20] (1734) 3 P. Wins. 277.

[21] (1798) 2 Esp. 643.

[22] "Then the Lord Chancellor started another point, viz., that this was a criminal prosecution; and the agreement being to stifle a criminal prosecution, was therefore not to be executed in equity" (see (1734) P. Wms. 277 at 279). After further argument by counsel, however, the report states simply that "this objection was no further insisted on".

[23] (1844) 6 Q.B. 308 (Court of Queen's Bench); (1846) 9 Q.B. 371 (Court of Exchequer Chamber).

[24] (1844) 6 Q.B. 308 at 395.

[25] (1844) 6 Q.B. 308 at 322.

[26] See also *Collins v Blantern* (1767) 2 Wils. 341 in which an agreement to slide a prosecution for the common law misdemeanour of perjury, "a crime most detrimental to the commonwealth", was held to be illegal.

[27] (1890) 45 Ch. D. 351.

[28] cf. *Fallowes v Taylor* (1798) 7 T.R. 475.

[29] See (1890) 45 Ch. D. 351 at 362.

Valid compromises.[30]   In a sense, of course, all criminal offences are, by   **8–07**
definition, matters of public interest.[31] In practice, however, very minor offences
will not result in a prosecution unless the victim chooses to press charges. It
would be surprising if a system as pragmatic as the common law did not permit
such victims deliberately to refrain from bringing criminal proceedings, in return
for the promise of reparation. Even in *Keir v Leeman* Tindal CJ accepted that the
victim "in the case of an assault . . . may . . . undertake not to prosecute on behalf
of the public".[32] In *Fisher v Apollinaris*[33] it was held that a prosecution, which
had been brought by a company for the false use of its trade mark, had been
validly compromised. "This is one of those misdemeanours", said James LJ,[34]
"where the person injured has the choice between a civil and a criminal remedy".
He continued: "Offences of this kind are indictable, but it is not against the policy
of our law to allow the injured person to enter a compromise with regard to
them".[35]

Kerridge v Simmonds.   Although *Fisher v Apollinaris* has not gone   **8–08**
uncriticised,[36] it was adopted emphatically by the High Court of Australia, just
over a hundred years ago, in what is probably the most important twentieth
century consideration of the point by an appellate court in a common law
jurisdiction. In *Kerridge v Simmonds*[37] the defendant agreed under seal to make
monthly payments to a former mistress, one of the conditions of the deed being
that the claimant would withdraw criminal proceedings, apparently for libel,
which she had instituted against him. When the claimant sought to enforce the
agreement, the defendant argued that it was one to "compound a prosecution" and
hence illegal; he emphasised that *criminal* libel involves "a strong element of
public injury, the danger of provoking a breach of the peace".[38] Nevertheless the
High Court held unanimously that there was no objection to the compromise of
the prosecution, and that the deed was therefore enforceable. "I am of the
opinion", said Griffith CJ, "that it is not unlawful for a person defamed, or who

---

[30] In "Contracts to Stifle Prosecutions" (1974) 3 Anglo-American Law Review 472, I argued that the
distinction between "public" and "private" offences was untenable, but I am now persuaded that this
view was wrong: see A. H. Hudson "Compromises of Criminal Liability" (1980) 43 M.L.R. 532,
especially at 538.
[31] The distinction between public and private offences has been rejected in New Zealand. See
Polymer Developments Group v Tilialo [2002] 3 N.Z.L.R. 258 in which a contract to stifle a
prosecution was held to be an illegal contract, but in which relief was granted under the New Zealand
Illegal Contracts Act 1970. On this Act see below, Ch.20.
[32] See (1846) 9 Q.B. 371 at 395.
[33] (1875) 10 Ch. App. 297.
[34] (1875) 10 Ch. App. 297 at 302.
[35] (1875) 10 Ch. App. 297 at 303, per Mellish LJ: "Such compromises are constantly made before
criminal Courts in cases of assault or libel . . . and it has never been considered that there was
anything wrong in such transactions".
[36] For criticism of an oblique dictum of James LJ, relating to indictments for highway nuisances, see,
per Stirling J at first instance in *Windhill Local Board of Health v Vint* (1890) 45 Ch. D. 351 at
359–360.
[37] (1906) 4 C.L.R. 253.
[38] See, per counsel, *arguendo*, in [1906] 4 C.L.R. 253 at 255.

has sustained purely personal injury, to withdraw a prosecution already instituted for such an offence, or to agree not to initiate such a prosecution".[39]

8–09 **Small number of cases.** In practice the number of cases in which compromises will be accepted by the courts as having given rise to valid contracts, with an enforceable quid pro quo, is likely to be very small; and any potential uncertainty inherent in the distinguishing of "public" from "private" offences is unlikely to be significant. Nevertheless, the existence of the possibility at least means that those defendants, who might have otherwise have been able to avoid legitimate agreements on a technicality, will be unable to do so.[40] Moreover, since the right surrendered by the compromise is normally limited to the freedom to bring a private prosecution, with the rights of the public prosecuting authorities unaffected,[41] there is no danger of serious criminality going unpunished as a result of compromises.[42]

(c) Concealing an Arrestable Offence

8–10 **"Making good of loss or injury".** The Criminal Law Act 1967 s.5(1) provides that:

> "Where a person has committed a relevant offence,[43] any other person who, knowing or believing that the offence or some other relevant offence has been committed, and that he has information which might be of material assistance in securing the prosecution or conviction of an offender for it, accepts or agrees to accept for not disclosing that information *any consideration other than the making good of loss or injury caused by that offence, or the making of reasonable compensation for that loss or injury*, shall be liable on conviction on indictment to imprisonment for not more than two years."[44]

This section was passed in order to replace, by a new offence, the old offences of misprision of felony and compounding of felony, which had been abolished as a result of the assimilation of the law relating to felonies to that relating to misdemeanours.[45] The crime of misprision was apparently committed by any person who, with knowledge of the fact that a felony had been committed, merely refrained from disclosing that information to the authorities.[46] It was not necessary for the defendant to have accepted any consideration, in return for his silence, before this offence could be committed and misprision was, therefore, of no interest to the law of contract. The offence of compounding, on the other hand, was only committed by a person who did accept consideration as the price of

---

[39] [1906] 4 C.L.R. 253 at 260.
[40] cf. per Higgins J in *Kerridge v Simmonds* [1906] 4 C.L.R. 253 at 263: "I am glad to find that, in spite of the industrious research of counsel for the appellant, no case has been found which obliges us to hold that which is against common sense".
[41] See, per Griffith CJ in *Kerridge v Simmonds* [1906] 4 C.L.R. 253 at 259.
[42] See A. H. Hudson, "Compromises of Criminal Liability" (1980) 43 M.L.R. 532.
[43] Section 4(1A) of the Act provides that a "relevant offence" is one for which the sentence is fixed by law or for which an offender can be sentenced to five years imprisonment:
[44] Italics supplied.
[45] i.e. Criminal Law Act 1967 s.1(2), see above.
[46] See *Sykes v DPP* [1962] A.C. 528; C.K. Allen, "Misprision" (1962) 78 L.Q.R. 40.

keeping his knowledge to himself,[47] and its relationship with the law of contract was therefore more direct. The offence created by s.5(1) is, however, noticeably narrower in scope than the old law on compounding which it replaces. It is not an offence to accept consideration, if this only takes the form of the making good of any loss or injury caused by the crime which is kept from disclosure.

Some contracts validated?   The careful limitation upon the extent of criminal liability raises the question whether s.5(1) may have validated impliedly some of those agreements to stifle prosecutions which amounted previously to illegal contracts.[48] On one view an agreement to stifle a prosecution will now be an enforceable contract, provided that the consideration consists only of making good the loss caused by the offence to the victim.[49] Moreover, this will be the case irrespective of the gravity of the offence in question. It is submitted that this is not the law. It is difficult to believe that the victim of a murder attempt, who agrees to accept compensation in return for his not going to the police, enters into a legally enforceable contract. It does not follow from the removal of criminal sanctions, that the bar on contractual enforceability has also been removed.[50] Whenever the court refuses, for reasons of "public policy", to enforce a contract, it is choosing to discourage undesirable activities indirectly when the legislature has declined to discourage them directly by the imposition of criminal liability. Such liability might be too harsh or inappropriate for other reasons.[51] Indeed the Criminal Law Act 1967 does itself illustrate, in another context involving illegality, the importance of the distinction between criminal and civil law. The Act abolishes criminal and tortious liability in respect of the old common law offences of maintenance and champerty.[52] It provides expressly, however, that this abolition is not to affect the common law whereby contracts involving maintenance and champerty are treated as unenforceable for illegality.[53] Section

8–11

---

[47] See Smith and Hogan, *Criminal Law* (London: Sweet & Maxwell, 1965), pp.543–544.
[48] See the various views expressed in *Chitty on Contracts*, 32nd edn (London: Sweet & Maxwell, 2015), para.16-046; Treitel, *The Law of Contract*, edited by Peel, 14th edn (London: Sweet & Maxwell, 2015), para.11-046 (pp.556-557); *Cheshire, Fifoot and Furmston on Contract*, edited by Furmston, 16th edn, (Oxford University Press, 2012), pp.470-471; *Anson's Law of Contract*, (30th edn, Beatson, Burrows and Cartwright eds., Oxford University Press 2016), p.421.
[49] See A.H. Hudson, "Contractual Compromises of Criminal Liability" (1980) 43 M.L.R. 532.
[50] See, per Mason J in *A. v Hayden* (1984) 156 C.L.R. 532 at 555–557 (High Court of Australia).
[51] For a very clear statement of the rationale of the law's refusal to enforce contracts which it deems to be contrary to public policy even though they do not contravene the criminal law see J. R. Lucas, *The Principles of Politics* (Oxford University Press, 1966), pp.346–351.
[52] Criminal Law Act 1967 s.14(1).
[53] Criminal Law Act 1967 s.14(2).

5(1) of the Criminal Law Act 1967 was intended simply to improve the criminal law and to reduce its severity.[54] There is no good reason for supposing that it has done anything more.[55]

(d)   Existing Liabilities

8–12   **Civil and criminal proceedings.**   In many of the cases in which an attempt to stifle a prosecution is alleged, the party seeking to avoid the contract on this ground will already owe money to the person who is seeking to enforce it. The defendant will typically have agreed to provide security to support an existing liability to the claimant, which he has incurred by way of criminal activity such as fraud or embezzlement. If the contract for the giving of security is supported by consideration which merely takes the form of an undertaking not to take civil action to recover the amount already due, it will clearly be valid and enforceable. Since, however, an undertaking not to proceed against a defendant in such circumstances will often be given in vague terms, it may be very difficult to decide whether or not the agreement did in fact extend to criminal as well as civil proceedings.

8–13   **"A just and bona fide debt".**   In *Ward v Lloyd*[56] the defendant had given security to the claimant for money which he owed to him. In an attempt to avoid this security, it was contended that it had been given in consideration of a promise not to prosecute the defendant for embezzlement. The claimant denied that he had made any such promise, however, and the attempt failed. Coltman J said[57]:

> "It is true that threats were used by the plaintiff, which may have influenced the defendant. It is possible that he may have hoped that, if he gave the security, he would not be prosecuted. In the absence, however, of an agreement, express or necessarily implied, to that effect, there is no ground for setting the warrant of attorney aside. Such an agreement is not to be inferred from hasty expressions used by a man when seeking to obtain security for a just debt."

Ward v Lloyd was applied in the similar case of *Flower v Sadler*,[58] in which Cotton LJ observed that "there is a distinction between getting a security for a debt from the debtor himself and getting it from a third person who is under no obligation to the creditor". His Lordship concluded that "the doctrine contended for does not apply, where a just and bona fide debt actually exists, where there is good consideration for giving a security, and where the transaction between the

---

[54] It might be suggested that the absence of any similar express provision in relation to the abolition of the offence of compounding implies, by contrast, that contractual unenforceability was intended to be abrogated. The better view, however, is that the legislature never addressed the effect of that abolition upon the law of contract, and that the matter should therefore be decided on general principles.

[55] The 7th report of the Criminal Law Revision Committee (Cmnd. 2659), which formed the basis of the 1967 Act, made no recommendation as to the law of contract in connection with the abolition of compounding.

[56] (1843) 6 Man. & G. 785.

[57] (1843) 6 Man. & G. 785, at 790. cf. *Wallace v Hardacre* (1807) 1 Camp. 45, per Lord Ellenborough at 46.

[58] See (1882) 10 Q.B. 572 at 576.

parties involves a civil liability as well as, possibly, a criminal act". It is submitted, however, that these last observations should be treated with caution. It is going too far to suggest that no transaction can ever be unenforceable for illegality merely because it relates to an existing debt between the parties. Obviously the debt itself, if genuine, will always provide the creditor with a cause of action against the debtor regardless of what he does to enforce it, but it does not follow that a separate transaction between the parties giving the creditor security, or quantifying the debtor's liability, will necessarily be devoid of any taint of illegality.

No bargaining about prosecution.   Whether any additional security, for example, was given by the debtor himself or by a third party, the crucial question is: was any bargain struck as regards prosecution? In *Whitmore v Farley*,[59] Fry J observed,[60] in reaching a decision later upheld by the Court of Appeal, that "in the cases of embezzlement by a servant . . . a master might have had an action for money had and received against the servant", but concluded that "the co-existence of a right of action with a private offence does not render a compromise of a public offence legal". *Whitmore v Farley* was a case in which the security held to be illegal had been provided by the debtor's wife, and not by the debtor himself. But in *Clubb v Hutson*[61] the principle seems to have been applied to defeat an action on a promissory note brought directly by the creditor against the debtor. The defendant alleged that he had given the note in consideration of the claimant's agreeing not to prosecute him for obtaining money by false pretences. Counsel for the claimant argued that, as the person injured by the commission of the offence, his client could sue on the promissory note; nevertheless the Court rejected the argument, holding that the offence was not one "in which the personal interest of the aggrieved party alone is concerned".[62]

8–14

A presumption?   On the whole, the courts do appear anxious that the special difficulties which face creditors in cases of this type should not go unrecognised. Such claimants can hardly be expected to go out of their way to emphasise that they do *not* intend to bring criminal proceedings when seeking, for example, to extract a promise of security. The better view would therefore appear to be that, where there is a valid civil debt owed by the defendant to the claimant, there is a presumption to the effect that any undertaking not to proceed against the defendant applied only to civil proceedings and not to criminal. This presumption can, however, be rebutted by clear evidence to the opposite effect.[63] In *Jones v Merionethshire Permanent Benefit Building Society*,[64] Bowen LJ put it as follows:

8–15

---

[59] (1880) 43 L.T. (N.S.) 192, per Fry J; (1881) 45 L.T. (N.S.) 99, CA.
[60] See (1880) 43 L.T. (N.S.) 192 at 197.
[61] (1865) 18 C.B. (N.S.) 414.
[62] (1865) 18 C.B. (N.S.) 414 at 417, per Erle CJ.
[63] See e.g. *Lound v Grimwade* (1888) 39 Ch. D. 605.
[64] [1892] 1 Ch:173 at 185.

> "It is a circumstance which may be lawfully taken into consideration that the offender has done his best himself, or with the assistance of his friends, to make good his wrong. But the test is, what is the moral duty of the person who has been injured to himself and others? He must make no bargain about that. If reparation takes the form of a bargain then, to my mind, the bargain is one which the court will not enforce."

8–16   **Third parties.**   Despite the broad language of Bowen LJ in this passage, with his reference to the assistance of friends, it would not seem appropriate to apply the presumption in favour of creditors to situations in which a promise is made to repay is made by a third party such as a relative or friend. On the contrary, such agreements are normally construed strictly in favour of the third party rather than the creditor. This is probably reflected in the actual decision in *Jones v Merionethshire Permanent Benefit Building Society* itself, in which a claim against relatives was dismissed.[65] The presumption may also be inapplicable, even as between claimant and original wrongdoer, if the offence was not a purely financial one but involved, for example, a crime of violence causing injury to the claimant.[66] It will usually be more difficult, in such circumstances, for the claimant plausibly to contend that the possibility of criminal proceedings never featured in any deliberations which took place between the parties; and evidence to support that contention would therefore seem to be needed.

(e)   Illegality and Duress

8–17   **"Never free agents".**   In *Mutual Finance v John Wetton*,[67] the claimants had threatened to prosecute a member of a family company who, they alleged, had forged the signature of the company on a guarantee. In response to this threat the company had given a new guarantee to the claimants, who were aware that this had only been forthcoming because the state of health of the father of the alleged forger was such that the prosecution of his son would endanger his life. An attempt to enforce the new guarantee failed, but did not do so on the ground of illegality as such. Porter J said that the defendants "were never free agents", and held that the guarantee was voidable at their option as having been obtained by undue influence. Similarly, in other cases which could have been treated as turning upon the illegality of stifling a prosecution, the concept of duress in equity, or undue influence, has been used instead to determine the question of enforceability.

---

[65] See also the recent case of *Newell v Royal Bank of Canada* (1997) 147 D.L.R. (4th) 268 in which The Nova Scotia Court of Appeal held that the claimant was not bound by an agreement with the Bank to accept responsibility for money withdrawn from his account by his wife, who had forged his signature and would have been prosecuted in the absence of the agreement. Hallett JA, referring to *Jones'* case, said: "One must ask the question, should different policy considerations apply in the 1990s than those that were applied in the 1890s. I tend to think that there are as many persons who are prepared to forge cheques today as there were a hundred years ago. The policy considerations that dictated the unwillingness of courts to enforce agreements founded on illegal consideration ought not to be changed" (280–281).
[66] cf. *Johnson v Musselman* (1917) 37 D.L.R. 162 (Can) (wilfully killing a horse).
[67] [1937] 2 K.B. 389.

Williams v Bayley. In the well-known case of *Williams v Bayley*,[68] the **8–18**
signatures on certain bills of exchange and promissory notes were forged. The
bank upon which the notes were drawn incurred loss as a result and threatened to
prosecute the forger. This threat induced the father of the alleged forger to
mortgage his own property to the bank, in order to secure the making good of the
loss. The security was held to be unenforceable, but the case is usually treated as
a leading authority not on illegality but on duress in equity or "pressure".[69] In the
three speeches delivered in the case itself, the language of equity is interwoven
with that of illegality. Lord Westbury said[70]:

> "There are two aspects of this case, or rather two points of view in which it may be regarded.
> One of them is: was the respondent a free and voluntary agent, or did he give the security in
> question under undue pressure exerted by the appellants? That regards the case with reference
> to the respondent alone. The second question regards the case with reference to the appellants
> alone: was the transaction, taken independently of the question of pressure, an illegal one, as
> being contrary to the settled rules and principles of law?"

Distinct concepts. Lord Westbury does at least distinguish, in this passage, **8–19**
between duress and illegality. In other cases, however, the question of whether or
not the parties struck a bargain on the possibility of prosecution appears to have
been treated, not as conclusive against enforceability in itself, but merely as an
incidental factor in determining whether or not there had been an inequitable
exercise of "pressure".[71] This is an unfortunate and potentially misleading
approach. Duress and undue influence is normally perceived to be a branch of the
general law of contract.[72] It defines the principles upon which relief may be
granted against agreements procured by grossly unfair means. It is therefore
concerned with the relationship of the parties to the contract towards each other
and not, except in the most general sense, with the public interest.

Protection of the public. Illegality, on the other hand, is concerned primarily **8–20**
with the protection of the public rather than with the protection of the parties
from each other.[73] No doubt in many cases the result will be the same whichever
approach is adopted. But it is still important that the relevance, and distinctive
characteristics, of illegality are not obscured. Unlike duress, it is beyond the
control of the parties and may be invoked by the court against their wishes. It can
usually be relied on even if it was not pleaded.[74] An important area in which there
could still be differences between the two sets of principles is that of unjust
enrichment. In the absence of illegality, a victim of duress will normally be
entitled to restitutionary relief. It is true that this relief normally remains available

---

[68] (1866) L.R. 1 H.L. 200.

[69] See e.g. *Cheshire, Fifoot and Furmston on Contract*, edited by Furmston, 16th edn, (Oxford University Press, 2012), p. 399.

[70] (1866) L.R. 1 H.L. 200 at 216.

[71] See *Haywood v Whitaker* (1887) 3 T.L.R. 537 and *McClatchie v Haslam* (1891) 65 L.T. 691. See also, per Vaughan Williams J at first instance in *Jones v Merionethshire Permanent Benefit Building Society* [1891] 2 Ch. 587 at 597–598.

[72] For an apparent exception see *Kaufman v Gerson* [1904] 1 K.B. 591, discussed in Ch.10, below.

[73] See the illuminating judgment of Palles CB in *Rourke v Mealy* (1879) 41 L.T. 168 (Ir. Ex. Div.) in which illegality and duress are separated and carefully distinguished.

[74] cf. *Seear v Cohen* (1882) 45 L.T. (N.S.) 589 (duress).

even if the claimant was pressured into entering into a contract to stifle a prosecution.[75] Traditionally, this was on the basis that oppression was a recognised exception to the notion encapsulated in the maxim *in pari delicto potior est conditio defendentis*.[76]

8–21 **Undeserving cases?** There may be situations, however, in which the illegality was so grave that the generosity normally afforded to victims of oppression would not be extended to the particular victim in question.[77] It is not illogical that the law might be more reluctant to relieve a party who has allowed himself to be pressured into a contract which is detrimental to the public at large, than it is to relieve a party who has merely been pressured into an agreement which is contrary to his own interests.[78] At the very least, the legitimacy of drawing such a distinction is an issue which merits rational debate; and yet it is one which can only be concealed from view by an approach which regards duress and illegality as two sides of the same coin. Moreover, situations can arise in which a contract to stifle a prosecution is entered into without any pressure being exerted at all.[79] In some cases, for example, the offender or his friends may themselves take the initiative in bargaining for the avoidance of criminal proceedings.[80] It would be unfortunate if any confusion regarding the scope of restitutionary relief, caused by the interweaving of duress and illegality in cases where the choice of concept made no difference to the outcome, enabled such claimants fortuitously to benefit from relief which they perhaps ought not to receive. It must be admitted, however, that the likelihood in practice of a conflict arising between the two concepts has now been greatly reduced by the decision of the Supreme Court in *Patel v Mirza*,[81] which radically widened the scope of relief for unjust enrichment in illegality cases. Nevertheless the importance of clarity in helping to prevent potential confusion should never be underestimated. The majority in *Patel v Mirza* favoured a flexible approach to relief based upon an examination of relevant policy issues.[82] It is not still not entirely inconceivable that situations might arise in which the public interest could necessitate denial of relief even to a victim of duress.

---

[75] See generally, Ch.17, below.

[76] See e.g. *Atkinson v Denby* (1862) 7 H. & N. 934; *Smith v Cuff* (1817) 6 M. & S. 160.

[77] cf. *Callaghan v O'Sullivan* [1925] V.L.R. 664, at 668, per Irvine CJ in the Supreme Court of Victoria: ". . . the position that the parties are not *in pari delicto* where there is coercion exercised by the person taking the money over the person taking it . . . has never been laid down as a principle of general application. Indeed, if it did it would enable money paid to stifle a prosecution to be *in all cases* recoverable" (italics supplied).

[78] It is significant that, in the law of contract in general, the notion of "pressure" is comparatively wide in scope, whereas in the criminal law the defence of duress is narrow: see *Smith and Hogan's Criminal Law*, Ormerod and Laird (eds), 14th edn, (Oxford University Press, 2015), Ch.12, para.12.2 (p.387 et seq.).

[79] See, e.g. *Lound v Grimwade* (1888) 39 Ch. D. 605. cf. *Howard v Odham's Press* [1938] 1 K.B. 1.

[80] cf. *Re Mapleback Ex p. Caldecott* (1876) 4 Ch. D. 150.

[81] [2016] UKSC 42.

[82] See below, Chs 17 and 18.

CHAPTER 9

MAINTENANCE AND CHAMPERTY

1. INTRODUCTION

Nature of maintenance and champerty. In the Court of Appeal in *Trendtex* **9–01**
Trading Corporation v Credit Suisse,[1] Oliver LJ said:

> "Maintenance is a very ancient concept and its history is one of a progressive alleviation of a
> strictness which at one time even forbade the giving of evidence except under subpoena. It
> may be defined as the rendering by one person, improperly, of assistance to another in
> prosecuting or defending proceedings in which the person so rendering assistance has no
> legitimate interest. Champerty was merely an aggravated form of maintenance and was
> constituted by an agreement between the maintainer and the maintained for the division of the
> proceeds of the suit."

Until 1967 both maintenance and champerty were crimes and torts, although
criminal liability was rarely imposed in modern times. Successful opponents of
impecunious litigants whose suits had been unlawfully maintained did, however,
sometimes sue the maintainer in tort to recover as damages sums equivalent to
the costs of the litigation which the other party to it had been unable to pay.[2] The
Criminal Law Act 1967 made such actions impossible in future: s.13 abolished
the old common law offences of maintenance and champerty, and s.14(2)
removed the liability in tort which hitherto existed in favour of those who could
prove that they had suffered damage in consequence of litigation having been
unlawfully maintained.

Contractual rules unaffected. Section 14(2) of the 1967 Act, however, **9–02**
contained an important proviso as follows:

> "The abolition of criminal and civil liability under the law of England and Wales for
> maintenance and champerty shall not affect any rule of that law as to the cases in which a
> contract is to be treated as contrary to public policy or otherwise illegal."

Accordingly, it is still the case that an agreement to engage in maintenance or
its aggravated form, champerty, can be unenforceable for illegality by one or both
of the parties to it. Moreover, notwithstanding the abolition of tortious liability,
the enforceability or otherwise of such agreements may still be a matter of
interest to third parties. The extent of a third party's liability may depend upon the

---

[1] [1980] Q.B. 629 at 663; [1980] 3 All E.R. 721 at 749.
[2] See, e.g. *Wiggins v Lavy* (1928) xliv T.L.R. 721, CA. cf. *Neville v London Express Newspapers*
[1919] A.C. 368.

enforceability of the contract between the maintainer and the maintained,[3] and the court may occasionally even be persuaded by a third party to stay, as an abuse of the process of the court, an action being brought against him by a maintained litigant.[4] Indeed, most of the modern reported cases concerned with maintenance and champerty have come before the court by a somewhat oblique route, often involving third parties. Many of these decisions are apt to illustrate the *limitations* on the concepts; the original reasons for their existence being perceived as diminished in importance in modern circumstances.

9–03   **Background.**   In the Court of Appeal in *Giles v Thompson*,[5] Steyn LJ, acknowledging his debt to a seminal article on the subject,[6] said the following about the circumstances which led to the development of maintenance and champerty:

> ". . . it seems that one of the abuses which afflicted the administration of justice was the practice of assigning doubtful or fraudulent claims to royal officials, nobles or other persons of wealth and influence, who could in those times be expected to receive a very sympathetic hearing in the court proceedings. The agreement often was that the assignee would maintain the action at his own expense, and share the proceeds of a favourable outcome with the assignor. Often these disputes involved a claim to the possession of land, and the subsequent sharing of land if the action was successful. Two factors contributed to the growth of these abuses. First, detachment and disinterestedness was not the hallmark of the mediaeval judiciary. There was in truth no independent judiciary. Secondly, the civil, justice system was not yet developed, and it was not capable of exposing abuses of legal procedure and giving effective redress."[7]

With the emergence of an independent judiciary, and the development of effective court procedures, the abuses which maintenance and champerty were intended to redress have largely disappeared.

9–04   **Degree of approval.**   Indeed, in the very different circumstances of the contemporary legal system the maintaining of litigation, and even champertous agreements to divide the proceeds of an action in the event of it succeeding, have come to be regarded with a degree of approval rather than automatic condemnation. This is due to the recognition that, without financial assistance, many people of modest means will in practice be excluded from access to the courts.[8] Moreover, it is now government policy, enshrined in legislation, to

---

[3] See, e.g. *Giles v Thompson* [1994] 1 A.C. 142; [1993] 3 All E.R. 321.
[4] See, e.g. *Re Oasis Merchandising Services* [1997] 1 All E.R. 1009, CA.
[5] [1993] 3 All E.R. 321 at 328.
[6] See Winfield, "The History of Maintenance and Champerty" (1919) 35 L.Q.R. 50.
[7] See also the graphic description of mediaeval proceedings by Jeremy Bentham in his *Works* (Bowring ed., 1843), vol.3, pp.19–20. quoted by Steyn LJ in *Giles v Thompson*: "a man might buy a weak claim, in hopes that power might convert it into a strong one, and that the sword of a baron, stalking into court with a rabble of retainers at his heels, might strike terror into the eyes of the judge upon the bench".
[8] "In current conditions, the denial of access to justice for want of financial resources may fairly be regarded as a more potent threat to the well-being of society than the risks of perverting the administration of justice which rightly exercised our mediaeval forebears": per Sir Thomas Bingham MR in *Giles v Thompson* [1993] 3 All E.R. 321 at 348, CA.

encourage "no win, no fee" schemes by barristers and solicitors[9]: arrangements which would formerly have been both champertous and a serious breach of professional discipline. This policy has been accompanied by drastic curtailment in the scope of public funding for litigation by means of legal aid.

High Court of Australia.   In *Campbells Cash & Carry Pty v Fostif Pty*[10] the   **9–05** High Court of Australia in 2006 subjected maintenance and champerty to an extensive review. The majority, emphasising the importance of access to justice, held that the doctrines are effectively obsolete in Australia.[11] Two justices did, however, express strongly a dissentient view,[12] maintaining that "(t)he facilitation of access to justice ... is not to be treated as having absolute priority over traditional principle".[13]

2.   LAWFUL MAINTENANCE

"Common interest".   The maintenance of another person's litigation was   **9–06** never regarded as illegal irrespective of the circumstances. If the maintainer had a "common interest" in the litigation, with the person who was actually a party to it, the maintenance would not be unlawful.[14] Moreover, there were a number of "exceptions" to the general rule of illegality, which could render the maintenance lawful even in the absence of "common interest". These exceptions, which apparently included kinship, charity and master and servant, were however ill-defined, as was the scope of the concept of common interest itself. Although the detailed structure of the law was therefore obscure, it was clear that maintaining litigation could be unlawful in many cases.

Trade rivals.   As long ago as the early years of the twentieth century, however,   **9–07** this very restrictive approach had begun to disintegrate. The 1908 decision of the Court of Appeal in *British Cash and Parcels Conveyors v Lamson Store Service Co*[15] seems to have represented a significant turning point. The claimant and the defendants were trade rivals for the same customers. The claimant sued the customers on the ground that they had broken subsisting contracts with the claimant when entering into contracts with the defendants, who in turn agreed to indemnify the customers against any damages and costs awarded against them. The claimant alleged that the indemnities constituted unlawful maintenance, which was then a tort, and sued the defendants. Their claim failed. The Court reviewed the authorities as they then stood, and pointed out that contracts of indemnity were in common use and were frequently the subject of insurance

---

[9] See the Courts and Legal Services Act 1990 s.58 (as inserted by the Access to Justice Act 1999 s.27).
[10] [2006] HCA 41. See also *Mobil Oil Australia Pty v Trendlen Pty* [2006] HCA 42.
[11] See per Gummow, Hayne and Crennan JJ in [2006] HCA 41 at [66]–[95].
[12] See per Callinan and Heydon JJ in [2006] HCA 41 at [249] et seq.
[13] See ibid. at [256].
[14] See *Bradlaugh v Newdegate* (1883) II Q.B.D 1 at 11, per Lord Coleridge CJ See also *Plating Company v Farquharson* (1881) 17 Ch.D. 49.
[15] [1908] 1 K.B. 1006; [1908–10] All E.R. Rep. 146.

contracts, the validity of which was generally assumed. Sir Herbert Cozens-Hardy MR considered that the defendants "had a business interest, a commercial interest, which fully justified the indemnities or guarantees which they gave".[16] Fletcher Moulton LJ emphasised that "the old common law of maintenance [was] to a large extent obsolete". He continued, "To say that a tradesman is to submit to the loss of a customer because of threats by a rival of bringing unfounded claims against that customer, and that he may not legitimately extend his business by indemnifying the customer who is desirous to employ him against such claims, is to my mind ridiculous".[17]

9–08   **The *Martell* case.**   This decision of the Court of Appeal in the *British Cash and Parcels* case featured prominently in the judgment of Dankwerts J, itself upheld by the Court of Appeal, in what is still the leading modern authority on maintenance: *Martell v Consett Iron Co.*[18] In this case an action by riparian owners, for alleged pollution of the River Derwent, was supported by a body known as the Anglers' Co-operative Association, membership of which was open to anyone interested in angling who paid a small annual subscription. The defendants in the action claimed that this support enjoyed by the claimants constituted unlawful maintenance, but their contention was rejected. Dankwerts J observed that the doctrine of maintenance "which was evolved to deal with cases of oppression should not be allowed to become an instrument of oppression, which it must be if humble men are not allowed to combine or to receive contributions to meet a powerful adversary".[19] Earlier in his judgment he had expressed himself as follows[20]:

> "This case happens to be about the interests of anglers, but the principle involved is of much greater importance. It would be disingenuous to disregard the difficulties which the man of small resources (not confined to the legal aid class) faces in present-day conditions in defending such rights as he may have against infringement by powerful commercial corporations or adversaries who may draw their strength from the rates or the National Exchequer. If such a man may not avail himself of the help of sympathisers, his condition may be serious indeed."

In the Court of Appeal Jenkins and Hodson LJJ examined the notion of "common interest" for the purposes of the law of maintenance as traditionally understood. Jenkins LJ said that, in his view, "the range of interests is potentially of great width",[21] while Hodson LJ considered the "common interest" formula to be "elastic".[22]

9–09   **Broader modern approach.**   In the older cases libel actions were apt to be regarded as being exclusively of concern to the parties to them, so as to render

---

[16] See [1908] 1 K.B. 1006 at 1012; [1908–10] All E.R. Rep. 146 at 149.
[17] See [1908] 1 K.B. 1006 at 1013–1015; [1908–10] All E.R. Rep. 146 at 150.
[18] [1955] Ch. 363.
[19] [1955] Ch. 363 at 386.
[20] [1955] Ch. 363 at 375.
[21] [1955] Ch. 363 at 418.
[22] [1955] Ch. 363 at 427.

financial support from others particularly likely to constitute maintenance.[23] But a decision of the Court of Appeal in 1967 illustrated that the very much broader modern approach, to the legitimacy of externally supported litigation, could apply to those actions also. In *Hill v Archbold*[24] the claimant, a member of a trade union, attempted unsuccessfully to prevent the funds of the union being used to support its officials in libel actions which the officials brought in respect of allegations that they had lied in the course of their work for the union. The Court of Appeal held that the union had a "real interest" in defending the reputation of their officers, so that its funding of the litigation was lawful. Lord Denning MR said[25]:

> "Much maintenance is considered justifiable today which would . . . [formerly] have been considered obnoxious. Most of the actions in our courts are supported by some association or other, or by the state itself. Comparatively few litigants bring suits, or defend them, at their own expense. Most claims by workmen against their employers are paid for by a trade union. Most defences of motorists are paid for by insurance companies. This is perfectly justifiable and is accepted by everyone as lawful."

Present position.   The present position is probably that the concept of   9–10
maintenance retains, for what it is worth, its original structure so that a maintainer must, if illegality is to be avoided, either have a "common interest" with the litigant, or come within a recognised exception whereby maintenance will be lawful without such an interest. Accordingly, it may occasionally still be convenient for a situation which falls within one of the exceptions to be identified as so doing, in order to avoid the need to prove the existence of a "common interest".[26] In practice, however, the latter concept is now so broad that there can be few situations in which unlawful maintenance will be established successfully. In any event unlawful maintenance is not in itself a defence to the action being "maintained".[27] Overall, it is of interest that "crowdfunding" of litigation has now become an accepted means of securing access to justice.[28]

3.   CHAMPERTY[29]

Dividing line between maintenance and champerty.   Assisting someone else   9–11
with the funding of their litigation is one thing, but seeking in addition to profit from the proceedings is another. "There can be no champerty if there is no maintenance", Millett LJ observed recently, "but there can still be champerty even if the maintenance is not unlawful".[30] This proposition is illustrated by *Cole*

---

[23] See *Alabaster v Harness* [1895] 1 Q.B. 339. CA; *Oram v Hun* [1914] 1 Ch. 98. CA; *Baker v Jones* [1954] 1 W.L.R. 1005.
[24] [1968] 1 Q.B. 686.
[25] [1968] 1 Q.B. 686 at 694–695.
[26] See, e.g. *Condliffe v Hislop* [1996] 1 W.L.R. 753; [1996] 1 All E.R. 431, CA (kinship).
[27] See para.9–26 below.
[28] See e.g. the website *www.crowdjustice.org* [accessed 28 February 2017].
[29] See Adrian Walters. "A Modern Doctrine of Champerty?" (1996) 112 L.Q.R. 560.
[30] See *Thai Trading Co v Taylor* [1998] Q.B. 781, at 786; [1998] 3 All E.R. 65, at 69. cf. per Lord Neuberger MR in *Sibthorpe v Southwark LBC* [2011] EWCA Civ 25 at [55] (". . . it appears to me that

v Booker.[31] The claimant lent the defendant, an old friend who was "in reduced circumstances", a sum of money to enable him to bring an action for malicious prosecution following the dismissal of a criminal charge which had been brought against him. The claimant stipulated not only that the loan should be repaid if the action was successful, but also that an additional sum should be paid to him out of any damages awarded. The action duly succeeded but the defendant refused to pay the claimant, who sued him. Bailhache J held that the maintaining of the action was lawful as it came within one of the recognised exceptions to maintenance, that of "charity". But the claimant could not recover the additional sum stipulated for since the agreement had been champertous.[32] This case was decided in 1913. Today champerty is no longer regarded with the same degree of disapprobation as formerly, and the courts are certainly not eager to extend the doctrine. On the contrary, "its scope is to be curtailed rather than expanded".[33] Thus the Court of Appeal has held that it is not champertous for a solicitor merely to undertake to indemnify his client against liability for the defendant's costs if he *loses*, with no corresponding *gain* to the solicitor if he wins.[34] And as the following case illustrates, the courts will not allow technical arguments based upon champerty to render legitimate commercial arrangements unlawful.

9–12   ***Giles v Thompson.***   In *Giles v Thompson*[35] car-hire companies hired out vehicles to motorists, whose cars had been damaged in road accidents without fault on their part, for the period while their own vehicles were off the road being repaired. If as expected, but only if, the motorists' claims against the other drivers involved in the accidents succeeded, the motorists would then be obliged to reimburse the car-hire companies out of the proceeds. The car-hire companies would manage the cases on the motorists' behalf, usually using solicitors chosen by the companies themselves; and the claims would necessarily involve, in addition to the repairs and any personal injuries, damages for the cost of hiring a substitute vehicle. The scheme proved a great commercial success for the car-hire companies, but it was met with markedly less enthusiasm by the insurers of negligent motorists. The latter found themselves footing the bill for a type of claim which, although well-established as a matter of law, few accident victims deprived of their vehicles had, in practice, bothered to bring until the entrepreneurial initiative of the car-hire companies gave them the incentive to do so. The insurers' response was to seek to undermine the schemes by alleging that they champertously involved the companies intervening in, and seeking to profit from, disputes to which they were not parties. The Court of Appeal and House of

---

the law has developed, perhaps unconsciously, so that, at least when it comes to agreements with those who conduct litigation . . . there can be champerty without maintenance.").
[31] (1913) T.L.R. 295.
[32] [1915] T.L.R. 295 "Charity may be indiscreet, but must not and, indeed, cannot be mercenary": per Bailhache J.
[33] See *Sibthorpe v Southwark LBC* [2011] EWCA Civ 25 at [44] per Lord Neuberger MR.
[34] See *Sibthorpe v Southwark LBC* [2011] EWCA Civ 25 (". . . if one considers the various judicial definitions of champerty, they all envisage a gain if the action concerned succeeds" ibid. at [43] per Lord Neuberger MR).
[35] [1994] 1 A.C. 142; [1993] 3 All E.R. 321.

Lords unanimously rejected the insurers' contention.[36] Lord Mustill observed that the law on maintenance and champerty could "best be kept in forward motion by looking to its origins as a principle of public policy designed to protect the purity of justice and the interests of vulnerable litigants".[37] He continued[38]:

> "The car hire company makes its profits from the hiring, not from the litigation. It does not divide the spoils, but relies upon the fruits of the litigation as a source from which the motorist can satisfy his or her liability for the provision of a genuine service, external to the litigation. I can see no convincing reason for saying that, as between the parties to the hiring agreement, the whole transaction is so unbalanced, or so fraught with risk, that it ought to be stamped out. The agreement is one which in my opinion the law should recognise and enforce."

Factortame and access to justice. In 1988 the Government legislated to **9–13** prevent certain fishing companies from fishing in British waters. In famous and protracted litigation the relevant legislation was ultimately held to be contrary to EU law, and it became apparent that the fishing companies would be entitled to substantial compensation from the Government. The assessment of this compensation was, however, an extremely complex matter potentially requiring yet more litigation between the companies and the Government. The former, however, had been impoverished by the situation and did not have the means to pay for the professional accountancy advice and assistance which was necessary. A leading firm of accountants therefore agreed, in 1998, to provide that advice and assistance in return for 8 per cent of the proceeds if the fishing companies succeeded in their claims. The claims were ultimately settled in favour of the companies and the accountants were duly paid. When, however, the companies sought to hold the Government, as the unsuccessful party, liable for their costs, the Government attempted to deny liability for the sums paid to the accountants on the ground that the arrangement for their services had been champertous. When this issue reached the Court of Appeal, in *Factortame v Secretary of State for the Environment (No.2)*,[39] Lord Phillips MR quoted at length from the judgments in *Giles v Thompson* and said[40]:

> "This decision abundantly supports the proposition that, in any individual case, it is necessary to look at the agreement under attack in order to see whether it tends to conflict with existing public policy that is directed to protecting the due administration of justice with particular regard to the interests of the defendant".

Applying this approach to the case before them, the Court attached importance to the fact that the accountants had been scrupulous not to act as *experts* in the dispute,[41] and had appointed *other* accountants for this purpose; that 8 per cent was "not extravagant"; and that not being solicitors or barristers the accountants

---

[36] For a more successful avenue of attack by the insurers see the subsequent case of *Dimond v Lovell* [2000] 2 All E.R. 897, HL.
[37] See [1994] 1 A.C. 142 at 164; [1993] 3 All E.R. 321, at 360.
[38] See [1994] 1 A.C. 142 at 165; [1993] 3 All E.R. 321 at 361.
[39] [2002] EWCA Civ 932; [2002] 4 All E.R. 97. See also *Golden Eye International v Telefonica* [2012] EWHC 723 (reversed in part, but not on this point, in [2012] EWCA Civ 1740); *Mansell v Robinson* [2007] EWHC 101 (QB); *Papera Traders v Hyundai Merchant Marine, The Eurasian Dream (No.2)* [2002] EWHC 2130 (Comm).
[40] [1994] 1 A.C. 142 at 44.
[41] See below, para.9–27.

were not bound by the elaborate statutory rules applicable to conditional fee agreements. Moreover, without the arrangement with the accountants, the companies could not have pursued their claims. Lord Phillips MR concluded[42]:

> "The Claimants had been brought low by the initial wrong done to them and by the costs and stress of prolonged litigation in which no quarter was given. They were faced with an extraordinarily complicated task in proving the damage that they had suffered and there was a real risk that lack of funds might result in their losing the fruits of their litigation. The 1998 agreements ensured that they continued to enjoy access to justice. They did this without putting justice in jeopardy. The 1998 agreements were not champertous."

9–14   **Where the concept is inapplicable.** Since champerty involves "trafficking in litigation", it cannot have any application to agreements which do not relate to disputes as such. In *Savill Brothers v Langman*[43] the Court of Appeal held that an agreement to support an application to licensing justices, for a licence for a new public house, could not be attacked as champertous. When magistrates sit as licensing justices they are discharging administrative functions. "Here", said Collin LJ, "there is no stirring up of suits or quarrels because the application for a licence is not in any sense litigation. Therefore it is impossible that there can be champerty in relation to the application for a licence".[44] *Savill's* case was followed in the much more recent case of *Picton Jones & Co v Arcadia Developments*.[45] Here it was alleged that chartered surveyors had acted champertously in attending local authority planning committees, and planning inquiries before inspectors, in support of applications by developers to build and run amusement arcades. In addition to their hourly rate, the surveyors were to be paid a substantial fee in the event of the project being successful. Judge J rejected the allegation and held that the fee was recoverable. "Whatever else they may have been", he said, "the applications for gaming permits and planning permissions were not, in my judgment, a *lis* or litigation or even contentious proceedings".[46]

4. ASSIGNMENT[47]

9–15   **Choses in action.** One specific area in which maintenance and champerty have cast a long shadow is that relating to the assignment of choses in action. A chose in action, such as a debt or other legal obligation, is a right defined and recognised by law but incapable of being reduced into physical possession. In earlier times fear of "trafficking in litigation" led to such assignments being regarded with caution. Before 1873 choses in action were not assignable at all at common law; and although their assignability was recognised and enforced in equity, it was apparently still subject to restrictions. Nevertheless, at first glance, the wording of the well-known provision in s.136 of the Law of Property Act

---

[42] See [2002] EWCA Civ 932; [2002] 4 All E.R. 97 at 91.
[43] (1898) 79 L.T. 44.
[44] (1898) 79 L.T. 44 at 48.
[45] [1989] 1 E.G.L.R. 43.
[46] [1989] 1 E.G.L.R. 43, at 44.
[47] See Y. L. Tan, "Champertous Contracts and Assignments" (1990) 106 L.Q.R. 656.

1925, which dates back to the Supreme Court of Judicature Act 1873, appears to sweep away any surviving restrictions. Subsection 1 provides that:

> "Any absolute assignment in writing under the hand of the assignor . . . of any debt or other legal thing in action, of which express notice in writing has been given to the debtor . . . is effectual in law . . ."

In fact, however, cases decided in the years following the passing of the 1873 Act,[48] combined with much more recent authorities,[49] have made it clear that, in some circumstances, the doctrines of maintenance and champerty will still render assignments invalid notwithstanding the wording of the section. But unfortunately, the precise nature of those circumstances has tended to remain somewhat obscure.

"Bare right to litigate".   One familiar proposition is that an assignment of a **9–16** "bare right to litigate"[50] will be invalid whereas the assignment of a right of property will be valid, "even although that property may be incapable of being recovered without litigation".[51] But as McCardie J once somewhat laconically observed, "to effect such an analysis and to differentiate between the two things" is not exactly straightforward.[52] One possible interpretation of the proposition might be that the assignment would be invalid if litigation was contemplated, at the time of the assignment, as being necessary to enforce the right. But it became apparent that this proved too much, otherwise a debtor could render an otherwise indisputable debt unassignable simply by refusing to pay it.[53] Another interpretation of the proposition might be that rights of action in tort are not assignable,[54] but this too has been perceived as far too wide to make commercial sense,[55] even if it might hold good for personal claims such as assault.[56] In

---

[48] See, e.g. *May v Lane* (1894) 64 L.J.Q.B. 236, CA; *Defries v Milne* [1913] 1 Ch. 98, CA. cf. *Glegg v Bromley* [1912] 3 K.B. 474, CA.

[49] See *Laurent v Sale & Co* [1963] 1 W.L.R. 829; *Trendtex Trading Corporation v Credit Suisse* [1982] A.C. 679.

[50] "No single phrase has given rise to greater confusion than the rule . . . that you cannot assign a 'bare right to litigate'": per Lloyd LJ in *Brownton v Edward Moore Inbucon* [1985] 3 All E.R. 499 at 507.

[51] See *Dawson v Great Northern and City Railway* [1905] 1 K.B. 260 at 271, per Stirling LJ, CA.

[52] See *County Hotel and Wine Co v London and North Western Railway* [1918] 2 K.B. 251 at 261. See also, per Oliver LJ in the Court of Appeal in *Trendtex Trading Corporation v Credit Suisse* [1980] Q.B. 629 at 663; [1980] 3 All E.R. 721 at 749: "I question whether, in the year 1980, our jurisprudence ought still to have room for distinctions, which owe more to sophistry than to logic, between choses in action and what are described as 'bare' rights of action or between strictly proprietary and purely commercial or financial interests".

[53] See *County Hotel and Wine Co v London and North Western Railway* [1918] 2 K.B. 251 at 258, per McCardie J; *Camdex International v Bank of Zambia* [1998] Q.B. 22; [1996] 3 All E.R. 431, CA. cf. *Fitzroy v Cave* [1905] 2 K.B. 364, CA. See also, per Oliver LJ in the Court of Appeal in *Trendtex Trading Corporation v Credit Suisse* [1980] Q.B. 629 at 671; [1980] 3 All E.R. 721 at 755: "What logical dividing line is there between the innocent assignee of a contract and the champertous assignee of the right to sue for damages for its breach? Why is it to be assumed that the former will behave with total rectitude whilst the latter may suppress evidence, suborn witnesses and advance inflated and unsustainable claims?"

[54] See *Defries v Milne* [1913] 1 Ch. 98, CA. See also *Glegg v Bromley* [1912] 3 K.B. 474, CA.

[55] See *Compania Colombiana de Seguros v Pacific Steam Navigation Co* [1965] 1 Q.B. 101.

Simpson v Norfolk and Norwich University Hospital NHS Trust[57] the Court of Appeal held that a right of action in tort for negligence causing personal injury was not assignable since, on the facts of the case, the assignee had no sufficient interest in the outcome.[58]

9–17 **The *Trendtex* case.**   The current law, which is still by no means as free from doubt as could be wished, is essentially to be derived from a trio of cases decided in the past thirty years or so.[59] In *Trendtex Trading Corporation v Credit Suisse*[60] the claimant company was owed a substantial sum by a Nigerian company and was, in its turn, heavily indebted to its bankers, Credit Suisse. The claimants therefore assigned their Nigerian claim to Credit Suisse, the defendants, for a heavily discounted sum. The latter then promptly re-assigned it to a mysterious third party for a somewhat larger figure. The claimants were shocked to discover that the third party then succeeded in recovering from the Nigerian company a sum ten times greater than the maximum which the claimants had been led to believe, at the time of their original assignment, was likely in practice to be obtainable. The claimants suspected that they had been defrauded and challenged the validity of the assignments as champertous. Although the actual decision in the case was on a procedural point, on which all the judges who heard the case were unanimous, the House of Lords differed from the Court of Appeal on the champerty point.

9–18 **Agreements invalid.**   The Court of Appeal considered the assignments to be unobjectionable, whereas the House of Lords held that, in English law, they had been invalid. Lord Roskill said[61]:

> "I am afraid that, with respect, I cannot agree with Lord Denning M.R. when he said in the instant case that 'The old saying that you cannot assign a "bare right to litigate" is gone'. I venture to think that still remains a fundamental principle of our law. But it is today true that in English law an assignee who can show that he has a genuine commercial interest in the enforcement of the claim of another and to that extent takes an assignment of that claim to himself is entitled to enforce that assignment unless by the terms of that assignment he falls foul of our law of champerty."

---

[56] See, per Lord Denning MR in the Court of Appeal in *Trendtex Trading Corporation v Credit Suisse* [1980] Q.B. 629 at 656; [1980] 3 All E.R. 721 at 743. But see criticism by Tan, "Champertous Contracts and Assignments" (1990) 106 L.Q.R. 656 at p.667, who argues that the proposition that "there never could be a legitimate and genuine interest in an assignment of an action in respect of a personal tort" seems "contrary to the widely accepted practice of liability insurance". He suggests that "rights under non-intentional torts should be assignable if there is a genuine commercial interest in the assignment", cf. *Glegg v Bromley* [1912] 3 K.B. 474, CA (the fruits of an action can be assigned when the right of action itself cannot).

[57] [2011] EWCA Civ 1149.

[58] She was seeking support for a campaign against the hospital for its alleged failure to control MRSA infection:" . . . in my view it would be damaging to the administration of justice and unfair to defendants for the law to recognise an interest of that kind as sufficient to support the assignment of a cause of action for personal injury" per Moore-Bick LJ in [2011] EWCA Civ at [24].

[59] See *Laurent v Sale & Co* [1963] 1 W.L.R. 829; *Trendtex Trading Corporation v Credit Suisse* [1982] A.C. 679; *Camdex International v Central Bank of Zambia* [1998] Q.B. 22; [1996] 3 All E.R. 431, CA.

[60] [1982] A.C. 679.

[61] [1982] A.C. 679 at 703; [1981] 3 All E.R. 520 at 531, HL.

Applying this "genuine commercial interest test", his Lordship considered that while Credit Suisse would have been entitled to take an assignment of Trendtex's claim, "for the purpose of recouping themselves for their own substantial losses", it was not legitimate for them to devise a scheme whereby the claim was, from the outset, "to be sold on to the anonymous third party to obtain what profit he could from it, apart from paying to Credit Suisse the purchase price". Lord Roskill thus expressed his conclusion as follows[62]:

> "Such an agreement, in my opinion, offends, for it was a step towards the sale of a bare cause of action to a third party who had no genuine commercial interest in the claim in return for a division of the spoils. Credit Suisse taking the fixed amount which I have already mentioned."

"Genuine commercial interest".   The present position therefore appears to be   9–19
that the assignee must have a "genuine commercial interest" for the assignment to be valid. But what constitutes a "genuine commercial interest"?[63] In *Brownton v Edward Moore Incubon*,[64] which was decided a few years after the *Trendtex* case, the Court of Appeal emphasised that the mere fact that the parties to the assignment expected to profit from the transaction is not, in itself, enough to render an assignment champertous. In so far as the remarks of Lord Roskill just quoted might be taken to give the opposite impression, it would clearly be a misinterpretation since otherwise few assignments would ever be valid.[65] Nevertheless Sir John Megaw did suggest in the *Brownton* case that "if there were a prospect of some excessive profit, that might properly be a factor in deciding whether the commercial interest was genuine".[66] This appears to be one factor in an inquiry which should "look at the transaction as a whole".[67]

Routinely accepted transactions.   Thus the validity or otherwise of an   9–20
assignment is likely to turn largely on the facts of each case. This cannot be regarded as wholly satisfactory, although it may be that champertous assignments are easier to recognise than to define, and that the commercial world does not find the apparent uncertainty to be a serious issue in practice. The courts certainly appear to apply the "genuine commercial interest" test with a presumption in favour of the validity of routinely accepted transactions. In *Camdex International v Bank of Zambia*[68] the claimants took an assignment of a debt owed by the

---

[62] [1982] A.C. 679 at 703; [1981] 3 All E.R. 520 at 531, HL.
[63] See Y. L. Tan, "Champertous Contracts and Assignments" (1990) 106 L.Q.R. 656, especially at p.664 (discussing *Bourne v Colodense Ltd* [1985] I.C.R. 291).
[64] [1985] 3 All E.R. 499, CA.
[65] See, per Sir John Megaw in [1985] 3 All E.R. 499 at 506, CA. See also, per Hobhouse LJ in *Camdex International v Central Bank of Zambia* [1998] Q.B. 22 at 35; [1996] 3 All E.R. 431 at 442: ". . . why else should a commercial entity purchase a debt?"
[66] See [1985] 3 All E.R. 499 at 506. cf. Tan, "Champertous Contracts and Assignments" (1990) 106 L.Q.R. 656, at pp.671 et seq., especially at p.674: "It is suggested that the Court of Appeal in *Brownton v Edward Moore Inbucon* was right to play down the importance of the profit element. It is not as distinctive of champerty as it might seem to be. For example, a contract to maintain could be the result of pure intermeddling and harassment; whereas a champertous contract could be the result of cold, commercial calculation, the element of profit-making actually marking out the case as more acceptable".
[67] See *Brownton v Edward Moore Inbucon* [1985] 3 All E.R. 499 at 509, per Lloyd LJ, CA.
[68] [1998] Q.B. 22; [1996] 3 All E.R. 431, CA.

defendant bank, at a time when it was evident that the debt would not be recovered without litigation. The claimants obtained summary judgment against the defendants, but the latter attacked the validity of the assignment claiming that it was champertous. The Court of Appeal held that the attack would fail. The prospect of litigation did not invalidate the assignment. "All this", observed Hobhouse LJ, "is the stuff of wholly unobjectionable debt collection and discloses nothing which is contrary to the policy of English law".[69]

5.   THE LEGAL PROFESSION

9–21   **Conditional fees.**   "Modern public policy", said Lord Denning MR in 1980,[70] "condemns champerty in a lawyer whenever he seeks to recover not only his proper costs but also a portion of the damages for himself, or when he conducts a case on the basis that he is to be paid if he wins but not if he loses". The principle embodied in this dictum, which not only rendered agreements which contravened it unenforceable at common law but also made the lawyers involved liable to be subjected to professional disciplinary proceedings, is familiar and of long-standing. The years since Lord Denning spoke have, however, seen radical changes, both in the underlying common law and in the statutory provisions regulating the conduct of barristers and solicitors. Recognition of the extent to which arrangements such as "no win, no fee" have facilitated access to justice in other countries, especially the US, has led to their limited recognition in this country. This has been notwithstanding the countervailing arguments based on the importance of ensuring that the integrity of justice, and the lawyer's overriding duty to the court, is not compromised. The initial statutory breakthrough came with s.58 of the Courts and Legal Services Act 1990, which legitimised conditional fee agreements in proceedings to be specified by the Lord Chancellor by order. It was not until 1995 that an order was made, so that it was only in that year that s.58 became operative. The current version of s.58 was inserted into the 1990 Act by s.27 of the Access to Justice Act 1999, and was further amended by s.154 of the Coroners and Justice Act 2009 and s.45 of the Legal Aid, Sentencing and Punishment of Offenders Act 2012.[71] Alongside, but separate from, the statutory developments the last five years of the twentieth century saw some striking, if at times chaotic, changes in the case-law on the enforceability at common law of novel funding arrangements.

9–22   *Thai Trading.*   In the 1995 case of *Aratra Potato v Taylor Johnson Garrett*,[72] Garland J applied the established orthodoxy and held that an agreement whereby a large and well-known firm of London solicitors agreed to a 20 per cent

---

[69] [1998] Q.B. 22 at 40; [1996] 3 All E.R. at 446. See also, per Peter Gibson LJ at 446: "It is a normal, and for many in business an essential, incident of modern commercial life that debts are bought and sold, and it would be highly unfortunate it such everyday transactions were to be held to be champertous, save in wholly exceptional circumstances not present here".

[70] See *Trendtex Trading Corporation v Credit Suisse* [1980] Q.B. 629 at 654, CA.

[71] These further amendments significantly introduce "Damages-based agreements" whereby persons providing advocacy services can stipulate for payment out of the damages awarded if the claim is successful: see s.58AA of the 1990 Act.

[72] [1995] 4 All E.R. 695.

reduction in their fee if they lost a case was champertous, and unenforceable at common law. The solicitors were therefore unable to sue for their fees. Just under three years later, however, the Court of Appeal purported to overrule *Aratra Potato* in *Thai Trading Co v Taylor*.[73] In that case a solicitor agreed to charge no fee if the case was unsuccessful. Millett LJ with whom Hutchison and Kennedy LJJ agreed, had "no hesitation" in concluding that "it is not improper for a solicitor to agree to act on the basis that he is to be paid his ordinary costs if he wins but not if he loses".[74] His Lordship also went so far as to question whether such an arrangement had "ever" been "contrary to public policy".[75] Very shortly afterwards Sir Richard Scott VC followed and extended *Thai Trading* by holding that not merely could a solicitor or barrister properly accept a reduced fee in the event of failure, but also that it was lawful to negotiate an uplift on the normal fee in the event of success.[76] The decision in *Thai Trading* itself had been particularly striking in that the arrangement held to be lawful was clearly contrary to the Solicitors Practice Rules 1987. The response of Millett LJ to this point had been to assert that "the fact that a professional rule prohibits a practice does not of itself make the practice contrary to law" and that, in any event, "the Solicitors Rules are based on a perception of public policy derived from judicial decisions the correctness of which is in question in this appeal".[77]

Flawed reasoning.   Unfortunately, however, 10 months later the reasoning of the Court of Appeal on this point was held by the Divisional Court to have been flawed; with the consequence that, in effect, *Thai Trading* had been decided *per incuriam*.[78] And a year later the validity of this criticism was accepted by the Court of Appeal itself.[79] The problem was that a 1982 decision of the House of Lords,[80] which had not been cited to the Court in *Thai Trading*, had held that the Solicitors Practice Rules were to be treated as having the full force of statute; so that the arrangement which had been entered into had actually been the subject of a legislative prohibition, and not merely of an arguably outdated principle of common law.   9–23

Section 58.   On a less technical level than the validity of the decision itself, however, *Thai Trading* may be said to have won the argument. The new version of s.58 of the Courts and Legal Services Act 1990 was said by the Lord Chancellor, when what is now s.27 of the Access to Justice Act 1999 was being considered in committee, to be intended "to bring the effect of the judgment of the Court of Appeal in *Thai Trading* into statute law".[81] Although the legislature has therefore now removed the prohibition on "no win, no fee" agreements, and   9–24

---

[73] [1998] Q.B. 781; [1998] 3 All E.R. 65.
[74] See [1998] Q.B. 781 at 790; [1998] 3 All E.R. 65 at 72.
[75] See [1998] Q.B. 781 at 788; [1998] 3 All E.R. 65 at 71.
[76] See *Bevan Ashford v Yeandle* [1999] Ch.239; [1998] 3 All E.R. 238.
[77] See [1998] 8 Q.B. 781 at 785–786; [1998] 3 All E.R. 65 at 69.
[78] See *Hughes v Kingston upon Hull City Council* [1999] Q.B. 1193.
[79] See *Awwad v Geraghty & Co* [2001] Q.B. 570; [2000] 1 All E.R. 608.
[80] See *Swain v Law Society* [1983] 1 A.C. 598.
[81] See Hansard, HL. vol.596 col.960 (quoted in Dr J. Williams' commentary on the Access to Justice Act 1999 in *Current Law Statutes* (1999)).

agreements for increased fees in the event of success, it has only done so subject to conditions; and, in relation to "success fees", specific restrictions on the level of increase which can lawfully be charged.[82] Moreover, s.58(1) now provides as follows:

"A conditional fee agreement which satisfies all of the conditions applicable to it by virtue of this section shall not be unenforceable by reason only of its being a conditional fee agreement; but ... any other conditional fee agreement shall be unenforceable."

Although the subsection therefore legalises conditional fee agreements, provided the conditions are observed, its second limb, which was not present in the original 1990 version, specifically renders unlawful conditional fee agreements which do not satisfy those conditions.[83] Thus it will no longer be possible for the courts to develop the rules of public policy, as the Court of Appeal attempted to do in *Thai Trading*, so as to hold that novel forms of conditional fee arrangement, which do not satisfy the statutory requirements, might nevertheless be lawful.[84] At the same time, however, the statutory requirements only apply expressly to persons "providing advocacy or litigation services", and the Court of Appeal has held that the statutory limitations do *not* apply by implication to others who assist in the litigation process.[85]

9–25   **Expert witnesses.**   In *Factortame v Secretary of State for the Environment (No.2)*[86] the Court of Appeal considered, obiter, the question whether it is ever permissible for expert witnesses, who are not covered by the statutory conditional fee arrangements, to have a financial interest in the outcome of the litigation in which they give evidence. While the Court did not consider that professional employees of one of the parties should necessarily be prevented from giving evidence,[87] it did indicate that any scheme which gave the expert a direct financial interest in the outcome of the litigation would rarely be acceptable. Lord Phillips MR said[88]:

"To give evidence on a contingency fee basis gives an expert, who would otherwise be independent, a significant financial interest in the outcome of the case. As a general proposition, such an interest is highly undesirable. In many cases the expert will be giving an authoritative opinion on issues that are critical to the outcome of the case. In such a situation the threat to his objectivity posed by a conditional fee agreement may carry greater dangers to the administration of justice than would the interest of an advocate or solicitor acting under a similar agreement. Accordingly, we consider that it will be in a very rare case indeed that the court will be prepared to consent to an expert being instructed under a contingency fee agreement."

---

[82] See the Courts and Legal Services Act 1990 s.58(3) as inserted by the Access to Justice Act 1999 s.27.

[83] See e.g. *Rees v Gateley Wareing (A Firm)* [2014] EWCA Civ 1351; [2015] 1 W.L.R. 2179.

[84] See *Sibthorpe v Southwark LBC* [2011] EWCA Civ 25 at [34]–[41] per Lord Neuberger MR.

[85] See *Factortame v Secretary of State for the Environment (No.2)* [2002] EWCA Civ 932; [2002] 4 All E.R. 97.

[86] [2002] EWCA Civ 932; [2002] 4 All E.R. 97.

[87] See *Field v Leeds City Council* [2000] 1 E.G.L.R. 54 (CA). cf. *Liverpool Roman Catholic Archdiocese Trustees Inc v Goldberg (No.2)* [2001] 4 All E.R. 950; [2001] 1 W.L.R. 2337.

[88] [2002] EWCA Civ 932; [2002] 4 All E.R. 97 at 73. cf. *Hamilton v Al Fayed (No.2)* [2002] EWCA Civ 665; [2002] 3 All E.R. 641, per Chadwick LJ at 70.

6. THE EFFECTS OF MAINTENANCE AND CHAMPERTY

Not a defence in itself. It is clear that the mere fact that a claimant's action is being unlawfully maintained does not, of itself, constitute a defence to the action.[89] Nor does such maintenance provide grounds for the action to be stayed[90]; not least because it would seem to follow that unlawfully maintained defendants would also have to be deprived of the opportunity of defending themselves, an outcome which would clearly be inappropriate.[91] This latter anomaly cannot occur in relation to champerty, which by its very nature can only involve claimants. Nevertheless, the courts insist on the importance of access to justice, and it is not a defence in itself that the claimant is being supported champertously.[92] Nor, unless the proceedings are a calculated attempt to contaminate the "purity of justice",[93] and an abuse of process, will the action be stayed.[94] Indeed in one context, that of insolvency, liquidators are authorised by statute to enter into agreements which would otherwise be champertous; enabling them to finance the bringing of claims on behalf of the company.[95] In general the modern approach is to promote access to justice where possible, and the commercial practice of agreeing to fund litigation in return for a share in the proceeds if it is successful is now well-established. There is even a body called the Association of Litigation Funders. It is nevertheless probably desirable that, apart from satisfying themselves as to the chances of success, such funders do not actively intervene in the conduct of the litigation if allegations of champerty are to be avoided.[96] In practice, however, such agreements are more likely to come to the notice of the courts when the latter make costs orders directly against the funders after the claim they funded has failed.[97]

9–26

---

[89] See *Skelton v Baxter* [1919] 2 K.B. 544. cf. *Neville v London Express Newspaper* [1919] A.C. 368.

[90] See *Martell v Consett Iron Co* [1955] 1 Ch. 363. See also *Abraham v Thompson* [1997] 4 All E.R. 362, CA (security for costs).

[91] See *Martell v Consett Iron Co* [1955] 1 Ch. 363, CA. per Jenkins LJ at 422 and, per Hodson LJ at 429.

[92] See *Stocznia Gdanska SA v Latvian Shipping Co* [1999] 3 All E.R. 822; see also *Wild v Simpson* [1919] 2 K.B. 544, per Atkin LJ at 564, CA.

[93] See, per Lord Mustill in *Giles v Thompson* [1994] 1 A.C. 142 at 164; [1993] 3 All E.R. 321 at 360.

[94] See *Stocznia Gdanska SA v Latvian Shipping Co* [1999] 3 All E.R. 822. In *Grovewood Holdings Plc v James Capel & Co*, Lightman J held that champerty would normally constitute abuse of process but his view has been heavily criticised: see, especially, *Abraham v Thompson* [1997] 4 All E.R. 362 at 378, per Millett LJ.

[95] See, e.g. *Ramsey v Hartley* [1977] 1 W.L.R. 686; [1977] 2 All E.R. 673, CA. See also *Stein v Blake* [1996] 1 A.C. 243; [1995] 2 All E.R. 961; *Norglen v Reeds Rains Prudential* [1999] 2 A.C. 1. cf. *Re Oasis Merchandising Services* [1997] 1 All E.R. 1009, CA; *Ruttle Plant v Secretary of State for Environment Food and Rural Affairs (No.2)* [2008] EWHC 238 (TCC); [2009] 1 All E.R. 448. For criticism of the insolvency exception see Adrian Walters, "A Modern Doctrine of Champerty?" (1996) 112 L.Q.R. 560 at p.566: "Clearly, the judges who developed the exception perceived champerty as an obstacle to the efficient administration of bankruptcies and company liquidations in the interests of creditors. Nevertheless, it is far from clear why this laudable policy objective was elevated at the expense of other equally meritworthy objectives such as the impartial administration of civil justice".

[96] See *Excalibur Ventures LLC v Texas Keystone Inc* [2016] EWCA Civ 1144 per Tomlinson LJ at [31].

[97] See eg *Excalibur Ventures LLC v Texas Keystone Inc* (previous note). See also *Arkin v Borchard Lines Ltd* [2015] 1 WLR 3055.

9–27 **Agreements unenforceable.** Situations in which merely the funding of the litigation is unlawful must, however, be distinguished from those in which the issue itself is whether a party acquired enforceable rights under an agreement which was unlawful by reason of champerty or maintenance. In *Aratra Potato Co v Taylor Johnson Garrett*[98] Garland J held, in accordance with the general principles relating to illegal agreements, that a champertous contract cannot be enforced by either party to it. It followed, on the facts of that case, that solicitors who had entered into a champertous agreement with their clients could not recover their fees but, neither could the clients contend that the illegality enabled them to recover the fees already paid.[99] Similarly, if an assignee only obtained his title under an assignment which was unlawful, by reason of maintenance or champerty, any claim to vindicate that title by action will necessarily fail.[100]

7. IMPLICATIONS FOR PUBLIC POLICY GENERALLY

9–28 **When circumstances change.** In general, the law relating to maintenance and champerty provides a striking example of how the scope of public policy, as expounded by the judges, can alter as circumstances change. In relation to the assignment of choses in action, however, it also illustrates how public policy is capable of "crystallising" into specific rules which can acquire a technical life of their own, and be resistant to alteration even when the reasons for their origin are all but forgotten.[101] Even in the context of more broadly expressed doctrine, however, there can be significant judicial disagreement as to the legitimacy of innovation to reflect changes in the world at large.[102]

9–29 **Relationship with statute.** The area also highlights the complex nature of the relationship between legislation on the one hand, and public policy as developed by the common law, on the other. At least three different aspects of, or even approaches to, that relationship may be identified in the recent debates surrounding the methods of remunerating those involved in legal and similar processes. First, judges anxious to develop the law can point to the policies underlying legislation and extend their application, by analogy, to situations outside the scope of the statute itself.[103] The reasoning of Millett LJ in *Thai Trading Co v Taylor*[104] and of Sir Richard Scott VC in *Bevan Ashford v*

---

[98] [1995] 4 All E.R. 695.

[99] In so far as the judgment in this cases concerned unjust enrichment it must now be read in the light of the decision of the Supreme Court in *Patel v Mirza* [2016] UKSC 42.

[100] See *Laurent v Sale & Co* [1963] 1 W.L.R. 829; [1963] 2 All E.R. 63.

[101] *Giles v Thompson* [1994] 1 A.C. 142 per Lord Mustill at 164; [1993] 3 All E.R. 321 at 360.

[102] In *Martell v Consett Iron Co* [1955] 1 Ch. 363 at 414 Dankwerts J said, in relation to the decision of the House of Lords in *Neville v London Express Newspapers* [1919] A.C. 368, that "what may have been the last word on public policy in 1919 is not necessarily the test in 1954". In the Court of Appeal, however, Jenkins LJ said ([1955] Ch. at 414) that he would "find it impossible to hold that we would be justified in regarding ourselves as no longer bound" by two earlier decisions "on the strength of the changes in public policy or in social or economic conditions since those cases were approved in the year 1918 by a majority of the House of Lords".

[103] See generally, J. Beatson, "The Role of Statute in the Development of Common Law Doctrine" (2001) 117 L.Q.R. 247, especially at pp.256–258.

[104] See [1998] Q.B. 781; [1998] 3 All E.R. 65 at 73, CA.

Yeandle,[105] provide striking examples of this technique. Secondly, the converse approach may be adopted by those anxious to preserve the status quo as far as the common law is concerned: if legislative intervention has recently occurred it should be assumed that Parliament addressed itself to all the relevant issues and that further judicial development of the law would therefore be inappropriate.[106] Thirdly, the legislature itself may have acted against the background of the existing common law and the values which it happened to embody at a particular time. The question may then arise as to how far that has had the effect of codifying those values and inhibiting their further development.[107] This issue is perhaps particularly prone to arise in relation to subordinate legislation, and to become interwoven with questions relating to vires. The controversy surrounding the status and effect of the Solicitors Practice Rules in the "no win, no fee" cases may be said to illustrate this aspect of the problem.[108]

Room to manoeuvre.   At least in theory, these three approaches are not conflicting alternatives. Statutes obviously differ in their scope and background. Nevertheless, in practice there will often be uncertainty about the precise intentions of the legislature, with a consequent degree of judicial room to manoeuvre between the three approaches. It is submitted that the first approach could be deployed in these circumstances rather more frequently than the innate conservatism of the judiciary is apt to allow. Of course unambiguous wording and clarity of intention will sometimes effectively rule out creative use of statute to develop the common law by analogy with legislative changes and policies. Where this is not the case, however, imaginative use of ideas derived from statute may provide an opportunity for the judges to develop the law at a time when naked assertion of a policy-making role, by the common law itself, would clearly be regarded as illegitimate.

9–30

Public policy's policy.   The need for careful evaluation of underlying policies, and their limits, is not confined to statutes. It also applies to the established common law heads of public policy themselves. In *Giles v Thompson*"[109] the defendants, who sought to defend the claims against them by alleging champerty, argued that the arrangements to which the claimants had come with the car-hire companies were not, in fact, in the best interest of the claimants themselves. In the Court of Appeal, Steyn LJ described this as "an argument, seductively presented, which was calculated to divert the judicial eye from following the ball". He continued[110]:

9–31

---

[105] See [1999] Ch. 239 at 251; [1998] 3 All E.R. 238 at 248.
[106] See, e.g. *Awwad v Geraghty & Co* [2001] 1 Q.B. 570, per May LJ at 600; [2000] 1 All E.R. 608 at 634–635. cf. *Factortame v Secretary of State for the Environment (No.2)* [2002] EWCA Civ 932; [2002] 4 All E.R. 97. See also *Sibthorpe v Southwark LBC* [2011] EWCA Civ 25 at [47] per Lord Neuberger MR.
[107] *Awwad v Geraghty & Co* [2001] 1 Q.B. 570 per Schiemann LJ at 576–577; [2000] 1 All E.R. 608 at 611.
[108] See *Hughes v Kingston upon Hull City Council* [1999] Q.B. 1193; [1999] 2 All E.R. 49.
[109] [1994] 1 A.C. 142; [1993] 3 All E.R. 321.
[110] [1993] 3 All E.R. at 336.

"The relevant head of public policy exists to protect public justice and courts have always focused on the protection of the party confronted with maintained litigation . . . In the context of the present cases the head of public policy does not exist to protect the plaintiffs. It exists to protect the interests of the defendants. The undesirable features which are alleged to operate against the interests of plaintiffs are outside the existing head of public policy which condemns champerty."

Even where heads of public policy have apparently crystallised into specific rules of law, analysis of their original purpose may facilitate a less deferential attitude towards their continuance in changed circumstances.[111] Of course caution will be necessary where the rules have been relied upon in the making of long-term dispositions. Nevertheless, in an area such as the assignment of choses in action, there is still scope for greater judicial boldness and clarity in expounding the law in a manner appropriate to the modern commercial world.

---

[111] cf. Adrian Walters, "A Modern Doctrine of Champerty?" (1996) 112 L.Q.R. 560 at 567: ". . . a liberal approach to champerty is required which promotes the access to justice ideal and eschews the perpetuation of arbitrary distinctions".

CHAPTER 10

PEACE AND WAR

1. INTRODUCTION

International dimension. Public policy issues are not confined to purely **10–01** municipal contracts. Not infrequently contracts which it is sought to enforce in England have an international dimension, usually because one or both of the parties lives abroad. Two broad questions may be distinguished, as far as contractual relationships in peace-time are concerned. First, to what extent will English law decline to enforce a contract, governed by English law, on the ground that the agreement or its performance could involve contravention of the law of another, friendly, state. Secondly, to what extent will English concepts of public policy be applied to a contract, sought to be enforced in England, which is governed by a different law under which it is unobjectionable. The answer to the second question depends upon the relevant principles of the conflict of laws; which, since the passing of the Contracts (Applicable Law) Act 1990, have been those embodied in the EEC Convention on the Law Applicable to Contractual Obligations 1980, known as the Rome Convention. Questions of both kinds can arise in the course of international trade in peace-time. If, however, hostilities should break out, between the UK and another state, a very different body of doctrine may fall to be applied to contracts made between parties resident in the opposing countries. In this chapter the peace-time principles based upon international comity will be considered first, and then the authorities on "trading with the enemy" will be examined. The latter offer general insights into the approach of the courts to the resolution of illegality issues, which are not confined to the particular war-time situations which gave rise to the cases.

2. INTERNATIONAL COMITY

(a) Contracts Governed by English Law

Illegality at the place of performance. English law will not normally enforce **10–02** a contract, governed by English law, if its performance would involve the contravention of the law of another State where that performance is to take place. In *Ralli Bros v Campania Naviera Sota Y Aznar*[1] a charterparty governed by English law provided for the carriage of a cargo from India to Spain, and for payment to be made in Spain. The level of payment stipulated happened,

---

[1] [1920] 2 K.B. 287.

however, to exceed a statutory maximum which had been prescribed by the Spanish government as part of a scheme to regulate the cost of imports, in order to keep down domestic prices. A unanimous Court of Appeal held that an action could not be brought in England to secure payment at the higher contractual level, and indicated that any older authorities apparently to the contrary were wrongly decided.[2] "This country should not", said Scrutton LJ, "assist or sanction the breach of the laws of other independent States".[3] Similarly, in *Regazzoni v K. C. Sethia (1944) Ltd*,[4] the House of Lords held that a contract to ship goods from India, with the intention that they should eventually reach South Africa, was unenforceable; the Government of India having statutorily prohibited the export from India of goods "destined for any port or place in the Union of South Africa". Lord Keith of Avonholme said[5]:

> "In the present case I can see no escape from the view that to recognise the contract between the appellant and the respondent as an enforceable contract would give a just cause for complaint by the Government of India and should be regarded as contrary to conceptions of international comity. On grounds of public policy, therefore, this is a contract which our courts ought not to recognize."

10–03   **Exceptional cases.**   Lord Reid said in *Regazzoni v K. C. Sethia (1944) Ltd*[6] that he could "imagine a foreign law involving persecution of such a character that we would regard an agreement to break it as meritorious".[7] Lord Somervell also made an observation to the same effect.[8] No hypothetical illustrations were provided. It is to be hoped, however, that an agreement, for example, to contravene a ban on the importation of books and newspapers, imposed by a tyrannical regime, would not be regarded with disfavour by the courts.

10–04   **Revenue laws.**   Lord Mansfield once famously remarked, well over two centuries ago,[9] that "no country ever takes notice of the revenue laws of another". In practice, however, that view has long been outdated. In *Regazzoni v K. C. Sethia (1944) Ltd*[10] Lord Keith of Avonholme observed that Lord Mansfield's proposition was "too widely expressed", and required "fuller examination and elucidation". The Court of Appeal in that case was more emphatic in its rejection of the eighteenth century jurisprudence on this point,[11] and Lord Somervell in the

---

[2] e.g. *Barker v Hodgson* (1814) 3 M. & S. 267.

[3] See also *Walton (Grain) v British Italian Trading Co* [1959] 1 Lloyd's Rep. 223 (especially at 236), in which Diplock J followed "the classic judgment" of Scrutton LJ in the *Ralli Bros* case; and *Gillespie Management Corp v Terrace Properties* (1989) 62 D.L.R. (4th) 221 (British Columbia Court of Appeal).

[4] [1958] A.C. 301. See *Mahonia v JP Morgan Chase* [2003] EWHC 1927, per Colman J at 12–33.

[5] [1958] A.C. 301 at 827.

[6] [1958] A.C. 301 at 325.

[7] cf. *Oppenheimer v Cattermole* [1976] A.C. 249.

[8] "There may, of course, be laws the enforcement of which would be against 'morals'. In such a case an exception might be made to the general principle" [1958] A.C. 301 at 330. See also Dicey, Morris & Collins *The Conflict of Laws*, edited by Collins, 15th edn (London: Sweet & Maxwell, 2012), p.1876.

[9] See *Holman v Johnson* (1775) 1 Cowp. 341 at 343.

[10] [1958] A.C. 301 at 328.

[11] [1956] 2 Q.B. 490, especially, per Denning LJ at 515–516. See also, per Kerr LJ in *Euro-Diam v Bathurst* [1990] 1 Q.B. 1 at 40, CA.

House of Lords said specifically "that the courts of this country should not today enforce a contract to smuggle goods into or out of a foreign and friendly state".[12] Thus in *Soleimany v Soleimany*[13] the Court of Appeal held that a contract which involved smuggling carpets out of Iran would be unenforceable for illegality. There is, nevertheless, a sense in which illegality cases involving revenue laws can give rise to special problems, and these are not confined to contravention of the laws of other states, but can occur in situations simply involving breach of municipal revenue law. Since the contravention of such provisions is rarely an end in itself, difficult issues can arise as to the effect upon the rights of the parties,[14] which may suffer disproportionately if the principles of illegality are applied with insufficient precision or analysis. Thus Lord Reid, in *Regazzoni*'s case,[15] was careful to reserve his opinion about the "difficult questions" which can arise "where parties agree to deal with goods which they both know have already been smuggled out of a foreign country", or "where the seller knows that the buyer intends to use the goods for an illegal purpose or to smuggle them into a foreign country". Lord Keith of Avonholme also suggested that some of the decisions, on apparent failure to take notice of the revenue laws of other states, might be "supported on the view that the transaction in question was unaffected by the illegality" because one party simply had "no concern, or reason to be concerned" with the intentions of the other; or because "the illegality had been exhausted and new rights and liabilities had emerged which did not call for any recognition of the illegality".[16]

Scope of "performance".   The ease with which the authorities on unenforce-   **10–05**
ability by virtue of foreign law can involve primarily more general aspects of the law relating to illegal transactions, rather than just the international comity point, is illustrated by the well-known decision of the Court of Appeal in *Foster v Driscoll*.[17] In this case the Court held, by a majority, that a complicated arrangement to run whisky into the US, during the period of prohibition in that country, was unenforceable for illegality. Although Scrutton LJ differed from his brethren, he only did so on a factual point which has arisen in other cases not involving a foreign element: in effect the distinction between knowledge and participation.[18] The contract had not actually been performed, and it was apparently possible that performance could have taken the form of transferring the whisky to a third party in Canada; from where the third party would smuggle it into the US. Since mere knowledge of another's unlawful intention is normally insufficient to implicate an otherwise innocent party in an illegal scheme, Scrutton LJ considered that awareness of the whisky's ultimate destination did not render the contract illegal. This reading of the facts of the case by Scrutton LJ was, however, considered to be wholly unconvincing by Lawrence and Sankey

---

[12] [1958] A.C. 301 at 330.
[13] [1999] Q.B. 785.
[14] See, e.g. *Geismar v Sun Alliance and London Insurance* [1978] Q.B. 383.
[15] [1958] A.C. 301 at 323–324.
[16] [1958] A.C. 301, at 328. cf. *Euro-Diam v Bathurst* [1990] 1 Q.B. 1.
[17] [1929] 1 K.B. 470.
[18] See Ch.4, above.

LJJ. The elaborate transaction had clearly been, in the words of the former,[19] a "partnership formed for the main purpose of deriving profit" from the high prices which contraband whisky could yield as result of prohibition. Whatever the formal position relating to "performance", the partners were therefore participants in the illegal scheme. An actual obligation to break the law is not a necessary condition of illegality. Sankey LJ correctly expressed the position as follows[20]:

> "In my view, an English contract should, and will, be held invalid on account of illegality if the *real object and intention* of the parties necessitates them joining in an endeavour to perform in a foreign and friendly country some act which is illegal by the law of such country, notwithstanding the fact that there may be, in a certain event, alternative modes or places of performing, which permit the contract to be performed legally."

10–06 *Foster v Driscoll* **confirmed.** Scrutton LJ's dissenting interpretation of the facts in *Foster's* case did not find favour with the unanimous House of Lords in *Regazzoni v K. C. Sethia (1944) Ltd*,[21] which held *Foster v Driscoll* to have been rightly decided. These two cases were recently relied upon by the Court of Appeal in *Royal Boskalis Westminster NV v Mountain*[22] in which an agreement, the effect of which was to breach legislation passed in several countries implementing United Nations sanctions against Iraq, was held to be unenforceable for illegality. Elaborate attempts by counsel to defend the agreement by analysing minutely the knowledge and intention of the parties, somewhat similar to the approach of Scrutton LJ in *Foster v Driscoll*, were rejected as unconvincing. It was as "plain as a pikestaff", said Phillips LJ,[23] that if the objective of the parties was to be achieved, "sanctions legislation would have to be breached".

10–07 **Contrary to public policy at the place of performance.** In *Lemenda Trading Co v African Middle East Petroleum Co*[24] the defendants wished to secure the renewal of an oil supply contract between themselves, and the national oil company of the state of Qatar. To that end they engaged the services of the claimant who agreed, for payment, to use his influence with the leading personnel of the Qatar company. The renewal was duly secured, but the defendants refused to pay the claimant on the ground that agreements, such as theirs with him, were treated in Qatar as being contrary to the public policy of that state and unenforceable. It so happened, however, that the particular agreement between the claimant and the defendants was governed not by the law of Qatar, but by English law. Moreover, even though the agreement was to be performed in Qatar, there was no suggestion that the agreement was formally illegal in that state, as

---

[19] [1929] 1 K.B. 470 at 510.
[20] [1929] 1 K.B. 470, at 521–522 (italics supplied).
[21] [1958] A.C. 301.
[22] [1999] Q.B. 674.
[23] [1999] Q.B. 674, at 733.
[24] [1988] Q.B. 448; [1988] 1 All E.R. 513.

distinct from being merely unenforceable on grounds of public policy. Phillips J held that the principle in the *Ralli Bros* case was therefore not directly applicable. He said[25]:

> "There is a clear distinction between acts which infringe public policy and acts which violate provisions of law. I have been referred to no decided case that supports the proposition that the English courts should, as a matter of comity, refuse to enforce an English law contract on the sole ground that performance would be contrary to the public policy of the country of performance. The public policy of Qatar cannot, of itself, constitute any bar to the enforcement of the agreement in this case."

Where public policies coincide. Phillips J nevertheless went on to hold, **10–08** however, that the claimant's claim was unenforceable. He did so on the ground that English public policy also looked with disfavour on agreements to use influence, in return for payment, so as to procure benefits from third parties.[26] The fact that the public policy of the law by which the contract was governed happened to coincide with the public policy of the place of performance, was regarded as decisive. He said[27]:

> "In my judgment, the English courts should not enforce an English law contract which falls to be performed abroad where (i) it relates to an adventure which is contrary to a head of English public policy which is founded on general principles of morality and (ii) the same public policy applies in the country of performance so that the agreement would not be enforceable under the law of that country. In such a situation international comity combines with English domestic policy to militate against enforcement."

(b)   Contracts Governed by Foreign Law

"Ordre public". It is implicit in the reasoning of Phillips J in the *Lemenda* **10–09** case, based as it was upon the common approach of English law and the law of Qatar, that English law's conceptions of public policy are not applied automatically to every contract sought to be enforced in England, irrespective of the law governing the contract or the law of the place where it is to be performed. In fact it is clear that they are not so applied. Thus in *Lemenda* itself, Phillips J inclined to the view that the moral objection to the "practice of exacting payment for the use of personal influence" was not "so weighty as to lead an English court to refuse to enforce an agreement regardless of the country of performance and regardless of the attitude of that country to such a practice".[28] Although the contract in the *Lemenda* case was governed by English law, the question of the applicability of English law notions of public policy arises acutely where the contract is *not* governed by English law, and is not objectionable under the law by which it *is* governed. The general principle is stated by art.16 of the Rome Convention as follows:

---

[25] [1988] Q.B. 448 at 456; [1988] 1 All E.R. 513 at 519.
[26] See *Parkinson v College of Ambulance* [1925] 2 K.B. 1; *Montefiore v Menday Motor Components Ltd* [1918] 2 K.B. 241; *Norman v Cole* (1800) 3 Esp. 253. For discussion, see Ch.7, above.
[27] [1988] Q.B. 448 at 461; [1988] 1 All E.R. 513 at 523.
[28] [1988] Q.B. 448 at 461; [1988] 1 All E.R. 513 at 523.

"The application of a rule of the law of any country . . . may be refused only if such application is manifestly incompatible with the public policy ('ordre public') of the forum."[29]

Thus a contract which is governed by foreign law, under which it is unobjectionable, can nevertheless be unenforceable in England if it offends against some aspect of public policy which English law considers to be of overriding importance.[30] It is not entirely clear, however, which aspects of public policy fall into this category, and the matter will inevitably fall to be decided on a case by case basis.

10–10   **Fraud.**   Contracts which involve the fraudulent deception of third parties are, however, likely to be regarded as invalid on this ground. In *Mitsubishi Corporation v Aristidis I. Alafouzos*[31] it was alleged that the price stated in a contract to build a ship in Japan, for a Greek owner, had been artificially inflated in order to secure necessary permits from the Japanese authorities, with the true price being included in a side agreement between the parties.[32] Steyn J, before whom the case came on an interlocutory application, indicated that if the allegation was proved the contract would be unenforceable in England, notwithstanding that the conduct in question may not have been unlawful under the law of Japan. He said[33]:

> "It would be extraordinary if public policy, in the context of international business transactions, condemned such conduct in this country but allowed the coercive power of the state to be enlisted if the deception was practised abroad. I hold, without hesitation, that the public conscience does not permit our Courts to show a larger tolerance to the enforcement of a deceiving transaction if it took place abroad."

Although the contract in the *Mitsubishi* case was in fact governed by English law, it would seem to be clear from the emphatic wording of Steyn J that his approach would have been the same even if the contract had been governed by Japanese law.

10–11   ***Kaufman v Gerson.***   In the difficult case of *Kaufman v Gerson*,[34] enforceability of a contract governed by French law, to be performed in France, was refused in England. The defendant had been coerced into entering the contract by a threat to prosecute her husband for a criminal offence, and the consideration for the agreement was that the husband would not be prosecuted if his wife made good the loss which the commission of the offence had caused to the claimant. The latter brought an action in England to recover the sum due under the agreement.

---

[29] See also art.7(2): "Nothing in this Convention shall restrict the application of the rules of the law of the forum in a situation where they are mandatory irrespective of the law otherwise applicable to the contract".

[30] cf. per Lord Halsbury LC in *Re Missouri Steamship Co* (1889) 42 Ch. D. 321 at 336: "Where a contract is void on the ground of immorality . . . then the contract would be void all over the world, and no civilised country would be called on to enforce it". See also *Vervaeke v Smith* [1983] A.C. 145, especially at 156–157 (Lord Hailsham LC) and 164 (Lord Simon).

[31] [1988] 1 Lloyd's Rep. 191.

[32] cf. *Alexander v Rayson* [1936] 1 K.B. 169.

[33] See [1988] 1 Lloyd's Rep. 191 at 195.

[34] [1904] 1 K.B. 591.

At first instance Wright J found in his favour, holding that although such a contract would probably have been unenforceable for illegality under English law, on the ground that it was one to stifle a prosecution, that illegality should not lead the courts to decline enforceability of a foreign contract.[35] It is interesting that the Court of Appeal was inclined to agree with Wright J on this point, so that the case strongly suggests that the public policy which discourages the stifling of prosecutions in England will not usually be regarded as so fundamental as to warrant international application. The real significance of the case, however, lies in the fact that the Court of Appeal reversed Wright J, and found for the defendant, on the ground that the contract would have been additionally unenforceable in England, but not in France, as having been procured by duress.[36] "In my opinion", said Sir Richard Henn Collins MR,[37] "it is a universal principle of the courts of this country that they will not enforce any contract which has been brought about by coercion"; and Romer LJ indicated that "to enforce such a contract would be to do something conflicting with the essential moral interests of the community".[38] This decision has been much criticised,[39] and does seem questionable on its particular facts.[40] Nevertheless the broad principle that, if severe pressure is exerted upon a party, the resulting contract will be unenforceable in England, must be correct. The application of physical violence, or the threat of such violence, will clearly have that effect.[41]

Other forms of pressure. Thus in *Royal Boskalis Westminster NV v Mountain*[42] the Court of Appeal held that a contract procured, inter alia, by a threat of hostage-taking, would be unenforceable in England, despite apparently being valid by the governing law of the contract in that case.[43] Where less extreme forms of pressure are concerned, it must inevitably be a question of degree, to be decided in relation to the circumstances of the case,[44] whether they will have an overriding effect. Accordingly, it appears that English law will be content to allow the proper law of the contract to determine the validity, or otherwise, of a contract procured by the use of economic "pressure" in an industrial relations dispute, notwithstanding that such pressure would have an

10–12

---

[35] [1903] 2 K.B. 114. For contracts to stifle prosecutions see Ch.8, above.

[36] See also *Rousillon v Rousillon* (1880) 14 Ch.D. 351.

[37] [1904] 1 K.B. 591 at 599 (wording as quoted is from 90 L.T. 608 at 610).

[38] [1904] 1 K.B. 591, at 599–600 (wording as quoted is from 90 L.T. 608 at 611).

[39] See *National Surety Co v Larsen* [1929] 4 D.L.R. 918 in which the British Columbia Court of Appeal declined to follow *Kaufman v Gerson*.

[40] cf. Dicey, Morris & Collins, *The Conflict of Laws*, 15th edn (London: Sweet & Maxwell, 2012), pp.1873; and also p.1877 (Illustration 4).

[41] cf. per Mathew LJ in *Kaufman v Gerson* [1904] 1 K.B. 591 at 600: "The facts show that moral torture, and nothing less, was applied to the defendant . . ." (wording as quoted is from 90 L.T. 608 at 611).

[42] [1999] Q.B. 674.

[43] ". . . there remains a class of duress so unconscionable that it will cause the English court, as a matter of public policy, to override the proper law of the contract" [1999] Q.B. 674 at 729.

[44] cf. *Israel Discount Bank of New York v Hadjipateras* [1984] 1 W.L.R. 137 per Stephenson LJ; [1983] 3 All E.R. 129 at 134, CA: "I do not doubt that an agreement obtained by undue influence, like an agreement obtained by duress or coercion, may be treated by our courts as invalidating a foreign judgment based on the agreement, or as a ground for not enforcing it as contrary to the distinctive public policy of this country".

invalidating effect under English common law.[45] On other hand, the proposition, associated with *Kaufman v Gerson*, that the stifling of prosecutions will *not* be regarded as sufficiently serious to infect all contracts sued upon in England, cannot be absolute. It is difficult to believe, for example, that the English courts would ever enforce an agreement to prevent a prosecution for murder, in return for money.

10–13   **Other cases.**   It appears that the general principle, which denies enforceability to a contract entered into with the *intention* of contravening the law of another state,[46] is also one which will normally be insisted upon by the English courts, irrespective of whether or not English law happens to be the governing law of the contract in question.[47] On the other hand, it is now doubtful whether the specific rule associated with *Ralli Bros v Compania Naviera Sota Y Aznar*,[48] that a contract will not be enforced in England because its performance happens to be illegal by the law of another country, where it is to be performed, will be insisted upon if the contract is governed by the law of yet another country—which has no such rule and would regard the contract as unobjectionable. Although long regarded as an overriding rule of English public policy, the preferred view now appears to be that the rule in the *Ralli Bros* case is merely a rule of English municipal law, which is only to be applied to contracts governed by that law.[49] In general, the need for an intuitive judicial response to the facts of the particular case, in determining whether some aspect of English public policy should be applied to contracts governed by foreign law, can never be wholly eliminated. Fortunately, this response is likely to be fairly uniform. It is clearly important, however, that in as much as other jurisdictions may legitimately reflect cultural differences in their attitudes to familiar situations, the approach of the English courts should be both informed and sensitive.

---

[45] This appears to be implicit in the decision of the House of Lords in *Dimskal Shipping Co v International Transport Workers Federation* [1992] A.C. 152.
[46] See *Foster v Driscoll* [1929] 1 K.B. 470 and *Regazzoni v K. C. Sethia (1944) Ltd* [1958] A.C. 301, discussed above.
[47] See *Royal Boskalis Westminster NV v Mountain* [1999] Q.B. 674 at 692, per Stuart-Smith LJ. See also *Dicey, Morris & Collins, The Conflict of Laws*, edited by Collins, 15th edn, (London: Sweet & Maxwell, 2012), p.1838–1840.
[48] [1920] 2 K.B. 287, see para.10–02, above.
[49] See *Dicey, Morris & Collins, The Conflict of Laws*, edited by Collins, 15th edn (London: Sweet & Maxwell, 2012), p.1838–1840. See also Reynolds, "Illegality by Lex Loci Solutionis" (1992) 109 L.Q.R. 553. Paradoxically, art.7(1) of the Rome Convention could have made the *Ralli Bros* rule one of general application even if it had not been previously, but that Article is not part of English law: see the Contracts (Applicable Law) Act 1990 s.2(2).

3.   TRADING WITH THE ENEMY[50]

(a)   The Principles

Continuing importance.   The two world wars of the twentieth century,   **10–14**
preceded by major conflicts during the eighteenth and nineteenth centuries,
generated a not inconsiderable body of case-law concerning the invalidity, on
public policy grounds, of contracts which involved "trading with the enemy".
Fortunately, the likelihood of the UK becoming involved in yet another major
conflict, on the same scale as the wars of 1914–18 and 1939–45, currently seems
remote. When hostilities do occur, as over the Falkland Islands in 1982, military
operations are likely to claim authorisation from resolutions of the United
Nations[51]; without war ever being formally declared. Such conflicts may well
give rise to specific legislative provisions governing various aspects of
commercial activity, albeit on a more limited scale than the Trading with the
Enemy Acts of 1914 and 1939. The common law principles exist independently
of any legislative provisions which may accompany the outbreak of hostilities,
however, and remain important.[52] They may assist in clarifying the precise effect
upon contracts of any legislative provisions relating to a future conflict; and they
may even be directly applicable to contracts made subject to English law when
war, not involving the UK itself, happens to break out in the place of
performance.[53]

Insights into illegality generally.   For the purposes of the present work,   **10–15**
however, the cases warrant attention primarily for any insights which they may
provide, beyond their immediate context, into the working of the common law
principles of public policy generally. It is therefore appropriate, once the basic
common law doctrine relating to trading with the enemy has been outlined, to
examine the cases from this more general perspective. The issues touched upon
include the tension, in the public policy context, between certainty and flexibility;
and the status of contractual terms which seek apparently to provide for the
impact of illegality upon the agreement. Some of the judgments also consider the
nature and difficulty, in the context of illegality, of such distinctions as that
between contractual and proprietary interests, and between executed and
executory contracts.

---

[50] See McNair and Watts, *The Legal Effects of War*, 4th edn, (Cambridge University Press, 1966),
especially Chs 3 and 4.

[51] cf. the 2003 invasion of Iraq.

[52] cf. *McNair and Watts*, The Legal Effects of War, 4th edn (1966), at p.49: "When the United
Kingdom becomes a party to an armed conflict not amounting to the technical state of war, the
automatic consequences of war such as enemy status, abrogation of most contracts, prohibition of
intercourse, etc., are absent. Nevertheless, there are many acts, particularly within the sphere of
contract or transfer of property, which, while normally free from objection, would become illegal on
the ground that their performance during the armed conflict would be contrary to public policy as
recognized by the common law".

[53] cf. *Arab Bank v Barclays Bank* [1954] A.C. 495.

10–16   **The doctrine.**   "In my opinion", said Sir William Scott"[54] in the well-known case of *The Hoop*[55] "there exists such a general rule in the maritime jurisprudence of this country by which all trading with the public enemy, unless with the permission of the sovereign, is forbidden". The lengthy judgment in this case, which concerned the importation of goods from the continent of Europe during the French revolutionary war, shows that the doctrine which it enunciates was already considered to be well-established before the end of the eighteenth century. Although itself a decision in Admiralty, Sir William Scott found it "difficult to conceive" that the position at common law could "by any possibility be otherwise, for the rule in no degree arises from the transaction being upon the water, but from principles of public policy and of public law, which are just as weighty on the one element as on the other".[56] That the common law rule is indeed the same was confirmed by the Court of Exchequer Chamber, half a century later in *Esposito v Bowden*[57] at the beginning of the Crimean war. A charterparty, by which a cargo of grain was to be carried from Odessa to Falmouth, was held to be dissolved by the subsequent declaration of war upon Russia, which rendered Odessa a hostile port. The "declaration of war", said Willes J delivering the judgment of the Court,[58] "imports a prohibition of commercial intercourse and correspondence with the inhabitants of the enemy's country, and that such intercourse, except with the licence of the Crown, is illegal".

10–17   **Residence.**   The first major exposition of the doctrine in the twentieth century is to be found in the important judgment of a seven-member Court of Appeal, delivered by Lord Reading CJ in *Porter v Freudenberg*,[59] early in the First World War. Lord Reading said[60]:

> "This law was founded in earlier days upon the conception that all subjects owing allegiance to the Crown were at war with subjects of the State at war with the Crown, and later it was grounded upon public policy, which forbids the doing of acts that will be or may be to the advantage of the enemy State by increasing its capacity for prolonging hostilities in adding to the credit, money or goods, or other resources available to individuals in the enemy State. Trading with a British subject or the subject of a neutral State carrying on business in the hostile territory is as much assistance to the alien enemy as if it were with a subject of enemy nationality carrying on business in the enemy State, and, therefore, for the purpose of the enforcement of civil rights, they are equally treated as alien enemies. *It is clear law that the test for this purpose is not nationality but the place of carrying on business.*"

Accordingly, British subjects resident in enemy territory cannot have access to our courts during wartime,[61] whereas subjects of the enemy state lawfully resident in this country *are* able to sue. In *Schaffenius v Goldberg*[62] the claimant,

---

54   Later Lord Stowell.
55   See (1799) 1 Ch. Rob. 196 at 198.
56   (1799) 1 Ch. Rob. 196, at 217.
57   (1857) 7 El. & Bl. 763.
58   (1857) 7 El. & Bl. 763, at 779.
59   [1915] 1 K.B. 857.
60   [1915] 1 K.B. 857, at 868 (italics supplied).
61   cf. *Bevan v Bevan* [1955] Q.B. 227.
62   [1916] 1 K.B. 284, CA.

who was German by birth but had lived in England for 22 years, was able to enforce a contract of loan even though he had been interned as a civilian prisoner of war.[63]

Corporate claimants.[64]   Determining the status of corporate claimants, for the   **10–18** purposes of the rule, sometimes gave rise to difficulty. In *Daimler Co Ltd v Continental Tyre and Rubber Co (Great Britain) Ltd*[65] a company registered in England had German directors who were resident in Germany, where most of the shares were also held. When the company sought to enforce a trade debt during the First World War, an eight-member House of Lords, while striking out the case on other grounds, found itself to be sharply divided as to whether or not the company was an alien enemy. Lord Halsbury LC was emphatic that it was, whereas Lords Shaw and Parmoor considered that "a company registered in this country, and which is not carrying on business in an enemy country, is not an enemy company ... whatever may be the nationality of its directors and corporators". Lord Parker, with whom Lords Mersey, Kinnear and Atkinson agreed, observed that "something more than the mere place or country of registration must be looked at"; and concluded that the "acts of a company's organs, its directors, managers, secretary, and so forth ... are the company's acts and may invest it definitively with enemy character". Companies registered in England held to have acquired enemy status on these principles necessarily remain English companies bound by English law, including the prohibition on trading with the enemy.[66] A company will not acquire an enemy character merely because some of its shareholders are enemy aliens, but any attempt by those shareholders to vote by proxy at a meeting of the company will be disallowed.[67] Companies registered in friendly states will nevertheless acquire enemy status if their country is overrun, and effectively controlled, by the enemy.[68]

Actions against enemy aliens.   The principle that prevents enemy aliens from   **10–19** suing in the courts does not have the effect of conferring immunity from suit upon them for the duration of the war. In *Porter v Freudenberg*[69] Lord Reading CJ said:

> ". . . there seems no possible reason why our law should decree an immunity during hostilities to the alien enemy against the payment of just debts or demands due to British or neutral subjects. The rule of law suspending the alien enemy's right of action is based upon public policy, but no considerations of public policy are apparent which would justify preventing the enforcement by a British or neutral subject of a right against the enemy."

---

[63] See also *Re Man: Duchess of Sutherland* (1915) 31 T.L.R. 394, CA; *Schostall v Johnson* (1919) 36 T.L.R. 75.
[64] See McNair and Watts, *The Legal Effects of War*, 4th edn (1966), Ch.9.
[65] [1916] 2 A.C. 307.
[66] See *Kuenigl v Donnersmarck* [1955] 1 Q.B. 515; [1955] 1 All E.R. 46.
[67] See *Robson v Premier Oil and Pipe Line Co* [1915] 2 Ch.124.
[68] See *Sovfracht (V/O) v Van Udens Scheepvart En Agentur Maatschappi* [1943] A.C. 203.
[69] See [1915] 1 K.B. 857 at 880

Indeed "to hold otherwise", as Bailhache J put it in a decision which was approved in *Porter*'s case,[70] would "injure a British subject and . . . turn a disability into a relief". Thus in *Halsey v Lowenfeld*[71] an action by a landlord against an enemy alien tenant, for unpaid rent, was allowed to proceed. An alien enemy who is sued will be allowed to defend himself, and if necessary to appeal,[72] but should he be successful he will be unable to recover until after the war any costs which might be awarded.[73]

10–20   **Not confiscatory.**   In *Hugh Stevenson and Sons v Aktiengesellschaft Fur Carton-Nagen-Industrie*[74] Lord Finlay LC said:

> "It is not the law of this country that the property of enemy subjects is confiscated. Until the restoration of peace the enemy can, of course, make no claim to have it delivered up to him, but when peace is restored he is considered as entitled to his property with any fruits which it may have borne in the meantime."

In that case a partnership between an English company and a German company was dissolved by the outbreak of the First World War, but the English company continued to trade using the assets of the partnership. Atkin J held that the German company was entitled to receive its share of the value of the assets as at the date of the dissolution, but not to any of the wealth generated by those assets during the subsequent trading. Nevertheless, a majority of the Court of Appeal, itself upheld by a unanimous House of Lords, reversed his decision and held that the German company was entitled to a share of the profits created subsequently during the war. Their assets had been held by the English company in a fiduciary capacity, and they were entitled to an account of the proceeds. On the other hand, it follows from the dissolution of contracts by the declaration of war that purely contractual payments which would have accrued to an alien enemy, if the dissolution had not occurred, are necessarily lost to it forever. The principle in the *Hugh Stevenson* case is therefore confined to proprietary interests, which in some situations can be difficult to distinguish from mere contractual rights.

(b)   Questions of General Relevance to Illegality

(i)   Policy and Flexibility

10–21   **Rigid approach.**   In several of the leading cases on trading with the enemy, and on the status of enemy aliens in litigation, the courts were prompted to examine the nature of public policy itself, as a doctrine of the common law. In particular, they considered the extent to which it might afford the judges freedom to manoeuvre in response to the circumstances of each individual case. An early

---

[70] See *Robinson v Continental Insurance Co of Mannheim* [1915] 1 K.B. 155.
[71] [1916] 1 K.B. 143. See McNair and Watts, *The Legal Effects of War*, 4th edn, (1966), pp.292–293.
[72] See *Porter v Freudenberg* [1915] 1 K.B. 857 at 883, per Reading CJ.
[73] See *Robinson v Continental Insurance Co of Mannheim* [1915] 1 K.B. 155 at 162, per Bailhache J.
[74] [1918] A.C. 239.

denial of any substantive discretion is to be found in *The Hoop*,[75] in which Sir William Scott conceded that the unsuccessful parties deserved "great indulgence" because they had relied upon misleading assurances given to them by the authorities. But he nevertheless concluded that "if there is a rule of law on the subject binding the court, I must follow where that rule leads me; though it leads to consequences, which I may privately regret". A similar denial of flexibility is to be found in *Janson v Driefontein Mines*,[76] the circumstances of which were somewhat unusual in that the party which was seeking a less rigid approach did so in an attempt to broaden, rather than narrow, the scope of the applicable doctrine. The facts of the case have been given in an earlier chapter.[77] An underwriter sought to avoid liability on an insurance policy by arguing that the common law doctrine which invalidates contracts with the "enemy" should extend to situations in which war was "imminent"; and not be confined merely to the period following the formal declaration of war. A unanimous House of Lords upheld the decision of the trial judge, and the majority in the Court of Appeal, in favour of the claimants' right to enforce the policy. In criticising the defendant's argument, Lord Halsbury LC expressed himself as follows:

> "Instead of a known and ascertained rule which makes it clear whether a contract is unlawful or not, the intending parties to a contract must look all around the political horizon and form a judgment whether in some one, or more contingencies the fulfilment of it may be injurious to their own country in the event of war . . . I cannot imagine worse public policy than this."

Relaxation of rigidity.   In a subsequent case decided shortly before the end of   **10–22** the First World War, however, the House of Lords was sharply divided on the extent to which a supposedly rigid rule could be relaxed; with those favouring rigidity being in the minority. In *Rodriguez v Speyer Bros*[78] a partnership, dissolved at the outbreak of war, had consisted of six partners; one of whom had, by virtue of the war, become an enemy alien. In the process of dissolution the partnership sued for a debt which it was owed, and the question arose whether the action was properly constituted in that, since it was brought in the names of all the partners, an enemy alien was included as a co-claimant. There was little likelihood of the latter benefitting from the action,[79] and the majority of the House upheld the claim; accepting the argument that to do otherwise would simply inflict hardship on the British partners, and therefore be counter-productive. Lord Haldane, who was in the majority, posed the question thus[80]:

> "Is the rule which prevents an enemy alien from suing in the King's courts a crystallised proposition forming part of the ordinary common law so definite that it must be applied without reference to whether a particular case involves the real mischief to guard against which the rule was originally introduced? Or is the rule one of what is called public policy, which does not apply to a particular instance if that instance discloses no mischief from the point of view of public policy?"

---

[75] (1799) 1 Ch. Rob. 196.
[76] [1902] A.C. 484.
[77] See Ch.6, above.
[78] [1919] A.C. 59. See also Ch.6, above.
[79] But cf. in [1919] A.C. 59 at 114, per Lord Sumner, dissenting.
[80] See [1919] A.C. 59 at 77 ([1918–19] All E.R. Rep. 884 at 894).

10–23 **Crystallisation or underlying purpose?** In concluding that the rule should not be applied in the instant case, Lord Haldane contended that the rules relating to the status of enemy aliens could be applied flexibly with due regard to their underlying purpose. Lord Haldane's approach did, however, provoke Lord Atkinson and Lord Sumner to dissent in strong terms. The latter asserted that public policy applied to contracts "in order to disable, not in order to enable"; and that he had "never heard of a legal disability from which a party or transaction could be relieved because it would be good policy to do so".[81] Lord Atkinson said[82]:

> "This rule of our law, like many other of our rules of law, was, no doubt, originally based upon and embodies certain rules of public policy; but in this case, as in many others, the principles of public policy so adopted have, as numerous authorities conclusively show, crystallised, as it were, into strict and rigid rules of law."

10–24 **Certainty and pragmatism.** In *Sovfracht (V/0) v Van Udens Scheepvart En Agentuur Maatschappij*[83] which was decided during the Second World War, the House of Lords had to consider whether a company, registered in a friendly country, had become an alien enemy when the country in question had been overrun by the enemy. The company, citing the judgments of the majority in *Rodriguez v Speyer Bros*, urged that a pragmatic approach should be adopted, and that it should not automatically be regarded as an enemy alien. The House nevertheless decided unanimously that it should be so regarded, and that it therefore would not be allowed to pursue a claim for a pre-war debt. Lord Porter said that "whether a given act is against public policy must . . . be decided on general principles". It was "not permissible to say that a particular act will not in fact assist the enemy", if it belonged to "a class which is likely to assist him".[84] The observations of Lord Wright are of particular interest to the resolution of public policy issues beyond the specific context of trading with the enemy. He drew a distinction between, on the one hand, "the familiar rules of public policy" which "deal with internal affairs, contracts, dispositions of property, morality and the like", and on the other, "matters of national policy, of affairs of state in international and belligerent relations". The latter "should be regulated by a settled rule of law".[85] The proposition that the attainment of certainty should be accorded higher priority in some areas of public policy, and lower priority in others, is in principle an attractive one. This is not to say, however, that the distinction should simply be between municipal issues and those with an international dimension. A high degree of certainty has, for example, always been regarded as desirable where "dispositions of property" are concerned.

---

[81] [1919] A.C. 59 at 125 ([1918–19] All E.R. Rep. 884 at 917–918).
[82] [1919] A.C. 59 at 90 ([1918–19] All E.R. Rep. 884 at 899).
[83] [1943] A.C. 203. " . . . the most important of the war decisions given in the War of 1939 to 1945": McNair and Watts, *The Legal Effects of War*, 4th edn, (1966), p.375.
[84] [1943] A.C. 203 at 251–252.
[85] [1943] A.C. 203 at 234.

(ii) Conceptual Issues

Property and performance.   Since illegality differs from the rest of the law of   **10–25**
contract by focusing upon the public interest rather than the interests of the
parties, it will often attach significance to aspects of a transaction which might in
other circumstances have been of little importance. In illegality generally the
capacity of "illegal" contracts to transfer property,[86] despite being otherwise
unenforceable, may make it important to determine whether a particular
agreement was one which could give rise to proprietary interests and, if so,
whether it had reached an appropriate stage in its performance for such rights to
have arisen. In the particular context of trading with the enemy, the principle that
all contracts with the enemy are dissolved at the outbreak of war, but that the
property of the enemy is not confiscated, led to a number of disputes. In *Tingley
v Muller*,[87] decided during the First World War, the Court of Appeal attached
importance to the rule that "a contract for the sale of land . . . at once gives the
purchaser an equitable interest in the land",[88] when upholding the validity of a
contract to sell a house on behalf of an enemy alien. In the Second World War
case of *Schering Ltd v Stockholms Enskilda Bank Aktiebolag*[89] a majority of the
House of Lords held that a pre-war contract with a German company, which had
effectively become one for "the discharge of an accrued debt by instalments",[90]
remained enforceable. Lord Porter said[91]:

> "It is, no doubt, generally true that the further performance of contracts made before the
> outbreak of war and not fully performed on either side is prohibited as contrary to public
> policy provided that such performance involves intercourse with an enemy or benefits him . . .
> There are however exceptions and limitations upon this doctrine. So far at any rate as concerns
> benefit to the enemy, the further performance of contracts which have been completely
> performed on one side and in which all that remains is payment by the other are suspended,
> not dissolved, and in the same category are to be placed certain contracts particularly those
> which are really concomitants of the rights of property though still executory."[92]

Executed and executory contracts.   The distinction between executory and   **10–26**
executed contracts is often important in illegality. If the law has actually been
contravened, the position of one or both of the parties to a contract may be very
different from what it would have been at an earlier stage. Formerly the so-called
locus poenitentiae doctrine insisted that a party who sought restitutionary relief
from a contract affected by illegality had to withdraw before performance was
undertaken.[93] Even though a much more relaxed attitude is now taken to the
granting of such relief, as a result of the decision of the Supreme Court in *Patel v
Mirza*,[94] there can be no doubt that the distinction between those situations in

---

[86] See Ch.16, below.
[87] [1917] 2 Ch.144.
[88] [1917] 2 Ch.144, at 165. per Warrington LJ; see also, per Cozens-Hardy LJ at 157 ([1916–17] All
E.R. Rep. at 480 and 474–475).
[89] [1946] A.C. 219.
[90] [1946] A.C. 219, at 242, per Lord Thankerton.
[91] [1946] A.C. 219, at 258–259.
[92] See also *Ex p. Boussmaker* (1806) 13 Ves. 71.
[93] See Ch.18, below.
[94] [2016] UKSC 42.

which the law was actually broken and those in which it was not will continue to be significant. Thus a party who was promised that steps would be taken to ensure legality might have a right to damages if those steps are not taken; but that right will normally be lost if he proceeds to perform irrespective of whether or not a breach of the law will actually take place as a result.[95] Some of the cases on trading with the enemy nevertheless provide a reminder that, as Lord Macmillan put it in *Schering Ltd v Stockholms Enskilda Bank Aktiebolag*,[96] "the distinction between an executed and an executory contract is not always easy to draw". Where the obligations on both sides are complex, and especially if they are divided into apparently separate stages, it may be far from easy to decide which obligations are dissolved by the outbreak of war; and which give rise to accrued rights, the enforcement of which is merely suspended while hostilities continue.[97] In *Schering's* case[98] Lord Thankerton quoted with approval the words of Sir Arnold McNair, in his work on the *Legal Effects of War*,[99] who said "that the distinction between 'executed' and 'executory' contracts may not be very helpful in this connection". Although the context of the cases on trading with the enemy is an unusual one, they do illustrate the importance, in illegality generally, of avoiding purely mechanistic deployment of distinctions such as that between executed and executory agreements.

10–27   **Need for precise analysis.**   The salutary invocation of the dissentients in *Rodriguez v Speyer Bros*, against resolving public policy cases on a purely ad hoc discretionary basis, does not obviate the need for precise analysis of the relationship between the type of contract in question, and the mischief at which the particular rule of public policy is aimed. Lord Dunedin emphasised in one case that "it is not every contract that is abrogated by the war, it is only a contract which is still executory *and which for its execution requires intercourse between the English subject and the enemy*"[100] An enlightened approach to the problem is to be found in the relatively recent case of *Bevan v Bevan*.[101] The question in this case was whether a husband's obligation to pay maintenance instalments to his wife, under a separation agreement, was abrogated by the outbreak of the Second World War. The wife, who had become an enemy alien by virtue of having chosen voluntarily to live in enemy territory throughout the war, subsequently sued in peace-time for the instalments which the husband had ceased to pay at the outbreak of the war. It was conceded on the wife's behalf that the contract had been executory: the separation agreement had not conferred anything resembling a proprietary right to the instalments, which were simply contractual payments which became due from time to time. Sellers J considered the authorities on trading with the enemy, and expressed the view that the courts had "throughout dealt with each case as it has arisen and viewed it from the standpoint of public policy rather than rigid precedent or rule". He concluded that "public policy did

[95] See Ch.2, above.
[96] [1946] A.C. 219 at 257–258.
[97] cf. *Arab Bank v Barclays Bank* [1954] A.C. 495.
[98] [1946] A.C. 219 at 240.
[99] See 2nd edn, p.93. The passage is now in the 4th edn, p.128.
[100] See *Ottoman Bank v Jebaru* [1928] A.C. 269 at 276 (italics supplied).
[101] [1955] 2 Q.B. 227.

not require that this contract should terminate on the outbreak of war".[102] The minimal degree of intercourse with the enemy, constituted by the theoretical need for the husband's bank to transmit the funds to the wife's bank, was insufficient to abrogate the agreement.[103]

Illegality and the terms of the contract.   The contention is occasionally   **10–28**
advanced in illegality cases that the parties have themselves provided in their contract for the impact of public policy upon their agreement, and done so in such a manner as successfully to preclude judicial denial of the validity of the contract. The notion of a "warranty of legality" is, for example, sometimes invoked in cases arising out of situations in which a licence is required for a particular trade or activity, but where one was not obtained in the case in question. The confusion implicit in this notion has been examined in an earlier chapter.[104] The underlying principle is that illegality is beyond the reach of the parties, and its incidence cannot be made the subject of allocation by them. But the application of this principle in particular cases will not always be straightforward; and may call for precision in delimiting the scope and purpose of the illegality. The issue arose in the context of trading with the enemy in relation to clauses which purported to *suspend* the operation of the contract during events such as war.[105] When one party alleged that public policy had abrogated the contract permanently at the outbreak of war, the other would respond that, since the agreement itself had prevented any continuing involvement between the parties while they were enemies, the rule of public policy did not apply.

Suspension disallowed.   At first the courts managed to avoid confronting the   **10–29**
issue directly by construing the suspensory clauses narrowly and concluding that, on their own terms, they were inapplicable; with the result that the full force of public policy applied to the contract in any event.[106] But where it was impossible to apply this approach, careful analysis of the situation would sometimes lead the court to conclude that to permit the continued existence of the contract, even in a suspended state, might assist the enemy's capacity to prosecute the war, and hence necessitate dissolution.[107] Thus in *Ertel Bieber & Co v Rio Tinto Co*[108] a contract to sell iron ore to a German firm, made before the outbreak of the First World War, was not saved by a suspensory clause since a guarantee that supply would be renewed after the war would, inter alia, give the enemy greater freedom to deploy his existing stocks in the prosecution of the war. Against that factual background Lord Sumner, in the House of Lords, dealt with the conceptual aspect as follows[109]:

---

[102] [1955] 2 Q.B. 227, at 245.
[103] In practice statutory machinery under the Trading with the Enemy Act 1939 obviated the need for such transmission by providing for the making of payments to the Custodian of Enemy Property.
[104] See Ch.2, above.
[105] See McNair and Watts, *The Legal Effects of War*, 4th edn, (1966), pp.128–131 and 298–301.
[106] See, e.g. *Zinc Corporation v Hirsch* [1916] 1 K.B. 541, CA.
[107] See, e.g. *Clapham Steamship Co v Handels-En-Transport-Maatschappij Vulcaan of Rotterdam* [1917] 2 K.B. 639.
[108] [1918] A.C. 260.
[109] [1918] A.C. 260, at 285–286.

"What the law forbids is impossible of performance to those who owe obedience to that law, and this higher public obligation discharges any private obligation to the contrary . . . If upon public grounds the law interferes with private executory contracts on the outbreak of war by dissolving them, how can it be open to a subject for his private advantage to withdraw his contract from the operation of the war and to claim to do what the law rejects, to suspend merely where the law dissolves?"

The force of the *Ertel Bieber* principle is illustrated by the fact that the House of Lords held subsequently that another case was indistinguishable from it despite an enormous disparity, in the later case, between the likely length of the war and the intended duration of the contract[110]: a fact which caused one member of the House to express reservations.[111] The agreement had been formed in 1873, and had been due to last for 99 years, but was held to have been dissolved in 1914.

---

[110] See *Fried Krupp Aktiengesellashaft v Orconera Iron Ore Co* [1918] 88 L.J. Ch. 304.
[111] See [1918] 88 L.J. Ch.304 at 311, per Lord Finlay. cf. per Lord Shaw at 313.

PART 3

RESTRAINT OF TRADE

CHAPTER 11

NATURE OF THE DOCTRINE

1. INTRODUCTION

Origins.[1] "The law with regard to restraint of trade", observed Lord Reid in   **11–01**
Esso Petroleum v Harper's Garage,[2] "is of ancient origin. There are references to
it in the Year Books, and it seems to have received considerable attention in the
time of Queen Elizabeth I". The modern law on the subject could almost be said
to date from 1711, when Parker CJ (later Lord Macclesfield) delivered in *Mitchel
v Reynolds*[3] a judgment referred to in a twentieth century case as "penetrating"
and as "one of the most outstanding and helpful authorities . . . which seems to fit
and rule many very modern conditions".[4] Parker CJ said[5]:

> "To conclude, in all restraints of trade where nothing more appears, the law presumes them
> bad; but if the circumstances are set forth that presumption is excluded and the court is to
> judge of those circumstances, and determine accordingly. If on them, it appears to be a just and
> honest contract, it ought to be maintained."

This statement of principle was echoed by Lord Macnaghten in *Nordenfelt v
Maxim Nordenfelt Guns and Ammunition Co*[6] a decision of the House of Lords in
1894 which remains the single most important authority on the subject. He said[7]:

> "The public have an interest in every person's carrying on his trade freely; so has the
> individual. All interference with individual liberty of action in trading, and all restraints of
> trade themselves, if there is nothing more, are contrary to public policy, and, therefore, void.
> That is the general rule. But there are exceptions. Restraints of trade and interference with
> individual liberty of action, may be justified by the special circumstances of a particular case.
> It is a sufficient justification, and indeed, it is the only justification, if the restriction is
> reasonable—reasonable, that is, in reference to the interests of the parties concerned and

---

[1] On the doctrine of restraint of trade see, generally, J. D. Heydon, *The Restraint of Trade Doctrine*,
3rd edn, (LexisNexis Butterworths, 2008). See also Michael Jefferson, *Restraint of Trade* (Wiley,
1996).
[2] [1968] A.C. 269 at 293; [1967] 1 All E.R. 699 at 704.
[3] (1711) 1 P.Wms. 181.
[4] *Herbert Morris Ltd v Saxelby* [1916] A.C. 688 at 717 per Lord Shaw ([1916–17] All E.R. Rep. 305
at 314). See also the still valuable survey of the history of the restraint of trade doctrine and of its
modern role by Harlan M. Blake, "Employee Agreements Not To Compete" (1960) 73 Harv. L.R. 625
at 630–631: "There is very little in the modern approach to the problem for which a basis cannot be
found in Macclesfield's opinion".
[5] See (1711) 1 P. Wins. 181 at 197; [1558–1774] All E.R. Rep. 26 at 33.
[6] [1894] A.C. 535.
[7] [1894] A.C. 535 at 565.

reasonable in reference to the interests of the public, so framed and so guarded as to afford adequate protection to the party in whose favour it is imposed, while at the same time it is in no way injurious to the public."

11–02   **Competition.**   At the heart of the doctrine of restraint of trade is a tension between freedom of contract on the one hand, and freedom to trade or work on the other.[8] It would appear from the foregoing quotations that, in so far as this tension is irresoluble, the law puts freedom of contract in the subordinate position. Nevertheless, there is a paradoxical sense in which, if the law did not adopt that position, freedom of contract could theoretically stifle itself to death by subjecting ever-increasing numbers of people to restraints: "freedom to contract now [could] be used to fetter freedom to contract in the future".[9] Thus a belief in the virtue of economic freedom may be said to be the single value preference which underlies the doctrine of restraint of trade. Accordingly, even in situations in which the courts are least likely to strike down agreements, those involving organisations dealing at arm's length, covenants aimed at restraining competition as such, without any specific justification such as the protection of the goodwill of a business sold by the covenantor to the covenantee, will be void.

11–03   **Bare covenant not to compete.**   In *Vancouver Malt and Sake Brewing Co v Vancouver Breweries*[10] the appellants were licensed to brew beer but had never in fact done so, having confined themselves to the brewing of a Japanese liquor called sake. They entered into an agreement with the respondents, in return for a substantial sum, that they would not begin brewing beer in the future for up to 15 years. The appellants were apparently anxious to raise finance for their business which was going through a period of difficulty, and the respondents, whose business was confined to brewing beer, wished to eliminate a potential rival. At the instance of the appellants, who wished to be free of the covenant which they had freely entered into seven years before, the Privy Council reversed the Canadian courts below and held that the covenant was void. A representative of the respondents had conceded, in cross-examination, that they had paid the appellants simply for the purpose of preventing them "from competing with you".[11] Lord Macmillan, delivering the judgment of the Judicial Committee of the Privy Council, said[12]:

> "The restrictive covenants in the present agreement . . . are at once seen to present unusual features. They are not inserted as being reasonably necessary to render effectual a sale in the interests of both parties, for there is no transaction of sale to be protected. Nothing has been sold . . . It is simply a case of the appellants undertaking to the respondents in consideration of a sum of money to them that they will not for fifteen years carry on a particular branch of business. That is the whole substance of the agreement. If there was any sale, it was a sale by the appellants of their liberty to brew beer and a purchase by the respondents of protection against the possible competition of the appellants in the brewing of beer . . . and so far as their Lordships are aware there is no case in the English Law Reports, and certainly none was cited at the Bar, in which a bare covenant not to compete has been upheld."

---

[8] See, e.g. *Herbert Morris v Saxelby* [1916] 1 A.C. 688 at 716 per Lord Shaw ([1916–17] All E.R. Rep. 305 at 314).

[9] See P. L. Davies, "Post-Employment Restraints: Some Recent Developments" [1992] J.B.L. 490.

[10] [1934] A.C. 181.

[11] [1934] A.C. 181 at 189; [1934] All E.R. Rep. 38 at 41.

[12] See [1934] A.C. 181 at 190; [1934] All E.R. Rep. 38 at 41.

2. CONCEPTS AND CATEGORIES

Flexible categorisation and judicial intuition.   If, unlike *Vancouver Malt and*   **11–04**
Sake Brewing Co v Vancouver Breweries, there has been a genuine sale of the
goodwill of a business, the courts are disposed to view a covenant restricting the
vendor's right to compete with the business which he has sold with greater favour
than they regard covenants extracted from employees not to compete with their
former employer, after their employment with him has ended.[13] Indeed, in
situations of the latter type freedom to compete cannot as such be restricted at all:
an employer can seek validly only to protect his "trade secrets", or confidential
information, and his base of customer contacts. These matters are explored in
detail in the following pages of this Part of the book. The doctrine is not,
however, confined to situations involving what may loosely be termed "vendor
and purchaser" cases on the one hand, and "employer and employee" cases on the
other; even though these two categories have generated the majority of the cases.
In *Esso Petroleum v Harper's Garage*,[14] in which the House of Lords applied the
doctrine to so-called "solus" ties involving exclusive trading agreements between
garages and petrol suppliers, their Lordships were at pains to emphasise that the
doctrine is not subject to immutable boundaries or rigid categorisation.[15] Indeed,
since any contract necessarily entails some sacrifice of freedom on the part of the
parties to it, the doctrine has the potential to change the face of the law of contract
by legitimising levels of judicial activism never previously seen.[16] Such a
massive increase in the scope of the doctrine has not yet occurred. But this is due
more to a shared judicial intuition as to the appropriate scope of judicial
interference with contractual activity, than to any formal, and analytically
watertight, limitations on the scope of the doctrine itself.

Public interest and the interests of the parties.[17]   As is made clear in the   **11–05**
well-known passage, quoted above, from Lord Macnaghten's speech in the
Nordenfelt case, the notion of public interest is central to the doctrine of restraint
of trade. Nevertheless, the conventional exposition of the doctrine is apt to draw a
sharper distinction between the public interest, and the interests of the parties,
than Lord Macnaghten probably intended. According to the conventional
approach, every allegedly unenforceable covenant has to be examined in two
separate stages. First, to see whether it is unreasonable in the interests of the
parties themselves: the onus of showing that it is not unreasonable being on the

---

[13] "Unlike a restraint accompanying a sale of good will, an employee restraint is not necessary for the employer to get the full value of the thing being acquired—in this case, the employee's current services": Harlan M. Blake, "Employee Agreements Not To Compete" (1960) 73 Harv. L.R. 625 at 647.
[14] [1968] A.C. 269; [1967] 1 All E.R. 699.
[15] See [1968] A.C. 269 at 295; [1967] 1 All E.R. 699 at 706 (Lord Reid); 306 and 713 (Lord Morris); 332–333 and 730 (Lord Wilberforce).
[16] cf. *A. Schroeder v Macaulay* [1974] 1 W.L.R. 1308; [1974] 3 All E.R. 616, HL, discussed in Ch.15, below.
[17] See also Ch.12, below.

covenantee rather than the covenantor.[18] Secondly, to see whether it is contrary to the public interest: the onus of showing that it is thus contrary being on the party claiming that to be the case, usually the covenantor.[19] So sharp a distinction between the interests of the parties on the one hand, and the public on the other, is, however, somewhat misleading. The burden of proof is insufficient to justify the two-pronged approach since its incidence is in truth rarely significant: whether or not a covenant is void on account of the doctrine of restraint of trade is one of law, with questions of fact rarely being in issue.[20] But more importantly, the very existence of the first stage of the analysis itself reflects the predominance of considerations of public policy.

11–06   **Public interest is multi-faceted.**   The law of contract does not normally insist on determining whether an agreement can objectively be said to be in the best interests of the parties to it. On the contrary, parties are usually free to make their own bargains free from judicial intervention. Thus, in *Esso Petroleum v Harper's Garage*,[21] Lord Pearce said:

> "Although the decided cases are almost invariably based on unreasonableness between the parties, it is *ultimately* on the ground of public policy that the court will decline to enforce a restraint as being unreasonable between the parties ... There is not, as some cases seem to suggest, a separation between what is reasonable on grounds of public policy and what is reasonable between the parties. There is one broad question: is it in the interests of the community that this restraint should, as between the parties, be held to be reasonable and enforceable?"

While this is undoubtedly correct at a general level, it does not follow that the conventional dichotomy is valueless.[22] The public interest is multi-faceted, and it is convenient to highlight the fact that there can be situations in which the court will decline to enforce a contract even if it was evidently in the interests of both parties at the time when it was entered into. Thus in *Vancouver Malt and Sake Brewing Co v Vancouver Breweries*, considered above, no attempt was made to evaluate the interests of the parties.[23] The court simply insisted that the public interest in the promotion of competition required that the contract should be void.

11–07   **Substance not form.**   "Whether a particular provision operates in restraint of trade is to be determined not by the form the stipulation wears", observed Lord Wilberforce in *Stenhouse Australia v Phillips*,[24] but "by its effect in practice". In that case an insurance agent's contract of employment stipulated that if

---

[18] See *Herbert Morris v Saxelby* [1916] A.C. 688 at 700 ([1916–17] All E.R. Rep. 305 at 309), per Lord Atkinson. But cf. per Viscount Maugham in *Connor Bros v Connors* [1940] 4 All E.R. 179 at 192–193, PC.

[19] See fn.18, above.

[20] See *Esso Petroleum v Harper's Garage* [1968] A.C. 269 at 319; [1967] 1 All E.R. 699 at 721, per Lord Hodson. But for an unusual case in which the burden of proof was relevant see *The Pharmaceutical Society of Great Britain v Dickson* [1970] A.C. 403; [1968] 2 All E.R. 686. See also Heydon, *The Restraint of Trade Doctrine*, 3rd edn, (LexisNexis Butterworths, 2008), pp.33 et seq.

[21] [1968] A.C. 269 at 324; [1967] 1 All E.R. 699 at 724 (emphasis in original).

[22] See Ch.12, below.

[23] See, per Diplock LJ in *Petrofina v Martin* [1966] Ch. 146 at 182; [1966] 1 All E.R. 126 at 139, CA.

[24] [1974] A.C. 391 at 402; [1974] 1 All E.R. 117 at 124.

commission-earning business was placed with an insurance company other than his former employer, within five years of his employment ceasing, he would pay one-half of the commission earned to the former employer. When the validity of the covenant was questioned the covenantee argued that the provision was merely "a profit-sharing agreement",[25] and not subject to the restraint of trade doctrine.[26] The Judicial Committee of the Privy Council rejected this argument and held that the clause was unreasonable and hence unenforceable.[27]

3. SANCTIONS AND BENEFITS

Liquidated damages. While an injunction is the form of relief most commonly sought in respect of breach of a valid restraint covenant, damages, whether liquidated or unliquidated, will also be available in appropriate cases.[28] An early example of the recovery of liquidated damages is provided by *Galsworthy v Strutt*.[29] A solicitor covenanted on the dissolution of his partnership with the claimant that he would not practise within 50 miles for the next seven years, and would not solicit clients of the former partnership. He also covenanted that, in the event of breach, he would pay £1,000 by way of liquidated damages. In reply to an action for an admitted breach of the covenant the defendant paid £50 into court, and contended that the £1,000 was a penalty. His contention was unsuccessful: the covenant could be broken in many different ways with varying degrees of seriousness and the sum stipulated for, which was payable once only, was a reasonable pre-estimate of possible damage.[30] Similarly, in *English Hop Growers v Dering*[31] a price maintenance agreement was held by the Court of Appeal not to be unreasonable[32]; and an attack upon a clause for its enforcement by way of liquidated damages, on the ground that sum stipulated was a penalty, was unsuccessful. The damages were "impossible to foresee or forecast",[33] and the particular sums stipulated for were appropriate.[34]

11–08

---

[25] [1974] A.C. 391; [1974] 1 All E.R. 117.

[26] cf. *Prudential Assurance Co v Rodrigues* [1982] 2 N.Z.L.R. 54.

[27] "The clause in question here contains no direct covenant to abstain from any kind of competition or business, but the question to be answered is whether, in effect, it is likely to cause the employee to refuse business which otherwise he would take; or, looking at it in another way, whether the existence of this provision would diminish his prospects of employment. Judged by this lest, their Lordships have no doubt that the clause operates in restraint of trade": [1974] A.C. 391 at 402–403; [1974] 1 All E.R. 117 at 124, per Lord Wilberforce.

[28] For a detailed example of the assessment of unliquidated damages see *H. & R. Block v Sanon* [1976] 1 N.Z.L.R. 213.

[29] (1848) 1 Exch. 659.

[30] "It cannot be said what damage a person may sustain by another setting up in business within a limited period of time or distance, nor how much he may be injured by the loss of one of his clients. The loss may be either great or small and, therefore, in order to avoid all dispute, the parties are content to fix a certain sum": per Parke B in (1848) 1 Exch. 659 at 663. See also, per Alderson B at 666–667.

[31] [1928] 2 K.B. 174.

[32] It would, of course, now be unenforceable.

[33] [1928] 2 K.B. 174 at 189, per Sankey LJ.

[34] cf. *H. F. Clarke v Thermidaire Corp* (1974) 5 D.L.R. (3d) 385 (penalty) (Supreme Court of Canada). For discussion of what constitutes a penalty see, generally, the decision of the Supreme Court in *Cavendish Square Holding BV v Talal El Makdessi* [2015] UKSC 67, [2015] 3 WLR 1373.

11–09   **Conditional entitlements.**   "(T)here is no relevant difference", observed Mr Jonathan Sumption QC sitting as a deputy High Court judge at first instance in *Marshall v NM Financial Management Ltd*,[35] "between a contract that a person will not carry on a particular trade and a contract that if he does not do so he will receive some benefit to which he would not otherwise be entitled". In that case the claimant's contract as a sales agent with the defendant company provided that his entitlement to continuing commission, earned on business introduced during his employment, would continue after the termination of that employment. This was, however, subject to the proviso that, "within the period of one year after the date of such termination", he did not become employed by any "organisation which may directly or indirectly be in competition" with the defendants. The Court of Appeal,[36] upholding Mr Sumption, confirmed that the claimant was entitled to the commission, notwithstanding his joining a competitor organisation immediately after leaving the defendants. Expressing the entitlement in terms of a condition did not prevent the clause from being subject to the restraint of trade doctrine, and being held unreasonable.[37] *Marshall's* case applied the well-known decision of the Court of Appeal in *Wyatt v Kreglinger and Fernau*,[38] in which the question had arisen of the application of the restraint of trade doctrine to a condition attached to a pension. On leaving the defendant's employment, the claimant had been granted a pension conditional upon his not undertaking employment "in the wool trade". The Court of Appeal held that this stipulation was void as an unreasonable restraint of trade.[39] Slesser LJ could not "in principle find any distinction", between a situation in which a person "expressly covenanted to exclude himself . . . from a trade", and one in which "he says he will give up a benefit which he would otherwise receive if he does enter into that particular trade".[40]

11–10   **Consideration.**   In *Wyatt v Kreglinger and Fernau* the defendants had ceased to pay the claimant his pension; and the determination of the Court of Appeal, that the clause in question was an unreasonable restraint of trade, had the unfortunate effect of holding in their favour that they were entitled so to do. Apart from the clause there had been no consideration to support the grant of the pension, which was in consequence held to have been a gratuitous promise[41]: there having been no pension scheme operative during the claimant's employment. Although this was an extreme case, the effect of holding similar clauses to be unenforceable in other cases has raised the question of whether there was sufficient consideration, apart from the clause, to support the claim to the benefit. The courts not unnaturally lean in favour of upholding the claim in such cases, on the basis that

---

[35] [1995] 1 W.L.R. 1461 at 1465; [1995] 4 All E.R. 785 at 791.

[36] [1997] 1 W.L.R. 1527; [1997] I.C.R. 1065.

[37] See also *Sadler v Imperial Life Assurance Co of Canada* [1988] I.R.L.R. 388. cf. *Spence v Mercantile Bank of India* (1921) 37 T.L.R. 745, CA.

[38] [1933] 1 K.B. 793.

[39] See also *Bull v Pitney-Bowes* [1967] 1 W.L.R. 273; *Taylor v McQuilkin* (1968) 2 D.L.R. (3d) 463 (Manitoba).

[40] [1933] 1 K.B. 793 at 809. See also, per Scrutton LJ at 807.

[41] cf. *Vancouver Malt and Sake Brewing Co v Vancouver Breweries* [1934] A.C. 38, PC.

NATURE OF THE DOCTRINE

adequate consideration remained.[42] In one case the Court of Queen's Bench even held that an annuitant who had agreed, as consideration for the annuity, that he would not, in effect, compete with the defendants "in any district whatsoever" could enforce the annuity regardless of whether the condition was an unreasonable restraint of trade or not.[43] The basis of the decision appears to have been that since the claimant had, in fact, complied with the condition and submitted voluntarily to the restraint, he was "clearly entitled to recover the consideration due in respect of it".[44] This not unattractive decision by a strong court[45] was subsequently subjected to criticism in the Court of Appeal in two cases,[46] on the orthodox conceptual ground that a void provision could not provide consideration to support a promise. The second of the two cases was *Wyatt v Kreglinger and Fernau* itself, in which the unsuccessful claimant had understandably sought to reply upon it.

Pragmatism rebuked.   There is a familiar tension, within the cases on the   **11–11** doctrine of consideration generally, between the approach which seeks to preserve the conceptual integrity of the doctrine, and a more pragmatic approach which is anxious to prevent the doctrine from causing injustice.[47] It is not surprising that this tension is reflected in restraint of trade cases, since it will often in practice be difficult to disregard the question of sufficiency of consideration when determining the "reasonableness" of the agreement as between the parties to it.[48] The tension is illustrated vividly in a case decided as long ago as 1837. In *Hitchcock v Coker*[49] the Court of King's Bench declined to enforce a restraint, observing that "the consideration for this agreement appears to have been trifling".[50] But their decision was reversed by the Court of Exchequer Chamber, which insisted sternly that it was not the court's duty to determine "whether the consideration is equal in value to that which the party gives up or loses by the restraint under which he has placed himself". The court was not to determine whether "the party restrained has made an improvident bargain", but merely whether "there actually is a consideration for the bargain,

---

[42] See, e.g. *Marshall v NM Financial Management Ltd* [1995] 1 W.L.R. 1461; [1995] 4 All E.R. 785 (affirmed); [1997] 1 W.L.R. 1527; [1997] I.C.R. 1065; *Sadler v Imperial Life Assurance of Canada* [1988] I.R.L.R. 388; *Wallis v Day* (1837) 2 M. & W. 273. See also *Re Prudential Assurance Co's Trust Deed* [1934] Ch. 388.

[43] See *Bishop v Kitchin* (1868) 38 L.J.Q.B. 20.

[44] (1868) 38 L.J.Q.B. 20 at 20–21, per curiam.

[45] Cockburn CJ, Lush, Hannen and Hayes JJ.

[46] See *Joseph Evans v Heathcote* [1918] 1 K.B. 418 and *Wyatt v Kreglinger and Fernau* [1933] 1 K.B. 793.

[47] See, e.g. *New Zealand Shipping Co v A. M. Sarterthwaite & Co, The Eurymedon* [1975] A.C. 154. See also *Ward v Byham* [1956] 1 W.L.R. 496; *D and C Builders v Rees* [1966] 2 Q.B. 617. See generally, Atiyah, *Essays on Contract* (1986), Ch.8: "Consideration: A Restatement".

[48] cf. per Waller LJ in *Turner v Commonwealth & British Minerals* [2000] I.R.L.R. 114 at 117: "In most employer and employee situations, no further or specific consideration is paid in order to gain the employee's agreement to be bound by a restrictive covenant, and it does seem to me that in considering the interests of the parties *it is a legitimate factor to take into account that the employees were being paid something extra for the covenant they agreed to sign* ..." (italics supplied).

[49] (1836) 6 Ad. & El. 438.

[50] (1836) 6 Ad. & El. 438 at 446, per Lord Denman CJ delivering the judgment of the court.

and that such consideration is a legal consideration and of some value".[51] Although statements such as these could appear legitimately in a contemporary exposition of the law of contract without seeming out of place, some of the modern authorities have adopted a more realistic approach to the doctrine of consideration.

11–12   **Realism.**   In some restraint of trade cases this realism has come to the aid of covenantees; enabling them to defeat attempts to invoke the technicalities of the doctrine, against the merits, to evade legitimate restrictions.[52] In others, notions akin to that of unconscionability have in effect enabled the inadequacy of consideration to be taken into account, to the advantage of covenantors.[53] In the 1991 case of *Briggs v Oates*[54] the claimant was responsible for terminating the defendant's five-year term of employment after four years. When the claimant sought subsequently, unsuccessfully, to enforce a restraint against the defendant, Scott J observed that[55]: "One year out of five is certainly not de minimis. The defendant was deprived . . . of the full consideration in exchange for which he accepted the cl.8 restriction. In such a case, in my opinion, he is not bound by the restriction".[56] Even if this approach were to commend itself in other cases, however, the indulgence will almost certainly be confined to situations involving covenants between employer and employee, and those closely analogous.[57] A suggestion in a case which involved the sale of the goodwill of a business, that the court should ensure "proportionality" between the interests of the parties, and thereby effectively consider the adequacy of the consideration, was forcefully condemned by Millett J.[58]

---

[51] (1836) 6 Ad. & El. 438 at 457, per Tindal CJ delivering the judgment of the court.
[52] See, e.g. *PCO Services v Rumleski* [1963] 38 D.L.R. (2d) 390 ("past" consideration). See also *Spink (Bournemouth) v Spink* [1936] 1 Ch. 544; [1936] 1 All E.R. 597.
[53] cf. *Schroeder Music Publishing Co v Macaulay* [1974] 1 W.L.R. 1308, HL, discussed in Ch.15, below.
[54] [1991] 1 All E.R. 407.
[55] [1991] 1 All E.R. 407 at 417.
[56] See also *Gledhow Autoparts v Delaney* [1965] 1 W.L.R. 1366 at 1377; [1965] 3 All E.R. 288 at 295, per Diplock LJ; and *Cantol v Brodi Chemicals* (1969) 94 D.L.R. (3d) 265 at 272, per Goodman J (Ontario). But cf. *Lawrence David Ltd v Ashton* [1989] I.C.R. 123 at 130; [1991] 1 All E.R. 385 at 391, per Balcombe LJ (apparently welcoming a concession by counsel that the relative brevity of the employment could not be a basis for attacking the validity of a subsequent restriction).
[57] cf. *Brown v Brown* [1980] N.Z.L.R. 484 at 489–490, per Cooke J.
[58] See *Allied Dunbar v Weisinger* [1988] I.R.L.R. 60 at 65: "In my judgment this is a novel and dangerous doctrine . . . or perhaps more accurately a revival, in modern dress, of an obsolete and discredited theory . . . It . . . calls upon the court to perform a balancing exercise which is not in reality capable of being carried out and which is best left to the parties to resolve by the process of negotiation". See also Heydon, *The Restraint of Trade Doctrine*, 3rd edn, (LexisNexis Butterworths, 2008), pp.174–184, for a forceful defence of the orthodox view that the court will not investigate the adequacy of consideration.

4. CONTINUING RELATIONSHIPS

No clear limits on the scope of the doctrine. In *Esso Petroleum v Harper's*   **11–13**
Garage[59] Lord Morris observed that "counsel for the respondents did not shrink
from the assertion that *every* contract of personal service is a contract in restraint
of trade". The assertion was advanced in opposition to a central contention of
Esso Petroleum which was, in effect, that the doctrine of restraint of trade had no
application to covenants which sought to govern the activities of the parties
during continuing contractual relationships, as distinct from those which sought
to limit the activities of one of the parties *after* the *termination* of their
relationship. The full implications of the respondents' argument were spelled out
clearly by Lord Pearce[60]:

> "Since any man who sells the whole, or even a substantial part, of his services, his output, his
> custom or his commercial loyalty to one party is thereby restraining himself from selling to
> other persons, it might be argued that the court can investigate the reasonableness of any such
> contract and allow the contracting party to resile subsequently from any bargain which it
> considers an unreasonable restraint on his liberty of trade with others."

The House was clearly not disposed to commit itself to this argument, with its
potential for a massive expansion of judicial activism in the law of contract as a
whole.[61] At the same time, however, the actual decision of the House in favour of
the applicability of the restraint of trade doctrine, and the reasonableness test, to
the "solus" tie in the case itself necessarily implied rejection of the rival
contention: that the doctrine was limited to the typical situation of covenants
constraining only post-relationship activities, as distinct from contemporaneous
ones. It follows that "there must", in the words of Lord Pearce, "be a line between
those contracts which are in restraint of trade and whose reasonableness can,
therefore, be considered by the courts, and those contracts which merely regulate
the normal commercial relations between the parties and are, therefore, free from
the doctrine".[62] But the House declined to "attempt to define the dividing line".[63]

Absolute exemption unattainable. Thus Lord Reid was content to observe   **11–14**
that the application of the doctrine "ought to depend less on legal niceties or
theoretical possibilities than on the practical effect of a restraint in hampering that
freedom which it is the policy of the law to protect".[64] Lord Wilberforce was

---

[59] [1968] A.C. 269 at 307; [1967] 1 All E.R. 699 at 713 (italics supplied).
[60] [1968] A.C. 269 at 324–325; [1967] 1 All E.R. 699 at 724.
[61] "I cannot think that either authority or logic requires acceptance of so extreme a view" [1968] A.C.
269 at 307; [1967] 1 All E.R. 699 at 713, per Lord Morris.
[62] [1968] A.C. 269 at 327; [1967] 1 All E.R. 699 at 726.
[63] See [1968] A.C. 269 at 298–299; [1967] 1 All E.R. 699 at 707 per Lord Reid. See also, per Lord
Wilberforce at 332 and 729: "No exhaustive test can be stated—probably no precise, non-exhaustive
test". For recent discussion of the threshold of the restraint of trade doctrine by the High Court of
Australia see *Peters (WA) v Petersville* (2001) 205 C.L.R. 126, and the same Court in *Maggbury Pty
v Hafele Australia Pty* (2001) 210 C.L.R. 181.
[64] [1968] A.C. 269 at 298; [1967] 1 All E.R. 699 at 707. cf. per Lord Morris at 306 and 713: "In some
cases it matters not whether it is said that the doctrine does not apply or whether it is said that a
restraint would so obviously pass the test of reasonableness that no one would be disposed even to
seek to invoke the doctrine".

prepared to accept that some contracts "may be found to have passed into the accepted and normal currency of commercial or contractual or conveyancing relations" so as not to require "justification under a public policy test of reasonableness".[65] Nevertheless his Lordship went on to add the following significant caveat[66]:

"Absolute exemption . . . is never obtained: circumstances, social or economic, may have altered, since they obtained acceptance, in such a way as to call for a fresh examination: there may be some exorbitant or special feature in the individual contract which takes it out of the accepted category: but the court must be persuaded of this before it calls on the relevant party to justify a contract of this kind."

11–15 **Negative stipulation cases.** In the familiar line of cases, relating to the enforcement by injunction of negative stipulations in contracts of personal service, the courts rarely considered that the restraint of trade doctrine constituted a significant argument against awarding an injunction.[67] It was implicit in the approach adopted that breach of an agreement to work exclusively for one employer will give rise to an action for damages at common law; without that doctrine being perceived, at least in most cases, to be of relevance.[68] Similarly, in the old case of *Morris v Colman*[69] Lord Eldon rejected a contention that a contract prohibiting a playwright engaged by the Haymarket Theatre from writing also for other theatres, was invalid as being in restraint of trade.[70] It would clearly be quite wrong to assume, however, that that line of cases effectively precludes the application of the restraint of trade doctrine to contracts for personal services during the employment period.

11–16 **Power to intervene.** On the contrary, the well-known decision of the House of Lords in *Schroeder v Macaulay*,[71] which is discussed in a later chapter,[72] illustrates that the courts are prepared to call for justification of any terms that appear to be exceptionally restrictive or oppressive; and to deny enforceability if satisfactory justification is not forthcoming. *Schroeder*'s case was decided after *Esso Petroleum v Harper's Garage*, and dicta in *Harper*'s case were cited in

---

[65] [1968] A.C. 269 at 333; [1967] 1 All E.R. 699 at 729.
[66] [1968] A.C. 269 at 333; [1967] 1 All E.R. 699 at 730.
[67] Whether a negative stipulation is enforced by injunction depends, inter alia, on the degree of financial hardship likely to be suffered by the employee if he declines to return to work for the employer. This is a question of fact in each case: see eg *Sunrise Brokers LLP v Rodgers* [2014] EWCA Civ 1373. In practice employers seeking such injunctions nowadays often undertake to pay the employee during the injunctive period whether he works or not: see eg *Elsevier Ltd v Munro* [2014] EWHC 2648 (see also per Underhill LJ in *Sunrise Brokers LLP v Rodgers* [2014] EWCA Civ 1373 at [28]).
[68] See *Lumley v Wagner* (1852) 1 De G.M. & G. 604; *Warner Bros Pictures Inc v Nelson* [1937] 1 K.B. 209. cf. *Warren v Mendy* [1989] 1 W.L.R. 853.
[69] (1812) 18 Ves. 437.
[70] "I cannot perceive any violation of public policy in this provision . . . In partnership engagements, a covenant that the partners shall not carry on for their private benefit that particular commercial concern in which they are jointly engaged, is not only permitted but is the constant course". See also *Bouchard Servais v Prince's Hall Restaurant* (1904) 20 T.L.R. 574, CA.
[71] [1974] 1 W.L.R. 1308; [1974] 3 All E.R. 616.
[72] See Ch.15.

support of the decision reached.[73] But the same approach can also be found in much earlier cases. Thus in *Young v Timmins*,[74] which was decided in 1831, the Court refused enforceability where an employee agreed to work exclusively for his employer, but without the latter being obliged reciprocally to furnish an adequate quantity of work and consequent remuneration. Lord Lyndhurst LCB observed[75] that the agreement placed the employee "entirely at the mercy of the Messrs Timmins", and rejected the specific argument of the latter's counsel that it had "never been supposed" that "common contracts of hiring and service", which "must always exclude the working for anybody else", could be "void as being in restraint of trade".[76] Over a century and a half later, the Court similarly rejected a submission that a standard form agreement between a professional boxer and his manager was analogous to an "ordinary contract of employment", and hence "not subject to the restraint of trade doctrine".[77] In *Watson v Prager*[78] Scott J held that the potential for conflict of interest, when the manager was also promoter of the contests in which the boxer appeared, meant that the terms of the agreement "easily enable[d] enforcement in an oppressive manner".[79] The contract was therefore in unreasonable restraint of trade, and unenforceable by the manager. Accordingly, in so far as a broad assumption, to the effect that the restraint of trade doctrine was inapplicable, underlay the "entertainer" cases, the reasoning in those cases is obviously untenable.[80]

Garden leave.   In *Esso Petroleum v Harper's Garage* Lord Pearce observed   **11–17**
that the non-applicability of the restraint of trade doctrine "to ordinary commercial contracts ... during the existence of the contract" only held good "*provided* that any prevention of work outside the contract viewed as a whole is directed towards the absorption of the parties' services and not their sterilisation".[81] This approach may be said to underlie the attitude of the courts towards what have come to be known as "garden leave" clauses. In recent years employees who have given their employers notice are sometimes put on "leave" to prevent them from working during their period of notice, notwithstanding their

---

[73] [1974] 1 W.L.R. 1308 at 1314; [1974] 3 All E.R. 616 at 622. See also *Proactive Sports Management Ltd v Rooney* [2011] EWCA Civ 1444.
[74] (1831) Cr. & J. 331. In so far as the reasoning turned upon the inadequacy of consideration it would no longer be considered valid, but in *Esso Petroleum v Harper's Garage* Lord Reid considered that the actual decision had been correct: see [1968] A.C. 269 at 294; [1967] 1 All E.R. 699 at 705.
[75] (1831) Cr. & J. 331 at 339.
[76] (1831) Cr. & J. 331 at 335, per counsel *arguendo*.
[77] See *Watson v Prager* [1991] 1 W.L.R. 726 at 742; [1991] 3 All E.R. 487 at 501, per Scott J referring to the argument of counsel.
[78] [1991] 1 W.L.R. 726; [1991] 3 All E.R. 487.
[79] [1991] 1 W.L.R. 726 at 747; [1991] 3 All E.R. 487 at 506, per Scott J.
[80] In *Warner Bros Pictures Inc v Nelson* [1937] 1 K.B. 209 at 214; [1936] 3 All E.R. 160 at 163. Branson J said: "Where, as in the present contract, the covenants are all concerned with what is to happen whilst the defendant is employed by the plaintiffs and not thereafter, there is no room for the application of the doctrine of restraint of trade". This dictum is, however, clearly now incorrect: see Heydon, *The Restraint of Trade Doctrine*, 3rd edn (LexisNexis Butterworths, 2008), pp.72–73. See also *Chitty on Contracts*, 32nd edn, (London: Sweet & Maxwell, 2015), para.16–125, fn.767 ("... can no longer be relied on").
[81] [1968] A.C. 269 at 328; [1967] 1 All E.R. 699 at 727 (italics supplied).

remaining on full pay.[82] The objective is to prevent employees in sensitive areas from having access to information or customers at a time when their loyalty to their employer is likely to be diminished. If a long period of such leave has already elapsed this may affect the extent to which the employer is able subsequently to enforce a restrictive covenant, should the employer seek further protection even after the employee has finally departed.[83] More significant for present purposes, however, is the approach adopted by the court if the employer seeks to enforce by injunction the negative stipulation in a "garden leave" clause, so as to prevent the employee from doing "outside" work prior to his departure.[84] The Court of Appeal has noted that an "employee has a concern to work and a concern to exercise his skills", and that this can apply not only to "artists and singers who depend upon publicity" but also "to skilled workmen and even to chartered accountants".[85] Accordingly, any injunctive relief granted to the employer, whether sought under the general law or under an actual "garden leave" clause, may well be limited in scope.[86] Moreover, an employer does not have an automatic right to put an employee on "garden leave"; whether such a right exists will depend upon the construction of the contract. Such a right will only arise by necessary implication if the contract does not confer upon the employee a right to exercise his skills, but only a right to remuneration.[87] If the contract gives the employee a "right to work", an express term authorising "garden leave" will be necessary before such leave can be imposed by the employer.[88] In the absence of such an express term an employee with a right to work may, however, still be put on garden leave if he or she has been in breach of duty to the employer.[89]

11–18   **Refusing "consent".**[90]   A clause which was, perhaps, a precursor of the "garden leave" technique was contained in a covenant considered by Danckwerts J in *Marchon Products v Thornes*.[91] A 12-month restriction upon a former employee was expressed to be subject to the condition that the employer had refused "consent" to the employee taking up a proposed new post. It was also provided that such consent should not be "unreasonably withheld" and, if it were

---

[82] See *Provident Financial Group v Hayward* [1989] I.C.R. 160; [1989] I.R.L.R. 84; [1989] 3 All E.R. 298, CA. See also *Ashcourt Rowan Financial Planning Ltd v Hall* [2013] EWHC 1185 per Andrew Smith J at [35].

[83] See *Credit Suisse Asset Management v Armstrong* [1996] I.C.R. 882 at 894; [1996] I.R.L.R. 450 at 455, per Neill LJ. But cf. *Ashcourt Rowan Financial Planning Ltd v Hall* [2013] EWHC 1185.

[84] See e.g. *J M Finn & Co v Holliday* [2013] EWHC 3450 (negative covenant enforced for full twelve-month garden leave period prior to expiry of defendant's contract).

[85] See *Credit Suisse Asset Management v Armstrong* [1996] I.C.R. 882 at 893; [1996] I.R.L.R. 450 at 454, per Neill LJ, quoting Dillon LJ in *Provident Financial Group v Hayward* [1989] I.C.R. 160 at 168; [1989] I.R.L.R. 84 at 86.

[86] cf. *Provident Financial Group v Hayward* [1989] I.C.R. 160; [1989] I.R.L.R. 84; [1989] 3 All E.R. 298, CA.

[87] See, e.g. *S.B.J. Stephenson v Mandy* [2000] I.R.L.R. 233 at 241.

[88] See *William Hill Organisation v Tucker* [1999] I.C.R. 291, CA, especially at 301, per Morritt LJ.

[89] See *S.G.&R. Valuation Service Co v Boudrais* [2008] EWHC 1340 (Cranston J).

[90] See Heydon, *The Restraint of Trade Doctrine*, 3rd edn, (LexisNexis Butterworths, 2008), pp.173–174.

[91] (1954) 71 R.P.C. 445. See also *Kerchiss v Colora Printing Inks* [1960] R.P.C. 235. But cf. *J.W. Chafer v Lilley* [1947] L.J.R 231.

withheld, the employee would become entitled to half his former salary for a period of 15 months. Danckwerts J observed that the clause was "rather unusual", and appeared to be favourably impressed by its capacity to ensure that "the blow and the possible damage to the employee is softened".[92] On the facts, he held that consent had not been unreasonably withheld, and enforced the covenant. The tactical value of such clauses, in making restrictive covenants more palatable to the courts, should perhaps not be underestimated.[93] If a covenant is indubitably too wide, however, a provision for continuing post-employment payments to the covenantor will not protect it from invalidity.[94]

5. LEGISLATIVE PROMOTION OF COMPETITION

(a) Nature of the Statutory Provisions

Relationship with the common law. The principles of the common law   **11–19**
relating to contracts in restraint of trade are, in themselves, largely unaffected by the major legislative steps taken in recent decades to remove barriers to effective competition in the national economy and beyond. The importance of avoiding the restriction of economic activity, especially on the part of those immediately concerned, clearly underlies the common law doctrines in this area. Nevertheless, the focus of the court in any given case is necessarily upon the particular situation before it. It would be neither practicable, nor in accordance with modern notions of democratic legitimacy, for the English judiciary to pursue macro-economic policies of their own devising. A loose analogy drawn from another branch of the law may serve to illustrate the approximate relationship between the statute and common law in this area. The law of private nuisance adjudicates on disputes between adjacent occupiers when their respective uses of land interfere with each other's enjoyment. In doing so it also concerns itself, at a rudimentary level, with the interest of the community at large when considering which localities are appropriate for particular activities, and which are not.[95] Since the middle years of the twentieth century, however, the broad and politically-sensitive questions of land-use allocation have been governed by statutorily-based planning law.[96] Although nuisance and planning law occasionally come into contact,[97] for the most part they function effectively in their respective spheres largely in isolation from each other. Like planning law, the regulation of competition is a vast subject in its own right. Any attempt at detailed exposition is therefore beyond the scope of this book, and appropriate specialist works should be consulted.[98] At the same

---

[92] (1954) 71 R.P.C. 445 at 448.

[93] For a relatively recent example of a covenant containing such a clause being held to be enforceable see *S.B.J. Stephenson v Mandy* [2000] I.R.L.R. 233 (soliciting employees).

[94] See *T.S.C. Europe (UK) v Massey* [1999] I.R.L.R. 22 at 29.

[95] See, e.g. *St Helen's Smelting Co v Tipping* (1865) 11 H.L.C. 642.

[96] The first comprehensive statute was the Town and Country Planning Act 1947. See now the Town and Country Planning Act 1990.

[97] See *Gillingham B C v Medway (Chatham) Dock Co* [1993] Q.B. 343 (relevance of planning permission to a common law nuisance action).

[98] See e.g. Whish and Bailey, *Competition Law*, 8th edn, (Oxford University Press, 2015); Bellamy and Child, *European Union Law of Competition*, 7th edn (Oxford University Press, 2013).

time, however, brief mention of the main provisions is appropriate in order to delineate the respective spheres of the common law and statute in this field.

11–20   **Eurolaw and the Competition Act 1998.**   The promotion of common rules on competition within the Community is, of course, one of the main objectives of the EU.[99] Two Articles of the Treaty on the Functioning of the European Union are of central importance. The first, art.101 (formerly art.85),[100] deals with "agreements between undertakings" which restrict or distort "competition within the common market". The second, art.102 (formerly 82 of the Rome Treaty), deals with "abuse by one or more undertakings of a dominant position within the common market". These Articles are supplemented by regulations and an extensive body of case-law. This regime does, of course, apply in the UK to all matters which fall within its scope.[101] As far as competition law solely within the UK is concerned, a regime dating back to the immediate post-war years, and including such familiar legislative landmarks as the Restrictive Trade Practices Act 1956 and the Monopolies and Mergers Act 1965, was comprehensively and fundamentally overhauled by the Competition Act 1998. This legislation expressly moulds domestic competition law on the same principles as those applicable, in the European context, under Community law. A subsequent enactment, the Enterprise Act 2002, made important structural reforms to the way in which competition is regulated within the UK, including changes to the organisation of the existing institutions such as the Office of Fair Trading and the Competition Commission. Yet more recent legislation, the Enterprise and Regulatory Reform Act 2013, has provided for the abolition of the Office of Fair Trading and the Competition Commission and the transfer of their functions to a new Competition and Markets Authority. But the 1998 Act still contains the greater part of the substantive law relating to the legislative control of competition.

11–21   **Purpose of the 1998 Act.**   Sections 60(1) and (2) of the Competition Act 1998 provide as follows:

> "(1)   The purpose of this section is to ensure that so far as is possible (having regard to any relevant differences between the provisions concerned), questions arising . . . in relation to competition within the United Kingdom are dealt with in a manner which is consistent with the treatment of corresponding questions arising in Community law in relation to competition within the Community.
>
> (2)   At any time when the court determines a question arising under this Part, it must act . . . with a view to securing that there is no inconsistency between–
>
>   (a)   the principles applied, and decision reached, by the court to determine that question; and
>
>   (b)   the principles laid down by the Treaty and the European Court, and any relevant decision of that Court, as applicable at that time in determining any corresponding question arising in Community law."

---

[99] At the time of writing (December 2016) the UK is still a member of the EU. Its anticipated eventual departure will necessarily affect, to a greater or lesser extent, UK competition law.

[100] Originally known as Article 81, the Article was renumbered as 85 by the Treaty of Amsterdam was which incorporated into English law by the European Communities (Amendment) Act 1998.

[101] See the European Communities Act 1972. For valuable discussion of an important respect in which EU competition law may indirectly limit the scope of the restraint of trade doctrine in domestic law see Mary Catherine Lucy "Europeanisation and the restraint of trade doctrine" (2012) 31 LS 623.

The Act does not, of course, introduce Community law, *as such*, into areas of domestic law into which it has not already intruded. Moreover, some of the issues important in Community law, such as integration into a single market, are not relevant in domestic law. The Government's objective, in securing the Act, was rather to ensure that the same *principles*, and body of case-law, should, wherever possible, apply in domestic as in Community law. The idea is that businesses should no longer "have to worry about two different *approaches* to competition policy".[102] Nevertheless, for the very limited purposes of the present thumbnail sketch, the introduction of a common approach does mean that it suffices to focus on the Competition Act,[103] without dealing formally in addition with Community law.

(b)   Prohibited Agreements

"Chapter I prohibition".   Section 2(1) of the Competition Act 1998 provides that: **11–22**

> ". . . agreements between undertakings, decisions by associations of undertakings or concerted practices which—
> (a)   may affect trade within the United Kingdom, and
> (b)   have as their object or effect the prevention, restriction or distortion of competition within the United Kingdom, are prohibited . . ."

Sub-section 2 provides that the prohibition applies, in particular, to price-fixing; limiting and controlling production and investment, or markets; and applying "dissimilar conditions to equivalent transactions with other trading parties, thereby placing them at a competitive disadvantage". Subsection 4 provides that prohibited agreements will be "void", and s.36 provides for the imposition of penalties for infringement which may be up to "10 per cent of the turnover of the undertaking". Sections 3–16 of the Act deal with exclusions and exemptions from the very general provisions of s.2, and consequently include much of the detail of competition law. The wording of s.2 itself, which is to be known as "the Chapter I prohibition",[104] is virtually identical with that of art.101 of the Treaty. A few general points arising out of the application of the Article in Community law, in so far as they cast light upon the relationship between the statutory regimes on the one hand, and the common law on the other, are therefore worth noting briefly.

Position of employees.   Since both the Ch.I prohibition and art.101 are directed at "agreements between undertakings", most restrictive covenants between individual employees and their employers, with which the majority of common law restraint of trade cases are concerned, are outside the scope of the   **11–23**

---

[102] See the speech of Lord Simon of Highbury, introducing the second reading of the Competition Bill into the House of Lords as Minister of State, Department of Trade and Industry: Hansard, HL Vol. 582, col. 1145 (italics supplied).
[103] I am indebted to the Commentary on the Act by Stephen Corry and Barry J. Rodger in the *Current Law Statutes Series* (1999).
[104] See s.2(8).

prohibition.[105] Nevertheless, agreements between employers relating to employment practices could presumably fall within it,[106] and other Articles of the Treaty may be of assistance to employees in particular cases.[107] The operation of the "transfer" system affecting professional footballers is one area which has given rise to controversy.[108]

11–24   **"Small agreements".**   Section 39 provides that parties to "small agreements" may enjoy "immunity" from the financial penalties for infringement of the Ch.I prohibition authorised by s.36, except where price-fixing was involved. The precise criteria for enjoyment of the immunity are to be defined by delegated legislation, taking into account such factors as "the combined turnover of the parties" and "the share of the market affected by the agreement". In a somewhat similar fashion, the case-law of the European Community has established that agreements which affect only a very small proportion of the overall market will not be prohibited by art.101.[109] In the case of the domestic legislation, however, it is clear that the immunity can only apply to the financial penalties and that the offending agreements will still be "void".

11–25   **Exclusive dealing arrangements.**   It is clear that exclusive dealing arrangements, such as the "tied-house" system between breweries and public houses, can contravene art.101 of the Treaty.[110] But when such so-called "vertical" agreements, between undertakings at different levels of the supply chain, are challenged on competition grounds, the question is apt to prove more difficult to answer than when "horizontal" agreements, such as price-fixing cartels between businesses competing directly in the same market-place, are involved. Under Community law, a number of exclusive dealing arrangements have been granted block exemption from art.101 pursuant to the provision, in the article itself, that the prohibition may "be declared inapplicable" in respect of agreements which in fact contribute "to improving the production or distribution of goods or to promoting technical or economic progress, while allowing consumers a fair share of the resulting benefit".[111] In England the most litigated exclusive trading arrangements have been those involving "solus" ties between garages and petrol companies.[112] The complexity of the issues relating to "vertical" agreements

---

[105] See Treitel, *Law of Contract*, edited by Peel, 14th edn (London: Sweet & Maxwell, 2015), para.11-07 (pp.595-596), citing *Suiker Unie v Commission* [1975] E.C.R. 1663 at 2007.

[106] cf. *Kores Manufacturing Co v Kolok Manufacturing Co* [1959] Ch.108.

[107] See, e.g. art.39 (of the Treaty of Rome as renumbered by the Treaty of Amsterdam): free movement of workers.

[108] See *Union Royale Belge des Sociétés de Football Association ASBL v Bosman* [1996] All E.R. (E.C.) 97, decided under Art.48 (as it was then numbered). See generally, P. E. Morris, S. Morrow, and P. M. Spink, "EC Law and Professional Football: Bosman and its implications", (1996) 59 M.L.R. 893, cf. *Buckley v Tutty* (1971) 125 C.L.R. 353; and *Eastham v Newcastle United Football Club* [1964] Ch. 413.

[109] See *Volk v Ets Vervacke SPRL* [1969] E.C.R. 295.

[110] See *Delimitis v Henninger Brau* [1992] 5 C.M.L.R. 210. See also *Passmore v Morland Plc* [1999] I.C.R. 913; [1999] 3 All E.R. 1005, CA. cf *Crehan v Inntrepreneur Pub Co CPC* [2006] UKHL 38; [2006] 4 All E.R. 465.

[111] Article 101(3). One controversial block exemption was that granted in respect of motor vehicle distribution and servicing arrangements: see Reg.123/85.

[112] See Ch.12, below.

generally proved too difficult to resolve for the incorporation of a specific provision in the Competition Act. Equally difficult issues surround the extent to which agreements controlling the use of land should be viewed from a competition perspective, and considered to be objectionable, given the existence of important alternative perspectives; including those reflecting an environmental standpoint. Indeed the difficulty of avoiding incidental destabilisation of the law governing restrictive covenants affecting land was one of the problems with which the House of Lords attempted to grapple in *Esso Petroleum v Harper's Garage*.[113] In the event, s.50(1) of the Competition Act left it to delegated legislation to make provision, "with such modifications as may be prescribed", for the application to "vertical agreements and land agreements", of the general prohibitions contained in the Act; and such delegated legislation has duly been forthcoming.[114]

(c) Abuse of Dominant Position

"Chapter II prohibition". Section 18(1) of the Competition Act 1998 provides that "any conduct on the part of one or more undertakings which amounts to the abuse of a dominant position in a market is prohibited if it may affect trade within the United Kingdom". The section, to be known as "the Chapter II prohibition"[115] is based upon the similarly worded art.102 of the Treaty on the Functioning of the European Union (formerly art.82 of the Treaty of Rome). The article and the Act provide that abuse may "in particular" consist in the imposition of unfair prices; limiting production to the detriment of consumers; "applying dissimilar conditions to equivalent transactions"; and making contracts conditional upon the acceptance of other, unrelated, obligations.[116]

11–26

---

[113] [1968] A.C. 269.

[114] See e.g. the Competition Act (Land Agreements Exclusion Revocation) Order 2010 No.1709 (which brings land agreements within the prohibition).

[115] Competition Act 1998 s.18(4).

[116] For an example of an (unsuccessful) claim under s.18 see *Chester City Council v Arriva Plc* [2007] EWHC 1373 (Ch).

CHAPTER 12

FRONTIERS OF PROTECTION

1. CONFIDENTIALITY AND SECRECY

(a) Scope of Protection

Overlapping issues.   In *Greer v Sketchley Ltd*[1] Lord Denning MR said:

> "One must remember that in the cases between master and servant the master cannot protect himself from competition at the hands of an outgoing servant. He cannot prevent the outgoing servant from using the skill and experience he has acquired over the years, perhaps in the master's business. Those are the servant's own property. He is not to be denied the use of his own skill and experience even though he acquired them in the course of the master's business. He can be prevented from soliciting the master's customers or trade connections. He can be prevented from using the employer's trade secrets. Also the master can be protected from the servant using confidential information which he acquired in the course of the master's business."[2]

The law relating to contractual restraints upon soliciting a former employer's customers are dealt with in a later chapter. The cases on attempts to prevent use of the employer's trade secrets, or confidential information, reveal two central, and overlapping, issues. First, there is the question of what can, and what cannot, validly be made the subject of a restrictive covenant. This involves consideration of the fundamental distinction between an employee's own skill and experience, which he cannot be prevented from putting at the service of a new employer, and "genuine" secret or confidential information which can be protected by an appropriate covenant. Secondly, there is the question of the relationship between this branch of the law and the jurisdiction to restrain breaches of confidence, irrespective of the absence of an express covenant.

"Skill and experience".   In *Herbert Morris Ltd v Saxelby*[3] the claimants sought to prevent the defendant, who had spent 14 years as a specialist draftsman and engineer with the claimants, from working in the same specialist area for another employer. The wording of the covenant was detailed and specific,[4] but the House of Lords indicated that the claimants were really claiming that it was

---

[1] [1979] I.R.L.R. 445 at 446–447.

[2] See also the classic, and still frequently cited, statement to the same effect by Lord Parker of Waddington in *Herbert Morris Ltd v Saxelby* [1916] 1 A.C. 688 at 709. For a convenient recent general summary of the law see *Brakes Bros v Ungless* [2004] EWHC 2799, per Gloster J at para.15.

[3] [1916] 1 A.C. 688.

[4] The employee covenanted not to "be concerned or assist . . . in the sale or manufacture of hand overhead travelling cranes, pulley blocks, or hand overhead railways . . ."

their systems and methods of working, rather than any technical solution or formula, which actually constituted "trade secrets". The claim failed. Lord Atkinson said"[5]:

> "The respondent cannot . . . get rid of the impressions left upon his mind by his experience on the plaintiffs' works; they are part of himself; and, in my view, he violates no obligation express or implied arising from the relation in which he stood to the appellants by using in the service of some persons other than them the general knowledge he has acquired of their scheme of organisation and methods of business."

Just as an employee cannot be prevented from taking the benefit of his experience with his former employer elsewhere, the same applies necessarily to skills thus acquired. As Lord Shaw put it in *Saxelby*'s case, "a man's aptitudes, his skill, his dexterity, his manual or mental ability . . . are not his master's property; they are his own property; they are himself".[6]

(b) Trade Secrets

12–03 **Need to avoid being "blinded by science".** The most obvious types of situation in which restraints can validly be imposed involve highly technical scientific formulae developed by employers for their own manufacturing processes; the early disclosure of which to competitors could be highly damaging to market advantages legitimately acquired by expensive research and development. Thus industrial chemists, and those engaged in similar occupations, not unnaturally feature prominently in the reported examples of successful restraints.[7] But even in cases of this kind courts need to be conscious of the danger of being "blinded by science" by employers: even mundane or commonplace scientific knowledge can be made to appear esoteric to a layman.[8] And scientists are as entitled as other employees to benefit from the inevitable improvement in their knowledge and skills as their careers progress.[9]

12–04 **"Recognisable body of objective knowledge".** In *FSS Travel & Leisure Systems v Johnson*[10] the claimants, who specialised in producing computer software for the travel industry, sought to enforce a restrictive covenant restraining one of their programmers from joining a rival firm which operated in the same market. The defendant had helped to develop several thousand programs, and to solve difficult problems which had occurred in the course of

---

[5] [1916] 1 A.C. 688 at 703–704.
[6] [1916] 1 A.C. 688 at 714.
[7] See, e.g. *Kerchiss v Colora Printing Inks Ltd* [1960] R.P.C. 235. See also *Commercial Plastics v Vincent* [1965] 1 Q.B. 623 (covenant unenforceable on other grounds); *Caribonum Co Ltd v Le Couch* (1913) 109 T.L.R. 385, affirmed (1913) 109 T.L.R. 587.
[8] cf. *Lock International Plc v Beswick* [1989] 1 W.L.R. 1268 at 1281; [1989] 3 All E.R. 373 at 384 per Hoffman J: ". . . alleged confidential knowledge of technical processes described in technical language . . . may look like magic but turn out merely to embody a principle discovered by Faraday or Ampere".
[9] cf. *Printers and Finishers v Holloway* [1965] 1 W.L.R. 1 at 9; [1964] 3 All E.R. 731 at 736, per Cross J.
[10] [1998] I.R.L.R. 382.

that work. The trial judge[11] held that the claimants did have "trade secrets" which could be protected by the covenant, but he was reversed by the Court of Appeal[12] on this point.[13] Mummery LJ said that the claimants' evidence had really related to the defendant's knowledge "as to how to do his job and to the acquisition of skill and experience by him in the doing of it". That evidence had been "lacking in concrete examples and in solid relevant detail, identifying a separate and specific recognisable body of objective knowledge". The solutions to software development problems, which the claimants saw as "specific" knowledge, were "too vague and indefinite to constitute trade secrets protectable by the restrictive covenant".[14] Similarly, knowledge acquired by extensive reading of existing, but obscure, scientific literature cannot amount to "trade secrets" which an employee can be prevented from using in the service of a subsequent employer.[15] Of course, while a person is actually employed, his implied contractual duty of fidelity to his employer will subject him to much more stringent obligations with respect to the non-disclosure of his employer's activities generally. But the principles applicable in that context should not be confused with the quite separate ones appertaining to attempts to restrain employees after the employment has ceased, when they need to earn their living elsewhere.[16]

Liability for misuse of trade secrets is not strict.   A defendant cannot be   **12–05** liable for disclosing the claimant's trade secrets, whether by virtue of a contractual restrictive covenant or the equitable jurisdiction to restrain breaches of confidence, if he was unaware that the information in fact belonged to the claimant. The Supreme Court so held in *Vestergaard Frandsen A/S v Bestnet Europe*.[17] Although the defendant was a former employee of the claimants, and subsequently worked alongside other former employees in a new company they founded which in fact used the claimant's trade secrets, she herself had not had access to the trade secrets when she was employed by the claimants. Although the other former employees had done so, and were indeed in breach of their obligation of confidentiality, the defendant herself was unaware of this and had assumed that the information being used by the new company had been obtained legitimately. Although the case was decided on this relatively narrow ground, Lord Neuberger, who delivered the only judgment in the Supreme Court (with which the other Justices agreed), took the opportunity to look at the case "a little more broadly" and expressed himself as follows[18]:

---

[11] Ronald Walker QC sitting as a deputy High Court judge.
[12] Lord Woolf MR, Millett and Mummery LJJ.
[13] He had actually found in favour of the defendant but on another point. His decision was therefore affirmed on other grounds.
[14] See also *Balston Ltd v Headline Filters Ltd* [1987] F.S.R. 330 at 351, per Scott J. ("Technologically based industries abound. All have what they regard as secrets").
[15] See *Triplex Safety Glass Co v Scorah* [1938] 1 Ch.211 at 215–216; [1937] 4 All E.R. 693 at 697–698, per Farwell J. cf. *Stephenson Jordan & Harrison Ltd v McDonald & Evans* [1952] 1 T.L.R. 101.
[16] See *Faccenda Chicken v Fowler* [1987] Ch. 117 at 135–136; [1986] 1 All E.R. 617 at 625, per Neill LJ. See also *J. A. Mont (UK) Ltd v Mills* [1993] F.S.R. 577 at 590, per Glidewell LJ.
[17] [2013] UKSC 31.
[18] See ibid. at [44]–[45].

"Particularly in a modern economy, the law has to maintain a realistic, and fair balance between (i) protecting trade secrets (and other intellectual property rights) and (ii) not unreasonably inhibiting competition in the market place. The importance to the economic prosperity of the country of research and development in the commercial world is self-evident, and the protection of intellectual property rights, including trade secrets, is one of the vital contributions of the law to that end. On the other hand, the law should not discourage former employees from benefitting society and advancing themselves by imposing unfair potential difficulties on their honest attempts to compete with their former employers".

His Lordship concluded that it would have been "inconsistent with maintaining that balance", as well as "oppressive" on the defendant, to have imposed what would have amounted to strict liability for use of the claimant's trade secrets.

(c)   Confidential Information

12–06   **Less technical than trade secrets.**   In so far as protection of both "confidential information" and "trade secrets" can, in appropriate cases, justify valid restraints it is not necessary to make a formal distinction between the two expressions. Either term may therefore be used to denote the whole field which an employer can seek legitimately to protect.[19] Nevertheless, since they have rather different meanings in ordinary speech, clarity is promoted by referring to them separately as Lord Denning MR did in the passage quoted above from his judgment in *Greer v Sketchley Ltd*. "Confidential information" would therefore typically include minutes of meetings relating to proposed commercial developments, whereas "trade secrets" would be confined to more technical matters.

12–07   ***The Littlewoods Organisation v Harris.***   A reported example of non-technical confidential information being protected successfully by a restrictive covenant is provided by *The Littlewoods Organisation v Harris*.[20] The defendant had played a key role in the development of the claimants' mail-order marketing strategy for the following year, and the Court of Appeal enforced a covenant restraining him from joining a rival organisation immediately after his employment ceased. In the fast-moving contemporary business environment, commercially confidential information will often be more important to companies than "trade secrets" as such.[21] The latter expression tends to evoke a bygone age, when both technology and business moved more slowly.[22]

---

[19] cf. *Lansing Linde Ltd v Ken* [1991] 1 W.L.R. 251 at 260; [1991] 1 All E.R. 418 at 425–126, Slaughton LJ, CA. See also, per Butler-Sloss LJ, in the same case, at 270 and 435.

[20] [1977] 1 W.L.R. 1472. For discussion see M. W. Bryan, "Restraint or Trade: Back to a Basic Analysis" [1980] J.B.L. 326.

[21] See, e.g. *S.B.J. Stephenson v Mandy* [2000] I.R.L.R. 233 (details of customers, etc.).

[22] See Harlan M. Blake, "Employee Agreements Not To Compete" (1960) 73 Harv. L.R. 625 at 667 et seq: "The concept of the trade secret ... has its roots in an era when business technology was less complex and dynamic than it is today. The formula of a patent medicine or a secret process was often the cornerstone of a business whose methods and product remained unchanged for decades".

(d)   Relationship to Breach of Confidence

Jurisdiction in the absence of a covenant.   Even in the absence of a restrictive   **12–08**
covenant, the court has jurisdiction to prevent breaches of confidence. This
jurisdiction was examined at length by Goulding J, and by the Court of Appeal, in
Faccenda Chicken Ltd v Fowler.[23] In this case a former employee of the plaintiff
firm, which sold fresh chickens to the retail and catering outlets, set up a rival
organisation in direct competition with the claimant. There was no restrictive
covenant, but the claimant contended that the defendant had abused the
claimant's confidence by making use of detailed information relating to
customers and prices, acquired during the period of employment. In rejecting the
claimant's claim, Neill LJ, delivering the judgment of the Court of Appeal, spoke
as follows in relation to the breach of confidence jurisdiction[24]:

> "In our judgment the information will only be protected if it can properly be classed as a trade
> secret or as material which, while not properly to be described as a trade secret, is in all the
> circumstances of such a highly confidential nature as to require the same protection as a trade
> secret *eo nomine*."

Since similiar phraseology is used in the restrictive covenant cases, the
question arises as to whether or not the scope of the two doctrines is the same,
thereby potentially rendering restrictive covenants superfluous in this area. Some
uncertainty can be detected on this point in the cases. In *Printers and Finishers v
Holloway*,[25] Cross J rejected a breach of confidence claim, but clearly envisaged
a separate role for restrictive covenants. He said:

> "If [the plaintiff's managing director] is right in thinking that there are features in his process
> which can fairly be regarded as trade secrets and which his employees will inevitably carry
> away with them in their heads, then the proper way for the plaintiffs to protect themselves
> would be by exacting covenants from their employees restricting their field of activity after
> they have left their employment, not by asking the court to extend the general equitable
> doctrine to prevent breaking confidence beyond all reasonable bounds."[26]

In *Faccenda Chicken v Fowler*, Neill LJ cited this dictum with apparent
approval, but in an immediately preceding passage in the judgment of the court
he appeared to deny that a restrictive covenant could in fact extend the scope of
an employer's protection beyond that afforded by the general breach of
confidence jurisdiction.[27]

---

[23] [1987] Ch. 117; [1986] 1 All E.R. 617 (affirming [1985] 1 All E.R. 724). cf. *Generics (UK) Ltd v
Yeda Research & Development Co Ltd* [2012] EWCA Civ 726.
[24] See [1987] Ch. 117 at 137; [1986] 1 All E.R. 617 at 626.
[25] [1965] 1 W.L.R. 1.
[26] [1965] 1 W.L.R. 1 at 6. cf. *The Littlewoods Organisation v Harris* [1977] 1 W.L.R. 1472 at 1479,
per Lord Denning MR. See also, per Scott J in *Balston Ltd v Headline Filters Ltd* [1987] F.S.R. 330 at
351–352: "Employers who want to impose fetters of this sort on their employees ought in my view to
be expected to do so by express covenant. The reasonableness of the covenant can then be subjected
to the rigorous attention to which all employee covenants in restraint of trade are subject".
[27] See [1987] Ch. 117 at 137; [1986] 1 All E.R. 617 at 626 expressing disagreement with observations
of Goulding J at first instance in [1985] 1 All E.R. 724 at 731.

12–09 **Covenant can extend protection.**   The clearest exposition of the issue is now to be found in the judgment of Scott J in *Balston Ltd v Headline Filters Ltd*.[28] The case concerned an attempt to invoke the breach of confidence jurisdiction, which Scott J rejected. His Lordship treated that jurisdiction as based upon an implied term in the employment contract, in contrast to the express term represented by a restrictive covenant. He addressed the apparent ambiguity in the judgment of the Court of Appeal in the *Faccenda Chicken* case, and pointed out that the breach of confidence jurisdiction was potentially far harsher upon the former employee than an express covenant, and should therefore be exercised with a degree of caution even greater than that adopted in determining the validity of restrictive covenants. He pointed out that an implied term would normally "be unlimited in time and probably in area as well". It would be difficult, for example, to conceive of an *implied* term that operated for "one year only or restrained use in, say, the Home Counties" whereas "an express covenant against use or disclosure is very likely to be limited both as to time and as to area". He therefore concluded as follows[29]:

> "In short, express restricted covenant and implied term raise to my mind quite different considerations and I decline to read the *Faccenda* judgment as holding that confidential information that could not be protected by an implied term *ipso facto* could not be protected by a suitably limited express covenant."[30]

Similarly, in *Caterpillar Logistics Service (UK) Ltd v de Crean*[31] the Court of Appeal declined relief for an alleged breach of confidentiality because, inter alia, the claimant could have required the defendant to enter into an express covenant but had failed to do so.[32]

2.   "PUBLIC INTEREST"

(a)   The Issues

12–10 **Three aspects.**   Lord Macnaghten famously observed, in *Nordenfelt v Maxim Nordenfelt Guns and Ammunition Co*,[33] that to be justifiable a restraint must be "reasonable ... in reference to the interest of the parties concerned and reasonable in reference to the interests of the public". On numerous occasions since this formula was developed, courts have been exercised by the problem of determining precisely what is to be understood by the concept of "public interest" in the present context. It is perhaps helpful to identify three aspects of the matter

---

[28] [1987] F.S.R. 330. See also *Force India Formula One Team Ltd v Aerolab SRL* [2012] EWHC 616 per Arnold J at [229]–[230] (decision affirmed on other grounds in [2013] EWCA Civ 780).
[29] [1987] F.S.R. 330 at 348.
[30] See also *Systems Reliability Holdings v Smith* [1990] I.R.L.R. 377 at 384, in which Harman J expressed his agreement with the criticisms by Scott J of the dicta of the Court of Appeal in *Faccenda Chicken* on this point.
[31] [2012] EWCA Civ 156.
[32] See per Stanley Burnton LJ ibid. at [61]–[64]. cf *Personnel Hygiene Services v Rentokil Initial UK Ltd* [2014] EWCA Civ 29 in which an injunction to protect confidential information was granted: the defendants sought unsuccessfully to rely on the *Caterpillar* case but it was distinguished on the facts.
[33] [1895] A.C. 535 at 565, quoted at length in Ch.11, above.

for consideration. First, what exactly is the conceptual nature of the relationship between the interests of the public, and those of the parties themselves, for the purpose of applying the "reasonableness" test? Secondly, in what actual circumstances will the "public interest" provide a distinct basis for a finding that a restraint is unjustifiable? Thirdly, how widely can the court range appropriately in its selection of relevant criteria when assessing what is, or is not, in the public interest?

(b)   Relationship to the Interests of the Parties

Reasonableness.   Since the overall context of the restraint of trade doctrine is   **12–11**
that of "public policy", there is a sense in which even consideration of the parties' interests alone comes under that general umbrella. Nor is the matter merely semantic. The fact that the court is even prepared to embark upon an examination of the "reasonableness" of the contract as between the parties to it indicates that an interventionist approach is being adopted which is quite distinct from that which governs the enforceability of contracts generally.[34] Accordingly, judges have sometimes attempted to conflate the two, apparently separate, limbs of Lord Macnaghten's test: either by suggesting that "reasonableness" in the interests of the parties is really the only substantive issue involved[35] or, conversely, that the "public interest" is the single overriding consideration.[36] It is submitted that neither suggestion is particularly helpful, and that Lord Macnaghten's dichotomy is to be preferred. No doubt it is true that, as Lord Atkinson observed in *Herbert Morris v Saxelby*,[37] where an individual is subjected to a restraint which is against his own interests, "the general public suffer with him", for they are deprived of the benefits of his skill and experience. In this sense, the public interest and that of the covenantor "if they are not conterminous certainly overlap". But notwithstanding that the distinction between the two categories may ultimately be perceived as one of degree, the differences at the opposing ends of the spectrum are sufficiently great as to render over-zealous wielding of Occam's razor more likely to confuse than to enlighten.

Both limbs necessary.   Thus, in situations in which individual employees have   **12–12**
been subjected to oppressive covenants, the primary focus of the court will in practice be protection of the employee's own interests. Where businesses have dealt at arm's length with each other, on the other hand, they can usually be regarded as adequate guardians of their own interests.[38] In cases such as the latter, however, the possible impact of the bargain upon third parties, or upon the public

---

[34] See Ch.11, above.

[35] See e.g. per Lord Parker of Waddington delivering the judgment of the Judicial Committee of the Privy Council in *Att.-Gen. of the Commonwealth of Australia v Adelaide SS Co* [1913] A.C. 781 at 795: "Their Lordships are not aware of any case in which a restraint though reasonable in the interests of the parties has been held unenforceable because it involved some injury to the public".

[36] See *Esso Petroleum v Harper's Garage* [1968] A.C. 269 at 324; [1967] 1 All E.R. 699 at 724 per Lord Pearce: "one broad question" (quoted at length in Ch.11, above).

[37] [1916] 1 A.C. 688 at 699.

[38] "Where two experienced traders are bargaining on equal terms and one has agreed to a restraint for reasons which seem good to him. the court is in grave danger of stultifying itself if it says that it

generally, may often call for careful judicial scrutiny.[39] Thus there is "an obvious public benefit" that inventors of new medical equipment "should not be restricted".[40] Moreover, not all situations can readily be classified as "employee" or "business" cases.[41] Clarity of analysis in each case that arises is therefore more likely to be facilitated by preservation of both limbs of Lord Macnaghten's exposition.[42]

(c) Circumstances in which Public Interest will Invalidate

12–13   **Public interest as more correct ground.**   "I think", said Lord Reid in *Esso Petroleum v Harper's Garage*,[43] "that in some cases where the court has held that a restraint was not in the interests of the parties it would have been more correct to hold that the restraint was against the public interest". As his Lordship proceeded to point out, the decision of the Court of Appeal in *Kores Manufacturing Co v Kolok Manufacturing Co*[44] is a good example of this process. The claimants and defendants were competing firms manufacturing typewriting supplies. They occupied adjoining factories in Tottenham, North London, and agreed that they would not employ each other's ex-employees. The objective was to promote stability in their respective labour forces, and supposedly to protect "trade secrets". When one of the firms broke the agreement, the Court of Appeal held that it was unenforceable on the ground that it was "unreasonable in the interests of the parties to it".[45] The Court therefore found it unnecessary "to form any conclusion on the question of reasonableness in the public interest".[46] It is submitted, however, that even if the agreement *had* been in the interests of the parties to it (as they evidently considered it to have been when they entered into it) it would clearly have been unenforceable on grounds of

---

knows that trader's interest better than he does himself": per Lord Reid in *Esso Petroleum v Harpers Garage* [1968] A.C. 269 at 300; [1967] 1 All E.R. 699 at 709.

[39] See *McEllistrim v Ballymacelligott Co-operative Agricultural & Dairy Society* [1919] A.C. 548, per Lord Birkenhead LC at 562: "It is . . . not difficult to conceive of a case in which a contract in restraint of trade might be adjusted to safeguard the reasonable interests of the contracting parties, and yet might be opposed to the public interest". See also *Tank Lining Corp v Dunlop Industrial* (1982) 140 D.L.R. (3d) 659 at 668 et seq. (Ontario Court of Appeal).

[40] See *Dranez Anstalt v Hayek* [2002] EWCA Civ 1729; [2003] FSR 32 at [21] per Chadwick LJ.

[41] See, e.g. *Deacons v Bridge* [1984] A.C. 705; [1984] 2 All E.R. 19, especially at 714 and 22, per Lord Fraser (partnership agreement between solicitors). See also *Dawnay Day & Co v De Braconier D'Alphen* [1998] I.C.R. 1068 at 1106; [1997] I.R.L.R. 442 at 446, per Evans LJ, CA.

[42] "A contract which is in restraint of trade cannot be enforced unless (a) it is reasonable as between the parties; (b) it is consistent with the interests of the public . . . Every contract therefore which is impeached as being in restraint of trade must submit itself to the two standards indicated. *Both still survive*": per Lord Birkenhead LC in *McEllistrim v Ballymacelligott Co-operative Agricultural & Dairy Society* [1919] A.C. 548 at 562 (italics supplied).

[43] [1968] A.C. 269 at 300; [1967] 1 All E.R. 699 at 709.

[44] [1959] Ch. 108.

[45] [1959] Ch. 108 at 125; [1958] 2 All E.R. 65 at 73, per Jenkins LJ delivering the judgment of the court.

[46] [1959] Ch. 108 at 127; [1958] 2 All E.R. 65 at 75 per Jenkins LJ.

public interest.[47] It sought indirectly to impose restrictions on the choice of employment of third parties, which could not validly have been imposed on those parties directly.[48]

Neville v Dominion of Canada News Co.   A very different type of situation   **12–14** resulted in an agreement being held unenforceable on, inter alia, restraint of trade grounds in *Neville v Dominion of Canada News Co.*[49] The defendant proprietors of a newspaper owed money to the claimant who was a prominent financier. In return for his foregoing half the debt, the defendants agreed never to comment upon the claimant's activities in the financial columns of their newspaper, despite their avowed intention of providing impartial and independent investment advice in those columns. When the defendants broke the agreement by publishing material to which the claimant objected, the latter sued for the balance of the debt, but he was unsuccessful. Lord Cozens-Hardy MR saw the agreement as "plainly a covenant in restraint of trade", and had "no hesitation insaying that it was not reasonable'".[50] Again, the Court of Appeal was hesitant to refer openly to the public interest in contradistinction to that of the parties, but rightly concluded that the transaction involved bribery and could not "be regarded as otherwise than against public policy".[51]

(d)   Criteria for Assessment

Conservative approach.   The reluctance of the courts overtly to engage in   **12–15** consideration of the public interest is understandable. They are anxious not to overstep the proper limits of the judicial function, either in practical or in constitutional terms. In *Texaco v Mulberry Filling Station*,[52] Ungoed-Thomas J expressed himself as follows in the course of holding that the particular covenant before him was prima facie valid:

> "But what is meant by reasonableness with reference to the interests of the public? It is part of the doctrine of restraint of trade which is based on and directed to securing the liberty of the subject and not the utmost economic advantage. It is part of the doctrine of the common law and not of economics. So it must, of course, refer to interests as recognisable and recognised by law. But if it refers to interests of the public at large, it might not only involve balancing a mass of conflicting economic, social and other interests which a court of law might be ill-adapted to achieve; but, more important, interests of the public at large would lack sufficiently specific formulation to be capable of judicial as contrasted with unregulated personal decision and application—a decision varying, as Lord Eldon L.C. put it, like the length of the chancellor's foot."

While insistence that only interests of the public "recognisable and recognised by law" should be judicially protected might seem to be thoroughly proper, it can

---

[47] cf. *Mineral Water Bottle Exchange & Trade Protection Society v Booth* (1887) 36 Ch.D. 465. CA.
[48] [1959] Ch. 108 at 125–126; [1958] 2 All E.R. 65 at 74 per Jenkins LJ.
[49] [1915] 3 K.B. 556, CA.
[50] [1915] 3 K.B. 556 at 564.
[51] [1915] 3 K.B. at 564 per Lord Cozens-Hardy M.R. See also Ch.7, above.
[52] [1972] 1 W.L.R. 814 at 827; [1972] 1 All E.R. 513 at 526. See also *Stephens v Gulf Oil Canada Ltd* (1975) 65 D.L.R. (3d) 193 at 212–214 (Ontario Court of Appeal).

also provide a pretext for circular reasoning and for unwarranted judicial conservatism. Outdated doctrines may be preserved beyond their sell-by date.[53]

12–16   **Facilitating movement?**   Fortunately, the determination of how far trade should be regulated in the public interest is now largely a matter for the legislature.[54] But public policy does not stand still, and there is no easy or straightforward guide enabling judges to determine whether and when the law should move on, and to what extent facilitating movement is an appropriate part of the judicial function. The cases indicate that restraint of trade is rooted in the notion that competition is in the public interest,[55] and that monopolies are to be discouraged.[56] Nevertheless, the courts have sometimes been prepared to support price-fixing agreements,[57] and agreements to limit the re-sale of second-hand cars.[58] In other cases factors as diverse as the desirability of discouraging practice by unqualified estate-agents,[59] and of "facilitating the assumption by established solicitors' firms of younger men as partners",[60] have been taken into account under the umbrella of "public interest". A lack of professional people in a particular locality has sometimes been put forward in other jurisdictions as a reason for invalidating a restraint. The Second American *Restatement of Contracts*, for example, suggests that a shortage of doctors in the area in question could have that effect.[61]

3.   VENDOR AND PURCHASER

12–17   **Covenants more favourably regarded.**   "I think it can be regarded as settled", said Jenkins LJ in *Ronbar Enterprises v Green*,[62] "that the court takes a far stricter and less favourable view of covenants in restraint of trade entered into between master and servant than it does of similar covenants between vendor and purchaser." He continued[63]:

---

[53] For further discussion of the approach of Ungoed-Thomas J in this case see John Bell, *Policy Arguments in Judicial Decisions* (Oxford University Press, 1983), pp.171–175.

[54] See, e.g. the Competition Act 1998.

[55] See *Vancouver Mall and Sake Brewing Co v Vancouver Breweries* [1934] A.C. 181. See also Ch.11, above.

[56] "The chief evil thought to be entailed by a monopoly ... was the rise in prices which such monopoly might entail. The idea that the public are injuriously affected by high prices has played no inconsiderable part in our legal history" per Lord Parker of Waddington in *Att.-Gen. of Australia v Adelaide SS Co* [1913] A.C. 781 at 796; [1911–13] All E.R. Rep. 1124.

[57] See e.g. *English Hop Growers v Dering* [1928] 2 K.B. 174, CA. cf. *Att.-Gen. of Australia v Adelaide SS Co* [1913] A.C. 781; [1911–13] All E.R. Rep. 1124.

[58] See *British Motor Trade Association v Gilbert* [1951] 2 T.L.R. 514; [1951] 2 All E.R. 641.

[59] See *Scorer v Seymour-Johns* [1966] 1 W.L.R. 1419 at 1423; [1966] 3 All E.R. 347 at 349, per Sellers LJ, CA.

[60] See *Deacons v Bridge* [1984] A.C. 705 at 718; [1984] 2 All E.R. 19 at 25, per Lord Fraser, PC.

[61] At para.188, Illustration 14. The cases cited in the Reporter's Note, however, suggest that the argument rarely succeeds in practice (p.51). See also *Green v Stanton* (1969) 6 D.L.E. (3d) 680 (British Columbia Court of Appeal) affirming (1969) 3 D.L.R. (3d) 358; *Baker v Lintott* (1981) 141 D.L.R. (3d) 571 (Alberta Court of Appeal) reversing (1980) 117 D.L.R. (3d) 465.

[62] [1954] 1 W.L.R. 815 at 820; [1954] 2 All E.R. 266 at 270, CA.

[63] [1954] 1 W.L.R. 815 at 820–821.

"In the case of a covenant between vendor and purchaser, the court recognises that it is perfectly proper for the parties, in order to give efficacy to the transaction, to enter into such restrictive provisions as regards competition as are reasonably necessary to enable the purchaser to reap the benefit of that which he has bought; and restrictions of that kind are regarded as necessary, not only in the interests of the purchaser, but in the interests of the vendor also, for they not only preserve the value to the purchaser of that which he buys, but also enable the vendor to realise a satisfactory price. It is obvious that in many types of business the goodwill would be well-nigh unsaleable if it was unlawful for the vendor to enter into an adequate covenant against competition."[64]

Nordenfelt case.   The classic authority on the enforceability of restrictive covenants between vendor and purchaser is still *Nordenfelt v Maxim Nordenfelt Guns and Ammunition Co.*[65] In that case the defendant sold his weapons manufacturing business to the claimants, and covenanted that he would not "carry on business" in such a manner as to compete with his former company for 25 years. The consideration was not insubstantial for an agreement concluded in 1886; consisting of £237,000 and £50,000 in shares in the purchaser company. The covenant was unrestricted in area and was therefore effectively worldwide, an aspect which was in the forefront of the defendant's attack upon its validity. The attack failed. The House of Lords held that in view of "the nature of the business . . . the class and number of customers" the covenant was reasonable, and there was nothing to lead to the conclusion that it was "injurious to the public interest".[66]

12–18

Question of degree.   The more favourable approach of the courts towards the enforceability of restrictive covenants between vendor and purchaser is not confined to the direct sale of undertakings, but will also apply to the sale of a majority shareholding by those responsible for controlling the company sold.[67] Indeed, in borderline cases the distinction between vendor and purchaser covenants on the one hand, and covenants between employer and employee on the other, may well become a question of degree.[68] In *Spink v Spink*[69] the defendant sold his substantial shareholding in a small private company to his brother, and resigned simultaneously as a director and a manager. He also agreed not to be interested in a similar business within a radius of 10 miles for five years; only to contend subsequently that this covenant was an invalid restraint upon a

12–19

---

[64] On the nature of the "goodwill" of a business, and the position of a purchaser in the absence of an express covenant, see *Trego v Hunt* [1896] A.C. 7. See also Heydon, *The Restraint of Trade Doctrine*, 3rd edn (LexisNexis Butterworths, 2008), Ch.8.

[65] [1894] A.C. 535.

[66] [1894] A.C. 535 at 559; [1891] All E.R. Rep. 1 at 14 per Lord Ashbourne.

[67] See, e.g. the *Nordenfelt* case itself, see also *Connor Bros v Connors* [1940] 4 All E.R. 179 at 190–191, per Viscount Maugham delivering the judgment of the Privy Council. In *Cavendish Square Holdings BV v El Makdessi* [2012] EWHC 3582 the High Court declared a restriction of eight and a half years duration in a vendor and purchaser covenant to be valid.

[68] cf. per Harman J in *Systems Reliability Holdings v Smith* [1990] I.R.L.R. 377 at 382: "The courts have always to try and apply the test of reasonableness to the circumstances and facts of the particular case before them, and classifying them as master and servant cases or vendor and purchaser cases is convenient . . . but is not a useful thing for the court which has got to sit down and say: 'What is reasonable in this particular deal?' ". See also *Dawnay Day & Co v de Braconier d'Alphen* [1998] I.C.R. 1068 at 1106; [1997] I.R.L.R. 442 at 446, per Evans L.J., CA.

[69] [1936] 1 Ch. 544; [1936] 1 All E.R. 597. See also *Alliance Paper Group v Prestwich* [1996] I.R.L.R. 25.

former employee. His contention failed and the covenant was enforced. Luxmoore J doubted whether the agreement was "really in the nature of an agreement between an employer and an employee at all", but added that it did not seem to him "to make much difference which way it [was] looked at" as "in all cases where there is something of a nature of a goodwill, covenants . . . are looked at with less stringency".[70] Similarly, in *Allied Dunbar v Weisinger*[71] a retiring salesman of financial services covenanted that, in return for a very substantial payment from the company with which he had been associated, he would effectively withdraw completely from the market for two years. The covenant was treated as one for the protection of goodwill on the sale of a business, and enforced.[72] Franchise agreements are also regarded as more akin to vendor and purchaser agreements than to agreements between employer and employee.[73]

12–20   **Reality of the agreement.**   Conversely, some contracts involving a sale of goodwill may in reality be closer to an agreement between employer and employee. In *D. Bates & Co v Dale*[74] the defendant ran a business giving tax advice to a few dozen clients. He sold the goodwill of the business to the claimants, a large firm of accountants, for £40 but continued to act as a manager of the business on behalf of the claimants. He covenanted that he would not set up in business as an accountant within a radius of 15 miles for 15 years after leaving the claimants' employment. Clauson J had no hesitation in holding this covenant to be invalid, without classifying it formally as one between employer and employee or between vendor and purchaser. It was enough that it conferred "far more" protection upon the claimants than was "reasonably adequate in the circumstances of the case".[75] In *Systems Reliability Holdings v Smith*,[76] on the other hand, a covenant entered into on the sale of shares in a company was held to come within the category of the sale of goodwill, and as such to be enforceable, even though the shareholding represented less than two per cent of the value of the company and had been acquired by the covenantor while he was an employee. A submission on the latter's behalf, that the covenant was in substance one between employer and employee, was rejected by Harman J.

12–21   **Protection limited to business sold.**   The readiness of the court to accord greater scope to freedom of contract, where covenants between vendor and purchaser are concerned, is subject to an important limitation. The protection accorded by the covenant must be confined to the business actually sold. Thus covenantees cannot absorb firms which were in competition with only part of

---

[70] [1936] 1 Ch. 544 at 547; [1936] 1 All E.R. at 600. See also *Stevens v Allied Freightways* [1968] N.Z.L.R. 1195.

[71] [1988] I.R.L.R. 60 (Millett J.).

[72] See also the decision of the Canadian Supreme Court in *Elsey v J. G. Collins Insurance Agencies* (1978) 83 D.L.R. (3d) 1, in which the covenantee sold his insurance business to the covenantee and became the latter's employee. The fact that an employment relationship had existed subsequent to the sale did not prevent the covenant from being enforced as one for the sale of goodwill.

[73] See *Carewatch Care Services Ltd v Focus Caring Services Ltd and Others* [2014] EWHC 2313 per Henderson J at [127] and cases there cited.

[74] [1937] 3 All E.R. 650.

[75] [1937] 3 All E.R. 650 at 655.

[76] [1990] I.R.L.R. 377.

their business, and seek protection from the vendors against any competition with the full range of their activities prior to the acquisition. In *British Reinforced Concrete Engineering Co v Schelf*[77] the defendant owners of a small business sold the business, and a patent which it owned, to the claimant company. The defendants also covenanted that they would not become involved "in the business of the manufacture or sale of road reinforcements in any part of the United Kingdom". The claimants never exploited the patent, which was for a different road reinforcement process from their own pre-existing one. In effect the claimants had sought merely to eliminate the sale of a rival system. When one of the defendants subsequently obtained employment with a firm dealing in reinforced concrete the claimants brought proceedings against him for breach of covenant. Their claim failed. Younger LJ, sitting as an additional judge of the King's Bench Division, expressed himself as follows[78]:

> "The plaintiffs' claim here is based on the hypothesis that the legitimate subject of protection is the plaintiffs' business; and there can, I think, be no doubt that the restrictive covenant is framed with reference to the requirements of that business, and of no other. Its extravagance in range as applied to the altogether insignificant business sold, hardly requires statement . . . It is the business sold which is the legitimate subject of protection, and it is for its protection in the hands of the purchaser, and for its protection only, that the vendor's restrictive covenant can be legitimately exacted . . . A covenant in gross against trading, however great the consideration, is void. A covenant only exacted for the protection of a business with which the covenantor has never had any connection is, for this purpose, no better than a covenant in gross."

Vendor restrained from taking paid employment.   Although in *Schelf's* case   **12–22**
the attempt to restrain the defendant from taking up salaried employment failed on other grounds, there is no objection in principle to the vendor of a business being restrained by a suitably drafted covenant from taking paid employment after sale of the business, if that employment involves competition with the business sold. Moreover, the more relaxed attitude to severance adopted by the court with regard to vendor and purchaser covenants may sometimes come to the assistance of purchasers to ensure that the covenant is sufficiently limited in scope as to satisfy this requirement.[79] Both aspects of the more sympathetic approach of the court to covenants of this type, as distinct from those between employer and employee, are illustrated by the decision of the Court of Appeal in *Ronbar Enterprises v Green*.[80] The defendant published a weekly sporting newspaper which was sold to the claimants. The defendant covenanted not to be "engaged or interested in any business similar to or competing with" the business sold. When the defendant accepted paid employment on a rival newspaper the Court of Appeal granted the claimants an interlocutory injunction to enforce the covenant, having first severed the words "similar to or"; unless removed those words rendered the covenant unlimited in area and hence, in the circumstances, too wide to be valid.

---

[77] [1921] 2 Ch. 563.
[78] [1921] 2 Ch. 563 at 574–576; [1921] All E.R. Rep. 202 at 211–212.
[79] On the doctrine of severance see generally Ch.19, below.
[80] [1954] 1 W.L.R. 815; [1954] 2 All E.R. 266.

12–23   **Relevance of patent legislation.**   In appropriate cases the scope of patent legislation can be relevant to the determination of the reasonableness of a covenant from the perspective of public interest. In *Dranez Anstalt v Hayek*, in which the Court of Appeal declined to enforce a covenant against an inventor in the medical science field, Chadwick LJ said[81]:

> "The grant or registration of a patent confers a monopoly. The statutory monopoly can be justified on the grounds that it is necessary (for a limited time) in order to encourage inventors, and those who fund them, to apply their skills and resources in developing products and processes from which the public will benefit. But the balance between the benefits which will accrue to the public from permitting monopolies in order to encourage invention and the detriment which may be suffered by the public from monopolistic practices is struck by the patent legislation. A case in which it could be justified as reasonable in the interest of the public to superimpose further contractual restraints on invention, going beyond what Parliament has thought necessary, must be regarded as exceptional."

4.   EXCLUSIVE SUPPLY CONTRACTS

12–24   **"Solus agreements".**   The decision of the House of Lords in *Esso Petroleum v Harper's Garage*[82] saw one of the most significant extensions of the restraint of trade doctrine for decades. The House established unambiguously that the doctrine is not confined to the traditional categories of employee restraints and sales of businesses, but extends to contracts whereby one business binds itself to obtain all its supplies exclusively from another business. Lord Reid explained the background to the *Esso* case as follows[83]:

> "When petrol rationing came to an end in 1950 the large producers began to make agreements, now known as solus agreements, with garage owners under which the garage owner, in return for certain advantages, agreed to sell only the petrol of the producer with whom he made the agreement. Within a short time three-quarters of the filling stations in this country were tied in that way, and by the dates of the agreement in this case over ninety per cent had agreed to it. It appears that the garage owners were not at a disadvantage in bargaining with the large producing companies as there was intense competition between these companies to obtain these ties. So we can assume that both the garage owners and the companies thought that such ties were to their advantage; and it is not said in this case that all ties are either against the public interest or against the interests of the parties. The respondents' case is that the ties with which we are concerned are for too long periods."

The proposition that "solus" ties might be subjected to the "reasonableness" tests of the restraint of trade doctrine was met at the outset with the argument that the ties did not limit any individual's freedom to trade, but merely the use to which a particular piece of land—the garage subject to the tie—could be put.[84] Moreover, restrictions upon land use by restrictive covenants or covenants in leases, usually aimed at preserving amenity, are a very long-established feature of

---

[81] See [2002] EWCA Civ 1729; [2003] F.S.R. 32 at para.25.

[82] [1968] A.C. 269; [1967] 1 All E.R. 699.

[83] [1968] A.C. 269 at 301; [1967] 1 All E.R. 699 at 709–710.

[84] See the reversed decision of Mocatta J at first instance in *Esso Petroleum v Harper's Garage* [1966] 2 Q.B. 514; [1965] 2 All E.R. 933.

the law of real property. Might not the law relating to such covenants become subject to undesirable destabilisation if the fluid restraint of trade doctrine gained a foothold in the area?[85]

Arguments against invoking the doctrine rejected.   The House of Lords   **12–25** refused to be intimidated by the novelty of applying the restraint of trade doctrine in virgin territory. The argument that freedom to trade as such was unaffected was rejected as unrealistic: an individual whose energy and resources had been wholly committed to one garage was hardly in a position to open another one in order to escape the "solus" tie. Their Lordships countered the fears of a general destabilisation of the law relating to covenants affecting land with, broadly speaking, two main arguments. First, it was contended that a distinction could be drawn between, on the one hand, the surrendering by means of a "solus" tie of a freedom to trade which the covenantor had previously enjoyed and, on the other, the acquisition of a piece of land subject to pre-existing restrictions which the covenantor accepted voluntarily as a condition of the acquisition.[86] Secondly, covenants which had "passed into the accepted and normal currency of commercial or contractual or conveyancing relations" would not usually call for "justification under a public policy test of reasonableness".[87] While neither argument is free from difficulty, the four decades or so since *Esso Petroleum v Harper's Garage* was decided cannot be said to have witnessed any significant erosion of stability which can plausibly be attributed to that decision.

Mortgages and leases.   A common advantage which garage-owners obtain   **12–26** from "solus" ties is the provision of financial assistance to acquire or develop their businesses. In *Harper's* case itself the covenant was contained in a mortgage which was irredeemable for the period of the tie. A defence argument that it should therefore be exempt from scrutiny from a restraint of trade perspective, so as to avoid any conflict with the law relating to redemption of mortgages, was rejected. Their Lordships showed greater circumspection with respect to ties contained in leases since, unlike mortgages which are essentially commercial in nature, leases frequently contain provisions legitimately restricting land use. In any event, the possible applicability of the restraint of trade doctrine to leases did not arise for decision. Subsequent cases, however, have made it clear that "solus" ties in leases will not be exempt from the restraint of trade doctrine, any more than those in mortgages or in straightforward contracts.[88]

Scope of relief.   In *Alec Lobb v Total Oil GB*,[89] Dillon LJ said[90]:   **12–27**

---

[85] cf. *Quadramain Pty v Sevastopol Investments* (1975–6) 133 C.L.R. 390.
[86] See *Cleveland Petroleum Co v Dartstone* [1969] 1 W.L.R. 116; [1969] 1 All E.R. 201 in which observations of the House of Lords on this point in *Esso Petroleum v Harper's Garage* were applied by the Court of Appeal.
[87] [1968] A.C. 269 at 332–333; [1967] 1 All E.R. 699 at 729 per Lord Wilberforce.
[88] See *Amoco Australia Pty Ltd v Rocca Bros Motor Engineering Co Pty Ltd* [1975] A.C. 561; [1975] 1 All E.R. 968, PC. cf. *Cleveland Petroleum Co v Dartstone* [1969] 1 W.L.R. 116; [1969] 1 All E.R. 201, CA.
[89] [1985] 1 W.L.R. 173; [1985] 1 All E.R. 303. CA.
[90] See [1985] 1 W.L.R. 173 at 178–179; [1985] 1 All E.R. 303 at 309.

"The decision in *Esso v Harper's Garage* has been generally taken as laying down a rule of thumb that a petrol supply restraint, requiring a dealer to take all his petrol from one petrol company, is reasonable and valid if it will last no longer than five years, but if it will last for significantly more than five years, e.g. for twenty-one years, it is unreasonable and invalid unless the petrol company can prove that a tie for the longer period is an economic necessity for it."

In *Harper*'s case itself the respondents owned two garages, one of which was subjected to a tie of four years and 10 months and the other to a tie of 21 years. The longer tie was combined with a mortgage which could not be redeemed otherwise than by instalments during the same 21 year period as the tie. The Court of Appeal held that both covenants were unenforceable as being in unreasonable restraint of trade,[91] but the House of Lords held that only the longer tie was unenforceable and reversed the Court of Appeal with respect to the shorter one. The House of Lords emphasised, however, that it was impossible to lay down any general rule since every case would depend upon the evidence put forward by the parties. Lord Reid refused expressly to express "any opinion as to the validity of ties for periods mid-way between the two periods" considered in *Esso Petroleum v Harper's Garage*[92] itself.[93]

12–28   **Contrasting cases.**   The contrasting cases of *Petrofina (Gt. Britain) Ltd v Martin*[94] and *Alec Lobb (Garages) v Total Oil GB Ltd*[95] illustrate how the circumstances surrounding "solus" ties can differ. In the *Petrofina* case the tie was for 12 years, but would continue even after the expiry of that period if the quantity of petrol bought from Petrofina had not reached a stipulated minimum. Although Petrofina could escape from the agreement if circumstances beyond their control prevented them from supplying petrol there was no equivalent provision for the garage-owner, who could be compelled to keep the garage open even if it became impossible to do so otherwise than at a loss: he could only escape by persuading someone else to buy the garage and continue the tie. The Court of Appeal held, in a decision which was reached before *Harper*'s case but was apparently approved by the House of Lords in that case,[96] that the tie was unenforceable. Diplock LJ said[97] of the restrictions that they created:

"a new commercial serfdom from which the garage proprietor can obtain manumission only on finding a substitute serf. To this the courts of twentieth-century England will not lend their aid".

In the *Alec Lobb* case, on the other hand, the Court of Appeal upheld a 21 year tie as valid. The evidence showed that the agreement had actually been urged

---

[91] [1966] 2 Q.B. 514; [1966] 1 All E.R. 725.
[92] [1968] A.C. 269 at 304; [1967] 1 All E.R. 699 at 711.
[93] It is important to note that undertakings given by the petroleum industry to the Government, following a Report on the industry in 1965 by the then Monopolies Commission, have a significant impact on the way in which "solus" ties are operated in practice. The undertakings are now within the responsibility of the Competition and Markets Authority.
[94] [1966] Ch. 146; [1966] 1 All E.R. 126, CA.
[95] [1985] 1 W.L.R. 173; [1985] 1 All E.R. 303, CA.
[96] [1968] A.C. 269 at 304; [1967] 1 All E.R. 699 at 711, per Lord Reid.
[97] [1966] Ch. 146 at 190–191; [1966] 1 All E.R. 126 at 144.

upon a reluctant petrol supplier by the garage proprietors, in a desperate attempt to raise finance to turn round a failing business. Moreover, there were break clauses during the tie period at seven and 14 years. Dunn LJ said that it seemed to him "that public policy should encourage a transaction which enabled trading by the [garage] to continue, and preserved an outlet for [Total's] products".[98] He concluded, along with Dillon and Waller LJJ, "that in the special circumstances of [the] case Total [had] established that the covenants in restraint of trade were reasonable"'.[99]

Other contexts.   Although the context in which the House of Lords established that the restraint doctrine applies to exclusive supply agreements related to the sale of petrol,[100] there can obviously be many other contexts in which such agreements can be entered into. For example, the concept of "tied-houses" was a feature of the brewery industry for well over a century, apparently without any tie being held to be in restraint of trade.[101] In *Queensland Co-operative Milling Association v Pamag Pty*[102] the High Court of Australia considered the application of the doctrine to a contract whereby a baker covenanted to obtain all its flour from one miller. Although the covenant was upheld on the facts, the case contains an important discussion of the special issues raised when the doctrine is applied to exclusive supply arrangements; especially the difficulty of applying in such cases the notion that attempts to gain protection from "competition" are, as such and without more, to be disallowed automatically.[103]

12–29

Sole agency agreements.   Another context in which the question of the reasonableness of a requirement of exclusivity during the period of the contract can arise is that of sole agency agreements. In *OMM v Ria Financial Services and Wasilewski*[104] the defendant agreed to work exclusively as agent for the claimant financial services company in a particular area. This restriction was upheld by the Court of Appeal notwithstanding a contention that the contract was one-sided because the claimants had not undertaken *not* to appoint an additional agent during the defendant's tenure. Longmore LJ quoted at length from the speeches of Lord Pearce and Lord Wilberforce in *Esso Petroleum v Harper's Garage* and derived the proposition that "since sole agencies [are] a normal and necessary incident of commerce, the doctrine of restraint of trade should not apply to them unless in some way the agent's ability to work could be said to be sterilised in that he could only work for a party who might not choose to absorb his output."[105]

12–30

---

[98] [1985] 1 W.L.R. 173 at 186; [1985] 1 All E.R. 303 at 315.
[99] [1985] 1 W.L.R. 173 at 186; [1985] 1 All E.R. 303 at 315.
[100] Purely as a matter of terminology, the expression "solus tie" appears to have been confined to the petrol cases.
[101] See, e.g. *Catt v Tourle* (1869) 4 Ch. App. 654; *Biggs v Hoddinott* [1898] 2 Ch. 307.
[102] (1973) 133 C.L.R. 260.
[103] (1973) 133 C.L.R. 260 at 265; per Menzies J, and 277; per Stephen J.
[104] [2015] EWCA Civ 1084.
[105] See ibid at [7].

CHAPTER 13

CONSTRUCTION AND SCOPE OF COVENANTS

1. INTERPRETATION: LITERAL OR CONTEXTUAL?

Construction affected by policy considerations. When the cases on the actual interpretation of restrictive covenants are examined, a tension can be perceived between two factors, especially where covenants between employer and employee are concerned. On the one hand there is the desirability of ensuring that "contractual documents are nowadays construed", in the words of Lord Hoffman in a different context, in accordance with "the common sense principles by which any serious utterance would be interpreted in ordinary life".[1] On the other hand there is the great importance, specific to restraint of trade cases, of ensuring that employers are not given any encouragement to impose restrictive covenants in unenforceably wide terms; in the hope that the cost and uncertainty of defending a legal action will in practice secure compliance from ex-employees.[2] This latter consideration led to a number of decisions which, if read in isolation and without regard to the underlying policy reasons, are apt to seem highly artificial and legalistic.[3] Far-fetched hypothetical situations, which were unlikely ever to have been in the contemplation of the parties, would be referred to in order to demonstrate that, taken literally, the covenant could apply to them; and that it was therefore too wide.[4] Moreover, the weight attached to this policy factor seemed, until relatively recently, to have become so great that the courts would construe restrictive covenants strictly against all employers, regardless of whether or not the individual employer in question had sought to act oppressively. Thus, in one case[5] the Court of Appeal expressed regret at considering itself obliged to reach a decision adverse to the claimants who did "have important confidential information, for which they might reasonably [have claimed] protection by a suitably limited restrictive provision". Their "home-made" covenant had been "offered and accepted in good faith between commercial men and [had] not [been] in the least intended to be oppressive".[6]

13–01

---

[1] See *Investors Compensation Scheme v West Bromwich Building Society* [1998] 1 W.L.R. 896 at 912; [1998] 1 All E.R. 98 at 114, HL. See also *Chartbrook v Persimmon Homes* [2009] UKHL38, [2009] 4 All ER 677; *Rainy Sky SA v Kookmin Bank* [2011] UKSC 50, [2012] 1 All ER 1137; *Arnold v Britton* [2015] UKSC 36. [2016] 1 All ER 1.

[2] cf. *Mason v Provident Clothing and Supply Co* [1913] A.C. 724 at 745, per Lord Moulton (severance). See also *Scully UK Ltd v Lee* [1998] I.R.L.R. 259, CA.

[3] See, e.g. *Whitmore v King* (1918) 87 L.J. Ch. 647, CA.

[4] See, e.g. *Routh v Jones* [1947] 1 All E.R. 758, CA and *Lyne-Perkis v Jones* [1969] 1 W.L.R. 1293, CA (medical practitioners). But cf. *Clarke v Newland* [1991] 3 All E.R. 397, CA.

[5] See *Commercial Plastics v Vincent* [1965] 1 Q.B. 623.

[6] [1965] 1 Q.B. 623 at 647, per Pearson LJ delivering the judgment of the court.

13–02   **Less rigidity.**   In the last 30 years or so of the twentieth century, however, a move away from the rigidity of the highly benevolent (as far as employees were concerned) approach began to be seen. In *Home Counties Dairies Ltd v Skilton*[7] a milk roundsman was subjected to a covenant restraining him from selling "milk or dairy produce" to those customers of his former employer with whom he had dealt in the last six months of his employment. The defendant contended that the wording would prevent him from accepting employment in a grocer's shop in case he inadvertently sold butter or cheese to a former customer, or serving behind the counter in a milk-bar which such customers might frequent. These arguments persuaded the trial judge that the covenant was too wide to be enforceable, but his judgment was reversed by the Court of Appeal. Harman LJ said[8]:

> "It is the first principle in construing written documents . . . to consider the circumstances at the time they were made and the position of the parties to them. Now the first thing to observe here is that this is an agreement between a dairyman and one of his roundsmen then operating a milk round on his behalf. It may therefore be supposed to be concerned with the employer's trade as a dairyman and the employee's as a milk roundsman . . . I am therefore of opinion that, on a true construction of the agreement, it has nothing to do with any commodity not such as is dealt with by the employee in the course of his round . . . If it were so, he could not be employed in a restaurant, and this seems to me to be outside the scope of the agreement altogether. It is in fact, on its true construction, an agreement not to serve an employer as a milk roundsman calling on the customers of the old milk round whom he has served in the last six months. This is precisely the area which, to my mind, the employer is entitled to protect."[9]

13–03   **Context of the business.**   Similarly, in *Marion White Ltd v Francis*[10] the Court of Appeal reversed the trial judge so as to enforce a covenant preventing a young hairdresser from being "in any way engaged or concerned or interested in the business of a Ladies' Hairdresser within one half mile" of her former employers for 12 months after her employment ceased. The defendant argued that the covenant was too wide as it could include a variety of activities unrelated to hairdressing as such, but this contention was rejected. Buckley LJ said[11]:

> "[A]n agreement of this kind and a clause of this kind must be read in the context of the business in relation to which the covenant is entered into and of the relation between the parties; and I think for myself that it is giving too wide an interpretation to this covenant to say that it would extend to any such activities as being employed as a bookkeeper or as a cleaner or anything of that sort".

13–04   **The Court of Appeal across a century.**   One of the more significant of the later twentieth century cases in this context is the 1978 majority decision of the Court of Appeal in *The Littlewoods Organisation Ltd v Harris*.[12] A covenant restraining a senior executive from joining a rival company within 12 months was enforced, again reversing the judge at first instance. Among the contentions rejected by the Court of Appeal was one to the effect that the covenant in question

---

[7] [1970] 1 W.L.R. 526, CA.
[8] [1970] 1 W.L.R. 526 at 533; [1970] 1 All E.R. 1227 at 1231.
[9] See also *Plowman (G. W.) & Son v Nash* [1964] 1 W.L.R. 568, CA.
[10] [1972] 1 W.L.R. 1423; [1972] 3 All E.R. 857, CA.
[11] [1972] 1 W.L.R. 1423 at 1430; [1972] 3 All E.R. 857 at 863.
[12] [1977] 1 W.L.R. 1472 (Lord Denning MR and Megaw LJ, Browne LJ dissenting).

was too wide as it could, in theory, have extended to the new employer's subsidiaries on the other side of the world, which posed no threat to the claimants. The Court reviewed the authorities on the interpretation of restrictive covenants,[13] and placed particular emphasis on a trio of earlier decisions of the Court of Appeal at the end of the nineteenth century[14]; decisions which had been partially lost sight of in the earlier years of the twentieth century when strict construction of such covenants against employers was in the ascendancy. In all three cases the Court had been led by Sir Nathaniel Lindley (either as a Lord Justice or as Master of the Rolls) and in one of them he had expressed himself as follows[15]:

"Agreements in restraint of trade, like other agreements, must be construed with reference to the object sought to be attained by them. In cases such as the one before us . . . the Court ought not to hold a just and honest agreement void, even when to enforce it would be just, simply because the agreement is so unskilfully worded as apparently, or even really, to cover some conceivable case not within the mischief sought to be guarded against. Public policy does not require so serious a consequence to be attached to a mere want of accuracy in expression. To hold such an agreement wholly illegal and void is to lose all sense of proportion, and is not necessary for the protection either of the defendant or of the public."

Almost exactly a century later Waller LJ, also in the Court of Appeal, expressed himself as follows[16]:

"There is in my view some interconnection between the question of construction and the doctrine of restraint of trade. That, as it seems to me, must be so for at least one reason. If a particular construction was to lead to the view that the clause was unenforceable, then an alternative view, which did not lead to the same result if legitimate, ought to be preferred."[17]

Wide terms still struck down.   Despite the revival of interest in the earlier   **13–05** authorities, and the move in the more recent cases away from artificially rigid "literal" interpretation, it would be an oversimplification to suppose that the pendulum has swung decisively in favour of employers. Although a restrictive covenant will now "be construed in its context, and in the light of the factual matrix at the time when the agreement was made",[18] the court will still not hesitate to strike down any covenant which is clearly too wide on its terms. Thus in *Greer v Sketchley Ltd*[19] the Court of Appeal, distinguishing *The Littlewoods Organisation v Harris*, declined to enforce a covenant which sought to restrain a senior executive from joining a rival firm for 12 months. The wording of the

---

[13] See also *Beckett Investment Management Group v Glyn Hall* [2007] EWCA Civ 613 per Maurice Kay LJ at paras 1–20.
[14] See *Mills v Dunham* [1891] 1 Ch. 576; *Moenich v Fenestre* (1892) 67 L.T. 602: *Haynes v Doman* [1899] 2 Ch. 13. On "the rule in *Mills v Dunham*" see R. N. Gooderson, "Restraint of Trade in the Field Code" (1963) 79 L.Q.R. 410 at pp.425 et seq.
[15] See *Haynes v Doman* [1899] 2 Ch. 13 at 25–26. See also *Clark v Electronic Applications* [1963] R.P.C. 234.
[16] See *Turner v British & Commonwealth Minerals* [2000] I.R.L.R. 114 at 116.
[17] See also *PSG Franchising Ltd v Lydia Derby Ltd* [2012] EWHC 3707 at [45] per Males J: ". . . the restriction has been carefully limited as to both period and territorial scope . . . To hold the clause to be void because of the mere possibility that in some as yet unidentified circumstances it might operate unreasonably would be wrong".
[18] See *Clarke v Newland* [1991] 1 All E.R. 397 at 402, per Neill LJ, CA.
[19] [1979] I.R.L.R. 445.

covenant expressly made it applicable to "any part of the United Kingdom", whereas the activities of the employers were at that time largely confined to London and the Midlands, with no presence at all in substantial parts of the country. Shaw LJ observed[20] that it was not possible "to qualify the plain language" of the clause "except by distortion and deformation of the clause itself", and that was "something a court ought not to seek to do to save a restraint of trade from ineffectiveness".[21] Similarly, a covenant will not be enforced if it refers specifically to an interest which the claimant is not entitled to protect, even though it might have been enforceable if a different, and legitimate, interest had been specified instead.[22]

13–06   **Continuing importance of protecting employees.**   A particularly robust assertion of the continuing importance of protecting employees, from potentially oppressive restrictive covenants, is to be found in the 1992 decision of the Court of Appeal in *J.A. Mont (UK) Ltd v Mills*.[23] The claimant employers had been granted an injunction on a much narrower basis than the wide restrictive covenant on which it was based; the judge having expressed the view that a "more relaxed, flexible or practicable" approach now applied in restraint of trade cases. But a strong and unanimous Court of Appeal reviewed the authorities carefully, and had no hesitation in reversing his decision. Simon Brown LJ said[24]:

> "If the court here were to construe this covenant as the plaintiffs desire, what possible reason would employers ever have to impose restraints in appropriately limited terms? ... Thus would be perpetuated the long-recognised vice of ex-employees being left subject to apparently excessive restraints and yet quite unable, short of expensive litigation and at peril of substantial damages claims, to determine precisely what their rights may be."

The Court of Appeal adopted a similarly robust approach in *Prophet plc v Huggett*.[25] Striving to render a wide and complicated restraint clause enforceable, the draftsman added a proviso which was intended to have a narrowing effect but which, read literally, negated the main clause and deprived the employer of any protection. At trial the judge was persuaded, in effect, to depart from literal interpretation so as to avoid this (from the employer's perspective) absurd result. But his decision was reversed by the Court of Appeal. "It was not for the judge",

---

[20] [1979] I.R.L.R. 445 at 448.
[21] See also *Willow Oak Developments Ltd v Silverwood* [2006] EWCA Civ 600; [2006] I.C.R. 1552, per Buxton LJ at para.33: "The [*Harris*] doctrine's application in our case, to employees in comparatively modest positions who might well move to other parts of the country, would be a matter of some difficulty".
[22] See *Office Angels v Rainer-Thomas* [1991] I.R.L.R. 214, especially at 219, per Sir Christopher Slade.
[23] [1993] F.S.R. 577. See also *Scully UK Ltd v Lee* [1998] I.R.L.R. 259, CA. cf. *Hanover Insurance Brokers v Schapiro* [1994] I.R.L.R. 82 at 87, per Nolan LJ, noting "an apparent difference between the unsympathetic approach ... adopted towards the construction of restrictive covenants of excessive width [in *J A. Mont (UK) Ltd v Mills*] and the more flexible and supportive approach adopted [in *The Littlewoods Organisation v Harris*]".
[24] [1993] F.S.R. 577 at 584.
[25] [2014] EWCA Civ 1013.

said Rimer LJ, "to re-make the parties' clause … bargain. [The employer] made its clause … bed and it must now lie on it".[26]

Discretion.   The reality of the current position would appear to be that a reluctance to resort to strained and artificial interpretative techniques in fact co-exists, perhaps rather uneasily, alongside a continued insistence that employers should not be allowed to rely on loose drafting to act oppressively towards their former employees. In practice, this appears to leave the court with a good deal of covert discretion. It enjoys a high degree of freedom to adopt an approach towards the construction of any particular covenant which accords with its perception of the merits of the case before it.[27]

    13–07

Date for determination of validity.   The reasonableness, and hence validity, of a covenant has to be determined as at the date when it was entered into.[28] Thus a clause which was too wide at that time cannot be validated subsequently if the covenantor acquires wider responsibilities which would have made the original width of the covenant legitimate: employers seeking protection need to ensure that they extract a new covenant at the time of the promotion.[29]

    13–08

2.   AREA COVENANTS

Close scrutiny.   Restrictive covenants imposed upon employees often seek to restrict the covenantor's activities, after the employment has ceased, within a specific area; usually defined in terms of a measurable distance from the covenantee's place of business. It must not be forgotten,[30] however, that a former employer is only entitled to protection against disclosure of genuine "trade secrets" or confidential information and against soliciting of his former customers or persons in a similar commercial relationship with him.[31] Area covenants are therefore only permitted in so far as they represent a convenient way of protecting those interests without specifying them with greater precision, which may well not be practicable. But the courts tend to approach area covenants with

    13–09

---

[26] See ibid at [28].

[27] See, e.g. comments in *Marion White v Francis* [1972] 1 W.L.R. 1423 at 1428; [1972] 3 All E.R. 857 at 861 ("The conduct of the defendant ethically is really quite inexcusable"); *Home Counties Dairies v Skilton* [1970] 1 W.L.R. 526 at 532; [1970] 1 All E.R. 1227 at 1230 ("a flagrant breach of his covenant"), cf. *Greer v Sketchley Ltd* [1979] I.R.L.R. 445 at 446, of successful employee ("He did a very courteous and sensible thing which I have never come across before in these cases").

[28] See *Commercial Plastics v Vincent* [1965] 1 Q.B. 623 [1965] 1 Q.B. 623 at 644, per Pearson LJ delivering the judgment of the court.

[29] See *PAT Systems v Neilly* [2012] EWHC 2609 at [32]–[40] per Underhill J (citing *Gledhow Autoparts v Delaney* [1965] 1 W.L.R. 1366 at 1377; [1965] 3 All E.R. 288 at 295 per Diplock LJ, CA).

[30] See Ch.12, above.

[31] e.g. the relationship between a pool of temporary office-workers and their employment agency see *Office Angels v Rainer-Thomas* [1991] I.R.L.R. 214 at 219, per Sir Christopher Slade (the observations on this point were obiter, since the decision concerned the relationship between the claimant employment agency and its clients—i.e. those who employ the temporary workers).

caution, and to scrutinise them closely, to ensure that the covenant does not in truth represent an illegitimate attempt by the former employer to protect himself against competition as such.[32]

13–10 **Specific restriction preferable.** In *Office Angels v Rainer-Thomas*[33] the Court of Appeal held that an area covenant which sought to preclude departing senior employees of an employment agency from opening a rival agency, in an area which included most of the City of London, was too wide. While the claimant agency had a legitimate interest in preventing the defendants from taking advantage of the contacts which they had acquired with one hundred or so of the claimant's clients, the area in question included many thousands of potential clients as well as several hundred other employment agencies. Moreover, many of the existing clients, with respect to whom protection would have been legitimate, operated by telephone from outside the prescribed area. The covenant would therefore not actually have afforded the claimant the only protection to which they would have been entitled. It merely "placed a disproportionately severe restriction on the defendants' right to compete with the claimant after leaving its employment",[34] and was unenforceable. If it is possible for them to do so, covenantees are therefore well advised to stipulate, not for an area covenant, but for a specific restriction against approaching customers whom the employee dealt with during the course of the employment. In cases in which area covenants have been held to be too wide and hence invalid, the courts have frequently observed that a suitably drafted covenant against solicitation would have been upheld.[35]

13–11 **Nature of employment.** If an area covenant is required, the size of the area likely to prove acceptable to the courts will depend upon the nature of the work carried out by the covenantee during the period of employment. In *Mason Provident Clothing Co*[36] the defendant was employed by the claimants as a "canvasser" and debt collector to persuade customers to subscribe to an arrangement whereby they could purchase goods from local shops, effectively on credit supplied by the claimants, and pay for them by weekly instalments. The defendant, who worked in Islington, London, was one of about 1,000 canvassers employed by the claimants who divided London into 15 districts. After leaving the claimants' employment the defendant obtained canvassing work, with a similar company, about two miles from the area in which he had worked for the claimants. The latter thereupon sought to enforce a restrictive covenant under which the defendant had agreed not to assist in the carrying on a similar business "within twenty-five miles of London". The House of Lords held that the covenant was far too wide to be enforced. Viscount Haldane LC said[37]:

---

[32] See *Office Angels v Rainer-Thomas* [1991] I.R.L.R. 214 at 222, per Sir Christopher Slade.
[33] [1991] I.R.L.R. 214, CA.
[34] See [1991] I.R.L.R. 214 at 222, per Sir Christopher Slade.
[35] See, e.g. *Gledhow Autoparts v Delaney* [1965] 1 W.L.R. 1366; [1965] 3 All E.R. 288, CA. See also *Mason v Provident Clothing Co* [1913] A.C. 724; *Dickson v Jones* [1939] 3 All E.R. 182; *S.W. Strange v Mann* [1965] 1 W.L.R. 629; [1965] 1 All E.R. 1069.
[36] [1913] A.C. 724.
[37] [1913] A.C. 724 at 734.

"The success of the canvasser depended . . . mainly on his natural aptitude. No doubt he might acquire, in the course of his employment, lists of actual or possible customers in the district in which he had canvassed. I think that under a properly limited clause the employers would have been entitled to restrain him from canvassing such customers. But that is not the clause which the respondents in this case did frame. They have chosen to try to bind the appellant to an extent which might be necessary for their protection if they had been carrying on a business of a different kind."

Where customers are listed. In *S.W. Strange v Mann*[38] an attempt was made to enforce a covenant restraining the manager of a bookmaker's shop from being similarly employed within 12 miles of Cheltenham, the town in which he had been employed by the claimants. Again, the covenant was held to be unenforceable. It was argued on behalf of the defendant that, since the business operated entirely on a credit basis with the customers' names and addresses being recorded, any area covenant was necessarily illegitimate since the claimants' interests could have been effectively protected by a covenant against dealing with the persons listed in the company's books. Stamp J considered the argument to be "a logically attractive one", but was not ultimately prepared to accept the submission "that in relation to exclusively credit business an area restriction, however narrow its radius, must always be more than adequate".[39] Nevertheless, Stamp J made it clear that he regarded the credit nature of the business as a relevant point in leading him to the conclusion that the twelve mile restriction was too wide: the claimants' interests would have been adequately protected by a covenant against solicitation combined with "a covenant not to carry on business in Cheltenham itself".

13–12

Unidentified cash-payers. If the situation is one in which the customers of the former employer are not formally listed, but pay cash and had dealings with the employee personally, an area covenant will normally be the only practicable form of protection. But even here the courts will be zealous to ensure that any covenant is no wider than can be justified. Thus in *Empire Meat Co v Patrick*[40] the manager of a butcher's shop covenanted not to be concerned with a similar business within a distance of five miles. The Court of Appeal accepted that, since the majority of the claimants' customers were cash-payers who were "very difficult to identify", an area agreement was legitimate in principle. Nevertheless, since the evidence was to the effect that most of the customers came from within two miles, the Court held, reversing the trial judge, that the claimants had not "satisfied the onus which rests upon them of establishing that the five miles radius was necessary for the protection of their business".[41]

13–13

Shorter the better. A covenant is therefore likely to be looked upon more favourably if the claimant can point to a recurring, but not formally recorded,

13–14

---

[38] [1965] 1 W.L.R. 629; [1965] 1 All E.R. 1069.
[39] [1965] 1 W.L.R. 629 at 639–640; [1965] 1 All E.R. 1069 at 1077. cf. P.L Davies. "Post Employment Restraints: Some Recent Developments" [1992] J.B.L. 490 at p.493: "In the case of business connections, it has perhaps too easily come to be accepted that it is very difficult to provide adequate protection except through an area covenant".
[40] [1939] 2 All E.R. 85.
[41] [1939] 2 All E.R. 85 at 93, per Finlay LJ delivering the judgment of the Court (the unsuccessful counsel for the claimants was A.T. Denning, KC).

customer base within the area in question, and one with which the employee had close personal contact. Even in such cases, however, the court will need to be persuaded that the actual distance can be supported. Thus in one case involving a solicitor,[42] and another involving a tax adviser,[43] covenants of 15 miles were held to be too wide on the facts. On the other hand, the House of Lords allowed a solicitor to enforce a seven mile covenant in one case,[44] and the Court of Appeal allowed an estate agent to enforce a five mile covenant in another.[45] Employers should therefore think carefully about the nature of their business before seeking to define the relevant area for the purposes of a restrictive covenant. In the case of a local "high street" operation half a mile may be an appropriate limit. The Court of Appeal upheld covenants based on that distance in one case involving a tailor,[46] and another involving a hairdresser.[47]

13–15 **Method of calculation.** It has been clear since the 1872 decision of the Court of Exchequer Chamber in *Mouflet v Cole*[48] that, in the absence of specific words to the contrary in the covenant, the appropriate measure of distance for the purpose of enforcing an area covenant is by drawing a circle with an appropriate radius. In *Mouflet's* case the claimant succeeded, on this basis, even though the defendant contended that any feasible route actually travelled between the two points would have put him beyond the scope of the covenant. The distance is therefore to be measured, not on the basis of actual travel, but "as the crow flies".[49]

3. DURATION

13–16 **Subordinate issue?** In 1984 Lord Fraser, delivering the judgment of the Privy Council in *Deacons v Bridge*,[50] said that there "appears to be no reported case where a restriction which was otherwise reasonable has been held to be unreasonable solely because of its duration". The limitation as to covenants "otherwise reasonable" necessarily introduces a degree of circularity into this statement. Moreover, there are reported judgments in which duration has been mentioned as a relevant factor,[51] and at least one in which it appears to have been decisive.[52] Nevertheless, there is some truth in the statement in the sense that duration usually appears to be regarded as a subordinate issue with other factors

---

[42] See *Dickson v Jones* [1939] 3 All E.R. 182. See also Ch.14, below.
[43] See *D. Bates & Co v Date* [1937] 3 All E.R. 650.
[44] See *Fitch v Dewes* [1921] 2 A.C. 158. See also Ch.14, below.
[45] See *Scorer v Seymour-Johns* [1966] 1 W.L.R. 1419; [1966] 3 All E.R. 347. See also *OMM v Ria Financial Services and Wasilewski* [2015] EWCA Civ 1084.
[46] See *Putsman v Taylor* [1927] 1 K.B. 741.
[47] See *Marion While Ltd v Francis* [1972] 1 W.L.R. 1423; [1972] 3 All E.R. 857.
[48] (1872) L.R. 8 Exch. 32.
[49] (1872) L.R. 8 Exch. 32. See also *Ernest's Char Pit v Demendeiros* (1970) 15 D.L.R. (3d) 663 (Ontario).
[50] [1984] A.C. 705 at 717; [1984] 2 All E.R. 19 at 24.
[51] See, e.g. *Whitehill v Bradford* [1952] Ch. 236; [1952] 1 All E.R. 115, discussed below. See also *Sir W C. Leng & Co v Andrews* [1909] 1 Ch. 763; CA, especially per Fletcher Moulton LJ at 771.
[52] See *M & S Drapers v Reynolds* [1957] 1 W.L.R. 9; [1956] 3 All E.R. 814, CA, discussed below.

such as area and the nature of the activity to which the covenant relates providing the primary focus in the determination of validity or invalidity.[53]

Life-long covenant on senior employee. It has long been clear that, in cases involving the sale of a business, the vendor may subject himself validly to restrictions lasting many years, or even of unlimited duration.[54] If such covenants were not permitted it could be much more difficult to realise the goodwill of a business as a saleable asset.[55] The position is different where covenants between employer and employee are concerned. There can be situations, however, in which the relationship between the parties, although nominally that of employer and employee, bears some resemblance to that of vendor and purchaser. Particularly in the case of very senior employees, the protection of the value of the goodwill of the business as a whole may be a legitimate objective of the covenantee. In such cases much longer restrictions may be upheld than would be permitted in situations involving less exalted employees. In *Gilford Motor Co v Horne*[56] the defendant, who had been managing director of the claimant company, covenanted not to solicit any customers who had dealt with the company during his period as managing director. The covenant was effectively for the duration of the defendant's life, and at first instance Farwell J appears to have attached importance to this factor in holding that the covenant was too wide to be enforced.[57] The Court of Appeal, however, reversed his decision. Lawrence LJ emphasised that the defendant was "not in a subordinate position, but in a highly responsible and confidential position, being placed in actual charge of the business of the company". The claimant company was therefore acting legitimately, and not seeking "to gain a special advantage which it could not otherwise secure",[58] in attempting to enforce the covenant against the defendant who had subsequently created a new, rival, motor business.

13–17

Other employees: *Horne's* case distinguished. *Gilford Motor Co v Horne* was, however, distinguished by the Court of Appeal in *M & S Drapers v Reynolds*.[59] In this case the defendant had been employed by the claimants, on a weekly wage, as a salesman and collector in their credit drapery business. He had covenanted that he would not, after leaving the claimants' employment, solicit their customers. The covenant was only of five years duration and, when attempting to enforce it, the claimants argued that this rendered theirs an a fortiori case when compared with the life-long covenant in *Home*. But the Court of Appeal observed, in the words of Hodson LJ,[60] "that the circumstances of that case were entirely different", and that a "restriction for as long as five years" was

13–18

---

[53] See, e.g. *Stevens v Allied Freightways* [1968] N.Z.L.R. 1195 at 1200.
[54] See, e.g. *Connors Bros v Connors* [1940] 4 All E.R. 179, PC (unlimited duration); *Nonlenfelt v Maxim Nordenfelt Guns & Ammunition Co* [1894] A.C. 535, HL (25 years).
[55] See *Nordenfelt v Maxim Nordenfelt Guns & Ammunition Co* [1894] A.C. 535 at 552; [1891–94] All E.R. Rep. 1 at 11, per Lord Watson.
[56] [1933] Ch. 935. See also *Spink (Bournemouth) Ltd v Spink* [1936] 1 Ch. 544; [1936] 1 All E.R. 597.
[57] [1933] Ch. 935 at 949; [1933] All E.R. Rep. 109 at 112.
[58] [1933] Ch. 935 at 963; [1933] All E.R. Rep. 109 at 118.
[59] [1957] 1 W.L.R. 9; [1956] 3 All E.R. 815.
[60] [1957] 1 W.L.R. 9 at 13; [1956] 3 All E.R. 815 at 817.

"for a man in the position of the defendant unreasonable". As Denning LJ put it[61]: "A managing director can look after himself. A traveller is not so well placed to do so. The law must protect him".

13–19   **Partners.**   A rather different type of case from that of either vendor and purchaser, or employer and subordinate employee, is that of a departing partner in a firm where the goodwill of the partnership is owned by all the partners.[62] In *Deacons v Bridge*[63] a former partner in a firm of solicitors covenanted that he would not act for clients of the firm for five years after leaving. The Privy Council held that this covenant was enforceable, its duration "being in no way unreasonable".[64] Moreover, in the earlier case of *Whitehill v Bradford*[65] a covenant restraining a departing partner in a medical practice from practising within a 10-mile radius of the partnership for 21 years was held to be enforceable by the Court of Appeal. Sir Raymond Evershed MR said[66]:

> "Twenty-one years, of course, is a long time, and in practice might, no doubt, well be equivalent to a life banishment from the area concerned, but . . . I am not persuaded that in a case of this kind there is anything vicious in so long a period of time. The partnership . . . was intended to continue for a long period. A man like the defendant, with his professional qualifications, is a relatively mobile person and the whole of the rest of the United Kingdom is open for the application by him of his professional skill. I am not, therefore satisfied that twenty-one years is over long."

The decision in this case seems to be a harsh one as far as the defendant was concerned, and it may be doubted whether it provides a reliable indication as to the outcome of a similar case nowadays.[67] In *Jenkins v Reid*,[68] another case involving a medical partnership and one which was decided before *Whitehill v Bradford*, Romer J refused to enforce an area covenant, with a five-mile radius, which was to be lifelong. His Lordship declared himself "very much impressed by the fact that the restriction is to go on for as long as the plaintiff lives", and in the absence of clear evidence he was certainly not prepared to "infer that such a long restriction was in the least necessary for the preservation of the goodwill of the practice".[69]

13–20   **Months not years?**   Other things being equal, the shorter the duration of a restrictive covenant the greater are the chances of it proving acceptable to the courts.[70] The rate of change in the commercial world, both with respect to "trade

---

[61] [1957] 1 W.L.R. 9 at 19; [1956] 3 All E.R. 815 at 821.
[62] See *Geraghty v Minter* (1979) 142 C.L.R. for discussion by the High Court of Australia of the application of the restraint doctrine to partnerships, and of the concept of "goodwill" in such cases.
[63] [1984] A.C. 705; [1984] 2 All E.R. 19.
[64] [1984] A.C. 705 at 717; [1984] 2 All E.R. 19 at 24. For covenants restricting solicitors see further below, Ch.14.
[65] [1952] Ch. 236; [1952] 1 All E.R. 115.
[66] [1952] Ch. 236 at 251; [1952] 1 All E.R. 115 at 119–120.
[67] For covenants restricting medical practitioners see further Ch.14, below.
[68] [1948] 1 All E.R. 471.
[69] See [1948] 1 All E.R. 471 at 480.
[70] ". . . as the time of the restriction lengthens and the space of its operation extends, the weight of the onus on the covenantees grows," per Hodson LJ in *M & S Drapers v Reynolds* [1957] 1 W.L.R. 9 at 12; [1956] 3 All E.R. 814 at 816.

secrets" and to the stability of customer bases, is such that decisions from earlier times, imposing long restrictions in ordinary employer and employee cases, no longer provide an effective indication as to what would be acceptable today.[71] Everything depends necessarily upon the circumstances of the individual situation. Nevertheless, it is likely that justifying a restriction for longer than two or three years at the most in an "ordinary" employment case,[72] bearing in mind the need in any event to prove confidential information or customer contacts, is likely to prove a very demanding forensic task.[73] In practice covenants will nowadays need in most cases to be limited to months rather than years to have a realistic chance of being enforced. In reported cases involving the financial services sector the Court of Appeal has, in recent years, enforced covenants limited to periods of six[74] and 12 months.[75] A 12 month covenant has also been enforced against a former employee involved in pharmaceutical sales.[76] When enforcing a covenant whereby a motor-vehicle repair technician had undertaken not to solicit his former employer's customers for six months, the Court of Appeal noted that "the brevity of the restraint period" was an important factor in the covenant's favour.[77]

4. MODIFICATION BY STATUTE IN OTHER JURISDICTIONS

(a) New Zealand

Deletion or modification. The New Zealand Illegal Contracts Act 1970 s.8 provides as follows: **13–21**

> "
> **Restraints of trade—**
> (1) Where any provision of any contract constitutes an unreasonable restraint of trade, the Court may—
>> (a) Delete the provision and give effect to the contract as so amended; or

---

[71] See, e.g. *Haynes v Doman* [1899] 2 Ch. 13, CA (lifelong restriction within a 25 mile radius on a 24-year-old junior clerk).

[72] In *Scorer v Seymour-Johns* [1966] 1 W.L.R. 1419; [1966] 3 All E.R. 347, the Court of Appeal enforced a three--year restriction on an estate agent. See also *G.W. Plowman v Ash* [1964] 1 W.L.R. 568; [1964] 2 All E.R. 10, CA (sales representative).

[73] cf. *Duarte v The Black and Decker Corporation* [2007] EWHC 2720, per Field J at [109]: "Counsel have been able to find only three cases in which a 2 year covenant was upheld . . . To say the least, if a 2 years non-compete covenant is going to be upheld in English law, the scope of the balance of the covenant has got to be narrowly drawn, which is not the case here".

[74] See *OMM v Ria Financial Services and Wasilewski* [2015] EWCA Civ 1084; *Credit Suisse Asset Management v Armstrong* [1996] I.C.R. 882; [1996] I.R.L.R. 450. See also *TFS Derivatives v Morgan* [2004] EWHC 3181 (QB).

[75] See *Dawnay Day & Co v De Braconier D'Alphen* [1998] I.C.R. 1068; [1997] I.R.L.R. 442. See also *Beckett Investment Management Group v Glyn Hall* [2007] EWCA Civ 613; *Thomas v Farr* [2007] EWCA Civ 118; *Romero Insurance Brokers Ltd v Templeton* [2013] EWHC 1198; *Croesus Financial Services v Bradshaw* [2013] EWHC 3685 cf. *PAT Systems v Neilly* [2012] EWHC 2609 at [44]–[45] per Underhill J (12 month covenant too wide whereas a six month one would probably have been enforceable).

[76] See *Norbrook Laboratories (GB) v Adair* [2008] EWHC 978.

[77] See *Dentmaster (UK) Ltd v Kent* [1997] I.R.L.R. 636 at 638, per Waite LJ. See also *Brake Bros v Ungless* [2004] EWHC 2799 (six month covenants enforced against buyers in the catering industry).

(b) So modify the provision that at the time the contract was entered into the provision as modified would have been reasonable, and give effect to the contract as so modified; or

(c) Where the deletion or modification of the provision would so alter the bargain between the parties that it would be unreasonable to allow the contract to stand, decline to enforce the contract.

(2) The Court may modify a provision under paragraph (b) of subsection (1) of this section, notwithstanding that the modification cannot be effected by the deletion of words from the provision."

This provision was applied in *H. & R. Block v Sanott.*[78] The case concerned an area covenant by a former employee, which extended to 25 miles with a stated duration of five years. The contract was in the covenantee's standard form, and Somers J considered whether enforceability should simply be denied on the ground "that the terms were not the result of any deliberate bargaining or really any genuine pre-estimate of need".[79] In the end, however, he modified the covenant by reducing its radius to five miles, and its duration to three years, and enforced it in its modified form. In a subsequent case the New Zealand Court of Appeal applied the provision to what was, in effect, a vendor and purchaser covenant: the area was reduced in extent, and the duration was reduced from 20 years to 12.[80]

(b) New South Wales

13–22   **"Beneficial surgery".**   The New South Wales Restraints of Trade Act 1976 s.4(1) provides as follows:

"A restraint of trade is valid to the extent to which it is not against public policy, whether it is in severable terms or not".

Section 4(3) goes on to empower the Court to order that a restraint should be:

". . . altogether invalid or valid to such extent only (not exceeding the extent to which the restraint is not against public policy) as the Court thinks fit . . ."

It would appear to be clear that the Act removes the "blue pencil" test, whereby severance of an unlawful provision is only permitted when the offending words can be excised cleanly without leaving the literal meaning of the remaining words unclear.[81] Instead "beneficial surgery"[82] is permitted, whereby a "discretion is enlivened by the Act to permit the Supreme Court to order that the restraint be altogether valid or valid to an extent defined".[83] On the other hand, the Act does not allow the court to build an entirely fresh covenant for the parties according to its own notions of reasonableness. As the Court of Appeal of New South Wales observed recently, "amputation is directed but reconstruction is

---

[78] [1976] 1 N.Z.L.R. 213.
[79] [1976] 1 N.Z.L.R. 213 at 219.
[80] See *Brown v Brown* [1980] 1 N.Z.L.R. 484.
[81] For the "blue pencil" test, and the doctrine of severance generally, see Ch.19, below.
[82] *Wright v Gasweld Pty* (1991) 22 N.S.W.L.R. 317 at 339 per Samuels JA.
[83] *Wright v Gasweld Pty* (1991) 22 N.S.W.L.R. 317 at 337 per Kirby P.

not".[84] The Act has, however, been held to facilitate so-called "cascading" restraint clauses whereby several alternative possibilities for geographical scope and periods of enforcement are provided, in effect leaving the court to choose the appropriate options.[85]

"Imaginary breaches".   The Act's abrogation of the rigidity of the common   **13–23** law is not, however, confined merely to removal of the "blue pencil" test. It also appears to have effected a loosening of the approach which sometimes enabled defendants to resist enforcement of restrictions, in circumstances in which such enforcement would have been entirely reasonable, merely because far-fetched situations could be envisaged in which the covenant in question would have operated unreasonably. In *Orton v Melman*,[86] McLelland J referred, in order to determine the mischief at which the legislation had been directed, to the Report of the New South Wales Law Commission on *Covenants in Restraint of Trade*,[87] which had preceded the Act. He concluded[88]:

> "The mischief or defect was that in determining the validity of a restraint the courts were bound to consider all possible breaches within its terms (after any possible severance) and determine whether public policy was infringed by the restraint of all such breaches, rather than by the actual or threatened breaches proved in the particular case; or, as stated succinctly in the report (para. 12): 'The Court does not consider the actual breach, it considers imaginary breaches'."

It is interesting to note that, as the cases discussed earlier in this chapter illustrate, the English common law also effected a similar move away from a highly artificial approach to the construction of restrictive covenants, and did so at about the same time as the legislative intervention in New South Wales.[89]

---

[84] See *ICT Pty v Sea Containers* (1995) N.S.W.L.R. 640 at 674. See also *A. Buckle & Son Pty v McAllister* (1986) 4 N.S.W.L.R. 426 at 434, per Needham J: "I do not think [the Act] empowers the court to create a valid restraint out of an invalid one unless that can be done by a reading down process", cf. per Austin J in *K.A. & C. Smith Pty v Ward* (1998) 45 N.S.W.L.R. 702 at 725: "The question is, what (if any) are the limits to the re-drafting process?"
[85] See e.g. *OAMPS Insurance Brokers Ltd v Hanna* [2010] NSWSC 781 (affmd [2010] NSWSCA 267).
[86] [1981] 1 N.S.W.L.R. 583. See also *K.A. & C. Smith Pty v Ward* (1998) 45 N.S.W.L.R. 702 at 724–728, per Austin J.
[87] L.R.C. 9 (1970).
[88] [1981] 1 N.S.W.L.R. 583 at 587.
[89] See, especially, *The Littlewoods Organisation v Harris* [1977] 1 W.L.R. 1472.

CHAPTER 14

CUSTOMERS, RIVALS AND THE PROFESSIONS

1. INTRODUCTION

Related issues. This chapter is devoted to several distinct, but related, issues.   14–01
The first two sections are concerned with covenants which are more specific in
their avowed objectives than the "area" covenants which have been considered in
the previous chapter. These are covenants against solicitation of the claimant's
former customers, and covenants against joining a rival employer of the claimant.
Covenants which seek to impose restraints upon the subsequent activities of
professional people, such as medical practitioners and solicitors, are particularly
likely to be directed towards preventing loss of the claimants' existing patients or
clients to "rival" practices or firms; even if "area" covenants are in practice
sometimes used. It is therefore appropriate that the final sections should focus
specifically upon restrictive covenants in the medical and legal contexts.

2. SOLICITATION OF CUSTOMERS

Must be justified as reasonable. Since covenants against solicitation of the   14–02
claimant's clients or customers are less indiscriminate in their effect than
covenants which seek to restrict the defendant's activities on an area basis, they
are apt to be looked upon with less disfavour by the courts. Nevertheless, their
enforceability can never be taken for granted,[1] and the burden is still on the
covenantee to justify the restraint as reasonable in the circumstances.

"Customers". Difficulty has sometimes arisen with respect to the degree of   14–03
particularity, and freedom from ambiguity, with which expressions such as
"customer" need to be characterised. In *Express Dairy Co v Jackson*,[2] for
example, McCardie J refused to enforce a non-solicitation covenant which
referred merely to "customers belonging to the [plaintiff's] business", on the
ground that that wording could include persons who only became customers after
the defendant had left the claimant's employment. His Lordship held, choosing
not to follow earlier dicta in the Court of Appeal,[3] that this rendered the covenant
too wide. A covenant may also fail if the departing employee had had contacts of
his own, which he may have brought to the employer, and the wording used could

---

[1] See generally Heydon, *The Restraint of Trade Doctrine*, 3rd edn (LexisNexis Butterworths, 2008),
pp.161–165.
[2] (1929) 99 L.J.K.B. 181.
[3] See *Dubowski & Sons v Goldstein* [1896] 1 Q.B. 478, per Lord Esher MR and Rigby LJ.

be taken to mean that the covenantor was henceforth precluded from taking advantage even of those contacts. This point arose in *M & S Drapers v Reynolds*,[4] in which Denning LJ expressed himself as follows[5]:

> "I do not see . . . why the employers should be able to forbid him to call on the people whom he already knew before he worked for them—the people whom I will call 'his customers'. His knowledge of these people, and his influence with them, were due to his own efforts—or at any rate they were nothing to do with his employers. His goodwill with those customers belonged to him, and cannot reasonably be taken from him by a covenant of this kind. Any other view would mean that, soon after employing him, they could dismiss him at a fortnight's notice and could then prevent him . . . thereafter from calling on those persons who had been his customers long before he entered the employment. When I find that the clause is so wide as to cover 'his customers', . . . I think that it is an unreasonable restraint of trade."[6]

14–04 **Habitual purchasers.** On the other hand, in *Gilford Motor Co v Horne*[7] an attack upon a covenant, alleging insufficient particularity, was unsuccessful. The wording in that case prohibited the defendant from soliciting not only any persons or firms who were "customers", but also those who were "in the habit of dealing with" the claimants, during the period of the defendant's employment. Although Farwell J considered the covenant thus phrased to be too vague and ambiguous to be enforced, the Court of Appeal disagreed. The claimants were entitled to be protected from the solicitation of persons who habitually purchased from them, but "whose names have not yet been inscribed upon any register of customers".[8] It is therefore not essential to the validity of a non-solicitation covenant that the customers to which it applies should be readily identifiable on a list kept by the covenantee.

14–05 **Discontinued custom.** *Horne*'s case was applied and extended by the Court of Appeal in *G. W. Plowman v Ash*.[9] In that case a covenant was attacked unsuccessfully on the ground, inter alia, that its wording could include customers who had ceased to trade with the claimants after the defendant had left their employment. But the Court, reversing the trial judge,[10] held that the employers were "entitled to retain the possibility that those who at one time during the employee's employment placed orders with the employer and [had] discontinued their custom might come back again".[11] Thus even if a former customer is emphatic that they will not return to the claimants in any event, the latter are still

---

[4] [1957] 1 W.L.R. 9; [1956] 3 All E.R. 815. See Ch.13, above.

[5] [1957] 1 W.L.R. 9 at 18; [1956] 3 All E.R. 815 at 821.

[6] cf. *Hanover Insurance Brokers v Schapiro* [1994] I.R.L.R. 82, CA (covenant preventing contact with pre-existing customers may be enforceable if the covenantor was a highly paid employee who had, in effect, been paid for introducing them to the covenantee). See also *Stevens v Allied Freightways* [1968] N.Z.L.R. 1195.

[7] [1933] Ch. 935. For another aspect of this case see Ch.13, above.

[8] [1933] Ch. 935 at 959; [1933] All E.R. Rep. 109 at 116, per Lord Hanworth MR.

[9] [1964] 1 W.L.R. 568; [1964] 2 All E.R. 10.

[10] Coincidentally, Plowman J.

[11] [1964] 1 W.L.R. 568 at 573; [1964] 2 All E.R. 10 at 13, per Davies LJ See also *Home Counties Dairies Ltd v Skilton* [1970] 1 W.L.R. 526; [1970] 1 All E.R. 1227, CA. In *Coppage v Safety Net Security* [2013] EWCA Civ 1176 the Court of Appeal enforced a covenant against soliciting "any individual or organisation who has during your period of employment been a customer of ours, if the purpose of such an approach is to solicit business which could have been undertaken by us."

entitled to have that customer included within the scope of an injunction granted to enforce a valid non-solicitation covenant upon a former employee.[12]

No personal knowledge.   The covenant in *G. W. Plowman v Ash* was also   **14–06**
challenged on the ground that its wording could include customers of whom the defendant could have had no personal knowledge, since they were not situated in the particular area within which he had, in fact, operated. This objection was not fatal to the validity of the covenant either, and the claimants were awarded an interlocutory injunction. The employer could "legitimately protect itself"[13] against the defendant's solicitation anywhere within the area in which he could have been required to work, even if his actual area was narrower. Nor was it considered that the absence of personal knowledge should cause difficulty to the defendant. "When calling on anybody", the employee should simply, in order to avoid breaking the covenant, "ascertain first whether he was a customer of the employer in the relevant period; and if he finds that he was such a customer, then he must say 'Goodbye'".[14]

Some interchange essential.   It is therefore clearly not a necessary condition of   **14–07**
validity that the employee should have dealt personally with the customers in question. On the other hand the employer himself, or someone else acting on his behalf, must actually have done so. That is to say, a non-solicitation covenant must actually refer to the employer's "customers" or "clients", etc.[15] Such a covenant cannot validly prevent an ex-employee from approaching anyone with whom he might, on account of his geographical responsibilities and the nature of the product, have had dealings on his employer's behalf regardless of whether or not he or anyone else in fact did so.[16] A restraint of that type can only be imposed, if at all, as an area covenant in compliance with the tight restrictions on the scope of such covenants.[17] An impossibly wide area covenant cannot be made effective by couching it in language similar to that used in non-solicitation covenants.[18] Nevertheless, two members of the Court of Appeal have suggested, obiter, that the term "customer" may not be construed so narrowly as to require an actual contract to have been concluded, and that "persons on whom [the employee] had called"[19] might validly be included. Moreover, if a non-solicitation covenant is genuinely limited in its scope in terms of the persons whom the former employee is forbidden to approach, it may be capable of extending legitimately over a much

---

[12] See *John Michael Design Plc v Cooke* [1987] 2 All E.R. 332, discussed in Ch.15, below.
[13] [1964] 1 W.L.R. 568 at 572; [1964] 2 All E.R. 10 at 13, per Harman LJ.
[14] [1964] 1 W.L.R. 568 at 575; [1964] 2 All E.R. 10 at 15, per Russell LJ.
[15] cf. *Norbrook Laboratories (G.B.) v Adair* [2008] EWHC 978 ("prospective customers" held to be too wide: "prospective" severed).
[16] See *Gledhow Autoparts v Delaney* [1965] 1 W.L.R. 1366; [1965] 3 All E.R. 288, CA. See also *Marley Tile Co v Johnson* [1982] I.R.L.R. 75; *WRN Ltd v Ayris* [2008] EWHC 1080.
[17] cf. *Office-Angels v Rainer-Thomas* [1991] I.R.L.R. 214, CA.
[18] See, e.g. *Gledhow Autoparts v Delaney* [1965] 1 W.L.R. 1366; [1965] 3 All E.R. 288, CA.
[19] *Gledhow Autoparts v Delaney* [1965] 1 W.L.R. 1366 at 1377; [1965] 3 All E.R. 288 at 295, per Diplock LJ See also, per Sellers LJ at 373 and 292.

wider area than is normally permissible in cases of actual area covenants.[20] At the same time, the more narrowly and specifically a covenant is expressed the greater will be its chances of being enforced.[21]

3.   RIVAL EMPLOYERS

(a)   Covenants Against Joining Other Organisations

14–08   *The Littlewoods Organisation v Harris.*   Instead of, or more usually in addition to, area covenants and non-solicitation covenants, an employer may seek specifically to restrain employees from joining rival organisations after their departure. In *The Littlewoods Organisation v Harris*[22] the claimant organisation secured a covenant from the defendant, who was one of their senior executives, that within 12 months of leaving their service he would not enter "into a Contract of Service . . . with Great Universal Stores Limited". Great Universal Stores were the claimants' main rivals in the business of mail order retailing. By a majority the Court of Appeal held that, in the words of Lord Denning MR, the relevant provision was "a perfectly good clause and it should be upheld by the courts".[23] The defendant had contended unsuccessfully that the clause was too wide because, unlike Littlewoods which was a UK company, Great Universal Stores had subsidiaries worldwide to which the covenant would apply literally even though employment outside the UK could not harm the claimants. But the Court of Appeal felt able to construe the clause "by relation to its object",[24] and hence limit its scope to the UK alone. The object of the covenant had been to protect the confidentiality of the claimants' marketing strategy, and mail order catalogue, which the defendant had played a key part in producing. The Court, reversing the court below, held that the claimants had demonstrated legitimate confidential information which they were entitled to protect.[25]

14–09   **"Competitors".**   Covenants against joining a rival employer are, of course, like all restrictive covenants between employer and employee, governed by the fundamental principle that covenantees are only entitled to protection of their customer base and their trade secrets or confidential information. Indeed, covenants against joining rival employers are, by their very nature, apt to be subjected to even greater than usual scrutiny by the courts to ensure that they are not illegitimate attempts by the claimants merely to protect themselves against

---

[20] See *G.W. Plowman & Son v Ash* [1964] 1 W.L.R. 568, CA; *Business Seating (Renovations) v Broad* [1989] I.C.R. 713; *Dentmaster (UK) Ltd v Kent* [1997] I.R.L.R. 636, CA.

[21] See, e.g. *Stenhouse Australia v Phillips* [1974] A.C. 391, PC. See also *Coppage v Safety Net Security* [2013] EWCA Civ 1176 at [19] per Sir Bernard Rix: "One might debate matters such as the extent to which a non-solicitation clause is drafted in terms which go no wider than the legitimate protection required by an employer's proprietary interests: but if the restraint period is as short as six months, that must be a powerful factor in assessing the overall reasonableness of the clause".

[22] [1977] 1 W.L.R. 1472.

[23] See [1977] 1 W.L.R. 1472 at 1483; [1978] 1 All E.R. 1026 at 1037.

[24] [1977] 1 W.L.R. 1472 at 1483; [1978] 1 All E.R. 1026 at 1037, per Lord Denning MR. See also Ch.13, above.

[25] See Ch.12, above.

competition.[26] It follows that if the word "competitor" is used in the drafting of such covenants, particular care should be taken to qualify it so as not to create an unfortunate impression, and thereby detract from the substance of what might be a legitimate covenant. In *Commercial Plastics v Vincent*[27] the defendant's letter of appointment said that, "in view of the highly technical and confidential nature of this appointment you have agreed not to seek employment with any of our competitors ... for at least one year after leaving our employ". Although the clause included a phrase limiting the scope of the word "competitors" to a particular type of activity, the Court of Appeal construed the limitation very literally and held that it was not narrow and specific enough. It followed that the covenant was too wide and unenforceable. The Court expressed regret at the decision which it felt obliged to reach, observing that the claimants' case had "underlying merits", and that it was "unfortunate" that a clause agreed in good faith had "to be ruled out and declared void in a court of law for lack of the necessary limiting words".[28]

Inauspicious prospects.   In the somewhat similar earlier case of *Vandervell Products Ltd v McLeod*[29] the defendant covenanted with his employers that he would not, for two years after his employment ceased, "enter into the employment of any competitor of your company in business". Morris LJ observed that a clause thus worded had "somewhat inauspicious prospects",[30] in view of the long-established position that the courts will not enforce covenants by employees against competition alone. It appeared from the evidence that the target of the covenant was one particular rival firm, the Glacier Metal Co, which was in fact the defendant's new employer. The Court of Appeal appeared to accept that a covenant naming that company, or otherwise defining more specifically the *particular* activity of a competitor against which protection was sought, may well have been valid.[31] But as it stood, the covenant, which was in a standard form and had not been drafted with reference to the nature of the work which the defendant had been employed to do, was too wide to be enforced.

14–10

Competition as a necessary condition.   While it is clearly not a sufficient condition of validity that a restrictive covenant of this type should restrain an employee from joining his former employer's competitors, it *is* a necessary condition. A covenant which can be construed as seeking to restrain an employee

14–11

---

[26] A lower degree of scrutiny is appropriate where the employer is merely seeking to restrain an employee who is seeking, in breach of contract, to work for a competitor while still employed by the claimant and the doctrine of restraint of trade is therefore inapplicable: see *Elsevier Ltd v Munro* [2014] EWHC 2648. cf. para.11–17 above (garden leave).
[27] [1965] 1 Q.B. 623.
[28] [1965] 1 Q.B. 623 at 647; [1964] 3 All E.R. 546 at 555, per Pearson LJ delivering the judgment of the court. In *The Littlewoods Organisation v Harris*, Lord Denning MR indicated that, in his view, *Vincent's* case should have been decided the other way: see [1977] 1 W.L.R. 1472 at 1481; [1978] 1 All E.R. 1026 at 1036. See also, per Megaw LJ at 1489 and 1042.
[29] [1957] R.P.C. 185.
[30] [1957] R.P.C. 185 at 196.
[31] [1957] R.P.C. 185 at 192 (Lord Evershed MR); at 195 (Hodson LJ); and at 196 (Morris LJ).

from joining businesses which are not in competition with the covenantor at all will go beyond the protection of the latter's legitimate interests, and hence be unenforceable on that account.[32]

14–12   **Particularity.**   The approach of the Court of Appeal in *The Littlewoods Organisation v Harris* to the construction of the covenant in that case was significantly more relaxed, and hence more favourable to the claimant employer, than that adopted in *Commercial Plastics v Vincent* and *Vandervell Products v McLeod*. Nevertheless, the flexibility which the courts in practice enjoy when construing restrictive covenants means that it cannot be assumed that a more rigid approach will not commend itself once again, especially if such an approach were to lead to a result more in accordance with the court's perception of the merits of the particular case.[33] It is therefore clear that, in so far as any guidance can be extracted from the authorities as to the drafting of successful covenants, those against joining rival employers should be drafted with as much precision and particularity as circumstances permit.[34] And the employer or employers, which the covenantee wishes to prevent the covenantor from joining, should if possible be named specifically.[35] Moreover, even if a list is provided, it will still be too wide if it consists simply of the names of large, multi-faceted organisations, some activities of which would be unrelated to the those which the covenantee was concerned to protect.[36]

(b)   "Poaching" by Former Employee

14–13   **Subject to reasonableness test.**   It is not uncommon for contracts of employment nowadays to include a stipulation that the covenantor will not, after leaving the covenantee's employment, seek to persuade his former colleagues also to leave the claimant's employment and join him in a rival organisation, which will typically be a new business subsequently created by the covenantor.[37] Such covenants appear to fall within the restraint of trade doctrine, thereby enabling the court to subject their enforceability to the test of "reasonableness".[38] The well-known decision of the Court of Appeal in *Kores Manufacturing Co v Kolok Manufacturing Co*[39] is relevant by analogy. It will be recalled that in that case a covenant between two pre-existing rival employers not to recruit each other's employees was held to be invalid. Assuming that the doctrine does also

---

[32] See *Scully UK Ltd v Lee* [1998] I.R.L.R. 259, especially per Sir Richard Scott VC at 266: "A clause which bars the employee from involving himself in businesses which do not compete with the business of the previous employer ought not, in my judgment, to be upheld". See also, per Aldous LJ at 263–264.

[33] cf. *Ashcourt Rowan Financial Planning Ltd v Hall* [2013] EWHC 1185.

[34] See, e.g. *Ashcourt Rowan Financial Planning Ltd v Hall* (previous note) in which enforceability was denied. cf. *Putsman v Taylor* [1927] 1 K.B. 637.

[35] cf. *Norbrook Laboratories (GB) Ltd v Adair* [2008] EWHC 978 (covenant held to be too wide). See also *Ashcourt Rowan Financial Planning Ltd v Hall* [2013] EWHC 1185.

[36] See *Duarte v The Black and Decker Corporation* [2007] EWHC 2720.

[37] See, e.g. *Hanover Insurance Brokers v Schapiro* [1994] I.R.L.R. 82, CA.

[38] See P. J. Sales, "Covenants Restricting Recruitment of Employees and the Doctrine of Restraint of Trade" (1988) 104 L.Q.R. 600.

[39] [1959] Ch. 108, discussed in Ch.12, above.

apply to non-recruitment covenants by former employees, the question arises as to how their "reasonableness" will be tested.

Stable workforce? Obviously each covenant will stand or fall on its individual   **14–14**
merits. Nevertheless, while the courts have shown some awareness of the need to protect investment in staff training and development,[40] the mere desirability of maintaining a stable workforce would seem unlikely, *in itself* to constitute an interest which an employer is entitled to protect.[41] In *Hanover Insurance Brokers v Schapiro*,[42] in which the Court of Appeal declined in interlocutory proceedings to enforce a covenant against poaching employees, Dillon LJ said[43]:

> ". . . the employee has the right to work for the employer he wants to work for if that employer is willing to employ him . . . [Counsel for the plaintiff] submits that an insurance broker depends on its staff, and that the goodwill of an insurance broker's business depends on its staff. So in a sense it does, as with any other company, but that does not make the staff an asset of the company like apples or pears or other stock in trade."

Nevertheless, in cases decided since *Schapiro*, restraints against poaching have been held to be, in principle, enforceable.[44] Such covenants are regarded with greater favour if they are restricted specifically to senior staff,[45] and the covenantor knows specifically which employees he is not allowed to approach.[46] Where groups of senior employees have defected to rival organisations which they have themselves created, in breach of their contractual and fiduciary obligations, the courts have shown an increasing readiness to grant their former employer so-called "springboard" injunctions to deprive the new organisation of the competitive advantage which it would otherwise have gained.[47]

---

[40] cf. *Bridge v Deacons* [1984] A.C. 705.

[41] See Sales, "Covenants Restricting Recruitment of Employees and the Doctrine of Restraint of Trade" (1988) 104 L.Q.R. 600, at pp.613 et seq.

[42] [1994] I.R.L.R. 82.

[43] [1994] I.R.L.R. 82 at 84.

[44] See *Alliance Paper Group v Prestwich* [1996] I.R.L.R. 25; and, per Evans LJ in *Dawnay Day & Co v de Braconier d'Alphen* [1998] I.C.R. 1068 at 1111; [1997] I.R.L.R. 442 at 448: ". . . an employer's interest in maintaining a stable, trained workforce is one which he can properly protect within the limits of reasonableness". See also *S.B.J. Stephenson v Mandy* [2000] I.R.L.R. 233 at 238–239, and the unreported decision of the Court of Appeal in *Ingham v ABC Contract Services*, which is referred to in the *Dawnay Day* case.

[45] In *Alliance Paper Group v Prestwich*, see fn.42, above, the clause enforced was one confined to employees "in a senior capacity", cf. *TSC Europe (UK) v Massey* [1999] I.R.L.R. 22, in which a clause not restricted in the same way was held to be invalid.

[46] See *CEF Holdings Ltd c City Electrical Factors Ltd* [2012] EWHC 1525 at [40]–[49] per Silber J (covenant held invalid).

[47] See, especially, *QBE Management Services v Dymoke and others* [2012] EWHC 80 (Haddon-Cave J). See also *Dorma UK Ltd v Bateman and Others* [2015] EWHC 4142.

4. MEDICAL PRACTITIONERS

14–15 **Types of practice distinguished.** The law relating to the enforceability of restrictive covenants, on the breakdown of professional relationships between persons practising medicine together, has been the subject of judicial consideration on several occasions. In *Routh v Jones*[48] the claimants, who practised in partnership as general medical practitioners, employed the defendant as their medical assistant. The latter covenanted that, on the termination of the appointment, he would not "practise in any department of medicine surgery or midwifery", within 10 miles of the practice for five years. When the defendant began subsequently to practise as a general practitioner on his own account, in breach of the covenant, the Court of Appeal held that it was unenforceable. Its wording was wide enough to preclude the defendant from accepting an appointment as a hospital consultant, even though such an appointment could not possibly have an adverse effect upon the plaintiffs' general practice. *Routh v Jones* has been followed in several cases involving covenants with similar wording. Thus in *Lyne-Pirkis v Jones*[49] the defendant had covenanted not to "engage in practice as a medical practitioner". But since this case was also concerned exclusively with general practice, Edmund Davies LJ said that he had "come to the conclusion that the . . . phrase is capable of embracing practise as a consultant", and he concluded: "It is accordingly too wide and that in itself sounds the death-knell of the validity of this restrictive clause".[50] It is possible, however, that the approach adopted in these cases will need to be reconsidered in the light of the move away from rigid, literal, construction of restrictive covenants in favour of a more contextual approach.[51]

14–16 **Covenants enforced.** *Routh v Jones* was distinguished in *Whitehill v Bradford*,[52] in which earlier general words in a restrictive covenant were qualified by a later provision, confining the restriction "to a retiring or outgoing partner carrying on or being interested or concerned in the profession of a general medical practitioner". The Court of Appeal decided that this limitation narrowed the scope of the covenant sufficiently to render it enforceable. Similarly, in the 1991 case of *Clarke v Newland*[53] the Court of Appeal felt able to grant an interlocutory injunction to enforce a restrictive covenant on the breakup of a partnership between two general practitioners. The covenant in that case was, in some respects, worded rather generally enabling counsel for the defendant to contend strongly that *Routh v Jones* and *Lyne-Pirkis v Jones* were indistinguishable. But the Court of Appeal attached importance to the description of the practice, in the early part of the covenant, as being one "of general medical practitioners"; this was treated as confining the covenant to the context thus described, resulting in its validity.

---

[48] [1947] 1 All E.R. 758.
[49] [1969] 1 W.L.R. 1293.
[50] [1969] 1 W.L.R. 1293 at 1301; [1969] 3 All E.R. 738 at 744. See also *Jenkins v Reid* [1948] 1 All E.R. 471; *Peyton v Mindham* [1972] 1 W.L.R. 8; [1971] 3 All E.R. 1215.
[51] See Ch.13, above.
[52] [1952] Ch. 236.
[53] [1991] 1 All E.R. 397.

Area of restriction. In one case Stamp J doubted whether an area covenant 14–17
could ever be reasonable in the case of a medical practice, since all the names of
the patients are recorded so that a covenant not to attend those patients should be
sufficient to protect the practice.[54] None of the relevant authorities had been cited
to Stamp J, however, and it is clear that area covenants can, in principle, be valid
in medical cases. A practice is entitled to protect its goodwill,[55] and the
expectation of new patients within its area. In *Whitehill v Bradford*[56] an area
covenant was enforced which was notable for its breadth: not to practise within a
10 mile radius for 21 years.[57] It is very unlikely that such a covenant would find
favour with the courts today.[58] The covenant enforced in *Clarke v Newland*[59] was
limited to three years and confined to a specific area of south west London, the
boundaries of which were defined by the river Thames and three named roads. In
Lyne-Pirkis v Jones the covenant, which was unenforceable for other reasons,[60]
had been for five years and covered a radius of 10 miles. All the existing patients
were to be found within a five mile radius, and the Court of Appeal was divided
as to whether the covenant would have been invalid in any event on the ground of
excessive territorial width. Russell LJ thought that it would have been, whereas
Edmund Davies and Fenton Atkinson LJJ were less inclined to condemn the
covenant on that account.[61] In *Kerr v Morris*[62] the Court of Appeal granted an
interlocutory injunction to enforce a covenant not to "carry on the profession of
General Medical Practitioner within a radius of two miles" from the premises of
the practice; the duration of the covenant being limited to two years. Such a
covenant probably provides a more realistic indication of what would nowadays
be considered reasonable than some of the earlier decisions. Nevertheless, it is
obviously impossible to generalise about appropriate territorial width: a rural
practice, for example, will inevitably cover a larger area than an urban one.

---

[54] See *Macfarlane v Kent* [1965] 1 W.L.R. 1019 at 1024; [1965] 2 All E.R. 376 at 381. For another
case in which Stamp J was inclined to favour the same approach in a different context see *S.W.
Strange v Mann* [1965] 1 W.L.R. 629; [1965] 1 All E.R. 1069, discussed in Ch.13. above.
[55] Statutory provisions prevent the goodwill of medical practices under the National Health Service
from being sold; but this does not have the effect of denying practitioners from protecting that
goodwill by a valid covenant in restraint of trade, since it remains a valuable asset: see *Kerr v Morris*
[1987] Ch. 90; [1986] 3 All E.R. 217, CA, overruling *Hensman v Trail, The Times,* 22 October 1980.
See also *Whitehill v Bradford* [1952] Ch. 236.
[56] [1952] Ch. 236. See Ch.13, above.
[57] See also *Green v Stanton* (1969) 6 D.L.R. (3d) 680 (British Columbia Court of Appeal) affirming
(1969) 3 D.L.R. 358.
[58] cf. *Jenkins v Reid* [1948] 1 All E.R. 471 in which a lifelong restriction upon a medical practitioner
was held to be invalid. See Ch.13, above.
[59] [1991] 1 All E.R. 397.
[60] [1969] 1 W.L.R. 1293; [1969] 3 All E.R. 738.
[61] See [1969] 1 W.L.R. 1293 at 1300; [1969] 3 All E.R. 738 at 743 (Russell LJ); at 1301 and 744–745
(Edmund Davies LJ); at 1302 and 745 (Fenton Atkinson LJ).
[62] [1987] Ch. 90; [1986] 3 All E.R. 217.

5.   SOLICITORS

14–18   **Protecting goodwill.**   It is clear that firms of solicitors are entitled to protect their goodwill by the use of restrictive covenants, subject to the usual requirements as to reasonableness. In *Deacons (A Firm) v Bridge*[63] the defendant, formerly a partner of the claimants, which was a large solicitors' firm in Hong Kong, had covenanted that for five years after leaving the partnership he would not act as a solicitor in Hong Kong for any persons or organisations which had been clients of the firm for three years prior to his departure from it. In an action against him to enforce the covenant the defendant argued that it was invalid. He pointed out that the firm had been divided into a number of departments, and that partners in each department often had little or no knowledge of clients of the firm whose contact was with other departments. He contended that a reasonable restriction should be limited to clients who knew him and for whom he had acted. The Judicial Committee of the Privy Council rejected this argument and held that the covenant was enforceable. The firm "had one single practice in which each of the partners had an interest".[64] It would be impracticable and unfair not to have a uniform covenant which applied to all partners equally, since the extent of client contact could vary considerably depending upon the nature of each partner's duties. It was also in the public interest to encourage the taking on of younger partners, which firms would be less enthusiastic about doing if a partner departing at the height of his powers could jeopardise the firm's goodwill.[65]

14–19   **Area covenants.**   The covenant in *Deacons (A Firm) v Bridge* was a non-solicitation covenant, such restrictions are usually looked upon with less disfavour than area covenants, but the courts have been prepared to enforce the latter against solicitors. In the 1921 case of *Fitch v Dewes*[66] the defendant had covenanted with the claimant, for whom he had worked for 15 years and to whom he had been articled, that on leaving the latter's employment he would not be "concerned in the office, profession, or business of a solicitor within a radius of seven miles of the town hall of Tamworth". There was no time-limit, so that the covenant was effectively life-long, and this formed the basis of the defendant's attack upon the validity of the covenant. The attack failed. The House of Lords held that, particularly having regard to what they considered to be the limited area of the covenant, it was not unreasonable for the goodwill of the firm to be protected permanently from the defendant, for the benefit of the claimant and any successors of his. *Fitch v Dewes* was distinguished in the 1939 case of *Dickson v Jones*[67] in which the defendant, who again had been articled to the claimant, covenanted that he would not "at many time hereafter practise as a solicitor within a radius of 15 miles from the Town Hall, Hanley". Farwell J observed that a non-solicitation covenant might have been enforceable, as would an area covenant limited to Stoke-on-Trent itself where the claimant had most of his

---

[63] [1984] A.C. 705; [1984] 2 All E.R. 19, PC. See also Ch.13, above.
[64] [1984] A.C. 705 at 717; [1984] 2 All E.R. 19 at 24, per Lord Fraser.
[65] See [1984] A.C. 705 at 718–719; [1984] 2 All E.R. 19 at 25. See also *Fitch v Dewes* [1921] 2 A.C. 158, HL at 165–166, per Lord Birkenhead, LC ([1921] All E.R. Rep. 13 at 17).
[66] [1921] 2 A.C. 158.
[67] [1939] 3 All E.R. 182.

clients. Even the 15 mile radius might have been acceptable if it had been for a limited period of time. But the combination of that radius with a lifelong restriction upon a young man was "very far beyond anything which may be said to be reasonably necessary for the protection of the plaintiff".[68] The approach adopted in this case is more likely to commend itself to a court nowadays than that in *Fitch v Dewes*, which may be thought to go to the limit of the law, and which would be treated as a decision very much on its own facts. Nevertheless area covenants are still enforced against solicitors. In 2000 the Court of Appeal enforced one, with a 10 mile radius and a twelve-month time-limit, against a young solicitor in the East Midlands who had been with his former employers for four years.[69] Such covenants will, however, only be appropriate for "high street" practices. Non-solicitation covenants, as in *Deacons (A Firm) v Bridge*, will be the only practicable means of protection for a modern commercial practice.[70]

"Brass plate" construction.   Even in the case of area covenants protecting "high street" practices, it has been contended persuasively by Spowart-Taylor and Hough that such covenants should be construed presumptively as mere "brass plate" covenants.[71] A covenant construed in this way would only prevent the covenantor from actually establishing his practice within the prohibited area, and leave him free to act for clients living within the area if they consulted him elsewhere.[72] As Spowart-Taylor and Hough put it: "This would serve to protect the goodwill by discouraging continued solicitor-client contact but the determined client would not actually be prevented from seeking out his solicitor".[73]

14–20

Sale of business.   If a solicitors' firm is sold as a going concern it is, of course, possible for the vendors validly to covenant that they will not compete with the business; such covenants being much broader than those permissible in the case of former employees or even partners. An example, albeit an extreme one, is provided by the old case of *Whittaker v Howe*.[74] The defendants sold their partnership to the claimants and agreed not to practice as solicitors in any part of Great Britain for 20 years without the claimants' consent. Lord Langdale MR held that the covenant was valid and awarded an injunction to enforce it.

14–21

Rejected heresy.   In *Oswald Hickson Collier & Co v Carter-Ruck*[75] Lord Denning MR suggested that the fiduciary nature of the relationship between solicitor and client meant that "it would be contrary to public policy that he

14–22

---

[68] [1939] 3 All E.R. 182 at 189.
[69] See *Hollis & Co v Stocks* [2000] I.R.L.R. 712.
[70] See e.g. *Allan Janes LLP v Johal* [2006] EWHC 286 (Ch) in which an attempt to enforce an area covenant failed but a covenant against dealing with former clients of the claimant firm was upheld.
[71] See Ann Spowart-Taylor and Barry Hough, "The Client and Restraint of Trade" (1984) 47 M.L.R. 745 at p.750.
[72] On the meaning of "brass plate" covenants see, per Russell LJ in *Lyne-Pirkis v Jones* [1969] 1 W.L.R. 1293 at 1299–1300; [1969] 3 All E.R. 738 at 742–743 (medical practice). See also *Lu v Lim* (1993) 30 N.S.W.L.R. 332.
[73] See Ann Spowart-Taylor and Barry Hough, "The Client and Restraint and Trade" (1984) 47 M.L.R. 745.
[74] (1841) 3 Beav. 383.
[75] [1984] A.C. 720 (Note) at 723; [1984] 2 All E.R. 15 at 18, CA (decided in 1982).

should be precluded from acting for a client when that client wanted him to act for him". This proposition, which would invalidate all restrictive covenants involving solicitors, was shortly afterwards rejected "emphatically" by the Privy Council in *Deacons (A Firm) v Bridge*[76] as inconsistent with clear authority to the contrary, including a decision of the House of Lords.[77] It is of interest, however that Lord Denning's view echoed doubts expressed long ago by Lord Eldon,[78] and by Lord Langdale MR.[79] Moreover, the emphasis in *Deacons (A Firm) v Bridge* upon the reasonableness of protecting the interests of the firm, thereby "disregarding completely client interest", has not gone uncriticised.[80] Particularly in cases of pending litigation, where the solicitor may already have done a considerable body of detailed work for the client, there is much to be said for allowing the particular solicitor-client relationship to continue, notwithstanding the covenant.[81]

---

[76] See [1984] A.C. 705 at 719; [1984] 2 All E.R. 19 at 26, per Lord Fraser delivering the judgment of the Board.

[77] i.e. *Fitch v Dewes* [1921] 2 A.C. 158. See also per Bernard Livesey QC, sitting as a Deputy High Court Judge, in *Allan Janes LLP v Johal* [2006] EWHC 286 (Ch) at paras [52] and [58].

[78] See *Candler v Candler* (1821) Jac. 225 at 231.

[79] See *Whittaker v Howe* (1841) 3 Beav. 383.

[80] See Ann Spowart-Taylor and Barry Hough, "The Client and Restraint of Trade" (1984) 47 M.L.R. 745.

[81] See Ann Spowart-Taylor and Barry Hough, cited at fn.76 at p.750. Lord Denning MR himself referred to "pending litigation" in *Oswald Hickson Collier & Co v Carter-Ruck* itself: see [1984] A.C 720 (Note) at 723; [1984] 2 All E.R. 15 at 18.

CHAPTER 15

OPPRESSION, REPUDIATION AND INTERIM INJUNCTIONS

1.   INTRODUCTION

Three types of situation.   In this chapter we examine three different types of   **15–01**
situation in which it is contended that claimants alleging breaches of restrictive
covenants should be denied relief. The first type of situation is that in which the
stipulations which the claimant seeks to enforce, usually in a subsisting contract,
are said to be to be too oppressive to be tolerated. The second is where the
claimants themselves had, or are alleged to have, repudiated the contract which
contained the restraint. The third situation is that in which the particular form of
relief sought by the claimant might, if it were granted, have the effect of denying
the defendant an effective opportunity to challenge the enforceability of the
restrictive covenant on its merits. This is an issue which can arise in relation to
applications for interim injunctions.

2.   OPPRESSION

Far-reaching implications?   In the well-known case of *A. Schroeder Music*   **15–02**
Publishing Co v Macaulay,[1] Lord Reid said:

> "A contract by which a person engages to give his exclusive services to another for a period
> necessarily involves extensive restriction during that period of the common law right to
> exercise any lawful activity he chooses in such manner as he thinks best. Normally the
> doctrine of restraint of trade has no application to such restrictions: they require no
> justification. *But if contractual restrictions appear to be unnecessary or to be reasonably
> capable of enforcement in an oppressive manner, then they must be justified before they can be
> enforced.*"

In theory, the final sentence of this dictum could have presaged a far-reaching
jurisdiction to subject the terms of all contracts, or at least contracts of personal
service, to an open-ended reasonableness test.[2] While the doctrine of restraint of
trade has long warranted deliberate interference by the court with the bargain
agreed by the parties, the jurisdiction has largely been confined to covenants
which, by their very nature, take effect *after* the main period of activity governed
by the contract has ended; typically with the termination of an employee's
service. Any widespread extension of this jurisdiction to the continuing rights and
duties imposed by subsisting agreements would radically undermine traditional

---

[1] [1974] 1 W.L.R. 1308 at 1314; [1974] 3 All E.R. 616 at 622 (italics supplied).
[2] See Ch.11, above.

[245]

assumptions about the law of contract as a whole, and the judicial role in relation to it. The House of Lords was concerned with this conceptual issue in the earlier case of *Esso Petroleum v Harper's Garage*,[3] in which subsisting "solus" ties requiring garages to obtain all their petrol from one supplier for a long period, were held to be subject to the restraint of trade doctrine. Lord Pearce suggested that it might be possible to limit the applicability of the doctrine by asking whether "any prevention of work outside the contract viewed as a whole is directed towards the absorption of the parties' services and not their sterilisation"[4]; "absorption" being acceptable but "sterilisation" providing a justification for judicial intervention. This distinction is not free from difficulty,[5] however, and no watertight definition of the scope of the restraint of trade doctrine has ever emerged, nor is one likely to do so.[6]

15–03   **Pragmatism?**   In practice, however, the four decades that have passed since the House of Lords decided the *Schroeder* and *Esso* cases have not witnessed any significant destabilisation of freedom of contract. With its usual pragmatism the common law has managed to preserve certainty by abstaining from intervention in the great majority of cases, while simultaneously retaining jurisdiction to do so in exceptional situations. The decision in the *Schroeder* case does not appear to have opened the floodgates to large numbers of claims by parties seeking to escape from subsisting contracts for personal services. The key to the success of the balancing act in that context no doubt lies in the nature and rarity of the situations in which the jurisdiction is invoked. "Oppression" means what it says.

15–04   **Oppression in practice.**   In *A. Schroeder Music Publishing Co v Macaulay*[7] itself, the claimant was a young song-writer who had yet to establish himself. The defendants were music publishers who engaged the exclusive services of the claimant for five years. In return for modest royalties the defendants were to be entitled to the copyright of all the claimant's compositions, but were not under any obligation to publish any of them. If the royalties reached a certain minimum level the agreement would extend automatically for a further five years, although the defendants could terminate the agreement at any time by giving the claimant a month's notice. There was, however, no provision entitling the claimant to terminate the agreement at all. The House of Lords had no hesitation in holding this "one-sided agreement" to be unenforceable as being in unreasonable restraint of trade. Since the decision might be perceived, from a strictly orthodox perspective, to have been heretical, it is notable that all the judges who heard the case, at every level, were in agreement. The House of Lords unanimously upheld

---

[3] [1968] A.C. 269; [1967] 1 All E.R. 699. See Ch.11, above.
[4] [1968] A.C. 269; [1967] 1 All E.R. at 727.
[5] See per Russell LJ delivering the judgment of the Court of Appeal in *Schroeder*'s case; sub nom. *Instone v A. Schroeder Co Ltd* [1974] 1 All E.R. 171 at 177. See also J. D. Heydon, *The Restraint of Trade Doctrine*, (3rd edn, (LexisNexis Butterworths, 2008), pp.67 et seq.).
[6] cf. Maureen B. Callahan, "Post-Employment Restraint Agreements: A Reassessment" (1985) 52 U. Chi. L. Rev. 703, who argues that the doctrine should be abolished as it "would make contract law more coherent" to leave "protection against employer misbehavior" to "the generally applicable doctrine of unconscionability" (p.707).
[7] [1974] 1 W.L.R. 1308; [1974] 3 All E.R. 616.

the Court of Appeal which had itself upheld a decision in favour of the claimant at first instance.[8] Nearly four decades after the decision in *Schroeder's* case the Court of Appeal applied the doctrine of restraint of trade in somewhat similar circumstances to uphold the trial judge who had invalidated a sole agency contract between a well-known professional footballer and a company which had agreed to promote his "image" in relation to such matters as advertising and product endorsement. In *Proactive Sports Management Ltd v Rooney*[9] the footballer had been only 17 years old when he entered into the contract, which was to be of eight years duration and entitled the company to 20 per cent commission. Eight years was a substantial period when compared with the usual length of a professional footballer's career, and combined with the other factors, including the footballer's youth and the fact that he had not taken legal advice, was sufficient to render the contract oppressive.

Long-standing approach. The judicial instinct reflected in *Schroeder's* case did not suddenly manifest itself in 1974; on the contrary, it is of long standing. The Court of Appeal reacted with particular vehemence against an oppressive agreement in the 1916 case of *Horwood v Millar's Timber and Trading Co.*[10] By way of security for a loan of £42 and £31 interest on it, a clerk assigned to the claimant an insurance policy on his life, and agreed that his salary as a clerk should be subject to a first charge in favour of the claimant. He also agreed that he would never leave his job without the claimant's consent, and that he would not sell his house, any of his furniture, or borrow money or buy goods on credit. In holding unanimously the agreement to be unenforceable, as being in unreasonable restraint of trade. Warrington LJ said that it was "very seldom" that "so oppressive a contract" ever came before the court; while Scrutton LJ found it difficult to express his judgment "in language of sufficiently judicial modera-tion". Lord Cozens-Hardy MR observed that it was "the most extraordinary deed" that it had ever been his "fate to read", and that it "savour[ed] of serfdom". He spoke as follows[11]:

15–05

> ". . . considerations of public policy must be had regard to and . . . it is no answer to say that an adult man, as to whom undue pressure is not shown to have been exercised, ought to be allowed to enter into any contract he thinks fit affecting his own liberty of action. I think that is not the law. It seems to me that if as a matter of construction I come to the conclusion that the contract is one which puts the covenantor in the position . . . of adscriptus glebae, as the villein used to be called in mediaeval times, on the ground of public policy the law will not recognise such a thing. No one has a right so to deal with a man's liberty of action as well as his property, and the law says it is contrary to public policy."

Distinct from equitable relief. The exceptional cases in which the common law will declare a subsisting contract to be unenforceable on restraint of trade grounds must not be confused with those situations in which a party seeks relief from a contract by invoking equitable principles, such as those relating to undue

15–06

[8] See also *Clifford Davis Management Ltd v WEA Records Ltd* [1975] 1 W.L.R. 61; [1975] 1 All E.R. 237, CA.
[9] [2011] EWCA Civ 1444.
[10] [1917] 1 K.B. 305.
[11] [1917] 1 K.B. 305 at 311.

influence.[12] In restraint of trade cases the contract will speak for itself; it will not be necessary to point to any extraneous factors, such as impropriety on the part of the other party, or failure by him to draw attention to the need for independent legal advice. Nor is any inequality in the position of the parties a necessary condition of intervention. Thus an "oppressive" agreement is not necessarily one that has been procured by malpractice, but merely one the actual terms of which are grossly one-sided. In practice, however, some degree of questionable imbalance in the relationship between the parties will often have been present if such a contract has been entered into,[13] and the same situation may therefore give rise to overlapping claims for relief on both equitable and restraint of trade grounds.[14]

3. REPUDIATION

15–07   ***General Billposting v Atkinson.***   Ever since the 1908 decision of the House of Lords in *General Billposting Co v Atkinson*[15] it has been taken to be the law that, where the employer is guilty of a repudiatory breach of the contract of employment, and that repudiation is accepted by the employee,[16] the latter is discharged from any obligation to comply with restrictive covenants contained in the contract. In *Atkinson's* case the employee secured damages for wrongful dismissal, but was himself then sued for breach of a restrictive covenant. Although this latter action succeeded at first instance, both the Court of Appeal and House of Lords held unanimously that it would fail. "(T)he conduct of the employers here in dismissing the defendant in deliberate disregard of the terms of the contract", said Lord Collins,[17] meant that he "was thereupon justified in rescinding the contract and treating himself as absolved from the further performance of it on his part".

15–08   **Three questions.**   The doctrine in *General Billposting* may be said to give rise to three questions. First, what is the position if the employer is not in breach, but the restrictive covenant was so drafted as apparently to enable him to enforce it even if he *had* been? Secondly, in the light of modern developments in the law of contract generally, is the doctrine itself still good law? Thirdly, in what circumstances will an employer's breach actually have the effect, either under the *General Billposting* rule or otherwise, of precluding the enforceability of restrictive covenants? The important case of *Rock Refrigeration v Jones* is central to all three questions.

---

[12] cf. *Lloyds Bank v Bundy* [1975] Q.B. 326; [1974] 3 All E.R. 757, CA.

[13] cf. per Lord Diplock in *A. Schroeder Music Publishing Co v Macaulay* [1974] 1 W.L.R. 1308 at 1315–1316; [1974] 3 All E.R. 616 at 623–624. See also *Proactive Sports Management Ltd v Rooney* [2011] EWCA Civ 1444 at [100] per Arden LJ.

[14] cf. *Alec Lobb (Garages) Ltd v Total Oil GB Ltd* [1985] 1 W.L.R. 173; [1985] 1 All E.R. 303, CA.

[15] [1909] A.C. 118.

[16] On the need for acceptance to bring about termination of the contract see *Societe Generale, London Branch v Geys* [2012] UKSC 63, [2013] 1 All ER 1061. See also *MSC Mediterranean Shipping Co SA v Cottonex Astalt* [2016] EWCA Civ 789.

[17] [1909] A.C. 118 at 122.

Widely drafted covenants. In *Briggs v Oates*,[18] decided in 1989, Scott J expressed himself, obiter, as follows:

15–09

> "It is well settled that the reasonableness of a restraint clause is to be tested by reference to the position as at the date of the contract of which it forms part . . . A contract under which an employee could be immediately and wrongfully dismissed, but would nevertheless remain subject to an anticompetitive restraint, seems to me to be grossly unreasonable. I would not be prepared to enforce the restraint in such a contract."

Prior to this dictum, it never appears to have occurred to anyone to argue that the inclusion of wording which could be interpreted as having sought, in effect, to exclude the *General Billposting* doctrine, might be fatal to the validity of the entire clause by rendering it automatically "unreasonable" ab initio; whatever the actual circumstances in which it was invoked. Subsequently, however, Laws J applied the dictum in 1995 in *D v M*,[19] an interlocutory case, and held that a covenant which purported to bind the employee after termination of the employment "for any reason whatsoever" was unenforceable. "The short point", he said,[20] "is that where a covenant purports to confer on an employer rights to restrict his employee's conduct after termination of the contract even where the contract was unlawfully terminated by the employer, it is necessarily unreasonable".[21] One consequence of the new doctrine was the scope for debate on fine points of construction, to determine whether particular forms of words did or did not carry the fatal implication.[22] The need for this learning proved, however, to be short-lived. The new doctrine itself was roundly condemned by the Court of Appeal, in 1996, in the leading case of *Rock Refrigeration v Jones*,[23] and the decision in *D v M* was expressly overruled.

Rock Refrigeration v Jones. In this case the defendant employees themselves gave in their notice but the trial judge, following *D v M*, held that since the employment contracts provided that the restrictive covenants were to apply when the employment ended, "howsoever occasioned", they were unenforceable. The claimant employers appealed and succeeded in getting the decision overturned. Simon Brown and Morritt LJJ held that no contractual wording could ever be effective to prevent the rule in *General Billposting v Atkinson* from discharging an employee from all future obligations in the event of a repudiatory breach by his employer. In so far as the wording of any particular contract attempted to prevent this outcome, it would be "merely writ in water".[24] On this reasoning it followed, according to Simon Brown LJ, that "the law applicable to covenants and restraint of trade simply [had] no relevance" to such provisions.[25] Either they were unenforceable on a priori grounds (i.e. in the event of an actual employer's repudiation), or they should simply be ignored. The proposition that wording

15–10

---

[18] [1991] 1 All E.R. 407 at 417.
[19] [1996] I.R.L.R. 192.
[20] [1996] I.R.L.R. 192 at 197.
[21] See also the Scottish case of *Living Design v Davidson* [1994] I.R.L.R. 69 (Court of Session).
[22] See, e.g. *PR Consultants Scotland Ltd v Mann* [1996] I.R.L.R. 188 (Court of Session).
[23] [1997] I.C.R. 938; [1997] 1 All E.R. 1.
[24] [1997] I.C.R. 938 at 946; [1997] 1 All E.R. 1 at 8, per Simon Brown LJ.
[25] [1997] I.C.R. 938 at 948; [1997] 1 All E.R. 1 at 8.

which sought to preserve the enforceability of a covenant in all circumstances thereby infected the entire covenant, rendering it wholly unenforceable in any circumstances, was therefore stifled at birth by the Court of Appeal. This conclusion has the useful pragmatic result of denying employees a fortuitous means of escape from otherwise reasonable covenants, many of which will have been drafted long before the short-lived novel doctrine was thought of.[26]

15–11   **Is *General Billposting v Atkinson* still good law?**   The reasoning of Simon Brown and Morritt LJJ was based on the assumption that the *General Billposting* principle is itself still valid. It is important to note, however, that the third member of the court, Phillips LJ, questioned this assumption. He pointed out that, in the law of contract generally, the contemporary approach is to accord primacy to the construction of the actual agreement rather than to external principles of law imposed on the parties by the court.[27] Apart from *General Billposting*, he could therefore "see no principle of law which precludes the parties from validly agreeing to restraints that will subsist, even if the employment is brought to an end by repudiation".[28] Moreover, his Lordship considered that the *General Billposting* rule was not only inconsistent with "current legal principle", but was also out of accord "with the requirements of business efficacy". He said[29]:

> "Where an employer discloses to an employee confidential information, or otherwise puts the employee in a position to harm the employer's goodwill, it will usually be reasonable to impose negative restraints sufficient to protect those legitimate interests of the employer. Contracts of employment are now subject to complex statutory regulation, much of it designed to protect the employee. Cases of deliberate wrongful dismissal of employees, or repudiatory breach of the duties owed to them, are much less common than bona fide disputes as to whether or not there has been unfair or constructive dismissal. Employees who have been unfairly dismissed are entitled to statutory compensation. It does not seem to me necessarily fair or reasonable that an employer who is held liable to pay such compensation should also be at risk of losing the protection that is reasonably necessary to safeguard his confidential information or goodwill."

15–12   **Employers' breaches.**   The immediate practical importance of *Rock Refrigeration v Jones* is necessarily that, in circumstances in which there is no question of the employer having been in breach, the employee can no longer argue that an otherwise reasonable restrictive covenant is unenforceable because it purported to apply even if the employer *had* been in breach. If, however, the employee alleges that there *was* a repudiatory breach by the employer, the position is rather less

---

[26] *Rock Refrigeration v Jones* [1997] I.C.R. 938 at . . . per Morritt LJ; [1997] 1 All E.R. 1 at 10: ". . . covenants in . . . similar terms are frequently employed in contracts of employment but have only recently been found to be invalid on this ground. Counsel for Rock have drawn our attention to no fewer than 12 reported cases decided between 1964 and 1991 in which covenants in similar terms were not alleged or found to be invalid on this ground; nine of them were decisions of the Court of Appeal and one was an advice of the Privy Council".
[27] See, especially, *Photo Productions Ltd v Securicor Transport Ltd* [1980] A.C. 827.
[28] [1997] I.C.R. 938 at 960; [1997] 1 All E.R. 1 at 20. cf. *Explora Group Plc v Hesco Bastion Ltd* [2005] EWCA Civ 646, per Rix LJ at paras 83–84.
[29] [1997] I.C.R. 938 at 959; [1997] 1 All E.R. 1 at 20. See also *Praxis Capital Ltd v Burgess* [2015] EWHC 2631 at [72] per Judge Hodge QC (sitting as a judge of the High Court).

clear.[30] In such circumstances the fundamental difference between the approach of Simon Brown and Morritt LJJ on the one hand, and Phillips LJ on the other, could be significant. Since the majority view would still give free rein to the rule in the *General Billposting* case, an employee who proved a repudiatory breach by his employer would automatically be discharged from any obligation to comply with restrictive covenants. But if the approach of Phillips LJ is correct it would be possible for the employer to contend that, on its true construction, the covenant still applied after a repudiatory breach by the employer, and that this accorded with the intention of the parties at the time the contract was formed.

Two extremes. It is submitted that both the majority and the minority views in *Rock Refrigeration* represent extreme positions, and that neither is wholly correct. The approach of Simon Brown and Morritt LJJ, which would apparently result in a repudiatory breach having automatic consequences regardless of the construction of the contract, does seem to be inconsistent with the modern approach to contractual questions generally. The approach of Phillips LJ would appear to be preferable on this point. Nevertheless, there is also a sense in which, overall, the approach of Phillips LJ proves too much. While it is true that the modern law of contract accords great weight to matters of "construction", this approach cannot apply without qualification to the distinctive area of restraint of trade; which remains one in which the law reserves the right to interfere with the enforceability of contracts according to its own perception of "reasonableness" and the public interest. Accordingly, even if the "construction" approach were to be adopted, the question whether a particular restrictive covenant survived a repudiatory breach might in practice depend, not only upon the interpretation of the agreement, but also upon the court's perception of its "reasonableness" in all the circumstances. **15–13**

Factual circumstances. Paradoxically, the situation may not be very different under the ostensibly more straightforward, *General Billposting* approach, since a factual inquiry into the circumstances surrounding the alleged breach may still be necessary to determine whether it was, in truth, sufficiently serious to trigger automatic discharge of the employee's obligations. In *Lawrence David v Ashton*[31] the Court of Appeal had to decide whether to grant an interlocutory injunction to enforce a restrictive covenant. Balcombe LJ enumerated some of the factors relevant to this decision as follows[32]: **15–14**

> "... was there here a repudiatory breach of the contract which has been accepted by the defendant? This raises issues of fact, for example the precise manner of his dismissal, how and

---

[30] See the differing views expressed in the Canadian case of *Globex Foreign Exchange Corp v Kelcher* (2011) 337 DLR (4th) 202, 2011 ABCA 240 (Alberta Court of Appeal) in which the majority (Hunt and Martin JJ) concluded that *General Billposting v Atkinson* is still good law and that an employer's repudiatory breach would render any restrictive covenants unenforceable, whereas Slatter J dissented adopting the "construction" approach favoured in *Rock Refrigeration v Jones* by Phillips LJ. (*Globex Foreign Exchange Corp v Kelcher* is discussed by Francis Dawson in (2013) 129 LQR 508).
[31] [1989] I.C.R. 123; [1991] 1 All E.R. 385. Cf. *S.W. Strange Ltd v Mann* [1965] 1 W.L.R. 629; [1965] 1 All E.R. 1069.
[32] [1989] I.C.R. 123 at 133; [1991] 1 All E.R. 385 at 394.

when the defendant left and whether he has now been paid that to which he is entitled. It also raises an issue of law: was this a repudiatory breach-since not every breach of contract is repudiatory. We were referred to *W. Dennis & Sons Ltd v Tunnard Bros and Moore* (1911) 56 S.J. 162, a case at first instance, which certainly suggests that not every dismissal of an employee without proper notice may be repudiatory. On this point there is clearly a serious question to be tried."

The conclusion would therefore seem to be that, whichever approach is adopted, situations in which an employee contends that a restrictive covenant is unenforceable on account of a repudiatory breach of contract by his employer, will frequently involve the court in a precise examination of the factual circumstances of the particular case.[33]

4. INTERIM INJUNCTIONS[34]

15–15   *Cyanamid* **case.**   In the well-known 1975 case of *American Cyanamid Co v Ethicon*,[35] the House of Lords held that the decision whether to grant or refuse an interlocutory injunction should depend upon an assessment of the "balance of convenience". This marked a departure from previous practice, in which claimants who sought such injunctions had often been required to show that it was more likely than not that they would succeed at trial. The new approach placed emphasis upon the claimant's undertaking in damages, as a means of avoiding injustice to a defendant against whom an interlocutory injunction turned out to have been wrongly awarded. The objective was to make interlocutory injunctions somewhat easier to obtain and avoid the need for the court, in effect, to try the case at the interlocutory stage, on affidavit evidence.[36] The greater availability of such injunctions came, however, to be perceived to be a source of potential hardship to defendant employees subjected to restrictive covenants in restraint of trade cases. This is because the period during which an employer can realistically expect to restrict the future activities of former employees is likely, in modern conditions, to be a relatively short one.[37] A lengthy delay before the full hearing of the case could therefore mean that the grant of an interim injunction would effectively deny the defendant the opportunity to contest the enforceability of the restrictive covenant on its merits; as a result of the brevity of the restriction, the injunction could expire before the case was heard.[38] But provided

---

[33] See, e.g. *Maxwell v Gibsons Drugs* (1979) 103 D.L.R. (3d) 433 (British Columbia): payment in lieu of notice pursuant to a termination provision in the contract held not to be a repudiatory breach, employer therefore entitled to enforce covenant. See also *S.B.J. Stephenson v Mandy* [2000] I.R.L.R. 233 at 241.

[34] The term "interim injunctions" has replaced "interlocutory injunctions" by virtue of the Civil Procedure Rules (see CPR r.25.1(1)(a)). The older terminology is, however, used in the text when it was used in the cases (i.e. those which preceded the Rules).

[35] [1975] A.C. 396.

[36] For the more cautious approach adopted by the court in the less common cases where a *mandatory* (as distinct from the more usual *negative*) interim injunction is sought see *Warm Zones v Thurley and Another* [2014] EWHC 988 per Silber J at [27] and cases there cited.

[37] See Ch.13, above.

[38] See *Office Overload v Gunn* [1977] F.S.R. 39 at 43, per Lord Denning MR.

this will not occur, there is no objection in principle to the grant of interim injunctions against former employees in restraint of trade cases.[39]

"Disabusing the profession". In *Lawrence David Ltd v Ashton*,[40] which was decided in 1988. Balcombe LJ said:

> ". . . both counsel appear to have been of the view that [the *American Cyanamid*] approach is not relevant where an interlocutory injunction is sought to enforce a contractual obligation in restraint of trade. We were told that this is a view widely held in the profession, if so, it is time that the profession is disabused."

In the *Lawrence David* case the defendant had covenanted that he would not be involved in similar activities to those of the claimants, his former employers, for two years following the end of his employment with them. The claimants' appeal against refusal of an interlocutory injunction pending trial was heard by the Court of Appeal four months after the date on which the defendant had left the claimants' employment, and immediately accepted a post elsewhere, which was allegedly in breach of the covenant. The appeal was allowed. Balcombe LJ observed[41] that "cases of this kind are singularly appropriate for a speedy trial",[42] and asserted that "where the application of the *American Cyanamid* case indicates the desirability of an interlocutory injunction" the courts would "adapt their procedures" to ensure such a trial. In the instant case the Court's own inquiries suggested that a date could be found within the following three months. It is only where "the action cannot be tried before the period of the restraint has expired, or has run a large part of its course, that the grant of the interlocutory injunction will effectively dispose of the action". Accordingly, it is only in those circumstances that a recognised "exception to the rule in *American Cyanamid*" will apply[43]; enabling the judge properly "to consider the prospects of the plaintiffs succeeding in the action",[44] before granting an injunction.[45]

15–16

Lansing Linde v Kerr. The dicta of Balcombe LJ in the *Lawrence David* case: to the effect that the strength of the claimants case could properly be assessed where the interlocutory decision would operate in practice as a final judgment, were approved and applied by a differently constituted Court of Appeal in *Lansing Linde v Kerr*.[46] In this case the restraint on the defendant employee was for a twelve-month period, which would have virtually expired before the earliest date on which the action could be tried. Moreover, there was reason to suppose that the width of the covenant could prove an obstacle to the claimant's eventual

15–17

---

[39] See, e.g. *Polymasc Pharmaceuticals v Stephen Alexander Charles* [1999] F.S.R. 711 at 720–721, per Laddie J, for a reported example of judicial reasoning in applying the balance of convenience test.
[40] [1989] I.C.R. 123; [1991] 1 All E.R. 385, CA.
[41] [1989] I.C.R. 123 at 134; [1991] 1 All E.R. 385 at 395.
[42] See also *Dairy Crest v Pigott* [1989] I.C.R. 92 at 98.
[43] For the "exception" see the decision of the House of Lords in *NWL Ltd v Woods* [1979] 1 W.L.R. 1294.
[44] See [1989] I.C.R. 123 at 135; [1991] 1 All E.R. 385 at 395–396, per Balcombe LJ.
[45] See also *John Michael Design Plc v Cooke* [1987] I.C.R. 445; [1987] 2 All E.R. 332.
[46] [1991] 1 W.L.R. 251; [1991] 1 All E.R. 418. See also *Cayne v Global Natural Resources Plc* [1984] 1 All E.R. 225, CA; *Ashcourt Rowan Financial Planning Ltd v Hall* [2013] EWHC 1185.

success. In those circumstances an interlocutory injunction was held to have been rightly refused. Staughton LJ summarised the position as follows[47]:

> "If it will not be possible to hold a trial before the period for which the plaintiff claims to be entitled to an injunction has expired, or substantially expired, it seems to me that justice requires some consideration whether the plaintiff would be likely to succeed at trial. In those circumstances it is not enough to decide merely that there is a serious issue to be tried. The assertion of such an issue should not operate as a lettre de cachet, by which the defendant is prevented from doing that which, as it later turns out, he has a perfect right to do, for the whole or substantially the whole of the period in question. On a wider view it may still be right to impose such a restraint, but not unless there has been some assessment of the plaintiff's prospects of success. I would emphasise 'some assessment', because the courts constantly seek to discourage prolonged interlocutory battles on affidavit evidence ... Where an assessment of the prospects of success is required, it is for the judge to control its extent."

Butler-Sloss LJ added[48] that while "applications for injunctions to restrain an employee ... are [not] in a category of their own", they are "likely to have special features which may affect the balance", including the "length of the period of restraint and the time when the case may come to be heard".

15–18 **Danger of non-compensatable loss.** An important factor, in assessing the "balance of convenience" under the *Cyanamid* rule, is the extent to which the claimant's undertaking in damages will adequately compensate the defendant, if an interim injunction turns out to have been wrongly granted and the defendant succeeds at trial. This can be a particular source of concern in employee restraint of trade cases. While lost income during the period of restraint can easily be calculated, a greater difficulty is, in the words of Balcombe LJ in *Lawrence David Ltd v Ashton*,[49] "any long-term damage which [the defendant] may suffer by being kept out of the employment market for a period". Such damage "may not be easy to establish or, if established, to assess in monetary terms". The older the covenantor, the more critical this factor is likely to be. It reinforced the case for an early trial in the *Lawrence David* case itself, in which an injunction was granted against a 48-year-old defendant, even though the court found "his evidence that he may find difficulty in obtaining suitable employment, although not tested in cross-examination, [was] prima facie credible".[50] In *Lansing Linde v Kerr*, in which an injunction was refused, Beldam LJ observed[51] that the defendant would not "be adequately compensated by an award of damages" if he were to be deprived of the "right to take advantage of the unique opportunity of employment he has been offered".

15–19 **Claimant entitled to full protection of the covenant.** If, after careful scrutiny, the court decides that an injunction should be granted against an ex-employee, the claimant will prima facie be entitled to the full protection of the covenant which

---

[47] See [1991] 1 W.L.R. 251 at 258; [1991] 1 All E.R. 418 at 423–424, per Staughton LJ. See also *CEF Holdings Ltd v City Electrical Factors Ltd* [2012] EWHC 1525 at [28] per Silber J.
[48] [1991] 1 W.L.R. 251 at 269; [1991] 1 All E.R. 418 at 434.
[49] [1989] I.C.R. 123 at 134; [1991] 1 All E.R. 385 at 395.
[50] [1989] I.C.R. 123 at 134; [1991] 1 All E.R. 385 at 395.
[51] [1991] 1 W.L.R. 251 at 266; [1991] 1 All E.R. 418 at 431.

is being enforced. In *John Michael Design Plc v Cooke*[52] an interlocutory injunction was awarded against the defendants who were former employees of the claimants who had set up in business on their own account. The covenant was in respect of non-solicitation of the claimants' customers, but on "balance of convenience" grounds the judge had excluded one particular customer from the scope of the injunction. He was unwilling to deprive the defendants of contracting with that customer when that customer was emphatic that, in any event, it would no longer continue to do business with the claimants. The Court of Appeal allowed the claimants' appeal, and held that the injunction would extend to all customers within the scope of the covenant. O'Connor LJ pointed out[53] that "the plaintiff does not need protection against customers who are faithful to him: it is only in respect of his customers who may be coaxed by his ex-employees to transfer their allegiance". Nicholls LJ expressed himself as follows[54]:

> "The mere fact that a particular customer no longer wishes to remain a customer of the plaintiff but wishes in future to deal with the defendant is not *per se* a sound reason for excluding that customer from the scope of the injunction. With a non-dealing covenant, in practice the plaintiff will often only need protection when a customer of his has decided to change horses and go with the defendant. To regard the change of allegiance as *per se* a sufficient reason for refusing an injunction would be tantamount to refusing the court's assistance in giving a plaintiff protection in precisely the circumstances where that assistance is needed and for which the covenant was designed."

---

[52] [1987] I.C.R. 445; [1987] 2 All E.R. 332, CA.
[53] [1987] I.C.R. 445 at 448; [1987] 2 All E.R. 332 at 334.
[54] [1987] I.C.R. 445 at 449; [1987] 2 All E.R. 332 at 335.

PART 4

RELIEF FROM THE CONSEQUENCES

CHAPTER 16

THE ENFORCEABILITY OF PROPRIETARY INTERESTS

1. PASSING OF PROPERTY

Can pass despite illegality. It has frequently been held that property which   **16–01**
was transferred pursuant to an illegal transaction can vest in the transferee,
notwithstanding the illegality. Thus in *Feret v Hill*[1] a lessee was able to maintain
ejectment against his lessor notwithstanding that the lessee had acquired the
premises in order to run a brothel; and in *Ayerst v Jenkins*[2] the court refused to set
aside a settlement of property which had been made in anticipation of immoral
cohabitation. The clearest modern statement of the principle is, however, to be
found in the decision of the Judicial Committee of the Privy Council in *Singh v
Ali*.[3] The defendant sold a lorry to the claimant but, pursuant to a scheme between
the parties to defraud the licensing authorities, the defendant registered the lorry
in his own name; the defendant being entitled, under regulations in force at the
time, to a permit to operate the lorry, while the claimant was not so entitled. The
defendant detained the lorry without the claimant's consent, and refused to return
it to him. The Privy Council held that property in the lorry had passed to the
claimant, notwithstanding the illegality of the contract of sale, and that he could
therefore sue the defendant in detinue and trespass. Lord Denning, delivering the
judgment of the Board, said:

> "Although the transaction between the plaintiff and the defendant was illegal, nevertheless it
> was fully executed and carried out: and on that account it was effective to pass the property in
> the lorry to the plaintiff."[4]

---

[1] (1854) 15 C.B. 207.
[2] (1873) L.R. 16 Eq. 275.
[3] [1960] A.C. 167. See also *Patel v Mirza* [2016] UKSC 42 at [110] per Lord Toulson.
[4] [1960] A.C. 167 at 176. See also *Webb v Chief Constable of Merseyside* [2001] 1 All E.R. 209,
especially per May LJ at 220–221; *Gordon v Metropolitan Police Commissioner* [1910] 2 K.B. 192
(money obtained as a result of illegal dealings vests validly in the recipient and cannot be confiscated
by the police without specific statutory power); *Costello v Chief Constable of Derbyshire
Constabulary* [2001] 3 All E.R. 150, CA. For another recent application of the principle, see
Macdonald v Myerson [2001] EWCA Civ 66 (profits gained on a sale of properties belonged to their
owner notwithstanding that the original acquisition of the properties had involved the perpetration of
a mortgage fraud); see also *Mortgage Express v McDonnell* [2001] EWCA Civ 881.

16–02   **Arbitrariness.**   Although the proposition that property can pass under an illegal contract appears to be well-established,[5] it has not gone unquestioned.[6] The precise logical basis upon which an otherwise unenforceable agreement can be effective for this purpose is unclear, and it can lead to arbitrary results from a policy perspective. In *Singh v Ali*, Lord Denning expressed satisfaction with the outcome, on the ground that "if the law were not to allow the claimant to recover in this case, it would leave the defendant in possession of both the lorry and the money he received for it".[7] But in other cases the attractiveness of the result has been more questionable. Thus an unpaid seller of goods on credit is presumably unable to recover the goods back, if the contract is unenforceable for illegality, just as he cannot sue for the price. To hold otherwise would be tantamount to enforcing the illegal contract, but it does mean that the buyer gets the goods for nothing.

16–03   **Delivery unnecessary.**   Moreover, actual delivery of the goods to the buyer is unnecessary: the contract being effective in itself to transfer title to him. In *Belvoir Finance Co v Stapleton*[8] the claimants bought a motor-car from dealers and, without taking possession of the car themselves, let it out on hire-purchase to a firm of which the defendant was a manager. The original contract of sale between the dealers and the claimants, and the contract of hire-purchase between the claimants and the defendants' firm, were both considered to be illegal for contravention of relevant statutory restrictions.[9] The Court of Appeal nevertheless held that the claimants could sue the defendant for conversion when he fraudulently sold the car, which was subject to the illegal hire-purchase agreements, to innocent purchasers. The Court held that although "the plaintiffs obtained the car under a contract which was illegal, nevertheless, in as much as the contract was executed and the property passed, the car belonged to them and they can claim it".[10]

2.   THE "NO-RELIANCE" DOCTRINE AND ITS DEMISE

(a)   At Common Law

16–04   ***Bowmakers v Barnet Instruments.***   If an agreement considered to be unenforceable for illegality purports to transfer an interest in property which is temporary, or otherwise limited, the question may arise whether the property can be recovered back in accordance with the limitations expressly or impliedly laid down in the contract. Prior to the decision of the Supreme Court in *Patel v*

---

[5] See *The Illegality Defence* (2010) Law Com No.320 at 3.42–3.47 in which the Law Commission accepts that "where a legal interest is transferred under a contract that involves some element of illegality, ownership of the property passes" and expressly recommends that there should be *no* change in this position.

[6] See Higgins, "The Transfer of Property under Illegal Transactions" (1962) 25 M.L.R. 149.

[7] [1960] A.C. 167 at 178.

[8] [1971] 1 Q.B. 210. See also *Belvoir Finance Co v Harold G. Cole* [1969] 1 W.L.R. 1877.

[9] cf. *Bowmakers v Barnet Instruments* [1945] K.B. 65, discussed below.

[10] [1971] 1 Q.B. 210 at 218, per Lord Denning M.R.

Mirza[11] the orthodox view was that property rights could be enforced, in circumstances otherwise affected by illegality, *only* if it could be done without "reliance" on the illegality. This doctrine was usually associated with the well-known decision of the Court of Appeal in *Bowmakers v Barnet Instruments*.[12] The defendants hired certain machine-tools, from the claimant finance company, under hire-purchase agreements which contravened statutory regulations imposing price restrictions and licensing requirements. The contracts were therefore assumed to be unenforceable for illegality. In breach of the agreements the defendants sold some of the machine-tools to third parties and, although retaining the others, refused to pay to the claimants the hire-purchase sums due to them. The Court of Appeal held the defendants liable to the claimants for conversion in respect of *all* the machine-tools, du Parcq LJ, delivering the judgment of the court said[13]:

> "In our opinion, a man's right to possess his own chattels will as a general rule be enforced against one who, without any claim of right, is detaining them, or has converted them to his own use, even though it may appear either from the pleadings, or in the course of the trial, that the chattels in question came into the defendant's possession by reason of an illegal contract between himself and the plaintiff..."[14]

Bowmakers' case has not escaped criticism. At least with respect to the machine-tools which the defendants were merely detaining without paying for, if not also with respect to those which they had sold, the decision of the Court of Appeal seems to have been equivalent to actual enforcement of the illegal hire-purchase contracts.[15] Moreover, in several earlier cases involving leases, landlords were apparently held to be able neither to recover back the premises demised, nor to sue for rent, during the period of a letting which had been entered into for illegal purposes.[16] Nevertheless *Bowmakers v Barnet Instruments* has never been overruled and in *Patel v Mirza* its correctness was emphasised by the Supreme Court.

Criticism of the reasoning. The members of the Supreme Court were not, however, in agreement as to the validity of the reasoning used to reach the decision in *Bowmakers'* case. While Lord Sumption, effectively dissenting, accepted the "no reliance" reasoning,[17] the majority rejected it. Lord Toulson, speaking for the majority, expressed his agreement with the "general rule" in the passage from the judgment of du Parcq LJ quoted above, but went on to reject the words "provided that the plaintiff does not seek, and is not forced, either to found his claim on the illegal contract or to plead its illegality in order to support his

16–05

---

[11] 2016] UKSC 42.
[12] [1945] K.B. 65. See Coote, "Another Look at *Bowmakers v Barnet Instruments*" (1972) 35 M.L.R. 38.
[13] [1945] K.B. at 71, per du Parcq LJ delivering the judgment of the court.
[14] cf. *Thomas Brown & Sons v Fazal Deen* (1962) 108 C.L.R. 391 (claim necessarily founded on illegal contract).
[15] See Hamson, "Illegal Contracts and Limited Interests" 10 C.L.J. 249.
[16] See *Alexander v Rayson* [1936] 1 K.B. 169 at 186, per Romer LJ delivering the judgment of the court. See also *Feret v Hill* (1854) 15 C.B. 224. cf. *Gas Light and Coke Co v Turner* (1840) 5 Bing. N.C. 666 at 677, per Tindal CJ.
[17] See [2016] UKSC 42 at [234]-[236].

claim" with which du Parcq LJ had qualified the general rule. Lord Toulson noted that this "proviso" has been criticised because it "makes the question whether the court will refuse its assistance to the claimant to enforce his title to his property depend on a procedural question and…has led to uncertain case law about what constitutes reliance".[18] Finally, Lord Toulson expressed his agreement with the following passage from the judgment of du Parcq LJ:

> "We are satisfied that no rule of law, and no considerations of public policy, compel the court to dismiss the plaintiffs' claim in the case before us, and to do so would be, in our opinion, a manifest injustice."[19]

Lord Toulson considered that "That conclusion, rather than the answer to a procedural question, should have been the end of the illegality defence, since it is based on public policy".

16–06 **Exceptional cases?** After *Patel v Mirza* the applicability of the illegality defence will depend in all situations on a "trio of necessary considerations", including "the underlying policy of the prohibition which has been transgressed"and "any other relevant public policies", along with "a due sense of proportionality".[20] Where a claimant is seeking to enforce proprietary rights these considerations are perhaps less likely to lead to the defence of illegality being upheld than in situations involving only contractual enforceability or unjust enrichment. Nevertheless it is not inconceivable that they might apply in rare cases to defeat proprietary claims. The decision in *Bowmakers'* case can be contrasted with that of the Court of Queen's Bench in *Taylor v Chester*.[21] The claimant deposited a bank-note with the defendant, as security for payment for wine and food consumed by him in a brothel. The claimant sought to recover the note by relying on his property in it, but was held unable to do so since in order to defeat the defence that the note had been validly pledged, the "was obliged to set forth the immoral and illegal character of the contract on which the half-note had been deposited. It was, therefore, impossible for him to recover except through the medium and by the aid of an illegal transaction to which he was himself a party".[22] It is perhaps significant that *Taylor v Chester* and *Bowmakers v Barnet Instruments* involved very different types of wrongdoing.[23] In the latter case the Court of Appeal suggested that their "general rule" could be subject to an exception where "the goods claimed are of such a kind that it is unlawful to deal in them at all, as for example, obscene books".[24] And in *Patel v Mirza* itself Lord

---

[18] See [2016] UKSC 42 at [111].

[19] See [1945] K.B. 65 at 72.

[20] See [2016] UKSC 42 at [101] per Lord Toulson.

[21] (1869) L.R. 4 Q.B. 309.

[22] (1869) L.R. 4 Q.B. at 314, per Mellor J, delivering the judgment of the Court.

[23] "The result might well have been very different if the court had been moved to indignation at the plaintiff's conduct, as it might have been had the facts similar to those of *Taylor v Chester* been before it": Hamson, "Illegal Contracts and Limited Interests" (1949) 10 C.L.J. 249 at p.255.

[24] [1945] K.B. 65 at 72. See also, per May LJ in *Webb v Chief Constable of Merseyside* [2001] 1 All E.R. 209 at 222 (controlled drugs), cf. *Costello v Chief Constable of Derbyshire Constabulary* [2001] 3 All E.R. 150 at 164, CA, per Lightman J "… when considering the observations of du Parcq LJ … it is important to bear in mind that they were made at a time when the question was very much alive

Toulson said that "there may be circumstances in which a court will refuse to lend its assistance to an owner to enforce his title as, for example, where to do so would be to assist the claimant in a drug trafficking operation".[25]

(b)   In Equity

Not confined to common law.   The *Bowmakers'* principle of the enforceability   **16–07**
of proprietary rights is not merely a common law doctrine, it has been applied to
the enforcement of equitable interests such as resulting trusts. In the Australian
case of *Blackburn v YV Properties Ltd*[26] the legal title to land was transferred,
without consideration, pursuant to a fraudulent scheme to deceive the planning
authorities. The idea was to enable the transferee to object, as an ostensibly
independent party, to planning permission for a hotel on land nearby. In fact the
objection was to further the interests of the transferor, who was a commercial
rival of the company seeking the permission. Since the transfer had been without
consideration, it gave rise to a resulting trust in favour of the transferor. The Full
Court of the Supreme Court of Victoria, by a majority, held that the transferor
could enforce this trust to recover the title, despite the fraudulent scheme.[27]

(i)   Resulting Trusts

Tinsley v Milligan.   The application of the enforceability principle to resulting   **16–08**
trusts was confirmed by the House of Lords in the important, but difficult, case of
Tinsley v Milligan.[28] The appellant and respondent were co-habitees who bought
a house using both their resources. The house was, however, put solely in the
appellant's name to enable the respondent fraudulently to assert that she was
without means, and that she was the appellant's lodger. The proceeds of the fraud
were used by both parties; but the appellant relied on the illegal scheme in an
attempt to defeat the respondent's claim to a share of the proceeds of sale on a
disposal of the property, after the parties had fallen out. A bare majority of the
House of Lords[29] upheld a majority decision of the Court of Appeal,[30] which had
confirmed the finding of the trial judge in favour of the respondent; the latter's
claim was therefore not barred by illegality.[31] If there had been no question of

---

how far a court should protect a wrongdoer in asserting his rights of ownership . . . The House of
Lords in *Tinsley v Milligan* . . . held that law and equity must now speak with one voice in protecting
. . . ownership based on possession".

[25] See [2016] UKSC 42 at [110].
[26] [1980] V.R. 290.
[27] See also *Coplan v Coplan* (1958) 14 D.L.R. (2d) 426 (Can.) (manipulation of share transfer to
deceive the revenue).
[28] [1994] 1 A.C. 340. See Enonchong, *Illegal Transactions* (Lloyd's of London Press, 1998), pp.181
et seq.
[29] Jauncey, Lowry and Browne-Wilkinson LJJ; Keith and Goff LJJ dissenting.
[30] See [1992] Ch. 310 (Lloyd and Nicholls LJJ, Ralph Gibson LJ dissenting).
[31] See also *Lowson v Coombes* [1999] Ch. 373. A man and his mistress both contributed to the
purchase of a house, but it was put solely into the name of the mistress to avoid any potential claim by
the man's wife. Applying *Tinsley*'s case, the man was able to enforce a resulting trust on the sale of the
property, notwithstanding that the parties' intention to defeat any claim by the wife gave rise to an
illegality by virtue of the Matrimonial Causes Act 1973 s.37.

illegality the respondent's contribution to the purchase price would have created a resulting trust in her favour,[32] and Lord Browne-Wilkinson, in the leading majority judgment, held that that trust should be enforceable, notwithstanding the illegality, under the principle in *Bowmakers v Barnet Instruments*.

16–09 **Same rule to apply.** Since *Bowmakers'* case had confirmed that property rights could be acquired under illegal transactions, and enforced at common law, by a party able to make out a claim without "relying" on the illegality, Lord Browne-Wilkinson contended that the same principle should apply to the respondent's equitable interest in the proceeds of sale in *Tinsley*'s case. To establish her claim she only had to prove her contribution to the purchase money; it was the appellant who had to "rely" on the fraudulent scheme in order to try and defeat her claim. The appellant was obliged to argue, on the basis of the maxim that "he who comes to equity must come with clean hands", that the rules governing the acquisition and enforcement of property rights at common law differed from those in equity, and hence that the *Bowmakers* principle was inapplicable. His Lordship considered that "to draw such distinctions between property rights enforceable at law and those which require the intervention of equity would be surprising". In his view: "If the law is that a party is entitled to enforce a property right acquired under an illegal transaction . . . the same rule ought to apply to any property right so acquired, whether such right is legal or equitable". He accordingly concluded that[33]:

> "In my judgment the time has come to decide clearly that the rule is the same whether a plaintiff founds himself on a legal or equitable title: he is entitled to recover if he is not forced to plead or rely on the illegality, even if it emerges that the title on which he relied was acquired in the course of carrying through an illegal transaction."

(ii) Presumption of Advancement

16–10 **Ground of distinction.** The dissentients in *Tinsley v Milligan* pointed to a number of cases in which attempts to recover property in situations, apparently similar to that in *Tinsley*'s case, had failed for illegality because the transfer had been to promote an unlawful scheme. In the view of the majority, however, many of these could be distinguished on the ground that they had involved the operation of the presumption of advancement.[34] Thus in *Chettiar v Chettiar*[35] an illegal scheme was facilitated by a "gift" of land from father to son. Lord

---

[32] In *Stack v Dowden* [2007] UKHL 17; [2007] 2 All E.R. 929 the House of Lords held that the beneficial interests of an unmarried cohabiting couple in their former home should henceforth be determined, on the collapse of their relationship, by the application of a constructive trust approach rather than one based on the concept of the resulting trust. See also *Jones v Kernott* [2011] UKSC 53; [2012] 1 AC 776.

[33] [1994] 1 A.C. 340 at 376.

[34] For recent application of the presumption, see e.g. *Antoni v Antoni* [2007] UKPC 10. cf. *Lavelle v Lavelle* [2004] EWCA Civ 223. See now "Abolition of the presumption of advancement" below. See also interesting discussion of the scope of the presumption by the Supreme Court of Canada, involving a difference of judicial opinion, in *Pecore v Pecore* [2007] 279 D.L.R. (4th) 513 and *Madsen Estate v Saylor* [2007] 279 D.L.R. (4th) 547.

[35] [1962] A.C. 294.

Denning, delivering the judgment of the Privy Council, was emphatic that the father should not recover the land back[36]:

> "He cannot use the process of the courts to get the best of both worlds—to achieve his fraudulent purpose and also to get his property back. The courts will say: 'Let the estate lie where it falls'."

In *Tinsley*'s case no presumption of advancement in the appellant's favour was raised by the respondent's contribution, had it been otherwise the case would apparently have been decided differently. Lord Browne-Wilkinson said[37]:

> "A party to an illegality can recover by virtue of a legal or equitable property interest if, but only if, he can establish his title without relying on his own illegality. In cases where the presumption of advancement applies, the plaintiff is faced with the presumption of gift and therefore cannot claim under a resulting trust unless and until he has rebutted that presumption of gift: for those purposes the plaintiff does have to rely on the underlying illegality and therefore fails."

The majority in *Tinsley v Milligan* therefore applied not merely the "general rule" in *Bowmakers v Barnet Instruments*, relating to the enforceability of proprietary claims, but also the reasoning in that case based on the concept of "reliance".

Technicality and anomaly.   The effect of the reasoning of the majority in **16–11** *Tinsley v Milligan* was accordingly to make the decision in that case depend on narrow and technical grounds. Several commentators pointed out that that reasoning would entail apparently similar cases being decided differently, but without there being any convincing policy reasons to justify the distinctions.[38] Thus, because of the operation of the presumption of advancement, the result would have been different, that is to say the contributor's capital would have been forfeit to the other party, if the parties had been married instead of co-habitees and the house had been in the wife's name with the husband the contributor.[39] It would, however, have been the *same*—with the wife being able to recover her contribution—if the house had been put in her husband's name. It is not easy to see why the presence or absence of marriage should be relevant, when deciding what the consequences for the parties should be of their jointly committing a fraud on a third party.[40] These arguments finally helped to demolish *Tinsley v*

---

[36] [1962] A.C. 294 at 302–303. See also *Collier v Collier* [2002] EWCA Civ 1095.

[37] [1994] 1 A.C. 340 at 375.

[38] See Kodilinye, "A Fresh Approach to the Ex Turpi Causa and 'Clean Hands' Maxims" (1993) *Denning Law Journal* 93 at p.102; Stowe, "The 'Unruly Horse' has Bolted" (1994) 57 M.L.R. 441 at p.446; Buckley, "Law's Boundaries and the Challenge of Illegality" in Buckley (ed.), *Legal Structures* (1996), pp.233–234. cf. Enonchong, "Illegality: The Fading Flame of Public Policy" (John Wiley & Sons, 1994) 14 O.J.L.S. 295 at 299. See also Martin in [1992] Conv. 158.

[39] cf. *Re Tucker, Tucker v Gillis* (1988) 53 D.L.R. (4th) 688 (New Brunswick Court of Appeal). A father registered a boat in his daughter's name to deceive the revenue. The presumption of advancement applied and his estate was unable to recover ownership of the boat after his death.

[40] cf. per Robert Walker LJ in *Lowson v Coombes* [1999] Ch. 373 at 385: "The importance attached by the majority [i.e. in *Tinsley's* case] to the presumption of advancement does to my mind create difficulties, because the presumption has been cogently criticised both as out of date in modern social and economic conditions . . . and as being uncertain in its scope".

Milligan. In *Patel v Mirza* the Supreme Court was unanimous in overruling it. Although the actual decision was considered to be correct, the reasoning underlying it was not. Although the minority, led by Lord Sumption, would have retained the "no reliance" principle, they considered that it had been wrongly applied on the facts.[41] This in itself might be thought to demonstrate the vague and uncertain nature of the "reliance" principle, which the majority rejected in favour of a policy based approach as already explained.

(iii)   Windfalls

16–12   **Struggling with *Tinsley*.**   Although the potential for anomaly inherent in the reasoning in *Tinsley v Milligan* has now been consigned to history, it is instructive to see how the courts struggled to avoid applying it in the years before the case was finally overruled. The decisions in question not only help to highlight the unsatisfactory nature of the "reliance" principle, but also illustrate the kinds of situation with which the new policy based approach may have to grapple in the future. Soon after *Tinsley v Milligan* was decided both the High Court of Australia, and the Court of Appeal in England, had occasion to confront the implications of that decision in situations to which, unlike *Tinsley's* case itself, the presumption of advancement *did* apply. In both *Nelson v Nelson*[42] and *Tribe v Tribe*,[43] the supposedly temporary transfer of the formal ownership of property had originally been undertaken in order to deceive a third party as to the extent of the transferor's resources. In both cases the transferees had accepted the gratuitous transfer with full knowledge of its purpose. They nevertheless sought subsequently to gain windfalls by invoking illegality to resist the transferors' claims, made on the basis of a resulting trust, for the re-transfer which had originally been the agreed intention of the parties. In *Nelson v Nelson* the claimant transferred the title of her house to her daughter in order to deceive the Commonwealth of Australia, when purchasing a further house, as to her entitlement to participate in a statutory scheme which enabled widows of war veterans to purchase homes at specially subsidised rates provided they did not own homes already. After a further house was purchased at the subsidised rate the original house was sold, as had been planned, and the claimant sought to recover the proceeds of sale from her daughter. The latter argued that the presumption of advancement operated to make the transfer a gift from her mother, and that she could not rebut the presumption without relying on her own illegality. The High Court held at the outset that the presumption of advancement could apply to transfers by mothers to their children, and that the traditional view that it is confined to such transfers by fathers should no longer be followed "in the present social context".[44] It followed that the question whether the mother could recover the proceeds of sale, by disclosing the true purpose of the transfer, arose directly for decision.

---

[41] See [2016] UKSC 42 at [236] (Lord Sumption).
[42] (1995) 184 C.L.R. 538. See Rose, "Reconsidering Illegality" (1996) 10 *Journal of Contract Law* 47.
[43] [1996] Ch. 107. See Rose (1996) 112 L.Q.R. 386.
[44] (1995) 184 C.L.R. 538 at 585, per Toohey J.

Tribe v Tribe. In the English case of *Tribe v Tribe* a father transferred his **16–13**
shares in the family company to his son, without consideration, as part of a
scheme to deceive his creditors as to the extent of his resources. As it happened
an agreement was reached subsequently with the creditors without the need for
any deception to be practised on them. Nevertheless when the father sought
subsequently the return of the shares his son, like the daughter in *Nelson's* case,
invoked illegality in an attempt to defeat the claim. He argued that it followed
from *Tinsley v Milligan* that recovery would not be permitted in presumption of
advancement cases if revealing the true purpose of the transfer, in order to rebut
the presumption, would necessarily involve disclosing the illegality.

(iv)   Presumption of Advancement Rebutted

Recovery back despite illegality. In both *Nelson v Nelson* and *Tribe v Tribe* **16–14**
the argument that the parent should be barred by illegality from recovering back
the property was rejected,[45] and the presumption of advancement was held to
have been effectively rebutted. Both the High Court of Australia and the English
Court of Appeal criticised *Tinsley v Milligan* for the potential arbitrariness,
implicit in the judgments of the majority, that that case would have been decided
the other way if the presumption of advancement had applied. Such an approach,
"unusually for equity", elevated form over substance, and encouraged "a quest
for mitigation by the drawing of further line distinctions and exceptions whereby
recovery will be permitted".[46] In other respects, however, the reasons advanced
by the two courts in support of their decisions were very different. Two strands
are present in the judgment of the High Court in *Nelson v Nelson*, both of which
anticipate the reasoning of the majority in *Patel v Mirza*. One was that it was not
part of the intention of the statute, which created the subsidy scheme, to bar
recovery in situations such as that in question. The other was that to allow the
illegality argument to succeed would involve the infliction of a *disproportionate*[47] penalty upon the mother in the circumstances. The conclusion as to statutory
interpretation was reinforced by the provision of specific machinery in the
legislation for the recovery, by the Commonwealth, of payments made as a result
of deception; from which it could plausibly be inferred that further forfeiture was
not intended.[48]

No deception actually practised. In *Tribe v Tribe* the Court of Appeal **16–15**
emphasised that no deception had actually been practised, and held that the father
could take advantage of the principle that a claimant could be excused his
participation in an illegal scheme if he withdrew before the scheme reached
fruition. On this basis the Court of Appeal felt able to reject the argument based
upon *Tinsley v Milligan*, since the so-called *locus poenitentiae* doctrine had not

[45] cf. *Collier v Collier* [2002] EWCA Civ 1095 in which a parent's attempt to recover back his property *did* fail.
[46] (1995) 184 C.L.R. 538 at 558, per Deane and Gummow JJ. See also, per Nourse LJ in *Tribe v Tribe* [1995] 4 All E.R. 236 at 244.
[47] See also the Californian case of *Re Torrez* (1987) 827 F. 2d 1299 at 1301, cited by Deane and Gummow JJ in (1995) 184 C.L.R. 538 at 566.
[48] See the Defence Homes Act 1918 s.29 (Aus.) as inserted by an amending Act in 1988.

been in issue in that case. Millett LJ nevertheless drew attention to the unclear nature of the relationship between, on the one hand, the *locus poenitentiae* concept and, on the other, the supposed principle that a party can "enforce his property rights if he can do so without relying on the fraud or illegality".[49] This lack of clarity was also resolved by the decision of the Supreme Court in *Patel v Mirza*, which subjected the *locus poenitentiae* doctrine to a radical re-examination. This issue is discussed in the next chapter.[50]

16–16   **Abolition of the presumption of advancement.**   In view of the difficult illegality case law to which the presumption of advancement gave rise, after the decision in *Tinsley v Milligan*, it should be noted that the Equality Act 2010, s.199(1) provides that the "presumption of advancement . . . is abolished". In January 2017, however, this provision had yet to be brought into force. Moreover, s.199(2) of the Act provides that the abolition will not affect "anything done" or "any obligation incurred" before its commencement. Accordingly, had it not been for *Patel v Mirza* the potential for anomaly to which the presumption could have given rise, as a result of the reasoning in *Tinsley's* case, would be likely to have remained for some time to come. The Law Commission actually recommended that a statutory discretion should be introduced to enable the court, in "exceptional circumstances", to prevent a beneficiary from enforcing a trust which had been created "for a criminal purpose", such as the concealing of assets from creditors. Although obviously not confined to situations involving the presumption of advancement, such a discretion would have enabled the courts to limit the ability of the presumption to produce arbitrary results.[51] In 2012, however, the Government indicated that it did not intend to act on this recommendation. It is therefore fortunate that the reasoning of the majority of the Supreme Court in *Patel v Mirza* would appear to have given the court the necessary flexibility to deal with such situations without recourse to legislation.

3. CONCLUSIONS

16–17   **Sensible position.**   The proposition that property can pass under an illegal contract is a sensible one. The destabilising uncertainty, which would result from a general doctrine to the *opposite* effect, would almost certainly outweigh any conceivable benefits in terms of discouraging undesirable contractual activity. Nevertheless, the reasoning of the Court of Appeal in *Bowmakers v Barnet Instruments*, with its emphasis upon the claimant not being obliged "either to found his claim on the illegal contract or to plead its illegality in order to support his claim",[52] was at best mechanistic and at worst misleading.[53] The application of the same reasoning to resulting trusts in *Tinsley v Milligan* only added to the

---

[49] [1996] Ch. 107 at 124; [1995] 4 All E.R. 236 at 250.
[50] See Ch.17, below.
[51] See *The Illegality Defence* (2010) Law Com No.320, Part Two: "Illegality and Trusts". See, further, Ch.21 below.
[52] See, per du Parcq LJ in [1945] K.B. 65 at 71.
[53] For criticism of the confused nature of English law's former "no reliance" doctrine, from the perspective of Roman-Dutch law, see the decision of the Appellate Division of the Supreme Court of South Africa in *Jajbhay v Cassim* [1939] A.D. 537, especially, per Watermeyer JA at 554–557.

complexity. The decision of the Supreme Court in *Patel v Mirza*, confirming the existence of a general rule in favour of the enforceability of proprietary rights accompanied by a policy based ability not to apply it in exceptional cases, is therefore to be welcomed.

Position reversed in New Zealand.   In New Zealand the radical step has been   **16–18** taken of providing by statute that "no person shall become entitled to any property under a disposition" made by a contract unenforceable for illegality.[54] This is a reversal of the position assumed to exist in English law, but it is accompanied by a broad discretion enabling the court to grant "validation of the contract in whole or part or for any particular purpose".[55] There is much to be said for a statutory discretion in illegality cases, as the Law Commission originally, provisionally recommended.[56] Nevertheless, in the particular context of the enforceability of proprietary rights, it is submitted that the position reached by the common law in England is preferable to a presumption rendering such rights prima facie unenforceable.

---

[54] See the Illegal Contracts Act (N.Z.) s.6.
[55] See the Illegal Contracts Act (N.Z.) s.7. For the New Zealand Act, see Ch.20, below.
[56] See "Illegal Transactions; The Effect of Illegality in Contract and Trusts", Law Commission Consultation Paper No.154 (1999).

CHAPTER 17

ILLEGALITY AND RESTITUTION

1. INTRODUCTION

Development of the law of restitution.   If a contract is unenforceable for   **17–01**
illegality, it may sometimes be possible for one or both of the parties to recover
back money or property transferred pursuant to that contract. The basis of such
recovery will be the law of restitution, designed to reverse unjust enrichment,
which has developed around various common law and equitable remedies;
including the common law action for money had and received. This branch of the
law has seen substantial clarification and growth in recent years,[1] and cases in
which the contractual objectives of the parties have been stultified by illegality
represent an obvious source for its application. The availability of restitutionary
relief if a contract is merely void, as distinct from illegal, has been confirmed by
the celebrated series of cases arising out of the interest rate swap transactions
which were entered into in large numbers by local authorities in the 1980s,[2] until
the House of Lords held that they were ultra vires.[3]

Restitution in cases of illegality.   Where the contract was not merely void, but   **17–02**
unenforceable for illegality, English law formerly adopted a rather narrow view
of the scope of restitutionary relief. Indeed the application of the law of
restitution in this area was long inhibited by the fiction that restitution was
founded upon an "imputed promise": if the contract was unenforceable for
illegality it was difficult to see how there could be any basis for enforcing an
implied term.[4] But even after that fiction passed into history,[5] the courts remained
cautious about expanding the scope of restitution significantly in illegality cases.
This perhaps reflected a fear that its availability might provide an incentive to
perform the forbidden contract itself, in order to avoid having to restore benefits
received; or a belief that the contract was so abhorrent that the court should not
assist the parties to it in any way. On the other hand, it was notable that cases

---

[1] See, especially, *Lipkin Gorman (A Firm) v Karpnale* [1991] 2 A.C. 548.
[2] See, especially, *Westdentsche Landesbank v Islington LBC* [1996] A.C. 669; see also [1994] 4 All
E.R. 890 (Hobhouse J and the Court of Appeal); *Kleinwort Benson v Lincoln City Council* [1999] 2
A.C. 349; [1998] 4 All E.R. 513, HL.
[3] See *Hazell v Hammersmith and Fulham LBC* [1992] 2 A.C. 1.
[4] cf. *Sinclair v Brougham* [1914] A.C. 398.
[5] See *Westdeutsche Landesbank v Islington LBC* [1996] A.C. 669; [1996] 2 All E.R. 961, especially at
710 and 992–993, per Lord Browne-Wilkinson.

adopting a more flexible approach to recovery could be found in other jurisdictions such as Scotland[6] and South Africa.[7]

17–03　　*Patel v Mirza.*　　In 2016 English law itself put the scope of restitutionary relief for unjust enrichment on a much wider basis than heretofore and apparently rendered much of the prior learning in the area obsolete. In *Patel v Mirza*[8] the parties entered into an agreement to engage in betting on share prices on the basis of inside information, which is unlawful. Their agreement amounted to a criminal conspiracy.[9] The claimant transferred £620,000 to the defendant for this purpose, but when the expected inside information failed to materialise, preventing the betting from taking place, the defendant failed to return the money to the claimant. The latter therefore brought an action for unjust enrichment. He failed at first instance but succeeded in the Court of Appeal and before a nine-member Supreme Court. The fact that the Supreme Court was unanimous in the result it reached, against the background of the more restrictive approach which applied previously (as accurately reflected in the decision at first instance), demonstrates vividly in itself that the law has now changed and that restitutionary relief is to be granted more widely in situations involving illegality. Nevertheless the precise extent of the change is not easy to state in detail. This is because the nine Justices differed in their reasons. Those who focused specifically on unjust enrichment were in a minority. The majority used their judgments to restructure the law relating to illegality generally, so that their frame of reference extended well beyond unjust enrichment and the situation in the particular case. This restructuring involved, as explained earlier in this book, the adoption of an overtly policy-based approach to which the minority were opposed. In practice, however, it seems unlikely that this difference of approach, although it might be fundamental in other contexts involving illegality, will often lead to different results in the context of restitution. But this cannot be guaranteed so early in the redevelopment of the law commenced by *Patel v Mirza*. The safest course is therefore still to consider the earlier authorities but to do so in the light of the changes to be expected in the light of the judgments in *Patel's* case.

2.　WHERE RESTITUTIONARY RELIEF WAS FORMERLY DENIED

17–04　　**Relationship with *locus poenitentiae*.**　　In the gravest cases of illegality there was formerly no question of any assistance being given to either party, for the purposes of restitution or otherwise. As the old case of *Everet v Williams*[10] illustrates vividly, the court would not order an account between parties whose

---

[6] See *Cuthbertson v Lowes (1870) 8 M 1073* (referred to in *Dowling & Rutter v Abacus Frozen Foods Ltd (No.2)* 2002 SLT 491).

[7] See the decision of the Apellate Division of the Supreme Court of South Africa, administering Roman-Dutch law, in *Jajbhay v Cassim* [1939] A.D. 537, especially at 545, per Stratford CJ: ". . . where public policy is not foreseeably affected by a grant or a refusal of the relief claimed, . . . a Court of law might well decide in favour of doing justice between the individuals concerned and so prevent unjust enrichment".

[8] [2016] UKSC 42.

[9] See the Criminal Justice Act 1993, s.52.

[10] (1725). For details of the case, drawn from the original records, see (1893) 9 L.Q.R. 197.

business happened to be highway robbery. Similarly, a hired assassin who was paid in advance was unlikely to be ordered to repay his fee, on the ground of failure of consideration, if his victim escaped his grasp. In cases as serious as these, it would have been surprising if even a party who repudiated the illegal purpose before performance could have secured restitution by invoking the so-called *locus poenitentiae* doctrine; which favoured those who withdrew from unlawful transactions. On the other hand, however, it was implicit in that doctrine that there was an intermediate category of illegality situations, deemed too serious for any relief to be granted at a later stage, in which restitutionary relief could nevertheless be granted if the unlawful scheme was abandoned at an appropriately early point. It is clear that at least some cases involving plans to commit fraud on third parties came within this latter category.[11]

Radical change in the law. In *Patel v Mirza* several of the Justices appeared to favour a prima facie rule that unjust enrichment claims should be permitted in illegality cases on an extraordinarily wide basis. They emphasised the importance of the distinction between enforceability of the contract and restitution. Thus Lord Sumption observed that[12]: **17–05**

> "... the courts will not give effect to an illegal transaction or to a right derived from it. But restitution does not do that. It merely recognises the ineffectiveness of the transaction and gives effect to the ordinary legal consequences of that state of affairs. The effect is to put the parties in the position in which they would have been if they had never entered into the illegal transaction, which in the eyes of the law is the position which they should always have been in."

From this starting point the Lords Neuberger and Sumption expressly contemplated restitutionary claims being permitted even if the contract had been fully performed, and even if it involved very serious crimes such as murder. The rationale was that allowing such claims would normally be in accordance with policy since it would discourage criminality and, where a crime had taken place and been paid for, help to deprive the criminal of his ill-gotten gains. Lord Neuberger said[13]:

> "... if the claimant paid a sum to the defendant to commit a crime, such as a murder or a robbery, it seems to me that the claimant should normally be able to recover the sum, irrespective of whether the defendant had committed, or even attempted to commit, the crime. If the defendant had not attempted the crime, the Rule would generally apply. If he had actually succeeded in carrying out the crime, he should not be better off than if he had not done so."

Lord Sumption expressed himself in very similar terms, expressly rejecting the suggestion "that there may be some crimes so heinous that the courts will decline to award restitution in any circumstances".[14] It is important to remember that these observations were obiter: in *Patel's* case the illegal purpose had not actually been put into effect, and that purpose was, in any event, hardly in the same

---

[11] See Ch.18, below.
[12] See [2016] UKSC 42 at [250].
[13] See ibid at [176].
[14] See [2016] UKSC 42 at [254].

category as murder. Moreover the majority, who favoured a more policy-oriented approach to the facts of each case, were necessarily more cautious and did not commit themselves to such extreme propositions. Thus Lord Toulson, who delivered the leading speech of the majority, did not "exclude the possibility that there may be particular reason for the court to refuse its assistance to the claimant",[15] and appeared to contemplate that drug-traffickers might fall into that category. Nevertheless even he favoured replacing the complexity of the law as it then stood with the proposition that "a person who satisfies the ordinary requirements of a claim in unjust enrichment will not prima facie be debarred from recovering money paid or property transferred by reason of the fact that the consideration which has failed was an unlawful consideration".[16] Thus although further judicial development of the law in this area is awaited, it seems to be clear that the position has changed very radically from one in which a complex set of rules embodied a limited approach to recovery to one in which there is a strong presumption in favour of restitutionary relief with, possibly, little or no regard to the gravity of the illegality or the extent to which it had been put into effect.

3. MISTAKE, FAILURE OF CONSIDERATION AND OPPRESSION

17–06   **Established situations.**   Even before the decision in *Patel v Mirza*, when restitutionary relief was still limited in scope and confined to various categories, such as that associated with the concept of *locus poenitentiae*, there were a number of situations in which it was already established that relief would be available when a contract could not be lawfully performed. These included cases involving mistake, failure of consideration and oppression. The relevant decisions are still important since they will presumably remain good law even if the new law on unjust enrichment in this area eventually turns out to be somewhat narrower in scope than the widest dicta in *Patel v Mirza* apparently suggest. This must, however, be subject to the caveat that all disputes involving illegality are now to be resolved by explicit consideration of the underlying policy issues in the particular situation.

(a)   Mistake

17–07   **Mistake of fact.**   It has long been clear that restitutionary relief may be available to a party who entered into an illegal transaction as a result of a mistake as to the facts constituting the illegality. Thus in *Oom v Bruce*[17] insurance premiums paid in ignorance of an outbreak of war, which made the contract unlawful as it involved trading with an enemy, were held to be recoverable. In the similar case of *Hentig v Staniforth*,[18] Lord Ellenborough said:

> "In the present case, a state of facts was supposed to exist, and reasonably so supposed, under which, if the expectation of the parties had been realised, the voyage would have been legal.

---

[15] See ibid at [116].
[16] See [2016] UKSC 42 at [116].
[17] (1810) 12 East. 225.
[18] (1816) 5 M. & S. 122 at 125–126.

Unfortunately for the plaintiff his expectation was disappointed, and he lost the benefit of his insurance; but he contemplated a legal voyage and a legal contract. And we think, therefore, that he is not a party to a violation of the law, and is entitled to recover back his premium, as money paid without any consideration."

Demise of the mistake of law rule. Until the decision of the House of Lords in **17–08**
Kleinwort Benson v Lincoln City Council,[19] a mistake of law, as distinct from one of fact, could not afford a basis for restitution. In the absence of fraud or culpable misrepresentation, a wholly innocent party who had entered, as a result of a mistake of law, into a contract unenforceable for illegality could not secure the return of any money which he had paid. A well-known line of authority, going back to the 1802 decision of the Court of King's Bench in *Bilbie v Lumley*[20] was overruled in *Kleinwort*'s case. Lord Goff said that[21]:

> ". . . the mistake of law rule should no longer be maintained as part of English law, and that English law should now recognise that there is a general right to recover money paid under a mistake, whether of fact or law, subject to the defences available in the law of restitution."[22]

Kleinwort Benson v Lincoln City Council was one of the cases arising out of the entry by local authorities into ultra vires interest rate transactions.[23] It therefore concerned contracts which were merely void and not illegal. Provided the party seeking relief was genuinely and excusably ignorant of the law, however, the reasoning should be equally applicable to resources transferred under contracts unenforceable for illegality. The much criticised decision of the Court of Appeal in *Harse v Pearl Life Assurance Co*,[24] in which the innocent claimant was unable to recover back the premiums which he had paid on an illegal life insurance policy, would therefore now be decided differently.[25]

(b)   Failure of Consideration

Nature of failure of consideration. In *Westdeutsche v Islington London*   **17–09**
Borough Council,[26] another of the interest rate "swap" cases, Hobhouse J suggested that "absence" of consideration might be a more appropriate concept where void contracts are concerned,[27] in order, apparently, to overcome a perceived difficulty that the notion of consideration itself may be meaningless if

---

[19] [1999] 2 A.C. 349. See also *David Securities Pty v Commonwealth Bank of Australia* (1992) 175 C.L.R. 353.
[20] (1802) 2 East. 469.
[21] [1999] 2 A.C. 349 at 375; [1998] 4 All E.R. 513 at 533.
[22] See also *Deutsche Morgan Grenfell v Inland Revenue Commissioners* [2006] UKHL 49; [2007] 1 A.C. 558.
[23] See also *Haugesund Kommune v Depfa ACS Bank* [2010] EWCA Civ 579, [2011] 1 All ER 190.
[24] [1904] 1 K.B. 558.
[25] cf. the American Law Institute's *Second Restatement of Contracts*, which suggests restitution should be allowed in the event of "excusable ignorance . . . of legislation of a minor character, in the absence of which the promise would be enforceable" (para.198).
[26] [1996] A.C. 669. See also [1994] 4 All E.R. 890 (Hobhouse J and the Court of Appeal). The actual decision of the House of Lords in the *Westdeutsche* case, on the principles governing the award of interest in restitution cases, was narrowly distinguished by the House itself in the case of *Sempra Metals v Inland Revenue Commissioners* [2007] UKHL 34.
[27] [1994] 4 All E.R. 890 at 924.

the contract was never enforceable.[28] The approach of Hobhouse J was, however, doubted in the same case by Lord Goff in a dissenting speech in the House of Lords, who contended that "the concept of failure of consideration need not be so narrowly confined".[29] He inclined to the view that the notion of failure of consideration could apply to contracts which had never been enforceable, and also emphasised the desirability of escaping "from the unfortunate effects of the so-called rule that money is only recoverable at common law on the ground of failure of consideration where the failure is *total*".[30] He referred to a series of old cases on void annuities in which, even though "payments had been made . . . both ways", the courts had ascertained "the balance of account between the parties" and ordered the repayment of that balance.[31] Lord Goff therefore considered that the court should therefore adopt a broad view of restitutionary relief,[32] subject to the defences available,[33] and not take a narrow view of the scope of failure of consideration. It is now clear that Lord Goff's view has been adopted.[34]

17–10   **Illegality as a defence: corrupt motive?**   Even if a situation is one which would normally give rise to a right to restitutionary relief, the circumstances surrounding the contract could still prevent such a claim from succeeding. A corrupt motive for entering into the agreement did so in *Begbie v Phosphate Sewage*.[35] The defendants had patented in England a special process for the utilisation of sewage. In the honest belief that their process had also been patented in Berlin, they agreed to sell the exclusive right to use the process in that city to the claimant for £15,000. It so happened, however, that under the applicable law it was impossible to obtain an exclusive right to use the process in Berlin. The defendants had therefore purported to sell something which did not, and could not, exist. The claimant sought to recover back the £15,000 on the ground of total failure of consideration, but his action was unsuccessful.[36] It appeared that he, unlike the defendants, had actually been aware that no exclusive right could be obtained to use the process in Berlin. His only purpose in entering into the contract had been fraudulently to attract investment in a company which he proposed to form. He had intended to represent to prospective shareholders

---

[28] See *Fibrosa Spolka Akeyjna v Fairbairn Lawson Combe Barbour* [1943] A.C. 32 at 48, per Viscount Simon LC ("wiped out altogether"), sed quaere. An opposite argument, to the effect that if a contract was always unenforceable the consideration had *necessarily* failed, is also "unreal": see, per Garland J in *Aratra Potato v Taylor Johnson Garrett (A Firm)* [1995] 4 All E.R. 695 at 710.
[29] [1996] A.C. 669 at 683; [1996] 2 All E.R. 961 at 967. See also Birks, "No consideration: Restitution after Void Contracts" (1993) 23 U.W.A.L.R. 195; Frederick Wilmot-Smith, "Reconsidering 'Total' Failure" [2013] CLJ 414.
[30] [1996] A.C. 669 at 682; [1996] 2 All E.R. 961 at 967 (italics supplied).
[31] See [1996] A.C. 669 at 683; [1996] 2 All E.R. 961 at 967. The cases are cited in the judgment of Hobhouse J at first instance: see [1994] 4 All E.R. 890 at 921–922.
[32] A broad view of the nature and scope of restitutionary relief was also favoured by a majority of the House of Lords in *Sempra Metals v Inland Revenue Commissioners* [2007] UKHL 34.
[33] e.g. that of change of position; see *Lipkin Gorman (A Firm) v Karpnale* [1991] 2 A.C. 548; see also *Haugesund Kommune v Depfa ACS Bank* [2010] EWCA Civ 579, [2011] 1 All ER 190 especially at [106]–[130] per Aikens LJ.
[34] See per Lord Toulson in *Patel v Mirza* [2016] UKSC 42 at [13]. See also per Lord Sumption at [246]-[250].
[35] (1875) 10 Q.B. 491, affirmed (1876) 1 Q.B.D. 679.
[36] cf. *Berg v Sadler and Moore* [1937] 2 K.B. 158.

that, if the company were to purchase from him the "right" which he had acquired from the defendants, it would be in a strong and lucrative position. The Court of Appeal, upholding the Court of Queen's Bench, held that there had been no failure of consideration since the claimant had got what he paid for: a hollow right which he intended to use to commit fraud. It must be doubtful whether this case would be decided the same way after *Patel v Mirza*, with its emphasis on the desirability of unscrambling unlawful transactions with the motives of the parties apparently to be disregarded. Perhaps, however, on the unusual facts of the case it could be argued that the policy of discouraging fraud would favour denial of recovery.[37]

(c) Oppression

Not "in pari delicto". If a contract is procured by duress or undue influence, the victim of the pressure will normally enjoy restitutionary relief. In some cases, however, the pressure may take the form of a threat to prosecute the victim himself, or a close-friend or member of his family, for a criminal offence; typically in order to procure security for the repayment of money allegedly stolen from the promisee.[38] In others the promisee, owed money by the promisor, may refuse to agree to enter into a composition with the other creditors unless he is assured privately that his own claim will be met in full.[39] An attempt actually to enforce such an agreement by the person who made the threat will normally fail on the ground that the contract was an illegal one to stifle a prosecution, or to defraud the promisor's remaining creditors, or otherwise to interfere with the administration of justice. Nevertheless, if the victim of the pressure seeks to recover back any money or property transferred pursuant to the agreement, the question may arise whether his own claim to restitution should be defeated on the ground that, however reluctantly, he had himself been a party to an illegal contract. On the whole, however, the courts have long taken the view that the existence of the pressure meant that the victim was not *in pari delicto* with the other party, and hence that he could normally be awarded restitution despite the illegality.[40]

17–11

Relief granted. In *Smith v Cuff*[41] the claimant sought a composition with his creditors, but the defendant refused to enter the arrangement unless given promissory notes for the remainder of his debt. When a subsequent holder of one

17–12

---

[37] cf. per Lord Neuberger in *Patel v Mirza* [2016] UKSC 42 at [162]: "…there could well be no recovery (or only partial recovery) by a plaintiff where the defendant was unaware of the facts which gave rise to the illegality – especially if he had received the money and had altered his position so that it might be oppressive to expect him to repay it".

[38] See e.g. *Williams v Bayley* (1866) L.R. 1 H.L. 200; *Jones v Merionethshire Permanent Benefit Building Society* [1992] 1 Ch. 273; *Mutual Finance v John Wetton* [19371] 2 K.B. 389. See generally, Hudson, "Contractual Compromises of Criminal Liability" (1980) 43 M.L.R. 532; Buckley, "Contracts to Stifle Prosecutions" (1974) 3 An.-Am. L.R. 472. See also Ch.8, above.

[39] See *Smith v Cuff* (1817) 6 M. & S. 160; *Morton v Riley* (1843) 11 M. & W. 492; *Atkinson v Denby* (1862) 7 H. & N. 934.

[40] But see "Undeserving cases?" in Ch.8, above.

[41] (1817) 6 M. & S. 160.

of the notes enforced payment from the claimant it was held that the claimant could recover the sums from the defendant as money had and received. Lord Ellenborough CJ said[42]:

> "This is not a case of *par delictum*: it is oppression on one side, and submission on the other: it can never be predicated as *par delictum*, when one holds the rod, and the other bows to it. There was an inequality of situation between these parties: one was creditor, the other debtor, who was driven to comply with the terms which the former chose to enforce. And is there any case where money having been obtained extorsively, and by oppression, and in fraud of the party's own act as it regards the other creditors, it has been held that it may not be recovered back? On the contrary, I believe it has been uniformly decided that an action lies."

17–13 **Threat of prosecution.** In *Davies v London and Provincial Marine Insurance Co*[43] certain friends of an employee of the insurance company were led to believe that their friend was about to be prosecuted by the company for embezzlement. As a result they agreed to make payments to the company to replace the sums allegedly missing, in order to prevent the prosecution from taking place. It transpired subsequently that charges could not have been brought for embezzlement in any event, and the friends sought the return of the money which they had paid to the company. The claim was resisted on the ground that what had occurred had constituted an attempt to compound a felony, but Fry J nevertheless ordered recovery. In his judgment, in which duress and illegality were intertwined, he said[44]:

> ". . . it appears to me to be clear that illegality resulting from pressure and illegality resulting from an attempt to stifle a prosecution do not fall within that class of illegalities which induces the Court to stay its hand, but are of a class in which the Court has actively given its assistance in favour of the oppressed party, by directing the money to be repaid."[45]

4. RESTITUTION AND ENFORCEMENT

17–14 **Continuing uncertainty.** An area of continuing uncertainty concerns situations in which relief for unjust enrichment would resemble enforcement of the illegal contract.[46] An important case in this context is a decision of the Court of Appeal which preceded *Patel v Mirza*.

---

[42] (1817) 6 M. & S. 160 at 165.
[43] (1878) 8 Ch. 469.
[44] (1878) 8 Ch. 469 at 477.
[45] In one case the Court of Appeal held that there could be no relief where money had been transferred to stifle a prosecution for forgery, but there does not appear to have been any pressure on the facts: see *Re Mapleback Ex p. Caldecott* (1876) 4 Ch. D. 150.
[46] The level of remuneration awarded for unjust enrichment under a quantum meruit will not necessarily resemble that which would have been recoverable under the unenforceable contract: see *Proactive Sports Management v Rooney* [2011] EWCA Civ 1444 at [117]–[124] per Arden LJ. For discussion by the Supreme Court of the principles applicable in assessing remuneration under a quantum meruit see *Benedetti v Sawiris* [2013] UKSC 50.

Quantum meruit claim allowed.   In *Mohammed v Alaga & Co (A Firm)*[47] the   **17–15**
defendant firm of solicitors allegedly entered into an agreement with the
claimant, a member of the Somali community, who agreed to introduce Somali
clients to the defendants and to provide assistance, such as the translation of
documents, in the preparation of their cases. The claimant said that the solicitors
had promised, in return, to pay the claimant the equivalent of one-half of the
Legal Aid fees which they received as a result. The defendants denied the
existence of such an agreement but contended that it would, in any event, have
been unenforceable for illegality as being in contravention of the then r.7 of the
Solicitors' Practice Rules 1990. Those rules, which had statutory force,[48]
prohibited solicitors (subject to certain exceptions) from entering into fee-sharing
arrangements with other persons.[49] On the trial of a preliminary issue the judge
assumed, in the claimant's favour, that he had been unaware of the illegality, but
nevertheless held that the alleged agreement was unenforceable by either party;
the illegality was clearly based on a perception of the public interest and not upon
any intention to protect persons in the position of the claimant. The judge,
Lightman J, also held that restitutionary relief would not be extended to the
claimant since that would have the effect "of nullifying the statutory
prohibition".[50] The Court of Appeal, however, reversed the judge on this point,
and ordered that the claimant's claim, to be remunerated on a quantum meruit
basis, should be allowed to go forward.

Greater readiness to investigate culpability.   The situation was distinct from   **17–16**
one involving, say, an unenforceable contract of loan, in which restitution might
well be indistinguishable from enforceability.[51] Lord Bingham CJ said that the
claimant "was not seeking to recover any part of the consideration payable under
the unlawful contract".[52] Moreover, the solicitors should have known of the
prohibition,[53] but the claimant could not have been expected to be aware of it. In
the words of Robert Walker LJ[54]:

> ". . . the claimant may be able to establish at trial that he was not culpable, or was significantly
> less culpable than the defendant solicitors, and that they should not be unjustly enriched as the
> result of unremunerated services such as interpreting and translating actually performed by the
> claimant for the solicitors' clients. Remuneration which the plaintiff received on that basis
> would be a proper disbursement and would not, it seems to me, involve either a payment for
> introductions or the sharing of part of the solicitors' own profit costs."

---

[47] [2000] 1 W.L.R. 1815; [1999] 3 All E.R. 699, CA, reversing [1998] 2 All E.R. 720. See
Enonchong, "Restitution Following Illegal Fee-Sharing Agreement with a Solicitor" (2000)
Restitution Law Review 241.
[48] See *Swain v Law Society* [1983] 1 A.C. 598.
[49] But see now the Solicitors Regulation Authority Handbook and Code of Conduct 2016, Ch.9.
[50] [1998] 2 All E.R. 720 at 726.
[51] [2000] 1 W.L.R. 1815 at 1825; [1999] 3 All E.R. 699 at 708, per Lord Bingham CJ. cf. *Boissevain
v Weil* [1950] A.C. 327.
[52] [2000] 1 W.L.R. 1815 at 1825; [1999] 3 All E.R. 699 at 707.
[53] The solicitors could not themselves have recovered any payment for services rendered by them to
the claimant in such circumstances. cf. *Awwad v Geraghty & Co (A Firm)* [2001] Q.B. 570; [2000] 1
All E.R. 608, CA. See also *Birmingham City Council v Forde* [2009] EWHC 12 at [202]–[206] per
Christopher Clarke J.
[54] See [2000] 1 W.L.R. 1815 at 1827; [1999] 3 All E.R. 699 at 710.

The readiness of the Court of Appeal to permit investigation of the parties' relative culpability in this case, went beyond the crude assessment usually carried out on the basis of the *in pari delicto* maxim.[55] That would normally have treated the parties as equally "guilty"; the possibly greater moral blameworthiness of one of them not being considered to detract from their having entered into a contract which, for reasons of public interest, was prohibited.

17–17   **Similar approach adopted in Australia.**   At first instance in *Mohammed v Alaga*,[56] Lightman J discussed, but chose not to apply, a significant decision of the High Court of Australia which foreshadowed the approach favoured by the Court of Appeal in *Mohammed's* case. In *Pavey & Matthews Pty v Paul*[57] a claimant expressly prohibited from enforcing a contract was nevertheless granted restitutionary relief.[58] Deane J said[59]:

> "The quasi-contractual obligation to pay fair and just compensation for a benefit which has been accepted will only arise where there is no applicable genuine agreement or where such an agreement is frustrated, avoided or unenforceable. In such a case, it is the very fact that there is no genuine agreement or that the genuine agreement is frustrated, avoided or unenforceable that provides the occasion for (and part of the circumstances giving rise to) the imposition by the law of the obligation to make restitution."[60]

17–18   **Position after *Patel*.**   In *Patel v Mirza* counsel for the unsuccessful defendant argued before the Supreme Court that *Mohammed v Alaga* was either a case to be confined to its own facts or was wrongly decided. In response Lord Toulson, whose judgment represented the view of the majority, rejected this submission and expressly "affirm[ed] its correctness".[61] Lord Neuberger, however, was rather more cautious and considered that there would be "real room for debate in any particular case whether [a claimant] should be entitled to claim payment on a *quantum meruit* basis, even though he cannot enforce his right to contractual payment".[62] Lord Sumption declined to express a view "about cases in which an order for restitution would be functionally indistinguishable from an order for enforcement" but was "inclined to think" that "the traditional view…that if the law will not enforce an agreement it will not give the same financial relief under a different legal label" was "sound".[63] A degree of uncertainty on the point would

---

[55] cf. the approach of the Appellate Division of the Supreme Court of South Africa, administering Roman-Dutch law in *Jajbhay v Cassim* [1939] A.D. 537, especially, per Tindall JA at 558: ". . . according to our law our Courts are not bound to enforce rigidly in every case the general rule *in pari delicto potior est conditio defendentis* but may come to the relief of one of the parties where such a course is necessary in order to prevent injustice or to satisfy the requirements of public policy".

[56] [1998] 2 All E.R. 720 at 726.

[57] (1987) 162 C.L.R. 221.

[58] But cf. the more recent decision of the High Court of Australia in *Equuscorp Pty Ltd v Haxton* [2012] HCA 7 (noted by Elise Bant in (2012) 128 LQR 341) in which a majority of the Court (Heydon J dissenting) declined to award restitutionary relief on the ground that to do so would have undermined the policy rendering the contract between the parties unenforceable for illegality.

[59] (1987) 162 C.L.R. 221 at 256 (quoted by Lightman J in [1998] 2 All E.R. 720 at 726).

[60] cf. the American Law Institute's *Second Restatement of Contracts*, para.197, which allows for restitution in illegality cases, if its denial "would cause disproportionate forfeiture".

[61] See [2016] UKSC 42 at [119].

[62] See ibid at [180].

[63] See [2016] UKSC 42 at [255].

therefore seem to remain, not least because discussion of the issue in *Patel v Mirza* was in any event obiter. Nevertheless in view of the general approach to illegality adopted by the majority in that case it would seem that the outcome in any given situation, in this context as elsewhere, is now likely to depend upon consideration of the underlying policy factors.

5. FRAUD AND NEGLIGENCE

Deceit. In some cases, claimants able to prove fraud have been able to obtain relief, from the consequences of having entered into a contract unenforceable for illegality, by suing in tort for deceit. In *Hughes v Liverpool Victoria Friendly Society*[64] decided at a time when restitutionary relief for mistakes of law was not available, an innocent claimant who had paid premiums on an illegal contract of life insurance was held able to recover what she had paid; on the ground that the defendants had fraudulently misrepresented to her that the transaction was legal. In *Hughes'* case the fraud had related to the legality of the transaction itself, but this does not appear to be a requirement for success. In *Shelley v Paddock*[65] the defendants, who were resident in Spain, agreed to sell to the claimant, who was resident in England, a house in Spain. The claimant thereupon paid the purchase-price to the defendants, who represented that they were acting on behalf of the owners of the property. Unfortunately, the claimant failed to obtain Treasury permission to remit money to persons abroad, as was necessary at that time under the Exchange Control Act 1947. The reason for the omission was that the claimant was unaware of the existence of the Exchange Control Act, and therefore of the need to obtain Treasury permission. Subsequently it transpired that the defendants, who had since returned to England, were unable to make good title to the Spanish property and that they had, in fact, defrauded the claimant. The latter brought a successful action in tort for deceit, to recover back what she had paid. The defendants raised the illegality of the transaction by way of defence, and sought to rely on the supposed general rule that money paid under an illegal contract cannot be recovered back. This defence was rejected both by Bristow J[66] and by the Court of Appeal. Lord Denning MR observed that the defendants were "guilty of a swindle", and concluded that it was "only fair and just that they should not be allowed to keep the benefit of their fraud".[67] Similarly, in the earlier case of *Dott v Brickwell*,[68] Swinfen Eady J allowed an unlicensed moneylender to recover money lent under an illegal and unenforceable contract of loan, by suing in deceit in circumstances in which he had been induced to lend the money by fraudulent misrepresentation.

17–19

Tort and restitution. In both *Shelley v Paddock* and *Dott v Brickwell* the claimants were allowed to distinguish themselves from the defendants using the *in pari delicto* maxim, on the ground that they were victims of fraud. This does

17–20

---

[64] [1916] 2 K.B. 482.
[65] [1980] Q.B. 348.
[66] [1979] Q.B. 120; [1978] 3 All E.R. 129. See Buckley (1978) 94 L.Q.R. 484.
[67] [1980] Q.B. 348 at 357; [1980] 1 All E.R. 1009 at 1012.
[68] (1906) 23 T.L.R. 61.

not, however, appear to be entirely logical since in neither case did the fraud relate to the illegal nature of the transaction. In reality, redressing fraud was simply accorded priority to giving full effect to the supposedly rigid illegality rules.[69] It is to be hoped that developments in the law of restitution after *Patel v Mirza* will enable claimants in not dissimiliar circumstances to enjoy a measure of relief, without being forced to take the drastic step of attempting to prove fraud.

17–21   **Negligent misstatement.**   Nevertheless, the availability of tortious remedies may still be of benefit to claimants able to establish them, in circumstances in which the availability of restitutionary relief may be open to question. The remedies available for this purpose include not only deceit but also negligent misstatement, and the analogous cause of action under s.2(1) of the Misrepresentation Act 1967. The Court of Appeal in *Mohammed v Alaga*, in addition to holding that a claim in restitution was in principle maintainable, also allowed a late amendment enabling the plaintiff to include tortious negligence in his claim when the action was tried.[70]

---

[69] cf. *Neal v Avers*, (1940) 63 C.L.R. 524.
[70] [2000] 1 W.L.R. 1815 at 1826; [1999] 3 All E.R. 699 at 708.

CHAPTER 18

UNDOING THE TRANSACTION

1.   THE LOCUS POENITENTIAE DOCTRINE

The old law.   Prior to the 2016 decision of the Supreme Court in *Patel v Mirza*[1]   **18–01**
relief for unjust enrichment in cases involving illegality was constrained by the
need to bring the claim within the scope of a limited number of exceptions to the
proposition that "reliance" upon the illegality precluded such recovery. One of
those exceptions was the so-called "*locus poenitentiae*" doctrine. This permitted
recovery if the claimant repudiated the illegal transaction. There is some
indication from the eighteenth century cases that relief on this basis was wide in
scope,[2] but during the nineteenth century it narrowed significantly. It became
necessary to withdraw from the transaction before it was completed, and even for
the claimant's motive to be examined so that actual "repentance" from the
unlawful purpose could be demonstrated: mere "frustration" of that purpose by
forces beyond the control of the parties was insufficient. Delineating the precise
scope of these requirements gave rise to a body of difficult and uncertain
case-law. A brief summary of this jurisprudence is appropriate in order to put the
new law into context.[3]

Fulfiment, frustration and repentance.   In *Kearley v Thompson*[4] the   **18–02**
claimant, a friend of a bankrupt, made an unlawful payment to the solicitors of a
petitioning creditor in return for their undertaking not to appear at the bankrupt's
public examination, and not to oppose his discharge. The solicitors accordingly
did not appear at the public examination, but before the bankrupt had applied for
his discharge the claimant sued the solicitors for the return of the money which he
had paid to them. The Court of Appeal dismissed the claim. Fry LJ said:

> "… where there has been a partial carrying into effect of an illegal purpose in a substantial
> manner, it is impossible, though there remains something not performed, that the money paid
> under that illegal contract can be recovered back."[5]

The underlying lack of clarity in the cases as to what constituted partial
fulfilment of the unlawful purpose, within the doctrine in *Kearley v Thompson*,
highlighted the difficulty of attempting to impose a rigid structure upon an

---

[1] [2016] UKSC 42.
[2] See *Patel v Mirza* [2016] UKSC 42 at [97]-[98] (Lord Toulson), [147-149] (Lord Neuberger)
[194-196] (Lord Mance), [251] (Lord Sumption).
[3] For a fuller account see previous editions of this work.
[4] (1890) 24 Q.B.D. 742.
[5] (1890) 24 Q.B.D. 742 at 747.

infinite variety of differing factual situations.[6] It was unclear whether it would be too late for a party to withdraw as soon as he had done everything which the plan required of him, even if further steps still remain to be taken by others. The terminology of "executed" and "executory" contracts is ambiguous in this context: as is not infrequently the case, language appropriate elsewhere in the law of contract is less helpful when resolving illegality issues. One point upon which the cases spoke with somewhat greater clarity, however, was in their opposition to recovery by a party whose unlawful scheme had merely been frustrated. In *Alexander v Rayson*[7] a landlord attempted to deceive an assessment committee into making an inappropriately low valuation of certain premises, by disguising part of the rent he was receiving as payment for services. The deception was discovered before the committee made its final assessment, so that the rateable value was calculated ultimately using the true rental figure and not the false one. Nevertheless the tenant invoked the illegal scheme in order to avoid her obligations under the lease and the Court of Appeal, reversing du Parcq J, held that she could do so. The Court observed that[8]:

> "Where the illegal purpose has been wholly or partially effected the law allows no *locus poenitentiae*... It will not be any readier to do so when the repentance, as in the present case, is merely due to the frustration by others of the plaintiff's fraudulent purpose."[9]

Another source of uncertainty under the old law was the extent to which the court would insist literally upon "repentance" as a necessary condition for granting restitution. Particular emphasis was placed on the need for "repentance" in *Bigos v Bousted*.[10] A person who attempted to contravene the Exchange Control Act 1947, by depositing a share certificate with the other party in return for the promise of Italian currency being made available to his wife and daughter in Italy, was unable to recover the certificate when the other party reneged on the agreement and failed to supply the currency. Pritchard J said[11]:

> "... the law is that the court will help a person who repents, provided his repentance comes before the illegal purpose has been substantially performed ... I think, however, that this case falls within the category of cases which I call the frustration cases ..."[12]

Although the need for penitence was questioned in the Court of Appeal in a subsequent case,[13] in another decision the same Court felt obliged to apply the traditional view and decline restitution in circumstances in which it would have

---

[6] cf. Beatson, "Repudiation of Illegal Purpose as a Ground for Restitution" (1975) 91 L.Q.R. 313, contending that most of the actual decisions, as distinct from the judgments, can be explained on the basis "that recovery will only be allowed if judicial inactivity increases the probability of the illegal purpose being achieved" (pp.314–315).

[7] [1936] 1 K.B. 169.

[8] See [1936] 2 K.B. at 190, per Romer LJ delivering the judgment of the court.

[9] See also *Zimmerman v Letkeman* (1977) 79 D.L.R. (3d) 508 in which *Alexander v Rayson* was applied by the Supreme Court of Canada to somewhat similiar facts.

[10] [1951] 1 All E.R. 92.

[11] [1951] 1 All E.R. 92 at 100.

[12] cf. *Ouston v Zurowski* (1985) 18 D.L.R. (4th) 563 in which the notion of "repentance" was successfully applied (review of the authorities by the British Columbia Court of Appeal).

[13] See *Tribe v Tribe* [1996] Ch. 107 at 135; [1995] 4 All E.R. 236 at 259–260 per Millett LJ.

apparently preferred to have granted it.[14] Yet another source of confusion was the controversial decision of the House of Lords in *Tinsley v Milligan*[15] which could be interpreted as deciding that the limitations on the scope of recovery under the locus poenitentiae doctrine could simply be ignored by claimants able to rely upon a resulting trust, implying the existence of anomalous distinctions in this context between equity and common law.[16]

Limitations swept away. In *Patel v Mirza*, the facts of which were given in the previous chapter,[17] a nine member Supreme Court simplified the law and greatly widened the scope of relief. The Justices were divided on the question whether the law should continue to attempt to retain fixed "rules" to resolve illegality cases or, as the majority held, move to a policy based "range of factors" approach. Nevertheless in terms of the basic presumption which should henceforth govern claims for unjust enrichment, the Court spoke with one voice in sweeping away the often obscure refinements of the previous case law. Lord Toulson said[18]:

    18–03

> "A claimant ... who satisfies the ordinary requirements of a claim for unjust enrichment, should not be debarred from enforcing his claim by reason only of the fact that the money which he seeks to recover was paid for an unlawful purpose."

Lord Mance referred to the "parties normal entitlement to reverse the effects of an illegal transaction, where possible, even though the transaction may have been wholly or in part executed or carried into effect".[19] Lord Sumption observed that "the concept of penitential withdrawal leads to difficult distinctions and suggests an enquiry into a party's state of mind of a kind which the law rarely contemplates".[20] He concluded that: "the limitation to cases in which the unlawful purpose has not been carried out never was sound. The rational rule, which I would hold to be the law, is that restitution is available for so long as mutual restitution of benefits remains possible".[21] Finally, by overruling the reasoning in *Tinsley v Milligan* the Supreme Court made clear that there are no relevant distinctions in this context between common law and equity.

2. PROTECTION OF THE CLAIMANT

Underlying reason for the illegality. The *locus poenitentiae* doctrine was not the only context in which the recovery back of money or property transferred pursuant to an unlawful scheme was permitted. Recovery was also allowed if the

    18–04

---

[14] See *Collier v Collier* [2002] EWCA Civ 1095, and comment by Lord Mance in *Patel v Mirza* [2016] UKSC 42 at [187]. The case would now be decided differently, see per Lord Clarke, ibid, at [221] and per Lord Sumption at [238].

[15] [1994] 1 AC 340, [1993] 3 All ER 65.

[16] See the discussion by Millett LJ in *Tribe v Tribe* [1996] Ch.107 at 126; [1995] 4 All E.R. 236 at 252.

[17] See Ch.17 para.[17–03]

[18] [2016] UKSC at [121].

[19] See ibid at [202],

[20] See [2016] UKSC at [252].

[21] See ibid at [253].

claimant could show that the underlying reason, for the provision or doctrine giving rise to the illegality, was the protection of persons in the position of the claimant himself.[22] In *Browning v Morris*[23] Lord Mansfield said:

> "... where contracts or transactions are prohibited by positive statutes, for the sake of protecting one set of men from another set of men; the one, from their situation and condition, being liable to be oppressed or imposed upon by the other; there, the parties are not *in pari delicto*; and in furtherance of these statutes, the person injured, after the transaction is finished and completed, may bring his action and defeat the contract."

Notwithstanding the broadening in the scope of unjust enrichment generally, after the decision in *Patel v Mirza*, this line of authority remains of value. If a statutory provision was intended to protect one party to a transaction from another, this is clearly of potential significance both within and beyond the area of restitution. It may affect the readiness of the court to allow a quantum meruit claim by the person protected and, paradoxically, may be of importance in preventing the *other* party from himself relying on the new regime to seek restitution of benefits conferred by him.[24] It is therefore still appropriate to outline the established law on this topic.

18–05   **Criminality no bar to recovery.**   The Rent Acts provide a familiar example of class-protecting legislation, providing expressly that premiums charged illegally in return for tenancies can be recovered by the tenant. Moreover, the policy underlying those express provisions has even been applied in favour of tenants who claim restitution without relying on the specific statutory machinery. In one such case, *Gray v Southouse*,[25] Devlin J emphasised that the legislative policy warranted recovery notwithstanding that the tenants will often have themselves committed a criminal offence by aiding and abetting the landlord, with full knowledge of the law, in order to gain the tenancy. He pointed out that widespread knowledge of the Acts and their provisions meant that "cases of innocent tenants must be very rare", and he could therefore "hardly believe that Parliament intended the wide words of the statute to be restricted to those exceptional cases".[26] Similarly, in *Kiriri Cotton Co v Dewani*[27] the Privy Council ordered the return to the tenant of an illegally paid premium even though the Ugandan legislation in question, while making the taking of a premium a criminal offence, did not, unlike the English Rent Acts, expressly give the tenant a right to get his money back. Lord Denning, giving the judgment of the Board, emphasised that the claim, as one for money had and received, was "simply an action for restitution of money which the defendant has received but which the law says he ought to return to the plaintiff". Like Devlin J in *Gray v Southouse*,

---

[22] See, e.g. *Amar Singh v Kulubya* [1964] A.C. 142, PC. See also *Murray Vernon Holdings v Hassall* [2010] EWHC 7 at [66].

[23] (1778) 2 Cowp. 790 at 792.

[24] See per Lord Neuberger in *Patel v Mirza* [2016] UKSC 42 at [162]:"... where one of the parties, especially the defendant, is in a class which is intended to be protected by the criminal legislation involved, it may well be inappropriate to invoke the Rule [i.e. of restitutio in integrum]."

[25] [1949] 2 All E.R. 1019.

[26] [1949] 2 All E.R. 1019 at 1021.

[27] [1960] A.C. 192.

Lord Denning acknowledged that the claimant tenant had probably himself committed a criminal offence as an accomplice with his landlord but neither this, nor the fact that the contract had been executed, was an obstacle to recovery. Lord Denning concluded[28]:

> "Seeing . . . that the parties are not *in pari delicto*, the tenant is entitled to recover the premium by the common law; and it is not necessary to find a remedy given by the ordinance, either expressly or by implication."

Enforceability of contract still precluded. Even if the legislation is clearly   **18–06**
intended to protect the claimant, this will only facilitate restitutionary relief and will not enable the prohibited contract itself to be enforced. This is a potential source of difficulty in employment cases, where an action on the contract may be the only effective remedy.[29] In such cases it is desirable, whenever possible, that the court should construe the applicable legislation as striking only at the employer; thereby leaving the employee's contractual remedies unaffected.[30] Where the contract is unenforceable, however, the restitutionary remedy of quantum meruit may provide a source of relief for the employee.[31]

Protection of debtors. The principle of class protection also found a ready   **18–07**
application in cases decided under legislation prohibiting unlicensed moneylending.[32] An important issue which arose in that context was whether debtors, who sought the recovery of securities transferred pursuant to moneylending transactions within the legislation, could be put on terms as to the repayment of the sums borrowed. A decision to this effect was reached by Parker J in *Lodge v National Union Investment Co*.[33] Since the debtor had in substance been seeking equitable relief, his Lordship considered that it was not equitable that a claimant who was "relying on the illegality of the contract and the exception enabling him to sue notwithstanding such illegality, should have relief without being put on terms by which both parties may be restored to the positions they occupied before

---

[28] [1960] A.C. 192 at 205; [1960] 1 All E.R. 177 at 182.
[29] See, e.g. *Wylie v Lawrence Wright Music Co* (1932) T.L.R. 295 (shop assistant unlawfully employed during compulsory holiday period unable to recover damages in lieu of missed holiday). cf. the American case of *Nizamuddowlah v Bengal Cabaret* (1977) 399 N.Y.S. 2d 854 in which an illegal immigrant working unlawfully was allowed to sue in unjust enrichment, and was awarded a sum based on the statutory minimum wage. The case is referred to by Birks in "Recovering Value Transferred Under an Illegal Contract" [2000] *Theoretical Inquiries in Law*, Tel Aviv, 155 at p.174, and discussed by Lord Toulson in *Patel v Mirza* [2016] UKSC 42 at [63]-[66].
[30] cf. the unsatisfactory American cases of *Short v Bullion-Beck and Champion Mining Co* (1899) 20 Utah 20; and *Hill v Missouri Pacific Railway Co* 8 F.Supp (W.D.La 1933), discussed in Gellhorn, "Contracts and Public Policy" (1935) 35 Columbia L.R. 679. See also Furmston, "Analysis of Illegal Contracts" (1965) 16 Toronto LJ 267, at pp.280 et seq.
[31] cf. *Mohammed v Alaga & Co (A Firm)* [2000] 1 W.L.R. 1815; [1999] 3 All E.R. 699. CA, discussed in Ch.17. above. See also per Lord Toulson in *Patel v Mirza* [2016] UKSC 42 at [119] and per Lord Sumption at [243].
[32] See *Victorian Daylesford Syndicate v Dott* [1905] 2 Ch. 624; *Bonnard v Dott* [1906] 1 Ch. 740; *Chapman v Michaelson* [1909] 1 Ch. 238; *Cohen v Lester (J.) Ltd* [1939] 1 K.B. 504.
[33] [1907] 1 Ch. 300.

the transaction commenced".[34] This decision was, however, very narrowly distinguished in later cases on the ground that it conflicted with the underlying policy of the legislation to protect the borrower.[35] In *Kasumu v Baba-Egbe*[36] Lord Radcliffe pointed out that to allow a creditor who was in breach of the legislation to "put himself in the position that his borrower would have to resort to the court in order completely to undo the effect of the transaction" would mean in effect that he "would be protected by the court from parting with his security except on terms that rendered the unenforceable loan enforceable, either to its full effect or in some modified terms". It followed that a court which imposed terms as a condition of relief "would be expressing a policy of its own in regard to such transactions . . . in direct conflict with the policy of the Acts themselves".[37]

18–08 **Legislative purpose.**   Identifying the "purpose" of an enactment with sufficient clarity to predicate that it was passed in order to protect one class of contracting parties from another, will not always be straightforward. Similar questions can arise in relation to the action in tort for damages for breach of statutory duty.[38] In *Green v Portsmouth Stadium*[39] a bookmaker sought to recover back sums which he had been illegally charged for entry to a greyhound racing track, contrary to the Betting and Lotteries Act 1934. The Court of Appeal, reversing Parker J, held that the action would not lie since it would be inconsistent with the decision of the House of Lords in *Cutler v Wandsworth Stadium*.[40] In that case the House had held, in an action for breach of statutory duty, that the Act had not been passed in order to benefit bookmakers as a class.[41]

---

[34] [1907] 1 Ch. 300 at 312. The approach of Parker J has been viewed with favour in Australia and Canada: see the judgment of the Federal Court of Australia in *Farrow v Edgar* (1993) 114 A.L.R. 1 at 12–13, and references there cited.
[35] For the position where the legislation is not primarily intended to protect the borrower, see the decision of the Ontario Court of Appeal in *Sidmay v Whettam Investments* (1967) 61 D.L.R. (2d) 358 (illegality by mortgagees did not relieve mortgagors of their obligations).
[36] [1956] A.C. 539 at 550.
[37] See also *Orakpo v Manson Investments* [1978] A.C. 95, in which the House of Lords refused to allow the doctrine of subrogation to come to the aid of a moneylender who had been in breach of the statutory provisions, notwithstanding that the borrower's defence was technical and devoid of merit. For criticism see Bentson, "Unjust Enrichment and the Moneylenders Act" (1978) 41 M.L.R. 330. See also *Farrow v Edgar* (1993) 114 A.L.R. 1 at 19, per Lockhart, Gummow and Lee JJ.
[38] See Buckley, "Liability in Tort for Breach of Statutory Duty" (1984) 100 L.Q.R. 204.
[39] [1953] K.B. 190.
[40] [1949] A.C. 398.
[41] Quaere whether *Green's* case would now be decided differently in view of the decisions of the House of Lords on the law of restitution in *Woolwich Equitable Building Society v Inland Revenue Commissioners* [1993] A.C. 709 and *Kleinwort Benson v Lincoln City Council* [1999] 2 A.C. 349; [1998] 4 All H.R. 513. See Birks, "Recovering Value Transferred Under an Illegal Contract" [2000] *Theoretical Inquiries in Law*, Tel Aviv, 155 at 197. See also criticism, by Kitto J in *South Australia Cold Stores v Electricity Trust of South Australia* (1965) 115 C.L.R. 247 at p.258, of the approach of Denning LJ in *Green's* case. But cf. Beatson, "Restitution of Taxes, Levies and other Imposts" (1993) 109 L.Q.R. 401 at p.416.

CHAPTER 19

THE DOCTRINE OF SEVERANCE

1. INTRODUCTION

Integral part of illegality. "Questions of severability", observed Lord   **19–01**
Brightman delivering the judgment of the Privy Council in *Carney v Herbert*[1]
"are often difficult. There are no set rules which will decide all cases".[2] The
doctrine of severance is an integral part of the law relating to illegality in
contract. Far from being merely a technical appendix to more familiar principles,
it is permeated by the public policy factors which this branch of the law
embodies. In cases in which severance is in issue, it is usually decisive of the
outcome of the litigation. Nevertheless, even by the standards of illegality, this
branch of the law is complex and obscure. It is one thing to deny enforceability of
an agreement on grounds of public policy, it is yet another to *enforce* a contract
which is at variance with the one actually concluded by the parties.

Objectives unclear. Indeed, the reason why severance has become so   **19–02**
uncertain in its operation is that, once it is established that some aspect of the
agreement is objectionable, it is often unclear what the court is seeking to achieve
when determining the precise extent to which enforceability should be permitted.
Is it simply trying to perceive what the intentions of the parties would have been,
had they anticipated that one or more of their objectives might become
unobtainable; or is it still pursuing independent public policy objectives? In truth,
questions relating to the intentions of the parties are often interwoven with policy
issues, and the resulting mixture is apt to be both confused and confusing. N. S.
Marsh, in his magisterial study of the doctrine of severance,[3] over half a century
ago, wrote that Continental legal systems did "not appear to find great difficulty
in determining when parts of an illegal contract may be enforced".[4] This was in
contrast with English law, which "developing its contractual remedies out of
delictual conceptions, has never accepted the principle of freedom of contract
without qualifications".[5]

---

[1] [1985] A.C. 301 at 309; [1985] 1 All E.R. 438 at 442.
[2] See also, per Kitto J in *Brooks v Burns Philip Trustee Co* (1969) 121 C.L.R. 432 at 438, who first
coined the phrase.
[3] See Marsh, "Severance of Illegality in Contract" (1948) 64 L.Q.R. 230 at p.347. See also the same
author's "Severance and Public Policy—An Addendum" (1953) 69 L.Q.R. 111.
[4] (1948) 64 L.Q.R. 230.
[5] (1948) 64 L.Q.R. 230 at 231.

19–03   **Modern tests.**   In *Sadler v Imperial Life Assurance Co of Canada*,[6] Mr P. J. Crawford QC, sitting as a Deputy High Court Judge, said that "a contract which contains an unenforceable provision nevertheless remains effective after the removal or severance of that provision", when certain conditions are satisfied, which he identified as follows:

> "1.   The unenforceable provision is capable of being removed without the necessity of adding to or modifying the wording of what remains.
> 2.   The remaining terms continue to be supported by adequate consideration,
> 3.   The removal of the unenforceable provision does not so change the character of the contract that it 'becomes not the sort of contract that the parties entered into at all".[7]

In quoting this passage, when sitting as a Deputy High Court Judge at first instance in *Marshall v NM Financial Management Ltd*,[8] Mr Jonathan Sumption QC said: "To these three propositions there should perhaps be added a fourth, namely that the severance must be consistent with the public policy underlying the avoidance of the offending part". It is convenient to adopt the four-fold classification thus identified, so as to examine the authorities under the following headings: Wording of the Provision, Scope of the Consideration, Character of the Contract, and Policy Factors.

2.   WORDING OF THE PROVISION

19–04   **"Blue pencil test".**   The so-called "blue pencil" test originated, in the words of N. S. Marsh, "in the preoccupation of the courts in the earlier cases with instruments under seal". In litigation involving deeds, the court was "concerned to see that what was left remained a valid deed".[9] Early in the twentieth century, the test was stated by Lord Sterndale MR, in *Attwood v Lamont*,[10] as follows:

> "I think ... that it is still the law that a contract can be severed if the severed parts are independent of one another, and can be severed without the severance affecting the meaning of the part remaining. This has sometimes been expressed, as ... that the severance can be effected when the part severed can be removed by running a blue pencil through it. This is a figurative way of expressing the principle, and like most figurative expressions may quite possibly lead to misunderstanding ... I think it clear that if the severance of a part of the agreement gives it a meaning and object different in kind and not only in extent, the different parts of it cannot be said to be independent."

The thrust of these remarks appears to be that, while it is a necessary condition of severability that the offending parts can be deleted without altering the sense of what remains, this is not a sufficient condition.[11] It is not enough for the severed

---

[6] [1988] I.R.L.R. 388 at 391–392. See also *TFS Derivatives v Morgan* [2004] EWHC 3181 (QB); *East England Schools CIC v Palmer & Another* [2013] EWHC 4138.

[7] The final words are a quotation from the judgment of Buckley LJ in *Chemidus Wavin Ltd v Société pour la Transformation et L'Exploitation des Resines Industrielles SA* (1978) 3 C.M.L.R. 514 at 520.

[8] [1995] 1 W.L.R. 1461 at 1466; [1995] 4 All E.R. 785 at 792–793 (affirmed [1997] 1 W.L.R. 1527; [1997] I.R.L.R. 449, CA).

[9] (1948) 64 L.Q.R. 347 at 351–352.

[10] [1920] 3 K.B. 571 at 577–578. See also *Beckett Investment Management Group v Glyn Hall* [2007] EWCA Civ 613 at paras 33–44, per Maurice Kay LJ.

[11] See also *Francotyp-Postalia v Whitehead* [2011] EWHC 367.

covenant to make literal sense, if what remains constitutes a contract significantly different in scope from that which the parties envisaged.[12]

Severance refused.   Thus in *Attwood v Lamont* itself, in which deletion could easily have been effected leaving a perfectly intelligible covenant behind, the Court of Appeal nevertheless refused severance on the ground that to allow it would "alter entirely the scope and intention of the agreement". The long list of prohibited activities,[13] included in a covenant in restraint of trade in that case, indicated that the essential object of the covenant had been the illegitimate one of protecting the covenantee from competition, rather than protecting his trade secrets or his contacts with his customers; and it therefore fell *in toto*. *Attwood's* case concerned a covenant extracted from an employer by an employee, which the courts were reluctant, at least until relatively recently,[14] to sever too readily. If, however, the case does not come into that category, and the bargaining strength of the parties was less unequal, it is more likely that satisfaction of the so-called "blue-pencil" test may in practice create something like a presumption that severance should be permitted; unless other requirements remain unfulfilled.

19–05

Goldsoll v Goldman.   The classic example of the test being applied, so as to leave behind an enforceable covenant, is the well-known decision of the Court of Appeal in *Goldsoll v Goldman*.[15] The vendor of a business promised the purchaser that he would not, for a period of two years, become involved in a similiar business "in the county of London, England, Scotland, Ireland, Wales, or any part of the United Kingdom of Great Britain and Ireland and the Isle of Man or in France, the US, Russia or Spain, or within twenty-five miles of Potsdamerstrasse, Berlin or St Stefan's Kirche, Vienna". Without hesitation the Court of Appeal agreed to delete all the wording from, and including, "or in France"; and then to enforce the covenant, which was thus confined to the UK and the Isle of Man.

19–06

Severance of area covenants.   The decisions in *Attwood v Lamont* and *Goldsoll v Goldman* can be contrasted not only on the basis that the covenant in the former was between master and servant, and in the latter between vendor and purchaser, but also on the basis that *Goldsoll's* case was excessively wide in terms of area. Even in master and servant cases the courts are perhaps more ready to sever covenants which are excessively wide in simply geographical terms, provided that the "blue pencil test" is satisfied,[16] than those which multiply words

19–07

---

[12] cf. per Salter J in the Divisional Court in *Putsman v Taylor* [1927] 1 K.B. 637 at 640: "Severance', as it seems to me, is the act of the parties, not of the court". Sed quaere, see Marsh, "Severance of Illegality in Contract" (1948) 64 L.Q.R. 230 at pp.362–363.
[13] The covenantor undertook not to "carry on or be in any way directly or indirectly concerned in any of the following trades or businesses, that is to say, the trade or business of a tailor, dressmaker, general draper, milliner, hatter, haberdasher, gentlemen's, ladies', or children's outfitter".
[14] But see now *T. Lucas & Co v Mitchell* [1974] Ch. 129; [1972] 3 All E.R. 689, discussed below.
[15] [1915] 1 Ch. 292.
[16] cf. *Mason v Provident Clothing and Supply Co* [1913] A.C. 724: "within twenty-five miles of London" (not severable).

and phrases in order to extend the covenant in other ways.[17] Thus, in *Attwood v Lamont* a variety of supposedly different functions was specified which, on analysis, added nothing to a single improper attempt to prevent legitimate competition.[18] *Attwood's* case can conveniently be contrasted in this respect with the otherwise not dissimilar master and servant case of *Putsman v Taylor*.[19] The defendant covenanted for five years not to accept employment as a tailor within a half-mile radius of three specific and distinct parts of Birmingham, where his former employer had shops. The Divisional Court[20] held that two of the three could be deleted. Talbot J said"[21]:

> "The contract in the present case is (among other things) not to enter employment of a particular kind in either of three defined areas. Why is that not severable into three contracts each binding the defendant not to enter such employment in one of the three? It is difficult to see how, if any such contract is severable, this is not."[22]

19–08   **"Plainly severable".**   Similarly, in *Scorer v Seymour-Johns*[23] the former employee of an estate-agent covenanted not to accept, for three years, similar employment within five miles of his employer's offices "at 85, Fore Street, Kingsbridge or Duke Street, Dartmouth". The employee had only been employed in the Kingsbridge office, and contended that the covenant was therefore unreasonably wide. But the Court of Appeal severed the reference to Dartmouth and granted the employer an injunction. "The prohibition in respect of Kingsbridge", said Salmon LJ, "stands quite separately and I have no difficulty in saying that the covenant is plainly severable".[24]

19–09   **Availability of deleted phrases.**   There is an important qualification to the "blue pencil test" itself, which adds a measure of flexibility to the manner in which it operates in practice. Although the court will never "add to or modify the wording otherwise than by excision"[25]; it will sometimes be prepared to allow excised wording to "remain", in a limited adjectival sense, so as to prevent the undeleted wording from being deprived of meaning. Thus in *T. Lucas & Co v*

---

[17] cf. per Hodson LJ in *Ronbar Enterprises v Green* [1954] 1 W.L.R. 815 at 822–823; [1954] 2 All E.R. 266 at 271: "It is quite clear that in a vendor and purchaser covenant, *insofar as matters of geography are concerned*, it is quite legitimate to deal with the area by severance" (italics supplied).
[18] See also *Mason v Provident Clothing and Supply Co* [1913] A.C. 724.
[19] [1927] 1 K.B. 637 (divisional court); [1927] 1 K.B. 741 (Court of Appeal).
[20] The Court of Appeal held that the covenant was enforceable in its entirety, so that the severance point did not arise: see [1927] 1 K.B. 741.
[21] See [1927] 1 K.B. 637 at 644.
[22] cf. criticism of this case, by Marsh (1948) 64 L.Q.R. 347 at pp.362–363, for "refusing to treat severance as a matter involving anything except the intention of the parties, such intention, however, being arbitrarily assumed by a formal test".
[23] [1966] 1 W.L.R. 1419; [1966] 3 All E.R. 347.
[24] [1966] 1 W.L.R. 1419 at 1427; [1966] 3 All E.R. 347 at 353.
[25] See, per Russell LJ in *T. Lucas & Co v Mitchell* [1974] Ch. 129 at 135; [1972] 3 All E.R. 689 at 693.

Mitchell[26] the surviving part of the covenant included the phrase "supply any such goods", and reference to the deleted wording was permitted to identify the goods in question.[27]

3. SCOPE OF THE CONSIDERATION

Need for additional consideration. Until relatively recently, the courts were inclined to hold that when part of the *consideration* for the contract was illegal, as distinct from merely the *promises* contained in it, severance was impossible.[28] Marsh demonstrates that this principle rested on dubious historical grounds,[29] and it has now been superseded by a readiness to sever the consideration where this is appropriate.[30] As a result, however, the question may arise as to whether there is sufficient consideration, once the offending provision has been deleted, for the contract to be enforceable at all. In *Bennett v Bennett*[31] a divorcing husband and wife reached an agreement, before decree nisi, whereby the former agreed to make financial provision for the latter, and for their son, in return for the wife undertaking not to invoke the jurisdiction of the court in relation to maintenance. This undertaking was, however, void as an attempt to oust the jurisdiction of the court,[32] and since it constituted "the main consideration moving from the wife",[33] the Court of Appeal held that she could not enforce the husband's covenants. An action which she brought when he failed to make the agreed payments was therefore dismissed.[34] In *Alec Lobb v Total Oil GB*,[35] Dunn LJ reviewed, obiter, the relevant severance cases and expressed his conclusion as follows[36]:

> "The preponderance of those authorities seems to me to indicate that, if the valid promises are supported by sufficient consideration, then the invalid promise can be severed from the valid even though the consideration also supports the invalid promise. On the other hand if the invalid promise is substantially the whole or main consideration for the agreement then there will be no severance."

No objection that agreement would not have been reached. Provided that consideration to support the contract *does* remain, and provided also that

19–10

19–11

[26] [1974] Ch. 129; [1972] 3 All E.R. 689, CA.
[27] See also, per Younger LJ in *British Reinforced Concrete Engineering Co v Schelff* [1921] 2 Ch. 563 at 573.
[28] See, e.g. per Lord Esher MR in *Kearney v Whitehaven Colliery* [1893] 1 Q.B. 700 at 711: ". . . if the consideration, or any part of it, is illegal then every promise contained in the agreement becomes illegal also, because in such a case every part of the consideration is consideration for the promise". See also *Lound v Grimwade* (1886) 39 Ch.D. 605 at 613, per Stirling J: "As part of the consideration is illegal, it follows that the whole is bad".
[29] See (1948) 64 L.Q.R. 230 at 236, et seq.
[30] See, generally, N. S. Marsh, "Severance and Public Policy—An Addendum" (1953) 69 L.Q.R. 111. See also *Mansell v Robinson* [2007] EWHC 101 (QB) at para.16 per Underhill J.
[31] [1952] 1 K.B. 249.
[32] See *Hyman v Hyman* [1929] A.C. 601.
[33] [1952] 1 K.B. 249 at 258 per Somervell LJ.
[34] cf. the not dissimilar case of *Goodinson v Goodinson* [1954] 2 Q.B. 118, CA, in which the payments to be made by the husband were enforceable because additional consideration, separate from the invalid ouster clause, remained to support the agreement.
[35] [1985] 1 W.L.R. 173; [1985] 1 All E.R. 303, see below.
[36] [1985] 1 W.L.R. 173 at 188; [1985] 1 All E.R. 303 at 317.

severance does not alter the essential *character* of the agreement,[37] enforceability cannot be resisted simply because one of the parties would not have chosen to enter into the contract in the absence of the deleted clause. At first glance this might seem surprising, but the motives of the parties for entering into an agreement are distinct from the concluded contract itself.[38] Moreover, if the law were otherwise, the resulting denial of enforceability might sometimes lead to very unfair results.[39] In *Alec Lobb v Total Oil GB*[40] the Court of Appeal was concerned with a transaction between a petrol company and a garage which involved an allegedly invalid "solus" tie, a lease-back, and a mortgage. The Court held that the "solus" restraint was, in the circumstances, valid; but went on to consider what the position would have been had their decision been different, and the clause had been severed. Dillon LJ said[41]:

> "The contract is of course changed by the excision of the tie, and obviously Total would not have granted a lease-back which did not contain such a tie. But I do not think that is good enough to prevent severance and lead to the conclusion that the whole of the lease and lease-back is void. A mortgage to a petrol company containing a tie would, in my judgment, remain in all other respects valid despite the invalidity of the tie as an unreasonable restraint of trade, *although the petrol company would not have contemplated making any advance on mortgage to a dealer without a tie.*"

19–12   **Employer's contention rejected.**   This passage was quoted with approval by Millett LJ, in the Court of Appeal in *Marshall v NM Financial Management*.[42] In that case the claimant, who had been employed by the defendant financial services company as a sales agent, was entitled after his departure to continuing commission on business he had already introduced earlier to the defendants. This entitlement was, however, conditional upon his not joining a rival organisation within one year of his leaving the defendants, a condition which the claimant contravened. When the condition was held to be unenforceable, as being in unreasonable restraint of trade, the defendants argued that its deletion removed the consideration which supported the entitlement to post-employment commission. That contention was rejected. "(I)n substance", said the judge, "the consideration for the payment of renewal commission is not the acceptance by Mr Marshall of the proviso, but his services in procuring business before his resignation".[43]

---

[37] See below, paras 19.13–19.15.
[38] cf. *Blackburn Bobbin Co v Allen* [1918] 2 K.B. 467 (frustration).
[39] Especially in cases involving the payment of commission or pensions: see, e.g. *Marshall v NM Financial Management*, discussed below. See also *Re Prudential Assurance Co's Trust Deed* [1934] Ch. 338; *Bull v Pitney-Bowes* [1967] 1 W.L.R. 273. cf. *Wyatt v Kreglinger & Fernau* [1933] 1 K.B. 793. For further discussion see Ch.11, above.
[40] [1985] 1 W.L.R. 173; [1985] 1 All E.R. 303.
[41] [1985] 1 W.L.R. 173 at 181; [1985] 1 All E.R. 303 at 311 (italics supplied).
[42] [1997] 1 W.L.R. 1527 at 1532; [1997] I.R.L.R. 449 at 451, CA; affirming [1995] 1 W.L.R. 1461; [1995] 4 All E.R. 795.
[43] [1995] 1 W.L.R. 1461 at 1468; [1995] 4 All E.R. 785 at 794, per Jonathan Sumption QC (sitting as a deputy High Court judge). This passage was expressly adopted in the Court of Appeal: see per Millett LJ in [1997] 1 W.L.R. 1527 at 1534; [1997] I.R.L.R. 449 at 452. See also *IBM United Kingdom Holdings & Another v Dalgleish & Others* [2015] EWHC 389 at [115]–[121] per Warren J.

4.   CHARACTER OF THE CONTRACT

Different agreement.   Even if sufficient consideration would have remained   **19–13**
after severance, it may sometimes still be possible to contend that the doctrine
should not apply, thus leaving the contract wholly unenforceable. This contention
would be based on the argument that deletion had so altered the character of the
agreement that the courts would, in effect, be enforcing a different contract.[44] As
Younger LJ emphasised in *British Reinforced Concrete Engineering Co v
Schelff*,[45] the doctrine of severance "does not authorise the making of a new
contract for the parties". In that case the claimants' claim was dismissed when
severance was declined, despite satisfaction of the "blue-pencil" test, of a clause
described by the judge as "really a principal, if not the main . . . part of one entire
covenant in mosaic".[46] Similarly, in *Attwood v Lamont*,[47] Lord Sterndale MR said
that to sever the contract in that case would be "not merely to remove one of
several covenants . . . but to alter entirely the scope and intention of the
agreement".[48] The leading modern illustration of this aspect of the doctrine of
severance is probably the judgment of the Judicial Committee of the Privy
Council in *Amoco Australia Pty v Rocca Bros Motor Engineering Co*.[49] A "solus"
tie was held to be unenforceable as being in unreasonable restraint of trade; and
the Privy Council held that since the tie had been the "heart and soul"[50] of a lease
of the petrol station to the petrol company, that lease itself was also
unenforceable. Lord Cross of Chelsea, delivering the judgment of the Board,
pointed out that the question of whether or not the rest of the agreement remained
enforceable after severance involved a paradox; one which is not unfamiliar
elsewhere in the law of contract.[51] He said[52]:

> "The answer depends on the intention of the parties as disclosed by the agreement into which
> they have entered; but generally, of course, they have not foreseen that one or more of the
> provisions in their agreement will be unenforceable."

Matter of impression.   Although it is conventional to ascribe the outcome to   **19–14**
the "intention of the parties", the logical difficulties inherent in this approach
inevitably mean that the court cannot avoid bringing its own judgment to bear.[53]
In this respect it is important to note that, as explained above, the mere fact that
one party would not have chosen to enter into the agreement in the absence of the
deleted clause is not a sufficient reason in itself for concluding that the contract is
no longer enforceable. There is one passage in the judgment of Lord Cross in the

---

[44] See e.g. *Credit Suisse v Allerdale Borough Council* [1997] Q.B. 306 at 335, per Neill LJ.
[45] [1921] 2 Ch. 563 at 573; [1921] All E.R. Rep. 202 at 210.
[46] [1921] 2 Ch. 563 at 573.
[47] [1921] 3 K.B. 571 at 580; [1920] All E.R. Rep. 55 at 61.
[48] See also *Francotyp-Postalia v Whitehead* [2011] EWHC 367; *Canadian American Financial Corp
v King* (1989) 60 D.L.R. (4th) 293 (British Columbia Court of Appeal).
[49] [1975] A.C. 561.
[50] [1975] A.C. 561 at 578.
[51] See e.g. the doctrines of frustration and "mistake".
[52] [1975] A.C. 561 at 578.
[53] cf. per Denning LJ in *Bennett v Bennett* [1952] 1 K.B. 249 at 261 considering whether severance
left "a reasonable arrangement between the parties".

Amoco case which is open to the interpretation that it would be sufficient to show that that is the course which one of the parties, would have chosen.[54] But as Dillon LJ observed in *Alec Lobb v Total Oil GS*,[55] the nature of the agreement in *Amoco* was such that "the invalid tie was the sole object or subject matter of the contract", and the decision in the case itself should be regarded as having proceeded on that basis. The question of whether the underlying "character" of the contract would be irremediably altered by severance is therefore necessarily one to be determined by the court, in the light of the facts of each case, essentially as a matter of impression.[56]

19–15   **Role of the court.**   In one Scottish case[57] a clause was considered which appeared to represent an ingenious attempt to control the way in which the doctrine of severance itself operated, by expanding the role of the court in applying the doctrine.[58] Although the Court of Session appeared to be not unsympathetic to the clause,[59] it is submitted that it would have been unenforceable in England on a priori grounds either as constituting, in substance, an invitation to the court to rewrite the contract,[60] or as an illegitimate attempt to bring illegality within the reach of the parties.

5.   POLICY FACTORS

19–16   **Differing categories.**   In *Goodinson v Goodinson*.[61] Somervell LJ observed "that there are two kinds of illegality of differing effect". He continued:

> "The first is where the illegality is criminal, or *contra bonos mores*, and in those cases . . . such a provision, if an ingredient in a contract, will invalidate the whole, although there may be many other provisions in it. There is a second kind of illegality which has no such taint; the other terms in the contract stand if the illegal portion can be severed, the illegal portion being a provision which the court, on grounds of public policy, will not enforce."

The second of the two categories identified here includes, for example, covenants in unreasonable restraint of trade and, as in *Goodinson*'s case itself, agreements to oust the jurisdiction of the court. Even within this second broad category, however, severance should not necessarily be automatic even when the various tests relating to application of the "blue-pencil", the presence of additional consideration and the unchanged "character" of the contract are all satisfied. But the policy issues involved in such cases, which tend to be focused on the relative bargaining strengths of the parties, are rather different from those

---

[54] [1975] A.C. 561 at 578.

[55] [1985] 1 W.L.R. 173 at 180; [1985] 1 All B.R. 303 at 311.

[56] See e.g. *Brand Studio Ltd v St John Knits, Inc* [2015] EWHC 3143, [2015] All ER (D) 23 (Nov).

[57] *Hinton & Higgs (UK) v Murphy and Valentine* [1989] I.R.L.R. 519.

[58] "The restrictions . . . are considered reasonable by the parties, but in the event that any such restrictions shall be found to be void would be valid if some part thereof were deleted . . . such restrictions shall apply with such modifications as may be necessary to make them valid or effective".

[59] [1989] I.R.L.R. 519 at 520, per Lord Dervaird.

[60] cf. *Davies v Davies* (1887) 36 Ch.D. 359, CA.

[61] [1954] 2 Q.B. 118 at 120, CA. See also the same judge in *Bennett v Bennett* [1952] 1 K.B. 249 at 253–254.

relating to contracts tainted with criminality, or with objectionable provisions of equivalent seriousness. It is convenient to deal first with the second of the two categories as listed by Somervell LJ, in which the most prominent cases are those involving restraints of trade, and then to deal with those situations "where the illegality is criminal, or *contra bonos mores*".

(a)   Restraint of Trade

Employees unlikely to challenge covenants.   At least until relatively recently,   **19–17**
the courts attached considerable weight to an important policy issue surrounding the application of the severance doctrine to covenants extracted from employees by their employers. The former will rarely have the resources to mount an effective challenge to the validity of a restrictive covenant and may therefore easily be intimidated into compliance. If, in addition, severance is readily granted in favour of the employer, in the exceptional cases in which a legal challenge to a covenant of excessive width is mounted, employers will have little incentive not to draft unreasonably wide covenants. They will be able to rely either upon intimidation, or upon the doctrine of severance, to ensure that their former employees are restrained. The point was well put in a classic passage from the speech of Lord Moulton in *Mason v Provident Clothing and Supply Co*[62] when he said:

> "It would be ... *pessimi exempli* if, when an employer had exacted a covenant deliberately framed in unreasonably wide terms, the courts were to come to his assistance, and, by applying their ingenuity and knowledge of the law, carve out of this void covenant the maximum of what he might validly have required. It must be remembered that the real sanction at the back of these covenants is the terror and expense of litigation, in which the servant is usually at a great disadvantage, in view of the longer purse of his master."

Significant deterrent.   In *Mason's* case itself the covenant was vague as well   **19–18**
as too wide, and the apparent inapplicability of the "blue pencil" test might be thought to have ruled out severance irrespective of any other considerations. Unfortunately, it is not clear precisely what distinct further protection, if any, is in practice accorded to employees in situations in which the "blue pencil" test, along with the consideration and unchanged "character" requirements, is satisfied. In *Attwood v Lamont*[63] which was decided by the Court of Appeal in 1920. Younger LJ, with whom Atkin LJ agreed, apparently held that if a single restrictive covenant between employer and employee contained separate restrictions, the whole covenant would be void if one of the restrictions was invalid: the otherwise unobjectionable would fall alongside the bad one. This salutary, and not unattractive, doctrine would indeed subject employers to a significant deterrent against unreasonable behaviour. It would, in effect, confine severance in master

---

[62] [1913] A.C. 724 at 745; [1911–13] All E.R. Rep. 400 at 411.
[63] [1920] 3 K.B. 571 at 593 et seq. See also, per Neville J at first instance in *Goldsoll v Goldman* [1914] 2 Ch. 603 at 613.

and servant cases to situations in which there were separate covenants, as distinct from separate restrictions within a single covenant.[64]

19–19 **Different approach.** Half a century after *Attwood v Lamont*, however, the Court of Appeal appeared to adopt a very different approach, and one much more favourable to employers. In *T. Lucas & Co v Mitchell*[65] a single clause contained a restriction upon the employee's "dealing" in certain goods, and a restriction upon "supplying" such goods to the customers of his former employer. It was established that the restriction on "dealing" was unreasonably wide, but that on "supplying" was, in itself, reasonable. The defendant employee contended, in reliance on *Attwood v Lamont*, that even the restriction on supplying could not be enforced against him. His contention was unsuccessful. The Court of Appeal, reversing Pennycuick VC,[66] chose not to follow the reasoning of Younger LJ in *Attwood's* case, which it characterised as imposing a "third" requirement for severance. Russell LJ, delivering the judgment of the Court,[67] said[68]:

> "... if you find two restraints which as a matter of construction are to be regarded as intended by the parties to be separate and severable, and the excision of the unenforceable restraint being capable of being made without either addition or modification, there is no third question, *even in master and servant cases.*"

19–20 **Measure of control.** The language of the judgment in *T. Lucas & Co v Mitchell* seems to represent a return to an excessively formal approach, in which policy considerations are subordinated to formalistic criteria.[69] As a result of the reasoning in this case it is not easy to see how, if at all, employer and employee covenants are to be treated any differently from those between the vendor and purchaser of a business, which have traditionally been regarded less unfavourably by the courts.[70] Clearly, however, the "construction" requirement does itself confer a measure of control upon the court. An employer who wished, for example, to impose a 25 mile radial covenant, but who suspected that this would be too wide, could not include 25 separate clauses beginning at one mile and covering all the intermediate distances at mile-long intervals. The court could be relied upon to hold that this constituted, in substance, one covenant which could

---

[64] cf. *Business Seating v Broad* [1989] I.C.R. 729 at 735, per Millett J: "... there are not one but two separate covenants ... In my judgment, there is not only no difficulty grammatically in severing the two covenants but the severance leaves entirely unaffected the [enforceable] covenant".

[65] [1974] Ch. 129; [1972] 3 All E.R. 689, CA. See also *Scorer v Seymour-Johns* [1966] 1 W.L.R. 1419, CA.

[66] [1974] Ch. 129; [1972] 2 All E.R. 1035.

[67] Russell, Cairns and Stamp LJJ.

[68] [1974] Ch. 129 at 137; [1972] 3 All E.R. 689 at 694 (italics supplied).

[69] See, e.g. the decision of the Divisional Court in *Putsman v Taylor* [1927] 1 K.B. 637, discussed above.

[70] See, e.g. *Goldsoll v Goldman* [1915] 1 Ch. 292 at 300, per Swinfen-Eady LJ; *Ronbar Enterprises v Green* [1954] 1 W.L.R. 815 at 822; [1954] 2 All E.R. 266 at 271, per Hodson LJ. See also, per Lord Shaw in *Mason v Provident Clothing and Supply Co* [1913] A.C. 724 at 738; [1911–13] All E.R. Rep. 400 at 407: "... there is much greater room for allowing, as between buyer and seller, a larger scope for freedom of contract and a correspondingly large restraint in freedom of trade than there is for allowing a restraint of the opportunity for labour in a contract between master and servant or an employer and an applicant for work".

not be severed.[71] But this approach would presumably not be confined to employer and employee cases: it would surely be perceived, in any context, as an illegitimate attempt to invite the court to write the contract for the parties.[72]

Good faith?   In truth, neither the approach in *Attwood v Lamont* nor that in *T. Lucas & Co v Mitchell* is wholly satisfactory. The latter leaves employees with no real protection against oppression; while the former is apt to penalise arbitrarily employers who might genuinely have sought, albeit unsuccessfully, to confine their restrictions within permissible grounds. Sixty years ago Marsh contended persuasively that "at least in restraint of trade cases, there are now sound reasons in public policy and a considerable weight of authority for a firm rule that partial illegality avoids the whole contract, unless the party seeking to enforce the restraint can satisfy the court that the excessive part of the restraint is unlikely to have had an *in terrorem* effect".[73] The heart of the problem lies in the absence in English law of any machinery to distinguish overtly between employers who act in "good faith" when drafting restrictive covenants, and those who do not. Unless and until such machinery can be developed, the approach of Younger and Atkin LJJ in the earlier case is to be preferred to that of Russell LJ in the later one. It is more appropriate that the employer should bear the risk of injustice than that the employee should do so. **19–21**

(b) "Tainted" Contracts

Scope of the contamination?   In the Australian case of *McFarlane v Daniell*,[74]   **19–22**
Jordan CJ said[75]:

> "The exact scope and limits of the doctrine that a legal promise associated with, but severable from, an illegal promise is capable of enforcement, are not clear. It can hardly be imagined that a Court would enforce a promise, however inherently valid and however severable, if contained in a contract one of the terms of which provided for assassination."

It is evident that some terms, including the one postulated in this passage, will be so objectionable that they will contaminate the whole of the contract which contains them. They will therefore render unenforceable other provisions in the same agreement which, left to themselves, would be innocuous. Of course even in this area difficult questions may arise, in theory at least, as to what provisions are comprised in the same agreement as the objectionable one, and which form part of some separate and legitimate, but contemporaneous, agreement between the same parties. A hired assassin may buy medicine for his cough at the same time, and from the same source, as the poison for the assassination. As elsewhere

---

[71] cf. *Mason v Provident Clothing and Supply Co* [1913] A.C. 724. See also the main ground of decision in *Attwood v Lamont* [1920] 3 K.B. 571, as expressed by Younger LJ at 593: "Now, here, I think, there is in truth but one covenant for the protection of the respondent's entire business, and not several covenants for the protection of his several businesses".

[72] But quaere whether severance should not have been refused on this ground in *Goldsoll v Goldman* [1915] 1 Ch. 292, CA.

[73] See "Severance of Illegality in Contract" (1948) 64 L.Q.R. 347 at 371.

[74] (1938) 38 S.R. (N.S.W.) 337.

[75] (1938) 38 S.R. (N.S.W.) 337 at 346.

in illegality, care must be taken to ensure the presence of a rational link between the agreement and the impropriety. Even villains have rights. Should not the assassin be able to sue for impurities in the medicine?[76]

19–23   **Seriousness of the illegality.**   In practice, questions arising out of contemporaneous agreements between the same parties are less likely to occur than disputes as to whether the particular illegality in question was serious enough to contaminate the whole of the contract, of which it definitely formed a part. It is notable that until the judgments of Somervell LJ in *Bennett v Bennett* and *Goodinson v Goodinson*,[77] this question never really featured explicitly in the leading English judgments on severance. The English courts preferred to conceal their application of policy considerations behind verbal and formalistic distinctions. The position was different across the Atlantic. As Marsh points out, "the old distinction between illegal contracts which are *malum prohibitum* and those which are *malum in se*, [was] more precisely formulated and more robustly stated in American than in English law".[78] The English authorities since *Bennett v Bennett* remain scanty but, such as they are, they establish that the mere fact that a stipulation provides for the commission of a criminal offence, even one technically punishable by imprisonment, will not ipso facto contaminate the rest of the contract and render it unenforceable. The court will evidently exercise a measure of discretion, and will probably confine the rejection of severance, and total denial of enforceability, to provisions which contemplate the more serious varieties of criminality.[79]

19–24   **Company buying its own shares.**   In *Carney v Herbert*,[80] a Privy Council appeal from New South Wales, the defendant sought to avoid liability on a guarantee on the ground that part of the composite transaction, of which his guarantee formed another part, involved the provision of security for the purchase of shares in a company by one of its own subsidiaries. The transaction had therefore contravened a provision of company law, familiar in both Australia and England. The relevant legislation provided for the imposition of a fine of one thousand dollars, or imprisonment for three months, on the officers of defaulting companies.[81] The Privy Council held that this contravention had not contaminated the rest of the transaction, and was severable. The defendant was therefore liable on his guarantee since "the nature of the illegality" was *not*, in the words of Lord Brightman delivering the judgment of the Board,[82] "such as to preclude its

---

[76] Would it make a difference if suppression of the cough was necessary to avoid detection?
[77] [1954] 2 Q.B. 118, CA.
[78] See "Severance of Illegality in Contract" (1948) 64 L.Q.R. 347 at 368, and cases there cited. But see also Ch.4, above, for criticism of the distinction.
[79] Contracts which involve trading with the enemy will not be severed nor, apparently, will those analogous thereto: see *Royal Boskalis Westminster v Mountain* [1999] Q.B. 674 at 693, per Stuart-Smith LJ (breach of legislation giving effect to United Nations sanctions). cf. *Mahonia v JP Morgan Chase* [2003] EWHC 1927 per Colman J at para.68 (whether a letter of credit can be impugned for illegality in the underlying transaction may depend upon the seriousness of that illegality).
[80] [1985] A.C. 301; [1985] 1 All E.R. 438.
[81] See the Companies Act 1961 (N.S.W.) s.67.
[82] [1985] A.C. 301 at 314; [1985] 1 All E.R. 438 at 446.

enforcement 'on the ground of public policy'". In so holding, the Privy Council followed earlier authorities to the same effect in England[83] and Australia.[84]

Blameworthiness.   In one of the Australian cases, *Niemann v Smedley*,[85] the   **19–25**
Full Court of the Supreme Court of Victoria expressed itself as follows:

> "An illegal term . . . if it is of a kind involving a serious element of moral turpitude or is obviously inimical to the interest of the community so as to offend almost any concept of public policy . . . will so infect the rest of the contract that the courts will refuse to give any recognition at all to the contract, e.g. a promise to commit a burglary or to defraud the revenue or one *contra bonos mores*. But such classes apart, where the illegality has no such taint, the other terms will stand if the illegal portion can be severed."

The inclusion of defrauding the revenue in this passage is notable, and in *Carney v Herbert* the Privy Council itself observed[86] that in *Miller v Karlinski*[87] the Court of Appeal in England had held that schemes to avoid income tax, by paying bogus "expenses", could contaminate the rest of the employment contract. On the other hand, even in revenue cases it is clear that the courts will exercise a measure of flexibility.[88] Accordingly, the degree of blameworthiness of the party seeking to avoid the contract may be taken into account when deciding upon the denial of severance through "contamination". In *Fielding and Platt v Najjar*[89] the defendants, a Lebanese company, attempted to avoid liability on a contract on the ground that the claimant vendors had, at the defendants' own request, agreed to issue a false invoice. The attempt failed. Lord Denning MR said[90]:

> ". . . even if there was a term that these goods should be invoiced falsely in order to deceive the Lebanese authorities, I do not think it would render the whole contract void. That term would be void for illegality. But it can clearly be severed from the rest of the contract. It can be rejected, leaving the rest of the contract good and enforceable."

6.   CONCLUSION

Damaging reticence.   There is continuing scope for further judicial clarifica-   **19–26**
tion of the doctrine of severance in illegality cases. There is, of course, an unavoidable degree of uncertainty resulting from the need to consider each contract individually. Nevertheless, this is one of those areas where the persistent reticence of the English judiciary with respect to the overt discussion of policy issues is particularly damaging. The temptation simply to manipulate formalistic tests, in order to produce a desired result, still has the potential to cause additional, avoidable, uncertainty.

---

[83] See *South Western Mineral Water Co v Ashmore* [1967] 1 W.L.R. 1110, especially at 1120, per Cross J.
[84] See. e.g. *Thomas Brown & Sons v Fazal Deen* (1962) 108 C.L.R. 391 (High Court of Australia).
[85] [1973] V.R. 769 at 778.
[86] [1985] A.C. 301 at 311; [1985] 1 All E.R. 438 at 444.
[87] (1945) 62 T.L.R. 85. See Ch.7, above.
[88] cf. *Tinsley v Milligan* [1994] 1 A.C. 340. See also Ch.7, and cases there cited.
[89] [1969] 1 W.L.R. 357; [1969] 2 All E.R. 150. See Ch.4. above.
[90] [1969] 1 W.L.R. 357 at 362; [1969] 2 All E.R. 150 at 153.

PART 5

REFORM

CHAPTER 20

THE NEW ZEALAND ILLEGAL CONTRACTS ACT 1970

1. Introduction

Comprehensive reform. In 1970, New Zealand became the first, and so far the only, Commonwealth jurisdiction to enact legislation intended to bring about comprehensive reform of the law relating to illegality in contract. The Act and its working have been the subject of close scrutiny by law reform bodies in Australia, Canada and the UK. Some examination of the New Zealand legislation, and the cases which have been decided upon it, is therefore appropriate.[1]

20–01

2. Provisions of the Act

(a) Definition and Scope

Common law preserved. The inherently vague and undefined nature of such notions as "illegality" and "public policy" is a difficulty which confronts any attempt at statutory reform of this branch of the law at the outset. There is a danger that imprecise statutory wording could turn out to have unexpected consequences much wider than those intended. The approach to the problem of definition adopted in New Zealand is simply to adopt and preserve the relevant common law. Section 3 of the Act provides as follows:

20–02

> "3. **'Illegal contract' defined**—
>
> Subject to section 5 of this Act, for the purposes of this Act the term 'illegal contract' means any contract governed by New Zealand law that is illegal at law or in equity, whether the illegality arises from the creation or performance of the contract; and includes a contract which contains an illegal provision, whether that provision is severable or not."

This provision has been criticised on the ground that, as the common law is itself far from clear as to what constitutes an "illegal contract", it is an inappropriate basis for a statutory regime, and could be a potential source of destabilising uncertainty over a wide area of the law of contract.[2]

---

[1] The provisions relating to restraint of trade are dealt with separately: see Ch.13, above. Minor amendments to the 1970 Act were made by the Illegal Contracts Amendment Act 2002.
[2] See Furmston, "The Illegal Contracts Act 1970—An English View" (1972) 5 N.Z.U.L.R. pp.151 at 155 et seq. cf. Brian Coote. "Validation Under the Illegal Contracts Act" (1992) 15 N.Z.U.L.R. 80.

20–03 **"Performance".** In order to reduce the breadth of s.3, the Act does itself seek to limit the situations which the use of the word "performance" in that section could encompass. Section 5 thus provides as follows:

> "5. **Breach of enactment—**
> A contract lawfully entered into shall not become illegal or unenforceable by any party by reason of the fact that its performance is in breach of any enactment, unless the enactment expressly so provides or its object clearly so requires."

The qualification contained in this section does preclude the argument that *any* infringement committed in the course of performing a contract could have the effect of bringing the Act into play. But the technique of statutory interpretation which it adopts in order to do so is one which is apt to prove artificial and uncertain.[3]

(b) Nullification and Validation

20–04 **Enforceability.** The Act implements a radical approach to the problems surrounding the enforceability of contracts affected by illegality. Its technique is to declare every "illegal contract" invalid, but then to confer a broad discretion on the court to reverse that invalidity. Sections 6(1) and 7(1) provide as follows:

> "6. **Illegal contracts to be of no effect—**
> (1) Notwithstanding any rule of law or equity to the contrary, but subject to the provisions of this Act and of any other enactment, every illegal contract shall be of no effect and no person shall become entitled to any property[4] under a disposition made by or pursuant to any such contract: Provided that nothing in this section shall invalidate—
> (a) Any disposition of property by a party to an illegal contract for valuable consideration . . . if the person to whom the disposition was made was not a party to the illegal contract and had not at the time of the disposition notice that the property was the subject of, or the whole or part of the consideration for, an illegal contract and otherwise acts in good faith.
> (b) . . .
> 7. **Court may grant relief—**
> (1) Notwithstanding the provisions of section 6 of this Act, but subject to the express provisions of any other enactment, the Court may in the course of any proceedings, or on application made for the purpose, grant to—
> (a) Any party to an illegal contract; or
> (b) Any party to a contract who is disqualified from enforcing it by reason of the commission of an illegal act in the course of its performance; or
> (c) Any person claiming through or under any such party—
> such relief by way of restitution, compensation, variation of the contract, validation of the contract in whole or part or for any particular purpose, or otherwise howsoever as the Court in its discretion thinks just."

---

[3] See Ch.2, above, for criticism of the view that statutes which neither expressly, nor impliedly, refer to contracts can nevertheless "prohibit" them. See also Enonchong, *Illegal Transactions* (Lloyd's of London Press, 1998), Ch.1, pp.3–8.

[4] " 'Property' means land, money, goods, things in action, goodwill, and every valuable thing, whether real or personal, and whether situated in New Zealand or elsewhere; and includes obligations, easements, and every description of estate, interest, and profit, present or future, vested or contingent, arising out of or incident to property": s.2.

Width of approach is striking.   This combination of general nullification   **20–05**
accompanied by a power to "validate", and thereby enforce in full, all contracts
considered by the existing law to be "illegal" is striking. It has been criticised on
the ground that it is inappropriate for the court expressly to have the power to
enforce agreements which, *ex hypothesi* had previously been considered
undesirable by the common law or the legislature.[5] The width of the general
"definition" in s.3 means that the court has the power to disregard the reasons for
declining to enforce contracts across the whole field of illegality, from those
condemned by the common law concept of "public policy" to those prohibited by
the legislature.[6] In the context of statutory illegality in particular, the New
Zealand courts have not been hesitant in making full use of the powers conferred
on them by the Act.[7] Notwithstanding the criticisms, the domestic reception to the
activity of the courts in this respect appears broadly to have been favourable.[8]

(c)   Property Rights

Common law abrogated.   As discussed in an earlier chapter,[9] the proposition   **20–06**
that at common law property which was transferred pursuant to an illegal
transaction can vest in the transferee, notwithstanding the illegality, appears to be
well-established. The potential arbitrariness of this principle, particularly where
the transfer of limited interests is involved, has also been discussed above; along
with the artificial concept of "reliance" which has often featured in the relevant
cases. The New Zealand Act adopts a particularly radical approach to the
problem. The general principle that property can pass under an illegal contract is
itself abrogated by s.6(1) of the Illegal Contracts Act 1970,[10] and all dispositions
of property made under such contracts are prima facie ineffective except where

---

[5] The Act was criticised on this ground by the Law Reform Commission of British Columbia in its
1983 *Report on Illegal Transactions*, and by the Ontario Law Reform Commission in Ch.11 of its
1987 *Amendment to the Law of Contract*. Both these reports are discussed in Ch.21, below.
[6] The Act was prompted, at least in part, by difficulties experienced in determining whether failure to
comply with a statutory provision requiring a "warranty of fitness", to accompany the sale of a
motor-vehicle, rendered the contract of sale unenforceable for illegality. The issue led to a series of
sharply conflicting decisions: see *Dromorne Linen Co v Ward* [1963] N.Z.L.R. 614 and *Berrett v
Smith* [1965] N.Z.L.R. 460 (favouring illegality); and *Fenton v Scotty's Car Sales* [1968] N.Z.L.R.
929 (favouring enforceability). For comment see D. M. McCrae in 1968 N.Z.L.J. 424.
[7] See below for a brief review of the cases. It is of interest that those responsible for the Act expected
that a narrower interpretation would be put upon it than that actually adopted. The power to
"validate", in particular, has been used less sparingly than the framers of the legislation apparently
intended: see Brian Coote, "Validation Under the Illegal Contracts Act" (1992) 15 N.Z.U.L.R. 80.
Coote concludes (at p.145) that, "experience with the Illegal Contracts Act demonstrates that if a
limitation on a jurisdiction is intended it ought to be stated and not merely left to be inferred".
[8] See the New Zealand Law Commission, *Contract Statutes Review* (1993) pp.17–21 (cited by the
Law Commission in England in its 1999 *Consultation Paper on Illegal Transactions* (Law Com.
No.154), para.7.9). See also Andrew Beck, "Illegality and the Courts' Discretion: The New Zealand
Illegal Contracts Act in Action" (1989) 13 N.Z.U.L.R. 389. For recent consideration of the scope of
the Act in the New Zealand Supreme Court see *Hickman v Turner and Waverley Ltd* [2012] NZSC 72;
[2013] 1 NLZR 741 at [131]-[134] per Mitting J.
[9] See Ch.16. above.
[10] ". . . every illegal contract shall be of no effect and no person shall become entitled to any property
under a disposition made by or pursuant to any such contract".

made in favour of third parties who took for valuable consideration, without notice of the illegality. But s.7(5) then provides as follows:

> "(5) The Court may by any order made under subsection (1) of this section vest any property that was the subject of, or the whole or part of the consideration for, an illegal contract in any party to the proceedings or may direct any such party to transfer or assign any such property to any other party to the proceedings."

20–07 **Approach not favoured elsewhere.** The specific provision contained in this subsection is in addition to the general power under the Act to "validate" the contract,[11] and hence any dispositions of property made thereunder. The New Zealand approach has not found favour with law reform bodies elsewhere, which have generally preferred to recommend that any proposed reforms should operate against the background of the common law rule, relating to the transfer of property, remaining intact.[12] Criticism has focused upon the need for security of title, particularly with respect to the transfer of land. Attention has also been drawn to the potentially anomalous consequence of the New Zealand legislation that it apparently leaves title in the grantor, while simultaneously depriving him of a remedy to vindicate that title if he happens to have parted with possession.[13]

(d)   Discretion

20–08 **Relevant factors.** Section 7(3) of the Act provides as follows:

> "(3) In considering whether to grant relief under subsection (1) of this section the Court shall have regard to—
> (a) The conduct of the parties; and
> (b) In the case of a breach of an enactment, the object of the enactment and the gravity of the penalty expressly provided for any breach thereof; and
> (c) Such other matters as it thinks proper–but shall not grant relief if it considers that to do so would not be in the public interest."

The discretion thus conferred by the Act, combined with the power to regulate the disposition of property, is notable for its extreme width; and the guidance provided for its exercise by this subsection is expressed in very general terms. A significant consequence of such a broad formula is that it allows the court to apportion any losses occurring as a result of a contract being held to be unenforceable for illegality. Some of the cases considered below illustrate the use to which the New Zealand courts have put their discretion.

---

[11] See s.7(1)(c), discussed above.
[12] See Ch.21, below.
[13] See the *Report on Illegal Transactions* by the Law Reform Commission of British Columbia, 1983. pp.81–83.

3. THE OPERATION OF THE ACT

Statutory reform in practice. In so far as the relatively small number of cases reported during the 40 or so years of its existence is any guide, the Act has not generated the degree of uncertainty which some anticipated.[14] The cases on the Act are, however, of considerable interest; not least for those elsewhere considering statutory reform of illegality. A central issue surrounds the relationship between any new statutory jurisdiction in this area, and the rest of the law. Is there a danger of creating anomaly whereby parties to illegal contracts may paradoxically enjoy *preferential* treatment, as compared with those whose contracts fail for other reasons? One context in which this question arises concerns the desirability or otherwise of conferring a broad power to *adjust* the rights of the parties. Is there also a danger of undermining the legitimate policies and objectives of earlier legislation, or of the common law itself? The New Zealand experience provides a unique opportunity to view the response of judges to these issues in practice.

20–09

(a) Adjusting Rights

Flexibility. The New Zealand judiciary has not hesitated to take full advantage of the flexibility afforded by the wide language of s.7 of the Illegal Contracts Act to adjust the positions of the parties to an illegal contract when granting relief, occasionally even to prevent movements in the market from impacting harshly upon one party or the other. A possible objection to such adjustment is, of course, that such relief is not afforded to victims of unfortunate bargains by the general law of contract. The New Zealand decisions nevertheless demonstrate the advantages which such flexibility can provide, at any rate when illegality is considered in isolation from the rest of the law. In its absence, relief rigidly confined, for example, to "all or nothing" reversal of unjust enrichment, may occasionally produce results unattractively at variance with the parties' differing degrees of responsibility for, and guilty involvement in, the illegality itself.

20–10

Fraud. In *Duncan v McDonald*[15] a group of confidence-tricksters persuaded Duncan, a solicitor, to advance to them NZ $285,000 from an estate of which he was a trustee. The money would be used to bribe officials of a foreign government to over-invoice contracts with that government. Part of the very substantial proceeds of that over-invoicing would then be shared with Duncan. In order to protect the estate, Duncan persuaded the McDonalds to mortgage their property in the estate's favour, with the inducement that they also would benefit substantially. In fact the NZ $285,000 were irretrievably lost, and the proceeds never materialised. Although Duncan and the McDonalds were therefore themselves the victims of fraud, the arrangement into which they had entered was itself illegal, since it had contemplated the commission of a fraud upon the foreign government. Their degree of involvement had, however, differed. Duncan

20–11

---

[14] cf. Furmston 'The Illegal Contracts Act 1970—An English View" (1972) 5 N.Z.U.L.R. 151.
[15] [1997] 3 N.Z.L.R. 669.

was the instigator, and appears to have been fully aware of what was proposed. He represented to the McDonalds that the venture was "legal and risk-free"; but the trial judge found that the rate of return promised to them was such that they also must have realised that the mortgage was to further an illegal venture. The question arose as to how the loss of NZ $285,000 to the estate was to be made good. In the Court of Appeal Blanchard J, delivering the judgment of the court, said that "the just solution to the problem created for the estate by Mr Duncan's breach of trust would be that Mr Duncan should be the primary source of recoupment of the lost moneys and that the McDonalds should bear the lesser share".[16] In granting relief under the Illegal Contracts Act the Court declared the mortgage on the McDonalds' property to be valid to the extent of NZ $75,000, and held that the estate should look to Duncan for the balance for his breach of trust. If, however, Duncan proved unable to satisfy the claim against him, any shortfall would become recoverable from the McDonalds.[17]

20–12 **Illegal sales.** Several other cases in which relief has been granted under the Illegal Contracts Act concerned contracts for the sale of land, which had contravened statutory requirements. In validating the contracts the courts have been prepared to apportion any losses or gains, resulting from the delay pending validation, between the parties so as to reflect their differing degrees of responsibility for what had occurred.[18] A flexible approach has also been adopted when validating contracts involving motor-cars, which were illegal due to contravention of statutory restrictions on the supply of credit. In one such case, *Evans v Credit Services*,[19] in which a "glib but unreliable" car salesman was regarded as "the 'villain in the piece'", whereas the "uncomplicated" claimant's part had been "essentially one of quiescence",[20] McMullin J expressed himself as follows[21]:

> "In granting relief, there is no room for the award of punitive damages at the suit of a person who applies for the exercise of that relief. But that is not to say that the Court cannot, in deciding on the measure of relief, take account of the part played by each party ... A consideration of those matters may result in the grant of relief in one case and its refusal in another or it may reflect itself in the measure of relief granted."

In the result ownership of the motor-car was vested in the claimant, and he was also excused from making any further payments under the contract. At the same time, however, the courts have been alert to the danger, when granting relief in cases of this type, of allowing the Illegal Contracts Act to be used purely as a basis for affording escape from the terms of disadvantageous agreements.[22]

---

[16] [1997] 3 N.Z.L.R. 669 at 685.

[17] "The beneficiaries are entirely innocent of any involvement in the transaction. The McDonalds are not" per Blanchard J in [1997] 3 N.Z.L.R. 669 at 686.

[18] See, e.g. *France v Might* [1987] 2 N.Z.L.R. 38. See also *Bevin v Smith* [1994] 3 N.Z.L.R. 648.

[19] [1975] 2 N.Z.L.R. 560.

[20] [1975] 2 N.Z.L.R. 560 at 563–564, per McMullin J (quoting from the judgment of Woodhouse J in earlier proceedings).

[21] [1975] 2 N.Z.L.R. at 565. See also, per Woodhouse and Cooke JJ in *Broadlands Rentals Ltd v R. D. Bull Ltd* [1976] 2 N.Z.L.R. 595 at 600.

[22] See *Broadlands Rentals Ltd v R. D. Bull Ltd* [1976] 2 N.Z.L.R. 595 in which the order of the trial judge was varied as having been unduly favourable to "a rather unsophisticated individual" (per

(b)   Potential Conflict with Legitimate Policies

Danger of anomaly.   In one case a party who wished to prevent the grant of   **20–13**
relief under the Illegal Contracts Act argued that a transaction had merely been
"unenforceable" rather than "illegal"[23]; but the Court held that the contract had
been illegal, and that the Act could therefore be invoked. The point had been
noted by Cooke J[24] in one of the early cases decided under the Act, when he
observed that:

> "... anomalies ... may flow from the fact that the Illegal Contracts Act is in the main
> concerned with illegal contracts and not with contracts that are merely void by statute.
> Perhaps, in the absence of a corresponding power of validation, unfair results can still flow as
> regards contracts which are merely void."[25]

Nevertheless, in that case also the Court held that the contract had actually
been illegal so that the discretion was available.

Other enactments.   A more general question is whether, even where the   **20–14**
jurisdiction unquestionably exists, its exercise should be refused lest the purpose
of another statute would be subverted. In *Harding v Coburn*[26] Cooke J
emphasised that "it is no part of the purposes of the Illegal Contracts Act to
undermine the social or economic policies of other enactments".[27] In several
cases relief under s.7 of the Act has been refused on this ground.[28] One feature
which does emerge clearly from the cases on this aspect of the exercise of the
discretion is the highly ad hoc approach which is adopted: the court examines
carefully the precise contractual situation in question as well as the purpose of the
other statute. As a result, while relief will sometimes be refused on the basis that
it would undermine the purpose of another statute, in other cases involving the
same provision relief will be granted.[29] It is submitted that this is a useful

---

Chilwell J at first instance in [1975] 1 N.Z.L.R. 304 at 309). The Court of Appeal observed that the
Act "provides for a discretionary lifting of burdens, not for a distribution of windfalls", (per
Woodhouse and Cooke JJ in [1976] 2 N.Z.L.R. at 600).
[23] See *Howick Building Co Ltd v Howick Parklands Ltd* [1993] 1 N.Z.L.R. at 759–760.
[24] Now Lord Cooke of Thorndon.
[25] See *Harding v Coburn* [1976] 2 N.Z.L.R. 577 at 587. The point arises because s.7(1) of the Illegal
Contracts Act makes the availability of relief "subject to the express provisions of any other
enactment": see, e.g. *Parker v Rock Finance Corporation Ltd* [1981] 1 N.Z.L.R. 488 at 493; *Dreadon
v Fletcher Development Co Ltd* [1974] 2 N.Z.L.R. 11 at 19.
[26] [1976] 2 N.Z.L.R. 577 at 584–5.
[27] See also *Hurrell v Townend* [1976] 2 N.Z.L.R. 577 at 584–5.
[28] See *Euro-National Corporation v NZI Bank Ltd* [1992] 2 N.Z.L.R. 739; *Edwards v O'Connor*
[1989] 3 N.Z.L.R. 448; *Lower Hutt City Council v Martin* [1987] 1 N.Z.L.R. 321. *Leith v Gould*
[1986] 1 N.Z.L.R. 760.
[29] In several cases involving financial assistance by a company for the purchase of its own shares
(contrary to New Zealand Companies Act 1955 s.62) relief amounting to enforceability has been held
to be available: see *Catley v Herbert* [1988] 1 N.Z.L.R. 606; *Coleman v Myers* [1977] 2 N.Z.L.R. 225
at 378. But in other cases involving the same provision it has been denied: see *Euro-National
Corporation v NZI Bank Ltd* [1992] 2 N.Z.L.R. 739 and *Hoverd Industries Ltd v Supercool
Refrigeration, etc., Ltd* [1994] 3 N.Z.L.R. 300 (reversed on other grounds in [1995] 3 N.Z.L.R. 577).
Similarly, relief is frequently granted in cases involving New Zealand Land Settlement Promotion and
Acquisition Act 1952 s.52: see, e.g. *Bevin v Smith* [1994] 3 N.Z.L.R. 648; *Williams v Gibbons* [1994]

demonstration of the benefits which an overt statutory discretion can provide in illegality cases. The granting or refusal of relief often depends upon whether the illegality was the result of deliberation or oversight.[30] This in itself provides a sharp contrast with the confusion, and apparent rigidity, which has often appeared to prevail at common law.[31]

20–15   **Public policy.**   It was suggested judicially in one case that, notwithstanding the broad definition of an "illegal contract" in s.3, "it would be wrong in principle to apply the Act" so as "to validate a contract which was illegal from the outset as being contrary to public policy".[32] Although this dictum was subsequently disapproved,[33] and it has been emphasised judicially that the jurisdiction exists in all its plenitude in such cases,[34] it is perhaps significant that there appears to be no reported decision in which full "validation" of a contract illegal solely for reasons of public policy has actually been granted. The overwhelming majority of cases decided under the Act concern statutory illegality.

---

1 N.Z.L.R. 273; *Hurrell v Townend* [1982] 1 N.Z.L.R. 536. In another such case, however, *Leith v Gould* [1986] 1 N.Z.L.R. 760, relief was refused on the ground that "to validate the transaction would be totally to avoid the operation of the legislation and necessarily to vitiate the object of the enactment" (per Ongley J at 768).

[30] See, especially, *Euro-National Corporation v NZI Bank Ltd* [1992] 2 N.Z.L.R. 739 at 766–767.

[31] cf. per Devlin J in *St John Shipping Corporation v Joseph Rank* [1957] 1 Q.B. 267 at 283: ". . . the court will not enforce a contract which is expressly or impliedly prohibited by statute. If the contract is of this class it does not matter what the intent of the parties is; if the statute prohibits the contract, it is unenforceable whether the parties meant to break the law or not".

[32] See *Bardsell v Kerr* [1979] 2 N.Z.L.R. 731 at 737–738, per Quilliam J (contract to stifle a prosecution). See also *Peters v Collinge* [1993] 2 N.Z.L.R. 554 (contract to preclude a person from standing for Parliament).

[33] See *Phillips v Foster* [1991] 3 N.Z.L.R. 263 at 265–266, per Cooke P. See also *Polymer Developments Group v Tilialo* [2002] 3 N.Z.L.R. in which Glazebrook J applied the Act to grant relief in a situation involving a contract to stifle a prosecution.

[34] See *Mall Finance & Investment Co Ltd v Slater* [1976] 2 N.Z.L.R. 685 at 689, per Cooke J. But cf. the reversed decision of White J at first instance in [1976] 2 N.Z.L.R. 1.

CHAPTER 21

REFORM PROPOSALS IN COMMONWEALTH JURISDICTIONS

1. INTRODUCTION

Similarities and differences.[1]   In addition to New Zealand, where the **21–01** deliberations actually resulted in legislation, law reform bodies in several other Commonwealth jurisdictions have considered the desirability of change in the area of illegality.[2] These include reports by the Law Reform Commission of British Columbia in 1983,[3] the Ontario Law Reform Commission in 1987,[4] the Singapore Academy of Law in 2002,[5] and the Law Reform Committee of South Australia in 1977.[6] Moreover, in early 2009 the Law Commission in England issued a "Consultative Report" on *The Illegality Defence*,[7] followed in 2010 by a briefer final report with the same title, which reflected changes in the approach of the Commission since it published a previous consultation paper on the subject a decade earlier.[8] Indeed, in view of the complexity and difficulty of this branch of the law, it is not surprising that the various reports reveal important differences in approach as well as significant similarities. In this chapter the recommendations of the two Canadian reports will be summarised briefly, along with those from Australia and Singapore. Although none of these reports has yet been implemented formally, it does not follow that they have been without influence. Next, the recommendations of the Law Commission in England will be outlined. A later part of the chapter will look at cases which suggest that even the unimplemented reports from the other jurisdictions may already have had a positive effect on the development of the common law in those jurisdictions. A concluding section will briefly summarise the relevant developments in English law in recent times. These presented a rather confused and erratic picture prior to

---

[1] What follows is based in part on my article "Illegal Transactions: Chaos or Discretion?" (2000) L.S. 155.
[2] See Ch.20, above. Another jurisdiction, outside the Commonwealth, which has enacted legislation is Israel. Israeli Contract (General Part) 1973 s.31 confers an overt discretion upon the court to relieve against the consequences of illegality. For discussion, see Daniel Friedmann. "Consequences of Illegality Under the Israeli Contract Law (General Part) 1973" (1984) 33 I.C.L.Q. 81.
[3] See the *Report on Illegal Transactions* (hereinafter the *Report*).
[4] See *Amendment to the Law of Contract*, Ch.11.
[5] See Singapore Academy of law, "Relief from Unenforceability of Illegal Contracts and Trusts" (5 July 2002): available online at *http://lawnet.com.sg*.
[6] See the *Thirty-Seventh Report Relating to the Doctrines of Frustration and Illegality in the Law of Contract*.
[7] See Law Commission Consultation Paper No.189.
[8] See *Illegal Transactions: The Effect of Illegality on Contracts and Trusts*, Law Commission Consultation Paper No.154 (1999).

the ground-breaking decision of a nine-member Supreme Court in *Patel v Mirza*.[9] It is clear from the reasoning of the majority in this case that the various reform proposals, in this jurisdiction and elsewhere, have also had an influence on the formulation of judicial thinking in England.

2. BRITISH COLUMBIA

21–02   **Need for forthright approach.**   In its *Report on Illegal Transactions*, issued in 1983, the Law Commission of British Columbia reviewed the "common law governing the rights of parties to illegal transactions", including "not only contracts, but also non-contractual arrangements such as trusts and gifts". It observed that the existing common law position concealed the key question of "whether the effect of the contract is contrary to public policy" behind obscure technicalities and was "in disarray and, perforce, complex". It was instead "preferable that the issues involved in granting or denying relief [should] be reviewed objectively and forthrightly".

21–03   **Relief against the consequences of illegality.**   The model for legislative reform, favoured by the Commission, was the conferring upon the court of a discretionary power to give relief against the consequences of illegality. The power would operate against the background of the existing "general rule" of unenforceability, which would be preserved. The Commission was exercised, however, as to the relationship which should exist between the new discretionary power and those situations in which, by way of established "exceptions" to the "general rule", the common law itself permits enforceability. The Commission defined these[10] as including situations in which the "parties are not *in pari delicto*", the "plaintiff is a member of a protected class" and the "plaintiff need not rely on the illegal transaction". Correspondents to the Commission's working paper had been divided on the question whether these "exceptions" should be retained, with the new discretion fulfilling a supplementary role, or entirely replaced.

21–04   **Exceptions to be superseded.**   The conclusion reached on this point was to favour the latter view: the existing "exceptions" should be superseded by the new statutory discretion, on the ground that "much of the beneficial effect of reforming legislation would . . . be lost if the court is obliged to grant a remedy when it would be unjust to do so merely because the claimant falls within an exception to the general rule".[11] The same approach is adopted in the New Zealand Illegal Contracts Act.[12] The Commission did, however, consider that the existing common law on the effectiveness of illegal transactions actually to transfer title to property should not, as such, be abrogated by the proposed

---

[9] [2016] UKSC 42. See, generally, above, especially Chs 1, 17 and 18.
[10] See the *Report*, Ch.V.
[11] *Report*, p.58.
[12] "Subject to the express provisions of any other enactment, no Court shall, in respect of any illegal contract, grant relief to any person otherwise than in accordance with the provisions of this Act": s.7(7).

legislation.[13] On this issue it therefore differed from the New Zealand Act.[14] The court should, however, be given "a discretionary jurisdiction to vary property rights as appears just".[15]

Definition. The Law Reform Commission of British Columbia also considered the definition of "illegal contract" in the New Zealand Act to be unsatisfactory and recommended that the legislation, which it proposed, should incorporate a definition of an "illegal transaction"[16] in the following terms[17]:

21–05

> "... any transaction which is null, void, illegal, unlawful, invalid, unenforceable, or otherwise ineffective, or in respect of which no action or proceeding may be brought by reason of:
> (a)   an enactment or a provision in an enactment, or
> (b)   a rule of the common law or equity, relating to public policy, governing the formation, existence or performance of the transaction."

In view of the width of this definition the Commission recommended[18] that it should be supplemented by other provisions, so as to exclude transactions rendered unenforceable by factors such as frustration or limitation of actions. Invalidity on account of the doctrine of restraint of trade would also be excluded. The scope of statutory illegality would be limited by the use of phraseology similar to that in s.5 of the New Zealand Act but, unlike that Act, the statutory interpretation test would *not* be confined to cases of "performance" alone.[19] As far as "performance" itself was concerned, the British Columbia Commission was anxious not so much to *narrow* the scope of its proposed legislation as to prevent it from being *unduly* narrowed by "any jurisdictional argument based on the 'innocence' of the plaintiff".[20] The fear was that an action by such a claimant might be considered not to involve illegality at all, and hence to be outside the scope of the proposed Act; a consequence which the Commission considered would be unfortunate in view of the deliberately wide-ranging nature of the jurisdiction which it was proposed to confer upon the court.[21]

Remedies. In relation to remedies the Commission considered whether the court should merely be given the power to grant "such relief as appears just", or whether a specific list of remedies should be provided. It decided upon the latter, and recommended that the court should have the power to make an order for one

21–06

---

[13] "... the adoption of a provision barring the passing of title under an illegal transaction is not warranted": *Report*, p.81.

[14] cf. s.6(1), see Ch.20, above.

[15] *Report*, p.82.

[16] "We cannot agree with those of our correspondents who were of the view that it was unnecessary to define 'illegal contract' beyond affirming that the meaning of that term at common law is to govern": *Report*, p.67.

[17] *Report*, p.67.

[18] *Report*, p.73.

[19] "An Illegal Transaction Act should provide that a transaction not be regarded as an illegal transaction by reason that its *formation* or performance is in breach of an enactment, or contrary to the object of an enactment, unless the object of the enactment clearly so requires" *Report*, p.70 (italics supplied). See also *Report* at p.69: "... strictly speaking, the benevolent rule ... should apply equally to the formation of a transaction". For New Zealand Act s.5, see previous chapter.

[20] *Report*, p.70.

[21] See para.21–06, below.

or more remedies from a list which included restitution, compensation, a declaration and an order vesting property in any person.[22] The list also included, however, two provisions of special note. It included expressly power to order "apportionment of loss arising from the formation or performance of the transaction provided that no loss of profits shall be so apportioned".[23] By way of analogy the Commission referred to the legislative power to apportion in relation to frustrated contracts.[24] Moreover, the final item in the list read:

> "any other remedy the court could have granted under common law or equity had the transaction not been an illegal transaction."[25]

This suggested power is significant because it would seem to confer upon the court the power actually to *enforce* an illegal contract, whereas the draftsmen of the same report had earlier stated their hostility to an express power of enforcement.[26] This apparent tension within the recommendations is noted in the *Report* itself,[27] but the Commission nevertheless emphasised that the powers conferred should "include damages, declarations, injunctive relief, and specific performance". They conclude that while this may occasionally "amount to something akin to validation", in most cases it would not "be necessary for courts to go that far".[28]

21–07   **Discretionary factors.**   The Commission made detailed recommendations as to the factors which the courts should take into account when exercising the proposed statutory discretion. In so doing they gave specific consideration to the *locus poenitentiae* doctrine,[29] the only one of the Commonwealth law reform bodies to do so prior to the deliberations of the Law Commission in England. The *Report* noted that the Canadian courts were apparently prepared to allow withdrawal prior to "substantial performance", but also that interpreting this requirement, along with those of repentance and "magnitude of harm", involved the courts in "the exercise of a certain amount of discretion".[30] In recommending that the court should be given an overt discretion by statute to grant or deny relief in cases of illegality, the Commission proposed that "the extent to which the illegal transaction has been performed" should be one of the specific matters to

---

[22] *Report*, p.79.

[23] See *Report*, p.79, and the Draft British Columbia Illegal Transaction Act (Appendix E to the *Report*) s.5(l)(c). Such a power of apportionment has been provisionally rejected by the Law Commission in England (see below), but has been adopted in New Zealand (see previous chapter).

[24] *Report*, p.79.

[25] See s.5(l) of the Draft British Columbia Illegal Transaction Act (Appendix R to the *Report*).

[26] "If a transaction is illegal in the sense that it violates a statute, there is no justification for permitting courts to override completely the policy of the statute. Although we are more hesitant concerning transactions which are contrary to public policy, the reason such transactions fall within an Illegal Transaction Act in the first place is because, in the perception of the judge, enforcing that contract would have pernicious results. Preventing unjust enrichments or unfair results does not require going to the opposite extreme and ordering the very result which is said to be contrary to statute or harmful to society": *Report*, pp.74–75.

[27] *Report*, p.76.

[28] *Report*, p.76.

[29] See Ch.18 above.

[30] *Report*, p.23.

which the court should be required to have regard.[31] The list of factors recommended as relevant to the exercise of the discretion in general also included the public interest; the knowledge of the parties including any mistake of fact or law; and the object of any relevant statute, including the extent to which it may have been substantially complied with. The list concluded by suggesting that reference may finally be had to "the consequences to any person of denying relief" and "any other relevant factor".[32]

3.   ONTARIO

Similar to British Columbia.   The reform proposals of the Ontario Law   **21–08**
Reform Commission are to be found in Chapter 11 of its *Amendment of the Law of Contract*, published in 1987. Under the general heading, "Contracts that Infringe Public Policy", Ch.11 considers "contracts illegal at common law, and contracts illegal by statute",[33] including, in the former category, agreements in restraint of trade. The general approach of the Ontario Commission is broadly similar to that favoured by the Law Reform Commission of British Columbia, already outlined.

Unenforceability to be retained.   The Commission noted the anomalous   **21–09**
results sometimes produced by the general rule that, once a contract is found to be unenforceable for illegality, the court will not intervene to assist either party. In particular, it noted the propensity of this principle to cause hardship in cases of seemingly trivial statutory illegality, and cited the Ontario case of *Kingshott v Brunskill*.[34] In that case an "entirely technical" infringement of regulations relating to the grading of apples was invoked successfully, without merit, in a contractual dispute between two farmers as to the price of the crop sold, so as to prevent the seller from recovering the purchase price. At the same time, however, the Commission considered that it would be inappropriate to interfere with the existing law relating to the actual *unenforceability* of contracts affected by illegality. It referred to the nullification of illegal contracts, even for the purpose of transferring title to property, under s.6 of the New Zealand Illegal Contracts Act, and concluded that "there are dangers in this approach"; in particular because that approach involves, in the statutory sphere, the court being given the power to enforce contracts which the legislature had elsewhere intended should not be enforced; and "the problem of when a specific statute had the effect of displacing the general provision would be acute".[35] The Commission therefore concluded "that the wiser course is to omit any provision making ineffective the transfer of title to property and to omit any general power to declare valid, contracts that are illegal".

---

[31] See *Report*, at p.80. See also the draft British Columbia Illegal Transaction Act (Appendix E to the *Report*), s.6(1)(d).
[32] *Report*, p.80.
[33] *Amendment of the Law of Contract*, p.232.
[34] [1953] O.W.N. 133.
[35] *Amendment of the Law of Contract*, p.232.

21–10 **Consequences.** Alongside retention of the existing law relating to unenforce-ability, however, the Ontario Commission recommended, as their British Columbia colleagues had done earlier, that the court should be given power to relieve against the *consequences* of illegality: "in particular by granting an order for restitution and compensation for loss". The Commission considered that such a power would "enable the court to do justice in cases like *Kingshott v Brunskill* where, under the present law, injustices have occurred". Limited reform along these lines was considered to be "as much as can be expected of statutory reform in the area", but that was "an object well worth achieving".[36] The formal recommendation was expressed as follows[37]:

> "The existing common law doctrines with respect to illegal contracts should be retained, but the court should be given power to relieve against the consequences of illegality. Accordingly, legislation should be enacted to provide that, where a contract or any term thereof is unenforceable by reason of public policy (including the effect of any statutory provision) the court may grant such relief by way of restitution and compensation for loss or otherwise as it thinks just and as is not inconsistent with the policy underlying the unenforceability of the contract."

In exercising the proposed power the court would be expected to "take into account such factors as the gravity of the violation committed by the parties, whether it goes to the heart of the contract, and whether the parties knew or ought to have known that they were breaching the law".[38]

4. SOUTH AUSTRALIA

21–11 **1977 Report.** South Australia was the first common law jurisdiction after New Zealand in which proposals for reform of the law on illegality were formally advanced. The recommendations were published in 1977 in the "Thirty-Seventh Report" of the Law Reform Committee of South Australia, which related to the *Doctrines of Frustration and Illegality in the Law of Contract*.

21–12 **New Zealand approach with modifications.** The Committee's report summarised the existing law, with all the complexity which had "been fashioned by the Courts over the centuries", and concluded that "it is obvious that the common law rules need some statutory assistance".[39] The approach recom-mended was the implementation of legislation broadly following the framework of the New Zealand Act.[40] The Committee did, however, suggest various modifications to the wording of the New Zealand legislation, including expansion of the brief s.3 of the Illegal Contracts Act. The South Australian Committee considered that "it would be better to set out the various ways in which illegality

---

[36] *Report*, p.232.
[37] *Report*, p.234.
[38] *Report*, p.233.
[39] Thirty-seventh *Report*, p.23.
[40] "Once a new reform has been essayed by one Law Reform Committee and by one Parliament, it is easy to show how it could have been done differently but it does not necessarily follow that the different method so advocated would necessarily be better", Thirty-seventh *Report*, p.24.

may affect a contract in several subprovisions",[41] particularly in order to clarify the notion of illegality in *performance*. However, no actual draft of a possible expanded provision was in fact provided.

Common law to be left intact. The most fundamental departure from the New Zealand legislation, however, related to s.6 of that Act, which provides that "every illegal contract shall be of no effect". Instead of that section the Committee recommended that "there should be in our Act a section stating that the remedies in this Act are in addition to any remedy already given by the common law or by any other statute in relation to illegal contracts".[42] The proposed South Australian reform would therefore have left the common law intact, with legislation merely providing an additional source of relief.[43] The Committee's approach on this point was noted specifically by the Law Reform Commission of British Columbia which chose, however, to make the opposite recommendation for its own jurisdiction on the ground that "retaining the common law is fundamentally inconsistent with a discretionary power to grant relief".[44]

21–13

5. SINGAPORE

Wide-ranging discretion. In 2002 Singapore joined the list of Commonwealth countries which have published a report on reform of the law relating to illegality in contracts and trusts, along with a draft bill.[45] The starting point of the report is a recommendation that, unlike the New Zealand legislation, the existing law on what constitutes an illegal contract, or a contract affected by illegality, should be left *unchanged*, including the controversial notion of "reliance" and the capacity of an unlawful agreement to pass the title to property. But the court would be given a wide-ranging discretion to grant relief to the parties which would extend to adjusting their position by way of apportionment as well as enforcement of the contract, restitution, variation of the transaction or "compensation by way of damages or otherwise".[46] The factors to be taken into account in exercising the discretion were based in part upon those provisionally suggested by the Law Commission in England in its (now superseded) 1999 Consultation Paper, to which we now turn.

21–14

---

[41] Thirty-seventh *Report*, p.24.
[42] Thirty-seventh *Report*, pp.25–26.
[43] Accordingly, s.7(7) of the New Zealand Act (". . . no Court shall, in respect of any illegal contract, grant relief to any person otherwise than in accordance with the provisions of this Act") would be deleted for the purposes of the proposed Act: Thirty-seventh *Report*, p.27.
[44] See the British Columbia Law Reform Commission's *Report on Illegal Transactions*, 1983, p.58.
[45] See Singapore Academy of Law, "Relief from Unenforceability of Illegal Contracts and Trusts" (5 July 2002): available online at *http://lawnet.com.sg*.
[46] Singapore Academy of Law, "Relief from Unenforceability of Illegal Contracts and Trusts" (5 July 2002), draft "Illegal Transactions (Relief) Act" s.5.

6. PROPOSALS OF THE LAW COMMISSION IN ENGLAND

(a) Background

21–15 **Changing views.** In 2010 the Law Commission in England issued a final report on *The Illegality Defence*.[47] This had been preceded a year before by a "Consultative Report" with the same title.[48] Ten years earlier the Commission published a consultation paper on *Illegal Transactions; The Effect of Illegality in Contract and Trusts*.[49] The decade separating the two reports saw the Law Commission undergo a substantial change in its provisional view as a result of the responses it received to the first consultation paper and to a separate consultation paper on *The Illegality Defence in Tort*[50] published in 2001.

21–16 **The 1999 proposals.** In its first consultation paper the Law Commission provisionally recommended that a discretionary power to order the actual enforcement of certain types of contract, otherwise unenforceable for illegality, should be given by statute to the court. The power of enforcement would have been confined to situations "where the formation, purpose or performance of the contract" involved the "commission of a legal wrong".[51] The power would therefore not have extended to *other* illegal contracts, i.e. those considered by the common law itself to be "contrary to public policy" but which do not involve the commission of independently unlawful acts.[52] On the other hand, the provisional conclusions relating to the recovery back of money or property would have extended to contracts regarded as contrary to public policy, with the exception of contracts in restraint of trade. Again, a statutory discretion was favoured: the Commission expressed the "provisional view that a court should have a *discretion* to decide whether or not illegality should be recognised as a defence to a claim for the reversal of unjust enrichment in relation to benefits conferred under a contract which is unenforceable for illegality".[53] This would have enabled recovery to be more broadly-based than the then existing law, in which reversal of unjust enrichment was confined to situations involving mistakes of fact or law, unless the parties were not *in pari delicto*.[54] The statutory discretion would also have applied to those cases in which the claimant seeks to recover back money or property on the ground that he has withdrawn from an illegal transaction.[55] The Commission even recommended that the court should be given

---

[47] See Law Com No.320.
[48] See Law Commission Consultation Paper No.189.
[49] See Law Commission Consultation Paper No.154 (1999).
[50] See Law Commission Consultation Paper No.160.
[51] See Law Commission Consultation Paper No.154, para.7.10 (pp.95–96).
[52] See Law Commission Consultation Paper No.154, para.7.16 (p.98). See also para.7.13 (p.96): "In deciding whether or not a contract is contrary to public policy, the court is already effectively asking the question—would it be against the public interest to enforce the contract? Put another way, there is simply no scope for a discretion as regards enforceability which operates once the court has decided that a contract is contrary to public policy": Law Commission Consultation Paper No.154, para.7.13 (p.96).
[53] See Law Commission Consultation Paper No.154, para.7.22. (p.100) (italics supplied).
[54] But cf. *Mohammed v Alaga & Co (A Firm)* [1999] 3 All E.R. 699, CA discussed in Ch.17 above.
[55] See Ch.18, above.

discretion "to decide whether illegality should act as a defence to the recognition of contractually transferred or created property rights"[56] i.e. facilitating occasional disapplication of the principle that illegal contracts can be effective to pass property. The statutory discretion would have required the court to take into account five factors including the seriousness of the illegality, the claimant's knowledge, deterrence, the purpose of the rule violated by the contract, and the need for proportionality.[57] Unlike the Commonwealth law reform bodies, however, the Commission did not favour giving the court power to apportion losses between the parties.[58] Moreover, unlike the New Zealand legislation which adopts the opposite position,[59] the Commission favoured a presumption that all contracts affected by illegality, including even those involving the commission of serious crimes such as murder, should be "prima facie valid and enforceable"[60] unless and until the court decided otherwise.

(b)   2010 Recommendations

Rejection of wide-ranging statutory discretion.   In a very significant reversal   **21–17** of the approach provisionally favoured in its 1999 paper, and notwithstanding that a majority of respondents had favoured it, the 2010 Report no longer favoured a wide-ranging statutory discretion in illegality cases.[61] The earlier approach was rejected because of perceived difficulties in defining the scope of the discretion with sufficient precision to prevent it from having an unintended destabilising effect across a wide area of the law of contract.[62] Although legislative reform based upon a statutory discretion was still recommended for one specific area, that of trusts involving fraudulent concealment of assets from creditors or others, the approach recommended in 2010 for contractual situations raising illegality issues was reform by the judiciary itself.

Need for transparent approach.   The Commission considered that the courts   **21–18** generally managed to achieve acceptable results in situations involving illegality in contract, but contended that the process by which they did so could and should be made far more transparent and coherent without legislative intervention. In its 2009 Consultative Report the Commission proposed that the various "rules" manipulated in these cases should be regarded as being more in the nature of

---

[56] See Law Commission Consultation Paper No.154, para.7.26 (p.101). The illegality would not "invalidate a disposition of property to a third party purchaser for value without notice of the illegality", cf. New Zealand Illegal Contracts Act 1970 s.6(1).

[57] See Law Commission Consultation Paper No.154, paras 7.27–7.43 (pp.102–106).

[58] See below, cf. Ch.20, above (New Zealand).

[59] See the New Zealand Illegal Contracts Act 1970 ss.6 and 7, quoted in Ch.20, above.

[60] See Law Commission Consultation Paper No.154, para.7.49 (p.108).

[61] But see the views of Lord Sumption speaking extra-judicially in his 2012 address to the Chancery Bar Association: "Reflexions on the Law of Illegality" (available via the Supreme Court website). He argued that the Law Commission's "retreat [was] extremely unfortunate", and expressed the hope that the Government would eventually "prefer the more imaginative proposals which the Commission had put forward in its early consultation documents to the abandonment of the cause which is evident in its final report".

[62] See Law Commission Consultation Paper No.189, paras 3.104–3.122 (pp.49–54).

"guidance".[63] In deciding whether to uphold a defence of illegality when advanced against a claim for contractual enforcement, the court should expressly approach the case on the basis of the policies regarded as underlying the defence. In the same Report the Commission set these out as follows[64]:

> "(a) furthering the purpose of the rule which the illegal conduct has infringed; (b) consistency; (c) that the claimant should not profit from his or her own wrong; (d) deterrence; and (e) maintaining the integrity of the legal system.consistency;"

In its briefer 2010 final Report the Commission confirmed its adoption of the approach which it had proposed in the previous year's Consultative Report. It felt reassured by the reasoning of the House of Lords in two decisions, that the law was moving incrementally in the direction which it favoured. Although the two cases primarily concerned illegality as a defence in tort,[65] the Commission was sufficiently satisfied that the courts were beginning to adopt a more transparent and policy-based approach to decision-making in illegality cases generally, to conclude that legislative reform was not needed "outside the area of trust law".[66] The treatment of the Commission's Report in the first cases decided after its publication revealed a difference of opinion. In one case the Supreme Court in effect applied the flexible approach favoured by the Commission and decided the case by openly balancing the various policy factors in a way similar to that suggested by the Report.[67] In a subsequent case in the same court, however, one Justice expressly attacked the Commission's approach, declaring it "difficult to justify as an approach to authority or the proper development of the law".[68] Although the same Justice reiterated his view in his judgment in yet another case in the Supreme Court,[69] two other Justices in that case were evidently inclined to favour the Commission.[70] The same division of opinion was reflected in the reasoning of two members of the Court of Appeal in another decision handed down since the Commission's Report was published.[71] The conflict was not resolved until the majority decision of the Supreme Court in *Patel v Mirza*[72] in 2016.

21–19 **Balancing exercise.** According to the reasoning of the Commission, set out in full in the Consultative Report, application of its proposed guidelines should involve balancing them against the "legitimate expectation" of the claimant that

---

[63] See Law Commission Consultation Paper No.189 at para.3.40 (p.62).

[64] See Law Commission Consultation Paper No.189, para.3.142 (p.62).

[65] See *Gray v Thames Trains* [2009] UKHL 33 and *Stone & Rolls v Moore Stephens* [2009] UKHL 39. See also Law Com No.320 Pt 3, "Illegality and Other Claims" (pp.41–51).

[66] See Law Com No.320 para.340 (p.51).

[67] See *Hounga v Allen* [2014] UKSC 47; [2014] 1 W.L.R. 2889.

[68] See *Les Laboratoires Servier v Apotex* [2014] UKSC 55; [2014] 3 W.L.R. 1257 per Lord Sumption at [13]-[20],

[69] See *Bilta (UK) Ltd (in liquidation) v Nazir* [2015] UKSC 23; [2015] 2 All ER 1083 per Lord Sumption at [62]-[64] and [98]-[105].

[70] See *Bilta (UK) Ltd (in liquidation) v Nazir* [2015] UKSC 23; [2015] 2 All ER 1083 per Lord Toulson and Lord Hodge at [120]-[130] and [169]-[174]

[71] See *R (on the application of Best) v Chief Land Registrar* [2015] EWCA Civ 17 (compare the view of Sales LJ at [70] et seq. with that of Arden LJ at [111]-[112]).

[72] [2016] UKSC 42, see below.

the contract will be enforced and the need to ensure that the outcome is "proportionate" to any wrongdoing.[73] The focus should also be on the enforceability of *claims*, as such, rather than upon the conceptual notion of the "illegal contract" affecting both parties indiscriminately.[74] The difficult idea of "reliance" as a basis of decision-making in this area should also be abandoned.[75]

Unjust enrichment.   A similarly broad, transparent approach was also urged   **21–20**
upon the courts by the Commission when dealing with attempts to resist, on the basis of illegality, claims for the reversal of unjust enrichment. The court should again have regard to the policies underlying the defence of illegality in endeavouring to achieve "a just result, taking into account the relative merits of the parties and the proportionality of denying the claim".[76] In cases where a claimant seeks to invoke his or her withdrawal from an illegal scheme as the basis for recovery of money or property transferred pursuant to that scheme, the Commission was happy for "any future refinement of the law" to be "left to the incremental development of the case law"[77]; on the understanding that deterrence should be the primary rationale of the withdrawal doctrine.[78]

Passing of property.   Since the Commission had abandoned its earlier proposal   **21–21**
for a statutory discretion in the context of contractual enforcement, it followed a fortiori that it should also abandon it in the sphere of the transfer and creation of property rights.[79] The response of consultees to the 1999 paper had indeed indicated that introducing a discretion, with unavoidable uncertainty, into the field of property rights would be particularly controversial. Although the Commission expressed regret that the unsatisfactory language of "reliance" was still used in this area,[80] it nevertheless concluded that the law should be left as it is[81]; which the Commission summarised as being that "in relation to the creation, transfer or retention of legal property under a contract involving illegality, the illegality will be effectively ignored".[82]

Illegality and trusts.   In one area the Commission proposes, in the 2010 final   **21–22**
report, that legislation should be enacted to introduce a statutory discretion. This is a specific aspect of the law of trusts "when the trust arrangement is created in order to conceal the beneficiary's interest in the trust property in connection with a criminal purpose".[83] The Commission was concerned that the arbitrariness to

---

[73] See Law Commission Consultation Paper No.189, para.3.142 (p.62).
[74] See Law Commission Consultation Paper No.189, para.3.144 (p.63).
[75] See Law Commission Consultation Paper No.189 at para.3.148 (p.64).
[76] See Law Commission Consultation Paper No.189, para.4.44 (p.78).
[77] See Law Commission Consultation Paper No.189 at para.4.58 (p.83).
[78] See Law Commission Consultation Paper No.189, para.4.58 (p.83).
[79] See Law Commission Consultation Paper No.189, at paras 5.21–5.27 (pp.92–93).
[80] See Law Commission Consultation Paper No.189, para.5.26 (p.93).
[81] See Law Com No.320 para.3.47 (p.2).
[82] See Law Commission Consultation Paper No.189, para.5.26 (p.93).
[83] See Law Com No.320 para.2.32 (p.16). See also Law Commission Consultation Paper No.189, para.6.99 (p.126). The Commission recommended that the discretion should also apply, in limited circumstances, where a trust "*already created* is subsequently used to conceal beneficial ownership for a criminal purpose" (see Law Com No.320, paras 2.36–2.44 (pp.17–20) (italics supplied).

which the reasoning of the House of Lords in *Tinsley v Milligan*[84] could lead, with the outcome depending upon such irrelevant considerations as whether the situation happened to involve a resulting trust or the presumption of advancement,[85] could only be resolved by legislation. Unlike the areas of contractual enforcement, and unjust enrichment, where the Commission took the view that the fashioning of a more transparent and coherent approach should be achievable by the common law itself, the weight of a House of Lords decision was felt to preclude this option in the area covered by *Tinsley's* case.[86] Accordingly, the 2010 report included a draft Bill which would confer upon the court a statutory discretion "in exceptional circumstances" to deprive a beneficiary of his equitable interest where concealment has been involved and to declare who the interest should be vested in instead. In exercising the discretion the court would be enjoined to take any relevant factor into account including, inter alia, the conduct of all the persons involved, the value of the relevant equitable interest, and the possible deterrent effect of a particular order.[87]

7.   REFORM BY THE JUDICIARY

(a)   Canada

21–23   **Robust re-fashioning.**   Even before the English decision in *Patel v Mirza* it was possible to derive a degree of optimism about the viability of judicial reformulation of the law in this area from a trio of interesting Commonwealth cases. Thus two Canadian decisions, in both of which the British Columbia and Ontario Reports were referred to, provide striking evidence of how the law can be robustly and overtly re-fashioned by the judges themselves.

21–24   **The "modern approach".**   In *Re Still v Minister of National Revenue*[88] a legal immigrant into Canada believed, wrongly but in good faith, that she did not need a work permit before undertaking paid employment. Although she paid the required contributions during the tenure of her employment, the State denied her unemployment benefit, when she lost her job, on the ground that the absence of a work permit had rendered her contract of employment unenforceable for illegality. She sought judicial review of the refusal of benefit; and her application succeeded before the Federal Court of Appeal, which remitted her claim for reconsideration on the basis that her contract of employment had not been expressly or impliedly prohibited by the relevant immigration and employment legislation. In the course of a wide-ranging examination of the English and Canadian authorities on illegality in contract, the Court drew a distinction between what it described as the "classical model of illegality", and the "modern approach". Under the former, "the fact that the applicant acted in good faith [was]

---

[84] [1994] 1 A.C. 340.
[85] See above, Ch.16.
[86] See Law Commission Consultation Paper No.189, para.6.89 (p.123); see also para.1.15 (p.5).
[87] The Government announced in 2012 that it would not be acting upon the Commission's recommendation for legislation.
[88] (1997) 154 D.L.R. (4th) 229.

an irrelevant consideration"; whereas under the latter it was a material factor, along with the "purpose and object of [the] statutory prohibition".[89] Moreover, under the modern approach it was "open to ask whether the denial of unemployment benefits [was] a *de facto* penalty which [was] disproportionate to the statutory breach".[90]

Rejection of "doctrinal purity". A similarly robust rejection, of what was **21–25** described as "the traditional rule . . . that illegal contracts are unenforceable", had been seen earlier in the decision of the Alberta Court of Appeal in *Love's Realty and Financial Services Ltd v Coronet Trust*.[91] In this case an estate agent's claim for commission was met with the defence that he had been unlicensed at the material time. It was clear that his failure to obtain a licence had been due to an oversight, and he procured one subsequently. In enforcing the claim, and rejecting the defence, Kerans JA, delivering the judgment of the Court, quoted from the British Columbia Report and expressed himself as follows:

> "I see a . . . weakening of the traditional rule in its many exceptions. As with most applications
> of rules with harsh and apparently pointless effect save to preserve doctrinal purity, we should
> not be surprised to find bewildering 'exceptions' . . . I do not see the need for such confusing
> euphemism. I . . . say that . . . one can refuse to apply the traditional rule in a case when to
> apply it would have a harsh effect and is not required to affirm the legislative policy."[92]

(b) Australia

Re-formulation. The High Court of Australia has also taken the opportunity to **21–26** re-formulate the principles governing statutory illegality in view of its perception that "with the rapid expansion of regulation . . . the legal environment in which the doctrine of illegality operates has changed" rendering traditional formulations "too extreme and inflexible to represent sound legal policy in the late twentieth century".[93] In *Nelson v Nelson*,[94] which was discussed in detail in an earlier chapter,[95] the High Court implicitly rejected as artificial and arbitrary the use of "reliance" as the test for the recovery back of property in illegality cases.[96]

---

[89] (1997) 154 D.L.R. (4th) 229 at 246–247, per Robertson JA, delivering the judgment of the court.
[90] (1997) 154 D.L.R. (4th) 229 at 253. See also the judgment of Krever J, in the Ontario High Court in *Royal Bank of Canada v Grobman* (1977) 83 D.L.R. (3d) 415 at 431–432 which was quoted in *Re Still*: "As I understand the evolution of the current law of contract, modern judicial thinking has developed in a way that has considerably refined the knee-jerk reflexive reaction to a plea of illegality . . . The serious consequences of invalidating the contract, the social utility of those consequences and a determination of the class of persons for whom the prohibition was enacted, are all factors which the Court will weigh". For another case in which this passage was quoted, and the need for flexibility was emphasised, see the decision of the Ontario Court of Appeal in *William E. Thomson Associates v Carpenter* (1989) 61 D.L.R. (2nd) 1 at 10 et seq., per Blair JA, delivering the judgment of the Court.
[91] (1989) 57 D.L.R. (4th) 606 at 611.
[92] (1989) 57 D.L.R. (4th) 606 at 611 at 615–616.
[93] See *Nelson v Nelson* (1995) 184 C.L.R. 538 at 611, per McHugh J.
[94] (1995) 184 C.L.R. 538. See Rose, "Reconsidering Illegality" (1996) 10 J.C.L. 271 at 282 et seq.
[95] See Ch.16, above.
[96] See the *Report*, Ch.V.

21–27   **Coherent exposition.**   The significance of *Nelson v Nelson* for present purposes is the very explicit manner in which the Court sought coherently to expound the relevant principles. The following passage, from the judgment of McHugh J, is more reminiscent of the drafting of a statute than of conventional judicial language.[97]

> "... courts should not refuse to enforce legal or equitable rights simply because they arose out of or were associated with an unlawful purpose unless: (a) the statute discloses an intention that those rights should be unenforceable in all circumstances; or (b)(i) the sanction of refusing to enforce those rights is not disproportionate to the seriousness of the unlawful conduct; (ii) the imposition of the sanction is necessary, having regard to the terms of the statute, to protect its objects or policies; and (iii) the statute does not disclose an intention that the sanctions and remedies contained in the statute are to be the only legal consequences of a breach of the statute or the frustration of its policies."[98]

8.   CURRENT STATE OF ENGLISH LAW

21–28   **Setback to the struggle for reform.**   There are clearly significant differences between the various approaches to reform which have found favour elsewhere, either by way of judicial innovation or of legislative intervention (actual or proposed). Nevertheless, there appears to be a significant degree of consensus in favour of three broad themes. First, in the field of statutory illegality there is the rejection of literal interpretation, and strict liability, in favour of a broader "policy-orientated" approach. Secondly, there is the perceived need for a degree of judicial flexibility (either conferred by statute or developed by the common law itself) enabling such factors as proportionality and the states of the parties' minds to be taken into account. Thirdly, there is rejection (except in Singapore) of the notion of "reliance upon the illegality" as a test for the granting of relief, on the ground of its arbitrariness and artificiality. In England all these ideas struggled for judicial recognition in the final 15 years or so of the twentieth century. Apart from piecemeal legislation in one area, however, the struggle for reform suffered a serious setback with the decision of the House of Lords in *Tinsley v Milligan*.[99]

21–29   **Statutory illegality.**   In statutory illegality the tension between flexibility and policy, on the one hand, and literal interpretation and rigidity, on the other, was reflected in a series of cases concerning licensing provisions within the financial services industry, which were considered in an earlier chapter.[100] It is striking that the effect of these cases was to prompt the legislature into action to confer upon the court, albeit only in relation to one sphere of activity, the kind of statutory

---

[97] See (1995) 184 C.L.R. 538 at 613.
[98] See also the subsequent decision of the High Court of Australia in *Fitzgerald v F. J. Leonardt* (1997) 189 C.L.R. 215, in which the approach of McHugh J was applied.
[99] [1994] 1 A.C. 340.
[100] See *Phoenix General Insurance Co of Greece v Helvanon Insurance* [1988] Q.B. 216. See also *Bedford Insurance Co Ltd v Institutio de Resseguros do Brasil* [1985] Q.B. 966; *Stewart v Oriental Fire and Marine Insurance Co Ltd* [1985] Q.B. 988. Cf. *Hughes v Asset Managers Plc* [1995] 3 All E.R. 669; *Fuji Finance Inc. v Aetna Life Insurance Co Ltd* [1997] Ch. 173. See generally Ch.2, above.

discretion for which the authors of the various reform proposals have contended. The Financial Services and Markets Act 2000 s.28(3)[101] provides, with respect to agreements prohibited by the Act, that:

"If the court is satisfied that it is just and equitable in the circumstances of the case, it may allow—
(a)   the agreement to be enforced; or
(b)   money or property paid or transferred under the agreement to be retained."

In considering whether or not to exercise this discretion, the court is required to "have regard" to whether the person responsible for the illegality "reasonably believed" that he "was not contravening the general prohibition by making the agreement".[102] Unfortunately, since this provision was confined to the one area of financial services, uncertainty remained elsewhere as to whether the court would adopt a rigid or a flexible approach.

A false dawn.   Outside the area of statutory illegality in which the notion of   **21–30**
legislative "intention" is a complicating factor, a more flexible approach to questions of illegality involving the commission of unlawful acts was fashioned by the courts in a well-known series of cases decided between 1986 and 1993.[103] According to this approach, the court was enjoined to "keep in mind that the underlying principle is the so-called public conscience test", whereby it should "weigh, or balance, the adverse consequences of granting relief against the adverse consequences of refusing relief", in order to arrive at a "value judgment".[104] If this approach had survived, the English courts would in effect thereby have acquired, at least in one area of illegality, a judicial discretion to determine the outcome of cases by taking into account the relative culpability of the parties, and the extent to which forfeiture would be a sanction of inappropriate severity. This line of authority was, however, always fragile. As is often the case in illegality, its opponents could contend either that its relevance to the cases in which it was developed was oblique[105]; or that much narrower principles would have sufficed to reach the same, intuitively attractive, result in the particular situations in question[106]—albeit at a price in terms of the overall coherence and predictability of the law.[107] In the result, the unfortunate reasoning of the House of Lords in *Tinsley v Milligan* put an end to the promising "public conscience" test. At the same time, it entrenched even more deeply into English law the dubious notion of "reliance" upon illegality.

[101] See, formerly, the Financial Services Act 1986 s.132.
[102] See ss.28(4) and (5). See also s.28(6).
[103] See *Thackwell v Barclays Bank Plc* [1986] 1 All E.R. 676; *Saunders v Edwards* [1987] 1 W.L.R. 1116; *Euro-Diam v Bathurst* [1990] 1 Q.B. 1; *Howard v Shirlstar Container Transport Ltd* [1990] 1 W.L.R. 1292.
[104] See, per Nicholls LJ in the Court of Appeal in *Tinsley v Milligan* [1992] Ch. 310 at 319.
[105] See, *Tinsley v Milligan* [1994] 1 A.C. 340 at 359–361 per Lord Goff.
[106] See *Tinsley v Milligan* [1994] 1 A.C. 340 at 369 et seq. per Lord Browne-Wilkinson.
[107] I have called this elsewhere the "technique of evasive technicality": see R. A. Buckley, "Law's Boundaries and the Challenge of Illegality" in *Legal Structures* Buckley ed, (John Wiley and Sons, 1996), pp.232–234.

21–31   **Reform by the judiciary: *Patel v Mirza*.**   The decision in 2016 of a nine-member Supreme Court in *Patel v Mirza*[108] subjected English law on illegality to far-reaching change. The changes can conveniently be summarised as having three major aspects. First, the controversial decision of the House of Lords in *Tinsley v Milligan* was finally overruled. Secondly, a new and flexible approach to the resolution of illegality issues was introduced requiring overt consideration of relevant underlying policies and the proportionality of any given outcome. Thirdly, the law of unjust enrichment was subjected to radical simplification: the "reliance" test was abolished and a presumption introduced in favour of the undoing of transactions affected by illegality even when they had been completed. These aspects have been considered in detail in earlier chapters of this book.[109] It will be recalled that although there was unanimity as to the actual decision on the facts of *Patel's* case, the Supreme Court was divided in its reasoning with a minority registering opposition to the overt consideration of policy issues and the abolition of the "reliance" test. The reasoning of the majority has, however, clearly established the approach to be adopted for the foreseeable future. English law in this area has therefore embarked upon an exciting new phase.

---

[108] [2016] UKSC 42.
[109] See, especially, Chs 1, 17 and 18.

PART 6

CASES AND COMMENTS

CHAPTER 22

HYPOTHETICAL SITUATIONS INVOLVING ILLEGALITY

The purpose of this chapter. The purpose of this Chapter is to outline a   **22–01**
number of possible situations in which illegality issues might arise and to
comment upon how similar situations might be approached if they were actually
to occur. Although in practice every case is unique, it is hoped that these
examples might help to clarify how problems in this complex area of the law are
often analysed by the courts.

1. ILLEGALITY IN PERFORMANCE

While driving his own lorry in performance of a contract of carriage with the   **22–02**
defendant, the claimant caused a serious accident resulting in several fatalities.
He was subsequently convicted of causing death by dangerous driving and
sentenced to a long term of imprisonment. Despite the accident the defendant's
goods, which were being carried on the lorry, were undamaged and reached the
defendant safely. Nevertheless, appalled by what has occurred, the defendant
refuses to pay the claimant the charges due under the contract of carriage, and the
claimant sues him.

Comment. In *St John Shipping Corporation v Joseph Rank*[1] an attempt was   **22–03**
made to avoid charges due under a contract of carriage on the ground that the ship
had been overloaded contrary to statute. The attempt failed and the contract was
enforced. Having held that the doctrine of implied statutory prohibition (which is
not relevant in this hypothetical example) was not applicable, Devlin J held that
illegality in the *performance* of an initially unobjectionable contract could *not* (in
the absence of statutory illegality) prevent the "guilty" party from enforcing the
contract. He quoted a well-known dictum to the effect that "a plaintiff has [n]ever
been precluded from recovering by an infringement of the law, not contemplated
by the contract, in the performance of something to be done on his part".[2] This
dictum was again cited, and echoed in broad terms, by Browne-Wilkinson J in
Coral Leisure Group v Barnett[3]: "The fact that a party has in the course of
performing a contract committed an unlawful or immoral act will not by itself
prevent him from further enforcing that contract … " Unlike the hypothetical
situation here, however, the cases in which these statements were made did not
involve homicide (the *Coral Leisure Group* case concerned sexual misconduct).

---

[1] [1957] 1 Q.B. 267.
[2] See *Wetherell v Jones* (1832) 3 B. & Ad. 221 at 225 per Tenterden CJ.
[3] See [1981] I.C.R. 503 at 509.

There is some authority for the proposition that conduct which puts life or property at risk can prevent the enforcement of a contract of carriage by sea (see *Cunard v Hyde No.2*).[4] Moreover, a claimant convicted of manslaughter has been held unable to enforce a contract of indemnity in order to recover the damages awarded against him in favour of the widow of the deceased (see *Gray v Barr*)[5]; and claimants convicted of manslaughter have sometimes been held to forfeit benefits due under the will or intestacy of the deceased.[6] In the hypothetical situation here the claimant would no doubt argue that the road accident was conceptually separate from the contract of carriage, whereas the defendant would contend that it would be contrary to public policy to permit enforcement of the contract in these circumstances. This latter contention would be reinforced if, on the facts, it could be shown either that the claimant had been driving recklessly in order to fulfil a time stipulation in the contract (having needlessly wasted time earlier), or that the manner of his driving had jeopardised the safety of the goods and that it had only been by chance that they had escaped damage in the accident. The explicit consideration of policy factors favoured by the Supreme Court in *Patel v Mirza*[7] could facilitate arguments such as these.

2.   STATUTORY ILLEGALITY

22–04   Delegated legislation is introduced requiring vendors of new cars to provide the purchaser with a statement providing certain information as to the environmental impact of the vehicle. In one case the vendor fails to provide such a statement and the purchaser, having taken delivery of the car under a contract of sale, declines to pay the sums outstanding on the purchase relying on illegality.

22–05   **Comment.**   In *Anderson v Daniel*[8] a vendor of fertiliser who failed to provide documentation, as required by statute, when supplying the fertiliser was held to be prevented by illegality from enforcing the contract to recover the price.[9] On the other hand, in *Shaw v Groom*[10] a landlord who failed to provide his tenant with a rent book, as required by statute, was nevertheless permitted to sue for rent. In practice the courts are apt to ascribe their decisions in cases of this type to the intention of the legislature in the particular statute in question. This usually means that the level of penalty will be taken into account (e.g. a small fine might count against illegality), alongside the court's perception of the gravity of the context and the extent to which allowing contractual enforcement might thwart the statutory purpose. A series of cases involving facts close to those in the hypothetical situation here occurred in New Zealand (prior to the general statutory reform of illegality in that country), when vendors of motor-cars were required by statute to accompany the sale of the vehicles with a "warranty of

---

[4] (1859) 2 El. & Bl. 1.

[5] [1971] 2 Q.B. 554.

[6] See e.g. *Jones v Roberts* [1995] 2 F.L.R. 422.

[7] [2016] UKSC 42.

[8] [1924] 1 K.B. 138.

[9] See also *B&B Viennese Fashions v Losanne* [1952] 1 All E.R. 909.

[10] [1970] 2 Q.B. 504.

fitness". In some of these cases failure to supply the relevant document resulted in the contract of sale being held to be unenforceable for illegality,[11] whereas in others the contract was enforced.[12] Even if the contract of sale here is held to have been unenforceable for illegality it will still be effective to pass the property in the car to the purchaser.

3.   DEFRAUDING THE REVENUE

In an attempt improperly to take advantage of legislation imposing lower tax on cars with smaller engines a vendor, with the encouragement of the purchaser, equips a car with a larger engine than is usual for that type of vehicle and misrepresents the status of the vehicle to the licensing authorities. When the vehicle turns out to be defective, the purchaser brings an action against the vendor which the latter seeks to resist by invoking illegality.

22–06

Comment.   The Court normally takes a strict approach to cases in which the parties have conspired together to defraud the revenue authorities, and refuse to enforce the contract in favour of either party.[13] Occasionally, however, a more lenient view will be taken if one party is able to persuade the court that an obligation exists in his favour which can be regarded as conceptually distinct from the unlawful agreement. In practice, however, this argument is only likely to succeed in two types of case. First, if the loss caused to the party denied enforceability is perceived to be disproportionate to the seriousness of the illegality (irrespective of the conduct of the other party). This appears essentially to have been the reason for actual decision of the majority of the House of Lords in *Tinsley v Milligan*,[14] although the reasoning in that case was ostensibly based on more technical grounds since proportionality was not overtly accepted as a relevant factor in the law as it stood when *Tinsley's* case was decided. The reasoning (though not the actual decision) in *Tinsley's* case has, however, now been overruled by the Supreme Court in *Patel v Mirza*,[15] and "whether denial of the claim would be a proportionate response to the illegality"[16] is one of the factors to be taken into account when deciding on enforceability. Secondly, and potentially more promising for the purchaser in the hypothetical situation here, is if one of the parties to the contract was the victim of a separate fraud by the other party in the course of the same transaction.[17] Thus if, for example, the engine inserted in the vehicle by the vendor was one which he knew to be grossly defective it is conceivable that an action in deceit might succeed. Moreover, in cases falling short of fraud, claims based on misrepresentation may sometimes be allowed.[18]

22–07

---

[11]   See e.g. *Berrett v Smith* [1965] N.Z.L.R. 460.
[12]   See e.g. *Fenton v Scotty's Car Sales* [1968] N.Z.L.R. 929.
[13]   See e.g. *Miller v Karlinski* (1946) 62 T.L.R. 85.
[14]   [1994] 1 A.C. 340.
[15]   [2016] UKSC 42.
[16]   See per Lord Toulson, ibid, at [120].
[17]   See e.g. *Saunders v Edwards* [1987] 1 W.L.R. 1116; see also *Shelley v Paddock* [1980] Q.B. 348.
[18]   See e.g. *Mohamed v Alaga* [1999] 3 All E.R. 699 at 708–709 per Lord Bingham CJ.

4. BREACH OF LICENSING REQUIREMENTS

22–08   A carrier of goods delivers the goods safely pursuant to a contract of carriage but the goods owner refuses to pay the sums due under the contract after discovering that the vehicle in which the claimant had carried the goods had not been licensed for the purpose. The carrier sues the goods owner in attempt to recover his charges.

22–09   **Comment.**   The situation here is concerned with the doctrine of implied statutory prohibition of contractual rights. Since it appears unlikely that the contract identified a particular vehicle for the performance of the contract, the defendant will be unable to contend that the contract was incapable of lawful performance from the outset in order to resist enforceability. The issue will therefore turn upon whether the legislative intention, as embodied in the licensing statute, was to prevent carriers who performed their contracts in breach of its provisions from suing for their charges. In *Archbold's (Freightage) v S Spanglett*[19] a carrier attempted to avoid liability for losing the goods by relying on his own illegality in using an unlicensed vehicle. Not surprisingly this defence was rejected, but Devlin LJ dealt obiter with the type of hypothetical situation here when he said: "[The defendants] cannot themselves enforce the contract because they intended to perform it unlawfully with a van they knew was not properly licensed for the purpose".[20] This dictum would appear to be directly in point unless the carrier could persuade the court that he had several vehicles and that the use of the unlicensed one had been unintended or inadvertent. But even if this could be shown, it may be doubted whether this would enable the carrier to succeed since, despite Devlin LJ's reference to intention and knowledge, statutory illegality is normally strict. Indeed, Devlin J himself (as he then was) said in *St John Shipping Corporation v Joseph Rank*[21] that " . . . the court will not enforce a contract which is . . . impliedly prohibited by statute. If the contract is of this class it does not matter what the intent of the parties is; if the statute prohibits the contract, it is unenforceable whether the parties meant to break the law or not". The view that the claimant's action would fail is also reinforced by a Canadian decision on very similar facts to the hypothetical case here, and in which the carrier was unsuccessful in his attempt to recover his charges (see *Wasel Bros v Laskin*).[22] On the other hand, since the outcome will necessarily depend upon the construction of the particular statute there may be scope for the carrier to argue that the provision here did not intend to add contractual unenforceability to whatever penalties it provides. Factors such as the level of penalties imposed, and the frequency with which repetition constituted fresh offences, are among those which might be taken to cast light upon the statutory purpose. Where licensing provisions are in issue there is sometimes scope for the contention that their intention was generally to regulate a particular sphere of

---

[19] [1961] 1 Q.B. 374.
[20] [1961] 1 Q.B. at 388.
[21] [1957] 1 Q.B. 267 at 283.
[22] [1934] 2 D.L.R. 798; [1934] 2 W.W.R. 577.

business activity, rather than to invalidate every individual contract entered into in pursuance of that activity whenever contravention occurred.[23]

5.   EFFECT OF KNOWLEDGE OF OTHER PARTY'S ILLEGALITY

The claimant contracts for the carriage of a substantial load on the defendant's lorry. The charges set out in the contract are at a level normally to be expected for such carriage. Just before concluding the agreement the claimant asks for an assurance that the lorry is licensed to carry a load of the size in question and is assured that it does. When leaving the defendant's premises after signing the contract the claimant happens to see the defendant's lorry parked nearby and notices that it does not, in fact, possess an appropriate licence, but he nevertheless decides not to reopen the transaction. The lorry turns over while carrying the claimant's load, which is substantially damaged as a result. When the claimant sues for damages the defendant contends that the contract was unenforceable for illegality.

22–10

Comment.   In this situation the defendant is attempting to rely on his own illegality to avoid liability for damaging the claimant's load. Unlike *Defrauding the Revenue* above, however, the claimant was not aware, at the time when the contract was made, of what the defendant intended to do: so that the latter cannot contend that the contract was one in which both parties shared an unlawful intention when the contract was formed. The claimant did, however, become aware of the absence of an appropriate licence before performance actually started. This situation raises issues in both statutory and common law illegality. The possibility of statutory illegality arises because the defendant might contend that the relevant legislation imposed a duty on *both* parties to check the licensing position, so as to prevent the claimant from relying upon his initial ignorance. Should this contention fail, the defendant might argue that the claimant's knowledge of the situation prior to performance was sufficient at common law to preclude his enforcing the contract. As far as the statutory illegality point is concerned, licensing provisions in various contexts have occasionally been construed as requiring one party to check that the other is licensed for what he has agreed to do; enabling the unlicensed party to rely on his own illegality if the checks were not made.[24] Such decisions are relatively rare, however, and in one case in which a carrier attempted, as in the hypothetical situation here, to rely on his own illegality in using an unlicensed vehicle to resist a claim for damages, the attempt failed.[25] When approached from a common law perspective the situation here somewhat resembles that in *Ashmore, Benson, Pease & Co v A V Dawson*[26] in which a carrier succeeded in resisting a claim for damages from the goods owner by implicating the latter in the former's use of an illegally inappropriate vehicle for performance of the contract of carriage. Moreover, the fact that the

22–11

---

[23] See e.g. *Yango Pastoral Co Pty v First Chicago Australia* (1978) 139 CLR 410.
[24] See e.g. *Re Mahmoud and Ispahani* [1921] 2 K.B. 716; *Dennis & Co v Munn* [1949] 1 All E.R. 616.
[25] See *Archbold's (Freightage) v S Spanglett* [1961] 1 Q.B. 374, especially per Devlin LJ at 392.
[26] [1971] 1 W.L.R. 828.

otherwise "innocent" party only became aware of the other party's intentions *after* the formation of the contract will not necessarily be sufficient in itself to prevent the illegality defence from being successfully invoked against him (see *Cowan v Milbourn*).[27] Nevertheless, the claimant here may derive assistance from the emphasis in *Ashmore*'s case upon the claimant's *participation* in the claimant's performance in that case,[28] essentially by paying a much reduced price. Except in the gravest cases, mere *knowledge* of the other party's intention is unlikely to be sufficient. It may therefore be possible to distinguish the *Ashmore* decision here on the ground that the agreed charges were normal for the kind of carriage in question.

6.   DEFRAUDING INSURERS

22–12   The claimant's car was damaged in an accident. The repairs would normally cost £1,000 but the defendant vehicle repairer suggested that he should invoice the claimant's insurance company for £1,500, and that he and the claimant should then split the extra £500 equally between them. The transaction was carried out as agreed and the £500 was duly divided between the parties. Subsequently, however, the claimant discovered that the "repairs" had been merely cosmetic and that he had to pay £1,000 out of his own pocket to another repairer in order to have the work satisfactorily completed. When the claimant sued to recover this sum from the defendant, the latter alleged that the action was barred by illegality.

22–13   **Comment.**   A somewhat similar situation arose in *Taylor v Bhail*.[29] In this case a building owner suggested to a builder that the latter should artificially increase the price for remedial work after a storm, so as to enable the owner to deceive his insurance company into paying out more than the builder's actual charges. In return for agreeing to take part in the deception the builder would receive the contract for the work. A dispute subsequently arose between the parties, and the builder sued to enforce the contract. Although he had not initiated the fraudulent scheme, the Court of Appeal held that the builder's claim would nevertheless fail for illegality. (See also *Birkett v Acorn Business Machines*).[30] It is possible that this severe approach would also be applied here, to the detriment of the claimant. He might, however, try to persuade the court that policy factors favoured his claim[31] e.g. discouraging vehicle repairers from such initiatives. Moreover, if the defendant never intended to carry out the repairs, the claimant could contend that he had been the victim of (as well as a participant in) the defendant's fraudulent behaviour, and that an action in deceit should be allowed despite the illegality (see also *Defrauding the Revenue* above).

---

[27] (1867) L.R. 2 Exch. 230.
[28] See [1971] 1 W.L.R. 828 per Lord Denning MR and Scarman LJ.
[29] (1995) 50 Con. L.R. 70.
[30] [1999] 2 All E.R. Comm. 429.
[31] i.e. under the "range of factors" approach authorised by *Patel v Mirza* [2016] UKSC 42.

7.   TAX EVASION IN EMPLOYMENT

After some months in the defendant's employment the claimant noticed that the   **22–14**
net figure shown on her payslips was lower than the amount she actually
received. Anticipating that less tax had been deducted under the PAYE scheme
than ought to have been, she queried the payslips with her employer who replied:
"Oh, don't worry, leave it to me, the accounts department is in a mess. I'll sort it
out. If we have made a mistake the firm will pay the extra tax so you needn't
worry". Although she continued to receive the inaccurate payslips for some
months the claimant took no further action. She was subsequently dismissed by
her employer who responded to her claim for unfair dismissal by alleging that she
had been party to a scheme to defraud Inland Revenue and Customs of income
tax.

Comment.   There is no doubt that if employer and employee collaborate on   **22–15**
equal terms to defraud the Revenue and Customs, a subsequent attempt by the
employee to sue his employer for breach of the contract of employment will
normally fail for illegality (see *Miller v Karlinski*).[32] It is clear that, in principle,
this approach is not confined to common law actions on the contract but also
applies to claims for unfair dismissal.[33] Moreover, in one case decided in 1978,
the Employment Appeal Tribunal indicated that this robust approach would be
applied even where a "junior employee" had merely gone along with a tax fraud
initiated by his employer and was therefore the less blameworthy party (see
Tomlinson v Dick Evans "U" Drive).[34] Although this approach has never actually
been overruled, and each case will inevitably turn upon its own facts, more recent
decisions at Court of Appeal level seem to indicate that a more pragmatic and
lenient approach will sometimes be taken.[35] The hypothetical situation here is
somewhat similar to that in *Hall v Woolston Hall Leisure*[36] in which a claimant
who queried her payslips, but was content to accept her employer's inadequate
response, was able successfully to claim for sexual discrimination when the
defence of illegality was rejected. The Court of Appeal held that the employee
needed to have participated in the employer's fraud and not merely to have been
aware of it.[37] But even if situations such as that in this example are approached,
as *Hall*'s case suggests, on the basis of the distinction between knowledge and
participation, employees are likely to have their conduct carefully, even
sceptically, examined for any indication that they were content to "turn a blind
eye" to a fraud which they could have done more to question. In one recent case,
in which an employee successfully overcame a defence of illegality against her
claim for unfair dismissal, the Court of Appeal indicated that her success
depended upon the fact that as a foreign national her knowledge of tax
arrangements, and of the English language itself, was limited; and that such

---

[32] (1946) 62 T.L.R. 85.
[33] See e.g. *Salvesen v Simons* [1994] I.C.R. 409.
[34] [1978] I.C.R. 639.
[35] See e.g. *Hewcastle Catering v Ahmed and Elkamah* [1992] I.C.R. 626; [1991] I.R.L.R. 473, CA.
[36] [2001] 1 W.L.R. 225.
[37] [2001] 1 W.L.R. 225 at 236 per Peter Gibson LJ; and at 248 per Mance LJ.

leniency might not have been shown to an employee in otherwise similar circumstances but to whom those factors did not apply (see *Wheeler v Quality Deep Ltd*).[38]

8.   TRANSFERRING PROPERTY TO DECEIVE CREDITORS

22–16   In order to deceive her creditors a mother who was anticipating bankruptcy gratuitously transferred the ownership of a number of shares to her daughter. The deception was successful and the mother was able to secure a composition with her creditors on favourable terms. The mother subsequently sought return of the shares but the daughter refused.

22–17   **Comment.**   A transfer of property without consideration will normally give rise to a resulting trust in favour of the transferor. In *Tinsley v Milligan*[39] the House of Lords enforced such a trust even where the purpose of the transfer had been an illegal one, and had actually been put fully into effect. The actual decision of the House is now generally accepted as having been correct, notwithstanding that its reasoning was overruled by the Supreme Court in *Patel v Mirza*.[40] Nevertheless the claim of the mother here is not on all fours with the facts of *Tinsley v Milligan*, because the relationship between the parties might be held to give rise to the presumption of advancement. The House of Lords in *Tinsley's* case appeared to hold by implication that in such circumstances the claim of the transferor *would* be defeated by illegality since the claimant would be obliged to disclose the illegality in order to rebut the presumption of gift.[41] On the other hand, according to some authorities, a party who sought to deceive his creditors could still be permitted to revoke transactions entered into for that unlawful purpose, provided that the unlawful purpose was never carried through to fruition.[42] But according to the orthodox view, a party seeking relief on this basis had to show that they had actually "repented" of their unlawful intention, and not merely that the illegal scheme had become unnecessary or been "frustrated".[43] The mother in the hypothetical case here would, however, have been unable to benefit from this exception to unenforceability. She might nevertheless have attempted to outflank the requirements for the exception by contending that the presumption of advancement did not, in fact, apply so that she should could rely directly on the decision in *Tinsley v Milligan*. Traditionally the presumption of advancement applied to transfers by husbands or fathers to wives or children, and it is unclear whether it applies to transfers by mothers or wives.[44] The mother here could have submitted that the presumption of advancement is outdated and

---

[38] [2005] I.C.R. 265.
[39] [1994] 1 AC 340.
[40] [2016] UKSC 42.
[41] See e.g. *Chettiar v Chettiar* [1962] A.C. 294.
[42] See e.g. *Taylor v Bowers* (1876) 1 Q.B.D. 291.
[43] See e.g. *Bigos v Bousted* [1951] 1 All E.R. 92.
[44] The High Court of Australia has held that the presumption can apply to transfers by mothers to their children: *Nelson v Nelson* (1995) 184 C.L.R. 538.

should not be extended.[45] Since the decision of the Supreme Court in *Patel v Mirza*, however, the presence or absence of the presumption of advancement would appear to be irrelevant. The court held that claims for unjust enrichment would be permitted in cases involving illegality on a much broader base than formerly. In *Patel's* case itself the Court permitted the recovery of money transferred pursuant to an illegal scheme even though that scheme had merely been frustrated and there was no evidence of "repentance". Obiter dicta of several members of the court even asserted that re-transfer of benefits transferred in an illegal transaction should be permitted even if the scheme had been completed, on the ground that that would be more likely, on balance, to discourage entry into such transactions in the first place.[46] The ratio decidendi of the majority is, however, at once both more cautious and more flexible. Cases involving illegality now have to be resolved by consideration of a "range of factors" including whether denial of recovery would promote the policy underlying the prohibition, and whether it would be proportionate to the seriousness of the contravention.[47] This hypothetical case would therefore fall to be decided against these criteria. If the extent to which the creditors had been defrauded was relatively modest compared with the value of the shares transferred this *might* lead to the illegality being disregarded, but the decision could be otherwise if recovery were perceived as likely to encourage disregard of the requirements for lawful compositions with creditors.[48]

9.   RESTRAINTS UPON FORMER EMPLOYEES

The claimants' firm, based in London, produced computer software for GP's practices. The defendant was employed by them as a software designer. His contract included a covenant "not to accept employment with any organisation providing information technology services to the medical profession in England for six months" after leaving the claimant's employment. Three months after leaving the claimant's employment the defendant joined a firm in Newcastle which developed software for use in private hospitals, and the claimants sought an injunction to enforce the covenant.

22–18

Comment.   At the outset the claimants will need to satisfy the court that the defendant possesses "trade secrets" which they are entitled to protect, as distinct from professional skills which the defendant is entitled to use in his future career even if they were developed during his employment by the claimants. This distinction can be difficult to draw where highly technical or scientific activities are concerned, and the courts are apt to regard employers' submissions on the

22–19

---

[45] See discussion by the Supreme Court of Canada in *Pecore v Pecore* [2007] 279 D.L.R. (4th) 513. See also the Equality Act 2010 s.199 which will abolish the presumption, but which has yet to be brought into force.

[46] See per Lord Mance in [2016] UKSC 42 at [202], and per Lord Sumption ibid at [252]-[253].

[47] See, especially, per Lord Toulson in [2016] UKSC 42 at [120].

[48] A Law Commission recommendation for a *statutory* discretion to determine the effect of illegality upon trusts in circumstances such as these has not been implemented (see *The Illegality Defence* (2010) Law Com No.320).

point with a degree of scepticism. In *FSS Travel & Leisure Systems v Johnson*[49] an attempt by a specialist software firm to prevent a computer programmer from joining a rival organisation succeeded at first instance but failed on appeal. The evidence was considered to be insufficiently detailed, and to be without a clear indication of sophisticated and identifiably independent knowledge created by the defendant during the tenure of his employment with the claimant. If the claimants in the hypothetical case here succeed, unlike those in the *Johnson* case, in establishing the existence of "trade secrets", the next hurdle they will need to overcome is to satisfy the court that the words "information technology services to the medical profession" are no wider than necessary to protect the claimants. The claimants are not entitled to protect themselves from competition as such, but only from competition based upon use of their "trade secrets". The defendant may well be able to point to significant distinctions between different types of activity, within the medical profession as a whole, which could render the crucial words too vague and general. Thus clinical usage might be distinguished from administrative or organisational functions, and specialist clinical activity in the private sector might prove to be significantly different from that of general practice in the National Health Service. The court may well be unsympathetic to the claimants unless it can be satisfied that the covenant had been drafted with the highest degree of particularity which could reasonably have been expected.

The next issue to be addressed in relation to the covenant in this question is that of the *area* to which it relates. It is to be noted that the restraint extends to the whole of England. While the courts are traditionally somewhat sceptical of area covenants, the degree of scepticism will inevitably vary depending upon the nature of the employment. In the information technology field the court may well take the view that extending protection to the whole of England will not be unreasonable, unless it appears that the particular type of service offered by firms such as that of the claimants does, in fact, tend to be merely regional rather than national in terms of the customers which it attracts. Finally, if the claimants manage to succeed on all the above points, the *duration* of the covenant will fall to be considered. Although in former times covenants for much longer periods have been enforced, in the fast-moving contemporary commercial world valid restraints are likely to be months, rather than years, in extent. The fact that the claimants here only sought protection for six months (of which merely three months remain) is likely to render this aspect of the covenant unobjectionable.

10.   COVENANTS BETWEEN VENDOR AND PURCHASER

22–20   The defendant built up a business supplying farming equipment to the agricultural industry throughout the UK. He decided to sell the business and covenanted with the purchasers, who had ambitious expansion plans, not to "become engaged anywhere directly or indirectly in the provision of agricultural services" for 10 years following the sale. Within a year of the sale the defendant accepted appointment as Chief Executive Officer of an international company, with its headquarters in the UK, which not only sold agricultural equipment but

---

[49] [1998] I.R.L.R. 382.

also acted as a consultancy providing specialist advice to farms throughout the world. The purchasers of his firm brought an action attempting to restrain the defendant from accepting his new appointment.

Comment.   The courts are generally prepared to take a more favourable view   **22–21**
of covenants between the vendors and purchasers of businesses, for the purposes of enforceability, than of those between employees and their former employers.[50] Nevertheless, the protection must be limited to the business sold, and not be an attempt to protect the purchaser from future competition against activities which were not formerly carried out by the business acquired (see *British Reinforced Concrete Engineering Co v Schelf*).[51] Since the business sold only traded in England and Wales this principle might be relevant here in as much as the purchasers are attempting to prevent the defendant from working for an international company. On the other hand, since the *type* of activity of both the business sold and the international company are the same it is more likely that the crucial issue will be the general one of whether the covenant is too wide even given the more relaxed approach adopted towards vendor and purchaser covenants. The defendant might contend that the width of the covenant is excessive in terms of duration, geography, and the breadth of the phrase "agricultural services". He might also argue that the phrase "directly or indirectly" was too uncertain, and to point out that he has not started a new, rival, business, but merely accepted paid employment.

To take the last point first, it is clear that there is no objection in principle to a covenant between vendor and purchaser restraining the former from accepting a position as an employee. In *Ronbar Enterprises v Green*[52] the publisher of a newspaper was restrained from accepting an appointment with a rival paper, in breach of a covenant entered into with the purchasers of the paper he had formerly published. Furthermore, the phrase "directly or indirectly", which is not uncommon in covenants in restraint of trade, was expressly held not to be void for uncertainty by the Judicial Committee of the Privy Council when construing a covenant between vendor and purchaser in *Connor Bros, Ltd v Connors*.[53] The duration and geographical scope of the covenant perhaps provide more formidable obstacles to enforceability. In the very well-known case of *Nordenfelt v Maxim Nordenfelt Guns and Ammunition Co*[54] a covenant between vendor and purchaser was enforced even though it was worldwide in extent and of 25 years duration. Moreover, in *Gilford Motor Co v Horne*[55] a covenant preventing the former managing director of a business sold from soliciting former customers was enforced even though it was effectively for the duration of his life. Nevertheless, these cases were decided many years ago and, in the faster-moving circumstances of modern industry, defending a covenant of even ten years duration, as in the hypothetical case here, could prove to be a formidable forensic task. A covenant limited to, say, two years might have been a more prudent

---

[50] See e.g. *Ronbar Enterprises v Green* [1954] 1 W.L.R. 815, especially per Jenkins LJ at 820–821.
[51] [1921] 2 Ch. 563.
[52] [1954] 1 W.L.R. 815.
[53] [1940] 4 All E.R. 179.
[54] [1894] A.C. 535.
[55] [1933] Ch. 935.

stipulation for the covenantees. The choice of the word "anywhere" might also prove difficult to defend since, unlike the *Nordenfelt* case, the business sold traded only in England and Wales. In *Littlewoods Organisation v Harris*[56] the Court of Appeal felt able to put a narrow construction upon a covenant potentially of world-wide application, and confine it to the UK, thus rendering it enforceable. It is doubtful, however, whether such an approach could assist the covenantees in this example. In *Harris* it was possible to confine the covenant itself to employment within the UK, but since the activities of the defendant in his new appointment would apply seamlessly to both the UK and elsewhere it is difficult to see how the covenant could in practice be construed so as to confine it to the UK and eliminate other countries. A similar difficulty might occur in construing the phrase "agricultural services", which would appear to be too wide as it stands since it would encompass other activities in addition to the provision of actual equipment. Since the defendant's new appointment might include the giving of advice as well as the sa le of equipment it would be difficult to restrain the part of his activities which overlapped with those of his former business without inhibiting the legitimate consultancy aspect of his new post.

In conclusion it must be doubted whether the greater flexibility shown in the enforceability of covenants between vendor and purchaser, including greater readiness to apply the doctrine of severance,[57] would in practice avail the covenantees in this hypothetical example. If the covenant had, say, named the firm which the defendant subsequently joined, and sought to restrain him for a short period from working for it in any capacity which involved the selling of agricultural equipment within the UK, they might have stood a better chance of success.

---

[56] [1977] 1 W.L.R. 472.
[57] See e.g. *Goldsoll v Goldman* [1915] 1 Ch. 292.

INDEX

This index has been prepared using Sweet and Maxwell's Legal Taxonomy. Main index entries conform to keywords provided by the Legal Taxonomy except where references to specific documents or non-standard terms (denoted by quotation marks) have been included. These keywords provide a means of identifying similar concepts in other Sweet and Maxwell publications and online services to which keywords from the Legal Taxonomy have been applied. Readers may find some minor differences between terms used in the text and those which appear in the index. Suggestions to *sweetandmaxwell.taxonomy@tr.com*.

All references are to paragraph number

Abuse of dominant position
  competition, 11–25
Administration of justice
  compromising legal process
    access to justice, 8–02
    arrestable offences, 8–10—8–11
    contracts, 8–04
    duress, 8–17—8–21
    existing liabilities, 8–12—8–16
    felonies and misdemeanours, 8–05
    ousting jurisdiction, 8–02
    public and private offences, 8–06
    public policy, 8–01
    settlement, 8–03
    valid compromises, 8–07—8–09
Advancement *see* **Presumptions**
Agency agreements
  restraint of trade, 12–30
Arrestable offences
  compromising legal process, 8–10—8–11
  concealment, 8–10—8–11
Assignment
  choses in action, 9–15
  current law, 9–17—9–18
  genuine commercial interest, 9–19
  life insurance, 5–26—5–29
  right to litigate, 9–16
  routinely accepted transactions, 9–20
Australia
  law reform, 21–26—21–27
  restitution, 17–17
  South Australia, 21–11—21–13
Benefit from criminal conduct
  forfeiture, 5–40—5–42
Bigamy
  public policy, 6–17

Blue pencil test
  severance, 19–04—19–07
Breach of confidence
  restraint of trade, 12–08—12–09
Breach of statutory duty
  torts, 1–17
Bribery
  confidentiality agreements, 7–28
  corrupt bargains, 7–24
British Colombia
  illegal transactions, 21–02—21–07
Canada
  British Colombia, 21–02—21–07
  law reform, 21–23—21–25
  Ontario, 21–08—21–10
Champerty
  access to justice, 9–13
  applicable proceedings, 9–14
  approval, 9–04—9–05
  background, 9–03
  car hire cases, 9–12
  contracts, 9–02
  effects, 9–26—9–27
  maintenance distinguished, 9–11
  origins of concept, 9–01
  professional indemnity insurance, 5–18
  public policy, 6–34, 9–28—9–31
  scope, 9–14
Choice of law
  foreign law, 10–09—10–13
  fraud, 10–10
  hostage-taking, 10–12
  intention, 10–13
  morality, 10–09
  place of performance, 10–02—10–08

INDEX

Choses in action
assignment, 9–15
Cohabitation
public policy, 6–22
Comity
choice of law
English law, 10–02—10–08
foreign law, 10–09—10–13
fraud, 10–10
general rule, 10–01
hostage-taking, 10–12
intention, 10–13
morality, 10–09
ordre public, 10–09
place of performance, 10–02—10–08
public policy, 10–07
Revenue laws, 10–04
Common law
illegality
generally, I–06
importance, 2–06
statutory illegality distinguished, 1–10—1–14
Commonwealth
British Columbia, 21–02—21–07
differences, 21–01
Ontario, 21–08—21–10
similarities, 21–01
Singapore, 21–14
South Australia, 21–11—21–13
Competition
abuse of dominant position, 11–26
Chapter I prohibition, 11–22
Chapter II prohibition, 11–26
employees, 11–23
European law, 11–20
exclusive dealership agreements, 11–25
nature of statutory provisions, 11–19
prohibited agreements, 11–22—11–25
purpose of statutory provisions, 11–21
restraint of trade, 11–19—11–26
small agreements, 11–24
Compromising legal process *see* **Administration of justice**
Concealment
arrestable offences, 8–10—8–11
Conditional fee agreements
expert witnesses, 9–25
legal profession, 9–21—9–24
Confidentiality agreements
bribery, 7–28
confidential information, 12–06—12–07
fraud
bribery, 7–28
concealment of criminality, 7–32—7–34
libel, 7–29—7–31
public interest, 7–35—7–39
libel, 7–29—7–31
public interest, 7–35—7–39

restraint of trade
breach of confidence, 12–08—12–09
confidential information, 12–06—12–07
issues, 12–01
misuse of trade secrets, 12–05
scope of protection, 12–01
skill and experience, 12–02
trade secrets, 12–03—12–04
trade secrets
generally, 12–03—12–04
misuse, 12–05
Consent
restraint of trade, 11–18
Consideration
severance
additional consideration, 19–10
no agreement reached, 19–11
scope, 19–10—19–12
Conspiracy
crime, 1–18
statutory illegality, 1–18
Consultation documents
Law Commission, 21–15
Contract terms
knowledge, 4–13
trading with the enemy, 10–28—10–29
Contracts
champerty, 9–02
compromising legal process
felonies and misdemeanours, 8–05
issues, 8–04
fraud
finance, 7–08
fraud upon the public, 7–03
insolvency, 7–05
insurance contracts, 7–07
motive, 7–06
preferences, 7–04
Revenue and Customs, 7–09—7–23
maintenance, 9–02
Criminal law
conspiracy, 1–18
illegal contracts, 1–01
illegality, I–06
intention, 1–04
proportionality, 1–05
seriousness of offence
approach after Patel v Mirza, 1–05—1–08
deliberate acts, 1–02—1–04
proportionality, 1–05
uncertain facts, 1–09
Damages
exemplary damages, 5–19—5–22
liquidated damages
restraint of trade, 11–08
recovery of damages
awareness of claimants, 5–12
champerty, 5–18

compulsory insurance, 5–21
directly liable claimants, 5–20
exemplary damages, 5–19—5–22
intention, 5–14—5–18
misrepresentation, 5–11
motor insurance, 5–14—5–15
professional indemnity insurance, 5–18
public policy, 5–10—5–13
social interests, 5–10
third party protection, 5–13
vicarious liability, 5–19
victims, 5–17, 5–22
violent offences, 5–16
Deceit
restitution, 17–19
Diminished responsibility
manslaughter, 5–31
Discretion
judiciary, 6–27—6–33
public policy, 6–27—6–33
Doctors
restrictive covenants
area covenants, 14–17
enforceable covenants, 14–16
types of practice, 14–15
Domestic violence and abuse
forfeiture, 5–36
Duress
illegality, 8–17—8–21
Enforcement
proprietary interests
advancement, 16–10—16–11, 16–14—16–16
conclusion, 16–17—16–18
New Zealand, 16–18
no reliance doctrine, 16–04—16–14
resulting trusts, 16–08—16–09
transfer of property in goods, 16–01—16–03
Exclusive dealership agreements
competition, 11–25
Exclusive supply agreements
restraint of trade
leases, 12–26
mortgages, 12–26
petrol, 12–24—12–28
scope of relief, 12–27
sole agency agreements, 12–30
solus agreements, 12–24—12–28
sole agency agreements, 12–30
solus agreements, 12–24—12–28
tied-houses, 12–29
Executory agreements
failure of consideration, 3–07—3–10
mistake, 3–05—3–06
performance
abandonment of original intention,
3–02—3–03
failure of consideration, 3–07—3–10
ignorance of the law, 3–02—3–03

illegality confused with other concepts,
3–04—3–11
illegality irrelevant, 3–02—3–03
mistake, 3–05—3–06
restitution, 3–11
restitution, 3–11
trading with the enemy, 10–26—10–27
Exemplary damages
recovery of damages, 5–19—5–22
Expert witnesses
conditional fees, 9–25
Failure of basis
executory agreements, 3–07—3–10
performance, 3–07—3–10
restitution, 17–09—17–10
Failure of consideration *see* **Failure of basis**
Fault
penalties, 5–02
Fines
implied prohibition of contracts, 2–05
penalties, 5–05
size, 5–05
Foreign law
comity, 10–09—10–13
Forfeiture
benefit from criminal conduct, 5–40—5–42
common law, 5–30—5–34
diminished responsibility, 5–31
domestic violence, 5–36
flexibility requirement, 5–33
Forfeiture Act 1982, 5–35—5–38
Inheritance (Provision for Family and
Dependants) Act 1975, 5–39
issues, 5–01
legislation, 5–34—5–39
manslaughter by gross negligence, 5–32
rule, 5–30
suicide pacts, 5–37—5–38
Fraud
bribery
confidentiality agreements, 7–28
corrupt bargains, 7–24
comity, 10–10
confidentiality agreements
bribery, 7–28
concealment of criminality, 7–32—7–34
libel, 7–29—7–31
public interest, 7–35—7–37
public interest disclosure, 7–38
contracts
finance, 7–08
fraud upon the public, 7–03
insolvency, 7–05
insurance contracts, 7–07
motive, 7–06
preferences, 7–04
Revenue and Customs, 7–09—7–23
corrupt bargains, 7–24—7–27

fraud upon the public, 7–03
income tax, 7–12—7–18
insolvency, 7–05
insurance contracts, 7–07
libel, 7–29—7–31
motive, 7–06
preferences, 7–04
public interest disclosure, 7–38
public policy, 7–02
purpose of agreement, 7–01
Revenue and Customs
  blameworthiness, 7–19—7–23
  documents, 7–10—7–11
  illegal contracts, 7–09
  income tax, 7–12—7–18
whistleblowing, 7–38
Freedom of contract
implied prohibition of contracts, 2–04
Garden leave
restraint of trade, 11–17
Health and safety at work
implied prohibition of contracts, 2–09
HMRC
fraud
  blameworthiness, 7–19—7–23
  documents, 7–10—7–11
  illegal contracts, 7–09
  income tax, 7–12—7–18
Hostage-taking
comity, 10–12
Human Rights Act 1998
provisions, I–03—I–04
Ignorance
knowledge, 4–30—4–32
performance, 3–02—3–03, 4–30—4–32
Illegal contracts
crime, 1–01
labelling contracts, I–05
restraint of trade, I–07
Illegality
blunt instrument of contract law, I–02
common law, I–06
complexity, I–01
criminal law, I–06
duress, 8–17—8–21
examples, I–09
Human Rights Act 1998, and, I–03—I–04
law reform, I–08
protection of property, I–04
statutory illegality
  approach of courts, 1–12
  breach of statutory duty, 1–17
  categorisation, 1–11
  common law illegality distinguished,
    1–10—1–14
  conspiracy, 1–18
  contractual context, 1–15—1–16
  express statutory prohibition, 1–13

implied prohibition, 1–14—1–16
  necessary contemplation by statute, 1–15
  non-contractual activities, 1–16
  penalties, 1–13
  unenforceable contracts, 1–13
  void contracts, 1–13
trading with the enemy, 10–15
Implied prohibition of contracts
both parties affected, 2–03
carrying out contract, 2–12
common law, 2–06
conditional agreements
  compliance with legal requirements,
    2–19—2–22
  contractual allocation of responsibility,
    2–23—2–26
contract type, 2–10
contractual allocation of responsibility,
  2–23—2–26
contractual context, 2–01
fines, 2–05
freedom of contract, 2–04
health and safety at work, 2–09
individual contract penalties, 2–07
innocent parties, 2–11
insurance contracts, 2–12
interpretation, 2–05—2–09
literal interpretation, 2–12
merits, 2–02
practical application of doctrine, 2–10—2–13
presumptions, 2–17
protecting the Revenue, 2–08
public policy, 2–02
rationale, 2–04
scope, 1–19
secondary obligation, 2–13
statutory interpretation
  flexible approach, 2–15
  innocent parties, 2–16
  legislative purpose, 2–14
  presumptions, 2–17
  protection of party, 2–18
  taxation, 2–08
Income tax
fraud, 7–12—7–18
Indemnities
costs, 5–09
issues, 5–01
professional indemnity insurance, 5–18
recovery of criminal penalties
  bad meat, 5–04
  costs, 5–09
  fault, 5–02
  fines, 5–05
  refusal, 5–06—5–09
  uninsured drivers, 5–03
recovery of damages
  awareness of claimants, 5–12

champerty, 5–18
compulsory insurance, 5–21
directly liable claimants, 5–20
exemplary damages, 5–19—5–22
intention, 5–14—5–18
misrepresentation, 5–11
motor vehicle cases, 5–14, 5–15
professional indemnity insurance, 5–18
public policy, 5–10—5–13
social interests, 5–10
third party protection, 5–13
vicarious liability, 5–19
victims, 5–17, 5–22
violence, 5–16
suicide
assignment of policy, 5–26—5–29
enforceability by deceased's estate,
5–23—5–25
security, 5–26
surrender value, 5–27
vicarious liability, 5–19
victims, 5–17, 5–22
**Inheritance (Provision for Family and
Dependants) Act 1975**
forfeiture, 5–39
Injunctions
restrictive covenants
assessment of strength of case, 15–16
Cyanamid case, 15–15—15–16
full protection of covenant, 15–19
generally, 15–01
loss, 15–18
Insolvency
fraud, 7–05
Insurance contracts
fraud, 7–07
implied prohibition of contracts, 2–12
knowledge, 4–19—4–21
life insurance
assignment of policy, 5–26—5–29
enforcement of policy, 5–23—5–25
suicide, 5–23—5–29
Intention
comity, 10–13
crime, 1–04
Interim injunctions
restrictive covenants
assessment of strength of case, 15–16
Cyanamid case, 15–15—15–16
full protection of covenant, 15–19
generally, 15–01
loss, 15–18
Interpretation
area covenants
listed customers, 13–12
nature of employment, 13–11
permitted covenants, 13–09
specific restrictions, 13–10

unidentified cash-payers, 13–13
use, 13–09
implied prohibition of contracts, 2–05—2–09
restrictive covenants
context, 13–03—13–04
date for determination of validity, 13–08
discretion, 13–07
employee protection, 13–06
less rigid construction, 13–02
literal interpretation, 13–01
public policy, 13–01
wide terms, 13–05
Judiciary
see also **Public policy**
appointments, 6–32
discretion, 6–27—6–33
law reform
Australia, 21–26—21–27
Canada, 21–23—21–25
scrutiny, 6–31
Knowledge
actual facilitation of unlawful purpose, 4–10
after-acquired information, 4–26
assistance, 4–09—4–11
awareness, 4–04—4–06
categories, 4–01
claimant saving money, 4–08
contract terms, 4–13
degrees of knowledge, 4–22
extent of claimant's involvement
awareness, 4–04—4–06
contractual obligation, 4–12—4–13
participation, 4–07—4–11
related transactions, 4–14—4–21
gravely illegal schemes, 4–22—4–26
ignorance, 4–30—4–32
innocent party, 4–27—4–29
insurance contracts, 4–19—4–21
introduction, 4–01—4–03
loans, 4–17
mere awareness, 4–04—4–06
morality, 4–23, 4–24
motive, 4–16—4–18
participation
actual facilitation of unlawful purpose, 4–10
assistance, 4–09—4–11
claimant saving money, 4–08
contract terms, 4–13
insurance contracts, 4–19—4–21
knowledge insufficient, 4–07
loans, 4–17
motive, 4–16—4–18
profiting from illegality, 4–08
related transactions, 4–14—4–21
sharer in the illegal transaction, 4–09
tainting, 4–15
United States, 4–11

performance
  breach of promise, 4–29
  ignorance, 4–30—4–32
  innocent party, 4–27—4–29
  warranties, 4–33—4–35
profiting from illegality, 4–08
related transactions, 4–14—4–21
seriousness of offence, 4–22
source of illegality, 4–02
tainting, 4–15
United States, 4–11, 4–25
warranties, 4–33—4–35
Law Commission
consultation documents, 21–15—21–22
Law reform
  Australia, 21–26—21–27
  Canada, 21–23—21–25
  current law, 21–28—21–31
  illegality, I–08
  judiciary
    Australia, 21–26—21–27
    Canada, 21–23—21–25
  Law Commission, 21–15—21–22
Legal profession
conditional fees, 9–21—9–24
Libel
confidentiality agreements, 7–29—7–31
Life insurance
  assignment, 5–26—5–29
  enforceability by deceased's estate, 5–23—5–25
  suicide
    assignment of policy, 5–26—5–29
    enforcement of policy, 5–23—5–25
    security, 5–26
    surrender value, 5–27
  surrender value, 5–27
Liquidated damages
restraint of trade, 11–08
Literal interpretation
implied prohibition of contracts, 2–12
Loans
knowledge, 4–17
Locus poenitentiae
  criminality, 18–05
  debtors, 18–07
  frustration, 18–02
  generally, 18–01—18–03
  legislative purpose, 18–08
  old law, 18–01
  protection of claimant, 18–04—18–08
  repentance, 18–02
  restitution, 17–04—17–05
  underlying reason for illegality, 18–04
Maintenance
  background, 9–03
  champerty distinguished, 9–11
  contracts, 9–02
  effect, 9–26—9–27

lawful maintenance
  common interest, 9–06
  modern approach, 9–09
  present position, 9–10
  trade rivals, 9–07—9–08
origins of concept, 9–01
public policy, 6–34, 9–28—9–31
Manslaughter
diminished responsibility, 5–31
Manslaughter by gross negligence
forfeiture, 5–32
Marriage
  bigamy, 6–17
  brocage, 6–19—6–20
  premarital agreements, 6–18
  public policy
    anticipating death of spouse, 6–15
    bigamy, 6–17
    brocage, 6–19—6–20
    cohabitation, 6–22
    ignorance of existing marriage, 6–16
    premarital agreements, 6–18
    unmarried sexual partners, 6–21
    wills, 6–18
  wills, 6–18
Mistake
  executory agreements, 3–05—3–06
  performance, 3–05—3–06
  restitution
    factual mistake, 17–07
    introduction, 17–06
    legal mistake, 17–08
Morals and the law
  comity, 10–09
  knowledge, 4–23—4–24
  public policy
    ambiguities, 6–04
    flexibility, 6–05
    introduction, 1–01
    issues, 6–01—6–02
    nature, 6–03—6–10
    rigidity, 6–06
Motive
  fraud, 7–06
  knowledge, 4–16—4–18
Motor insurance
damages, 5–14—5–15
Negligent misstatement
restitution, 17–21
New South Wales
restrictive covenants, 13–22—13–23
New Zealand
  Illegal Contracts Act 1970
    adjustment of rights, 20–10—20–12
    conflict with legitimate policies, 20–13—20–14
    definitions, 20–02—20–03
    discretion, 20–08

fraud, 20–11
illegal sales, 20–12
nullification, 20–04—20–05
practical effect of reforms, 20–09
property rights, 20–06—20–07
public policy, 20–15
reform, 20–01
scope, 20–02
validation, 20–04—20–05
proprietary interests, 16–18
restrictive covenants, 13–21
Non-competition covenants
restraint of trade, 11–03
Non-solicitation covenants
customers, 14–03
discontinued custom, 14–05
habitual purchasers, 14–04
no personal knowledge of customers, 14–06
personal dealings with customers, 14–07
reasonableness, 14–02
use, 14–01
Ontario
illegal transactions, 21–08—21–10
Oppression
restitution, 17–11—17–13
restrictive covenants
examples, 15–04—15–05
generally, 15–01
implications, 15–02
pragmatic approach, 15–03
Participation *see* **Knowledge**
Partnerships
restrictive covenants, 13–19
Patents
restraint of trade, 12–23
Penalties
fault, 5–02
fines, 5–05
recovery of criminal penalties
bad meat, 5–04
costs, 5–09
fault, 5–02
fines, 5–05
refusal, 5–06—5–09
uninsured drivers, 5–03
statutory illegality, 1–13
uninsured drivers, 5–03
Performance
see also **Severance**
contracts governed by English law,
10–02—10–08
executory agreements
abandonment of original intention,
3–02—3–03
failure of consideration, 3–07—3–10
ignorance, 3–02—3–03
illegality confused with other concepts,
3–04—3–11

illegality irrelevant, 3–02—3–03
mistake, 3–05—3–06
restitution, 3–11
failure of consideration, 3–07—3–10
ignorance, 3–02—3–03, 4–30—4–32
innocent party, 3–18—3–21
knowledge
breach of promise, 4–29
ignorance, 4–30—4–32
innocent party, 4–27—4–29
warranties, 4–33—4–35
mistake, 3–05—3–06
party responsible for unlawful performance,
3–12—3–17
place of performance, 10–02—10–08
restitution, 3–11
unlawful performance
executory agreements, 3–02—3–11
failure of consideration, 3–07—3–10
ignorance of the law, 3–02—3–03
illegality confused with other concepts,
3–04—3–11
illegality irrelevant, 3–02—3–03
innocent party, 3–18—3–21
mistake, 3–05—3–06
primary object unlawful, 3–01
responsible party, 3–12—3–17
restitution, 3–11
warranties, 4–33—4–35
Performers
restraint of trade, 11–15
Petrol
exclusive supply agreements, 12–29
Place of performance
comity, 10–02—10–08
Precedent
public policy, 6–33
Preferences
fraud, 7–04
Pre-nuptial agreements
public policy, 6–18
Presumptions
advancement, 16–10—16–16
implied prohibition of contracts, 2–17
statutory interpretation, 2–17
Professional indemnity insurance
champerty, 5–18
Proportionality
seriousness of offence, 1–05
Proprietary interests
advancement, 16–10—16–16
enforcement
conclusion, 16–17—16–18
New Zealand, 16–18
no reliance doctrine, 16–04—16–14
presumption of advancement, 16–10—16–11,
16–14—16–16
resulting trusts, 16–08—16–09

transfer of property in goods, 16–01—16–03
  windfalls, 16–12—16–13
resulting trusts, 16–08—16–09
transfer of property in goods, 16–01—16–03

Prostitution
public policy, 6–22

Protection of property
Human Rights Act 1998, I–04
illegality, I–04

Public interest
confidentiality agreements, 7–35—7–39

Public policy
ambiguities, 6–04
appointments, 6–32
bigamy, 6–17
champerty, 6–34, 9–28—9–31
classes, 6–07
cohabitation, 6–22
comity, 10–07
compromising legal process, 8–01
confidence in judiciary, 6–31
consensus, 6–30
discretion, 6–27—6–33
factors to be taken into account
  question of degree, 6–11—6–13
  undesirable tendencies, 6–11—6–14
fraud, 7–02
implied prohibition of contracts, 2–02
influences, 6–29
issues, 6–01—6–02
maintenance, 6–34, 9–28—9–31
marriage
  anticipating death of spouse, 6–15
  bigamy, 6–17
  brocage, 6–19—6–20
  cohabitation, 6–22
  ignorance of existing marriage, 6–16
  premarital agreements, 6–18
  unmarried sexual partners, 6–21
  wills, 6–18
morality
  ambiguities, 6–04
  flexibility, 6–05
  introduction, 1–01
  issues, 6–01—6–02
  nature, 6–03—6–10
  rigidity, 6–06
philosophical framework, 6–28
precedent, 6–33
premarital agreements, 6–18
prostitution, 6–22—6–23
reliance in existing doctrine, 6–08—6–09
restraint of trade, 6–09—6–10, 11–05—11–06,
  12–10—12–16
restrictive covenants, 6–09—6–10,
  11–05—11–06, 12–10—12–16, 13–01
severance, 19–16—19–25
sexual services, 6–25—6–26

unenforceable contracts, 1–01
variability, 6–33

Purchasers
restraint of trade
  enforceability of covenant, 12–18—12–19
  general rule, 12–17
  paid employment, 12–22
  patents, 12–23
  reality of agreement, 12–20
  sale of businesses, 12–21

Repudiation
restrictive covenants
  basic rule, 15–07
  breach by employer, 15–12—15–13
  factual circumstances, 15–14
  generally, 15–01
  questions to be asked, 15–08
  widely drafted covenants, 15–09—15–11

Residence
trading with the enemy, 10–17

Restitution
Australia, 17–17
bar to relief, 17–04—17–05
deceit, 17–19
development of law, 17–01
executory agreements, 3–11
failure of consideration, 17–09—17–10
introduction, 17–01—17–03
locus poenitentiae, 17–04—17–05
mistake of fact
  generally, 17–07
  introduction, 17–06
mistake of law
  generally, 17–08
  introduction, 17–06
negligent misstatement, 17–21
oppression, 17–11—17–13
performance, 3–11
role, 17–14—17–18
torts, 17–20

Restraint of trade
see also **Restrictive covenants**; **Severance**
breach of confidence, 12–08—12–09
categorisation, 11–04
competition
  abuse of dominant position, 11–25
  Chapter I prohibition, 11–22
  Chapter II prohibition, 11–26
  employees, 11–23
  European law, 11–20
  exclusive dealership agreements, 11–25
  nature of statutory provisions, 11–19
  prohibited agreements, 11–22—11–25
  purpose of statutory provisions, 11–21
  small agreements, 11–24
conditional entitlements, 11–09
confidentiality agreements
  breach of confidence, 12–08—12–09

confidential information, 12–06—12–07
issues, 12–01
misuse of trade secrets, 12–05
scope of protection, 12–01
skill and experience, 12–02
trade secrets, 12–03—12–04
consent, 11–18
consideration, 11–10—11–11
continuing relationships
absolute exemption, 11–14
performers, 11–15
scope of doctrine, 11–13
exclusive dealership agreements, 11–25
exclusive supply agreements
leases, 12–26
mortgages, 12–26
petrol, 12–29
scope of relief, 12–27
solus agreements, 12–24—12–28
garden leave, 11–17
illegal contracts, I–07
justification, 11–16
liquidated damages, 11–08
misuse of trade secrets, 12–05
non-competition covenants, 11–03
origins, 11–01
patents, 12–23
performers, 11–15
public policy, 6–09—6–10, 11–05—11–06,
    12–10—12–16
realism, 11–12
severance, 19–17—19–21
solus agreements, 12–24—12–28
substance of provision, 11–07
trade secrets
generally, 12–03—12–04
misuse, 12–05
vendor and purchaser
enforceability of covenant, 12–18—12–19
general rule, 12–17
paid employment, 12–22
patents, 12–23
reality of agreement, 12–20
sale of businesses, 12–21
Restrictive covenants
see also **Restraint of trade; Severance**
area covenants
doctors, 14–17
duration, 13–14
length of covenant, 13–14
listed customers, 13–12
method of calculation, 13–15
nature of employment, 13–11
severance, 19–07
solicitors, 14–19—14–20
specific restrictions, 13–10
unidentified cash-payers, 13–13
use, 13–09

breach of confidence, 12–08—12–09
consent, 11–18
doctors
area covenants, 14–17
enforceable covenants, 14–16
types of practice, 14–15
duration
area covenants, 13–14
life-long covenants, 13–17
months, 13–20
partnerships, 13–19
senior employees, 13–17
status of employee, 13–18
subordinate issue, 13–16
garden leave, 11–17
interim injunctions
assessment of strength of case, 15–16
Cyanamid case, 15–15—15–16
full protection of covenant, 15–19
generally, 15–01
loss, 15–18
interpretation
context, 13–03—13–04
date for determination of validity, 13–08
discretion, 13–07
employee protection, 13–06
less rigid construction, 13–02
literal interpretation, 13–01
public policy, 13–01
wide terms, 13–05
joining other organisations, 14–08—14–12
life-long covenants, 13–17
medical practitioners
area covenants, 14–17
enforceable covenants, 14–16
types of practice, 14–15
New South Wales, 13–22—13–23
New Zealand, 13–21
non-competition covenants, 11–03
non-solicitation covenants
customers, 14–03
discontinued custom, 14–05
former employees, 14–13—14–14
no personal knowledge of customers, 14–06
personal dealings with customers, 14–07
reasonableness, 14–02
use, 14–01
oppression
equitable relief distinguished, 15–05
example, 15–04
examples, 15–04—15–05
generally, 15–01
implications, 15–02
pragmatic approach, 15–03
origins, 11–01
partnerships, 13–19
performers, 11–15
poaching employees, 14–13—14–14

public policy, 6–09—6–10, 11–05—11–06,
    12–10—12–16, 13–01
repudiation
  basic rule, 15–07
  factual circumstances, 15–14
  generally, 15–01
  questions to be asked, 15–08
  widely drafted covenants, 15–09—15–11
rival employers
  joining other organisations, 14–08—14–12
  poaching employees, 14–13—14–14
solicitation of customers
  customers, 14–03
  discontinued custom, 14–05
  no personal knowledge of customers, 14–06
  personal dealings with customers, 14–07
  reasonableness, 14–02
  use, 14–01
solicitation of former employees, 14–13—14–14
solicitors
  area covenants, 14–19—14–20
  'brass plate' covenants, 14–20
  goodwill, 14–18
  reasonableness, 14–22
  sale of business, 14–21
trade secrets
  generally, 12–03—12–04
  misuse, 12–05
Resulting trusts
  proprietary interests, 16–08—16–09
Revenue and Customs *see* **HMRC**
Sellers
  restraint of trade
    enforceability of covenant, 12–18—12–19
    general rule, 12–17
    paid employment, 12–22
    patents, 12–23
    reality of agreement, 12–20
    sale of businesses, 12–21
Seriousness of offence
  crime
    approach after Patel v Mirza, 1–05—1–08
    deliberate acts, 1–02—1–04
    intention, 1–04
    proportionality, 1–05
    uncertain facts, 1–09
  deliberate acts, 1–02—1–04
  knowledge, 4–22
  proportionality, 1–05
Settlement
  compromising legal process, 8–03
Severance
  see also **Performance**; **Restrictive covenants**
  area covenants, 19–07
  blue pencil test, 19–04—19–07
  character of contract, 19–13—19–15
  conclusion, 19–26

consideration
  additional consideration, 19–10
  no agreement reached, 19–11
  scope, 19–10—19–12
deleted phrases, 19–09
importance, 19–01
objectives, 19–02
plainly severable covenants, 19–08
public policy
  introduction, 19–16
  restraint of trade, 19–17—19–21
  tainted contracts, 19–22—19–25
restraint of trade, 19–17—19–21
tainted contracts, 19–22—19–25
tests, 19–03
uncertainty, 19–26
wording of provision, 19–04—19–09
Singapore
  illegal transactions, 21–14
Solicitors
  restrictive covenants
    area covenants, 14–19—14–20
    'brass plate' covenants, 14–20
    goodwill, 14–18
    reasonableness, 14–22
    sale of business, 14–21
Solus agreements
  restraint of trade, 12–24—12–28
South Australia
  illegal transactions, 21–11—21–13
Statutory illegality *see* **Illegality**
Statutory interpretation
  implied prohibition of contracts
    flexible approach, 2–15
    innocent parties, 2–16
    legislative purpose, 2–14
    presumptions, 2–17
    protection of party, 2–18
  presumptions, 2–17
Succession
  diminished responsibility, 5–31
  domestic violence, 5–36
  forfeiture
    common law, 5–30—5–34
    diminished responsibility, 5–31
    domestic violence, 5–36
    flexibility, 5–33
    Forfeiture Act 1982, 5–35—5–38
    Inheritance (Provision for Family and
        Dependants) Act 1975, 5–39
    manslaughter by gross negligence, 5–32
    rule, 5–30
    statute, 5–34—5–39
    suicide pacts, 5–37—5–38
  Inheritance (Provision for Family and
      Dependants) Act 1975, 5–39
  manslaughter by gross negligence, 5–32
  suicide pacts, 5–37—5–38

Suicide
indemnities
    assignment of life policies, 5–26—5–29
    enforceability by deceased's estate,
      5–23—5–25
life insurance
    assignment of policy, 5–26—5–29
    enforceability by deceased's estate,
      5–23—5–25
    security, 5–26
    surrender value, 5–27
suicide pacts, 5–37—5–38
Taxation
implied prohibition of contracts, 2–08
Tied pubs
restraint of trade, 12–29
Torts
agreement to commit, 1–01
breach of statutory duty, 1–17
restitution, 17–20
Trade secrets
restraint of trade
    generally, 12–03—12–04
    misuse, 12–05
Trading with the enemy
actions against enemy aliens, 10–19—10–20
conceptual issues, 10–25—10–29
confiscation, 10–20
contract terms, 10–28—10–29
corporate claimants, 10–18
doctrine, 10–16
executory agreements, 10–26—10–27
illegality, 10–15
importance, 10–14
performance, 10–25
principles, 10–14—10–20
property, 10–25
public policy, 10–21—10–24
residence, 10–17
Transfer of property in goods
proprietary interests, 16–01—16–03
Uninsured drivers
penalties, 5–03
United States
knowledge, 4–11, 4–25
Vicarious liability
indemnities, 5–19
Victims
indemnities, 5–17, 5–22
Violent offences
damages, 5–16

Void contracts
statutory illegality, blue, 1–13
War
comity
    fraud, 10–10
    general rule, 10–01
    hostage-taking, 10–12
    intention, 10–13
    morality, 10–09
    ordre public, 10–09
    place of performance, 10–02—10–08
    public policy, 10–07
    Revenue laws, 10–04
trading with the enemy
    actions against enemy aliens, 10–19—10–20
    conceptual issues, 10–25—10–29
    confiscation, 10–20
    contract terms, 10–28—10–29
    corporate claimants, 10–18
    doctrine, 10–16
    executory agreements, 10–26—10–27
    illegality, 10–15
    importance, 10–14
    performance, 10–25
    principles, 10–14—10–20
    property, 10–25
    public policy, 10–21—10–24
    residence, 10–17
Warranties
knowledge, 4–33—4–35
performance, 4–33—4–35
Whistleblowing
confidentiality agreements, 7–38
Wills
marriage, 6–18
public policy, 6–18
Withdrawal
illegal transaction
    criminality, 18–05
    debtors, 18–07
    frustration, 18–02
    generally, 18–01—18–03
    legislative purpose, 18–08
    old law, 18–01
    protection of claimant, 18–04—18–08
    repentance, 18–02
    restitution, 17–04—17–05
    underlying reason for illegality, 18–04